Queens and Mistresses of Renaissance France

Queens and Mistresses of Renaissance France

Kathleen Wellman

Yale
UNIVERSITY
PRESS
New Haven & London

Published with assistance from the foundation established
in memory of William McKean Brown.

Frontispiece: Gabrielle d'Estrées and her sister, the duchess of Villars. Fontainebleau school, late sixteenth century. Louvre/The Bridgeman Art Library.

Yale University Press books may be purchased in quantity for educational, business, or promotional use. For information, please e-mail sales.press@yale.edu (U.S. office) or sales@yaleup.co.uk (U.K. office).

Set in Electra type by Newgen North America.
Printed in the United States of America.

Library of Congress Cataloging-in-Publication Data

Wellman, Kathleen Anne, 1951–
Queens and mistresses of Renaissance France / Kathleen Wellman.
pages cm
Includes bibliographical references and index.
ISBN 978-0-300-17885-2 (cloth : alk. paper) 1. France—Kings and rulers—Biography. 2. Queens—France—Biography. 3. Mistresses—France—Biography. 4. France—History—15th century. 5. France—History—16th century. 6. Renaissance—France. I. Title.
DC112.A1W45 2013
944'.0209252—dc23

2012037490

A catalogue record for this book is available from the British Library.

∞ This paper meets the requirements of ANSI/NISO Z39.48–1992 (Permanence of Paper).

10 9 8 7 6 5 4 3 2 1

To my children, Elizabeth and Matthew

Contents

Preface

This book grew out of my experiences as co-director of the SMU-in-Paris summer program for more than a decade. Students who knew little about the French Renaissance were fascinated by the prominent figures who lived in chateaux of the Loire Valley and especially intrigued by the long-standing royal ménage à trois of Henry II, his wife, Catherine de Medici, and his mistress, Diane de Poitiers. As I considered how I might use that relationship to present this period, I discovered that queens and mistresses were much more central to the Renaissance than histories of the period acknowledge. The Renaissance court, focused on the person of the monarch, fused the familial and the political. As a result, it offered women of talent and determination opportunities to assume political and cultural roles through their intimate association with kings. Less rigidly organized than it would become under the absolutist kings of the seventeenth century, the Renaissance court proved more amenable to the influence of royal women. These queens and mistresses were also subjects and patrons of artists and writers, and two of them—Marguerite d'Angoulême and Marguerite de Valois—were important writers. They left a legacy in the paintings, histories, memoirs, legends, and myths they inspired, promoted, or even produced. This book thus makes queens and mistresses central to a narrative of the French Renaissance by exploring their roles in politics and culture from the designation of Agnès Sorel as the first official mistress in 1444 to the death in 1599 of Gabrielle d'Estrées, the mistress Henry IV planned to marry.

These women were not simply important to their time; they have had equally rich posthumous lives. They are important "sites of memory," as explored in Pierre Nora's important collection of essays on the places (construed broadly) where national memories coalesce. Each woman treated in this book has been used subsequently in a rich variety of ways: as a foil for the king or to elevate or condemn him; to fault the monarchy as a corrupt form of government or, antithetically, to praise it as an era of romance and grace; to argue against women's political activities or, very recently, to assert their importance to French culture. Ultimately, these women have played roles in defining the history and national character of France.

All of the women central to this project have been treated by historians, biographers, and polemicists from the sixteenth century to the present in French. They are prominent in fifteenth- and sixteenth-century primary sources, featured in poetry, memoirs, and political writings. Their stories became significant in political writings; French writers have used these women to take a position for or against the republic, the monarchy, or the Church. They occupy a place in Renaissance scholarship and modern popular history. Royal figures have attracted a resurgence of popular interest in France, just as they have in America. Biography too has enjoyed a revival in France as a kind of historical writing with widespread appeal. Most of these women have been treated in French popular biographies but are largely unfamiliar outside France, especially as compared to their better-known contemporaries—Henry VIII's six wives. But French queens and mistresses generally lived longer and were more politically active and culturally influential. Despite their prominence in their day, they are neither central to the conventional understanding of French history nor extensively treated in English-language texts, with two notable exceptions: Catherine de Medici's political career and Marguerite d'Angoulême's literary work.

The French Renaissance has, however, been a particularly fruitful period for both English-language scholars and their French counterparts, capturing the attention of accomplished and prolific historians such as Ivan Cloulas, Denis Crouzet, and R. J. Knecht. Several women featured here have attracted French scholars. Eliane Viennot's editions of Marguerite de Valois's works and biography of her, and Crouzet and Thierry Wanegffelen's works on Catherine de Medici are especially significant. French scholars Didier Le Fur, Anne-Marie Lecoq, and Nicole Hochner have studied the construction of the myths of Anne of Brittany, Francis I, and Louis XII, respectively. Art historians and literary scholars, including Cynthia Brown, Elizabeth L'Estrange, and Colette Winn, among others, have focused on the contributions of royal women to French patrimony as patrons and thus purveyors of images of both women and the monarchy. These works attest to the vibrancy of this field. This book is greatly indebted to recent studies of these women, in particular, and the culture of the Renaissance, women's history, and art history. I have also relied extensively on primary sources—some written by the women themselves, others by contemporaries commenting on them, the monarchy, or the culture of the day, and others writing later to define their histories, legends, and myths.

Mistress and queen, positions seemingly anachronistic in modern democratic culture, remain relevant to our more egalitarian political culture. We too have a culture enamored of celebrity, where young, beautiful women marry or consort with older, powerful, wealthy men. We too wonder about the influence women might exert in politics through "pillow talk." We, like men and women of the Renaissance, find the political influence of women, who have that influence only because of their personal relationships with powerful men, both intriguing and disturbing.

Like modern royalty or celebrities, Renaissance queens had access to funds and were able to define themselves through available media as politically important and culturally relevant, as complements to their husbands, and as integrally linked with the good of the country. All evidence to the contrary, they embody for some modern women expectations of an idyllic marriage and fairy-tale ending to a courtship. The royal mistress who attained immediate celebrity and high status has modern resonance. Lavish gifts to her often translated into great inheritable wealth for her family. Her precipitous rise gave her a hold on the popular imagination perhaps akin to that of the Hollywood actress: The public both wanted to know everything about her and, rather perversely, assumed that celebrity reflected virtue or merit. The modern allure of royalty or Hollywood celebrities has something in common with the Renaissance appreciation of queens and mistresses. The roles of queen and mistress were malleable enough to allow women to define them in dramatically different ways. Like an American First Lady, they had opportunities by virtue of their position. Their use of the position not only shaped their lives and influenced their historical reputations but also separated the great or influential queens or mistresses from those who simply held a distinctive status.

Despite their relevance to modern cultural concerns and important new scholarship on them, these queens and mistresses remain relatively unknown in the English-speaking world. My hope is that this book will make them more central to our understanding of the history of the French Renaissance, provoke further study, and introduce them to wider circles of scholars and, more generally, to interested readers.

To make this book more accessible to nonspecialist readers, I have translated, or used translations of, all quotations and titles of works. French titles can be found in the endnotes or in the complete bibliography available online (see **yalebooks.com/kwellman**). I have chosen to use the first names rather than the titles of major figures. Names are more consistent than titles, which often evolve to reflect changes in status or landholdings.

A general word about names and dates: The reporting of early dates was often inconsistent. The more important an event was, the more likely that we have more sources with greater consistency or a stronger subsequent consensus on how to date it. Less significant events are dated with less uniformity. Names are even more problematic. In this period, names often reflected place, especially for the nobility. Someone was "de," meaning "of," some place. But the nobility in this period often added estates, so they could be from several places or be named with one "de" followed by another "de." Sometimes an extra "de" specified a particular branch of the family. So for example, the royal house of Valois has the Valois d'Orléans and the Valois d'Angoulême branches. Ironically, better-known historical figures can be designated most simply, as they are in this book, by their first names. Less-well-known figures might require many place names to distinguish them from others of the same name or location. Inconsistencies remain as scholars now try to standardize and simplify usage by deciding which place should now correspond to our use of last names. For example, Philippe Duplessis-Mornay was "of," or from, both Mornay and Plessis. His last name is now given variously as Duplessis-Mornay, du Mornay, de Mornay de Plessis, with many different spellings to add to the confusion. I have tried to be consistent in my usage, but variants still occur, particularly in titles.

To make this rich but very complex period of French history from the mid-fifteenth century to the seventeenth century as clear as possible, there is a list of significant dates at the beginning of each chapter, and occasionally genealogical tables are included to make it easier to trace complex family and dynastic relations.

Much of the history of this period unfolded in the Loire Valley, in the chateaux built and redecorated by kings, queens, and mistresses. The chateaux discussed in this book are part of the French national patrimony and open for visiting. Most of them have Web sites for virtual visits.

ACKNOWLEDGMENTS

As I hope this book will find a receptive audience among nonspecialist readers, I have prevailed on many friends and colleagues to read it. I am especially grateful to the participants in a seminar of colleagues at SMU from a variety of specialties and disciplines—Janis Bergman-Carton, Edward Countryman, Dennis Cordell, James Hopkins, Thomas Knock, Beth Newman, and Carolyn Sargent—who read and commented on an early unwieldy draft, giving me much needed advice, particularly on how I might make this complex history clearer. Susan Branson tested it for an Americanist readership. Dena Goodman deployed her characteristic insightful criticism, provoking me to rethink crucial points and excise some irrelevancies. My colleague Jeremy Adams read the first two chapters to save me from egregious mistakes about the Middle Ages. I conscripted family members as well. My daughter Liz read several chapters, editing pen in hand. My mother, Mary Wellman, provided the educated general reader's perspective. My husband, Dennis Sepper, read it all thoroughly, and more importantly, has shared every step in its evolution—from inception to the technicalities of final submission. Even if I was unable to take advantage of all of their suggestions, the book's final form owes much to their thoughtful readings.

I appreciate the generous support of Southern Methodist University for my research, particularly from the Stanton Sharp and William P. Clements funds of the history department and the University Research Council, which supported the costs of reproducing images. Ian Aberle produced the genealogies, and Bill Nelson, the maps. The staffs of the Bibliothèque nationale de France and the interlibrary-loan office at SMU, especially Billie Stovall, were crucial in providing access to sources. The support of history department staff—Mildred

Pinkston, omniscient and indispensable administrative assistant, and Sharron Pierson, always-responsive departmental secretary—made it possible for me to complete this project while department chair.

This project has been especially enriched by my dozen years in the SMU-in-Paris summer program. My co-director, Carolyn Sargent, was gratifyingly intrigued by this project. Her stories of mistresses from her French school days made vividly clear how significant they remain in the popular imagination. David Freidel was always willing to share his appreciation of Renaissance art and kingship in the ten years we taught together. For the past several years, my colleague Dennis Cordell has pointed out traces of the Middle East on Renaissance France, and Michael Fuller has been unfailingly willing to hear yet another story about royal women. Isabelle Roynier, the director of the year-long SMU program, elucidated Renaissance sites we visited together, and Eric Waton facilitated local arrangements. Julia Gossard has shared in this project first as a student and now as assistant in the SMU-in-Paris summer program and Ph.D. candidate at the University of Texas. Conversations with all of them over many years have shaped this book.

I would also like to thank my editor, Laura Davulis, who not only read the entire manuscript but forced me to concede that it would be better if it were forty-five thousand words shorter—no matter how painful their excision. Christina Tucker has been exemplary as a responsive assistant editor, and Ann-Marie Imbornoni as a conscientious production editor. Kate Davis has been a gracious and punctilious copy editor. I appreciate their care and attention in shepherding this book through production. It has been a pleasure to work with Yale University Press.

Bringing this book to conclusion makes me realize just how much and how long I have been thinking, talking, and teaching about this project—with family, friends, colleagues, and students. Their enthusiasm and indulgence is much appreciated. All such projects are inevitably embedded deeply in family life, which makes all such work richer and more enjoyable, at least for the author. I have benefited, in too many ways to even imagine enumerating, from my shared personal and intellectual life with my husband, Dennis Sepper. He has shared in every part of this particular project in Paris summers and Loire Valley travels. The end result bears the mark of his encouragement, thoughtful comments, and editing and technical skills. My children, Liz and Matt Sepper, now accomplished adults, remain as always an unalloyed source of pride and delight. This book is dedicated to them with love.

Introduction

The painting of Henry IV's mistress Gabrielle d'Estrées on the frontispiece of this book illustrates quite dramatically some obvious and distinctive attractions of a royal mistress. This painting, by an unknown artist and now displayed in the Louvre, depicting Gabrielle with her sister at her bath, still takes stunned viewers aback as they try to determine what it conveys and how to respond to this unusual image. It is not simply the subjects' nudity that is disconcerting. Renaissance painters reveled in the freedom to portray the human body, but they did so most often under the guise of classical motifs. This painting, on the other hand, is overtly sexual. Its subjects directly engage the viewer. They seem to be actual women rather than the more usual nude figures—goddesses in a sylvan glade or allegorical representations. This painting instead shares features with the private art commissioned during the Renaissance by wealthy men for their enjoyment to celebrate the allure of courtesans.[1] In this case, both sisters, idealized sixteenth-century beauties, gaze directly at the viewer rather than with the downcast eyes or oblique regard of a respectable woman. Instead, the women invite the viewer into a private, intimate space. But the painting also points to a public space; the curtains and the drapery over a balustrade suggest a theater box where the women are clearly meant to be seen.

Elements of the background domestic scene point explicitly to Gabrielle's well-known circumstances. The painting of a nude male above the fireplace may invoke her royal lover, and the mirror behind the servant, reflecting nothing, may foreshadow an early death.[2] Gabrielle holds out the ring Henry IV received at his coronation and gave to her when he promised to marry her. Her sister, by pinching her right nipple, suggests that that she is pregnant with a male child.[3] The servant sewing in the background is likely working on a layette for the coming child. Most disconcerting is Gabrielle's overt sexuality, with its

Fig. i.1. Portrait of Catherine de Medici. French school, sixteenth century. Palazzo Pitti, Florence / The Bridgeman Art Library.

implicit power over the king. The painting does not merely bring the viewer into a domestic scene. It is also full of import for the king's relationship to his mistress and possibly for the future of France.

The portrait of Catherine de Medici, wife of Henry II, clearly depicted as queen, presents a more expected image. But it too conveys a message about her position (fig. i.1). It conforms to other, later portraits of sixteenth- and seventeenth-century queens and reinforces traditional expectations of them.[4] Like other such portraits, this one is almost full-scale. The queen's demeanor is formal, regal, and without any hint of sexuality. Her vertical and triangular shape reinforces both her physical and symbolic stability as a source of dynastic continuity. To note that her clothing is richly adorned is a considerable understatement; her dress is encrusted with pearls and jewels from hem to collar. The ermine identifies her as royal and ties her directly to the king; she reflects his majesty. Her oblique gaze suggests that this painting could well form a diptych with the king's portrait, pointing the viewer to their complementary relationship. Perhaps most telling, the woman is swallowed by the dress, the queen subsumed into the trappings of her position. These two images—the highly sexual mistress and the rigidly formal queen—point to conventional but different expectations of these two positions.

The queen of France was usually selected from the daughters of European monarchs or highest-ranking nobles to cement an alliance, seal a peace, or advance a king's political interests. The most fundamental decision about a queen's life was thus arranged to foster the monarchy into which she married. Political and dynastic considerations so predominated that they virtually precluded the personal interest of either party to the marriage. A prospective queen was often betrothed as an infant and negotiated away from her family to be raised in the nursery of the family into which she would wed. Marriages were arranged between spouses sight unseen, often with a great disproportion in their ages or without a language in common. Such marriages, not surprisingly, were often inharmonious, so much so that some kings resisted or were incapable of carrying out their conjugal duties.

The queen was also selected to bear heirs to the throne. As a result, her body was of great interest and subject to increasingly rigorous inspection to assess her likely success in this essential function.[5] Even the consummation of royal marriages or the births of royal children were quasi-public events, subject to scrutiny in the monarchy's interest. The sexual relationship between the king and queen was governed by distinct expectations. Unlike other women, who might delay marriage and thus reduce the number of risky pregnancies, royal women married as soon as they were nubile and were expected to bear children as soon and as frequently as possible to ensure the survival of the royal line against the high risk of infant mortality. A queen should produce sufficient heirs to guarantee male succession, but all additional children could be bartered in diplomatic exchanges. Although a queen often jeopardized her health with childbearing, failure to do so subjected her to the threat of repudiation. Divorce was forbidden, but marriages, especially royal marriages, could be annulled, and the failure of the queen to bear children was an acknowledged ground for annulment.

Although the production of heirs was her chief function, the queen played other significant roles. She participated in important ceremonies, presenting the monarch not simply as a ruler but also as a family man. She softened his image and cemented his relationship to his subjects. Constant public presentation was particularly important for the peripatetic kings of the Renaissance, a by-product of the contested kingship of the Hundred Years War (1337–1453), when there were rival claimants to the French crown. Subsequently, a king put himself on display to build loyalty to the crown by identifying his person with the country in events such as ceremonial entries into cities. Even events specifically dedicated to the queen—her marriage, coronation, and even her funeral—underscored the king's sovereignty. The queen was thus central to state occasions, and royal family events became quasi-public during the Renaissance.

Political ideology and iconography required a woman at the king's side to complement him and thus enhance his own positive qualities. The king filled military, political, and judicial functions; the queen was pious, good, and charitable. A king earned praise for his activities; a queen, for her qualities of character. To some degree, the success of the king and queen was gauged in terms of this complementarity. Her femininity enhanced his masculinity. And Renaissance artists developed an elaborate iconography to reinforce that relationship visually. By sustaining the familial persona of the king, the queen became more central, as political theorists increasingly described royal authority in terms of the patriarchal family. As the mother of royal children, she embodied the continued stability of the realm, with attendant hopes for peace and prosperity. She retained some status after the king's death—when she might be dowager queen, queen mother, or regent for a minor son. But her most important function, both in reality and ideology, was as bearer of royal sons.

A mistress, as the sexual image of Gabrielle d'Estrées confirms, was chosen for other purposes. A king singled her out for his own happiness, generally on the basis of a sexual attraction, obvious and remarked upon by the entire court. In the mid-fifteenth century, Charles VII's initial designation of an official favorite generated a great deal of comment, much of it negative. By the seventeenth century, an official royal mistress had become conventional, almost a royal norm. By then, as long as the king dutifully fathered heirs, there were few constraints on his sexual behavior. A king's fidelity to his queen could even be considered dangerous or highly suspect. From the time of the first officially designated royal mistress, a king's extramarital sexual activity could point to his virility, perhaps indicating that he was manlier than ordinary men. The mistress, whom a king selected for sexual pleasure or love, buttressed his masculinity. Her beauty sanctioned his choice, even if she provoked criticism.

The two introductory images convey something significant about the positions of queen and mistress, but they by no means tell the whole story. They lead one to expect that the royal mistress's role was always narrowly sexualized and the queen's strictly formal and equally narrow. One might assume that the two positions remained sharply distinct and that neither allowed women to operate outside these stereotypes. But the history of France from the mid-fifteenth until the seventeenth century suggests otherwise. During this period, powerful and influential queens and mistresses defied these expectations as well as established gender roles. They challenged overtly emerging patriarchal notions of monarchy as well.

Queens exercised political power under a variety of circumstances. The absence of men, at war, for example, opened up opportunities for women, sometimes in legally sanctioned regencies. Some royal women inherited and ruled their own territories. The widowed mother of a minor son often controlled land and wealth until his majority, usually at the age of fourteen. Weak men also created openings for royal women: Isabeau of Bavaria ruled when Charles VI was debilitated by madness, and Catherine de Medici, during her sons' minorities. Although stronger kings sometimes made less room for women in public arenas, strong women took advantage of every opportunity. Anne of Brittany, for example, promoted a political and diplomatic agenda because her husband made a public space for her, as Henry II did for his mistress Diane de Poitiers. In addition to occasions for direct political control, royal women—wives, daughters, sisters, mothers, and sometimes mistresses—were commissioned to carry out sensitive diplomatic missions.

Royal mistresses too were politically important, sometimes simply inspiring a king and reinvigorating a monarchy, other times taking more direct action. A king's close, personal relationship with his mistress sometimes made her his most important advisor. She might then exercise a greater effect on policy than his minister. She might also hold an official position, on the royal council, for example, or undertake political or diplomatic missions. The queen's political actions were often controversial, but a mistress's were even more unconventional and disconcerting. She not only destabilized the royal family but also, by inserting her supporters into a clear hierarchy, violated normal routes of noble advancement and thus disrupted the social and political order. Selected to serve personal purposes, a royal mistress nonetheless sometimes carved out a distinctive place in French history or even defined a king's reign.

Both queens and mistresses shaped Renaissance culture as well. Queens had great wealth at their disposal and used it to promote the arts and patronize artists. With patronage to dispense, mistresses too attracted intellectuals and artists and left an important legacy in Renaissance arts, texts, and artifacts. Women fostered Renaissance arts to a degree not sufficiently acknowledged. Just one telling example: The "Francis I wing" of the royal chateau of Blois was carried out under his wife Claude's direct supervision.

Thus queens did not remain confined to formal, ceremonial, and familial activities. Each queen shaped and adapted her position in a variety of ways. She married into a different situation, adapted to it, and modified it in ways that make her story worth telling. Nor did mistresses simply remain central to a king's private life; instead they regularly escaped from the sexual box to which they might have been consigned. Usually less conventional figures, mistresses were held to less rigid standards of behavior than queens. They could, especially when encouraged by the king, exercise broader social and political functions and place their personal qualities and interests on display. They had license to demonstrate great flair, both as patrons and models of the new Renaissance arts.

This book deliberately treats queens and mistresses together. It might seem an unwarranted blurring of categories to discuss the legally constituted queen and the sexually alluring mistress together, but this approach has several advantages. First, as noted, neither queen nor mistress remained confined to her expected role. Second, by discussing them jointly one can more completely consider the period from 1444 to 1599, where treating one or the other would offer a fragmented account. Sometimes the queen was the most prominent female figure; other times a mistress displaced her. Sometimes the two competed; other times both were challenged by other royal women—a mother or sister, for example. Third, the queen and the mistress occupied complementary positions: The queen had legitimate authority, while the mistress exercised power only through the king's favor; the queen was often foreign, while the mistress was almost always French; the queen had a sanctified marriage, tying her to morality and tradition, whereas the mistress's relationship was illicit and thus morally problematic; the queen was frequently dismissed as dull and unattractive, but the mistress was praised as beautiful and glamorous. Fourth, their lives were intertwined and lived in tandem to a surprising degree. Both not only had their public positions circumscribed by their relationship with the king but also shared a family life. If queen and mistress were both of childbearing age, they often bore children at the same time, and those children were then reared together. Even if a king was intensely involved with his mistress, he might nonetheless father legitimate children. Charles VII, reportedly besotted by his mistress, continued to produce legitimate offspring. Diane de Poitiers may have been the love of Henry II's life, but he fathered ten legitimate children and at least two illegitimate children by other women. The mistress frequently helped to rear royal children. Both the queen and the mistress belonged to the same tight social network of the royal court and sometimes worked together. Their common endeavors and shared interests complicate the traditional view, which reduces them to jealous rivals for a king's affection. Finally and most importantly, the designation of an official mistress created new relationships within both the royal family and the monarchy—with novel possibilities and permutations for the power structure, the status of women, Renaissance culture, and subsequent historical interpretation of the period. Women did not reign, but Renaissance kings consistently placed significant women at the head of the French state; which woman played that role varied from reign to reign.

These women's activities in politics, public life, and the culture of the day raised questions for their contemporaries and provoke us to examine the extent of that influence. These questions became particularly pressing for kings unremarkable for their abilities. But most importantly, during the fourteenth century, it had been contended and confirmed, in what came to be called the Salic law, that no royal daughter could inherit the crown and that no male heir could claim the crown by virtue of his descent from a royal daughter. That judicial argument was reinforced by many traditional claims of women's physical and mental weakness. If a mad king, like Charles VI, ceded power to the queen, or if the uninspiring Charles VII was goaded to action by his mistress, did women then control France? And if so, what did that say about the monarchy or France?

This book considers such questions by treating a set of royal women—from the designation of Agnès Sorel as official mistress in 1444 to the death in 1599 of Gabrielle d'Estrées, the mistress Henry IV promised to marry. It thus covers the period of the Renaissance construed broadly.

The Renaissance is best known from its development and manifestation in Italy. There it emerged in the late fourteenth century as city-states gained political and commercial vitality, requiring a more-literate and educated workforce and thus opening up new demand for notaries, scholars, diplomats, and bureaucrats. The artists and scholars, inspired by ancient texts and models, produced innovative arts and pathbreaking humanistic texts, their work supported by cities, religious orders, and wealthy citizens. New ideas rooted in both the classics and the greater economic and cultural opportunities for educated men gave rise to a renewed sense of the possible and inspired—as Jacob Burckhardt put it in his magisterial work *The Civilization of the Renaissance in Italy*, first published in 1860—the development of the individual. Burckhardt saw this new appreciation of the individual reflected most dramatically in distinctive manifestations of male culture—tyrant, military adventurer, artist, humanist.[6] The rediscovery of many previously unknown Greek and Roman texts reinforced this appreciation, revealing what man had accomplished in ancient times, raising the bar of human accomplishment higher for the Renaissance, and distinguishing its renewed sense of human possibility from its medieval past.

Burckhardt's iconic understanding of the Renaissance has been amplified, modified, and challenged by succeeding generations of scholars. Particularly significant for this book is the question posed by Joan Kelly-Gadol in her provocative article "Did Women Have a Renaissance?"[7] While she accepted that the Renaissance had opened up the world for men, Kelly-Gadol denied that women had benefited. Instead, she contended, women's lives became more constrained as the large kin-based family of the Middle Ages evolved into the nuclear family, with less protection for women, as the freedoms of courtly love were restricted by the patriarchal family and as jurists used precedents they found in Roman law to reduce women's legal status. While Kelly-Gadol's provocative question is still debated, much scholarship has corroborated her negative response, detailing, in particular, the ways classical texts at the heart of the Renaissance extolled a more sexually segregated model of public life than the medieval court.

This book answers Kelly-Gadol's question in the affirmative, but only for French women of the court. This is less arbitrary than it perhaps seems. One would not want to suggest that the average woman, any more than the average man, had a Renaissance. But the queens and mistresses as profiled in this book were sufficiently empowered by the new cultural movement to act in the political and cultural arenas. They did so not simply because their royal consorts allowed them to do so but also because of the distinctive character of the French Renaissance, most importantly its locus in the courts. Unlike its Italian counterpart, the French Renaissance did not unfold in the public sphere of the city, where women were generally unwelcome, but rather in the royal court, where they became increasingly important. Women may not have had a Renaissance, but these particular elite women played a crucial role in defining a distinctive French Renaissance.

As the Renaissance moved from Italy into the countries of northern Europe, it took a distinctive form in each of them. France, like other northern monarchies, was not receptive to the more representative forms of government of Italian city-states but rather adapted elements of the Italian Renaissance to its particular setting. French humanists focused far less on political philosophy. The classics served less as models of political engagement than they had for Italian scholars. Instead, in the French context, classical texts and artifacts provided a new, sophisticated frame of reference in allusion and symbol and offered rhetorical and stylistic models to be emulated and adopted. The French Renaissance did not spurn its medieval heritage as decisively as the Italian Renaissance had but rather grafted new cultural manifestations onto its traditions of courtly love and chivalry. Endorsed by the ruling elite, advanced by the crown, and located in the royal court, this Renaissance, socially narrower than its Italian counterpart, did not bring new groups to power and thus was less socially or politically iconoclastic. The crown continued to rely on traditional sources of its authority—its status as "most Christian" and its venerable connection to Roman law and feudalism, for example—but deployed new Renaissance arts to bolster those claims.

The arts in France grafted innovations onto the medieval Gothic, again connecting the traditional to the novel. But this fusion became more distinctive over time, as new artistic and literary forms—the Fontainebleau school of painting and the essays of Montaigne, for example—defined a characteristically French Renaissance. Ultimately French courts later set a model of new and effective uses of the arts and court ceremonies for later Italian princes to emulate.[8] Situated in elite court society, the Renaissance in France offered a new model of noble life as refined and cultured. Baldassare Castiglione's phenomenally successful *The Book of the Courtier* had described this new model of male and female elite behavior for the princely court of Urbino. This work was published in 1528 after many of the Italian states had evolved from republics into monarchies. And by the mid-sixteenth century, Italian humanism had narrowed its focus to scholarship, particularly philological studies, rather than to civic culture. But humanist political philosophers particularly appreciated Plato's idealized philosopher-king. This form of humanism, rooted in court culture and Platonic philosophy, came to be called courtly humanism and was ripe for export to the monarchies of northern Europe. The French court readily absorbed this strain of the Italian Renaissance and adapted it to its own context. But Castiglione puts us mid-Renaissance and gets ahead of the story.

In 1444, when this history begins, there were only glimmers of the Renaissance in France, although the movement was already well established in Italy. Charles VII (1422–1461)[9] was intrigued by Italian arts and goods, but the Hundred Years War kept his focus on the north and depleted his treasury of any funds to support the arts. (Charles's powerful uncles, rather than the king, cultivated the arts of northern Europe and began to acquire Italian goods.) Charles was too preoccupied with warfare to pursue the conquest of Italy, which in essence brought Renaissance arts to France during the reign of his grandson Charles VIII (1483–1498). Nonetheless, there were some early fifteenth-century intimations of the Renaissance. Greek and Roman texts with Renaissance commentaries began to filter into France and spread the ideas of the intellectual movement we call Renaissance humanism. Equally significant, the mid-fifteenth century marked the resolution of the Hundred Years War. This crucial turn in French fortunes made possible the beginnings of economic recovery and cultural development characteristic of the Renaissance. Peace allowed the monarchy to centralize power and reoriented French culture toward the monarchy and away from it rivals, the powerful dukes who had dominated during the Hundred Years War. (French historical periodization, recognizing this pronounced shift, begins the modern period here, as opposed to "contemporary," post-Revolutionary history.) Charles's designation of a royal favorite in 1444 allowed Agnès Sorel to exert the cultural influence that later Renaissance mistresses exploited more fully. Her selection not only put a woman into an influential and potentially powerful position in the French monarchy but also presented her in new ways that became increasingly significant over the course of the Renaissance.

The Renaissance was in full bloom in France when Protestant ideas emerged in the early sixteenth century. As a result, the French Renaissance was complicated by theological dissent, which increased over the course of the century. The second half of the sixteenth century was thoroughly blighted by religious warfare. War cast such a pall over more-secular cultural accomplishments that it is hard to associate the period with glorious artistic accomplishments of the Renaissance. Nonetheless, the Renaissance continued to develop despite war's pernicious effects. Catherine de Medici put an Italian imprint on French culture, introducing comedic theater, ballet, and Italian cuisine, the basis of what we now consider French cooking, for example.

When this story begins, France was not simply weaker; it was not even geographically recognizable as France. The domain of the French king was small and fragmented (fig. i.2). The king was territorially and politically weak and threatened throughout the Hundred Years War by strong dukes and the king of England. So too was it difficult to have any notion of France as a nation: Its frontiers were not demarcated; it had no common language or legal system. By 1599, when this book ends, France had a legal system, an established language, and nearly its modern boundaries.[10] It had also benefited from one hundred and fifty years of political and economic development, despite the setbacks of foreign and religious wars. Its king was committed to extending his control through military, bureaucratic, and fiscal means and was able to do so.

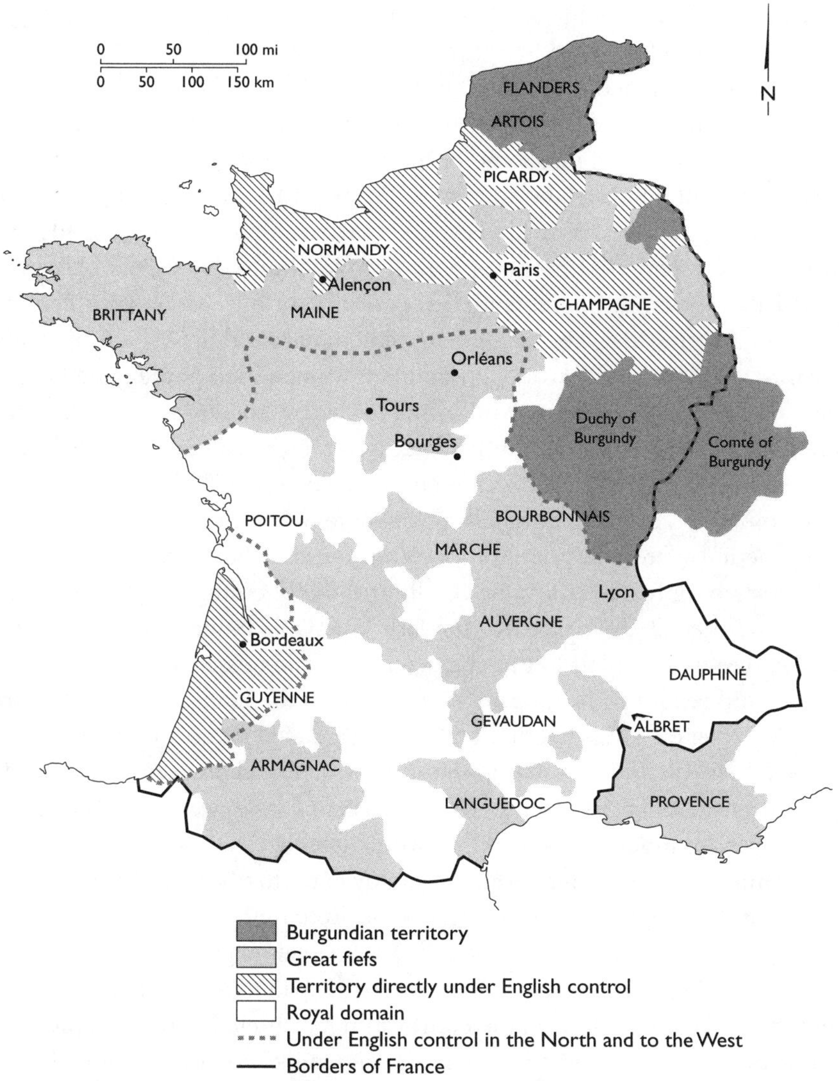

Fig. i.2. Map of French domain, ca. 1430, shows extent of the royal landholdings and of English control and influence, as well as the great fiefs. William L. Nelson.

The period treated in this book thus saw the immense transition from one of the weakest points of the French monarchy's power during the Hundred Years War to one of the strongest that emerged in the aftermath of the Wars of Religion. It begins when Charles VII was still trying to assert his claim to the throne and ends just as Henry IV had consolidated his. Charles VII relied on the messianic figure Joan of Arc to salvage his reign and on his mistress, Agnès Sorel, to enhance his image.

The date 1599 marks not only the death of Henry IV's mistress Gabrielle d'Estrées but also the year Henry took full control as king. He held the crown securely enough to promote some of the developments we associate with the centralization of politics, labeled as absolutism, and with the royal production of culture that fostered French classicism. Henry's reign consolidated royal power before a period of French political and cultural dominance. He inaugurated the powerful, bureaucratic French state of the seventeenth century, which would bring to power such preeminent ministers as Sully, Richelieu, and Mazarin, and equally noteworthy, prominent women such as the queen-regent Marie de Medici and the powerful mistress Madame de Pompadour, but they were forced to maneuver within the strictures of more centralized politics and culture. And Henry's legendary status emphasized explicitly his staunch masculinity, completely and appropriately devoid of female influence.

The period of recovery, expansion, and consolidation after the Hundred Years War not only made possible the flourishing of culture we associate with the Renaissance, it also proved particularly amenable to the influence of royal women, due in large part to the character of the Renaissance monarchy. The political and economic revitalization at the end of the Hundred Years War produced a greater openness to other cultures and generated the revenue necessary to cultivate the arts so essential to the Renaissance and often supported by female patrons. Perhaps as importantly, Renaissance kings were less constrained by bureaucracy and protocol than they would later become, which also allowed royal women to take greater advantage of any opportunity available to them.

The royal court, the venue in which the Renaissance emerged in France during political and economic expansion, was a locus of government somewhat more open to women (even if their active participation was always contested). Neither scholarly nor clerical, the court was not restricted to men, as medieval universities and Italian Renaissance academies and civic institutions had been. In a social hierarchy dominated by the hereditary nobility, the court functioned both as a forum of government and culture and as a site of the king's private, public, and political life. Kings recognized that they could assert greater authority and control over the nobility through the court and that the women of the court could enhance their image. The French Renaissance court—center of royal family life, governance, and high culture—created a more extensive public space for women and new opportunities for them to act.

Their exercise of power was often effective, their cultural roles significant, but every strong, active woman raised fears of a weakened monarchy. By the early seventeenth century, the concentration of power in the monarchy and control of the arts in male-dominated academies made it more difficult for women to play central intellectual and cultural roles. Exceptional queens and mistresses of the seventeenth and eighteenth centuries did so but against a well-developed tradition of opposition to politically engaged women. For their critics, sixteenth-century royal women presented powerful examples of the deleterious effect of women on monarchy.

Certain women—among them those featured in this book—played a fundamental part in delineating the Renaissance in France. Despite the best efforts of their contemporaries to thwart them or of subsequent writers to reduce them to romantic figures or even to write them out of history altogether, these women exercised political power and cultural influence. They did not simply *have* a Renaissance; they contributed to the new culture in such significant ways that they, as much as their male counterparts, *defined* the movement. Due in large part to their actions and accomplishments, the French Renaissance took its distinctive shape. The court's centrality and women's status in it made the French Renaissance more distinctively feminine than its Italian counterpart. Elite women—queens and mistresses in particular—were far better placed to advance this new cultural movement than were elite women in Italian city-states.

As we will see, the court setting also gave women distinct opportunities to promote their own agendas and to shape politics and culture. Agnès Sorel, the first officially acknowledged royal mistress, enhanced the sophistication of Charles VII's court and brought "new men" to power. As queen of France, Anne of Brittany insisted on propriety in her court and used it to mold elite women. During Francis I's reign, the court became more accessible to women, both politically and culturally. Henry II, his queen, and his mistress used a full array of Renaissance media both to enhance their own status and to present the monarchy in a favorable light. And Catherine de Medici, throughout the reigns of her sons, tried to use the court to consolidate power, forge loyalty to the crown, and build a cultural and political consensus. As the monarchy increased in power and wealth, the royal court became more important as a cultural venue, especially since Renaissance arts could be deployed so effectively to present the king and burnish his image. As patrons, models, and producers (of literary arts), queens and mistresses also deliberately and constructively used the arts to enhance their own status. Their imprint on the patrimony of France is evident in the artistic legacy of the Renaissance.

Historians of this period have generally focused on the rise of the monarch—his ministers, his politics, his wars. The Renaissance court has been less appreciated as the vehicle for the consolidation of royal power, and women's impact on it has been especially neglected. The model of Louis XIV's court—an obvious and compelling example of centralizing power—has cast the earlier period into relative obscurity. When the court is placed in the forefront of Renaissance culture, the centrality of royal women to the dynamic of power becomes more obvious. Their importance in defining the French monarchy and the character of the French Renaissance is made explicit. Each of the women treated in this book used her status somewhat differently, but each contributed to Renaissance culture, exerted a marked political and cultural influence, and inaugurated or modified public roles for women.

Each royal woman's life tells a particular yet revealing story within this larger history. As the first mistress with a public position to rival that of the queen, Agnès Sorel, the focus of the first chapter, set the standard for this position. It created opportunities for women to exercise power and encroach on male political power. This development took place against a backdrop of misogynistic polemics and contentious claims that women should not rule. Agnès's contemporaries used her to comment critically on the startling appearance of women in unexpected positions and to raise questions about the monarch, his relationship to both queen and mistress, and the nature of monarchy itself. Agnès occupies an enduring, if often romanticized, place in defining the monarchy and in interpreting French history.

Anne of Brittany, the subject of the second chapter, offers an example of the obstacles even an astute, territorially rich queen could face. Heiress to Brittany, Anne was the proposed bride for many different princes. Her marriage was deemed the best means to resolve the long-standing Breton-French conflict and save her duchy from the predations of war and military conquest. But it was ultimately intended to allow the French king to annex the duchy. As a result, her marriage contract with Charles VIII specified that if he predeceased her, she would marry the next claimant to the throne so that France could retain Brittany. Anne thus married two successive French kings and spelled out different contractual relations with each of them. In her first marriage, she had only a modest political role; in her second, she was powerful enough to pursue independent policies. Anne's many pregnancies, stillbirths, and miscarriages illuminate issues of fertility, childbearing, and maternal health, which shaped the lives of all Renaissance women but were more politically significant for a queen and often more physically dangerous. She also provides a striking example of the ways a queen could shape culture through her patronage of the arts.

The court of Francis I (1515–1547) epitomizes the full-blown realization of the Renaissance in France and vividly demonstrates the expanded activities of women in this setting. The third chapter features six women central to his reign. His mother, Louise of Savoy, acted as his regent and was so significant in his domestic and foreign policies that, in essence, she ruled with him during the first half of his reign. His sister, Marguerite d'Angoulême, was prominent at his court as his advisor and emissary and, in her own right, as a peer of the realm and as queen of Navarre.[11] She attained distinction both as a literary figure and an early supporter of new religious ideas. Both of Francis's queens, first Claude de France and then Eleanor of Austria, were background figures, who served traditional but important dynastic and diplomatic purposes and acted in those arenas. Francis designated two official mistresses, who often fulfilled the queen's public duties. Françoise de Foix was his partner in an idealized romantic relationship. Anne de Pisseleu, leader of a court faction, was a pivot of political power in the last fifteen years of Francis's reign.

Diane de Poitiers, Henry II's mistress and the subject of the fourth chapter, remains the most romanticized royal mistress, largely because she was so adept at using the arts to construct her image. The classical goddess Diana the Huntress became virtually synonymous with her. Over the course of Henry's reign, the court participated in the ritual reenactment of their romance, for that relationship in many ways shaped and elevated his reign. Shortly before Francis I's death, Diane and Anne de Pisseleu divided the court into two factions. Diane's case urges us to consider the royal mistress as a patroness of the arts and as a fundamental figure in the development of party politics, the construction of a monarch's myth, and the production of the lasting cultural legacy of his reign.

Catherine de Medici, the focus of the fifth chapter, is certainly one of the most controversial and powerful of French queens, even though, while her husband Henry II was alive, she was eclipsed by his mistress. Once widowed, Catherine became the powerful figure behind the thrones of her three sons, each of whom ruled during the period of the French Wars of Religion (1562–1598). Catherine tried to preserve the French crown by reconciling all groups to its authority in the face of religious and political divisions, with limited success. The Saint Bartholomew's Day Massacre, which decimated French Protestant leaders, has cast a dark shadow over her reputation. To some degree, the vituperation heaped upon her must be set in the context of the vociferous opposition to powerful, political women who violated norms of female behavior. Even though she was merely the figure behind the throne for the thirty years her sons reigned, Catherine was nonetheless one of the most powerful women of the sixteenth century.

Marguerite de Valois, the passionate and sophisticated daughter of Catherine de Medici and Henry II, is the focus of the sixth chapter. According to legend, she took lovers from all social ranks and thus flagrantly compromised sixteenth-century standards of appropriate female behavior. She was queen of Navarre and then queen of France by her marriage to Henry IV—although by the time he became king, she had clearly been shunted aside. Her marriage, intended to conciliate Protestants and Catholics, instead epitomized the political and cultural chaos of the second half of the sixteenth century, replete with religious conflict, shifting alliances, and sexual and political betrayal. Her wedding celebration was the occasion of the massacre of her husband's Protestant wedding guests. This inauspicious start foreshadowed the course of the marriage, which was eventually annulled. Even though Marguerite's sexual exploits were much exaggerated in her myth, her story affords an opportunity to explore the relationship between sex and politics in elite circles. Her legend has distorted her history by excluding her serious intellectual interests and undervaluing her political activities. Marguerite offers a compelling example of Renaissance self-fashioning, as she repeatedly rose phoenixlike from the ashes of disaster to attain prominence again and again.

Gabrielle d'Estrées, the subject of the last chapter, was a mistress Henry IV planned to marry, but she died on the eve of the ceremony, just as he had unquestionably solidified his claim to the throne. She demonstrates the extensive political activities that a mistress who had the full confidence of the king could assume. Theirs was a working political partnership as well as a romance. Henry presented Gabrielle as an appropriate future queen and, to the consternation of many, blurred the distinction between queen and mistress. Despite all of the activities Gabrielle undertook with Henry, she was readily expunged from the historical record immediately after her death. For Henry to have shared power with a mistress did not enhance his emerging legend. So in subsequent histories, Gabrielle was relegated to one of many women who merely attracted his sexual interest.

Each chapter focuses on a woman or a set of women. But each woman joined her life to that of a particular king, and her story must be set in his context as well. The issues a king faced largely circumscribed a royal woman's opportunities, which depended as well on his willingness to allow her to undertake them. And Renaissance kingship was fluid enough to be shaped by each particular king. As a result, there is great variety in the particular manifestations of Renaissance monarchy and its openness to women.

To attain her position, a queen or mistress often displaced another woman: A mistress frequently challenged a queen, and a queen sometimes came to power when another queen was set aside or exercised power after challenging a royal sister or mother. Women also wielded power through the female networks they cultivated. Thus royal women will be discussed in relation to other powerful women. Each chapter thus tells a somewhat different tale shaped by the particulars of the woman's relationship to a king, her distinctive opportunities, and the uses she made of them.

This book does not trace a progressive trajectory in the status of queens, mistresses, or women more generally. One cannot argue persuasively that queens or mistresses become stronger or that their positions evolved in a consistent direction. What ties this story together, beyond its chronological organization, is the way these women's lives and their use of their positions relate to the broader culture of the Renaissance. First, all of them benefited from the increased possibilities the relative flexibility of the Renaissance monarchy gave them. Second, they had a greater impact because the center of both politics and culture was the royal court in which queens and mistresses were central. To have an impact, these women had to act effectively within the fairly narrow social and political circle of the court. As government, located largely at court, was smaller, narrower, and closely connected to the royal family, these women had a disproportionately large influence. Third, they used the arts of the Renaissance to convey their messages to a noble elite, which was cohesive enough to appreciate their sophisticated use of images and allusions.

This book tells the story of this series of queens and mistresses through two complementary strands. It focuses first on their lives, particularly their political and cultural activities. These royal women have generally been overlooked, reduced to figures of romance, or, most often, relegated to brief mentions in conventional histories of the Renaissance. This book contends that they should be better integrated into such histories to reflect more accurately their varied and significant activities of statecraft and culture. Second is the history of how they have been used since their own day to critique the monarchy, to argue against women in power, and, in essence, to interpret the history of Renaissance France. That history begins with their effects on and contributions to the intellectual debate of their own day over the merits of women, called the "quarrel over women," and continues in their current uses in French popular culture.

Although many histories have overlooked these women, their contemporaries noted their prominence, and some complained vehemently. "The king of France is entirely ruled by women," complained the Milanese ambassador Prospero di Camulio about Charles VII's behavior. Nearly a century later, John Knox, the fiery Scottish Presbyterian leader, railed against the monstrous regiment of women—referring to the unusual spate of female rulers in the sixteenth century.[12] These complaints recognized that royal women were politically engaged, acting as advisors, diplomats, regents, and, particularly unnerving to many male commentators, even as rulers. For many of their contemporaries, the preeminence of women was unseemly—signaling a weak monarch or a corrupted or even imperiled monarchy. Intellectuals debated the worth of women more generally in the vituperative "quarrel over women," which raged from the fifteenth to the eighteenth century. Fears about the exercise of power by women were particularly intense in France, where Salic law excluded women from ruling. By extrapolation, as they were unfit for rule, women should be excluded from political and public positions, or so some argued. The involvement of women in the power structure and the culture of the Renaissance inevitably raised issues in the intense debate about the nature and value of women and often made royal women targets of attacks. Paradoxically, these attacks highlighted the distinctiveness and significance of women's contributions and exposed the gender dynamic at the heart of the French monarchy—so much so that some Renaissance women have been hailed occasionally in our day as early feminists.

In their own time, queens and mistresses elicited rare praise and frequent condemnation. Historians and polemicists of various stripes from their day to ours have invoked them to comment on the monarchy. Royal women thus occupy a very peculiar historical position; they have been intensely important to ideological debates but have generally been written out of standard narratives. But their lasting ideological significance has made them important in the subsequent understanding of the monarchy and even of the modern French nation. For many of the women featured in this book, their impact on the historiography of France is as significant, controversial, and richly textured as their actual lived lives. As each chapter documents, royal women served to interpret and reinterpret French history. That interpretation has been shaped critically by subsequent claims about the appropriate roles for women in the state and thus indicates just how thoroughly subsequent commentators thought royal women violated gender norms.

Records from the fifteenth century—the beginning of the story told here—offer rather scant commentary on royal women. Chroniclers, commissioned by kings and powerful nobles to record their exploits to their advantage, rarely remarked on royal women and, when they did, were usually critical. We thus have a better idea of how fifteenth-century queens and mistresses were perceived than what they actually did. These chroniclers sometimes condemned the failings of their patrons but were more likely to blame their patrons' enemies or the women associated with them. Royal women consistently made good scapegoats: Queens could be criticized for failing to serve the kingdom well, and mistresses for corrupting the king's morals and for the bad example they set.

When a woman attained power, her contemporaries considered her potential impact. Initially, they often assessed her looks to weigh her character or even abilities—an impulse even modern biographers sometimes cannot resist. Did she seem malleable or good tempered? Even if not overtly expressed, such discussions tried to determine whether she would likely retain the king's sexual interest and, if a queen, make legitimate offspring likely or, if a mistress, reliably channel his sexuality. Contemporary discussions acknowledge as well the disruptive influence women could have on the monarchy. This preoccupation with royal looks is explained too by the fact that there were few artistic depictions of royalty and most Frenchmen would never see their king or his image. The description of royals by contemporaries might have been more significant than we imagine.

As Plato's impact on the Renaissance increased, the assumption that exterior beauty reflected internal beauty became more pronounced and descriptions of royalty even more significant. This quest to interpret royal looks was not restricted to women. Chroniclers often scathingly described the physical shortcomings of French kings. But there was undeniably a gendered aspect to physical descriptions of royal women—beauty was the sine qua non. If she was a beauty, a royal woman often provoked contemporary appreciation. A mistress's stunning beauty might excuse a king's sexual straying from the marital bed. Later royal women astutely commissioned poets to praise their physical attributes in lyrical terms. Commentators also became self-serving enough to extol a royal woman's beauty, even if it was not in the eye of any beholder. The character her contemporaries ascribed to a royal woman often set her in opposition to her male consort. Charles VII's critics, for example, indicted his passivity but praised the verve and determination of his mistress, Agnès Sorel. Contemporaries hailed Louis XII as a man of the people but condemned his queen Anne of Brittany as haughty and remote. Their contemporaries delineated the parameters of the earliest assessments of royal women. Subsequent historians and commentators either followed their lead or rebutted them.

Even if a royal woman elicited her contemporaries' praise for her looks, her character, or her appealing contrast to her male consort, any political action she took almost inevitably provoked criticism. Only a queen like Francis I's first wife, Claude de France, who largely retreated into private maternity, received unalloyed praise. A queen's foreign birth often enmeshed her in political controversies. Her new country might remain at odds with that of her birth. The Hapsburgs, for example, warred with France even after Francis I married Eleanor, the sister of his Hapsburg rival Charles V. Under such circumstances, the queen could be denounced as disloyal, her political agenda or cultural impact condemned as foreign and unwelcome. A mistress could displace men in government. All such activities were deemed inappropriate.

At the beginning of this history, the French were nearing the end of their more than hundred-year war with England. They fought to maintain a contested claim to succession, insisting that the crown could be inherited only through direct male succession. But, as we will see, despite this exclusion, royal women became central political and cultural figures in the French court. But her presence was always controversial. A woman's appearance on the political scene inevitably raised pointed questions about the weakness of any monarch who relied on or empowered her, even if a regency (a government where someone else ruled in the stead of a minor, absent, or incapacitated king) conferred legitimate political authority on her.

The end of the Hundred Years War coincided with the advent of printing, which made possible the production of a larger number and greater array of texts commenting positively and negatively on kings and the women associated with them. New Renaissance literary forms were somewhat more inclined to portray royal women in a positive light, often as a deliberate strategy. Poets became fixtures at court, commissioned to produce lyrical portrayals of their patrons. With increasing skill, royalty began to use all media available to them—paintings, tapestries, pageants, festivals, music, and literature—to promote a positive image. The writings and artistic works commissioned by queens and mistresses became increasingly significant to their contemporary image and cultural legacy. Royal women deployed patronage to enhance their images just as effectively as their male counterparts did.

Stories circulated about royal women. The sixteenth-century biographer of the lives of women, Pierre de Bourdeille, lord of Brantôme, told some of the most enduring. Born in 1540 into an illustrious noble family, Brantôme followed the French court for more than thirty years as a man of letters. His work reported stories told in the court before his time (likely part of the lore of his family members who served the court) and those he heard firsthand.[13] His stories, which allowed immediately succeeding generations to peek into celebrity lives, remain some of those most consistently told about royal women's lives. His stories have thus proved especially significant in establishing and anchoring their historical reputations.

Even when these women were consigned to the distant past, they remained polemically useful. By the sixteenth century, attacks on fifteenth-century royal women had already become an effective way to indict a current monarch, as historians looked to the past to explain the weakness of their rulers. A former king and the women associated with him could be held up as a positive or negative model for a current monarch. How one portrayed royal women significantly shaped how one assessed particular kings and, by implication, the nature of the monarchy, the appropriate position of women in society, and beliefs about gender relations and moral issues.

In the sixteenth century, political polemics became even harsher as religious issues sharpened attacks on the monarch and the women associated with him. The almost four decades of religious warfare produced a culture of libel, sexual innuendo, and scurrilous attacks. And women, generally more associated than men with sexual failings in the Western tradition, were especially vulnerable to such attacks and increasingly targeted. Protestant commentators not only were more censorious about sexual morality, they also understood that attacking a king's morals undermined his authority, especially over questions of religion. They focused explicitly on royal women because Catherine de Medici was either the regent or the power behind the throne for most of the period of religious warfare. Protestant polemicists used the sexual indiscretions of kings and their mistresses to claim the moral high ground, arguing that the immorality of Catholic mistresses, such as Diane de Poitiers, subverted the state. A vast literature attacked the last Valois monarch, Henry III, for many forms of sexual deviance, many entirely imagined, in part because he had neither a mistress nor a politically engaged queen to be attacked in his stead. By the end of the sixteenth century, the court was more frequently in Paris, which afforded even greater opportunity for non-elites to comment critically on kings and the women associated with them. Some of the sharpest criticisms are found in Parisian texts, such as Pierre de L'Estoile's *Journal*. The polemical furor of the religious wars thus decisively shaped the subsequent historical treatment of royal women.

Even more importantly, after the ascent of the first Bourbon king, Henry IV, in 1589, Bourbon historians consistently disparaged the Valois to present a history favorable to the new dynasty at the expense of the old. These historians blamed many failures of Valois kings on the women associated with them. For example, Francis I's mother, Louise of Savoy, was held responsible for his failures, and Catherine de Medici for those of her sons.

Enlightenment *philosophes* made subversive use of royal women to attack the Church and the monarchy with wit and irreverence. Unlike some of their predecessors, the *philosophes* tended to be tolerant of or amused by royal sexual indiscretions. They used tales of queens and mistresses to shape their contemporaries' understanding of the past, particularly the monarchy, with humor and irreverence.

In contrast, nineteenth-century Romantics made their histories love stories. Romantic views of these liaisons persist, in part, because they make it possible for us to imagine the personal lives and passions of royalty. Changing notions—moral, political, and historical—help to explain why some royal mistresses, even if despised in their own day, have been subsequently appreciated or even venerated.

Many Romantic constructions were integrated into the popular nineteenth-century novels of Alexandre Dumas, which made larger-than-life sagas of monarchs, queens, and mistresses especially compelling. His novels were so successful that they took root in popular consciousness and popular education, making his stories about royal women virtually canonical. These women then became central to French history—in much the same way that Betsy Ross or Pocahontas hold iconic places in American history—places constructed more by myth than history.

Post-Revolutionary historians, on the other hand, denounced French kings but were even harsher in excoriating royal women; they found women who exercised power easy targets. Their intemperate assessments proved especially enduring in shaping the historical reputations of these women. The republic excluded women from its political culture and frequently blamed royal women for the most reprehensible aspects of the monarchy. For some post-Revolutionary historians, monarchy was a deplorable form of government but women's involvement corrupted it further. Royal women occupy an unusual interpretive position: They are praised to condemn a king but blamed to praise or rehabilitate him.

As this brief account suggests, the lives of these elite women, whether queens or mistresses, have consistently served as a canvas upon which many writers have painted some of their most cherished ideas. These women have been scapegoats, sources of inspiration, and models of virtue or depraved sexuality. They have been praised as helpmates or condemned as impediments to kings. They have been vilified or romanticized, or sometimes even romanticized into villains. But more often they have simply been passed over or written out of standard history.

The royal women featured in this book nonetheless remain enshrined in popular culture, especially in intriguing tales told about them and much enjoyed by subsequent generations. Such tales were incorporated into fictional works, and fictions in turn shaped histories. So while this book puts royal women into a narrative of Renaissance France, it also acknowledges the significance of the ways their contemporaries characterized them and historians subsequently used them.

Despite their surprisingly long and controversial lives in the historical record, these royal women have not been prominent in recent histories of women or treated by scholars pursuing social history or women's history—especially important areas of twentieth-century research. Elites were excluded from these new historical approaches largely because, insofar as women were included in histories of France before the mid-twentieth century, only elite women warranted mention. With its specific interest in recapturing the lives of women who had previously escaped notice, women's history focused on ignored groups—peasants, urban laborers, servants, and the like. Some of those writing about royal women after the French Revolution were reactionaries, hearkening back to the glories of monarchy. Such histories are tinged with hagiography or romance—qualities out of favor in serious histories.

Much of the history of women is written from a feminist perspective. Within that context, mistresses in particular are rather discomfiting subjects. Whether or not they used their feminine wiles to secure their position, they held it because of their sexual liaisons. In other words, they slept their way to the top. Nor did queens generally attain their positions because of great fortitude or qualities of mind. They were selected for the dynastic advantage they could bring to the monarch and the monarchy, an advantage due more to the accident of birth than to their abilities or efforts. Perhaps both mistress and queen have garnered so little attention in women's history because they did so little to warrant their status. Even if they surely confronted obstacles, they enjoyed the greatest privileges and resources afforded women of the day. Nonetheless, as this book contends, the relationship between a king and his queen and/or mistress exposes a fundamental gender dynamic at the heart of the French monarchy and should provoke more feminist scholarship.

But if recent histories have ignored royal women, the twenty-first century has witnessed a dramatic resurgence of interest in both the Renaissance and in biography. Renaissance scholarship sheds great light on the culture within which these women lived, and royal women have been the subjects of recent popular biographies in French as well. The appreciation of the confines and complexities of women's lives produced by women's history can be applied fruitfully to these royal women, as indeed very recent studies of both the court and queenship demonstrate. Questions of agency raised about women's lives by women's history enrich our understanding of royal women's lives as well. Although they owed their status to their relationship with the king, queens and mistresses could and did seize opportunities, act independently, carve out spheres of influence, and make a difference. A queen had opportunities by virtue of her position, but the uses she made of them, particularly the ways she overcame constraints and flouted conventions, separate the great or influential queens from those who simply occupied a place due to the status of their husbands. And the unusually public position of an officially designated royal mistress gave her extensive opportunities for self-fashioning as well. The lives of royal women enrich both our understanding of the history of women and of the French Renaissance. The following chapters put these particular elite women into a narrative of the period to both appreciate them and disentangle them from their historiography.

SIGNIFICANT DATES FOR CHAPTER 1

1403	Birth of Charles VII, February 22
1410	Birth of Agnès (by some accounts)
1415	French defeat at the Battle of Agincourt
1417	Charles becomes dauphin
1420	Treaty of Troyes denies Charles's right to kingship
1422	Death of Charles VI
	Birth of Agnès (likeliest date according to most recent evidence)
1429	Joan of Arc arrives at court
	Charles VII crowned king
1431	Trial and execution of Joan of Arc
1435	Treaty of Arras between Charles and the duke of Burgundy
1443	Record of gifts made to Agnès, including the chateau of Beauté
1444	Agnès presented as first official royal favorite by Charles VII
1450	Death of Agnès, February 9
1453	French victory in battle at Castillon ends the Hundred Years War
1456	Rehabilitation of Joan of Arc
1461	Death of Charles VII, July 22

1

Agnès Sorel

The First Official Royal Mistress

In 1444, Agnès Sorel became the first officially designated French royal mistress, when the forty-year-old king Charles VII (1422–1461) selected this extraordinarily beautiful, twenty-two-year-old young woman as his mistress. When he presented her to his court and gave her a position within it, he defined a new role for women and a new practice for French kings. This recognition not only brought Agnès into greater prominence than earlier mistresses had enjoyed but also gave her a quasi-official status. That status became common but was initially unique to France. Not all subsequent royal mistresses had an official status, but those who did had ever-greater opportunities, as the position of *maîtresse en titre,* or "titled mistress," evolved. Doubtless unintentionally, Charles's designation of Agnès had long-term ramifications, specifically for the roles of the king and queen and for their relationship. It created new opportunities for women to exercise power, ironically, when they had been explicitly excluded from ruling to settle the succession crisis of the Hundred Years War. This position also offered new ways for a king's contemporaries and subsequent historians to assess his reign.

The humanist scholar Aeneas Sylvius Piccolomini (later Pope Pius II) remarked on Charles's infatuation with Agnès: "He fell so much in love that he could not even spend an hour without her. Whether at table, in bed, at council, she was always by his side."[1] Charles's gift to Agnès of the chateau of Beauté led to her felicitous designation as "Mistress of Beauty"—a title befitting her reputation as the most beautiful woman of the fifteenth century. Blond, blue-eyed, pale and thin, with a narrow waist and high, round breasts, Agnès embodied the contemporary ideal of beauty. Her selection by a king passionately devoted to her and whom she inspired to valorous political and military feats seemingly made Agnès deserving of this elevation above others selected merely for sexual favors without such a privileged designation. Agnès has come to epitomize both a romantic love affair with a king and effective political engagement by a royal mistress.

We can only speculate about why Charles raised Agnès to such a privileged, public position: Perhaps it was simply her beauty and his infatuation; perhaps he considered her a fitting reward for his success in finally securing his throne; or perhaps he was asserting his independence from his uncle, mother, mother-in-law, and wife. Whatever his rationale, her new status allowed Agnès to set a standard for the royal mistress as a public celebrity and gave her unprecedented opportunities. Instead of being a partner in a hidden or merely private relationship, she assumed a prominent, public role.

More prominent as legend than historical personage, Agnès belongs to the history of royal mistresses, but the details of her life are less well known than those of later mistresses. Essential dates and developments of her life have been contested due to scant and contradictory documentary evidence from the fifteenth century. Chroniclers commented on her, but as they were usually clergymen attached to the crown or its opponents, they were often partisan and disapproving. Several remaining portraits of Agnès only offer enticing glimpses.

As a historical personage with clear name recognition but few concrete details to clutter a relatively blank slate, Agnès has proved irresistible to historians, artists, and poets, who have projected onto her life story widely divergent images and interpretations. She became a romantic heroine linked to a revitalized monarchy and ultimately to a French victory in the Hundred Years War. Conversely, she was excoriated as an immoral influence on the king, a woman who used her physical allure to lead him away from home, faith, and duty. Her historiography is as compelling as her biography, in part because her very presence in the monarchy was discomfiting. What, in essence, did her centrality say about the monarch and the monarchy? This new status gave a woman unusual access to a king, and his interest in her could give her power. Historical assessments range from crediting Agnès with almost complete control over Charles VII's political actions to dismissing her as important only in his personal life. Historians sometimes set Agnès in opposition to Joan of Arc, another notable woman in Charles VII's reign. If Joan's role was diminished, then Agnès's was heightened and vice versa.[2] As one historian baldly put it, "Agnès Sorel dominates the history of Charles VII's reign; Joan of Arc was but an episode."[3] Some, more comfortable with a sexual but secular inspiration for Charles VII's success than with Joan's heavenly voices, eagerly embraced Agnès as an anti-Joan.[4] But both Joan and Agnès made unconventional and discomfiting public uses of their sexuality: Joan assumed male garb and hair; Agnès put her sexual attraction on overt display with revealing clothes. For some historians, Agnès continued the liberation of France begun by Joan, although in many accounts, they were simply the most prominent of the women who rescued a feckless king. Strikingly, all these interpretations defined the monarch and his reign by them—Joan, Agnès, or both of them. Recent studies occasionally herald Agnès as a new Renaissance model of the feminine or even as an early feminist.[5]

THE HUNDRED YEARS WAR AND FRENCH SUCCESSION (1337–1435)

Agnès's prominence could scarcely have been predicted by her early life. Like many subsequent royal mistresses, Agnès was chosen as a young woman by a much older king. She had lived in youthful obscurity, while Charles had been deeply enmeshed in the political complexities of his age. His relationship with Agnès must thus be set within the context of both his long quest to wrest his crown from other members of the extended, royal family and, complex as it is, the Hundred Years War—a series of strikingly destructive wars fought between England and France from 1337 to 1453.[6]

At issue was succession to the French crown. On what grounds should competing claims to the throne be settled? What should the relationship between the crown and foreign princes who also controlled large territories within France be? The immediate and unsettling question was whether a noble with a blood claim to the French crown, who also happened to be the king of England, could claim France or whether this should be prevented at all costs.

Contested succession was the immediate provocation for the Hundred Years War. But it evolved into a fratricidal civil war and, combined with the arrival of the bubonic plague, precipitated not simply a political disaster but also an economic and demographic catastrophe. At the nadir of Charles VII's fortunes in the 1420s, when it seemed that the French claimant would not retain the kingdom, the population had declined to ten million from approximately twenty million in 1350 due to the combined devastations of war, famine, and plague. (France would not regain its prewar population for more than two hundred years.[7]) Serious though it was, Charles's political crisis thus pales in comparison to the devastation wrought during this protracted period of war.

The succession crisis emerged when Charles IV (1322–1328), the last of Philip IV's (1285–1314) sons, died without a surviving male heir (fig. 1.1). Two cousins then claimed the throne. One was Philip of Valois, the son of Philip IV's

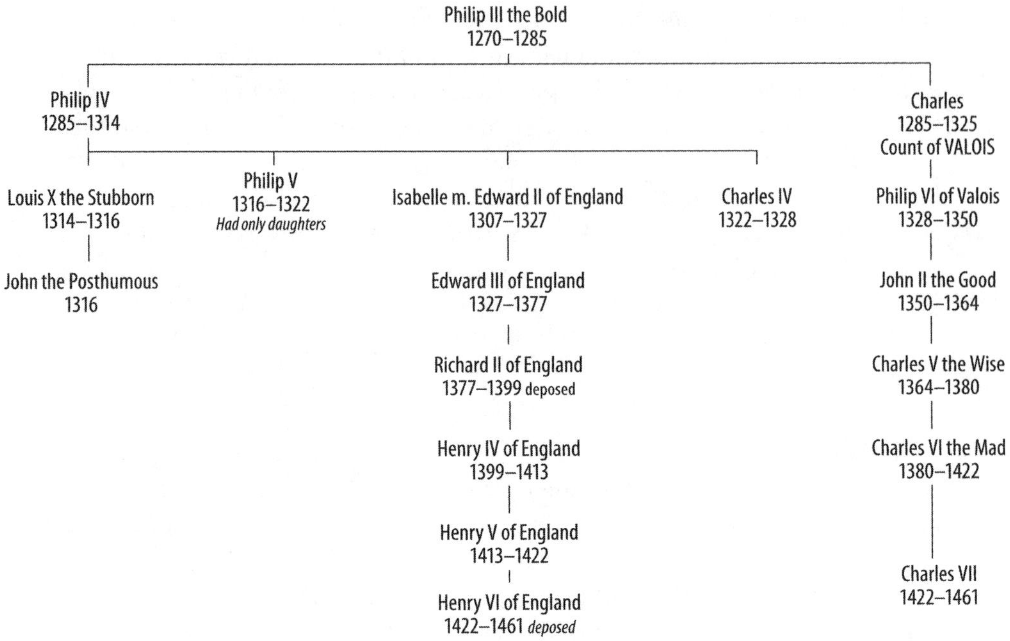

Fig. 1.1. Genealogy of contested claims to the French crown in the Hundred Years War, as the descendants of Philip the Bold, through his son Philip IV and his granddaughter Isabelle, wore the English crown and claimed France, while the descendants of his son Charles through the cadet branch (descent through a younger son) claimed France, citing the Salic law, which excluded the crown through female descent. Ian Aberle.

brother, Charles, count of Valois, and thus Philip IV's nephew. The other was Edward III, king of England, the son of Isabelle (the daughter of Philip IV), and thus Philip IV's grandson. Edward had the advantage of direct descent, which would have been respected ordinarily by the inheritance laws of both France and England. But in this case, the inheritance was the French crown and the heir was the king of England.

In response to these competing claims, French jurists insisted that the crown could not be alienated from France by descent through the female line. As the oldest and thus most venerable precedent sustained the most authoritative legal argument, jurists looked back to a legal code written for the Salian Franks at the time of Clovis (476–496) to ground their argument. This new piece of legal reasoning was explicitly designed to support the claims of the Valois (the name of the branch of the royal family now claiming the throne). But the term came to refer to a particular clause, added in 1413 by Jean de Montreuil, that distinguished male from female inheritance: Men inherited landed property, while women inherited only personal property and thus could not inherit the crown. The exclusion of women from ruling became the essential tenet referred to as the Salic law, instantly imbued with august antiquity and cited thereafter as a fundamental French law.[8]

Edward, as the son of a royal daughter, was ruled out when Parlement (the judicial branch of French government) supported Philip of Valois's claim. Although Philip was heir through the cadet branch (descent through a younger son), he was descended through a male line. He claimed the throne as Philip VI and thus inaugurated the Valois dynasty. This legal "precedent"—in this case, an argument designed to fit the existing political crisis—not only legitimated Valois claims to the throne but also reshaped the French monarchy by explicitly excluding female rule.

Claimants to the French throne during the Hundred Years War invoked or rejected this precedent. The first stage began when Edward III of England challenged Philip VI's claim. It was marked by French defeats at Crécy and Poitiers, where Philip's son, the next Valois claimant, John II the Good (1350–1364), was taken prisoner. This stage was settled in 1360 by the Treaty of Brétigny, whereby Edward attained almost one-third of French territory, including the large and wealthy province of Aquitaine, but ceded his claim to the French crown.

Charles V (1364–1380), the next Valois family standard bearer, had by the end of his reign successfully reasserted royal authority and recouped virtually all of the land formerly ceded to England. But these positive developments were completely undermined when his brothers challenged his twelve-year-old son and successor Charles VI (1380–1422), inaugurating the next long stage of the Hundred Years War. This stage was marked by fratricidal civil war, as first Charles VI's uncles, then his brother and cousins, and finally his nephew and all their supporters perpetuated the conflict, often allying with the English to undermine his claim (fig. 1.2).

Charles VI ultimately reasserted control but then suffered a severe mental breakdown (1392), during which he attacked his brother and killed five men before he was subdued. (Modern historians attribute his periods of madness to paranoid schizophrenia.[9]) The king's incapacity exacerbated tensions among feuding nobles and reignited civil war for control of the monarchy between two princes of the blood—Louis of Orléans, the king's younger brother, and John the Fearless, duke of Burgundy and cousin to both Louis and the king.[10] As their contest dragged on without a decisive victory, John determined to assassinate his rival. In 1407, his agents killed Louis as he left the queen's apartments. John admitted complicity but claimed he had acted only to prevent Louis's

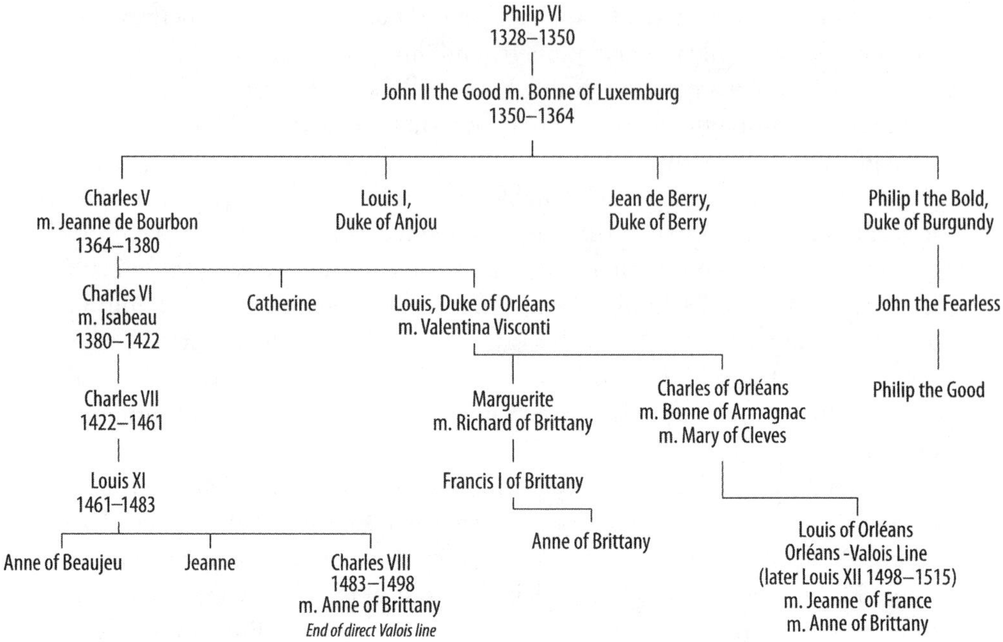

Fig. 1.2. Genealogy of Armagnac-Burgundian-Valois factions in the Hundred Years War. Ian Aberle.

treason. Louis's son, Charles, then allied with a faction of the Valois family led by Count Bernard VII of Armagnac (who was also Charles's father-in-law) to seek revenge and retain power. The two factions, Burgundians and Armagnacs, warred for control of France while Henry V of England reasserted his claim to France. At the Battle of Agincourt in 1415, he effectively pressed that claim with an overwhelming victory. From that time on, the English occupied much of France.

When Charles VI died in 1422, it seemed highly unlikely that his son Charles VII could assert his claim to a France devastated by both foreign occupation and civil war. The situation would have been a challenge for any nineteen-year-old prince, and Charles was not a compelling candidate for successful kingship. With what seems to modern readers appalling insensitivity, chroniclers commented on his physical failings, from his protruding lips and beady eyes to his long nose (fig. 1.3). He was undersized and sallow. The short tunics he wore exposed his bandy legs and uneven gait, making him look, as one tactless contemporary noted, deformed, although he conceded Charles looked more normal in long tunics.[11] On such an unimpressive physical specimen,

Fig. 1.3. Portrait of Charles VII by Jean Fouquet. Louvre, Paris / The Bridgeman Art Library.

the hopes of the French crown rested. His contemporaries were even harsher in analyzing his character. They expressed frustration with his vacillation and inaction and detailed his neuroses, which included his fear of strangers and of floors, a fear that seemed warranted when a palace floor collapsed killing several members of his court.[12] These comments reinforced doubts about Charles's prospects for kingship; nothing about his early life inspired confidence.

Charles VII was born in 1403 to Charles VI, better known as Charles the Mad, and Isabeau of Bavaria. As the fifth son, Charles was never expected to reign.[13] At the age of ten, he was engaged to Marie of Anjou, and as a son unlikely to inherit, he was sent to live under the tutelage of his future mother-in-law, Yolanda of Aragon. His early life had been shaped by the most violent events of the Hundred Years War. Charles was just twelve years old when the Battle of Agincourt decimated the French nobility and the English conquered much of France. Just two years later (1417), Charles, as Charles VI's only surviving son, became heir to a France divided by civil war and claimed by the English king Henry V. His mother and the duke of Burgundy, John the Fearless, allied to deny his claim and to defeat the Armagnacs who supported him. In 1419, Charles was complicit in the assassination of the duke of Burgundy, carried out by Charles's emissary during a meeting under truce with the Armagnacs. Although the Armagnacs considered the unscrupulous assassination a fitting revenge for John the Fearless's role in the assassination of Louis of Orléans, Charles seems to have been crippled by guilt for his role in John's death.[14] Needless to say, this escalation of hostilities did not bode well for a peaceful resolution of the Armagnac-Burgundian civil war. Subsequently a Parisian mob allied with Philip the Good (duke of Burgundy upon his father's assassination) slaughtered the Armagnacs. One of Charles's most vivid memories must have been of fleeing Paris to escape this particularly violent episode in the ongoing civil war. His claim to the throne was jeopardized further when Philip the Good allied with the English. But it was most decisively repudiated when, on December 23, 1420, Charles VI, constrained by the powerful Anglo-Burgundian alliance, proclaimed Henry V of England as his "heir and regent" and disinherited his son, Charles, because of his complicity in the "evil deed done to John of Burgundy."[15] Then Isabeau, in lieu of her husband (likely in the grip of madness), signed the Treaty of Troyes with the English, formally repudiating her son's claim to the throne.

Charles VI spent most of his reign confined in long periods of madness, emerging periodically, as the story went, to procreate his twelve children. This happy convention may well have arisen to refute any notion that Charles and his other siblings were illegitimate, especially since Isabeau later was suspected of adultery, including an affair with her husband's brother, Louis of Orléans. A foreign queen with a husband frequently incapacitated by madness, Isabeau was an easy target for scurrilous attacks and a scapegoat for the civil wars, deflecting criticism from her husband's feuding relatives. Recent studies document her rumored infidelity as Burgundian propaganda.[16] But Isabeau bore several children, including Charles, after her husband's initial period of madness, which doubtless fueled such rumors.[17] (To establish Charles's legitimacy, the nineteenth-century historian Gaston du Fresne de Beaucourt carefully correlated Isabeau's pregnancies with the dates when the king spent time with her.[18])

Most significantly for Charles, Isabeau's assent to the treaty explicitly rejected his claim to the throne because of "his horrendous crimes" and gave three-quarters of the royal domain to the English and their Burgundian supporters. Only some provinces south of the Loire and the territory held by the Armagnac faction recognized Charles as the legitimate heir. Isabeau arranged a marriage between Henry V of England and her daughter. After Isabeau disinherited Charles, the Burgundians went so far as to proclaim that he was not his father's son but a bastard.[19] Prospects for Charles's reign could hardly have been less auspicious. He lacked money and an army. His critics attacked his legitimacy both as his father's son and as claimant to the throne.

His kingship in question, Charles remained indecisive and ineffectual. His failure to respond to these serious threats to his reign may also have reflected his own doubts about his legitimacy as his enemies spread such rumors.[20] He surrounded himself with physicians, astrologers, and various court intriguers, none of whom could galvanize him to action.[21] His lassitude in these desperate circumstances has made him an almost irresistible target of modern psychoanalytic speculation. Yet fatalistic disengagement from events and pessimism about his prospects might have seemed an appropriate response. His parents had repudiated him and denied his claim; his allies had murdered his uncle. He had good reason to fear assassination, which was becoming an expedient to dispose of rivals. And three-quarters of the kingdom was held by the English allied with his cousin Philip the Good. Although Charles inherited the title of king at his father's death, he was facetiously pronounced the "King of Bourges," the town in the Loire Valley to which he retreated—an apt indication of just how little territory he controlled and authority he commanded (see fig. i.2).

When Henry V of England died in 1422 (the same year as Charles the Mad), Henry VI, like his father before him, claimed the thrones of both England and France. But Henry, an infant under the control of the duke of Bedford, who asserted the claim on his behalf, was not a convincing claimant. Furthermore, French discontent with the Treaty of Troyes had mounted, for the English had immediately violated their professed commitment to unite the two countries and instead treated the French as a conquered people. Even so, the French, divided by long-standing enmities, could not unite to challenge the English: Armagnacs and Burgundians remained more interested in fighting each other than in defeating the English.

The next year saw the birth of Charles's son (later Louis XI [1461–1483]), a development that reinforced his line. But Charles remained unwilling or unable to press his claim to the throne. In the early years of his reign, battles between the English and the French were decided by crushing French defeats at Cravant (1423) and at Verneuil (1424), which was even bloodier than Agincourt. These defeats drove Charles into greater apathy. The difficulties of these years of disastrous warfare were exacerbated by wretched weather. Chroniclers remarked on unusual freezes, storms, and flooding, which increased human misery and heightened a sense of impending doom.[22] But a disempowered king would be rescued by an unlikely heroine.

A SUPPORTING CAST OF WOMEN

At this low point for French fortunes, Joan of Arc appeared. In 1429, she walked into the king's chamber, picked him out among his councilors, and announced, "In the name of God, gentle prince, it is you and no other."[23] This statement was taken as recognition of Charles VII's royal qualities and his legitimacy. (Joan believed that the queen had borne illegitimate children and denounced Isabeau as "her who lost France."[24]) Joan affirmed that God had sent her to drive the English out of France. Despite her determination to restore Charles's rightful inheritance, she could not reverse French fortunes immediately. Indeed, the English besieged Orléans, further jeopardizing Charles's claim.

Despite his new champion, Charles remained apathetic and disengaged. He left his government to powerful feudal nobles, who were more intent on preserving their interests and avenging the massacre of the Armagnacs than on defeating the united English and Burgundians.[25] But on April 29, 1429, Joan successfully drove the English out of Orléans. Thanks to her, Charles claimed his throne and extended French territory. On July 17, 1429, he was consecrated in Reims, asserting his political legitimacy in a public and highly significant setting. Christine de Pizan, one of the most famous late-medieval writers, rejoiced in his success in her poem *The Tale of Joan of Arc:* "In 1429 the sun began to shine again. . . . And you Charles, king of France, this proof of divine intervention . . . for it was believed quite impossible that you should ever recover your country which you were on the point of losing. Now it is manifestly yours . . . and all this has been brought about by the intelligence of the Pucelle"[26] (the "Maid," a popular appellation for Joan). Joan's success saved Charles's reign but did not empower him; as one historian put it, "Joan arrived, and he disappeared."[27]

Joan was eager to follow up on her military victories by taking Paris, but she could not persuade Charles to take this decisive step. Unable to goad him to action, a frustrated Joan went north to join the fighting, where she was captured by a Burgundian lord. She could have been ransomed or even, after she had been turned over to the English, exchanged for an English prisoner. But Charles did nothing. He had failed to support Joan's campaign to take Paris, and now he abandoned her to the English, who turned her over to the Inquisition as a heretic.[28] Tried and convicted, Joan was burned in the marketplace in Rouen on May 30, 1431.

Joan's impact on Charles is unquestionable. She delivered a besieged Orléans to him, arranged to have him crowned, and led him in a triumphal march on Paris. But Charles did not follow up on these successes; he instead retreated to the chateaux in the Loire Valley. Despite the fact that he owed his crown to Joan, he did not intervene to save her from the English army or the fires of the Inquisition. Charles, as this example strikingly demonstrates, could betray those who served him well. Although he benefited from Joan's claim that God favored the French, her success may well have led him to fear her popularity or even to question whether her loyalty was to him. Joan's demonization of the English and their Burgundian allies also frustrated Charles's desire to make peace with the latter. Joan's defiance of accepted gender roles in insisting on wearing men's clothes, as well as her peasant status, made her a discomfiting royal ally.

After Joan's death, Charles again sank into indecision and did not emerge until four years later, likely as a result of the Treaty of Arras of 1435, which finally reconciled the Burgundians to the crown. Charles then waged war successfully against the English, took Paris, and, in 1444, settled the noble revolt against him with the Treaty of Tours.

Joan was just one of the powerful women who supported Charles. His early life story relegates him to a supporting role in a play dominated by powerful women. His mother was a key figure in Charles's youth, and she negotiated away his birthright. His mother-in-law, Yolanda of Aragon, took charge of him when he was just ten years old and gave him an education superior to that of most princes of the time. An able politician in her own right, Yolanda not only governed Anjou but also played a significant role in France, fostering Charles's claim to the throne. She brought aid to the besieged city of Orléans and took on the mission of demonstrating Joan's virginity.

Charles's queen, Marie of Anjou, might have been expected to play a more prominent role than she did. The daughter of Yolanda of Aragon and Louis II, duke of Anjou, Marie was engaged to Charles at ten and married him in 1422, when she was eighteen and he was nineteen. Marie has attracted scant historical interest, and she does not seem to have garnered much appreciation from her husband, despite the fact that she was a paragon of dynastic duty, bearing fourteen children. Contemporaries failed to acknowledge this prodigious fertility, commenting instead on her lack of beauty and charm and on her dull, pious court. One contemporary remarked scathingly that Marie "had a face which even scared the English."[29] Charles, perhaps understandably by these accounts, neither loved nor was inspired by her. Others, more sympathetically, commended Marie's resignation to her fate as a neglected wife in the interest of domestic harmony.[30] Most chroniclers, no doubt taking their cues from Charles, focused on his relationship with his mistress, although several chided him for neglecting his queen.

Negative comments about queens—as dull and unable to maintain the interest of their husbands—were likely intended, at least in part, to justify this new position of designated favorite, which put another woman into many of the queen's roles. Agnès, for example, would assume Marie's public functions, relegating her to a narrowly maternal role. After Agnès's death, when the king again reverted to debauchery, Marie presided over a lively court at Chinon and fostered the arts, suggesting that she likely warranted greater appreciation than she received.[31]

Accounts depicting Charles as the feckless pawn of one powerful woman or another are compelling. What we know of his character and early reign make such images credible. His contemporaries acknowledged that he was without great intelligence, power, or fortune; he was neither handsome nor appealing.[32] The portrait of Charles as king by Jean Fouquet, which hangs in the Louvre, seems to corroborate his contemporaries' low expectations and certainly depicts his lack of physical grace and charm (see fig. 1.3). Charles wears a large red velvet robe with a fur collar and cuffs. On his head sits a crown-shaped fur hat; his hands rest on a cushion; and he is framed by velvet drapery. His face presents an uninspiring picture of complete dejection: His small eyes are framed by the large bags under them; his nose is long, his lips large, and his expression morose. Strikingly, the diminutive Charles disappears into his hat and robe; his hands are swallowed by his sleeves. The clothing seems designed for a larger, more impressive figure despite the legend THE VERY VICTORIOUS KING OF FRANCE inscribed on it.[33]

Indeed, speculations about Charles's physiological and psychological limitations preoccupied nineteenth-century physicians. Believers in phrenology and other external evidence of mental capacity and disease, they examined his portraits and diagnosed various mental illnesses, ranging from degeneracy to neuropathology.[34] The modern writer Gonzague Saint Bris, building on the diagnoses of Charles in such histories, offered a more Freudian explanation. He attributed Agnès's power over Charles to her intuitive understanding of the psychological damage inflicted on him in childhood and claimed that the death of his mother in 1435 allowed Agnès to "liberate him from the chains that bound him."[35] Perhaps equally important, his powerful mother-in-law, Yolanda of Aragon, died in 1442, shortly before Charles elevated Agnès to official mistress.

The dominant role that women played in Charles's life not only exposed his weaknesses as king but also called into question the very viability of the monarchy. Either he was a weak king who allowed women to dominate him or, if he sanctioned the active roles taken by strong women—Joan, his mother, his mother-in-law, and later his mistress—he had weakened the monarchy. (His son, later Louis XI, likely in response to the preeminence of women in his father's reign, allowed women no role in his.)

Charles's obvious weaknesses and reliance on others, including strong women, led his contemporaries to look for a woman behind every positive development in his reign. After all, his success in gaining his throne was directly attributable to Joan. Only some twenty years after Joan's death did Charles reopen the Inquisition, which ultimately rehabilitated her, maintaining that her aid came from God, not the devil. Even though Charles offered limited, posthumous support for Joan, his relationship to the powerful women who aided him was generally to profit from their support. He is thus known, for good reason, as "Charles the Well-Served." When a revitalized Charles emerged after the Treaty of Arras (1435), they looked for a female source of inspiration. If his mistress had inspired Charles's decisive change in policy, what did her influence say about the monarchy, especially about the unsanctioned authority of any woman and, in this case, of a mistress exerting an illegitimate political power? To ask such questions raised the loaded proposition that women controlled the destiny of France through their influence over weak monarchs. Such questions were asked when Charles not simply took a mistress but gave her an unusually privileged status.

ENTER AGNÈS

The year 1444 saw the "joyous entry," during which Charles VII publicly designated Agnès Sorel as the first official royal favorite. The ceremonial entry developed from the feudal practice of a new lord receiving the homage of his vassals. Previously such events had been celebrated with tournaments, but it became more conventional for a king to make ceremonial entries into towns.[36] By choosing such an occasion to publicly present a favorite, Charles suggested that homage to him required a similar recognition of his mistress. Indeed, over the course of the Renaissance, formal entries into cities became an ever-more-significant way for a king to convey messages, including the importance of his mistress.

While Charles's presentation of his favorite in such a public setting was novel, that is not to say that previous kings of France had been models of conjugal happiness or fidelity. French kings had chosen women other than the queen as sexual partners from the time of the Merovingians (the reigning French dynasty from ca. 457 to 751). Dagobert I (629–639) was so notorious for his many sexual conquests that his biographer did not even list them, saying that it would take too many pages, and Charlemagne (768–814) had a long succession of concubines.[37] Unless such liaisons disrupted the royal marriage or succession, they were not noteworthy. But when Philip I (1060–1108) set aside his wife to marry his mistress, he was excommunicated.

Agnès offered a different model of the royal mistress and her role: She was not a king's fleeting sexual affair but rather was a central figure in Charles's court from the time he acknowledged her until her death. She did not simply contest a king's marriage. Instead she displaced the queen from many of her roles. Agnès thus began to define what this new status of official mistress entailed for the French monarchy. Her public role exposed a new gender dynamic at the heart of the French monarchy, which she and other royal women would exploit and their critics disparage.

Chroniclers noted her remarkable presence, all of them struck by her extraordinary beauty. "The king had recently elevated a gentlewoman named Agnès and placed her in such triumph and such power that her status was comparable to the greatest princess of the kingdom," Olivier de la Marche commented, adding that she was one of the most beautiful women he had ever seen. Jean Le Clerc acknowledged that "among the beautiful, she was the youngest and most beautiful in the world." And Thomas Basin, bishop of Lisieux and a critic of Agnès, nonetheless consistently referred to her as "beautiful Agnès."[38]

The designation as official favorite gave Agnès a highly visible status. She took her place at the king's side. She lived in the chateau of Loches in the Loire Valley, appeared frequently at court, traveled with the king, and gave birth to four daughters. Agnès's designation as royal mistress provoked both her contemporaries and later historians to wonder just how significant a role she played. For some, she became the inspiration or scapegoat for virtually all events of Charles VII's reign. For others, her public role was merely symbolic and her real role simply sexual.

In the sixteenth century, Brantôme claimed that Agnès inspired the king at decisive moments, provoking him to effective actions that redefined his reign. When Brantôme wrote about Agnès, he was reporting court events before his time and perhaps recounted by female family members who were ladies-in-waiting to queens. In one of those stories, Agnès told Charles that an astrologer had predicted that she would be associated with "the most valiant king." She then threatened to leave him for the English king, his enemy in the Hundred Years War. According to Brantôme, this threat goaded Charles to unprecedented feats of valor and produced his dramatic transformation, which led to his successes and ultimately ended the war.[39] Brantôme was one of the first to suggest that Agnès's influence over the monarch displaced that of Joan of Arc and was more significant in the ultimate French victory. Because of her association with at least the timing of these policies, he called her the "Lady of Peace." As the subsequent expansion of royal power coincided with her presence at the king's side, Agnès was frequently given credit for these important developments. Brantôme may have been the first to praise Agnès's positive political presence, but her contemporaries immediately recognized that Charles's love had given her unusual access and power.

Although her contemporaries frequently acknowledged her great beauty, her unusual status, and her beneficial effect on the king, little is known about Agnès's life. She was born, probably in 1422, to Jean Soreau or Sorel and Catherine de Maignelas, members of the provincial nobility. Male family members were men-at-arms or Church office holders. Many of the Sorels, including Agnès's four brothers, ultimately served Charles VII in positions gained through their sister's influence. Her father was a squire to Charles of Bourbon, an ally of the duke of Anjou. This connection likely led to Agnès's first publicly recorded position as lady-in-waiting to Isabelle, wife of René of Anjou.[40]

While Agnès's parents no doubt hoped to foster their daughter's prospects through this connection, one wonders how they responded to her selection as royal favorite. It put a daughter in a morally compromised position, but parents might nonetheless have hoped a king would single her out. Such a distinction later became one of the most effective routes to fame and fortune for the young woman, her offspring, and her extended family. By the seventeenth century, noble families deliberately paraded their daughters before Louis XIV's roving eye in hopes of attaining the benefits of having a royal mistress in the family. Prior to Agnès's elevation, a king's sexual interest sometimes yielded a small pension for a royal mistress, but the position had previously entailed neither a prominent role at court nor a lasting impact on French history. In Agnès's case, her elevated status made her more important and her position somewhat more secure but produced few lasting financial benefits.

The question of the extent of Agnès's political role has focused largely on the historiographical debate on just how early her relationship with Charles began.

The origins of the relationship remained murky, in part because, as the official court chronicler Jean Chartier reported, the relationship was remarkable for its discretion: "The king never touched her in public below the chin."[41] Most nineteenth-century historians and Agnès's modern biographer Robert Philippe contended that the relationship began as early as 1435, which made Agnès a key proponent of the peace of 1435 with the king's Burgundian adversaries.[42] The view of others that the relationship began in 1443, just before Agnès was elevated to official royal favorite, was corroborated in 2005 by forensic anthropologists who examined her skeletal remains. Their investigations revealed that Agnès was indeed born between 1422 and 1424 (thus supporting the later date of the relationship), that she had four pregnancies, was buried with the remains of an infant, and was indeed blond.[43]

Charles likely met Agnès in 1443. That year he had recaptured Toulouse, and René of Anjou (son of Yolanda and Louis II of Anjou) and his wife, Isabelle, duchess of Lorraine, came to salute him. This was the first time Charles met Isabelle, and among her ladies-in-waiting was Agnès. The official records show her income of ten *livres*, indicating that she had a less elevated rank than most of Isabelle's ladies.[44]

Agnès's presence as of April 8, 1443, is incontrovertible. Charles left his wife, pregnant with their twelfth child, to follow her. There were indisputable signs of Agnès's favor. Charles ceded the chateau of Beauté to her. This royal chateau, inhabited by Charles's Valois forebears, was the most beautiful chateau in the Ile de France (the territory including Paris and its environs), according to the *Journal of a Bourgeois of Paris.*[45] Agnès then became a lady-in-waiting to the queen, a development that may well have occurred at Charles's request and coincided with Agnès's selection as official favorite. Charles placed her in a position where, as a member of his wife's entourage, she would be accessible to him.

By 1443 there was a marked change in Charles. During the six years that he was unquestionably and very publicly tied to Agnès, Charles was an accomplished king. The most powerful barons had accepted his authority, and peace with England was signed shortly thereafter. His effectiveness was reflected in significant administrative developments. The French crown recouped considerable territory lost during the Hundred Years War. Charles reestablished courts of justice, reordered royal finances, and reformed the administration of government. By the end of his reign, Charles, this king from whom so little had been expected, bequeathed a larger and more powerful France to his heir.

Regardless of when the relationship began, Agnès wielded influence, unconventional for a royal mistress, on Charles's character and politics, inaugurating the tradition of the politically important French royal mistress. Admittedly, those dating their association back to 1435 gave her a longer period of influence, but even those who believed she had entered into the king's life as late as 1443 praised her for transforming him. As her biographer Pierre Champion put it, Charles, "A man of forty years, full of timidity, religion, and scruples, became, near the beautiful and vivacious Agnès, another Charles, worldly, bold, and gallant."[46]

With the later date more certain, it seems likely that Agnès was as much the beneficiary as the instigator of these changes in Charles's policies and demeanor. By 1443, his situation had changed in several respects that might have allowed him to woo and win the most beautiful young woman of the day. He had some important accomplishments to his credit. The conflict between the Burgundians and the Armagnacs, which had so blighted the history of France and his own personal saga, had been resolved, and he had retaken Paris. The long, bloody, interfamily dispute known as the Hundred Years War had come to a significant resolution. (There will be one more battle for Normandy.) Paradoxically, the long period of war had increased the power and prestige of the monarchy. An external enemy had fostered a sense of national identity and promoted the monarch as a source of unity. The end of war brought formerly rebellious princes into the king's government and made the court a stronger center of government. Perhaps personally significant to Charles, he was liberated from the control of both his mother and mother-in-law by their deaths. His selection of a royal mistress entailed, at some level, a rejection of that family as he pursued a relationship based on love and sexual attraction. But whether instigator or beneficiary, Agnès has received much credit for the positive direction of Charles's reign while he was involved with her. She was another woman who contributed to his appellation as "Charles the Well-Served." France had never before had an officially designated royal mistress. But Charles had gained the love of the most beautiful woman in France and was willing to raise her to an exceptional status.

AN AMBIGUOUS POSITION

Accounts of the period in which Agnès was the acknowledged favorite, from 1444 to her death in 1450, consistently recognize her personal importance to Charles, but the question of the extent of her political power remains. She undeniably exerted some political influence in advancing men who supported her to official positions. The chronicler La Marche acknowledged that role. Lamenting that "it was the time when women produced great noise in France," he

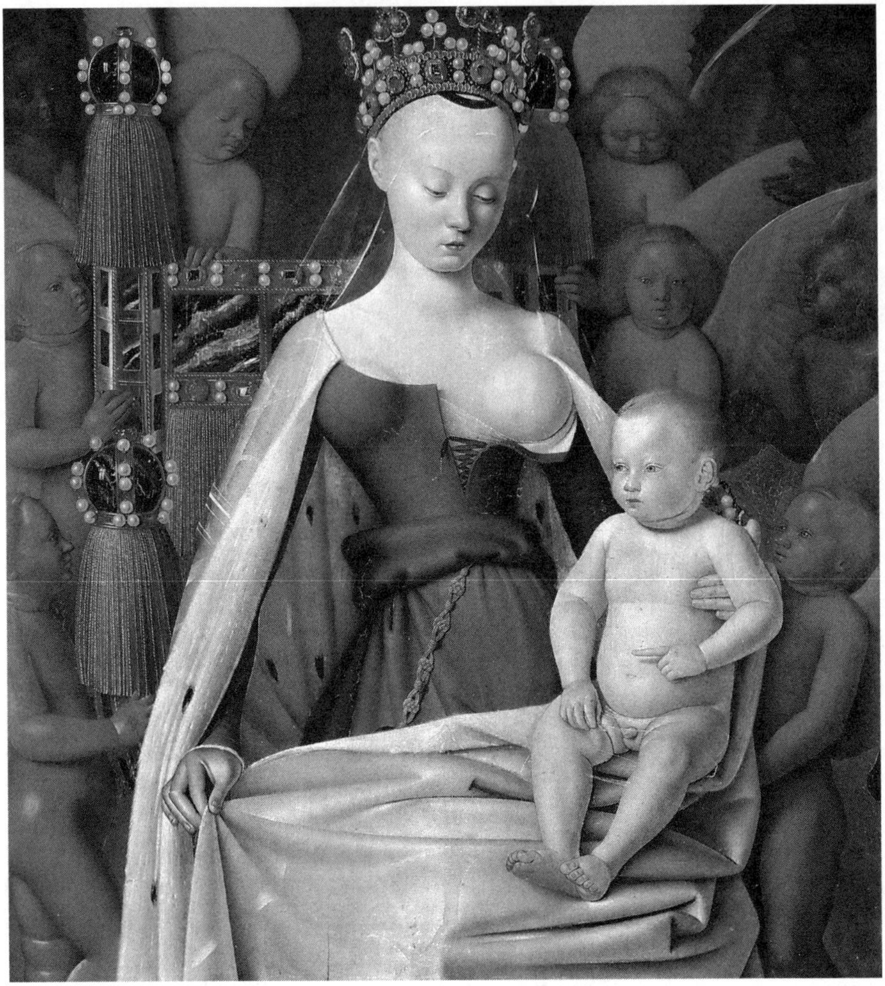

Fig. 1.4. Agnès Sorel as the model for the *Virgin Mary and Child Surrounded by Angels* by Jean Fouquet. Koninklijk Museum voor Schone Kunsten, Antwerp/The Bridgeman Art Library.

conceded that great benefits accrued to Charles because of his association with Agnès: "She advanced before the king young men-at-arms and gentlemen who ever since have served the king well."[47] Among them were Pierre de Brézé, who ultimately became royal commissioner of finance, and Etienne Chevalier, who served the king as councilor, first as ambassador to England and later as master of accounts and treasurer of France. An executor of Agnès's will, he also commissioned the famous image of her by Fouquet, who used her as his model for the Virgin Mary (fig. 1.4). Jacques Coeur, a wealthy entrepreneur with trading companies, who became keeper of the king's purse, not only used his new position to foster trade with the East to his own benefit but also deployed his personal wealth to underwrite Charles's military campaign in Normandy. Such men allied with Agnès, but their rise was contested, and the hostility they generated could tar the royal mistress as well.

Coeur's success, for example, attracted enmity. More than a year after her death he was accused of poisoning Agnès and was left to languish in prison for two years without being charged. Coeur was found guilty, not of poisoning Agnès but of treason for his financial speculations. (Kings increasingly used treason trials to consolidate their power at the expense of royal financiers.[48]) Coeur escaped from prison, sought religious asylum, became the pope's financier, and ultimately died fighting the Turks on the pope's crusade.

Coeur's example demonstrates both the problems and the opportunities an association with a royal mistress could offer. Her unconventional position allowed men of less privileged backgrounds to ally with her and thus rise to political prominence. A mistress might well attract a different sort of man, one more up-and-coming or of less-than-noble blood, who might not otherwise have attained such prominence. Agnès's relationship with these men inaugurated a pattern that later mistresses would deploy. Her status elevated them, and as their careers developed, her stature and influence increased. But their prominence provoked the traditional nobility's hostility, which was then increasingly directed at the mistress. The symbiotic relationship between Agnès and these new men undermined the traditional social hierarchy, especially within the court, and thus altered access to the king as well. Renaissance mistresses attached to the court the kind of men later kings, notably Louis XIII and Louis XIV, deliberately brought into royal service both to undermine the traditional aristocracy and to recruit able men, irrespective of social status. The court became more politically and culturally important under Charles VII, as the first official mistress made it more open and unconventional.

But Agnès did not simply foster the careers of young men who came to power due to her influence. Contemporaries, including her supporters Coeur and Brézé, who explicitly advanced this view, credited her with changing the direction of French politics toward peace and away from war. Their praise may well have advanced their own political agendas by attaching them to the royal mistress. Although her contemporaries praised Agnès as an advocate of peace, such claims, at least in part, simply recognized that the years of peace were those in which she held sway.[49]

To some degree, Agnès's contemporaries attacked her beauty for its ability to captivate the king. While all chroniclers noted the king's obvious interest, some saw her hold over him as a kind of sexual entrapment and condemned it. Contemporary critics recognized that the court not only shaped the domestic and personal life of the king but was also the primary political institution. They quite appropriately feared that Agnès's influence over Charles was not restricted to the personal. Even though Agnès is usually associated with the positive developments of peace following the long depredations of war, her contemporaries were disquieted that a woman exercised such a role or that a king's policies might be shaped by his love for a mistress.

But Agnès did not merely disrupt the political arena. Her fertility not only made her sexual relationship explicit, it highlighted the king's illegitimate sexual relationship to the detriment of the queen. While she was the designated mistress, Agnès bore four daughters; the first, born in 1444, was named Marie in honor of the queen. Marie too bore children throughout the period of her husband's relationship with Agnès. Surprisingly, in light of the many romanticized portrayals of Charles's relationship with Agnès, Thomas Basin repeated rumors of Charles's other liaisons and of Agnès's involvement with Brézé.[50] A hundred years later, likely following up on these rumors, Brantôme suggested that Charles even had reason to question whether one of Agnès's daughters was actually his.[51] Rumors of Agnès's sexual activity could discredit her and thus detract from her power. Such charges would be leveled against virtually every official mistress. They were effective because they underscored the sexual nature of her relationship and questioned her power.

Agnes's sexual relationship was evident when she attended Brézé's trial in Paris. He was compelled to answer far more serious charges of financial malfeasance, although witnesses also charged him with using Agnès to ensnare the king. He avoided condemnation for treason, largely because of the obvious support of Agnès, who attended his trial, clearly indicating that the king expected a favorable verdict. But Parisians received Agnès coolly, roundly criticizing her luxurious clothing as disrespectful of the queen. As the anonymous *Journal of a Bourgeois of Paris* reported: "There came to Paris a young lady, of whom it was publicly said that she was the *amie* [friend with a romantic connotation] of the king of France, without faith, without law, without truth to the good queen he married; and it even appears that she had great status like a countess or duchess. She came and went, often with the good queen of France, without shame of her sin, from which the queen had much sorrow in her heart."[52]

This mistress, as the *Journal* acknowledged, had undermined the queen's status by appropriating her public roles and relegating her to familial and maternal roles; Agnès was a sinner who had corrupted a king and led him away from his obligations to his family. Agnès's increasing prominence provoked not simply personal attacks or fears about her influence but also more generalized attacks on women in public life. Although some of her contemporaries praised her, Agnès inevitably tapped into the deep vein of criticism directed against women who participated in politics or assumed any public role. For critics, a mistress's sway over a king was identified with women's illegitimate power as she displaced men from their proper roles.

Agnès and her reputation must thus be set in the context of the fifteenth-century "quarrel over women," the long-standing and vehement debate about women's merits. Medieval fables detailing women's failings had been challenged by the influential thirteenth-century text the *Roman de la Rose*, which described the romantic courtship of an idealized woman in its first four thousand lines by Guillaume de Loris. But this positive presentation did not stand. The eighteen thousand lines subsequently added to this text by Jean de Meung incorporated misogynistic charges against women as he critiqued the hollowness of the chivalric tradition. Other contemporary texts were unequivocally hostile to women. The early fifteenth-century text *Fifteen Joys of Marriage*, for example, argued that marriage was invented to make men do penance on earth.[53] Then the famous Christine de Pizan entered the lists with her spirited defense of women as virtuous, intelligent, and able in *The Book of the City of the Ladies.*[54]

In times of crisis, texts attacking women became even more vociferous. Such literature seems imbued with a sense that, if the times were out of joint, the inappropriate and unnatural power of women was to blame. And fifteenth-century France indisputably presented compelling signs of a society in crisis. During the Hundred Years War, many nobles collaborated with the English against the Valois claimant to the throne; and in times of truce, they warred with each other. Artisans were impoverished, as few people had means to buy their goods in an economy disrupted by continuous war, and peasants faced famine. The social and economic problems engendered by decades of warfare unleashed particularly vehement criticisms of women, as some blamed their prominence for the problems France faced. As prominent a woman as Agnès could not fail to elicit criticism. Invectives against her thus belong to the literature that blamed women for social and economic disruption and denounced them for usurping positions traditionally and appropriately occupied by men.

Agnès's influence provoked growing hostility, court intrigues, and ultimately a confrontation between the king and his son, the dauphin (the heir apparent, so called because he held the territory of Dauphiné), the future Louis XI. Enguerrand de Monstrelet's *Chronicle* blamed Agnès explicitly for the hostility between father and son: "The hatred of Charles VII against Louis came from the fact that the prince had many times blamed and murmured against his father because of Beautiful Agnès who was in the good graces of the king much more than was the queen, a good and honorable woman. The dauphin was full of spite and through spite advanced her death."[55] The humanist Piccolomini reported that, in defense of his mother, Louis berated Agnès and then drew his sword and chased her to his father's bed.[56] Charles subsequently drove Louis into exile. While the immediate provocation for Louis's banishment may well have been his attack on Agnès, the more likely cause was his long history of plotting against his father, which continued long after Agnès's death.[57] (Louis likely deliberately slighted the memory of his father and his mistress when he turned Loches, the chateau most clearly connected to their relationship, into a prison.[58])

Despite contemporaries' criticisms and the dauphin's open rebellion, Agnès's position seemed virtually unassailable by 1449. She had been Charles's official favorite for at least five years and borne him three daughters. Her sway over the king and the court was obvious, and she occupied a position at the top of the social hierarchy on par with royal princesses. The year 1449 was also crucial for Charles, as the truce between the French and English was broken when the English allied with Brittany against France. Jean V de Bueil, an admiral and later the father-in-law of Agnès's daughter Jeanne, claimed that Agnès, concerned with fostering Charles's destiny, goaded him to renew hostilities against the English, saying "great kings conduct great business." If this were not inducement enough, she reputedly added, "You will find it easier still to exploit the virtue of beautiful women as much as you would like."[59]

As Charles prepared to besiege the English-held city of Rouen in Normandy, Agnès went to visit him despite her advanced pregnancy. There are conflicting explanations for this visit. Her detractors claimed that she went to Normandy because she was jealous and concerned to retain her sexual control over Charles. Others saw her as altruistic, contending that Agnès went to him to inspire Charles to greater feats of valor and to warn him of a plot against him.[60] Whatever her motives, most accounts concur that Charles did not welcome her, although he did install her at the abbey at Jumièges, near his military headquarters. The monks, who provided refuge, were doubtless even less eager to receive the king's very pregnant mistress. Exhausted by the trip, Agnès delivered another daughter. Several days later, she reported severe stomach pains and died on February 9, 1450. She had borne the king four daughters and was dead, likely at the age of twenty-eight. In the stuff of romantic legend, Agnès was credited with saving the king's life by warning him at the expense of her own.

Charles ordered a funerary monument built to her in Jumièges. Her heart was kept in the abbey, and the rest of her body buried, with that of her deceased infant daughter, in the abbey church.

Complications of childbirth were assumed to be the cause of Agnès's death, although, as with all sudden deaths of prominent figures, rumors of poisoning circulated throughout the centuries. In this case, forensic tests in April 2005 confirmed that Agnès died of mercury poisoning. Mercury was commonly used to treat intestinal worms from which, the forensic evidence shows, she suffered. The massive dose, however, suggests foul play. The strongest suspicion points to Louis, the future king, as the most likely perpetrator. As Le Clerc noted at the time of Agnès's death, "Some would say that the said dauphin had made die a young lady named Beautiful Agnès who was the most beautiful woman and completely in love with the king his father."[61] But Louis's complicity in this six-hundred-year-old mystery cannot be proved.

Despite her reputation as one of the principals in a famous fifteenth-century romance, Agnès was speedily replaced in Charles VII's affections by her cousin Antoinette. Popular chronicles emphasized Antoinette's youth at the expense of Agnès's age. The king's chronicler Chartier insisted Charles remained loyal to Agnès and that her cousin simply attended to his children.[62] But Antoinette was neither an official mistress nor simply a mistress. As chroniclers noted, she also acted as a procuress of beautiful young women who dressed like queens and lived in a grand and dissolute state.[63] As Chastellain noted, she "ascended that wheel of fortune higher than anyone at this time."[64] Like some later royal mistresses, Antoinette was married off by Charles to a compliant, richly rewarded husband. Despite romantic idealization of his relationship with Agnès, Charles was sexually promiscuous before he was involved with her and again afterward, according to his critics.

So Agnès's reputation remains that of a good mistress. While he was involved with her, Charles's life was characterized less by sexual excess and more by vitality and political engagement than during the rest of his reign. She thus provided the initial example of an argument that became conventional about the virtues of an official mistress. That is to say, she constrained a king's sexuality, or, with a good mistress, a king behaved better. Since Agnès's political allies too exerted a beneficial effect on royal politics, she was praised as a constructive political influence as well. She retains this positive reputation despite the fact that Charles's greatest success—driving the English out of France and ending the Hundred Years War—occurred shortly after her death.

The mere existence of an acknowledged favorite at court raised questions about the status she enjoyed on the royal stage. As the first mistress accorded this privileged status, Agnès defined its significant spheres of influence. With a practice novel for the day and perhaps in accord with her distinctive status, Charles legitimated his oldest daughter by Agnès on the eve of her marriage, and his son legitimated the other two. Her daughters later married men appropriate to their status as bearers of royal blood—marriages almost as advantageous as those arranged for Charles's legitimate offspring. Charles and, later, his son Louis XI used Agnès's daughters to cement the relationship between the crown and the new men brought to power under Charles.[65] Unlike later mistresses, Agnès neither showed personal interest in her daughters nor made efforts to advance their interests or ensure their futures. They were placed in noble households to be raised, as was customary with illegitimate royal offspring. Agnès had no subsequent involvement with them; they were not even mentioned in her will. (They were, of course, very young when she died.) Although her daughters would later enjoy the status royal blood conferred, Agnès's role was neither maternal nor familial. She instead remained identified with sexuality, beauty, and love.

Agnès inaugurated an improvement in the social and economic status of the mistress's family. She received significant material goods from Charles, including lucrative rents from the estates he gave her.[66] These gifts were more extensive than those previously given to royal mistresses, but they did not confer lasting wealth. Charles reclaimed many of her lands and goods after her death, and thus her family, unlike those of later mistresses, did not continue to reap the benefits of Agnès's status. Their financial gains were transitory and the family's benefit modest.

Agnès also set a model for the conspicuous consumption of luxury goods that later mistresses would follow. As the chronicler Jean Chartier remarked, she frequently wore exquisite necklaces of gold and favored long veils floating down to the ground.[67] Agnès was also one of the chief clients of Coeur, from whom she purchased large quantities of silk and cloth woven with gold. Her clothes were designed to create a spectacle; the trains on her dresses were so long (longer than those of other women) that her critics described them as tails. The fine quality of the goods with which she adorned herself set her above other ladies-in-waiting and must have also served as a constant reminder to the queen, the court, and the public of the king's sexual relationship with her. Parisian commentators explicitly objected to her status and wealth as marks of the king's favor. As Chastellain remarked, she had the best bedcovers, tapestries, jewels, and dishes. "She is the queen-*bis*, better treated, better housed, and better considered than the queen."[68] She even, he noted, lived in the queen's abode and had a better suite of rooms there. Her jewels were estimated to be worth 20,650 *écus*–an exorbitant sum for the period. Her ostentatious consumption, which also signaled her flagrant violation of the strictures on clothing that defined social rank, fueled her contemporaries' ire.[69] Nonetheless, through her cultivation of luxury goods, Agnès embodied a return to peace and prosperity.

SEX AND SANCTITY

Agnès, as her portraits attest, eschewed veils and wimples and instead dressed to reveal her neck, shoulders, and, above all, her breasts. This practice brought charges of immodesty and immorality and excoriations from Bishop Jean Juvénal des Ursins, perhaps because they made vividly obvious the sexual nature of her relationship with the king.[70] Agnès brought into fashion much more revealing dress, just as her sexual relationship with the king was placed in the forefront of public consciousness through her appearance at official royal functions. Chastellain severely criticized Agnès as a "student of vanity," and wrote: "From all that is of the ribaldry and the dissolution of manners, Agnès Sorel drew from them with open robes in the front where one sees her breasts. . . . Day and night she made up her face and studied only vanity so as to lead men astray and give a bad example to modest and honest women."[71] The medieval catalogue of the seven deadly sins made lust and luxury synonymous, particularly as applied to women.[72] For her contemporaries, Agnès was a vivid example of both.

Agnès's example shows both the positive and negative ramifications of a mistress's cultivation of fashion. Since she was almost invariably more attractive than the queen, her fashion sense and ability to wear clothes—particularly ostentatious or revealing clothes—could be construed as attacking the queen and flaunting her own immorality. A mistress's interest in fashion also demonstrated, especially for religious critics, her vanity and preoccupation with this life as opposed to the next.

Agnès's cultivation of luxury was her most obvious contribution to the evolution of court culture. Luxury was possible only because France was finally at peace. But expending resources on a mistress elicited sharp criticism: The largesse a king bestowed on her diverted funds from the kingdom's pressing needs. Juvénal des Ursins warned Charles that if he did not halt Agnès's conspicuous consumption, particularly the expense incurred by her dress, "he would draw upon himself the hatred of the people and the wrath of God."[73] Basin chided Charles for spending more on Agnès's vanity than on the queen and her court.[74] And Chastellain, who praised Agnès for giving Charles confidence, nonetheless warned him that her pursuit of luxury discredited him.[75]

Issues of sexual morality and questions of love complicated contemporary considerations of Agnès. Her relationship with Charles brought different understandings and expectations of love into conflict. The conventional view, sanctioned by the Church, held marriage indissoluble and sexual relations legitimate only within marriage. Poets extolled love as a way to elevate human thoughts and actions, although, according to many of them, love accorded ill with marriage. The idealization of love had reached its apogee in the courtly love tradition of the twelfth and thirteenth centuries. By the fifteenth century that tradition had become less important, but sixteenth-century Renaissance Neoplatonism will again extol love and beauty, and Agnès's reputation subsequently benefited from her association with both. Some of her contemporaries thus saw Agnès's striking beauty as a sign of her virtue and explained her power over Charles in terms of his love and her beauty. The official court chronicler Chartier, intent on presenting Charles as irreproachable, insisted that their relationship was not sexual.

Contemporary commentators found it difficult to determine how to discuss a woman who compromised conventional moral standards without criticizing, at least implicitly, the king. Some focused on Agnès's piety and charitable activities; she thus acquired something of a reputation for saintliness. They reported her gifts to the poor. Pope Nicholas V even granted her the special privilege of carrying a portable altar on her travels and sent her a papal absolution to be used at the hour of her death—no doubt to curry the king's favor.[76] Agnès donated to an abbey a statue of Mary Magdalene, one of the most popular fifteenth-century saints, perhaps acknowledging the comparability of a royal mistress to the repentant biblical prostitute.[77]

Agnès was the first royal mistress to elicit accounts of holiness during her life; the saintly status of royal mistresses came to be emphasized even more after their deaths. Chroniclers detailed deathbed reconciliations with the Church and praised mistresses' bequests to the Church. About Agnès, Chartier noted that she "made a good confession and repented of her sins" on her deathbed.[78] She bequeathed her worldly goods to the Collégiale Saint-Ours of Loches for masses for her soul. Her funeral monument at Loches depicted her praying and extending her heart to the Virgin Mary. (Protestants destroyed it during the Wars of Religion, as typifying both Catholic idolatry and the licentiousness of kings.) It violated the customs of the day by according a royal favorite the honor due more prominent figures. It was a significant acknowledgment of this first officially designated mistress's importance to her royal lover and his desire to have her recognized as such.

Even after death, Agnès's sexual role warred with her pious reputation. The battle between sexuality and sanctity has regularly disturbed her tomb, where she lies with hands folded in prayer, wearing a crown, with two angels at her head (fig. 1.5). In 1777, the canons of Loches, likely embarrassed by a royal mistress's prominence in their church, moved her tomb to a side chapel, claim-

Fig. 1.5. Tomb of Agnès Sorel, attributed to Jacques Morel, Chateau de Loches. The Bridgeman Art Library.

ing that it obstructed the choir. (When Agnès was exhumed at that time, those present remarked with disappointment that her hair was not *that* blond.) In 1793, French revolutionary troops destroyed her tomb. They may have had so little command of their history that they thought she was, in fact, a saint and therefore her tomb warranted the desecration reserved for artifacts of the

Catholic Church. Each time she was exhumed, some of her remains were removed, so that, for example, pieces of her bones and hair remain on display in a reliquary in the Museum of Chinon. In 1809, General François-René-Jean de Pommereul restored Agnès's mausoleum and then transferred it to the turret of the king's lodgings at Loches. Idealizing Agnès as a national heroine, he added an inscription to her tomb: THE ONLY MISTRESS WORTHY OF THE COUNTRY, AS THE PRICE OF HER FAVORS WAS EXPULSION OF THE ENGLISH FROM FRANCE. This epitaph was removed after the bishop of Tours objected to such lavish praise for a fallen woman.[79] After the most recent exhumation in April 2005, Agnès's remains were returned to the Collégiale Saint-Ours of Loches.

Agnès, like later designated mistresses, had a symbiotic relationship with artists of the day. Mistresses not only inspired but also commissioned works of art, which then garnered praise for both artist and subject. Beginning with Agnès's tenure, artistic representations became important in establishing a mistress's reputation and defining her legacy. Art confirmed Agnes's beauty and sanctity.

Agnès's modern reputation for beauty rests less on the avowals of her contemporaries than on her portraits. Late in her fourth pregnancy, she served as a model for Fouquet's *Virgin and Child Surrounded by Angels,* commissioned by Chevalier (see fig. 1.4). Fouquet depicted Agnès with all of the attributes of an ideal fifteenth-century beauty, from her blond hair and blue eyes to her high, round breasts. Her ideal coloring also connoted youth, purity, and virginity.[80] Agnès is ethereal, with fine features, downcast eyes, and a modest expression. (The photographic reconstruction of Agnès's face from her skeletal remains during the forensic work of the most recent exhumation conforms closely to Fouquet's painting.) In the style of fifteenth-century Madonnas, Agnès is shown with her breast exposed and holding a child. But in this case, her breast is unusually prominent and the child unusually remote from it and seemingly rather incidental to the beautiful woman. Nonetheless, the painter's depiction made the association between beauty and virtue concrete, while invoking the late-medieval devotion to the cult of the Virgin's breast.[81] Fouquet thus transformed Agnès into a model of spiritual beauty as well as sexual allure.

Fouquet's famous image of Agnès incorporates many of the conventional, iconographic associations of the queen with the Virgin Mary. Mary as the queen of heaven became a focus of religious devotion in the twelfth century, and in succeeding centuries, European queens were iconographically linked to her.[82] But the application of these images to a mistress must have been quite jarring, as indeed it still seems. Fouquet's painting depicts Agnès as the queen of heaven and thus appropriates not only the image of the Virgin Mary but also associations usually made with the queen. Fouquet cloaks Agnès in royal symbols, including the crown and the ermine. Agnès's appellation as "Mistress of Beauté" also allowed her to appropriate the term *beautiful*—a commonplace, conventionally applied to the queen.[83] Subsequently, the official favorite embodied this designation as well as the assumption that her physical beauty, rather than the queen's, reflected an inner virtue. And his mistress's beauty, rather than the queen's, enhanced a king's image.

A MISTRESS'S LEGACY

Immediately after Agnès's death, competing groups sought to control her story and its meaning for France—her family, the royal family, and local historians all claimed her.[84] Jean V de Bueil, Agnès's daughter Jeanne's father-in-law, praised her; favorable accounts of Agnès redounded to his family's credit. In the sixteenth century, Brantôme credited Agnès with both changing French policy and inspiring Charles.

Other sixteenth-century historians were more interested in Charles than Agnès. When they treated her, it was as a liability for Charles. François de Belleforest and Bernard de Girard Du Haillan, who wrote during the chaos of the Wars of Religion, were understandably rather pessimistic and inclined to moralize. They drew pointed political lessons from Agnès's prominence during Charles's reign: She had distracted him with the pursuit of pleasure, which led to the ruin of the kingdom. Du Haillan claimed that Charles did nothing but "amuse himself, making love to his fair Agnès . . . while the English marched through his kingdom."[85]

The poet Jean-Antoine de Baïf fostered the legend that Charles's love for Agnès caused his apathy and the troubles of his realm, although she ultimately forced him to act with honor. Agnès's death, in the fullness of youth and beauty, greatly impressed Baïf, who saw her as the heroic woman behind the throne—an enduring historiographical theme to the present.[86]

Another equally significant reading of the relationship between Charles and Agnès developed out of local histories and became prominent through the writings of Charles Sorel, a mid-seventeenth-century historian. His motives were largely personal. Although a Parisian bourgeois and no relation, he attached his name to Agnès to elevate his social standing. He articulated a fully developed view of Agnès as responsible for the restoration of the monarchy—the woman who persuaded Charles to take effective political and military action.[87]

But Sorel's laudatory depiction of Agnès's historic role was immediately undermined in Jean Chapelain's *The Maid, or the Heroic Poem of France Delivered.* ("Maid" was the name Joan of Arc used to refer to herself to highlight her status as virgin.) Published in 1656, this long epic poem enjoyed only a brief success but was influential for sharply contrasting Agnès with Joan of Arc. Joan was chaste and magnanimous; Agnès was an evil genius, inspired by demons. Chapelain described Agnès, in her chateau surrounded by ill-gotten goods, when her brother Roger persuaded her to return to the king to drive Joan from the kingdom after her triumph at Orléans. So Agnès, covered in jewels and sumptuous robes, distracted the amorous Charles, and Joan was ignominiously driven out. In this highly polemical and improbable account, Agnès went to Charles's Burgundian enemies to plot against Joan but then died after eating a poisoned apple meant for the king, becoming thus traitor and savior. Charles, on the verge of suicide to join her, was dissuaded by an angel.[88] This account clearly introduced many anachronistic and fictional elements into the story. Agnès was, after all, likely only seven years old when Joan appeared.

Voltaire poked fun at the entire legend in *La Pucelle* (*The Maid*).[89] Recognizing that Joan's virginity was understood as a source of her power, he presented a sexualized Joan who preserved her virginity only through the intervention of heavenly forces. The text deployed biting satire to attack both the clergy and the monarchy and, obscene as it is, became a scandalous success and a defining image of Joan. Agnès too received a sexualized treatment in Voltaire's text, as lovers and sexual predators pursued her thorough improbable, picaresque adventures. He made the liaison between Charles and Agnès a commonplace, readily committed to memory by generations of French school children.

Good king Charles, in the spring of his days,
At Easter time, in the city of Tours,
At a certain ball (this prince loved to dance)
Found, for the good of France,
A beauty named Agnès Sorel.
Never had Love formed such a one.[90]

In an especially notable line, Agnès seized control of the army from Joan, crying, "Long live love and France."[91] Ultimately Voltaire's Agnès was admirable—a great beauty who inspired a king.

Voltaire's contemporary, the historian Jean-François Dreux du Radier, was more cynical, citing the following anecdote: In 1750, he met a monk at Loches who had written a thousand sonnets praising Agnès's chastity. When Dreux du Radier responded that she had borne four children, the monk insisted that "it was an abominable calumny" refuted in his sonnets.[92] So unreasonably and extravagantly had Agnès come to be extolled.

Voltaire's readers could also see Agnès and Charles as an earlier incarnation of the eighteenth-century relationship between Madame de Pompadour and Louis XV. That correlation enhanced the political aspirations of Pompadour, the first officially designated mistress of bourgeois origins, who struggled throughout her tenure as royal mistress to gain acceptance by the nobility. Pompadour's association with Agnès gave her a noble and praiseworthy antecedent as designated favorite. It also correlated her role with the positive exercise of political power, even though her critics could charge that she was no Agnès Sorel.

Not surprisingly, given her reputation as an incomparable beauty, Agnès inspired nineteenth-century Romantics and proto-Romantics. Friedrich Schiller, in *The Maid of Orleans* (1801), made Agnès a romantic heroine who assured the French victory in the Hundred Years War by selling her jewels to pay soldiers. In this play, Charles proclaimed: "Here stands the heroine; I will win by my Agnès's love."[93] But Charles lost heart and retreated. For Schiller, like Voltaire, Joan, his romantic protagonist, was beset by suitors who assailed her virginity but ultimately was a tragic figure who renounced love for duty. Notably from the eighteenth century on, both women were consistently romanticized and sexualized. In his poem of 1827, "Charles VII at Jumièges," Ulrich Güttinger used Agnès's deathbed scene to predict the ultimate success of the French. Agnès's last words underscored her sanctity and commitment to France and Charles:

> Goodbye! Give me your hand, I am the love of France.
> Before leaving it, I see its deliverance,
> Your enemies conquered, your reign glorious,
> And I bring with me happiness from the heavens.[94]

When the nineteenth-century restoration of the monarchy produced a greater appreciation of the royal family and their associates, Agnès became the epitome of love and beauty, and her relationship with Charles a great romance. Some histories rehabilitated Charles at her expense: She became a woman who, by virtue of sexual attraction, distracted a king from his duties, reinvigorating Belleforest and Du Haillan's sixteenth-century theme; and the interpretation persists. In essence, they charged that because Charles played with Agnès, the English preyed on France.

The publication of documents in the nineteenth century brought historical personages into clearer view and produced the evidence behind the conflicting claims of when Agnès entered Charles's life and the extent of her influence.

Unlike eighteenth-century texts, which sexualized both Joan and Agnès, later work presented them as antithetical, explicitly associating Agnès with love, pleasure, and a more secular notion of the state. Importantly too, the nineteenth century defined the Hundred Years War as a national struggle analogous to their struggles against Prussia. In the twentieth century, Joan, beatified in 1909 and canonized in 1920, attained special status as a national heroine for post-WWI France, whether she was invoked as patriot or saint. Agnès, in turn, became less important, although she remains with Joan in the pantheon of heroines who unified and saved France.[95] Some modern writers have recently claimed Agnès as a feminist, a model more appropriate to post-WWII France. Her biographer Robert Philippe, for example, pointed to her clothing, particularly her décolletage, as "an exterior sign of the will of a woman to take on a new role in society."[96]

As Agnès's rich historiography attests, she remains evocative and controversial. It might well be argued that she is more vivid in the subsequent use made of her, both romantically and polemically, than in the glimpses of her available in fifteenth-century sources. Nonetheless, Agnès, the first official mistress, presents a telling example of the opportunities this new position offered. A prominent public woman, she was perceived as impelling a king first to pursue peace and then, when required, to war against the English, finally ending the Hundred Years War. Agnès is thus associated with a France restored to greater political power and enhanced by territorial gain. At the very least, her tenure as mistress coincided with these policies when Charles became a more effective ruler. The succession crisis of the Hundred Years War had been finally settled, placing the French crown firmly in the hands of the Valois and recouping territory previously forfeited to the English. The benefits of peace and prosperity redounded to Agnès's credit. She altered the character of the court by bringing new men into royal service and making it more dynamic and open to art and luxury. No doubt peace contributed greatly to the cultural changes associated with Agnès's preeminence. The chateaux of the Loire became more open, less the defensive structures of earlier times, for example. Agnès's fine silks attested to the new wealth of trade fostered by men such as her supporter Coeur and to the economic recovery after a long period of war. Her images and actions, ironically, solidified the crown as the legitimate political authority and the court as the source of political and cultural cohesion. Agnès also inaugurated the symbiotic relationship between artists and royal mistresses, later deployed most notably by Diane de Poitiers and Madame de Pompadour. From Agnes's time forward, the most prominent artists depicted mistresses in works commissioned by them or by the king on their behalf.

Insofar as Agnès contributed to the ongoing debate over women, she fueled denunciations of their immorality and their perfidious entrapment of men. In Christine de Pizan's pathbreaking *The Book of the City of the Ladies*, her most compelling defenses of female character praised sexual purity. But the strongest positive moral qualities her contemporaries ascribed to Agnès were charity and piety. They did not go so far as to associate her with sexual purity, except perhaps in portraying her as the Virgin Mary. Agnès instead offered a model of sexuality and secularism, controversial in her day but much appreciated by later commentators, most notably during the eighteenth century.

Although Agnès provoked some criticism for moral or political reasons, she was more often praised for her beneficial effect on the king and, by implication, the monarchy. Her example suggested that a royal mistress could be an asset to king and country. Agnès's prominence made the designated favorite a source of legend and myth, a significant subject for contemporary artists, and a focus for interpreting a monarch's reign and defining disparate visions of French history.

Agnès's contemporaries also laid out the elements of subsequent historical interpretations of royal mistresses. They set romance, love, and altruism against self-interest, lust, and venality as her motives and described her either as a saint bestowing charity or as a sinner inspiring immorality. She was a woman of refinement, cultivating the arts and fashion, or a profligate, wasting royal funds in pursuit of luxury and ostentation. She was a model of the effective use of power in the interest of France, or an interloper assuming roles from which all women should be barred. Contemporaries integrated Agnès's story into their worldview. For them, she epitomized changes in fifteenth-century culture, whether for good or ill. For subsequent historians and writers, she presents different ideas of France and, implicitly or explicitly, of the appropriate functions of women in the monarchy or public life. When she was seen primarily as the inspiration of a king and appropriately relegated to this supporting role, the royal mistress might generate less controversy than a queen, especially one as politically engaged as Anne of Brittany.

SIGNIFICANT DATES FOR CHAPTER 2

1462	Birth of Louis XII, June 27
1470	Birth of Charles VIII, June 30
1477	Birth of Anne of Brittany, January 25
1483	Death of Louis XI of France
	Anne of Beaujeu rules during Charles's minority
1484	Charles VIII crowned king of France
1485	"Crazy war" between France and Brittany
1486	Estates of Brittany recognize Anne of Brittany as heir
1488	Battle of Saint-Aubin-du-Cormier, July 28
	Treaty of Verger, August 19
	Death of Francis II, duke of Brittany, September 9
1489	Anne crowned duchess of Brittany, February 10
1490	Anne marries Maximilian of Austria by procuration, December 19
1491	Anne marries Charles VIII, December 6
1492	Anne crowned queen of France, February 8
	Birth of Charles-Orland, October 11
1495	Death of Charles-Orland, December 6
1498	Death of Charles VIII, April 7
1499	Anne marries Louis XII, January 8
	Birth of Claude, October 15
1504	Legal proceedings against Marshal Gié, June
	Anne again crowned queen of France, November 18
1505	Anne's visit to Brittany, June to September
1510	Birth of Renée
1514	Death of Anne, January 9
	Marriage of Claude to Francis d'Angoulême, May 18
1515	Death of Louis XII, January 1

2

Anne of Brittany

The Limits and Prospects of a Queen

Anne of Brittany was twice crowned queen of France by virtue of her marriage to two successive kings. The cases of Anne, a prominent queen, and Agnès, a famous mistress, can productively be juxtaposed to consider who had more choices or autonomy and what made one or the other "good" or effective. While one might assume that the status of queen would give a woman more power and authority than a mistress, the situation is not entirely clear. The fifteenth-century French queens immediately prior to Anne did not offer especially inspiring examples of political engagement or effective political or cultural influence. Isabeau of Bavaria controlled France during the periods of madness of her husband, Charles VI, but was also a foreign queen who undermined the monarchy by repudiating her son Charles VII's inheritance rights and by allying with England.[1] Although Charles VII's wife, Marie d'Anjou, was a dynastic model, bearing fourteen children, her husband neglected her for his mistress's company. His son, Louis XI, at odds with his father and Agnès, scorned women in general and his wives in particular, neither of whom enjoyed a public role.[2]

The marriage negotiated for a prospective queen largely defined her future, and convention, protocol, and obligation circumscribed her life. Some queens nonetheless carved out roles for themselves and maneuvered in their own interests or those of their children. With official status and access to funds, queens had greater potential to effect change than mistresses did, although they often depended on a king's encouragement of such activities. A queen's situation fundamentally differed from a mistress's. Almost inevitably she, as a princess, was a public person from birth and had a longer public history as well. Her family gave her status and some protection of her interests. But she also brought to her marriage the political context of the immediate negotiations that produced it. She inherited a role and, to some degree, an image. It was less incumbent upon her to form either, although the most successful queens did.

Royal marriages shared the social and economic pragmatism that underlay virtually all marriages of the period. For all social classes, marriage was essential to economic viability and success for most men and women, and marriages served the economic and social interests of the bride and groom and their extended families. But royal marriages were arranged for political and diplomatic ends as well, often cementing treaties, for example. While such marriages enhanced a king and his bride's families, ultimately his interests predominated. Almost invariably a French queen was uprooted from her home and forced to accommodate herself to a foreign court. Her entry into this setting was rarely accomplished with ease; an almost intrinsic opprobrium attached to her as a foreigner. Her loyalty to her new country remained questionable, especially if her marriage ended a war with her spouse's country. Her new countrymen were suspicious that her interests remained those of her native land.

A foreign-born queen rarely garnered favorable comments from her contemporaries, but Anne's case was particularly disquieting: She was not simply a foreign princess but remained duchess of Brittany. Even now, almost five hundred years after her death, Anne provokes debate about her loyalty. Historians of France frequently criticize her as a queen more concerned with preserving Brittany than advancing French interests; historians of Brittany praise her loyalty to her duchy.[3] Anne's Breton heritage shaped every aspect of her life and defined her historical reputation.

The queen's foreignness colored perceptions of her actions. With funds and patronage to dispense, she could promote high culture. If she shaped the culture of her adopted country by introducing arts or practices from her native land, as Anne did, she might be considered disloyal to France. If she did not leave a mark on French culture, she warranted criticism for her lack of style. In Anne's case, later critics condemned her for remaining mired in the Middle Ages instead of promoting Renaissance innovations; her admirers praised her for bringing sophistication to the French court.[4]

Contracted primarily to serve a political end, royal marriages rarely produced a congenial relationship between the king and queen. That personal relationship was a perennial subject of speculation, but rarely to the queen's credit. If relations between the king and the queen were contentious, the queen, not the king, was at fault. Contemporaries often blamed her for failing to interest him. Even Charles VIII, who was much disparaged by his contemporaries, was rarely criticized for his treatment of Anne, which included neglecting her to pursue a succession of indiscriminate sexual liaisons. A king's neglect rarely engendered sympathy for his wife.

As a result of Anne's position as queen of France and duchess of Brittany, her cultural innovations, and her difficult relationship with Charles VIII, her contemporaries and subsequent historians have assessed her in dramatically different ways. To understand this discrepancy, Anne must be placed in her Breton context; that context made her marriage to two French kings a political imperative. For Anne, like other queens, her personal history and her specific, political context defined her, and Brittany's political context was unusually complex and contested.

BRITTANY IN DISPUTE

Anne's birth on January 25, 1477, was heralded with relief and joy. Brittany finally had its heir; the continued rule of the Montforts, the ruling family of Brittany for the past 130 years, was now conceivable. When Anne was born, Francis II, her father and the duke of Brittany, was forty years old. His first wife had died without leaving any descendants; he had been married to his second wife for some time but had only fathered children by his mistress Antoinette of Maignelais (Agnès Sorel's cousin and Charles VII's former mistress, who had abandoned him for the young, handsome duke of Brittany). Francis neglected his wives for the company of Antoinette—a woman seventeen years his senior, whom "he cherished beyond measure, holding her in great estate, even higher than his wife"—charged the contemporary historian Bertrand d'Argentré, who also claimed that Francis's first wife, Marguerite of Brittany, had died of embarrassment at her displacement by her husband's mistress.[5] His second wife, Marguerite de Foix, objected less to her husband's extramarital relationship, but only after Antoinette's death did she give birth to Anne.

Unlike many of her royal contemporaries, Anne was educated to rule, no doubt because the duchy's future rested on her. Her education was entrusted to Françoise de Dinan, a prestigious Breton noblewoman. Anne was to be accomplished in the gracious arts appropriate to her station—singing, dancing, embroidery, and proper deportment. But she also received a literary education not only in French but also in Latin and Greek. Even if her education was rather extraordinary for a young girl, it cannot have been thorough, since it ended abruptly when she was just eleven.[6]

Anne's early life was shaped by her status as heiress to a rich duchy. She was used to negotiate international agreements to safeguard Brittany; a marriage alliance to a prince powerful enough to protect it was essential. Anne was an especially attractive marital prospect because of her duchy's allure for European rulers, especially since a daughter could inherit Brittany in the absence of a male heir. As a result, Anne was engaged at the age of four to Edward, the son of Edward IV of England. (Louis XI was blamed for preventing this politically advantageous match—brilliant for Brittany but disastrous for France.) Royal marriages could not be consummated until the age of sexual maturity, so Brittany had much time to use Anne to maneuver diplomatically. The duchy's vulnerable position made it central to international politics and made such negotiations crucial.

Brittany was a rich prize coveted by England, France, and the Hapsburg rulers of Austria; each wanted to prevent any other from controlling it. For French kings, Brittany was too close, enticing, and vulnerable not to be a target of their territorial aspirations. Brittany had no defensible frontier; many of its nobles were tied by feudal relationships to the French king. For three centuries, it had been involved in the wars between France and England. Now Brittany attracted the intense predatory interest of Louis XI. Jean Meschinot, the official court poet of Brittany (admittedly a biased source), described Louis as "a man without faith, without law, and without order, feigning innocence [but] completely full of malice."[7] Louis XI's determination to annex Brittany was the greatest threat it faced during Anne's youth.

Not only was Brittany in an increasingly perilous position vis-à-vis France but a historical precedent further jeopardized Anne's prospects for inheriting it. In 1341, when Jean III of Brittany died without a male heir, a fratricidal war between the Montfort and the Penthièvre families broke out. Brittany then became a battleground in the Hundred Years War, with the French king defending the rights of his vassal (a Penthièvre), and the English king supporting the Montfort claim. A treaty settled the contested claims in favor of the Montforts, with the stipulation that if the duke of Brittany died without a male heir, inheritance rights would revert to the Blois-Penthièvre family. The possible implementation of this clause loomed as long as Francis had no heir.[8]

Even after Anne's birth there was great cause for concern when Louis XI purchased the right to Breton succession from the female heiress of the Penthièvre family. Both the duchy and Anne's claim to it were continuously under assault by the French king. Louis certainly saw no political role for women and may have believed he could extend the exclusionary provision of the Salic law to Brittany. He had successfully applied that principle to annex Burgundy when it had no male heir in 1477 (fig. 2.1). However, the treaty had specified the succession of the duchy would not come to a woman *as long as* there was a

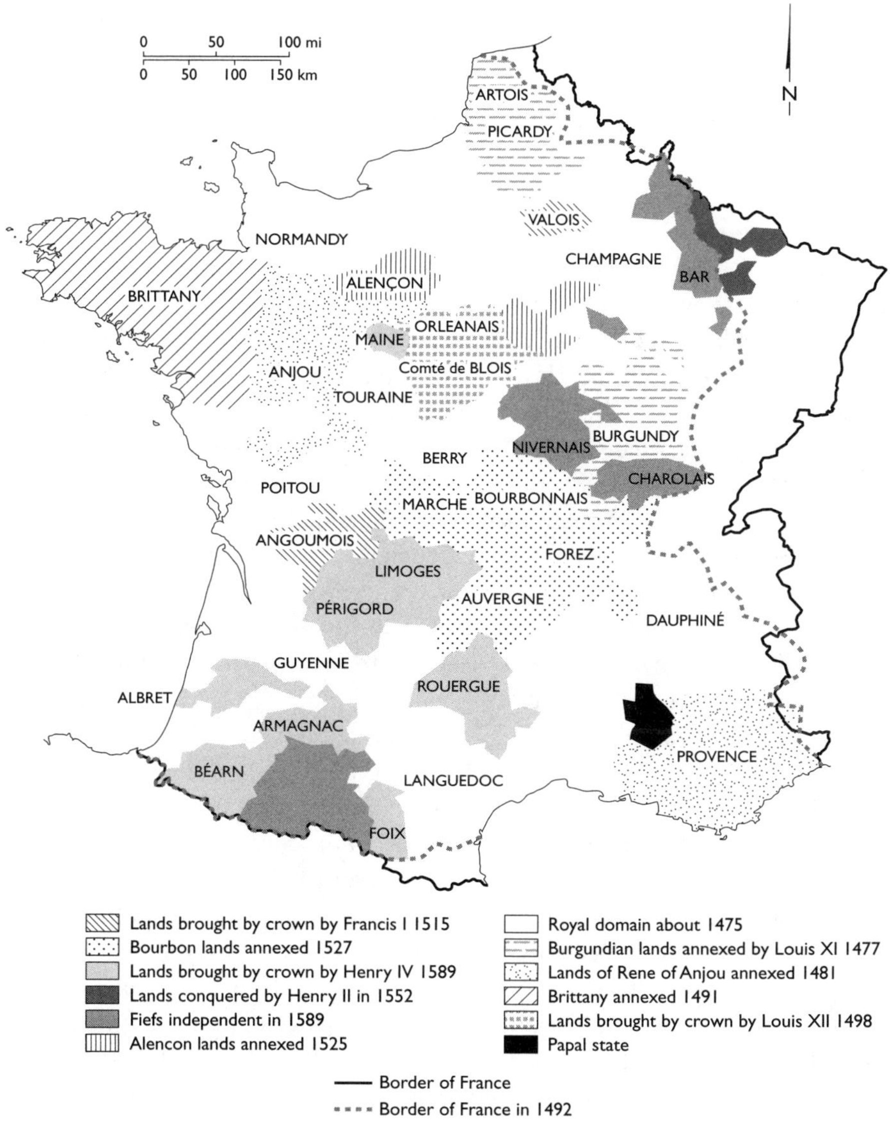

Fig. 2.1. Map of territories as they were added to French royal domain during the fifteenth and sixteenth centuries. William L. Nelson.

male descendant in the Breton line. As neither branch of the family had a male heir, Anne was unquestionably the legitimate successor, but the French king's purchase of the right of succession raised the specter that he might claim the duchy. Brittany therefore both prepared for war and pursued a foreign policy designed to avert this threat. It allied with Maximilian of Austria and Edward IV of England against France. Anne's early engagement to Edward, the English prince, reflected this foreign policy.

In 1461, these threats were realized when Louis XI tried to force the duke of Brittany to acknowledge him as his feudal overlord. Francis insisted that, as his power came directly from God, he was the highest authority in Brittany and not the French king's vassal.[9] His resistance reflected Brittany's fierce independence. (It paid homage but no taxes to the king of France, appointed its own judges, and had its bishops appointed by the pope.) The preservation of its traditional rights was the crucial issue in its dealings with the French monarchy.

The next year they were at war, and Francis organized a league committed to putting Edward IV of England on the French throne. When that war ended ten years later, Brittany was forced to accept a peace, which prohibited it from warring with France and tied its foreign policy firmly to that of France. Although Louis XI's death in 1483 delivered Brittany from its most dangerous enemy, France continued to threaten it.

After Louis's death, his intelligent and spirited daughter Anne of Beaujeu became de facto regent. Louis considered her the most capable of his children (two daughters and one son), grudgingly acknowledging her as "the least foolish of women."[10] It is ironic that as confirmed a misogynist as Louis XI left his daughter to rule. He was a devious, military man who allowed women no role in his reign. Not coincidentally, as a result of both his actions and this exclusion, no question was raised about his manhood or the efficacy of his rule.

In contrast, his son (eventually crowned Charles VIII) was discounted by his contemporaries as not simply young but also incapable of ruling, corroborating his father's sense of his limitations. Louis had left Charles's education to his wife because of his son's obvious weakness. Critics contended that it was misdirected by the reading of romances.[11] In other words, his mother's feminine cultural pursuits had emasculated Charles. Given his own rebellious plotting against his father, Louis likely deliberately kept his own son ignorant of politics and away from court.[12] In any case, Charles's contemporaries considered him neither intelligent nor well educated. The Milanese ambassador Agostino Calco warned that Charles "would not understand any communication written in Latin"—a clear sign of his inferior education.[13] The Renaissance historian and papal ambassador to France Francesco Guicciardini noted that Charles was not only "without any learning and skill but he hardly knew the letters of the alphabet."[14] Philippe de Commynes, chronicler and royal bureaucrat in the service of three French kings—Louis XI, Charles VIII, and Louis XII—characterized Charles as "a small man in body with little understanding."[15]

Contemporaries commented on Charles's physical failings as well, describing him as very short, ill-proportioned, with large eyes and a large beaked nose, and his mouth always hanging open. (His adenoids may have been the problem.) Guicciardini said that Charles was "very ugly . . . and his limbs so ill-proportioned that he seemed more like a monster than a man"[16] (fig. 2.2).

Fig. 2.2. Charles VIII shortly after his marriage to Anne. French school, sixteenth century. Chateau de Versailles / The Bridgeman Art Library.

Brantôme called him "our little king," and some modern historians insist that he was a dwarf.[17]

Charles's unprepossessing physical appearance and mental limitations led to his rivals, especially his cousin Louis of Orléans, to believe that he might be easily manipulated during his sister's regency. Charles was twelve years old when his father died and his sister assumed the authority to rule in his stead. Because of his weakness and her strength, Anne of Beaujeu controlled the government and determined domestic and foreign policy until she left the court in 1491.[18] She was thus a royal sister who acted most effectively to maintain her family's control of the crown. A strong regent, she challenged the duke of Brittany's control and its young duchess's right to inherit the duchy.

A king's minority presented great opportunities for women such as Anne of Beaujeu to exercise power. But regencies were generally unstable, as regents invariably faced challenges from other claimants to the throne and from nobles attempting to regain power at the crown's expense. A prince of the blood more usually became regent. As a young woman without the formal title, Anne was especially vulnerable to challenge. Many were eager to contest her authority, particularly Louis of Orléans, the prince of the blood with the best claim to the throne after Charles. Justifying her father's faith, Anne adroitly maneuvered the young Charles VIII, the Estates-General, and all opponents to preserve her control and to maintain her claim to rule in her brother's stead.[19]

Her treatment of the Estates-General revealed her political acumen. The Estates-General was a body with representatives of three distinct groups—clergy, the nobility, and the rest of the people. Kings called the Estates into session only when they needed some kind of support. They were reluctant to do so, since the Estates used such occasions to make demands in exchange for endorsing a king's request. But, as this particular session revealed, they could be manipulated by a clever ruler. When the Estates claimed to speak for the people against her, Anne exposed them as venal allies of her princely opponents, disassociating them from the common good they claimed to represent and thus undermining their attacks on her authority.

Louis of Orléans overtly challenged her regency and foreign policy by allying with Brittany and proposing to marry its young duchess. Romanticizers suggested that the twenty-two-year-old Louis was smitten by his first glimpse of the seven-year-old Anne of Brittany. This popular tale, a literary foreshadowing of their future relationship, nonetheless fueled the myth that developed after Anne's death.

Anne of Brittany's father too hoped to profit from the vulnerability of a French regency to reinforce Breton independence and to defeat French challenges to her right to succeed him. But Brittany was not well positioned to do so. French forces were far superior in number, and Brittany was in dire financial straits. And the Breton nobility was divided into anti- and pro-French factions. Breton nobles colluded with the French, accepting cash payments; French financial accounts reveal long lists of payments to "Breton pensioners,"[20] and Breton soldiers defected to the French. France lured discontented Breton nobles, and Brittany provided a haven for French nobles eager to challenge Anne of Beaujeu, most notably Louis of Orléans. These factors made Brittany ripe for interventionist aspirations from abroad and dissent from within. In 1484 a pro-French group of Breton nobles met with Anne of Beaujeu and swore to acknowledge Charles as the legitimate heir to Brittany if Francis died without a male heir.[21] In return, France agreed to respect Breton rights to administer justice and to arrange good marriages for Francis's two young daughters—Anne and her younger sister, Isabeau. At the same time, Louis of Orléans roused other French nobles to revolt against the regent.

Ultimately, Breton rebels joined French forces to fight against the duke of Brittany, and renegade French nobles joined Louis of Orléans in Brittany to war against France. The "crazy war," as it was called for obvious reasons, produced a French victory, but the causes for discontent and forces of disloyalty remained. Louis's ambition to foment a revolt against the regent was only temporarily thwarted, and, for France, Brittany remained a ripe target for annexation.

Francis convened the Estates of Brittany to demand that they recognize Anne as his heir and dangled her as a matrimonial prize to gain allies. An English alliance no longer seemed most advantageous; Henry Tudor (now Henry VII, having just deposed Richard III) was preoccupied with securing his throne. Maximilian, the Hapsburg ruler of the Austrian lands, seemed a more promising ally. He had just been elected king of the Romans and was likely to succeed his father as Holy Roman Emperor (as he did in 1489). Although Maximilian was too preoccupied with developments in his territory to come to Brittany's immediate aid, Brittany hoped that even the possibility of his intervention might deter French attacks. Alain d'Albret, who controlled extensive territory in the southwest of what is now France, was also offered Anne's hand in exchange for his military support.[22] At forty-seven, he was perhaps not the most appealing spouse for the ten-year-old Anne. Although Albret eagerly sought this marriage, French forces halted his troops, and he too was unable to come to Brittany's aid. A rather desperate Francis determined to marry Anne to Maximilian as the only ally who might eventually provide military support. As heiress and matrimonial prospect, Anne provided the most effective means to defend her duchy.

But this plan was immediately contested by Anne of Beaujeu, who berated Brittany for violating the treaty terms, which required French approval of any marriage proposed for the Breton heiress. Determined to quash the Breton-Hapsburg agreement, she allied with sixty Breton nobles, led by Marshal Rieux. She agreed to provide those nobles with an army sufficient to take Brittany but not to attack Francis directly—a specification perhaps intended to allay qualms the nobles might have had about their patent disloyalty. War was inevitable, although, as Georges Minois points out, it was again a strange war fought from strange positions: "The king of France allied with Breton nobles came to make war on a duke of Brittany defended by French princes."[23]

In May 1487, France invaded Brittany to punish rebellious French nobles and, more importantly, to insist that its authority be acknowledged. After a series of easy victories, Charles VIII, at the head of French troops, besieged Nantes, which roused even those Bretons supporting France to defend it. Rieux changed sides and recaptured most of the Breton towns under French control. But when Nantes fell, Francis's allies deserted him. He was so inept and indecisive in his later years that the sixteenth-century historian Bertrand d'Argentré noted, "By the weakness of age and sense, he no longer understood his affairs."[24] Modern historians speculate that Francis may have suffered from premature dementia.[25]

On July 28, 1488, Breton and French forces engaged in battle at Saint-Aubin-du-Cormier with disastrous results for Brittany: It lost six thousand men, and France fourteen hundred; Louis of Orléans was taken prisoner by the French; and Francis could only sue for peace. The decisive defeat sealed Brittany's fate, advanced Anne of Beaujeu's goal of annexing Brittany, and further jeopardized Anne of Brittany's right to inherit. The terms of the peace required Francis to send all foreign troops home and to gain the "advice, approbation, and consent" of France to any marriage proposed for his daughter.[26] Furthermore, a papal commission would examine Anne of Brittany's right to inherit the duchy.

Within weeks of signing the Treaty of Verger on August 19, 1488, acknowledging his defeat, Francis died, leaving the duchy in ruins, occupied by the French, and with an heiress not quite twelve years old. Charles VIII claimed his rights as Anne's guardian, but Rieux, appointed to this position by her father, refused to acknowledge them. The Breton crisis remained unresolved: Brittany asserted the young duchess's right to inherit, and France disputed it.

Anne faced grave difficulties upon her father's death. She was, however, able to withstand those who pressured her to take actions she saw as against her interests or those of Brittany—no mean feat for such a young girl. Even with the support of the guardians Francis had appointed, Rieux and Françoise de Dinan

(Albret's half sister), to shore up her political viability, Anne's first few years as duchess were difficult. Whatever her skills or her father's precautions, Anne was in a precarious position.

Although romantic biographies portray Anne as a political child prodigy able to assume power and manage this complex political situation in her duchy's interests, one must acknowledge the importance of the five men in charge of the government. They were Rieux, Albret, the count of Comminges, the count of Dunois, and Philippe of Montauban. They quickly split into two factions, disagreeing over which marital strategy for the young duchess would best allow Brittany to extricate itself from its untenable situation. Albret, Rieux, and Comminges once again favored her marriage to Albret. Montauban and Dunois favored a marriage to either Maximilian or Louis of Orléans.[27] Anne's attempt to inaugurate her rule by convening the Estates of Brittany elicited a sharp reproach from the French king. She could, he insisted, neither marry without his consent, nor use her title, nor conduct any official business until her right to the title had been confirmed by the pope.

Rieux tried to propel the marriage to Albret by producing Anne's supposed petition for a dispensation to marry Albret. (They were distantly related but close enough to require a papal dispensation.[28]) Anne, who emphatically opposed this marriage, swore before a papal court that she had sought neither the dispensation nor the marriage. She staunchly maintained that Albret, as a mere nobleman, was an unworthy spouse; only a king would be her husband.[29] The Breton historian Argentré praised her "courage and indomitable heart" and saw her resistance to matrimonial plans as a telling sign of her firm character.[30] His early history of Brittany praised Anne's ability to perceive her duchy's good and act accordingly.

Anne's categorical rejection of this marriage split her council, essentially creating rival governments. Montauban, who supported her, arranged her triumphal entry into Rennes and coronation as duchess of Brittany on February 10, 1489, two weeks after her twelfth birthday. Within five days, her official seal proclaimed ANNE BY THE GRACE OF GOD DUCHESS OF BRITTANY and depicted her armed with the sword of state.[31] Anne's authority was more illusory than real.

The duchy was again immediately plunged into war with France. Brittany sought help from foreign powers, which were increasingly concerned about its impending fall. Anne hoped that the arrival of Maximilian's troops would give her the advantage. But the war slowed to a stalemate as the French were unable to press their military advantage, and all parties had other concerns: Charles was contemplating a crusade, and Maximilian was distracted by problems at home. Both sides agreed to a truce, although it is worth noting that the truce was between Maximilian and Charles; Anne was not even party to the negotiations. Without consulting her, they determined that all foreign troops would leave Brittany; some Breton towns would be placed under the control of Pierre of Beaujeu (Anne of Beaujeu's husband); and Anne would have her rights to Brittany adjudicated by a papal commission.

The yearlong truce offered limited relief to Brittany. There was peace, but the rival governments in Nantes and Rennes each raided the treasury. Peace afforded an opportunity for the young duchess to tour the principal Breton towns, cementing her lifelong attachment to her duchy. This tour gave rise to her reputation as a populist, especially since she wore the wooden shoes of the poor when she walked in mud. This image still resonates in her popular appellation the "Good Duchess of the Wooden Shoes." Although the truce was implemented to resolve Charles VIII and Anne's competing claims to the duchy, the other European powers, allied against France, favored a marriage between Anne and Maximilian. Her advisors urged this marriage to save Brittany, as Maximilian had agreed that he would have no rights to Brittany. Thus it would not be subsumed into the Holy Roman Empire but would remain independent. This marriage alliance, intended to thwart French plans to conquer Brittany, Anne saw as preferable to any other.

On December 19, 1490, Anne married Maximilian by proxy in the cathedral of Rennes. According to the conventions of the day, Maximilian's emissary put his leg on her bed on the wedding night. This practice recognized the sometimes-pressing need for hastier marriages than contemporary conditions of travel allowed. In this case, haste was required by the great desirability of the political alliance the marriage would cement.

But this proxy marriage did not resolve the crisis; France had a grievance it intended to redress. Charles VIII strongly objected to the marriage, citing the critical clause of the Treaty of Verger that specified that Anne could not marry without France's consent—a provision France meant to enforce through war if necessary. Having determined that only military force would settle the Breton problem, Charles besieged Nantes, which quickly fell. Neither of the allies Brittany had relied on—the English or Maximilian—provided timely or sufficient reinforcements to prevent defeat. When foreign troops finally came to Brittany's aid in autumn 1491, they were poorly paid, badly organized, and of little help. The domestic situation further degenerated as hordes of brigands devastated Brittany. Only Rennes remained for the French to vanquish, but the outcome of the siege was a foregone conclusion; the only question was on what terms.

The Breton army had one-fourth as many troops as the French, and Brittany had been bled dry by war. Anne's advisors now recommended marriage to the French king to resolve the crisis.

When Charles came to officially request Anne's hand in marriage, he specified that she not assume the title "Duchess of Brittany." His father had purchased the inheritance rights to the duchy, and Charles insisted that he now held them. The dependence of the young duchess on the king of France was unequivocal; only his favor would allow her to retain any authority in Brittany. Although Charles's claims challenged Anne's authority and Breton autonomy, her marriage to him was the best resolution for Brittany.

Anne was required to present herself naked before French envoys to reassure the king that she was well made and would likely be able to bear a male child.[32] The body of the queen, especially with respect to her prospects for childbearing, would increasingly be scrutinized in the interest of the state. This practice, as well as the political ideology of queenship, negated her person and made her the vessel in which the king's seed might be planted.

Despite its political rationale, the marriage shocked contemporaries for several reasons. The fourteen-year-old duchess married a king who had been despoiling her country, and, perhaps most disconcerting, the count of Dunois fell dead from his horse as he rode off after negotiating the marriage—a strikingly inauspicious omen.[33] An immediate problem was that both Charles and Anne were already married. Charles had been married since 1482 to the very young Margaret of Austria, and Anne had married Maximilian by proxy. Both parties had to appeal to the papacy to release them from their previous entanglements. Anne's more clearly advantageous marriage to Maximilian would have to be set aside because of her duchy's dire necessity. In both cases, a marriage had been performed but not consummated. To marry Anne, Charles had to set aside his commitment to another young heiress.

Margaret, who had come to France at the age of three to be raised by Charles's sister Anne of Beaujeu, was now eleven and would be sent back to Austria. A great favorite in the French court, her tearful leave-taking was wrenching. As her case shows, princesses were not only hostages to diplomacy but also their fates could shift suddenly with changes of diplomatic alliances. Margaret had been considered an attractive match for Charles; her dowry was the rich territory of Artois and Franche-Comté. So advantageous was this alliance that the highly unusual step of performing a marriage ceremony with a three-year-old bride had been taken.[34] But now the surer prize of Brittany diminished Margaret's value to France.

The proposed marriage between Anne and Charles was an affront to Maximilian in two respects: The bride was his wife and the groom had returned his daughter. His agents conducted a vigorous propaganda campaign against the annulments, citing the double adultery of both parties and Anne's marriage to Charles as rape. As a result, the wedding ceremony between Anne and Charles was carried out clandestinely and in advance of the papal decree of annulment but with the full expectation that it would be forthcoming. This process was technically irregular but blessed by the three bishops who were present.

Confidence that popes could be relied upon to grant royal annulments was warranted. Despite the sacramental, permanent character of marriage according to Church teachings, a royal marriage could be set aside by the pope in the interest of any number of secular concerns: Popes were interested in making this process available to foster their own political agendas; European monarchs wanted a means to set aside infertile wives or, on occasion, wives whose political advantage had diminished. So, while an individual king might object to another king's annulment, as Maximilian did, or a pope might resist a particular royal annulment, all had a vested interest in the practice. But few annulments were as politically controversial as these, which offended the powerful Maximilian.

It is worth noting just how often Anne's marriage potential had been tapped in official engagements—at the age of four to the English heir Edward, at nine to Maximilian, at ten to Albret, and then again to Maximilian—with other proposals frequently on the table. No marriage would be performed until both parties had attained the age of sexual maturity, and no marriage contract was completely valid until the marriage had been consummated. Anne's contemporaries would have understood her many engagements as political alliances. As the political realities changed, the marriage agreements that cemented them were reconfigured. Anne's three engagements in the two years after her father's death, for example, offered Brittany its best defense. Even for the time, Anne's numerous engagements were excessive and demonstrate vividly that royal daughters, as pawns in dynastic power games, did not command their fates.[35] Like other young heiresses, Anne was captive to the political and diplomatic interests her lands could serve. She was especially vulnerable because of the predatory interests of France and her father's inability to protect the duchy, and because of Anne of Beaujeu's unwavering determination and effective mobilization of forces to annex Brittany.

Despite her precarious political position, Anne of Brittany acted to protect and preserve her own political autonomy insofar as she could. Her marriage contract with Charles resolved the immediate political crisis for Brittany but also gave her certain guarantees. It specified that the purpose of the union was a permanent and indissoluble peace between France and Brittany. It stipulated that jewels, furniture, other goods in Anne's possession at the time of the king's death, and, most importantly, her rights over Brittany would revert to her should Charles predecease her.[36] The king also committed to respect Breton rights—a commitment more symbolic than real. The marriage essentially confirmed Brittany's conquest.

Anne was clearly not in an advantageous position when this marriage was negotiated. Jurists drew up a contract to guarantee that the alliance between France and Brittany would be honored no matter what the circumstances. It also specified that if Charles predeceased Anne, she would marry his successor to the French crown to preserve this crucial alliance. If Anne did not marry Charles's heir, she would be required to remain a widow so that Brittany could not be attached to a rival of France through a second marriage. The initial indications for the future of the marriage were not propitious; the young king did not find the duchess attractive. "There is no demonstration of joy that this marriage has taken place, neither on the part of the king or any other," reported the ambassador Erasmus Brasca back to Milan.[37]

A ROYAL MARRIAGE

Despite her weak position, Anne's marriage to Charles afforded some protection of her rights in Brittany. Some Breton nobles had not been pleased to have an eleven-year-old girl as duchess and, as a result, allied with the French. Anne's marriage to the French king put an end to such alliances and maintained her position as duchess. Her new status as queen of France made her the most powerful queen in Europe by virtue of her husband's power and her own inheritance. After a childhood in which her own territories were despoiled and impoverished by war, Anne found wealth and security. This change in status might have made her grateful to Charles for providing these benefits. She was likely persuaded of the political necessity of the marriage. Personal happiness was a negligible consideration in such politically significant marriages.

Questions about the relationship between husband and wife in a royal marriage arise for the modern reader because of our own sense that the successful marriage rests on love. Their contemporaries too wanted kings and queens to have marriages that were at least harmonious enough to make offspring conceivable. Even though they recognized that such marriages were engineered by political necessity, they nonetheless speculated about their personal nature. They wondered if royal relationships engendered love and were reassured if they seemed at least affectionate. Royal marriages, the intimate relations of the most elite members of society, also intrigued their contemporaries. Venetian ambassadors, some of the nosiest members of any European court and the most loquacious commentators on the events that unfolded there, freely speculated on royal marriages. About Anne and Charles, the Venetian ambassador Zaccaria Contarini reported that, while Anne obviously desired Charles, he spent very few nights with her.[38] Charles preferred to spend more time with courtesans. Although he spared Anne the indignity of an official favorite, like Agnès Sorel, who might have usurped any number of her roles, Anne was no doubt as affronted by Charles's flagrant and indiscriminate pursuit of other women.

Historians usually describe the relationship between Anne and Charles in rather neutral terms. That is to say, since they fulfilled their primary function of producing offspring, their personal relations were of little import. Those who emphasize the couple's lack of harmony blame Anne for failing to allure her husband. Presumably, if she had not been so pious, dour, or even so Breton in temperament, she might have had a more successful marriage. Her biographers, generally more favorably inclined toward their subject, acknowledge that the relationship was not happy but contend that Charles was simply not good enough for Anne. Others insist that Charles succumbed to her charms despite his infidelities and point to clear signs of his favorable regard—she had four pregnancies within a thirty-month period, was consecrated as queen, and made a triumphal entry into Paris.[39]

As with other queens, contemporaries felt free to comment on Anne's physical attributes. Such physical descriptions were intended to indicate her character, but the descriptions and the attendant qualities of character they intended to convey varied widely. Anne enjoyed the conventional association of the queen with beauty, virtue, and the Virgin Mary, an association Agnès Sorel had temporarily broken. Conventional sources thus described Anne as "beautiful," reinforcing the assumption that her physical beauty reflected inner beauty and enhanced the king's image. Comparisons of the queen to the Virgin Mary emphasized her role as the mother of her people. They invoked the theology of marriage, where the royal relationship referred to the mystical union of Christ with his Church, an allusion reinforcing the king's religious status.[40] These associations affirmed Anne's status as queen, unchallenged by any other woman; all the iconographic elements supported her.

Conventional attributions of beauty and virtue tell us little about Anne. For more telling tales, one looks to the ambassadors from Italian cities who filed more explicit reports. The Venetian ambassador Contarini, for example, commented: "She is short, thin, with a visibly hunched back, although she wears shoes with a high heel to hide her deformity. She has a ruddy complexion and is pretty enough."[41] Her congenitally displaced hip caused some contemporaries to describe Anne as deformed, but even her critics conceded that she dressed attractively in Breton fashion. One of the earliest portraits of her by an unknown artist shows Anne at the time of her marriage and generally corroborates Contarini's rather lukewarm assessment of her looks. She is a very young girl with quite prominent features dressed simply and luxuriously in traditional Breton style (fig. 2.3).

Charles VIII's unimpressive physique was also the subject of contemporary discussion. Contarini was particularly uncomplimentary: With "a large and short torso, legs long and thin, the small king of France was a gnome. With large mouth, pendulous lips, bulging eyes, nonetheless he put forth an extraordinary seductiveness." He concluded: "In my opinion, which could be wrong, he is not worth much physically or intellectually."[42] One is left to wonder about these unflattering descriptions of the king, especially when they were intended to convey character traits. Although Anne was usually described in a fairly conventional way, her looks a mere indication of whether she might attract her husband, Charles's contemporaries worried that his looks indicated a lack of ability.

Despite her husband's seeming disinterest in Anne, the match was important for France; it secured its northwestern frontier from English control and attached the wealth of Brittany to the crown. In recognition of its significance, on February 8, 1492, Anne was not only crowned but also anointed as queen—an extraordinary privilege. On her entry into Paris, Brittany was allegorically represented as a "secure alliance" in tandem with France, as "peace" praised "divine wisdom" for bringing about the marriage. As part of the celebration, "justice," in an allegorical tableau, urged the people "to give thanks to God and the saints to see the lily (France) accompanied by the ermine (Brittany)."[43] Anne's public, quasi-religious coronation and anointing as queen might also have been intended to force the Vatican's hand to grant a speedier annulment. Pope Innocent VIII was still under considerable pressure not to do so, since her marriage to Charles had been constrained, or so Maximilian's representatives claimed.[44] And the young queen was already pregnant.

By the time the papal dispensation arrived, Anne had delivered a healthy son, Charles-Orland.[45] This rather unconventional name (a variant of Roland) invoked the famous warrior against the Saracens and hero of France's epic tale *The Song of Roland* and reflected Charles's interest in a crusade. His son would be a new Roland to save Christendom from the infidel.[46] To appease the princes of the realm who found the name too unconventional, Charles was added.

Fig. 2.3. Anne of Brittany at the time of her marriage to Charles. Bibliothèque nationale de France (BnF).

The birth of the young prince and heir to the throne did not enhance the marriage. Instead it freed Charles not only to seek physical pleasure elsewhere but also to travel, to conduct war, and to lead his own crusade. He could not have as readily pursued such activities without an heir, for a king without an heir who traveled or went to war left the kingdom prone to chaos should misfortune befall him.

In August 1494, Charles prepared to invade Italy with the dual goals of removing the occupier of the throne of Naples and launching a campaign for Jerusalem from there.[47] He wanted to increase his power and was eager for adventure and full of crusading zeal. The mission gave him an opportunity to fulfill his mythic notions of kingship as a royal crusader leading Christendom.

This campaign also signaled several important changes in French foreign policy. France had recovered sufficiently from the Hundred Years War to undertake an aggressive initiative. And it would be better for France that its wars would be fought on foreign soil during the Renaissance (except for the Wars of Religion). In addition, French foreign policy was redirected toward Italy—a development made possible largely because the attachment of Brittany made France less vulnerable to English attack. Equally important, this new policy signaled Charles's assumption of power from his sister.

Without a second male heir to "spare," Charles went to extraordinary lengths to preserve his son in good health; he was afraid of both disease and poison. (Charles was so personally cautious that, although he relished games of *jeu de paume* [a form of handball], he played only with protective headgear.) While his father was in Italy, Charles-Orland was sent to the chateau of Amboise so he would be exposed to fewer people. Despite these precautions, the young prince died of smallpox in December 1495 at the age of three. The courts of Europe breathed more easily realizing that, without an heir, Charles could not as readily pursue his designs on Italy.

The need to bear children, not only to guarantee the dynastic stability of France but also to provide heirs to Brittany, shaped Anne's entire adult life. Her early years as queen were spent in endless, largely unsuccessful childbearing. A year after Charles-Orland's birth, she miscarried a son at seven months. (This child may have been named Francis.) On the eve of Charles's departure for Italy, Anne miscarried a daughter. She bore another son in September 1496, called Charles, who lived a month. Her daughter Anne died immediately after birth in March 1498. Some sources cite a son named Francis born between these last two births, but, as Matarasso points out, that would be close to impossible.[48] From the age of fourteen to twenty-one, she had at least five known births with perhaps another birth and other early miscarriages.

Fig. 2.4. Tomb of Charles-Orland and his brother,
St. Gatien Cathedral, Tours. Photo by author.

The tomb she commissioned for two of her sons in the cathedral in Tours was one of the first to commemorate the death of young children (fig. 2.4). It attests to her grief and offers an individualized image of the two young princes—one is Charles-Orland and the other is likely the other son named Charles, who died a few weeks after his birth. Their garments are festooned with *fleurs de lys* and dolphins (*dauphin* is the French word for "dolphin" as well as the term for the royal heir apparent); their naturalistic effigies were sculpted by Guillaume Regnault. At their heads, angels hold pillows, and Renaissance artistic elements of garlands and putti decorate the sarcophagus.

Anne's record of childbearing misfortune is particularly striking but also reflects the considerable danger of childbirth for all mothers and children in this period. Miscarriages and stillbirths are not always explicable even today, and there are a number of possible medical explanations for Anne's difficulties. She could have suffered congenital defects, perhaps as a result of her displaced hip, which might have made carrying a child full term difficult. The gap in time between two successful pregnancies, with many intervening miscarriages and stillbirths, suggests the possibility of incompatible Rh factors.[49]

Although it is undeniable that the fundamental role of the queen was to produce an heir, one must wonder to what degree her life expectancy depended, because of the large number of high-risk pregnancies she might experience, on her ability to outlast the sexual interest of the king. Other couples would likely consider two heirs sufficient, as more could jeopardize the ability of inherited property to sustain them. But royal families could make political and diplomatic use of every child. More children made succession more secure and more diplomatic alliances possible. Royal women thus married earlier, bore children earlier and more frequently—all of which increased their chances of dying in childbirth.

AN ITALIAN TOUR

Charles's expedition required long preparation, but the court's stay in Lyon to plan and provision the Italian campaign must have severely disillusioned the young queen about her marriage. Charles's time there was a long drunken debauch—so much so that he convened his council in a brothel because of his avid interest in one of the inhabitants. In his recent biography of Louis XII, Bernard Quilliet comments: "Charles VIII spent his days at table, his nights in debauchery, until he fell to the ground in the early morning dead drunk, in his own vomit or that of his companions."[50] When Charles departed on campaign, he left behind his wife, who had recently miscarried and was again pregnant.

While Charles was in Italy, Anne thoroughly disappeared from the historical record; chroniclers followed Charles to Italy. A queen could exercise power in her husband's absence, but only if he allowed her to do so. And Charles appointed his sister Anne of Beaujeu as his regent instead of his wife. His wife's political impact was negligible; she had direct authority only over the several dozen women of her court. Her marriage robbed her of any active role in her duchy, which her husband also administered.

If Anne disappeared from the public record during this period, Charles launched himself on the world stage. His trip was heralded as an unalloyed triumph. News of an impending invasion of Florence led Piero de Medici, after a show of resistance, to turn the Signoria (the seat of the Florentine government) over to Charles. The arrival of the French seemed to replicate the Florentine civic legend that Charlemagne had liberated it. The Florentines now proclaimed Charles the new Charlemagne, freeing them from the Medici.[51] In each town the French passed through, they were welcomed by officials who gave them keys to the city, erected triumphal arches, and minted coins with Charles's image on them, largely to forestall the destruction they feared French forces might inflict.[52]

In December 1494, Charles arrived in Rome, seeking papal support for his claim to Naples. As his troops approached, the Neapolitans revolted, Ferrante II abdicated and fled, and Charles was again hailed as a liberator. But in their dealings with Neapolitan women, French troops contracted a disease they had never seen before; a new or more virulent form of syphilis had arrived in the port city with the return of Christopher Columbus's sailors from the New World.[53] Charles's march through Italy has been described as "Bacchus's procession," which left behind countless illegitimate children.[54] Charles himself spent time in Naples with a camp follower named "beautiful Guastalla." As Voltaire put it with trenchant wit, "When the French stubbornly went to Italy, they stunningly gained Genoa, Naples, and syphilis."[55] By 1497, the disease was epidemic in France, and a decade later in all of Europe.[56] One must also wonder whether some of Anne's subsequent difficulties in pregnancy were due to Charles's exposure to syphilis.

After Charles was proclaimed king of Naples and Jerusalem on May 12, 1495, he discovered that his allies were unwilling to support his crusade. More problematic, his triumphal romp through Italy had galvanized a league composed of Ferdinand of Aragon, Emperor Maximilian, and Pope Alexander VI. Determined to oust the French from Italy, they assembled forces to combat Charles at the alpine passes as he hastened to return to France. Greatly outnumbered, Charles was nonetheless victorious in the battle of Fornovo (1495). He so distinguished himself in battle that Commynes remarked "in height and general aspect, this young man appeared quite different from his usual self."[57] Despite his military success, Charles ultimately returned to France without having retained any Italian territory.

Charles likely left Italy believing that his mission had been a great triumph, but it was a disaster for Italy. His campaign unleashed a long period of unremitting foreign intervention. The Valois and the Hapsburgs would make Italy a battleground for their wars for European preeminence until the Treaty of Cateau-Cambrésis of 1559. This campaign inaugurated the calamitous period Niccolò Machiavelli described so vividly in *The Prince*. In the dire conditions and political chaos unleashed by foreign invasions, Machiavelli counseled, only a strong prince, acting by whatever means necessary, could salvage even a modicum of stability—the sine qua non of government.

Charles's expedition also destroyed any notion of the French as liberators. He acted more as an exploiting oppressor than a conquering liberator. He did not wear the mantle of Charlemagne well, and his campaign exposed him as a rather unimpressive character with no consistent policy in Italy other than its exploitation. While some Italian political theorists had cloaked the French king with the mantle of a mythic hero, they were disillusioned by Charles and found the conduct of the French in Italy deeply reprehensible. Charles's campaign began the largely fruitless quest by French kings for more than sixty years to gain authority and power in Italy.

Even if the campaign produced no lasting political gain, it had a marked impact on French culture. The treasures Charles brought back transformed Amboise into a luxurious chateau and whetted the appetites of subsequent kings for the new arts and luxury goods of the Italian Renaissance. The thousand volumes taken from the library of the Aragonese kings in Naples vastly expanded the royal library. Largely because of their appreciation for these new luxury goods, Anne and Charles began to develop a court that was quite different from Louis XI's.

Louis, renowned as a misogynist, had made no place for women in his court. He required that his queen, Charlotte of Savoy, and his many mistresses—none officially designated—be unobtrusive.[58] And his queen was, in fact, sequestered with his young son Charles at the chateau of Amboise throughout his reign. Louis's misogyny was likely influenced in part by his father's imposition of Agnès Sorel on the court. But, more importantly, it corroborated the notion that a strong king (unlike his father) ruled without relying on women or even tolerating their presence.

Charles too made little place for his queen and had to wrest power from his sister. But after his return from Italy, Charles's court allowed women a greater role, largely through the activities Anne fostered, although men and women tended to be segregated.[59] Charles and Anne refurbished Amboise in light of his exposure to Renaissance arts. Charles brought back some twenty-two artisans to carry out the renovation. Impressed by Italian gardens, he invited Pacello da Mercogliano to design some at Amboise and included *orangeries*, housing the first orange trees in France. Intrigued by the new arts he had seen in Italy, Charles "values neither Amboise nor any other place he had," Bishop Briçonnet wrote to Anne.[60] But Charles had little time to enjoy his Italian spoils of war or revel in his plans for Amboise. He was walking through the chateau when he struck his head on a low stone doorframe and died several hours later at the age of twenty-seven.[61]

His age at the time of death is worth emphasizing. Charles became king at the age of thirteen but remained, for the first eight years of his reign, largely under the sway of his able sister, who successfully gained Brittany for the crown. The Italian campaign was Charles's initiative, but its legacy was mixed. Charles's contemporaries admired his bravery in battle. Only later was it generally recognized that he had not achieved much as king and that he had set France on a course of engagement in Italy that netted little. If Charles's military leadership became somewhat promising, his personal conduct was much less so.

But one cannot determine what kind of king Charles might have become had he lived longer. After his Italian campaign, he renounced his former sinfulness (one wonders how much the fear of the new "Italian disease" might have had to do with this attack of conscience) and followed this resolve by clearing his court of prostitutes.[62] He also seemed to appreciate his young wife somewhat more. But his contemporaries' subsequent praise for his reformed character might have been provoked by his early, unexpected death. While Charles had inaugurated a new direction for French foreign policy and sought to reinvigorate a heroic model of a crusading king, he ultimately accomplished little in his short reign. His queen left even less of a mark on it.

Anne had occupied a central role in Brittany in her youth, but her marriage had sharply curtailed her power. Charles allowed her to exercise no role in either France or Brittany. Anne had virtually no contact with her duchy during his reign. The terms of her marriage set by French jurists and Charles's lack of interest in her restricted Anne; she was relegated almost entirely to childbearing. But without living children, she had no maternal role. Charles made no political place for her, and except for her coronation, Anne was not crucial to the ceremonies of his reign. At the time of Charles's death, Anne was just beginning to patronize the arts—a role that defined her essential contribution to the monarchy.

Despite their difficult relationship, Anne was grief stricken by Charles's untimely death. Only twenty-one years old, her life had been marked by great personal losses—her father, mother, sister, several children, and miscarriages. When she lost her husband, Anne also lost her position as queen of France. After the king's funeral, she returned to Brittany to reclaim her duchy and reassert her authority.[63] Resolved to rule, she secured control over Brittany's administration and revenues.

AN INCONVENIENT WIFE

Since Charles left no surviving heirs, Louis of Orléans, who had the best claim to the throne, became Louis XII (fig. 2.5).[64] The marriage agreement between Charles and Anne had specified that if Anne were widowed without having produced an heir, Charles's successor should marry her to keep Brittany joined to France. It is ironic that the beneficiary of this political foresight should be Charles's former rival, Louis of Orléans.

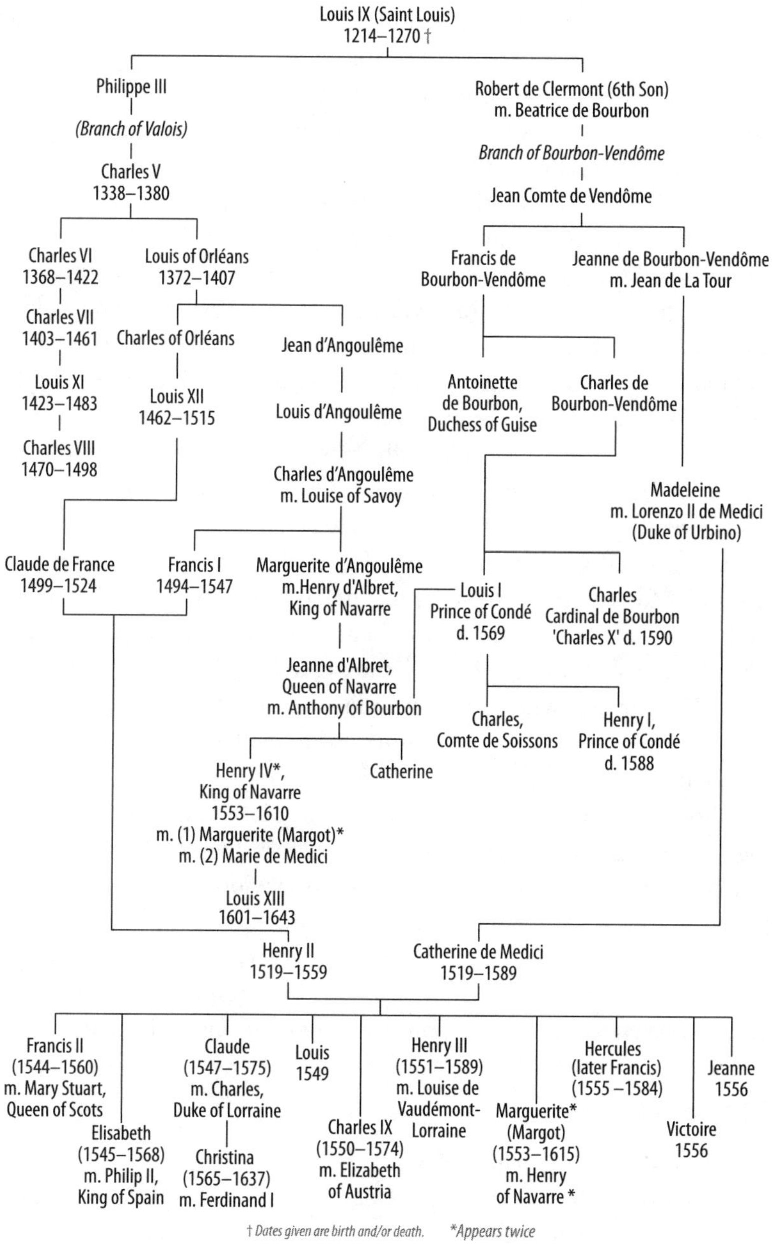

Fig. 2.5. A truncated genealogy of the royal family, showing the descent of both the Valois and Bourbon branches from Louis IX, with the Valois-Orléans and Valois-Angoulême branches as well as the Bourbon-Vendôme branch. Ian Aberle.

Although he was eager to marry Anne, Louis faced a significant obstacle to marrying her: He was already married to Jeanne of France (Louis XI's daughter and Charles VIII's sister). If Anne was a queen who had little role because of her husband's disinterest, Jeanne was a queen who suffered the active hostility of her spouse. Her situation reveals the limited power and vulnerability of royal daughters of France, particularly if they married, as was frequent in this period, other male members of the royal dynasty. Such marriages could mean that the grandson of the king who arranged the marriage would wear the crown, as indeed a surviving son born to Jeanne and Louis would have. But a royal daughter was particularly vulnerable after her father's death. Her marriage cemented no crucial alliance, and she would be unprotected, as indeed Jeanne was after her brother died and her husband came to the throne.

To retain Brittany and make heirs to the crown more likely, Louis XII initiated annulment proceedings against his queen. Over the course of their marriage, he had not spent much time with Jeanne. He asserted, in fact, that his marriage should be annulled on grounds that it had not been consummated, but his queen refused to corroborate his claim. The contested proceedings made Louis's quest for an annulment more complicated. Jeanne could have simply gone along with her husband's suit; some blame her for not doing so.[65] Ultimately the blame for the marriage with its messy ending belongs to Louis XI.

Jeanne was so severely deformed with a hunched back that she was assumed to be incapable of bearing children. Her father had married her to Louis of Orléans, his son's more charming rival with the next best claim to the throne. The marriage was initially arranged while Jeanne was just an infant, but as she grew and the extent of her deformities became more obvious, Louis XI believed that this marriage would bring an end to the Orléans line and became ever more committed to it. What better vengeance to heap on a rival! The reasons for the marriage expose the irrelevance of the interests of the principal parties. Jeanne was simply a pawn to her father's political machinations, as his letter shows:

> My Lord Grand Master,
>
> I have decided to go on with the marriage of my little daughter Jeanne with the little Duke of Orléans, *because I fancy that the children they will have together will not cost them much to rear.*[66] I advise you that I hope to accomplish this marriage, otherwise those who go contrary to me will have no assurance of life in my Realm, wherefore I am minded to carry out the whole according to my intention. . . .
>
> Louis[67]

While this letter seems too apt a proverbial "smoking gun," it was entered into evidence and authenticated during the proceedings.[68]

Louis of Orléans resented his marriage from the beginning. (During his wedding ceremony, he supposedly exclaimed to the bishop of Orléans, "My lord, better to be dead." [69]) Only the king's threats compelled him to visit his wife several times a year. When Louis threatened early in the marriage to end it, Louis XI imprisoned him. (Louis of Orléans was again later imprisoned for fighting against Anne of Beaujeu and Charles VIII in alliance with the Bretons.)

As noted, kings could confidently expect to procure annulments of their marriages, but Jeanne's refusal to endorse Louis's testimony about the nature of their marriage complicated this case.[70] It would have been clear-cut had she acceded to Louis's wishes or simply accepted the inevitability of his success in procuring the annulment. Instead she seemed to recognize with regret that her testimony refuted her husband's but insisted on her truthfulness and refused to swear that the marriage had not been consummated.[71] But the sworn testimony of a consecrated king was incontrovertible, and Louis received his annulment and a dispensation to marry Anne.[72]

The fate of the spurned queen and her subsequent historical reputation is worth mentioning. Jeanne remains much beloved, likely because of her religious devotion. After the annulment, she founded a religious group, the Order of the Blessed Virgin Mary, under the patronage of Our Lady of the Annunciation. When she died in 1505, Jeanne was wearing five nails embedded in her chest—a form of mortification of the flesh of the devout. Beatified in the eighteenth century and canonized in 1950, she is now known as Saint Jeanne of France.[73] She was and has remained a more popular queen than Anne, which raises questions about what makes a royal woman admirable: Was it Jeanne's unobtrusiveness, her long suffering in the face of her husband's flagrant disregard, or her religious devotion? A question beyond the scope of this book is, What made Jeanne a model for women and a candidate for sainthood in 1950?

This particular annulment also meant that both of Anne of Brittany's French marriages and subsequent reigns came at the expense of other women. Both required that the pope invalidate her spouses' previous marriages, although the annulment of Louis's marriage to Jeanne was obviously more problematic and controversial than Charles's unconsummated marriage to Margaret of Austria. But contemporaries worried that the contested annulment made Anne's marriage to Louis dubious and that, as a result, God would not favor them with a son. As Commynes commented about her marriage and infertility, "Whether or not the said marriages were according to ordinances of the Church . . . many doctors of theology told me no and many told me yes . . . but there is something in it that these ladies [Anne and Margaret of Austria] had so much misfortune in their children."[74]

A SECOND MARRIAGE AND REIGN

In marked contrast to Jeanne, Anne demonstrated realistic political awareness and self-interest, particularly evident in her decisiveness after Charles's death, as she secured Brittany as a sovereign province under her control. She stipulated that if Louis did not marry her within a year, the province would be separated from France. She reappointed her former chancellor Montauban and sought guidance from former allies. She presided over the Estates of Brittany and alerted its members that her "singular desire" was that "the poor people be favorably treated in good justice and tranquility."[75] Anne essentially removed herself from France and presented herself as the independent sovereign of Brittany, worthy of being courted by the French king.

Both Anne and Louis had to be acutely aware of the treaty stipulation that required the Breton duchess to marry *only* the French king or his heir, or remain a widow. Remaining a widow would not have been an attractive prospect for Anne, since it would have meant that she would bear no heir for Brittany. She was ambitious and wanted to remain queen of France. Now older, more experienced, and much more aware of her interests, Anne took an active role in these marriage negotiations. She was in a stronger position to dictate the terms, and she was dealing with an inexperienced king embroiled in a humiliating annulment case.

Anne and Louis could envision a future together despite their prior history. Louis had sought her hand or, more accurately, the duchy of Brittany when she was a child of seven and he was twenty-two.[76] He had also fought for Brittany or, more accurately, against Charles VIII and Anne of Beaujeu, for which he had spent three years in prison. Although Louis had reconciled with Charles, his behavior during Charles's reign and in his company was sometimes dissolute, and Louis came to power only because Anne's husband and sons were dead. For Louis, Brittany remained an advantageous acquisition. Marriage to Anne was also attractive because she had proved to be capable of bearing children, even though none were living.

On January 8, 1499, less than a year after Charles's death, Anne married Louis. Her new marriage contract corroborated her stronger position, stipulating that the duchy and its revenues would remain in her hands. It allowed for the independent status of Brittany by separating ducal succession from royal succession: If two sons were born to the marriage, the second would inherit Brittany; if there were only one son, that son's second child would inherit.[77] Anne also retained control over her dowry, and if the king predeceased her, it would revert to her.[78] The terms of the contract attest to Anne's greater power. She insisted on Breton independence and demanded the evacuation of French troops from the Breton towns of Brest and Saint-Malo. Anne's nominations of Breton officials would also be respected. Her second wedding ceremony took place in Nantes, underscoring her status as duchess of Brittany.

Despite her concern to protect Brittany, Anne relished her position as the queen of France and, with her second marriage, made a deliberate decision about where her best interests lay. She could have remained a powerful widow and ruler of Brittany. As Brantôme put it, "She would remain a king's widow rather than lower herself to one lesser than he . . . but thought that she might once again reign as the queen of France."[79] Furthermore, Anne could not guarantee the continued rule of her family in Brittany without children. By negotiating an advantageous relationship with a powerful king, she not only enhanced her own position but also that of any future children. She now attained what Charles had not given her—real, political power.

Her second tenure as queen of France raised many of the same issues as her first, but she enjoyed a much stronger position. This marriage was not a diplomatic solution to an acute crisis, as her first marriage had been; it instead reconfirmed the status quo by which Brittany had been brought into peaceful union with France. As a result, the marriage had more the character of a union freely entered into by both parties for their mutual peace and prosperity. Anne's role in this reign was much more active in both politics and the arts. She was also more involved in defining the images associated with this reign than she had been in her first marriage, as reflected in official ceremonies, emblems, and commissioned literature.

Anne's contemporaries wondered once again about the nature of her relationship with her new husband. Most recognized the political expediency that bound the couple and explained, at least initially, their relationship. Anne was twenty-two and likely somewhat jaundiced by her first marriage to the faithless Charles. She also had some reasons for hostility toward Louis. Even Claude de Seyssel, Louis's panegyrist, acknowledged that in his youth, Louis was "more nourished in lubricity and lasciviousness than in virtues and the things necessary to rule."[80] Anne, known for high standards of behavior, had disapproved of Charles's philandering and Louis's debauched youth. Nor had Anne been pleased when Louis had publicly rejoiced in the death of Charles-Orland because it made his own claim to the throne more secure.[81] Some of Louis's contemporaries initially dismissed him as soft in striking contrast to Anne's determination.

By the time Anne married him, Louis was frequently ill enough to be considered at death's door. He was small and thin, and his contemporaries considered him old, even though he was only thirty-six. Evidently his time in prison had aged him prematurely (fig. 2.6). But Louis had the great advantages of maturity and experience. His pronouncement when he came to power, "It would not be fitting for the king of France to avenge the wrongs done to the duke of Orléans," epitomizes the magnanimity for which he became known.[82] While not learned, he was a man of good sense with a practical turn of mind—an unpretentious man of the people, insofar as a king could be. Many Frenchmen responded favorably to Louis's common touch. Kind and good humored, he was popularly known as the "Father of His People," in part because his modest habits and policies of financial restraint allowed him to reduce taxes.[83] As a recent biographer put it, Louis was "a mediocre personality" but the "great good sense of the mediocre mind is sometimes worth more than the too ambitious programs of the exceptionally intelligent."[84]

Anne had a strikingly different personality. She was rigid—a quality both praised as determination and condemned as stubbornness. As Contarini noted, from the time of her arrival in France, once she made up her mind, she could not be dissuaded.[85] One of her devices (the graphic symbols and epigrams used to symbolize a person, dynasty, or family and promote identification with and loyalty to the monarchy[86]), "Non Mudera" (I will not be moved), reinforced this attribute, although it positively suggests her constancy.[87] Even her most partisan supporters acknowledge that she was completely humorless. She also spent lavishly on luxury goods, a practice that heightened some contemporary criticism, especially as compared to her husband's frugality. But her willingness to spend money enhanced her cultural legacy and that of her husband's reign.

This marriage was clearly more harmonious than Anne's first. It is difficult to assess the level of satisfaction in a marriage, but sources tell us something about Anne and Louis's relationship. Seyssel praised their compatibility, remarking that Anne gave "all pleasure and delights," no woman was "better treated or loved more" by her husband, and no other couple was as harmonious.[88] We know that the couple corresponded when separated and that Louis was solicitous of Anne. According to one story, when Anne met with ambassadors from another country, she tried to learn a few words in their language. When some courtiers taught her obscenities, Louis would not let the joke go forward. It was one thing to joke at his expense, he insisted, but quite another to target his wife, especially

Fig. 2.6. Louis XII by Jean Perréal. The Royal Collection, Her Majesty Queen Elizabeth II/The Bridgeman Art Library.

in light of her humorlessness.[89] The two were comfortable enough to disagree, most significantly over the marriage of their daughter. Perhaps, most strikingly, their reign suggested a true partnership in which Louis respected Anne and her political acumen enough to allow her to act in the political sphere. There she proved to be an asset, especially in dealing with foreign ambassadors. That partnership made their marriage unique among French royal marriages in this period and gave Anne greater opportunities as queen but also compromised Louis's subsequent reputation. A strong king could not, according to conventional wisdom, share his reign with a female partner.

The period of Anne's life that constituted her second reign as queen of France focused on three primary efforts—producing heirs to the kingdom, arranging an advantageous marriage for her daughter Claude, and supporting Louis's campaign in Italy as a prelude to launching a new crusade. Already in 1499, she was pregnant with Claude, and her husband was planning to claim Milan. It must have seemed that certain patterns of her life were repeating themselves.

In this new reign, Anne played a more direct role in political events. As the duchess of Brittany, she sent an ambassador to the Vatican. Just as her new marriage contract gave Anne more independent control of Brittany, so too her marriage created political opportunities in France. She served important official functions, presiding over feasts and receiving ambassadors. Louis consulted her about foreign affairs, even if her views did not always prevail. She negotiated with the Spanish, because of Louis's confidence in her and her connections through her mother to the Foix, princes in the Pyrenees.[90] Anne also intervened more directly in French policies, which provoked both contemporary opposition and generated her controversial historical reputation. Twice her intervention provoked particular affront—her position on the marriage of her daughter Claude and her role in the conflict with the papacy over French designs on Italy. In both cases, her views, critics contended, undermined French interests in favor of Brittany.

Anne's stance on her daughter's marriage was the most contentious issue of this reign; it put her at odds with both her husband and French policy. Claude was born to the couple during their first year of marriage, and marriage negotiations for her began almost immediately. Anne was more intent on making the most advantageous marriage for her daughter than on preserving Brittany for France. She therefore firmly resisted her husband's intention to marry Claude to Francis d'Angoulême, who would succeed him as king, if Louis and Anne were ultimately unsuccessful in producing a male heir. Anne did not share Louis's desire to shore up the legitimacy of Francis's claim to the throne by marrying him to a daughter of the direct royal line or to have a grandson possibly inherit the throne.[91] If Anne and Louis had a male child, then Francis would simply remain the duke of Angoulême. From Anne's point of view, such a match would not have enhanced Brittany's status and was highly undesirable for Claude; she would then have married a mere noble. It may have also seemed to Anne that Louis was willing to arrange Claude's marriage on the presumption that Anne would not bear a son. In any case, she was determined to marry Claude to Charles, who was at this point simply Philip of Castille's heir, although he ultimately ruled much of Europe as Emperor Charles V. Anne proposed that Claude's dowry consist not only of Brittany but also Naples, Milan, Asti, Burgundy, and Blois. This rich and controversial dowry could have given the Hapsburgs a claim to French territory. In 1501, when Claude was eighteen months old, Anne and Louis met with Philip and Juana of Castille to formalize an engagement between their children.

That same year, Pierre de Rohan, Marshal Gié, urged Louis to recognize his subjects' anxiety about his health and it implications for the kingdom's future. Gié maintained that a marriage between Claude and Francis would alleviate such concerns. It would give Francis's claim to the throne greater legitimacy and thus make succession more secure. Even though Gié belonged to a Breton noble family, he was firmly committed to the annexation of Brittany by France, and a marriage between Claude and Francis would secure it.[92] This issue became more pressing as the king planned his Italian campaign. Gié feared that in the event of the king's death, Anne would return to Brittany with her daughter and claim the French territories of Claude's dowry. These fears led Gié to advocate staunchly Claude's marriage to Francis, which put him at odds with the queen.

Louis never conceded that he would not have a son, but on April 30, 1501, he signed a secret agreement repudiating any marriage arrangement for Claude that was not with a French prince.[93] As Louis prepared for war, Gié developed a set of instructions specifying that if misadventure befell the king, Claude and Francis were to be taken immediately to Angers, where Gié was governor. The instructions were specifically intended to keep Anne from taking Claude to Brittany. Gié was persuasive enough that Louis incorporated these instructions into his will.

While his wife was most concerned about her daughter's future, Louis was preoccupied by the upcoming Italian campaign to enforce prior French claims to Naples and his more direct claim to Milan through his grandmother, Valentina Visconti. He too invoked the image of a crusading king and was encouraged in his quest by Anne's spiritual advisor, Francis de Paule. Once again, Anne was left behind in Lyon, and Louis, as on his previous campaign with Charles VIII, spent some time with women in Italy. He became involved with Tommasina Spinola in Genoa, although the chronicler Jean d'Auton insisted that this was an idealized, chivalric romance: "He pleased her so much that she became his *intendio* and he hers, that it to say, an honorable acquaintance." Auton did concede that Tommasina's infatuation with the king meant that she never again slept with her husband and died of chagrin. But Auton intended this example to underscore Louis's seductive charm.[94] The allure of Italian women for both of her husbands must have been galling to Anne, even if Louis was more faithful than Charles.

Louis's campaign, like Charles VIII's, began with a series of quick successes. He easily took Milan and Naples. But the French lost both territories almost as quickly as they had been gained. Ultimately, French defeats led to their withdrawal from Italy.[95] Exhausted and ill, Louis returned to France, where his dire state produced such grave concern that Gié attempted to detain the queen according to the instructions he had drawn up.

Despite Gié's advocacy of a French marriage, Louis continued to pursue, at least publicly, contradictory agendas with respect to Claude's marriage. In 1503, the parties to the marriage negotiation—Philip and Juana of Castille, and Louis and Anne—traveled to Lyon to reaffirm their children's future relationship. All realized that the king's illness made the issue pressing. The following year, Gié prevailed upon Louis to reconfirm the secret clause.

When Louis had recovered but was still quite weak, Gié's enemies, most importantly the queen, began legal proceedings against him for treason. Anne quite rightly saw him as a danger to her plans for Claude and took advantage of Louis's weakness to discredit Gié. Her *amour propre* must have been seriously offended by Gié's plans to detain her and her daughter if her husband died. Anne spared no effort to influence the proceedings, packing the court with her supporters. She wanted Gié punished for his advocacy of a French marriage for her daughter, and the first stage of the proceedings suggested that Gié would be condemned.

The same year, Anne was again crowned queen of France. The timing was no accident; the lavish public ceremony served several important political purposes. It showed the king's support for Anne; the ceremony included novel elements that were strikingly similar to the king's coronation and intended to emphasize her status. Anne received a spousal ring, an innovation in the queen's coronation. With the ring, she symbolically wed the kingdom, a gesture reinforcing her authority and its continuity should Louis's death make her Francis's regent.[96] The ceremony also countered the negative impressions of the monarchy produced by the initial proceedings against Gié. Some might well have seen him as having a clearer sense of French interests than this too-Breton queen. Anne understood the theatrical quality of politics and that public opinion, especially in Paris, shaped a monarch's image and authority. She relished her second coronation and triumphal entry into Paris.[97] She also announced another pregnancy, although this hope came to nothing.

In April 1505, Louis was again seriously ill. When doctors despaired for his life, Louis was forced to settle the question of his daughter's marriage. Ultimately, in May 1506, he announced as his final will that Claude should marry Francis. Over Anne's persistent and staunch objections, Claude, age six, was engaged to the eleven-year-old Francis, who was proclaimed Louis's heir. Louis specified that should he die before Francis attained his majority, a new council be appointed to advise the queen as regent and that under no circumstances should Anne be allowed to leave the kingdom. Even after Louis recovered, he made his wife promise to carry out his instructions.

To procure a public endorsement of his intentions, Louis deliberately manipulated public opinion in favor of a "French" marriage to Francis by convening the Assembly of Notables, which delivered the following remonstrance to him: "Sire, we have come here under your good pleasure to make a request of you for the general well-being of your kingdom, which is such that your humble subjects beg that it please you to give Madame Claude, your only daughter, in marriage to M. Francis, duke of Valois, here present, *who is all French*."[98] This ploy, produced by Louis's conniving, insisted on a French marriage and thus supposedly took the decision out of his hands.[99] The manuscript illumination shows the young couple before the king and the assembly with their supportive mothers in attendance (fig. 2.7).

Contrary to the image, the marriage alliance took Anne by surprise; she felt betrayed and set off for Brittany on the pretext of making a pilgrimage in gratitude for Louis's recovery. This issue had been the most divisive one between the couple, and its resolution was a decisive defeat for Anne. She had failed in her attempt to cement an alliance between Brittany and the Hapsburgs to preserve the independence of Brittany and to make an advantageous marriage for her daughter.

For Anne, the planned marriage did not end the issue. She pursued the case against Gié through an army of lawyers to ensure that he was punished for advocating this policy. When the royal council refused to convict Gié, Anne persuaded the king to move the proceedings to the Parlement of Toulouse, because it used Roman law, which was less advantageous for defendants—a change of jurisdiction against precedent.[100] Despite Anne's efforts to shape its decision, the Parlement of Toulouse convicted Gié not of treason but of "some excesses and faults."[101] This sentence, suspending his title and banishing him from court for five years, exposed the political nature of the proceedings against him. Given the seriousness of the charge and the queen's manipulation of the proceedings, the ambiguous verdict was a serious rebuff.[102] This case epitomized the negative character traits that Anne's contemporaries criticized:

Fig. 2.7. A meeting of the Assembly of Notables at Tours in 1506, witnessing the betrothal of Francis d'Angoulême (later Francis I) and Claude de France. Anne of Brittany and Louise of Savoy are assembled with their children and the women of their court. The image illustrates the *Chroniques de Louis XII* by Jean d'Auton. BnF.

She was stubborn, vindictive, and most concerned with Brittany. But she was also strong enough to bring legal proceedings for treason against a marshal of France and to pursue an independent foreign policy.

With his health improving and the kingdom on a more secure footing, Louis planned another Italian campaign. He allied with Pope Julius II, the king of Aragon, and the emperor against Venice. Anne opposed Louis's plans to go to war again; specifically she mistrusted his allies, who in fact later deserted him. After the French were initially successful against the Venetians at Agnadello, Julius II reconfigured his alliances to form the "Holy League" to stymie French advances.[103] Louis's dreams of Italian grandeur were now actively opposed by the pope—a great trial for the devout Anne, who redoubled her religious devotions in response.

In the face of papal opposition, Louis challenged papal authority on spiritual rather than political grounds. He convened a synod of French bishops, who called for a council to be held in Pisa to reform the Church. The pope then threatened to excommunicate Louis and put France under interdict—a punishment imposed by popes to censure rulers by prohibiting the sacraments and other religious rites in their kingdoms.

Despite these international setbacks, the royal family experienced some successes. In 1510 Louis toured Burgundy, where he was hailed as the Father of His People, and Anne gave birth to her daughter Renée. But her many pregnancies began to take an obvious toll on her. That same year, she had a serious health crisis and received last rites. Her subsequent recovery was heralded as a miracle, credited to Francis de Paule's intervention. By the end of the year, Anne was pregnant once again. Foreign ambassadors reported general jubilation because certain signs suggested that she was carrying a boy.[104]

Anne then faced an emotionally difficult situation: She was again pregnant and her husband remained at odds with the pope. She had opposed her husband's plans for Italy, in essence, taking the pope's position. She undoubtedly feared the excommunication of her husband, the interdiction of the kingdom, and, perhaps most of all, the ramifications of this religious opposition for her pregnancy. It was, after all, widely believed that her failure to bear a son indicated divine disapproval of her marriage. On January 21, 1512, Anne delivered her eleventh child, a boy who died immediately after birth. She can have had little cause for optimism, and she was ill enough after this delivery to spend the next five months in bed.

Despite heroic efforts to produce a male heir, Anne ultimately failed. In her first marriage, she had at least five pregnancies and perhaps several other early miscarriages. Her reproductive history with Louis was equally difficult. Claude was born in 1499. She had an early miscarriage in 1500 and miscarried a son in 1504. In 1507 a daughter was born prematurely; in 1510 Renée was born, and in 1512 a son was stillborn. Several other reported pregnancies likely ended in early miscarriages. Ultimately, only her two daughters survived. This was a great source of anxiety for the couple and the kingdom. Petrarch's famous text on *Remedies for Fortune Fair and Foul* illustrates the misfortune of having no heir, with an image of Louis before Lady Fortune, pointing to Anne holding their daughter Claude, who, of course, could not be his heir (fig. 2.8).

Anne's sorrow over failed pregnancies was exacerbated by hostility between her husband and the pope. When Louis convened the Council of Pisa, Julius II put France under interdict and ordered Louis to appear before the Lateran Council within sixty days. (Julius II had convened the Lateran Council to circumvent the Council of Pisa and to undermine any claim that laymen could convene a Church council.) Louis's hopes to acquire Milan were frustrated when French forces were decisively defeated at Novaro (1513). The political and religious crisis for France was alleviated only by Julius II's death, which allowed Louis to negotiate a truce with the Holy League. The election of Pope Leo X also improved French-papal relations enough so that the pope was willing to lift the interdict, if the king made amends. The religious crisis for France had been averted, but the aborted Italian campaign had netted it no territorial gains.

The issue of Claude's marriage reemerged in 1513 when Francis was nineteen and Claude fourteen, and thus of an age when one might consider a marriage between them. Anne continued to object. Her willingness to pursue a policy at odds with that of her husband reveals her independence and rests, at least in part, on her status as ruler of Brittany. Anne, fourteen years younger than Louis, might well have, in light of Louis's severe health crises, developed strategies to preserve Breton interests should he predecease her. But Anne too had serious and increasingly debilitating health problems, no doubt complicated by her many pregnancies. She suffered from kidney disease, with serious attacks in 1511 and 1514, and she had never fully recovered her health after the birth of her last stillborn son. Yet when Anne died in 1514 at the age of thirty-six, it was sudden and somewhat unexpected. Anne's funeral oration extolled her thirty-six virtues—one for each year of her life. Her Renaissance tomb at the Basilica of Saint-Denis, commissioned by Francis I and sculpted by Jean Juste, was the first of the elaborate, two-tiered Renaissance royal tombs. And she had the unusual distinction of a state funeral.[105]

Fig. 2.8. To illustrate Petrarch's *Remedies for Fortune Fair and Foul,* Louis XII appeals to Lady Reason and points to Anne of Brittany in the foreground holding her daughter, Claude de France. French school, sixteenth century. BnF/The Bridgeman Art Library.

A QUEEN'S IMPACT

Anne demonstrates that powerful queens, especially those who were entitled to rule their own territories, could act with some autonomy; her duchy endowed her with greater authority in France. She manipulated some political situations to her benefit, having set the terms of her second marriage negotiations to her advantage and extracted considerable financial and political concessions from Louis. In her second reign, Anne not only exercised greater political authority in Brittany and France but was also a more important political actor than in her first. If her first marriage proved to be an ordinary, rather miserable royal marriage, she forged an unusual partnership with her royal husband in her second. Most strikingly, she is the last pre-Revolutionary queen of France to have a political and personal partnership with her husband.

But Anne failed to fulfill her most essential goals: She left two daughters but no heir for France; she could not bring about the most advantageous Hapsburg marriage for Claude; and her initial support and later opposition to her husband's Italian campaigns did not alter his policies. But some of the policies Anne opposed were ultimately Louis's failures, and she was a partner in some of his successes.

Louis is generally regarded as a most successful king as a result of improving economic conditions—so much so that Machiavelli, who visited the couple at Blois, proclaimed that during Louis's reign "everyone was happy." Yet Louis failed in his foreign policy ventures. In *The Prince,* Machiavelli singled out Louis's Italian campaign as a striking example of what not to do when invading a foreign country.[106] Anne seems prescient in her assessment of the problems inherent in the Italian campaigns, although her objections were likely as much religious as strategic. Louis is praised for his diplomatic efforts in pursuit of peace, works of charity to ameliorate conditions for the poor, cultivation of commerce and industry, especially of textile and book manufacture, and promotion of French arts and culture. But Anne deserves some credit, for these were not simply Louis's interests; she shared them.

Anne, in the brief peace before her marriage to Charles, developed commercial fairs and encouraged the establishment of travelers' hotels to foster economic development in Brittany. As queen of France, she continued to support maritime commerce in Brittany.[107] Her earlier economic initiatives may have later inspired Louis's policies. She also worked with Louis to ensure the internal security of France by fostering alliances to protect its interests. In particular, Anne advocated a French-Hapsburg alliance—a forward-looking perspective.

This alliance would later be the most essential goal of French foreign policy, with treaties ratified by an exchange of children in marriage, just as Anne had proposed for Claude. Anne's policies also fostered an *ultramontane* (literally, "beyond the mountains") vision of the French Church. That is to say, she supported papal leadership of the French Church as opposed to a Gallican, or distinctively French, Church. This position put her at odds with Louis and subsequent French kings who favored instead a Gallican Church, which gave them greater control of Church property and offices.

Anne's promotion of Renaissance arts, especially through her cultivation of the decorative arts, remains evident, particularly in the chateaux of Amboise and Blois. Contemporary images portray Anne with the ambiguous symbol of two crowns, conveying both that she was queen of France and duchess of Brittany, and twice queen of France. During her two reigns as queen of France, Anne influenced two distinct manifestations of court culture. She left her mark on Amboise during her first reign. She had the chapel of Saint Hubert built overlooking the Loire. This model of flamboyant Gothic architecture celebrated the miraculous hunt of Saint Hubert, during which he encountered a stag with a crucifix set between its antlers and immediately converted to Christianity. The tympanum (a nineteenth-century restoration) shows both Anne and Charles praying to the Virgin Mary (fig. 2.9). The court Anne established at Amboise during her first reign was decisively Breton. She brought a Breton guard to France; she used her devices of the Breton ermine and the motto "Death before Dishonor" to reinforce visually her connections to Brittany. Her device of the knotted rope belt of the Franciscans presented an image of her virtuous and devout life. Anne patronized artists and writers such as Jean Meschinot and Jean Marot, and the illuminator Jean Bourdichon.[108]

With her second husband, Anne constructed a brilliant court at Blois. Perhaps reflecting her greater maturity, more-harmonious relationship with Louis, and greater exposure to the Italian Renaissance, this court attested to Anne's interest in the cultivation of art and manners. It inaugurated a revival of chivalric culture and announced the Renaissance in France—defining marks of Louis's reign—due largely to Anne's patronage. Anne was the first French queen to recognize that the court could enhance her status and authority. Castiglione, in his influential guide to Renaissance court behavior, extolled Anne as an exemplary woman of merit.[109] Anne changed the character of the court by emphasizing appropriate behavior and the cultivation of refined manners. Just one telling example of her insistence on better behavior was her prohibition of public urination; chamber pots were explicitly required.[110]

Fig. 2.9. Anne and Charles VIII on the tympanum of St. Hubert's Chapel, chateau of Amboise, a nineteenth-century reconstruction of the original, which was sculpted by Flemish artists brought to Amboise. Photo by author.

Anne's court was strikingly innovative in making a circle of young noble women central. Brantôme described it as "a very beautiful school for women, because Anne had them wisely nourished."[111] This circle grew dramatically. In 1492, there were sixteen women and eighteen girls, but by 1498 there were fifty-nine women and forty-one girls.[112] As many of these noble daughters were too impoverished to afford court attire, Anne incurred the considerable expense of clothing them. She not only insisted on maintaining a style of dress rigidly prescribed by rank but also demanded the highest standards of behavior from these women.[113] She strictly supervised them, censoring their reading matter and entertainment. Implacable toward those who disobeyed her, Anne was otherwise gracious and generous. She worked assiduously to find husbands for her unmarried ladies. She even had a special dispensation from the pope so that their marriages could be conducted without the delay of posting marriage banns. Yet her critics charged that her emphasis on virtue became prudery and that she exerted too rigid a control over these women's lives. Nonetheless, the marriages Anne arranged for her ladies were greatly advantageous by the terms of the day, providing them with increased status, wealth, and security. Perhaps even more significant, Anne arranged these marriages to forge diplomatic alliances for France. The eighteen-year-old Germaine de Foix married Ferdinand of Aragon, a fifty-four-year-old widower. Anne de Foix loved the Breton noble Dunois but married instead Ladislas, the forty-five-year-old widower king of Hungary. Both these diplomatically significant marriages took place against the will of the women involved, although the second produced a happy match and, importantly, cemented a crucial alliance against the Turkish threat to Europe.

Tragic tales of forced marriage and unrequited love at Anne's court found their way into Marguerite d'Angoulême's *Heptameron.* One tale described the sad fate of Rolandine (Anne of Rohan), one of Anne's ladies-in-waiting, who married her love, the illegitimate son of the house of Bourbon, clandestinely and without royal permission rather than agree to the queen's matrimonial plans for her.[114] Anne then arranged the annulment of the marriage, forced the young woman's father to keep her imprisoned at home, and turned the king against the young man involved. Anne de Rohan was not released until after the queen was dead and she was forty years old. Rather ironically, she married Gié's son—uniting two with a grievance against the queen.[115]

Anne's court, full of refined, virtuous women, had a profoundly feminine character. With its strong emphasis on propriety and virtue, it could be construed as a veritable realization of Christine de Pizan's *The Book of the City of the Ladies*, in which virtuous women constructed a city and governed it. Such a compelling example of the virtue and value of women surely contributed a positive argument to the ongoing battle over women in which members of her court actually participated. The writer Jean Marot, who defended women from the litany of charges against them in Jean de Meung's *Roman de la Rose*, was attached to her court and dedicated his *Truth-Telling Advocate of Ladies* to her, as did Octavien de Saint-Gelais in his *Twenty-one Epistles of Illustrious Ladies.* Anne was also Heinrich Cornelius Agrippa von Nettesheim's patron when he published his three-volume *Treatise on the Preeminence of the Female Sex.* Antoine Vérard presented her with an illustrated copy of Pizan's text with a prologue addressed to her. Her confessor, Antoine Dufour, wrote a *History of Famous Women* for her.[116]

Her contemporaries clearly saw her as receptive to texts asserting women's positive qualities and likely to support their works praising women.[117] Images of Anne show her accepting the works she commissioned from their authors (fig. 2.10). More importantly, her court put women into prominence and presented them as models of virtue. As it established more exacting standards of behavior, Anne's court advanced its civilizing function. Women would play these roles in the sexually integrated courts of later monarchs, where their impact would be even greater. But Anne's court also prefigured later, more-intellectual gatherings of women like that fostered by Marguerite d'Angoulême.

Anne enhanced the Bibliothèque nationale of France, which remains the ultimate beneficiary of royal book collecting. Jean Le Bon (1350–1364) purchased books during his captivity in England during the Hundred Years War. Charles V (1364–1380), who collected more than a thousand books, provided the embryonic form of the library. His sister and three brothers, all important nobles, added to the collection with illuminated manuscripts. Charles VIII's gifts to Anne, a more avid book collector than either of her husbands, of more than a thousand books looted from Italian collections brought important ancient and Renaissance texts into the royal collection.[118] Anne and Louis also fostered the nascent printing industry in France.[119]

Anne had wide-ranging intellectual interests, especially in history. She collected historical documents and commissioned histories of Brittany. Some of them, such as Jean Lemaire's *Illustrations of the Gauls and Singularities of Troy*, claimed that Brittany had been founded by the Trojans to argue for its exceptionalism and independence.[120] Louis, like many educated contemporaries, was captivated by ancient texts; Anne was more interested in contemporary events. She encouraged Pierre Choque to record the crusade against the Turks of 1501 in which he participated and Alain Bouchart to record events he had witnessed in her father's service, initiating *The Great Chronicles of Brittany*. Both Louis and Anne appreciated history for the moral lessons it provided.[121]

Anne was also devoted to Saint Anne, the mother of the Virgin Mary, an increasingly popular focus of fifteenth-century religious devotion, and to Francis de Paule, a favorite holy man for women with fertility problems. She multiplied forms of religious devotion over the course of her life. These practices could have been her response to her children's deaths and the serious illnesses and setbacks she and her husband faced. Some practices tied her to apocalypticism, that is to say, looking to the second coming of Christ. These beliefs were especially important to Charles VIII, who saw his crusade in Italy as an apocalyptic mission. Louis and Anne also both fostered alchemy; they believed specifically in talismans and in the power of gems, and Anne collected amulets and consulted astrologers.[122] These too would have been conventional means by which the royal couple and their contemporaries contended with the unpredictability

Fig. 2.10. Jean Marot presents his manuscript, *The Conquest of Genoa*, which praised Louis XII's expedition to Italy, to Anne of Brittany, accompanied by her ladies. Note the coffered ceilings characteristic of the Renaissance. Jean Bourdichon illuminated the manuscript. BnF.

of fortune. Some modern historians cite these interests to condemn Anne as backward, superstitious, or religiously bigoted. Such interests, however, were not retrograde in their day but, in fact, impelled Renaissance empirical studies of nature. Furthermore, such anachronistic charges do not properly appreciate Anne's role in promoting the cultural avant-garde of the fifteenth century.

Anne's two reigns as queen of France marked a transition from the Middle Ages to the Renaissance, as France enjoyed greater prosperity after the Hundred Years War. With her first husband, Anne became familiar with some Renaissance texts and arts and began to use them to promote her interests and define her image. In her second marriage, both she and her husband applied Renaissance decorative arts more thoroughly and began to invoke classical motifs in defining their image. The grafting of Renaissance arts and ideas onto High Gothic culture is perhaps most evident in this period. With the reign of Francis I, the Renaissance in its distinctive French manifestation largely displaced the Gothic and the medieval.

Comments by Anne's contemporaries provide a somewhat contradictory sense of her character, with assessments ranging from praise for her saintliness to denunciations of her vindictiveness. Some criticized her bad disposition and humorlessness. Others praised her morals and personal conduct as far above the standards of the day. The disparity illuminates the difficulty of "knowing" a historical personality, especially someone like a queen forced to live under the glare of the public eye. Those who reported on the queen, such as chroniclers and ambassadors, had official positions that gave them entrée but likely also constrained their reports. Anne, first as duchess and then twice as queen, was a quasi-public person her entire life. Her contemporaries witnessed Charles's flagrant infidelities, her children's deaths, her many failed pregnancies, and her quarrels with Louis.

Sources offer some consensus on Anne's general character, even if it has been interpreted somewhat differently. Her humorlessness and her insistence on rank made her seem haughty. When Anne was crossed, as she was by Gié, she pursued vengeance. She was implacable in protecting what she saw as her due or the interests of Brittany. Such resolve and strength of character were likely less appreciated in the fifteenth century than they might be in our own. But if her strength produced opposition and criticism, she was also elevated to mythic proportion as the "Good Duchess," a view that developed almost immediately after her death. André de La Vigne, who wrote *Epitaphs in Verse in Honor of the Queen*, described her as "the most virtuous, desirable, mourned, and regretted that has ever been."[123] The contemporary chronicler Saint-Gelais offered a double-edged assessment, noting that everyone was afraid to approach her, but when one did, "there was no one as soft, as humane, and as approachable."[124]

Praise or blame was likely the result of the way she redefined the role of queen. She acted in her own interest and those of her Breton domains, and on several issues, she had an agenda at odds with her husband's. These qualities would have stood Anne in good stead had she been an independent ruler of Brittany. She may well have understood the protection of Brittany as her responsibility as duchess and in the interests of her daughter Claude. Strength and independence were not attributes expected of a French queen, and they provoked some criticism even during her life. Commynes explicitly blamed her for Louis's failures: Because Louis consulted Anne, he failed to pursue the policies best for France.[125] The negative qualities ascribed to Anne became significant to the promotion of Louis's positive but antithetical image: He was genial, expansive, frugal, progressive, and ultimately the Father of His People. She was remote, extravagant, retrograde, and ultimately more duchess of Brittany than queen of France.

GOOD BRETON AND BAD FRENCH WOMAN

Modern interpretations of Anne have perpetuated and solidified the disparate views of her. She is praised as a ruler of Brittany who kept Breton interests firmly in mind and denounced for favoring Brittany at the expense of France. For her critics, she has the distinction of being a twice-crowned queen who nonetheless never made a commitment to France.[126] In large part, this distinction is due to the uses made of her by Breton partisans and historians from the time of her death to the present.

Ironically, Anne's cultivation of Breton history made her as significant as a Breton myth as a French queen. According to this myth, her actions all fostered a Breton agenda and thwarted its union with France. The formative work in defining this tradition was that of Argentré, great-nephew of Pierre Le Baud, whose history Anne had commissioned. Argentré asserted that Brittany had been independent until Anne's two marriages and that her intent was to preserve it as such. In Breton histories, Anne became a heroic orphan, working to undermine all threats to Brittany. Her marriage to Charles became a personal sacrifice to preserve Brittany, although it was harder to formulate a Breton rationale for her second marriage. These interpretations revived charges that Anne had been abducted by Charles and forced to repudiate the much preferable marriage to Emperor Maximilian.

After the French Revolution, when Brittany had lost its independent identity as a province, Anne became, in the historical retelling, a powerful example of resistance to the national government. The policies she defined in opposition to Louis XII became defining markers of a pro-Breton, anti-French agenda. In the nineteenth century, Anne became so prominent in local histories that she was recast as a figure of Breton folklore, featured in popular songs and depicted in wooden shoes and traditional dress. Images of her so attired are found throughout Brittany to this day.[127] This myth not only emphasized Anne's Breton interests and character, it also gave her a particularly active and important role in French history, even if often a destructive one.

French historians generally responded negatively to such appreciations of her influence, at least in part because they jeopardized Louis XII's heroic masculinity by making him dependent on his able wife. Several exceptions to this general trend include a seventeenth-century novel depicting Anne's relationship with Louis as a great romance and the seventeenth-century history by François Mézeray citing her effective political actions as a model for Anne of Austria's regency.[128] But insofar as Anne of Brittany was perceived as an effective agent, either culturally or politically, French historians generally construed her actions negatively. Culturally she was too retrograde, too religious, and her court exerted too strong a feminine influence. Politically too, she looked to the pope rather than to the French Church. In the eighteenth century, Anne became an example of the dangerous impact of women on politics because of their religiosity and superstition.

In the nineteenth century, when many historians appreciated the new, more-secular French Republic, Anne became an even more explicit target. Most notably, Michelet saw the traits so praised by Bretons as bad for France. She married Louis, he claimed, in vengeance for her first marriage, and then became the enemy within. Anne, badly married to Louis XII, then adopted the foreign policy agenda of the Emperor Maximilian, her former fiancé. For Michelet, her commitment to Maximilian's goals (even though she had never met him) completely undermined Louis XII's reign, for Anne functioned "as a true king of France." Every time Louis was ill, Anne attempted to betray France by implementing the pro-Hapsburg alliance. Only the fact that she predeceased Louis prevented her from committing the crime of giving France to Charles V through his marriage to Claude. But this alliance, disastrous as it would have been in Michelet's view, was not simply an alternative diplomacy but rather the product of Anne's evil character: "This bitter, haughty, solitary woman . . . [who] was all pride, loved nothing." With "her furious ambition," she wanted to be "empress of the world." For Michelet, Anne decisively changed the character of the French government from medieval collectivism to personal government by the royal family—from the nation's good to the power-mad queen's narrow interests: "All affairs were now personal, of family, favoritism, and gallantry. . . . France was ill, and Louis and Anne were the disease."[129] The historian François Guizot too criticized Anne. He saw her character as difficult and her relations with her two French royal husbands as uncongenial, dismissing romantic versions of her marriage to Louis XII. "Anne was haughty, imperious, sharp-tempered, and too much inclined to mix in intrigues and negotiations at Rome and Madrid, sometimes without regard for the king's policy," he claimed.[130] At the beginning of the twentieth century, these personal and political denunciations became entirely conventional once the influential historian Ernest Lavisse canonized them in his *History of France*, which proclaimed Anne "a good Breton and bad French woman."[131]

Many modern historians have generally adopted this view, but some, following Michelet's lead, are even more critical, seeing her as a narrow-minded, retrograde bigot.[132] Louis XII's recent biographer Bernard Quilliet described Anne as "authoritarian, egocentric, malicious, and obstinate."[133] For her critics, Anne's political actions and cultural interests were hostile to the new ideological and artistic currents from Italy. Indeed, her historical reputation has been so negative that some recent historians denounce it as systematic misogyny and rehabilitate her as a feminist before her time.[134] Doubtless her advocacy of women made Anne controversial and contributed to the misogyny underlying some accounts of her reign. Doubtless too her mythmaker's overt Breton advocacy elicited and continues to provoke a negative response from French historians.

Surprisingly, given the vehemence of the debate she provoked, Anne is generally neglected in histories of the Renaissance and noted most for her failure to produce an heir for France, although popular histories continue to either condemn her as a disloyal French queen or extol her as a Breton folk hero. As historians studying European women look at royalty through less resolutely nationalist lenses, Anne is likely to elicit more sympathetic treatments. Her political and diplomatic roles might be assessed more broadly and objectively. She is gaining the appreciation of some scholars for her importance in developing Renaissance culture, particularly through artistic and literary patronage.[135] She warrants greater consideration by practitioners of women's history as well. Bartered as a bride, she suffered through many miscarriages, stillborn births, and the deaths of infant children. Orphaned and widowed once, she died at an early age. Her courage in the face of adversity provides a model of a woman acting with resolve and intelligence within the confines of her situation—just the qualities historians of women find compelling.

Anne's iconography has evolved to emphasize modern concerns over her historical circumstances. Popularly lionized as the "Good Duchess of the Wooden Shoes" to reinforce her ties to Brittany and her identification with the common people, Anne is currently invoked on behalf of the campaign to preserve Breton traditions and language. Recent defenders use her to embody their fears about the possible effects of the European Union on regional interests. On the other side of this contemporary issue, Anne is heralded, because of the union between France and Brittany forged by her two marriages, as an early proponent of the European Union.[136] Ironically, the relative exclusion of Anne from the histories of France has allowed her to reemerge as acutely relevant to these conflicting modern concerns.

Anne's case is particularly revealing about what it meant to be queen of France. She most strikingly demonstrates the queen's primary role as a bearer of sons and the grave difficulties and health implications of this role, which entailed as many pregnancies as possible. But Anne also shows the significant impact of queens on culture. They had the means to collect goods of high culture and to patronize those who produced them. The cultural artifacts associated with queens now fill the national museums of France, while those of mistresses have been generally retained in private hands. Queens might, as Anne did, form a culture focused on women and exert influence through a network of women. Mistresses, as we saw with Agnès, were more likely to exercise power through men and often in opposition to other women, particularly the queen. Queens, like mistresses, are figures around whom the history of France has been constructed and reinterpreted over time, so much so that Anne can be revived as a scapegoat or invoked to serve modern purposes. As with later queens, their stories are also more central to French history than those of mistresses, although, as with Anne, they might be long overlooked in histories of the period and preoccupy primarily their biographers. Queens are more thoroughly embedded in the sources of the time and leave a more indelible mark on French history and in its records. As a result, they much less readily become one-dimensional figures of romance, as mistresses frequently do. Yet a queen may sometimes have an equally difficult time winning the war of public or historical opinion. Even if queens could not as easily capitalize on romantic or chivalric sentiments as mistresses such as Agnès Sorel had, they had a much greater potential to intervene in actual governance through their husbands or their sons. As a result, queens were more likely to become targets for xenophobia or misogyny. Any action taken by a queen might well raise these hackles either for her contemporaries or subsequent historians. But Anne's case reveals that a queen could, despite these significant obstacles, exert an important political and cultural influence. In the full flowering of the Renaissance under Francis I, the roles Anne played were developed more extensively by even more royal women, but it was a rare woman who assumed them all, as she had done.

SIGNIFICANT DATES FOR CHAPTER 3

1476	Birth of Louise of Savoy, September 11
1488	Marriage of Louise of Savoy to Charles d'Angoulême
1492	Birth of Marguerite d'Angoulême, April 11
1494	Birth of Francis, September 12
	Birth of Françoise de Foix
1496	Death of Charles d'Angoulême
1498	Birth of Eleanor of Austria, November 15
1499	Birth of Claude de France, October 13
1508	Birth of Anne de Pisseleu
1509	Marriage of Marguerite d'Angoulême to Charles, duke of Alençon
1514	Marriage of Claude de France and Francis, May 18
1515	Francis becomes king, January 1
	Battle of Marignano, September 13–14
1524	Death of Claude, July 20
1525	Battle of Pavia, February 24
	Death of Charles, duke of Alençon
1527	Marriage of Marguerite d'Angoulême to Henry d'Albret of Navarre
1528	Birth of Jeanne to Marguerite d'Angoulême to Henry d'Albret
1529	Peace of Cambrai, also known as the Ladies' Peace
1530	Marriage of Francis to Eleanor of Austria
1531	Death of Louise of Savoy, September 22
1534	Affair of the Placards, October 18
1537	Death of Françoise de Foix, October 16
1541	Marriage of Jeanne d'Albret and the duke of Cleves, June
1547	Death of Francis I, March 31
1549	Death of Marguerite d'Angoulême, December 21
1558	Death of Eleanor of Austria, February 25
1580	Death of Anne de Pisseleu

3

THE WOMEN OF THE COURT OF FRANCIS I

Wives and Mistresses, Sister and Mother

Francis I (1515–1547)—handsome, tall, imposing, richly attired—epitomizes the French Renaissance (fig. 3.1). When he came to the throne as a young man, his vitality offered a striking contrast to the enfeebled Louis XII and embodied hopes for a new reign. His court adapted Renaissance style to a French setting. He patronized the arts and built chateaux in a new, distinctive style. He brought artists of the Italian Renaissance, most notably Leonardo da Vinci, into a court enlivened by an endless chivalric pageant of feasts, balls, tournaments, hunting, sports, and court ceremonies. More than any previous king, Francis understood that royal pageantry enhanced his authority and that women were central to his court. They were not simply decorative embellishments of its many festivities. Instead, powerful, influential women shaped Francis's reign and were essential to its accomplishments. They too patronized artists and refurbished chateaux in Renaissance style. Not simply devoted to the study of classical texts, as were all proponents of the humanist culture of the Renaissance, some of them also wrote important texts of the French Renaissance. They were political actors and diplomats. Under Francis, "women were everything, even generals and captains," complained Marshal Gaspard de Saulx Tavannes in 1573, reflecting back on the court of his youth.[1] The women most closely associated with Francis were crucial in defining his reign and advancing the new culture of the court and thus in formulating his legacy—a distinctively French Renaissance.

Francis's claim that "a court without women is like a year without spring" is frequently cited, but the rest of the quotation is equally revealing. Without women, Francis maintained, a court "more resembles the court of a satrap or a

Fig.3.1. Francis I by Jean Clouet. Louvre/The Bridgeman Art Library.

Turk than that of a great Christian king."[2] Presumably a Christian court should more highly value women and include them in public life and court culture as the Turks and satraps did not. The comparison evoked the backwardness, heathenism, and authoritarianism Europeans associated with such governments. Instead, in Francis's estimation, a cultured court required women. The royal court, the venue in which the Renaissance emerged in France, was more hospitable to women than other new cultural sites, especially when the king promoted their participation.

Foremost were the women of Francis's family. His mother, Louise of Savoy, more than most royal mothers, lived through her son. She also acted with great competence as his agent in both domestic policy and international diplomacy. Francis and his mother essentially ruled together from his accession in 1515 until her death in 1531.[3] His sister, Marguerite d'Angoulême, who subsequently became queen of Navarre, was a renowned author, most notably of the *Heptameron*, her literary masterpiece.[4] She worked to reform the Catholic Church and was interested in the new religious ideas of both Christian humanists and early Protestant reformers. She thus attained distinction as a literary figure and religious thinker. One of Francis's closest advisors, especially after the death of their mother, Marguerite conducted political and diplomatic missions on his behalf. But in her personal life, she, like most royal women, was largely a hostage to her brother's interests. As a loyal sister, she was expected to subordinate her interests—public and personal, intellectual and political—to his.

Handsome and debonair, Francis was never at a loss for female companionship. His two officially designated mistresses were successively important. Françoise de Foix, duchess of Chateaubriant, and Anne de Pisseleu, the duchess of Estampes, frequently filled the public roles of the queen, presiding over some of the most lavish feasts associated with his reign. Françoise was beautiful and well educated; she and Francis exchanged romantic poems.[5] This relationship did not mask its sexual character. Instead, this mistress romanticized the king's extramarital relationship, casting their relationship in an idealized light. Anne, his official mistress for the last twenty years of his reign, led a political faction and thus became a polarizing figure. The prominence of these two mistresses attests to an evolution in court culture away from the emphasis on female virtue, which had characterized Anne of Brittany's court, to Francis's more libertine, sophisticated court. His court vibrantly reflected the rebirth of the classics in the revitalized culture of the French Renaissance.

Francis was also married twice. Given the greater visibility of women in his court, one might expect that his wives would be more prominent. But for different reasons, Claude de France and Eleanor of Austria played less important public roles. A queen was not always a significant figure, especially if she was not assertive enough to define a distinctive place for herself. Francis's queens failed to build on the legacy of Anne of Brittany, ceding power to other court women, remaining on the margins of public life, and, no doubt, making it more difficult for subsequent queens to reassert power. Claude's prodigious fertility ensured Francis's line. Through her, France finally attached Brittany permanently. Eleanor's marriage to Francis implemented a peace with the Hapsburg emperor Charles V, and she worked to maintain it. Francis's queens thus fulfilled traditional political purposes: The first added territory to France; the second produced peace with a recent enemy, which became the chief rationale for later royal marriages. Although Francis disparaged a court without women, those most central to his reign are rarely acknowledged for their extensive and varied contributions to the glory of his.

WIFE AND MOTHER

Louise of Savoy was an exemplary guardian of Francis's interests, assessing every situation for its possible impact on his future. From his birth, her greatest preoccupation was whether Anne of Brittany would have a son who would displace Francis as heir to the throne. With each of Anne's pregnancies, Louise privately rejoiced at the birth of a daughter or the death of a son. In 1512, she recorded in her *Journal*, "Anne at Blois . . . had a son, but he could not retard the exaltation of my Caesar; he was stillborn."[6] This journal, probably written about 1522, was essentially a catalog of the significant events of Louise's life, most of them revolving around Francis. Unlike a mistress or a wife who conformed to her royal consort's context, Louise, as Francis's mother, shaped a future king and set the stage for his reign.

When Francis became king, he turned to Louise for advice and assistance and relied on her to govern in his stead during his absences, certain that his own interests would be cultivated assiduously. Contemporary chroniclers acknowledged Louise's fundamental influence over the young king, and artists portrayed her solicitous care for the kingdom and her son (fig. 3.2). Louise's biographer, Paule Henry-Bordeaux, insists that she merited the title of "king" and recognition as one of the greatest "men of state" France has ever known.[7]

Louise's preeminence in Francis's court and, indeed, in the history of France was not foretold by her early circumstances. She was born in 1476 into a noble family, closely related to the royal family but relatively impoverished. Her father was Philip of Bresse, the younger son of the house of Savoy. (His sister was Charlotte of Savoy, Louis XI's much-despised wife). Her mother was Marguerite of Bourbon, the sister of the duke of Bourbon Jean II and of Pierre of Beaujeu, who married Anne, Charles VIII's sister. Louise was sent to be reared under the tutelage of her aunt, Anne of Beaujeu.[8] The most prominent member of that court circle of young women was Margaret of Austria, who was then Charles VIII's intended bride. The early relationship between Margaret and

Fig. 3.2. Louise of Savoy holds the young Francis's hand. In her other hand, she holds a compass, a symbol of prudence, the virtue most frequently associated with her. *Treatise on the Cardinal Virtues* by François de Moulins, illuminated by Guillaume Leroy. BnF.

Louise would prove fateful later in negotiating peace between Louise's son, Francis I, and Margaret's nephew, Charles V.

When Louise was only two years old, Louis XI selected Charles d'Angoulême as her spouse, not to promote her well-being but rather to prevent Charles from making a more advantageous marriage to Marie, heiress to the duchy of Burgundy, binding him instead to the politically insignificant and territorially impoverished Louise.[9] As with his own daughter's marriage to Louis of Orléans, Louis XI deliberately arranged this marriage to the disadvantage of his potential rival—a practice in keeping with his reputation as a malevolent meddler, nicknamed the "Spider King." After Louis XI died, Anne of Beaujeu, ruling in her brother's stead, insisted that Charles d'Angoulême, despite his objections, marry Louise partly to punish him for fighting in the "crazy war" on Brittany's side.

Thus at the age of eleven, Louise married a man seventeen years older than she and into a household she shared with her husband's long-standing mistress, Jeanne de Polignac, and their offspring. Jeanne took Louise under her wing in this unconventional domestic *ménage* at the chateau of Cognac, where both women raised their children together.[10] Although somewhat unconventional and impoverished, the household was also cultured. Charles was interested in music, painting, and his library. He inherited an extensive manuscript collection from his father and added appreciably to it. He retained Robinet Tesard, the most important sixteenth-century manuscript illuminator, and the two Saint-Gelais brothers; Jean later attained great renown as Louis XII's historian, and Octavien as a translator of ancient texts.[11] The Angoulême household thus was in the forefront of the French Renaissance in its appreciation of the ancients. Louise took advantage of its cultural riches and shared these interests; one of her devices would be "*Libris et Liberis*" (for my books and for my children).[12]

Louise's first child, her daughter Marguerite, was born in 1492. For Louise, as for other women of her station, her success as a wife required that she produce sons. To that end, she made a pilgrimage to consult with the holy man Francis de Paule, whose intercession was widely believed to ensure the birth of a son. He promised not only that Louise would have a son but also that he would be king. Louise's much-longed-for son, Francis, was named for him. She expressed her joy when "Francis, by the grace of God, King of France, my pacific Caesar, took his first sight of the light of day at Cognac, about ten hours after midday 1494, the 12th day of September."[13]

After the death of dauphin Charles-Orland (Charles VIII's and Anne of Brittany's son), Louise urged her husband to go to court to advance the family's interests, as they were now closer to the throne. When Charles became ill en route, she rushed to his side and nursed him for more than a month. "No one could have done more . . . and as his illness became more extreme, she had to be persuaded to leave the room, so that she would not die, as she already appeared more dead than alive," reported a contemporary.[14] Louise commented with characteristic succinctness, "The first day of the year 1496, I lost my husband."[15]

Charles's will expressed confidence in his nineteen-year-old widow. He designated her as guardian of his children and manager of his estates, but left her with only two thousand *écus* after his debts were paid. The young widow relied on Jean de Saint-Gelais to advise her. Louis of Orléans tried to nullify Charles's will, challenging Louise's rights on the grounds that the customary age for such control was twenty-five and she was only nineteen. Charles VIII settled the issue by granting Louise custody of her children but Louis of Orléans control of their business affairs. If, however, Louise remarried, she would lose her guardianship—a stipulation that might well explain her resistance to subsequent marriage proposals.

When Louis of Orléans became Louis XII, Louise went to court to reclaim some family lands now attached to the crown. Attaching lands to the crown through marriage was an important way the kingdom of France had gradually increased its territory. Royal relatives were granted land in *appanage* to give them a territorial base and income; such bequests would revert to the crown in the absence of a male heir. Thus Louise's suit was highly unorthodox and ultimately unsuccessful. Louis further ordered the family to move to the royal chateau of Amboise and placed it under the control of Gié, an act Louise deeply resented.[16] That enmity led Louise to make common cause later with Anne of Brittany in the court proceedings against Gié.

When Louis came to power, Louise was no doubt greatly encouraged about Francis's prospects. After all, Louis was married to Jeanne, by whom he had had no children and in whom he had little interest. Louise might well have begun to believe that Francis de Paule's prophecy would soon be fulfilled. If Louis had no heir, Francis would be the next king. But Francis's prospects were quickly jeopardized by Louis's annulment and subsequent marriage to Anne of Brittany.

The royal court, a model of decorum under Anne of Brittany, was rather horrified by Louise's entourage of her husband's former mistress, illegitimate children, and Saint-Gelais. He was considered to be such an adept advisor that, on Gié's advice, Louis XII detached him from Louise, so that Angoulême family interests could not be pursued independently of those of the crown. The king's appointment of Gié as Francis's governor allowed him to interfere further in Louise's affairs, beginning with the banishment of Saint-Gelais. Nonetheless, Louise continued to supervise Francis's education conscientiously. She instilled in him an appreciation for chivalric practices and humanist texts, and he owed his facility in Italian and Spanish to her. Knowledgeable and appreciative of the arts, Louise was likely responsible for cultivating her son's early interest in them.[17] Early exposure to these texts, languages, and arts formed the young man who would, of all European monarchs, most assiduously foster Renaissance culture.

The renowned humanist Castiglione later praised the exemplary quality of Francis's education: "I was told that he greatly loved and esteemed learning and respected all men of letters."[18] But Francis was not proficient in Latin—the sine qua non of humanist accomplishment. Thus the humanist Guillaume Budé reported to Erasmus, "This prince is not lettered (which I fear is too often the case with our kings), but he is endowed with natural eloquence; he has intelligence, tact, suppleness, and an easy and agreeable manner."[19] Despite Francis's reputation as an exemplarily educated Renaissance king, his sister profited more from their excellent education and became the scholar of the family.

Louise watched with trepidation Anne's many pregnancies and with hope each of the king's increasingly serious bouts of ill heath. Every setback for the royal family also brought Louise's matrimonial status to the fore, as Francis's future kingship seemed more likely. Several crowned heads of Europe requested Louise's hand in marriage, due to her son's expected ascent to the throne. She rejected both Ferdinand of Aragon and Henry VII, deferring her opportunities for an advantageous marriage to protect her son's interests.

Louise wielded the greatest authority over Francis until he made his first public appearance as Louis's heir in 1504 and moved beyond her direct tutelage. After the Assembly of Notables (1506) pleaded with Louis for a "French" marriage between his daughter Claude and Francis, the king formally recognized Francis as his heir and requested that he join his court. Louise commented, "My son went away from Amboise to be a courtier and left me all alone."[20]

With every passing year, Louise's expectations that Francis would become king increased. When Francis toured the kingdom in 1510 as the heir apparent, he was received with great enthusiasm. After the birth of yet another stillborn son to Anne in 1512, Francis was called popularly "Monsieur le Dauphin."[21] He attended council meetings and was elevated to captain of a hundred lances.[22] He acquitted himself well in his first military ventures, which may well have whetted his appetite for war. He belonged to the highest hereditary nobility, whose chief function was fighting. As descendents of the cadet branch of the house of Orléans, the Angoulême had grounds to intervene in Italy; Francis too could claim Milan through his great-grandmother Valentina Visconti. Like recent royal predecessors, Francis would spend much time and revenue pursuing the dream of control over Italy. Until her death, Louise would be the strongest advocate and most tireless negotiator for peace.

Francis became not only Louis's presumed heir but also his son-in-law. Louise and Anne, despite their mutual antipathy (Anne was all too aware that Louise rejoiced in the deaths of her male children), were united in opposing this marriage. Both hoped for other more-advantageous marriages for their children. When Louis was ill in 1505, he appointed both Anne and Louise as Claude's guardians. Before her death, Anne confided Claude's guardianship to Louise. A responsibility, Louise insisted, she carried out "honorably and amiably," although her claim that "everyone knows it; truth recognizes it; experience proves it; moreover common report proclaims it" might seem to protest too much.[23]

When Francis married Claude on May 18, 1514, the court was still in mourning for her mother. Nonetheless, the country rejoiced in its young, engaging presumptive heir. Francis immediately benefited from Claude's wealth; courtiers, who expected to profit from the association, flocked to him; and in June he requested the right to administer Brittany from his new bride. But Francis's fortunes were again cast into doubt by Louis's sudden marriage to the sixteen-year-old beauty Mary, the sister of Henry VIII of England. As Louise recorded, "King Louis XII, very old and debilitated, left Paris to go to his young wife. . . . October was the amorous wedding . . . they were married at 10 o'clock in the morning and went to bed together in the evening."[24] Written seven years after Francis became king, this entry seems tinged with bitter recognition that Louise's hopes for Francis might come to naught.

Louise was a more astute and effective protector of Francis's interests than he. According to Brantôme, Francis was not much interested in his young bride but intrigued by the new queen, even though such interest directly threatened his own prospects. When the courtier Jean de Grignols could not discourage Francis's pursuit of Mary, he informed Louise, who warned Francis that the birth of a male child to Mary would be his undoing.[25] Another serious threat was Mary's ongoing interest in the duke of Suffolk.[26] If Mary had borne a son, whether by Francis or the duke of Suffolk, Francis's claim to the throne would have been nullified. So those protecting Francis's interests kept the queen under constant surveillance until this threat to his future ended with Louis's death on January 1, 1515. Louise rejoiced in the realization of her hopes at long last: "My son was anointed and consecrated in the church of Reims. For this I hold myself grateful to the Divine Mercy, by which I am amply repaid for all the adversities and inconveniences, which came to me in my early years."[27] Louise had attained her greatest ambition; Francis was finally king of France, his interests preserved in no small measure because of her astute attention to them.

When Francis became king, Louise was thirty-eight years old. Antonio de Beatis, the secretary to the cardinal of Aragon, described her then as "an unusually tall woman, still finely complexioned, very rubicund and lively, and seems to me to be about forty years old but more than good, one could say, for another ten." Contemporaries recognized both Louise's ability and her influence on Francis. As Beatis noted, "She always accompanies her son and queen and plays the governess without restraint."[28] The duke of Suffolk warned Henry VIII: "Sir, it is she who runes [*sic*], all, and so may she well, for I never saw a woman like to her for wit, honor, and dignity. She has a great stroke in all matters with the king, her son."[29] The Venetian ambassador Zaccaria Contarini's account of Francis's schedule highlighted Louise's centrality in this new reign (and it is also revealing about how Francis spent his time): "He rises at eleven o'clock, hears Mass, dines, spends two or three hours with his mother, then goes whoring or hunting."[30] Louise unquestionably remained Francis's greatest political partner, but other women—Claude, his queen, and Françoise de Foix, his first designated mistress—were important at the outset of his reign.

"A PEARL OF A WOMAN . . . GOODNESS WITHOUT SIN"

The remark above is the chronicler of Anjou's description of the young queen, Claude de France, at the time of her death. She consistently received such praise from her contemporaries. She is extolled as an ideal queen, even though her public roles were minimal. Her character, according to contemporaries, compensated for her lack of beauty. The Austrian ambassador reported that Claude was "a retiring young girl with a pale complexion, thin, a little sickly, slightly hunchbacked, and rather unattractive," commenting further that "she was very small with a strange corpulence" but "her grace in speaking compensated greatly for her lack of beauty"[31] (fig. 3.3). Beatis remarked: "The Queen is young, and though small in stature, plain, and badly lame in both hips, is said to be very cultivated, generous, and pious."[32] Negative remarks on Claude's looks never connoted an attack on her character or actions; she is the *only* queen of France to provoke no adverse comment.

Claude's future, as we have seen, was determined by her father's desire to use her to cement Francis's claim to the throne by tying him more closely to the royal bloodline and enhancing his international stature. This marriage more firmly secured Claude's mother's legacy, the duchy of Brittany, as Francis acknowledged: "It goes to the regulations of the affair of Brittany to see to the

Fig. 3.3. Portrait of Queen Claude by Corneille de Lyon. Pushkin Museum, Moscow/The Bridgeman Art Library.

general interests of the kingdom. I esteem certainly this daughter of the king, but I could never love her. Nothing about her person seduces. But what matter! I see her, this child! Question of state! For love, there are others near by."[33] This frequently reproduced quotation seems to indicate a degree of self-knowledge on Francis's part and predicts the nature of his marriage to Claude, although like many too-apt quotations it may be fictional. In any case, immediately after the wedding, Francis abandoned her for the company of a Parisian woman.[34]

At twenty, Francis was already a well-known gallant. As Beatis noted, "The king is a great womanizer and readily breaks into others' gardens and drinks from many sources."[35] The Venetian ambassador Dandolo described him as a great hunter of deer and women.[36] Later Brantôme wrote about him: "King Francis loved too wildly and too much; for being young and free, he became involved first with one and then with another, for in that time, a man was not considered much of a gallant unless he whored every place without distinction."[37]

Although unable to provoke her husband's interest, Claude was amiable and largely unobtrusive. She neither challenged the king's mother for hegemony nor brought the literary accomplishments of her scintillating sister-in-law,

Marguerite, to court. Claude did not factionalize the court. She knew about her rivals for Francis's affection, for, as was usually the case, they were women of the court. Although she clearly suffered, Claude endured the situation.

Louis XII's death left Claude bereft of father and mother at fifteen and made her husband king of France. Shortly after Francis was crowned king, he prepared to assert his hereditary rights to the duchy of Milan. He also maneuvered to enhance his position on the European diplomatic stage. His daughter, born the year he became king, was immediately deployed to gain political advantage. She became part of diplomatic negotiations to marry her to Charles V (an earlier prospective spouse for Claude herself). Like many royal fathers, Francis was less than thrilled with a daughter's birth but appreciated her political uses.

Claude made few public appearances. In 1515, she made a pilgrimage to Sainte-Baume in southeastern France in hopes of bearing a son.[38] She was not consecrated as queen until 1517 because of the difficulties her pregnancies posed for her health and for travel. The next year, the dauphin Francis was born to great rejoicing. Claude's many pregnancies affected her health adversely, making her incapable of fulfilling her ceremonial role. That failure was almost imperceptible, so adroitly did her mother-in-law, sister-in-law, and her husband's mistress Françoise de Foix step in to fill it, presiding over court festivals and public functions of Francis's lavish court. She and Catherine of Aragon, Henry VIII of England's queen, attended the famous Field of the Cloth of Gold, the most spectacular of Renaissance fêtes, but both queens were self-effacing. On this occasion, the pregnant Claude was upstaged by her husband's mistress and his sister.

Claude's many pregnancies made it impossible for her to keep up with Francis's intensely peripatetic court as it moved from one royal chateau to another. She increasingly retreated to a largely private life at the chateau of Blois, where she played a significant role in overseeing the construction of what is now known as the Francis I wing. Like her mother, Claude too commissioned texts, and their illuminations suggest a complex dialogue between queen and illuminator about the roles of women and queen, such as her mother had.[39] So too she occupied herself with her ladies-in-waiting. Like many wronged wives, Claude sought comfort in religion, joining the Third Order Franciscans. The significant exception to this largely private life was the visit she made to Brittany in 1518. There, for perhaps the only time in her reign, Claude received an enthusiastic reception with full appreciation of *her* status, not as queen of France but as duchess of Brittany.

In her most essential role, Claude was almost the ideal queen, bringing seven children into the world in just under eight years. Five of her children lived to be adults. Her sons were Francis born in 1518, Henry born in 1519, and Charles born in 1522. Of her four daughters, two of them made diplomatically important marriages. Madeleine, born in 1520, married James V of Scotland, whom she captivated by posing as Botticelli's *Venus* in a fountain at Fontainebleau. Shortly after arriving in Scotland, she succumbed to pneumonia and died. Marguerite, born in 1523, married Emmanuel-Philibert of Savoy. Two of Claude's daughters died young: Louise at age two and Charlotte at seven.[40]

Claude more than fulfilled her most essential childbearing function, but her many pregnancies defined her tenure as queen. Although involved with other women, Francis did not neglect his conjugal duties, and he seems to have appreciated Claude's undemanding character. The king "holds his wife the queen in such honor and respect that, when in France and with her, he has never failed to sleep with her each night,"[41] reported Beatis. As an unfortunate byproduct of her frequent pregnancies, Claude became more obese and incapacitated with each one, and even more removed from public life. She had always limped, and her many pregnancies further deformed her hips. The last years of her life were spent in immobility and rather melancholy isolation at Blois. The birth of Marguerite in 1523 left her with little strength, and it became clear that her health was in serious decline, the deleterious effect of so many pregnancies. She may have also suffered the effects of syphilis contracted from Francis, who was likely infected very young.[42]

When Claude died at Blois on July 20, 1524, at the age of twenty-four, Francis was mobilizing for war. Although he did not return for Claude's funeral, he mourned her passing, writing to his mother, "I would never have thought that the tie of marriage joined by God would be so difficult to break."[43] Francis's friend Robert Fleuranges III de La Marck (1491–1537), marshal of France and historian, noted Francis's grief and said of Claude that never had there been a "more honest princess on earth, nor one more beloved in all the world, and everyone, young and old, believed that if she had not gone to paradise, then few would go."[44] The *Journal of a Bourgeois of Paris* reported, "It was said that, after her death, the gentle lady performed miracles."[45]

Claude's unobtrusiveness made her a shining example for the growing political ideology that asserted that the French queen was simply a site of passage for male offspring with little identity of her own. Ironically, Claude's "Frenchness," which made her so attractive to those supporting a French marriage, eroded her political identity. Brittany had been tied to France for some twenty-five years, and Claude did not use it as a base of independent political action and authority, as her mother had. Her marriage did, however, unite two branches of the Valois dynasty (see fig. 2.5). If marginal to the politics of Francis's reign, Claude admirably fulfilled the queen's most essential purpose: She was a fruitful wife who increased the likelihood of the continuation of Francis's line. As Brantôme wrote, she was "very good and very charitable, very sweet to everyone, and she never displeased or did harm to anyone either at court or in her kingdom."[46] But Francis preferred the company of his scintillating mistress Françoise.

A MISTRESS FOR THE RENAISSANCE

Early in Francis's reign, Françoise de Foix, his first official mistress, often appropriated the queen's public roles. Her relationship with Francis embodied romance. A royal mistress who captured the imagination, Françoise inspired romantic anecdotes, repeated in virtually every source that mentions her. She did not, as later mistresses, use her position to raise her own social standing or to shape politics; instead her relationship with the king seemed based on mutual attraction and love. This relationship may have also allowed Françoise to have a personally fulfilling relationship or evade an abusive husband. She also cloaked the king's extramarital relationship in chivalry and love.

A mistress of high social standing, Françoise was well able to preside over the glories of the royal court. The Foix were essentially princes of the Pyrenees. Françoise's brothers were renowned warriors in royal service during Louis XII's reign. Her husband's cousin Anne de Montmorency (Anne was a male as well as female first name in this period) was one of Francis's closest friends and most important officials and advisors. (Montmorency will play a central role in French government until his death in 1567.) Related to Anne of Brittany's family through Anne's mother Marguerite de Foix, Françoise entered the court as one of Anne's young ladies-in-waiting at the age of eleven, when she already gave promise of striking beauty. Renowned as a woman of spirit and intelligence, Françoise was also, as her correspondence with Francis attests, a poet of some accomplishment.

A particularly striking member of the court circle, Françoise immediately attracted the attention of Jean de Montmorency-Laval, count of Chateaubriant, although she was barely eleven and he was eighteen. He too was connected to Anne of Brittany (his grandmother Françoise de Dinan had been Anne's guardian) and attached to her court. His father had been chamberlain to Louis XII. Jean served first as page to the queen and then a member of Louis XII's military entourage. Anne, consistently involved in marriage arrangements for her ladies-in-waiting, favored a match between Françoise and Jean. The most serious impediment was the vast disparity of wealth between the two families: The Foix were venerable but impoverished nobility, but Jean was one of the wealthiest men of Brittany. So Anne dowered Françoise with twenty thousand *livres* from the Breton treasury.[47] The engagement was formally celebrated on September 8, 1505. The couple needed a dispensation to marry because the bride was so young and their families too closely related. Jean, apparently greatly enamored, persuaded Françoise to live with him without benefit of marriage—an unorthodox situation, which may have occurred because she lacked a father's protection. In any case, Françoise bore a daughter in 1508, but she did not, in fact, marry until 1509.[48] Françoise and Jean's highly unorthodox relationship also raises questions about the implications of her very early marriage and childbirth. Françoise bore her only child, Anne, when she was still just thirteen.

Despite the implacable rigidity Anne of Brittany often demonstrated with respect to the sexual morality of her ladies-in-waiting, most notably when they resisted her marriage plans for them, this unorthodox relationship does not seem to have provoked her ire. The couple remained in her good graces; they named their daughter after her, and Françoise was invited to attend the solemn inhumation of her cousin and Anne's mother, Marguerite de Foix.[49]

Françoise then spent nearly twelve years on her husband's extensive estates, occupying a position at the apogee of noble society, where she was renowned for her grace and beauty. Her husband's court was well known for the entertainments that characterized the Renaissance among the highest nobility of France—receptions, feasts, tournaments, and the visits of authors and artists. Both Françoise and her husband were interested in bringing a Renaissance style to their feudal chateau of Chateaubriant. This chateau, like the royal chateaux of Amboise and Blois, grafted new Renaissance architectural elements such as galleries and coffered ceilings onto medieval structures. Chateaubriant, like Blois, added a Renaissance wing to its Gothic structure. Despite its attractions, Chateaubriant was nonetheless provincial.

The court of the new king offered a more compelling model of Renaissance refinement. It was animated by a quest for pleasure, a spirit of chivalric romance, and an appreciation of wit and intelligence. Jean and Françoise were not initially called to this court, likely because of their strong attachment to Anne of Brittany and Louis XII. But when Francis attempted to ensure that Brittany remained firmly tied to France, he summoned the most powerful Breton nobles, including Jean. The lore surrounding their romance suggests that Francis called Jean to meet Françoise, an acclaimed beauty. It is much more likely that Francis needed Jean's support to hold his northern frontier. But Jean, evidently aware of Francis's reputation, forbade Françoise to join him at court unless he sent her a ring. If she received such a call without a ring, Françoise was to make her excuses. But after Jean told this story to his valet, who then told it to Francis, Francis had a jeweler make a copy of the ring and he sent it along with Jean's letter summoning her to court. When Françoise appeared, Jean was greatly dismayed to see her. Or so the often-cited story goes.[50]

This story not only has the intrigue of romance, it is also in keeping with what we know of Francis's character and his relationships with women. (It also suggests something about how powerful nobles dealt with a monarch's imperious demands.) There is little doubt that Jean was jealous and enamored of Françoise. He might not have been eager to have his wife join Francis's court with its appreciation of gallant women. But Francis likely found a jealous husband a challenge. He waged a campaign to seduce Françoise, feigning indifference, giving gifts to her husband (including a company of forty soldiers), and finally resorting to all-out pursuit. The letters they exchanged reveal the development of their relationship. Francis gave Françoise an extravagant piece of embroidered cloth. She responded with grace but tied her thanks to favors done for her husband and brothers. But ultimately she discreetly indicated her interest in a relationship.[51]

Because the king was attracted to Françoise, he brought her into his court as part of a small band of ladies who "appeared at court like goddesses from heaven,"[52] as Brantôme put it. Although Françoise had initially resisted Francis's advances, she eventually became his official mistress. She was touted as a great beauty even though she was a brunette and the fashion of the time favored blondes. The poet Clement Marot described her as "of great beauty, attractive grace, fine knowledge, [and] prompt intelligence."[53] Citing Solomon's *Song of Songs*, Françoise described herself, "black I am, but beautiful," referring to her brunette coloring. Her contemporaries acknowledged her beauty, but Francis was also attracted by her lively intelligence as well (fig. 3.4).

One can only speculate as to why Françoise abandoned her marriage and formed a liaison with the king. She already had great wealth and status as the wife of Jean, who had pursued her and then married her for love. Her marriage, unlike most, was not one of convenience, at least on her husband's part. Her correspondence indicates her growing love for Francis. By the time she became involved with him, she had lived for twelve years with Jean, a man who persuaded her to live with him without benefit of marriage and then married her when she was still very young.

We know rather more about her husband than is usually the case with a royal mistress. Although Jean had wooed and won Françoise, he was reputed to be

Fig. 3.4. Françoise de Foix, Madame de Chateaubriant. BnF.

serious and rather dour. Contemporaries detected something odd about him, although their remarks about the couple were made after his wife's affair with Francis had begun. Marguerite d'Angoulême suggested that Jean beat Françoise, and she referred to her as "the badly married one."[54] In a lawsuit over bequests after Jean's death, the lawyer remarked on "the disagreement between husband and wife."[55] To give Jean the benefit of the doubt, we cannot know whether that strangeness precipitated Françoise into an affair with the king or whether her infidelity soured Jean. After all, his wife's relationship with the king unfolded under the scrutiny of the court in which Jean was prominent.

No doubt Françoise was also aware that, although Jean persuaded her to take the socially risky step of living together without benefit of marriage, she had not suffered for taking it. Her earlier behavior suggests that even though she was very young, she was unusually willing to challenge accepted norms. She may well have considered that a relationship with the king posed less risk to her status than to have lived with Jean without benefit of marriage. And she had the young king's love and admiration. For Francis, this relationship was unlike his many other dalliances. Perhaps his many easy conquests had become stale and he had found something more in Françoise. He fell in love with her, as Francis acknowledged publicly and announced in verse. And Françoise responded by admitting that she too loved him:

> That which I want to reveal now
> It is that it please you to guard my honor
> Because I give you my love and my heart.[56]

Jean did not take the relationship with the good grace husbands in that position often demonstrated. Instead, he was angry enough over the alienation of Françoise's affections that he reportedly beat her.[57] Wife beating was not uncommon in the sixteenth century; a husband's control over his wife was virtually unlimited. As a popular saying put it, "Good horse, bad horse needs the spur. Good wife, bad wife needs the stick." That is not to say that women found this acceptable. Marguerite d'Angoulême, for example, explicitly argued that blows ended love.[58] A wife's infidelity with a king could, however, provide greater protection for her than other illicit relationships. Most men in Jean's position would have accepted their wife's relationship with the king, but Françoise and Jean's marriage was not conventional. Francis, Brantôme reported, went to Jean and threatened to have him beheaded if he ever beat his wife again.[59] Jean nonetheless benefited financially from his wife's position as royal favorite: He was first sent to Nantes to collect taxes, a position that gave him a lucrative income; he was rewarded with estates that added greatly to his domains and wealth. The duties of these positions also entailed more time away from court.

With an inconvenient husband directed elsewhere, the king and his new love pursued a romantic idyll. From August through October 1517, Francis traveled through Brittany with the smallest royal retinue possible, leaving no record of exactly where he was: The king was engaged in the pursuit of love. Françoise's new status was immediately obvious; she was given a place just behind the royal princesses at the baptism of Francis's son.[60] Such a position was tantamount to a public announcement of her status as an official favorite. Her presence was also on display at the lavish royal fête at the Bastille in December 1518 as reported by the *Journal of a Bourgeois of Paris*.[61]

When Francis spent Christmas at Romorantin, his mother's chateau, he insisted that a pavilion be set aside for Françoise. When he suffered a serious accident over the holidays (he was hit on the head with a lit torch), Louise made Françoise feel so unwelcome that she returned to Chateaubriant. Shortly thereafter, Françoise's only child died at the age of fifteen. As soon as he recovered from his own brush with death, Francis went to Françoise to console her. (The dynamics of this visit are difficult to imagine.) Françoise and her husband then both returned to the court, she as Francis's official favorite and as lady-in-waiting to the queen, and her husband as commander of a military garrison. Françoise was at the height of her influence, but Louise was not pleased with her importance to her son.

Françoise was especially prominent at the Field of the Cloth of Gold, the lavish spectacle Francis hosted to entertain and overwhelm Henry VIII as he attempted to recruit him as an ally against Charles V.[62] This event was a glorious example of Renaissance opulence during the early days of Francis's reign. To stage this event, Francis appointed a "minister of pleasure" to create a fairy-tale village on an empty plain—tents of cloth of gold for the king and the greatest lords, tents of cloth of silver for others. (Tent is clearly an inadequate word for the structures created—the king's tent, for example, had rooms and galleries, all richly decorated and furnished.) Not to be outdone, Henry VIII had transported from England tents of wood, cloth, and glass, with interiors decorated with silver and gold. Tournament viewing stands were constructed between the two royal encampments (fig. 3.5). After eight days of painstaking negotiations over

Fig. 3.5. *The Field of the Cloth of Gold.* English school, sixteenth century. The Royal Collection, Her Majesty Queen Elizabeth II/The Bridgeman Art Library.

questions of etiquette, all were entertained for twelve days by an endless array of tournaments, feasts, balls, and masquerades. Henry and Francis, obviously relishing their youth and status, had several unscripted meetings, including an exuberant, impromptu wrestling match. The Field of the Cloth of Gold seemed emblematic of the great potential of the young king's reign. It demonstrated Francis's facility in using Renaissance arts to define his image and to advance a diplomatic agenda through magisterial displays of wealth and power, which became a hallmark of his reign.

In many ways, Françoise was an ideal mistress in terms of the conventional expectations of the role. Chosen by a king to pursue a personal relationship, she did not meddle in politics. As a member of the highest nobility and married, she was socially appropriate and posed no threat to his marriage. But her story has had particular appeal for its romantic overtones and for the appreciation she garnered from her contemporaries for her intellectual accomplishment.

Françoise epitomized the distinctive character of the French Renaissance as an elite, predominantly secular movement at court. Her status, beauty, and intelligence seemed to affirm that a cultivated king should have a distinguished mistress. Unlike his queen, who was relegated to the private and largely maternal background, his mistress was placed in the cultural forefront. Unlike some other designated mistresses, Agnès for example, Françoise did not have a political impact; the king's mother filled that role throughout Françoise's tenure as mistress. Instead, Françoise polished Francis's image as a romantic, chivalric king. Her tenure as mistress and Claude's as queen coincided with the early, heady days of a young king whose potential and that of France seemed bright and full of promise. But for the hard political work of his reign, Francis relied on his mother.

A POLITICAL PARTNER

Louise functioned as Francis's full political partner from the beginning of his reign. As Francis's most recent biographer, Jean Jacquart, acknowledged, "She advised, she oriented, she proposed, and Francis's choices were often hers."[63] Louise worked to ameliorate the difficult relationship between the crown and Parlement. She demonstrated considerable expertise in implementing a foreign diplomacy designed to enable France to invade Italy. She negotiated a marriage agreement between Claude's sister, Renée, and Archduke Charles (the future Charles V), paid the king of England large sums to disengage from the hostilities, and persuaded Venice and Genoa not to impede the invasion.[64]

The Venetian ambassador Marino Sanuto acknowledged, "The Most Christian King's most illustrious mother would prove the greatest and most faithful friend Venice ever had" and advised that Venice ally "not with the nation, but with Madame the Regent, who seemed to have been charged with everything by the King her son."[65]

On June 28, 1515, having laid the diplomatic groundwork, Louise formally gave Francis the duchy of Milan. When Francis went to claim his inheritance, he appointed Louise as regent: "We have decided to leave the government of our realm to our well beloved and dear Lady and Mother . . . in whom we have entire and perfect confidence, who will, by her virtue and prudence, know how to acquit this trust."[66] Francis both proclaimed Louise's qualifications and explicitly empowered her to act with his full authority (fig. 3.6).

Despite Louise's successful reconfiguration of French alliances to make the military expedition possible, the French claim to Milan was challenged. The pope, the emperor, the king of Spain, and the duke of Milan responded with a counter declaration, uniting them to defend Italy. Francis, leading the largest French army ever assembled, crossed the Italian Alps on a mission to rival Hannibal's. Louise reported his triumph: "My son defeated the Swiss near Milan; and the battle began at five hours after noon and lasted all night and the next day until eleven hours before noon; and this very day, I left Amboise to go to Notre-Dame de Fountaines, to commend him whom I love more than myself, it is my glorious son and triumphant Caesar, subjugator of the Swiss."[67] When he defeated the combined Swiss and Milanese forces at the Battle of Marignano (1515), Francis was widely hailed as replicating Julius Caesar's triumph. Most important to his aspirations in Italy, he acquired Milan.

While her son campaigned abroad, Louise dealt with the diplomatic challenges of his reign. She was central to negotiations with the papacy over the Concordat of Bologna.[68] That agreement ultimately replaced the Pragmatic Sanction (1438), which had been promulgated by Charles VII to reform flagrant clerical abuses and to give the French Church greater control over Church offices.[69] After months of negotiation, as Chancellor Duprat worked assiduously behind the scenes under Louise's direction, Church and state agreed to a new arrangement.[70] It specified that some taxes would be paid to the pope and that the king would nominate candidates for clerical appointments. The Concordat was advantageous to the king, giving him a vast array of Church offices to award.[71] This power also ensured that the clergy, dependent on royal nomination, would be amenable to granting the "gifts" of cash the crown would henceforth request annually.[72] Although it was quite a coup for Louise to have negotiated

Fig. 3.6. Louise of Savoy is surrounded by representatives in a meeting of the Estates-General and the biblical heroines Judith and Esther. In *Hystoire aggrégative des annalles et cronicques d'Anjou* (1529) by Jean de Bourdigné. BnF.

the Concordat, Parlement objected to it as inferior to the Pragmatic Sanction, because it gave greater power of appointment to the king. Nonetheless, by its terms, the French Church retained some independence vis-à-vis the Vatican. Particularly important to Francis, the Concordat, by granting concessions to the Vatican, neutralized it as an opponent of his Italian campaign. With Parlement's ratification of the Concordat, Louise had successfully acted as head of state in her son's interest.

Generally, diplomacy during Francis's reign was a complicated dance between the two primary actors on the European stage—the Valois king of France and Charles, first the ruler of the northern Hapsburg territories, then of Spain, and finally of the Holy Roman Empire and large parts of the New World as well—with occasional appearances by Henry VIII of England and various popes and Italian princes. Francis was threatened by the Hapsburgs' growing power, best indicated by Charles's vast territorial holdings. Rivals, Francis and Charles considered any advantage for one a defeat for the other. They were profoundly different in temperament: Francis was debonair and a bon vivant; Charles was dour and religiously scrupulous. (Their differences became personal animus after Charles imprisoned Francis after the Battle of Pavia in 1525.) Their rivalry made war or preparations for renewed warfare between them the central international issue of the first half of the sixteenth century. Both Charles and Francis were committed to conquest of Italy.

In this contentious diplomatic context, Louise acted as Francis's agent. She worked specifically to increase his chances of being elected Holy Roman Emperor, sending an emissary to bribe the seven electors who would choose the emperor.[73] The Hapsburgs too were bribing electors in expectation of Maximilian's death, which came on January 12, 1519.

The election took place against the background of the challenges to the authority of the Church and empire posed by the earliest stages of the Reformation. (Just two years earlier Martin Luther had nailed his ninety-five theses attacking the Catholic theology and practice of penance to the Wittenberg cathedral door.) Both Charles and Francis saw the election as crucial to their own interests. If Charles became emperor, France would be encircled by Hapsburg territory. If Francis became emperor, Charles's territories would be isolated from each other and difficult to rule and his access to Italy restricted. Charles's ultimate success was a humiliating failure for France, especially in light of the sums expended on this fruitless quest. Louise commented that Charles was "elected King of the Romans in the town of Frankfurt. Would that it had pleased God to have left it empty longer, or rather that it had been left forever in the hands of Jesus Christ, to whom it belongs, and not to another."[74]

CONTENTIOUS CASES

Louise was also involved, at least indirectly, in two significant legal proceedings of the 1520s: the trials of Charles, the constable of Bourbon, and Jacques de Beaune, baron of Semblançay. These cases dealt with government finances and fundamental questions of inheritance of crown lands and defined legal and political precedents. They generated controversy in their day and shaped subsequent views of the Valois monarchy. These two cases gave Francis greater power at the expense of his financiers and the nobility, which provoked subsequent charges of incipient absolutism.

Charles of Bourbon's plot against the king is a complex tale of the accretion of power by a nobleman.[75] Its end marked an increase in royal power at the expense of the nobility. Charles of Bourbon served the king well until his attempts to extend his territory and power were checked. Then he committed treason.

Charles was Francis's distant cousin, and he married Suzanne of Beaujeu, the only child of Pierre and Anne of Beaujeu (Louis XI's daughter and Charles VIII's regent), an heiress with immense wealth and vast territorial holdings. Charles was so obviously intent on increasing his power that Henry VIII famously remarked to Francis, "If I had such a vassal, he would not long have his head attached to his shoulders."[76] Although Francis was close enough to Charles to be his son's godfather, their relationship degenerated over inheritance disputes.

Suzanne's death in April 1521 without living offspring precipitated a crisis with serious ramifications for the crown. She willed her immense territory to her husband. The fundamental question was whether she had any right to bequeath it or whether it should, in the absence of a male heir, have reverted to the crown. Suzanne's territory, combined with Charles's own, would have given him control of landholdings in the heart of France (see fig. 2.1).

Charles had long been involved in legal proceedings as he tried to retain the goods of relatives who had died without direct descendents. When he first pressed his claim to inherit from Pierre of Beaujeu, who too had died without a male heir, Louis XII advised Anne of Beaujeu to marry her daughter to him to settle that suit.[77] His marriage essentially deferred the contested inheritance to the next generation, when the inheritance was larger, more politically complex, and a greater threat to the crown. Although he allowed Suzanne to inherit these lands, Louis XII had stipulated that without a male heir, her properties would revert to the crown. As they had no children, Charles had his wife sign a will making him her heir and giving any children who might be born to his subsequent marriage the right to succeed him.[78] This clause made his claim to Suzanne's lands even more controversial.

The prospect of Bourbon control of all Charles claimed was not simply legally problematic but also potentially politically disastrous. Had the crown lost the Bourbonnais and the Auvergne, France might have fragmented into smaller states—a political configuration akin to the German principalities. To thwart Charles's quest to inherit his wife's territory, Louise as regent contested his claim both in her own interest and to preserve the French state.

Louise's involvement in this case has been complicated by the rumor that she had been Charles's mistress or intended to marry him. By the conventions of the day, Charles at thirty-one was in his prime and Louise at forty-four had entered old age.[79] A prior relationship or a future marriage between them may have been possibilities, although the memoirs and the correspondence of the sixteenth century are uncharacteristically silent. The only evidence is a dispatch from the emperor's ambassador, Jean de Saint-Mauris, reporting his secondhand conversation with Henry VIII: "There is great displeasure between the king, Francis, and the Duke of Bourbon, perhaps because he will not marry Madame the Regent who loves him much."[80] This report was not followed up on, as such sensational news about the regent surely would have been.[81] Such scant evidence, R. J. Knecht contends, does not "warrant succeeding generations of historians attributing the vilest motives to all of Louise's actions."[82] It may well have been easier to assign disreputable but personal motives than to credit Louise with astute responses to political crises.

In any case, Charles's matrimonial ambitions were loftier than the king's mother, and he no doubt hoped for offspring. He set his sights on Charles V's sister Eleanor, the recent widow of the king of Portugal. This marriage would have allied Charles and his considerable territory within France to the emperor, allowing Charles to challenge Francis for hegemony in Europe as well as France.[83]

The threat Charles posed loomed even larger when his mother-in-law, Anne of Beaujeu, died in 1522. She willed to him the rights of her husband, Pierre, and her inheritance from her parents, Louis XI and Charlotte of Savoy, and from her brother, Charles VIII. Her bequests would have further fostered the breakup of France. There is reason to wonder why Anne, who acted so ably as regent and so aggressively in trying to attach Brittany to France in the 1480s, would have made bequests that would have aided her son-in-law's quest to form a separate, powerful state within France. It is conceivable that she intended to engineer a coup—forcing Francis off the throne, by allying her powerful son-in-law to the emperor.[84] It is even more credible that Anne was most concerned to foster her family's interests. In other words, she may have seen her lands as her family's feudal estate, which her bequests would preserve. Her interests were no longer those of the crown, as her family no longer held it.

The crown vehemently contended that the Bourbon territory should revert to it as lands held by royal *appanage* but without a male heir. This claim sought to apply a practice inaugurated by Louis XI with respect to Burgundy in 1477 (see fig. 2.1). This practice allowed the royal family to provide lands and their revenues for minor sons and daughters without alienating those lands permanently from the crown.

More problematically, when the crown contested Charles's right to inherit, Louise filed a separate suit insisting on her rights, reclaiming the portion of Bourbon territory that had belonged to her mother, Marguerite of Bourbon.[85] But when Francis not only annulled Anne's will but also recognized Louise's claim, Parlement refused to register the decree.[86] Louise then commissioned the chancellor Duprat to contest Charles's claim before the Parlement of Paris in one of the most contentious trials of the day. In the end, Parlement asserted the crown's rights to the lands on the grounds that Francis was an heir in the direct line. Charles's claims were denied because he descended through a collateral line. Thus Parlement maintained the rights of the crown but on traditional grounds of family inheritance rights rather than on the state's claim to reattach lands held in *appanage*.

Charles was so aggrieved by the court decision that he entered into treasonable negotiations with Charles V and Henry VIII to invade and then divide France.[87] When initially informed of Charles's treachery, Francis offered him the chance to rejoin him, likely in deference to their long friendship.[88] Charles first denied his treachery and then fled to fight for the emperor, ultimately dying in the imperial sack of Rome in 1527.

The conflict between Charles and Francis is sometimes cast as the last feudal battle between a powerful vassal and his overlord or between the remnants of a feudal aristocracy and an emerging centralizing monarchy. But it also reflects a conflict between traditional inheritance practices and the intent of the crown to extend royal patrimony and authority.[89] Francis and Louise both considered it a battle that had to be won to preserve his power.

Louise was also involved in another deeply troubling and significant case during Francis's reign—the Semblançay affair. This case has proved decisive in the historical understanding of both Francis's reign and Louise's role in it. The problem came to light when Francis scrutinized royal finances closely because he was having serious problems funding his costly undertakings. The man who precipitated the crisis was Semblançay. His father, a successful cloth merchant from Tours, had lent money to Louis XI. Semblançay himself had a considerable fortune and increased it substantially by marrying an heiress. He administered the finances of important families, including the Angoulême and Orléans, and of large areas of France, including Languedoc and Provence. He had also been Anne of Brittany's treasurer. Louis XII had been a prudent manager of money, and Francis I was not, but the financier made money no matter what fiscal policy the king pursued. Early in Francis's reign, Semblançay was in such favor with Louise that she gave him the barony of Semblançay with its attendant title.[90] Always willing to lend money for royal ventures, Semblançay was an outstanding example of the class of men, which first emerged under Louis XI, who financed royal endeavors and enriched themselves at the same time. Downturns in a king's fortunes or a too-precipitous rise in a financier's could provoke royal scrutiny. When it did, Francis, much to Semblançay's surprise, chose to make an example of him.

In January 1518, Francis had given Semblançay almost unlimited power over French finances. When Francis again prepared for war, Louise wrote to Semblançay expressing her concerns over lack of revenue: "I implore you, without sparing any possible means in this world, to do the utmost."[91] The Italian campaign produced one financial crisis after another, as expenses outpaced the resources of the treasury. To deal with this perennial lack of funds, Semblançay resorted to ever-more-creative ways of financing the deficit. The kingdom devoured revenue, and it was convenient to have a banker who complained but somehow found the funds. When the king could borrow from no other source, he could tap Semblançay.[92]

Louise's letters begging for funds seemed to grant Semblançay license to procure them by any means. In 1521, as the financial situation was again pressing, she urged Semblançay to "do as one would do in such an extremity, my last hope."[93] By September of that year, she begged him to do the impossible to save "the person, honor, and state of the king." By October her requests became even more desperate: "We are at the end of our resources."[94] Although loans from Semblançay equipped the army, Milan was lost and inadequate funds for the troops were thought to have played a role. Little by little, the Italian territory conquered by Francis was being lost, and scrutiny fell on the financier. Louise had become suspicious and, by the end of 1522, claimed, "Without being able to substantiate it, my son and I were continually robbed by the financiers."[95]

Driven by the ever-greater difficulties in raising money, Francis undertook a massive reorganization of royal finances in 1523. When Semblançay was asked to submit accounts, he did not produce a single piece of paper. No doubt resentful of the implied wrongdoing, his impolitic resistance might have been motivated by fear that an audit would document his unconventional financial methods or suggest that his personal fortune should be at the crown's disposal.[96] When the controller general complained in February, 1524, that he had not received money to pay Swiss troops, Francis named a commission to examine the accounts. And Semblançay finally delivered his papers.

The initial proceedings against Semblançay, conducted in 1524, were inconclusive. He was simply ordered to separate the kingdom's finances from the regent's. But new legal proceedings in 1527 charged him with falsifying the king's accounts, diverting money from the royal treasury for his own use, and selling royal offices and pocketing the revenue.[97] Although Semblançay insisted that all monies could be verified, he was arrested, convicted of larceny and maladministration of royal finances, and condemned to be executed.[98] Ultimately Semblançay served as a scapegoat for financial dealings during Francis's reign; his hanging body was meant to deter profiteering financiers. Although Semblançay's conviction for dubious financial practices seems justified, Francis was uncharacteristically harsh in imposing such a severe penalty. Semblançay's case was the beginning of a broad attack on financiers by the king and the regent as they sought to make the kingdom's finances more secure and certain.

Semblançay's trial was significant in defining not only Francis's reign but also Louise's historical reputation. Part of an emerging entrepreneurial elite, Semblançay had been elevated by the regent. His trial has been used subsequently to indict Louise's lack of political acumen and to suggest that Francis's financial woes were due to her incompetence or greed. A story circulated that French military ventures failed because Louise insisted on repayment of her personal loan to the crown of four hundred thousand *écus*, and thus the troops were not paid.[99]

The story is not credible.[100] Such a demand would have countered Louise's lifelong practice of using her financial resources to foster Francis's success. Even more telling, Semblançay's defense made no use of such potentially exonerating material. His own records attest to Louise's willingness to put her funds at the king's disposal, and Francis affirmed that practice before the commission. The complex legal battle, due in part to the intermingling of the king's and the regent's funds, documented the serious financial crisis Francis's vast expenditures had produced. Despite her heroic efforts to fund his campaign, Louise was blamed for the financial crisis it produced. Her profound influence on Francis and her extensive involvement in his government made her an apt scapegoat.

By 1525, ten years into his reign, Francis had a number of important achievements to his credit, many of them advanced by his mother. With Louise's help, the young king's authority had been asserted against both Parlement and the Church. He had prevailed in legal challenges to both Semblançay and Charles of Bourbon. After Francis's first successful foray into Italy with his victory at Marignano, his reign was poised for greater achievement. As Francis prepared to sustain his claim to Italy and to prevent the incursion of the emperor, his mother would be required to play an even greater role.

THE GREAT REGENCY

After Francis departed for Italy, fearing to lose Milan to Charles V, Louise controlled the affairs of state in what is sometimes called the "great regency."[101] She consulted with Francis, but most of the initiatives during this period were hers. As Francis prepared to besiege the imperial forces occupying the fortress of Pavia, Louise wrote to Montmorency, expressing her concern that Francis "would advance too quickly before he assembled sufficient forces" and begged Montmorency "to prevent this effect."[102]

As Martin du Bellay reported in his *Memoirs*, Francis justified Louise's fears. The imperial commanders wanted to force the French to engage in battle because they were running out of money to pay their troops. When the French refused to attack, the imperial forces left their protected fortifications and marched toward them. The French then attempted to repulse them with heavy artillery fire, but imperial forces were out of range. When they took shelter in a hollow, Francis, assuming he had them on the run, charged. This move cut him off from the rest of his forces. He was counting too on the Swiss forces to back up the attack, but they fled when attacked by imperial forces. The French were then surrounded by the emperor's battalions. Although Francis fought valiantly, he was crushingly defeated. The French army was completely routed; the nobility suffered its greatest loss of life since Agincourt (1415); and Francis was captured and held for ransom.[103]

It is, of course, easier to second-guess any battle after the fact, but Francis's charge without sufficient backup seems rather strikingly ill-advised and perhaps reflects his impetuousness or youthful sense of inviolability, fueled by his success at Marignano and chivalric notion of kingship. Many of the closest friends of his youth died in the battle, and in its aftermath he himself had to endure the humiliation and rigors of imprisonment (fig. 3.7).

Francis immediately informed his mother of his capture: "Madame, in order that you may be acquainted with the rest of my misfortunes, *know that of all things there remains to me naught save honor and life which are safe.*" While the italicized phrase (Francis's emphasis) is frequently cited as evidence of his

Fig. 3.7. Louise of Savoy is shown steering the ship of state with a rudder, the image of her regency. She is guided by angels' wings, while Francis is shown languishing, presumably imprisoned in Spain. BnF.

chivalry, he continued in a more pragmatic vein: "And, so that in your adversity this news may bring you a little consolation, I have requested permission to write you this letter . . . begging you not to despair, but to employ your usual prudence; for I have hopes that in the end God will not abandon me, recommending your grandchildren and my children to your care.[104]

Louise's enemies expected her to concede anything to gain Francis's release, but she resisted making concessions to gain his freedom more quickly. (Francis was held for slightly more than a year, from February 1525 to March 1526.) Louise's position was daunting. She had to continue to both conduct a war and protect France from foreign aggression. In particular, Henry VIII was poised to take advantage of the French defeat at Pavia. Louise secured the frontiers, equipped the fleet, and enforced a policy of fiscal stringency. She made sure that the army was paid and prisoners ransomed. In response to a choice Charles V gave her, Louise settled on Francis's two young sons as his hostages rather than on Francis's oldest son and twelve peers of France; she realized that France could not wage war without its most powerful nobles.

Louise also worked to rectify France's weakened diplomatic position. She negotiated a peace with the English, presenting a French alliance as more advantageous than a Spanish one.[105] To contravene Charles V's growing influence, Louise sent a diplomatic mission to Constantinople, following up on a visit by Turkish ambassadors to Francis at his camp in Pavia. She also negotiated an alliance with Venice and the papacy.

Louise also faced opposition from Parlement.[106] Taking advantage of an enfeebled monarchy under a female regent, Parlement demanded that Louise repress heresy more vigilantly, abrogate the Concordat of Bologna, reform finances, and establish an independent judiciary—measures designed to increase its power at the crown's expense. Parlement specifically wanted Louise to persecute the followers of Guillaume Briçonnet, a religious reformer, at Meaux. When she refused, Parlement appealed to the king, who responded angrily, supporting his mother. Louise demonstrated a hardheaded pragmatism in dealing with both foreign and domestic pressures. The chancellor reassured the captive king, "Said lady has managed so well that the realm is on its accustomed footing."[107] Negotiations for Francis's release became urgent when he was struck with a "malignant fever."[108] His condition deteriorated until he was near death. His sister, negotiating in hopes of gaining his release, announced his dramatic recovery with joy: "By strong faith, death was defeated."[109]

The crucial stumbling block to Francis's release was Burgundy.[110] Charles reclaimed it on behalf of his grandmother, Mary of Burgundy, whose duchy had been annexed by Louis XI when the duchy was left to a female heir (see fig. 2.1).

Charles demanded it and the restoration of Charles of Bourbon's lands to him as conditions for Francis's release. Neither Francis nor Louise was willing to cede French territory. Francis signed documents indicating that he would abdicate in favor of his son rather than give up Burgundy.[111] He also refused to negotiate as a prisoner and turned authority over to Louise. Her ongoing diplomatic initiatives were designed to enhance France's position and so make Charles more amenable to peace. The stalled negotiations did pressure Charles: His agents in Italy warned him that if he wished to retain Milan and Naples, he should deal quickly with Francis.

Louise was most eager to have Francis released. She was worried about French finances, especially in light of the monies she had promised to their allies and the great cost of maintaining the kingdom ready for war.[112] She was also concerned about the mounting religious divisions, well aware that a king could adjudicate them more authoritatively. She faced increasing pressure to repress religious dissidents from both the theology faculty of the Sorbonne and Parlement. The Sorbonne claimed the right to decide theological issues for the kingdom and during the sixteenth century worked in concert with the Parlement of Paris to identify heresy and prosecute it. Even from prison, Francis supported Louise as much as he could. He wrote to the nobility of France, praising their obedience to Louise as proof they were "good Frenchmen."[113]

To end the stalemate with Charles V, Francis eventually accepted the terms of the Treaty of Madrid, ceding Burgundy and abandoning French claims in Italy. He further agreed to restore Charles of Bourbon's estates and to marry the emperor's sister Eleanor.[114] Francis asked to be released from prison before the treaty was actually signed, supposedly to persuade his subjects to relinquish Burgundy.

Francis immediately repudiated the treaty as nonbinding, because its promise had been extracted while he was imprisoned. The chancellor further informed the Spanish emissary that the king had no power to surrender French territory. Louise had advised Francis not to honor this unpalatable provision. Clement VII too sanctioned Francis's reneging, because it had been extorted by force.[115] Some historians have condemned Francis's action as unscrupulous, but his contemporaries saw it differently. Brantôme echoed their views and praised Francis: "Our king made the treaty of a very skillful prince."[116] In lieu of ceding Burgundy, Francis offered to pay two million crowns.

Louise's record during Francis's absence was strikingly successful despite the considerable domestic and international challenges she confronted. France had been threatened by English troops invading from the north and imperial forces from the south, but Louise had acted to reverse the dire situation. She paid off the English. (English kings were particularly amenable to cash payments, because Parliament was so resistant to funding their courts and military ventures.) Louise helped to negotiate the Concordat of Bologna with the papacy and instigated the anti-imperial alliance, the League of Cognac of 1526. She had broken up Charles V's alliances and reconfigured those of France. Louise returned to Francis a kingdom on a sounder footing.

Even after Francis's return, Louise retained the title and functions of regent: She remained at the center of French diplomacy; foreign ambassadors continued to consult with her; and Francis decreed that Louise would remain regent until her death.[117] Francis's return resumed shared governance between mother and son, although they sometimes worked at cross-purposes. The king pursued war, and his mother worked to engineer a lasting peace. As peacemaking was a role royal women often played, it might be tempting to pose a gendered dichotomy between men advocating war and women promoting peace. But women sometimes made war—Anne of Beaujeu, for example—and sometimes they eagerly supported the cause of war, as Francis's sister would. But Louise remained a consistent and effective advocate for peace.

THE RETURN OF THE KING (1526)

When Francis went to war, he left Françoise behind to wait for him. In response to her longing letters, he declared his love and hope that they would soon be reunited. When Francis was released from prison, Françoise was waiting at Chateaubriant, her husband's estate, expecting to be summoned to resume her place as Francis's designated favorite. This turned out to be a strategic mistake.

Francis's promise to marry Eleanor of Austria would certainly not have precluded his continuing a romantic relationship with Françoise. But his mother had been grooming another mistress for him, one more to her liking and, she thought, more amenable to her control.[118] Louise, who had always objected to Françoise's hold over her son, chose the beautiful, blond seventeen-year-old Anne de Pisseleu and arranged for her to be presented to him immediately upon his release from prison. Francis was hardly one to fail to succumb to such temptation. As Tavannes confided to his *Memoirs*, "Alexander [the Great] paid attention to women when he had no affairs of state; Francis tended to state affairs when there were no more women."[119]

Warned about a rival, Françoise rejoined the court, assuming she retained her status. Francis received her with courtesy and affection but with no greater enthusiasm than that. In response to her passionate letters, Francis became more evasive. Temporarily ceding the field to her rival, Françoise continued to write but shifted to verse (she and Francis had previously delighted in such a correspondence). With a confidence that in retrospect was clearly unwarranted, she disparaged her rival's pallid blondness:

The color white is easily effaced.
The color white is one of a past year.
The color white should be scorned . . .
But the dark complexion and the color black
Is of high price and great value.

This strategy did not restore her to Francis's good graces. Quite the contrary. Francis responded sharply:

If I had not held you so dear
For the time I spent with you,
I could say, "rest in peace."[120]

Francis likely expected to be able to enjoy the favors of both women. But Anne not only had the considerable advantages of youth and novelty on her side, she was acquiescent. Françoise insisted that, because of their love, she should be his only mistress, complaining, "You have made a change from one who loved you so much to a strange *amie*."[121] Between a demanding, former love and a new, compliant mistress, Francis chose with uncharacteristic cruelty.

Françoise's departure from court illustrates a mistress's difficulties when sexual attraction waned or when the king was no longer exclusively interested in her. The convention required that she withdraw gracefully. Without a king's favor, her future was murky. She might benefit from a generous royal remembrance or be dismissed without status or funds. She might, as Françoise did, return to an uncertain future with her husband.

Like other such relationships, Anne's triumph and Françoise's disgrace were enacted on the quasi-public stage of the court. Royal relationships were sources of gossip and entertainment. Such a contentious battle offered the spectacle of a long-running soap opera, since Françoise did not readily concede defeat. She ultimately resumed her position as chatelaine of Chateaubriant, taking care of her brother's orphaned children, fulfilling the responsibilities associated with her husband's positions, and taking an active role in the renovation of their chateau. Her husband remained in Francis's good graces; in 1531 Francis named him to the Order of the King and later appointed him governor of Brittany. Françoise and her family continued to enjoy the social and economic rewards of the king's favor.

Surprisingly, Francis's rejection of Françoise was not the end of their relationship. In the spring of 1532, Francis went to Brittany because it was customary for the Estates of Brittany to crown the presumptive heir to the duchy, in this case, his son Francis. For six weeks the king stayed at Chateaubriant, where he "hunted with his host [and] danced with his hostess."[122] Perhaps he saw in Françoise his youth and a lost love. For Françoise, it must have been a kind of affirmation of their previous relationship. While visiting, Francis behaved more as host than guest, organizing entertainments and consulting with Françoise's husband about his renovation projects. Françoise once again served as Francis's confidant, discussing the financial problems of the kingdom. She helped him write the "Declaration Regulating the Prices and Taxes of Provisions in Hostels and Taverns."[123] After his visit, Francis gave Françoise the chateau of Sucinio, a former summer residence of the dukes of Brittany and one of the richest domains of the duchy.[124]

Françoise appeared in historical records after the king's visit: Her signature is on a relative's marriage contract signed October 22, 1535, and she adjudicated a literary dispute about the merits of two contemporary poets.[125] This was just before her sudden and completely unexpected death on October 16, 1537, at the age of forty-three. Her death generated some widely circulated rumors that Jean had murdered her. Her husband aroused suspicion by arranging to have Francis's gift of Sucinio transferred to him a mere six days after her death. (It was, after all, a rich holding.) But Francis continued to promote Jean. It seems likely that if there had been any substance to these charges, Francis would have made sure that Jean was punished and Françoise avenged. The persistence and seriousness of the rumors provoked an official investigation; Francis sent Montmorency to investigate.[126] Although Montmorency concluded that Françoise had died of natural causes, Jean made Montmorency his heir, which again raised suspicion, even though Montmorency was a relative.[127] The final line of the poet Clement Marot's epitaph—"Here lies nothing where everything triumphed"—captured Françoise's dramatic rise and fall.

Françoise's relationship with Francis offers some telling conclusions about the status of a royal mistress. Most pointedly, it reveals that her lot was at best insecure and that any notion she might have of an enduring relationship with the king could be completely illusory, the relationship set aside by a monarch's wandering eye. A devoted mistress could endure a public repudiation. Without the king's support, a royal mistress could be subject to the control or even cruelty of her spouse.

The often-idealized relationship between Francis and Françoise shares with other glories of Francis's early reign some rather ephemeral qualities. Françoise was but a transitory figure, embodying the romance of the Renaissance court. The period after Francis's imprisonment posed more serious political challenges. To meet them, Francis relied on his mother. Louise remained unquestionably the most powerful woman of his reign and the most effective advocate for peace, even though the international situation was not conducive to it.

THE LADIES' PEACE (1529)

Francis's repudiation of the Treaty of Madrid greatly frustrated Charles V. He had mistakenly assumed that princely hostages would produce compliance with its terms. But Francis had no intention of ceding Burgundy and so did not negotiate the release of his sons. Despite this standoff, Charles was again poised to conquer Italy—a development Francis would not tolerate. In 1526 Francis allied with England, Venice, and the papacy to prevent it. While Francis prepared for war, Louise tried to find money for a renewed Italian campaign. Charles and Francis were both committed to war, frustrating Louise's diplomacy.

Louise looked to her sister-in-law, Margaret of Austria, the widow of her brother, Philibert, and Charles V's devoted aunt, to negotiate the release of Francis's young sons and effectively bind the two men in peace. Margaret played much the same, significant diplomatic role for her nephew as Louise did for Francis, but their negotiations were complicated by divergent agendas: Henry VIII wanted a divorce from Catherine of Aragon, but Pope Clement VII was essentially the prisoner of Catherine's nephew after his troops had sacked Rome (1527); Francis and Louise wanted to liberate Francis's sons; and Charles V still wanted Burgundy. Louise first sent an emissary pleading for better treatment of her grandsons and assured Margaret that "I am determined to use all of my influence with my son so that he should forget his grievance and desire only peace."[128] Both women sincerely desired peace, although Louise was more driven to attain it by her concern for her hostage grandsons. The two women could invoke their shared childhood under Anne of Beaujeu's tutelage as common ground.

Both Margaret and Louise worked for peace against the expressed interests of their more obdurate male relatives. Margaret had been successful in the past; she had signed a treaty of neutrality with the duchy of Burgundy, contrary to Charles's wishes. She had also worked to persuade Charles not to keep Francis a prisoner indefinitely by promoting marriage to Eleanor. The two women also found ways to speak to each other under the diplomatic radar; even the well-connected Italian ambassadors were unaware of their activities.

The peace Margaret presented to Charles V gave him clear advantages. If he no longer had to prepare for a French attack in Flanders, he could turn his attention to the Turkish leader, Suleiman the Magnificent. (When Charles eventually defeated him, he liberated Christian Europe from the Turkish threat by 1535.) The treaty also despoiled France of so much money that it would be unable to wage war again for years. Most critically, it ceded Italy to the emperor.

While more advantageous for Charles, the Ladies' Peace (formally called the Peace of Cambrai) was not a complete defeat for France. Charles renounced Charles of Bourbon's lands and agreed that his sister Eleanor would marry Francis, accompanied by the ransomed princes. The treaty largely reiterated the terms of the earlier Treaty of Madrid, but Francis retained Burgundy and the Bourbon lands. France negotiated from a weak position, and it was unquestionably a harsh peace with a negative impact on France's finances and political stature. The peace decisively altered the balance of power in Europe. Surrounded by the Hapsburgs, Francis then looked to the Turks as potential allies, shocking sixteenth-century Christendom. Aware of the obvious disadvantages of this peace, Louise nonetheless negotiated it as a calculated gamble designed to preserve France as a viable state in the face of continuing Hapsburg threats to its power.

After the treaty was signed, Louise sent a representative to check on her young grandsons while the vast ransom was raised. One might assume that the princes would be well treated, but that was not the case. As months passed, their conditions deteriorated, perhaps reflecting Charles's exasperation with Francis's seeming indifference to their plight. Louise's emissary returned with a heartbreaking report. Her grandsons were held in a dank cell; they had been deprived of their attendants; and they had forgotten how to speak French![129] Louise wrote to Charles asking him to restore the young princes' attendants. When Margaret heard of their condition, she interceded with Charles, appealing to his love for his own children.

When negotiations concluded, Louise attended the solemn ceremony in which Francis promised to marry Eleanor. But when the children were to be returned and Francis to marry Eleanor, Louise was incapacitated by gout and her newly remarried daughter Marguerite was pregnant. So she commissioned noblewomen to accompany the young princes and future queen to France, Diane de Poitiers among them—a portentous meeting for the young Prince Henry, as we will see, although this story too may be a popular foreshadowing.

Louise remained deeply involved in the politics and diplomacy of Francis's reign until her death in 1531. She was unswerving in her diplomatic efforts so that France could extricate itself from political difficulties. She took advantage of the weakness of any enemy and was both flexible and adept in pursuing French interests. She was Francis's most skilled political ally and agent. Francis acknowledged her as such when he gave her, against all precedent, a state funeral appropriate for a ruler.[130]

An uncrowned co-ruler during the first fifteen years of Francis's reign, Louise also had a great impact on the unfolding of subsequent political events. The Ladies' Peace gave France a seven-year hiatus in the duel for power with Charles V, which allowed it to deal with its shattered finances. The peace she negotiated with England survived until 1543. Because she recognized the advantages of pursing a foreign policy based on a balance of power, she encouraged Francis to ally with the Turks to both disconcert Charles V and threaten him from the east.[131] Francis paid tribute to his mother in the epitaph: "O heart which feels nothing of a woman but the name,"[132] no doubt intended to praise her competence and courage. Most importantly, when Louise died, she left her country at peace.[133]

Unquestionably, Louise had the most profound political impact on Francis and deserves considerable credit for many of the most positive developments of Francis's reign. She demonstrates the impact a woman empowered by her son could have on the highest levels of international diplomacy and domestic policy. Louise deserves great recognition as an especially effective regent under challenging circumstances. As her biographer Henry-Bordeaux put it, she was, "the keystone in the arch she formed with her son and daughter, but she had greater strength than either of them."[134] Her death ended Francis's youth and their reign together. Francis then increasingly relied on his sister, Marguerite, who took more central roles.

THE INCOMPARABLE AND ILLUSTRIOUS QUEEN OF NAVARRE

Marguerite had "the body of a woman, the heart of a man, and the head of an angel," proclaimed the poet Clement Marot.[135] Although she emerged as a key figure of the French Renaissance, Marguerite occupied a very different place in her mother's world than Francis did. Louise's *Journal* revolved around her "Caesar";[136] Marguerite was rarely mentioned. Her life was largely shaped by her status as the king's devoted sister (fig. 3.8). When Francis disagreed with her over issues such as the marriage of her daughter or the persecution of Protestants, she deferred to his wishes or retreated. Her life was shaped decisively by the limits imposed on elite women: A marriage was arranged for her to a man in whom she had no interest and with whom she shared no interests; when she

Fig. 3.8. Marguerite d'Angoulême by Jean Clouet. National Museums Liverpool / The Bridgeman Art Library.

made a second marriage for love, that beloved husband freely pursued sexual adventures; and Marguerite's relationship with her own daughter was largely defined by Francis's diplomatic agenda. Despite these constraints on her personal life, Marguerite was an intellectual luminary and political figure in Francis's court, and she attained great distinction as one of the most important writers of the French Renaissance.

Marguerite was born on April 11, 1492, into the Angoulême family, whose fortunes fluctuated as their expectations of inheriting the throne waxed and waned with Anne of Brittany's pregnancies and as Louis XII married his successive wives with greater or lesser prospects for fertility. Even more than the family's position vis-à-vis the throne, Marguerite's life was shaped by her position as moon to her brother's sun. We know little of her early life except that she followed her family's peregrinations from one royal chateau to another, spending time at her mother's chateaux at Cognac and Romorantin and at the royal chateaux of Amboise and Blois. Her early environment allowed her interests and abilities to flourish. She benefited from the excellent education available to her brother and, indeed, was the more apt pupil (fig. 3.9).

Marguerite grew up surrounded by the young men chosen by her mother as fitting companions for her brother and who later played important roles in

Fig. 3.9. An image of Marguerite d'Angoulême and Francis playing chess, used to illustrate the manuscript *Echecs des amoureux*. Not only did chess become popular in the sixteenth century, but the queen became more important to the game. BnF.

the history of France. Several of them, including Gaston de Foix, a young love of Marguerite's, and Guillaume de Bonnivet, died in Francis's wars. Charles de Montpensier became the constable of Bourbon and betrayed his king. The most important of them, Anne de Montmorency, was a political advisor and military leader who served Francis and Francis's son and grandsons.

Several of these young men had a marked impact on Marguerite. Her relationship with them, according to scholars' speculations, may be found, thinly disguised in fiction, in her best-known work, *Heptameron.* One story tells of a widow left with two children, a young prince and princess. Youthful love and trust was betrayed by assaults on the princess's virtue.[137] The princess Florinde fell in love with a stunningly handsome young prince who died in battle. Another young man, Amadour, consoled her and became her confidant. He married one of the princess's friends to remain close to her and then went to war. While he was away, the princess married another. When Amadour returned after the death of his wife, he first tried to persuade the princess that marriage made extramarital relationships permissible. He then tried to take her by force, despite her vociferous objections. She thwarted him again by deliberately bruising her face so badly that he would not find her attractive. When he nonetheless attacked her again, her cries brought her mother, and Amadour was forced into exile.

Another story tells of a similar attack.[138] In this version, the aggressor is housed in a room below the princess's, connected by a trapdoor. But the princess and her maid lie in wait for him. When he invades her room, they beat him so severely that he is forced to absent himself to avoid explaining his battered appearance.

Marguerite's biographers concede that these stories are not conclusively autobiographical. However, there seems to be sufficient correlation between her life and these stories to suppose that Foix was the handsome young prince, as he was both her early love and killed at the battle of Ravenna (1512), and that Bonnivet was the confidant turned attacker.[139] Whether autobiographical or not, these storied expose the vulnerability of women, even those like Marguerite at the top of the social hierarchy. Her personal experience of sexual assault may well explain the prominence of rape in the *Heptameron.*

Marguerite's personal life, like that of other royal women, was shaped by the marriage alliance made for her—a decision in which she actually had greater say than many of her contemporaries. Her situation was complicated by the fact that, during the years in which a marriage would likely be arranged, it was not clear whether she would be simply the sister of a prestigious but impoverished French nobleman or of the king of France. When marriage to Marguerite was proposed to Arthur, the oldest son of Henry VII of England, he preferred a king's daughter over a prospective king's sister and so chose Catherine of Aragon. After Arthur's death, Marguerite was proposed for his brother, the future Henry VIII, but it was still not certain that Francis would inherit the throne. A royal marriage for Marguerite would have given too much power to the Angoulême family if Francis were not the heir to the throne. Other marriages would have given undue influence to a mere nobleman should he then be married to a king's sister. Marguerite was not an entirely passive bystander. When Louis XII proposed the English Prince Henry, Marguerite objected to being sent to a foreign land. Surely, she contended, she could find a young, rich, noble husband without crossing the English Channel.[140]

Ultimately, the selection of Marguerite's husband was made in the crown's narrowest interests. In 1508, she married Charles, the duke of Alençon, a match Louis XII arranged to settle a legal dispute between the crown and the duke.[141] Charles derived great benefit from Marguerite's status. Once Francis became king, Charles had the status of second gentleman of the kingdom, with the attendant prerogatives.[142] Nothing about the arrangement served Marguerite's interests, and her situation was quite uncongenial. She was separated from home and family at the age of sixteen to go to her husband's estates in Normandy. Her spouse had been reared in relative poverty and isolation by a widowed mother. A feudal warrior with no intellectual interests, he was, by all accounts, remarkably undistinguished. Thus, Marguerite, a paragon of Renaissance learning and culture, married a feudal military man on whom the Renaissance had made no impression. She lived in the cultural backwater of Alençon, where the chateau was an austere feudal structure without the stylistic benefits or creature comforts of the Renaissance. Marguerite's devout mother-in-law had worked to preserve her son's estates, but their household was impoverished. Despite her difficult circumstances, Marguerite's exposure to this environment might well have awakened or heightened her religious devotion.

Marguerite's life dramatically changed with Francis's accession to the throne. He summoned her to court, where she became one of its greatest ornaments and a central figure in promulgating the Renaissance in a French setting. She also took on significant political missions, represented the king in the provinces, marshaled troops, and supervised construction projects. These activities demonstrated that Francis trusted her to act in his stead in a variety of contexts. An Italian ambassador acknowledged her influence: "The sister knows all the secrets but speaks little, what a most beautiful woman."[143] The duke of Suffolk advised his brother-in-law Henry VIII to write affectionately to Marguerite to curry her brother's favor.[144] She also received foreign ambassadors, as when the

English ambassador came to arrange a marriage between the newborn dauphin and Mary Tudor. Because Queen Claude was both retiring and frequently pregnant, Marguerite performed the public offices of her sister-in-law, often serving as Francis's official hostess. Marguerite played an important role in the royal household, overseeing the education of her nieces and nephews after Claude's death.[145]

In recognition of her many services, Francis settled a pension on Marguerite, which gave her a measure of financial independence.[146] Even more significant was his gift of the duchy of Berry and his elevation of that duchy to one conferring the status of peer of the realm on its holder. As there were only twelve peers at a time and very few of them throughout the sixteenth century were women, this position alone gave Marguerite an extraordinary official status. With a seat on the royal council, she was consulted by the king about the most important issues of the day. As her correspondence documents, she directed administrative and religious offices in her territories and acted as an effective patron of the nobles of her duchy.[147]

Marguerite's activities enhanced Francis's reputation as a paragon of the Renaissance. The famous Italian humanist Castiglione acknowledged Francis as "the mirror of graces and good education . . . much in contrast to the practices in France."[148] Francis was interested in humanism, but his sister was a scholar of true distinction and an outstanding exemplar of the roles women could play in courtly humanism. Castiglione's famous depiction of the court of Urbino in *The Book of the Courtier* not only made the court central to the transmission of humanism but also made women the crucial agents in moderating male culture by transforming the feudal warrior into the Renaissance man. While Anne of Brittany's court had a circle of devout women, it was not a venue where men and women enjoyed each other's company. Francis's distinctively Renaissance court appreciated women and made them central to its activities. Marguerite was a particularly apt French rendition of Castiglione's Elisabetta Gonzaga—a paragon of virtue and learning in a royal court. But Marguerite was not simply, on the Italian model, a woman who orchestrated the conversation of men; she pursued her own intellectual interests and defined the literature of the French Renaissance.

The early years of Francis's reign offer glimpses into Marguerite's interest in religious reform. Some of her ideas became central to the emergence of Protestantism in France. Initially, Francis gave her full rein. Intrigued by new ideas, he himself did not take a definitive stand until he perceived the reformers as a political threat. After hearing Guillaume Briçonnet, bishop of Meaux, preach, Marguerite corresponded extensively about theological issues with him. He became one of the most notable guides to her religious development. Briçonnet encouraged her interest in religious reform and urged her to get involved in nominating bishops, no doubt seeing her as a powerful ally for his reform-minded community.

Those who advocated the reform of the Church could remain completely orthodox, and many of them espoused ideas associated with the growing reform movement within the Catholic Church called Christian humanism. Christian humanists, like other Renaissance humanists, studied classical texts and applied philological methods to purify these texts of their medieval accretions; they focused particularly on early Christian texts.[149] Their studies revealed glaring inconsistencies between the practices, beliefs, and structure of the early Church and those of the Renaissance Church. While calls for reform based on this understanding of early Christianity could be and were launched from within the Church, espousing these ideas became more problematic once the Church had condemned Luther's ideas. Those committed to reform then found it more difficult to define a position distinct from Luther's. Calls for reform were increasingly construed as direct attacks on the Church.[150]

Marguerite was deeply sympathetic to both the ideas and the proponents of religious reform. She saw the new movement as a way to purify Catholicism and return it to its early, apostolic roots. She advocated the reform of monasteries and convents and had reformed several on her lands already by 1520.[151] She remained unflinchingly critical of the corruption of monasteries—a central theme of the *Heptameron.* Her strong commitment to charitable institutions led her to inaugurate a system of public assistance in hospitals in Alençon and in Paris. Marguerite was also formidable enough in debating the theological complexities underlying the Reformation to be perceived as a threat by the theology faculty of the Sorbonne.

Francis's defeat and subsequent imprisonment after Pavia propelled Marguerite into the arena of international diplomacy. Pavia also altered her personal circumstances. Not only did her husband fail to distinguish himself in battle, but, when wounded, he fled ignominiously and died in disgrace shortly thereafter.[152] (Many years later, Marguerite wrote a six-thousand-verse poem, *The Prisons,* commenting sympathetically on his disgrace.) As the affairs of state required Louise to remain in France, Marguerite went as the key negotiator with Charles V over the fate of Francis, then held in a Spanish prison. Marguerite found her brother unconscious and near death and warned her mother to expect the worst.[153] Constantly at prayer, she stayed by his side until his fever finally broke twenty-three days later. Marguerite negotiated with the emperor for more than three months. She allied with Charles's sister, Eleanor of Austria, who entertained a notion of Francis as a romantic hero. Marguerite played on this sentiment to gain better treatment for her brother and promoted the marriage between Eleanor and Francis to gain his release.[154] While she was in Spain, Francis decreed that if anything happened to his mother, Marguerite would be his regent. Although ultimately given safe passage, Marguerite was mistrustful enough to fear that the emperor might detain her as a hostage.[155]

While Marguerite was in Spain, religious hostilities in France increased. The group at Meaux took a more belligerent stance toward the Church, destroying a papal bull on indulgences and replacing it with a text criticizing the pope as the anti-Christ. The theology faculty of the Sorbonne took advantage of Francis's imprisonment to reassert its authority as a vigilant guardian of orthodoxy. It scrutinized the writings of advocates of Church reform, condemning as heretical the works of both Luther and the Christian humanist Jacques Lefèvre d'Etaples. Parlement was also mobilized to carry out the Sorbonne's wishes in the judicial venue, prosecuting those the Sorbonne condemned. Even though Francis had previously intervened on Lefèvre's behalf, Parlement forced him into exile for the duration of Francis's imprisonment. When Parlement condemned the celebrated humanist Louis de Berquin to death, he was saved only by Marguerite's personal intervention. (When Berquin was later convicted again, the death sentence was hastily carried out to prevent royal intervention.) Francis's eventual release from prison was a reprieve for reformers. Lefèvre, for example, was recalled from exile to serve as tutor to Francis's sons.

When Francis returned from Spain, he credited Marguerite with saving his life during his illness and with negotiating so conscientiously on his behalf.[156] He showered her with gifts, and she was clearly in very high standing.[157] As a widow and now undeniably the sister of the king of France, Marguerite could play a valuable diplomatic role in new marriage negotiations. But when she married again in 1527, she chose a husband for love—Henry d'Albret, the king of Navarre. This marriage afforded Francis only modest political advantage, shoring up the border between France and Spain. Likely Francis allowed this politically less-advantageous match in deference to Marguerite's personal feelings. Henry could be considered an appropriate husband for a royal princess, for he was a king, albeit a territorially disadvantaged one. He had lost much of his land when Ferdinand and Isabella of Spain seized part of Navarre in 1512, and Charles V took Béarn, another part of his territory. For a land-poor king, an alliance with the king of France's sister was a tremendous advantage; Henry became, as a result, one of the greatest lords of France. As queen in Navarre,

Marguerite continued to play a direct role in the politics and diplomacy and to correspond with many important European figures on both political and theological issues.

While this marriage was happier than Marguerite's first, it too had its humiliations. At the age of thirty-five, Marguerite was passionately in love with this new husband, twelve years her junior. Young and handsome, Henry had distinguished himself at the Battle of Pavia. He shared her interest in Renaissance arts, and they were bound by their mutual antipathy toward the emperor. Henry hoped marriage to the king's sister would lead to the recovery of his lost lands with Francis's support. (He had previously proposed marriage to Charles's sister Eleanor, expecting his lost lands as her dowry.) But Marguerite's marriage for love did not bring her great personal happiness, and she found her new situation less than ideal. The court in Navarre was provincial, and her husband was concerned most with protecting his remaining territory. After an initial period of happiness, she became disillusioned as Henry pursued sexual relationships with other women. Marguerite's correspondence documents her requests to ask others to bring him to heel.[158] Francis was forced to demand that he treat her as her rank required.[159]

Henry demonstrates some of these undesirable traits through the words Marguerite puts into the mouth of her character Hircan (a play on his name in Gascon, the language of Navarre) in the *Heptameron*. As the book's characters reflect on the meaning of the stories they told to their group of stranded travelers, Hircan inevitably asserts the greatest male prerogative and disdain for women. He is cynical about women's motives and the depth of their love, claiming, for example, that women act not from love but rather in women's ways, which are "resentful, bitter, and vindictive." He appreciates the cleverness of men in overcoming the scruples of women about sexual relations; if women resist, "men turn to trickery." Men have no call to defer to women, he insists, because "women are made for men."[160] Although other speakers challenge his views, Hircan presents a crass and overweening sense of male privilege, and his character seems to argue for Marguerite's increasing unhappiness in her marriage.

Despite the difficulties of her marriage, Marguerite gave birth to her daughter, Jeanne, in 1528 to her great joy. At the age of thirty-six, Marguerite was a rather old first-time, sixteenth-century mother. Her first marriage had been childless, and her second occurred after she had already likely entered a period of diminished fertility. In addition to her daughter, she bore a son in 1530 who died at the age of six months, and she had several recorded miscarriages. She grieved over the death of her son and desperately longed for more children. At the age of fifty, she fell ill but believed that she was again pregnant.[161]

When Jeanne was just two years old, Francis took her to be raised at the chateau of Plessis-les-Tours so that her father could not use her to recoup his Spanish territory through a Hapsburg marriage alliance for her. Well aware that this was his brother-in-law's greatest interest, Francis both wanted to prevent Henry from bartering his own daughter for his former lands and intended to use his niece instead to advance his own political agenda. As a result, Marguerite was separated from her daughter for most of her life.

While her mother was alive, Marguerite played important social, political, and cultural roles at her brother's court and acted as Louise's political and diplomatic agent, working with her to negotiate the Ladies' Peace. After her mother's death in 1531, Marguerite took over many of Louise's official functions. She traveled extensively, pursuing the king's as well as her own interests, going to Amiens to reform a Franciscan convent, to Normandy when the dauphin Francis was proclaimed governor, and to Rouen with the new queen, Eleanor, on her triumphal entry. Marguerite was greatly involved with Francis's children, especially in arranging marriages for them. She shared her brother's enthusiasm for building and commissioned two Renaissance chateaux at Nérac and Pau in Navarre. For the last sixteen years of Francis's reign, she was one of Francis's most significant confidants. The Venetian ambassador Matteo Dandolo praised Marguerite as the wisest of all (not merely the wisest woman). In 1540 he reported that she was constantly with the king and proclaimed "in the affairs and interests of state, one can have no surer discourses than hers."[162] Although Francis relied on Marguerite, she was sometimes at odds with him over politics or religion. These disagreements increasingly became serious enough that she periodically fled the court when she could not condone her brother's actions.

BROTHER AND SISTER AT ODDS

The religious situation in France became ever more contentious. The relationship between crown and Church was still evolving in response to the Concordat of Bologna. Objections to the Concordat united clergy, the theology faculty of the Sorbonne, and the Parlement against what they saw as royal encroachments on their power. The entrenched conservatism of the theology faculty also made them profoundly suspicious of Francis's interest in new ideas and learning; the faculty even proposed an interdiction on printing in France. They also objected to those Francis named to fill Church positions under the provisions of the Concordat. Their vigorous repudiation of Chancellor Duprat's proposed religious compromise founded on religious reform, tolerance, and Christian humanism exposed sharp divisions between guardians of orthodox Catholicism and those committed to religious reform and dimmed prospects of a theological accord or a common ground for reform of religious practice. In this atmosphere of mutual grievance and suspicion, virtually any incident could inflame religious passions. On May 30, 1528, a statue of the Virgin Mary on the rue des Rosiers in Paris was desecrated, an act that seemed to turn the tide of popular religious sentiment against the reformers. In response, Francis begged pardon of the Virgin and replaced the desecrated statue with a silver-plated one. His public piety in response to this violation reconciled Parisians to him and relieved their suspicions that he might foster heresy.[163] Despite heightened tensions, Marguerite remained committed to religious humanism and the reform of corrupt religious institutions. But she could offer only limited protection to some of her protégés. Even with her support, the position of the small community of religious reformers at Meaux became more tenuous.

Religious conflict created a politically charged situation for Francis. Interested in new ideas, he was first seen as being somewhat sympathetic toward those with Protestant leanings (so much so that some Loire Valley guides still proclaim him a Protestant). He sometimes allied with German Protestant princes against Charles V and was then more tolerant of French religious dissent. Most of the reform-minded in France had not yet broken with Rome, insisting that they simply wanted to return the Catholic Church to its apostolic character. The king had not yet taken a firm position.

There seemed to be renewed possibilities for religious reconciliation when Alexander Farnese, known as a humanist intellectual, was elected as Pope Paul III in 1534, but he too was unsuccessful in finding common ground to heal the religious divide or even to moderate the hardening theological views within the Catholic Church. Paul III appreciated Marguerite as a kindred spirit, recognizing her virtue, intelligence, and influence with her brother. He corresponded with her, seeking her assistance with Church positions in France and papal diplomatic efforts.[164] But over the course of his pontificate, his theological views too hardened.

Events that seemed to threaten the crown finally forced Francis to take a stand against the reformed religion. On the night of October 18, 1534, in the cities of Paris and Orléans, at the chateaux of Amboise and Blois, and even on the king's bedroom door, placards denouncing the Mass were posted. It is not clear who orchestrated this carefully coordinated event, but the placards were offensive on many levels. The content, intended to foment popular dissent, attacked both Church dogma and the clergy; the language was violent and vulgar.[165] The king was furious at what he saw as a direct attack on his authority. In early January 1535, accompanied by his three sons, Francis participated in a procession after which six people were burned as heretics. The *Journal of a Bourgeois of Paris* reported a series of such executions over the course of the year.[166]

Marguerite would likely have continued to play a central role in Francis's court, but her espousal of religious reform increasingly put her at odds with her brother.[167] Her earlier discussions with religious reformers had led to her writing career. She first explored theological questions with Briçonnet.[168] She then became an avid reader of poetry and an adept poet. In 1531, she wrote a small book of poems, *The Mirror of the Sinful Soul*, 160 verses, in which she explored theological ideas. A second edition of the text, published a few years later, galvanized the theology faculty of the Sorbonne to condemn the book. She found herself at odds with the Sorbonne again in Lent of 1533 when she called on her friend Gerard Roussel to preach. Roussel, Erasmus noted, "preached Scripture with much liberty."[169] (Erasmus was considered unorthodox enough by the Sorbonne.) Marguerite defended Roussel against the faculty—a controversial position for anyone, especially a woman, to take. At the same time, statues in a chapel on Marguerite's estates in Alençon were desecrated, provoking the Sorbonne to attack her even more vociferously.

Francis, given his invigorated defense of Catholicism after the Affair of the Placards, found religious dissenters in his court problematic. Montmorency, Marguerite's sometime ally no longer well-disposed toward her, said to Francis, "If your majesty wants to rid the country of heretics, you must begin with your sister."[170] Francis's reply—"Let us not speak of that; she loves me too much; she will never believe but what I believe, or take up a religion to the prejudice of my state"—demonstrated his rather arrogant confidence in her deference.[171] Marguerite avoided contention by leaving the court.

A return to Navarre gave Marguerite an opportunity to cultivate her religious ideas. She met with proponents of religious reform, including Christian humanists, some of the first Lutherans in France, and John Calvin and some of his earliest French followers, who became known as Huguenots. As these religious freethinkers began to be persecuted, Marguerite offered them refuge. It is a matter of debate whether Marguerite ever considered renouncing Catholicism, but she was unquestionably sympathetic to new religious views. Those sympathies might have influenced Francis to view reformers more favorably, but the Affair of the Placards had persuaded him that Protestants were dangerous, personally and politically. He opposed them thereafter, and even Marguerite became much more circumspect in her support. As Brantôme noted, Marguerite was suspected of Lutheranism, but "out of respect and love for her brother . . . she never made a profession or appearance of it."[172] But she remained deeply concerned about the growing persecution of dissenters. Lefèvre lived out his final days in her chateau at Nérac. She supported André Melancthon (a relative of Philip Melancthon, Luther's well-known associate) because she hoped that he could reconcile divergent religious views. And her religious writings reveal a turn toward mysticism, perhaps her response to the bitter theological dissension.

Marguerite's husband's quest to recoup his lost territory also complicated her relationship with her brother. Francis's attention was directed toward Italy rather than toward the small kingdom in the Pyrenees, but Navarre was Henry's chief preoccupation. In attempting to regain it, Henry negotiated with Charles V, which Francis regarded as double-dealing. Henry's actions cast a pall over Francis's relationship with his sister. Henry, on the other hand, considered himself forced to deal with Charles because Francis took no steps to regain his territory.[173]

When Henry and Marguerite returned to Navarre, they worked to develop it economically: They invited husbandmen from all over France to improve the land, bringing barren regions under cultivation.[174] Determined to establish good governance, they reformed the laws as well. Marguerite intended Navarre to be a site of virtue, a model Renaissance principality, but changes in international relations led to her return to Francis's court.

When Francesco II Sforza, the duke of Milan, died in 1535 without an heir, it was almost inevitable that Francis I and Charles V would resume their rivalry over Italy. Planning for war, Francis granted an amnesty to religious dissenters because he was now allied with German Protestant princes. When Francis prepared for a war, Montmorency argued for peace and so fell from favor. Francis called his sister back to court and again relied on her as his ally. He now appointed her as military governor of Guyenne.[175] Marguerite ardently supported her brother's war efforts, and her husband went to Gascony to raise troops. In pursuing war with the emperor, her husband and her brother were allied. In this context, the absence of Louise was most apparent—her strong voice for peace had not been replaced. But if Marguerite's husband and brother united in the pursuit of war, they were soon divided over the question of her daughter's marriage.

Against the backdrop of impending war, Marguerite's daughter, Jeanne, came of marriageable age. Her father wanted to use her to regain his Spanish lands. Henry had been gravely disappointed that his marriage to Marguerite had not led to the recovery of his territory. He hoped that Jeanne's marriage to Charles V's son, Philip, would recoup it. Marguerite was pleased at the prospect of such an advantageous marriage for her daughter. But Francis unequivocally opposed it, and Marguerite worried about the conflict it entailed between her interests as queen of Navarre and her duties as the king's sister. To placate his brother-in-law, Francis contended that the coming war with Spain would regain his territory. But Henry believed that his negotiations with Charles would more likely bear fruit. The situation put Marguerite and her husband's rights, as king and queen of Navarre, at odds with her obligation to the king of France. Marguerite worried that the situation was driving a wedge between her brother and her husband—one Charles V might well have deliberately exploited.[176]

Despite their prominence in Francis's court, women remained subject to the conventional marriage arrangements. Francis had no qualms whatsoever about using his niece for his political purposes, even over her vehement objections. He had Jeanne returned to Plessis-les-Tours so that her father could not use her to ally with Charles V. As Francis firmed up his alliance with the German princes, he insisted that she marry the duke of Cleves. Marguerite was not enthusiastic about this marriage, and the thirteen-year-old Jeanne vehemently objected. But when Francis emphasized the coming war as a means to reclaim his territory, Henry willingly signed his daughter's marriage contract. Marguerite was torn between the wishes of her husband and her brother and those of her daughter. In a letter to Francis, she both apologized for her daughter's resistance and expressed her desolation over the marriage: "Know that neither the king of Navarre nor I have any other desire nor intention other than to obey you, not only in a marriage but even if you would command our lives. But now, Monseigneur, having heard that my daughter, knowing neither of the great honor you make to her in deigning to visit her nor the obedience that she owes you, nor also that a daughter should not have a will, made such a foolish proposal that she should not have thought of it nor I have said it, except that I am ravaged by sorrow."[177]

The wedding took place, even though the bride had to be forcibly carried down the aisle, so opposed did she remain. But in deference to her youth, the marriage was not consummated. Jeanne wrote a letter protesting that she was married "against my will and intention."[178]

The war was fought on several fronts that had a direct impact on Marguerite: When Charles V attacked her husband's territory, Marguerite supported his efforts to protect it. Charles V's victory in Cleves altered her daughter's marital status. The duke of Cleves repudiated his alliance with Francis, including his marriage to Jeanne. Marguerite then wrote impassioned letters to the pope, urging her daughter's liberation from her never-wanted marriage. Swearing that she had been coerced, Jeanne was ultimately granted an annulment. In the face of military defeats, Francis became disillusioned with the advice of the pro-war party. Those at court who had advocated war, including Marguerite, lost favor, and Montmorency returned. Peace allowed Francis to turn his attention to the repression of heresy, which also put brother and sister at odds.

LITERARY LEGACY

Marguerite again returned to Navarre, where she cultivated her literary life and circle.[179] She gathered a court of distinguished ladies, among them Brantôme's mother and grandmother, who later recorded stories about it. This group of intelligent women discussed a range of ideas—philosophical, religious, and literary. Their gatherings foreshadow those of seventeenth-century salons.

In this period, Marguerite wrote the *Heptameron,* the work that established her place in French Renaissance literature. Literary scholars have identified the individuals who correspond to her characters, most notably Oisile, an anagram of Louise; Hircan, her husband; and Parlemente, Marguerite herself. The *Heptameron* weaves seven days of tales told by a group of stranded travelers. Each day focuses loosely on a theme; several characters tell stories illustrating the theme and then deduce moral lessons from them. Many of the stories, drawn from court life, offer an explicit window into views on love and sexual relationships of this social group. Other themes are particularly striking—the corruption of the Catholic clergy, especially the Franciscans, and the pitfalls of male-female relations.

The text not only has literary merit but also contributes to the ongoing "quarrel over women." By the time Marguerite considered these questions, some Renaissance humanists had considered women more sympathetically than their predecessors. The Renaissance revival of Platonic philosophy also played a significant role in this shift. By idealizing love and beauty, Neoplatonists opened the way for a new, more positive appreciation of women. Several members of Marguerite's court contributed directly to the "woman question." Antoine Héroët, a close friend, published *The Perfect Friend* (1542), which contended that women, by their goodness and intuition, could guide men.[180] Marguerite herself addressed this issue, insisting that women could lead men to Neoplatonic love in *The Distinction of True Love.*

Marguerite increasingly turned her attention to literary pursuits as Francis's peacetime repression of heresy alienated her. He carried out a violent massacre of the Vaudois, a remnant of the heretical thirteenth-century Albigensian sect. Although the Vaudois rejected what they considered medieval accretions in the Church, such as purgatory, the cult of the saints, and religious images, they outwardly conformed to Catholic practice. Their adherents were primarily peasants living in remote areas of Provence. Charles VIII had persecuted them. Louis XII sent tolerant examiners, who pronounced them good Christians. When the president of the Parlement of Aix warned Francis that the Vaudois intended to establish an independent republic, as Swiss Calvinists had, Francis signed the order of repression. The result: 3,000 people were massacred; 255 were executed after the massacre; about 700 men were sent to the galleys; and many children were sold into slavery.[181]

Although Francis accepted the political necessity of the persecution of Protestants in general and this massacre in particular, Marguerite found these practices abhorrent. They heightened her concern over the deteriorating religious situation in France. She was particularly distressed by the arrest of the humanist and printer Etienne Dolet. She had saved him before, but despite her personal entreaty to Francis, she could not now save him from being burned by order of the Inquisition. Even Marguerite was attacked: The bishop of Condom proclaimed her a heretic and urged her territories to revolt against her.[182]

Already strained over religious issues, Marguerite's relationship with Francis was again complicated by her daughter's marital prospects. Jeanne was now free to remarry after her annulment, and the issues that shaped her first marriage came to the fore. Her father still wanted to marry her to a son of Charles V. Francis, again intent on marrying her to serve his purposes, sequestered Jeanne at Plessis-les-Tours and kept her from her mother.

Despite these divisive issues between brother and sister, Francis called Marguerite to his side at the end of his life. He looked to her as his longest and most reliable ally; his son Henry was alienated from him, and his mistress worried most about her future. But Marguerite's health was not robust enough for her to hazard a winter journey. She planned to come in the spring, but Francis died on March 31, 1547.

Francis's death ended Marguerite's preeminence. A luminary and important advisor throughout her brother's thirty-two-year reign, she was reduced to political insignificance upon his death. Her allies were driven from Henry II's court, for Marguerite had supported the faction of the king's mistress, Anne de Pisseleu, during the last years of Francis's reign. Marguerite's decline in importance was strikingly demonstrated when Henry made his triumphal entry into Lyon: His mistress, Diane de Poitiers, was heralded and Marguerite unacknowledged. She even had cause for concern about her financial well-being, fearing that Henry would end the twenty-thousand-*livres* annuity that Francis had given her.

Marguerite also continued to worry about her daughter. Henry II planned to marry Jeanne to Anthony of Bourbon. Marguerite opposed this marriage because she and her husband still hoped for a Spanish marriage. But as adamantly as Jeanne had opposed her first marriage to the duke of Cleves, she was eager for this one. When Marguerite begged the dowager queen Eleanor and Diane de Poitiers to thwart the planned marriage, Henry declared that it would take place.[183] Marguerite left Henry's inhospitable court and returned to Navarre.

Toward the end of her life, perhaps in response to her brother's death and her own sense of mortality, Marguerite returned to religious mysticism. She wrote poems pointing to the vanity of the pursuit of empire, introducing Neoplatonic themes of love, and celebrating the Resurrection. She worked on a long poem, essentially an examination of conscience, which was clearly part of her preparation for death, which came in 1549.[184]

While Francis's sister and mother played important roles during his reign, his queens remained in the background. Claude had guaranteed the stability of his dynasty and commissioned works of art but was otherwise neglected and negligible. Eleanor, his second wife, was hostage to a treaty agreement, and her principle role was diplomatic. As queen of France, she attempted to foster peace between her husband and his most constant enemy, her brother Charles V.

A FOREIGN QUEEN

When Eleanor of Austria was initially proposed as Francis's bride as part of the Treaty of Madrid, the betrothal ceremony took place in his prison cell: He was too ill to leave his bed and she was represented by an emissary. Even though Francis had no intention of honoring the treaty, he played the gallant lover.[185] Eleanor was intrigued by her prospective husband, seeing him as a romantic figure—a valiant king and tragic prisoner. When Francis repudiated the treaty, the wedding was deferred for five years until the Ladies' Peace finally led to his sons' release.

Eleanor was born in 1498 to Philip the Fair and Juana the Mad of Spain. Despite her title, she had never set foot in Austria. After her father's early death and in light of her mother's mental instability, Eleanor was raised in the Low Countries by her aunt Margaret of Austria, one of the negotiators of the peace. Her grandfather Emperor Maximilian wanted to arrange a marriage for her to an important European king. He first pursued negotiations with Louis XII after Anne of Brittany's death, but Louis instead married Mary of York. As a young girl, Eleanor fell in love with Frederick of Bavaria, prince of the Palatinate, and against the expectations entailed by her value on the marriage market, pursued this relationship as if she controlled her own matrimonial destiny. This young prince had been welcomed in the Low Countries as one of the electors who would choose the next emperor, but his hereditary prospects were not promising. And Charles V did not consider him a fitting spouse for his sister. He instead married her to Manuel, the king of Portugal, who was infirm and thirty years older than she. During their three-year marriage, Eleanor bore a son, who died shortly after birth, and a daughter, who remained in Portugal, a hostage to international diplomacy. After Manuel's death, Charles first wanted to use Eleanor to consolidate his alliance with Charles of Bourbon and as booty for his treason. She instead became part of the diplomatic resolution of his battle with Francis I.

When Eleanor was betrothed to Francis, diplomats discussed her looks in great detail. They might have understood that Eleanor's prospects depended on her ability to attract Francis's renowned appreciation of female beauty (fig. 3.10). As a young girl, Eleanor had been considered attractive. When presented to the sixteen-year-old Eleanor, the English ambassador praised her as "beautiful and wise."[186] But at the time of her engagement, contemporaries assessed her looks in dramatically different ways. Perhaps reflecting national prejudice, the Spanish proclaimed her beauty; French commentators found her too short, too brunette, and not especially attractive. Brantôme gave the fullest, if rather peculiar, description of Eleanor: "When she was dressed, she seemed a very beautiful princess of rich and beautiful height but when she was undressed, the height of her body appeared so long one would have believed that she was a giant but so short were her legs and thighs, she made one think of a dwarf."[187] These somewhat negative descriptions may also have rationalized Francis's subsequent neglect.

Founded entirely on diplomacy, Eleanor's marriage reflected the issues of such marriages. A queen could both consolidate a peace treaty and play an ongoing diplomatic role. When a king warred, a queen could facilitate peace, especially if, like Eleanor, she had important family connections to exploit. A queen might conduct diplomatic missions, but her more common role was as a pawn in the diplomatic exchange that led to her marriage. Her marriage affirmed the prominence of her family but, more importantly, served her spouse's political agenda. In Eleanor's case, only a king was fit for a Hapsburg princess, and she, as Charles V's sister, was an appropriate queen to reinforce

Fig. 3.10. Portrait of Eleanor of Austria by Joos van Cleve. Museu Nacional de Arte Antiga, Lisbon / The Bridgeman Art Library.

Francis's status. Their marriage resolved Francis's immediate political contest with Charles.

When the Ladies' Peace was finally signed, Eleanor came to France in great state, escorting Francis's sons, Francis and Henry. She was presented to the court in lavish ceremonies in which she was allegorically depicted as peace and prosperity. She won the hearts of some Frenchmen for her role in the return of the young princes, but her triumph and her public roles were short-lived. Once her diplomatic purpose was served, a queen might essentially disappear from the historical record, described with laudatory but rather vague adjectives. Such was Eleanor's fate. She tried to exercise a productive role as queen, but Francis or the other powerful women of his court frustrated most of her efforts.

Eleanor's role as part of a diplomatic agreement did not endear her to her spouse; she was above all the sister of his long-standing enemy, and Francis neglected her, despite her obvious interest in him. The English ambassador reported: "Although the queen is very taken with her husband, no man is less pleased with his wife. For seven months he has scarcely seen her at all. I asked why? Because he does not find her pleasing to his appetite."[188] Eleanor remained largely imperceptible in the historical record. She did not attract Francis and had no logical entrée into court circles. A foreign queen, neglected by her husband, she was left without much of a role in her new country. Eleanor could not readily step into the possible public roles of the queen. Those roles were more than amply fulfilled by the king's new mistress, Anne de Pisseleu. The former queen, Claude, had more than fulfilled the dynastic function of a queen; her three sons seemed to guarantee succession to the throne by a direct, legitimate offspring. There was no necessity for Francis to seek out his new queen.

At Eleanor's coronation in 1531, Francis watched with his mistress, Anne de Pisseleu, who was as prominent in the festivities as the queen. At the celebration, a prize for beauty was awarded to Anne (although she had to share it with Diane de Poitiers). Notably, the queen received no prize. When Eleanor objected to Anne's constant presence, Francis elevated Anne by appointing her as one of Eleanor's ladies-in-waiting. Eleanor might have enjoyed her mother-in-law's support, but Louise died shortly after she arrived. Eleanor tried to occupy herself with her stepchildren, but they made no place for her. Indeed, her stepson Henry had a marked aversion to her as a reminder of his imprisonment. She might have allied with her sister-in-law Marguerite, but they shared few interests. Marguerite was much more intellectual and, more significantly, sympathetic to the reformed religion. Eleanor was a devout Catholic. Although unable to define a role in the royal household, Eleanor valiantly tried to reconcile her husband and her brother. Soon after her arrival, Francis used her as a vehicle to present the royal family to the people. As she traveled from town to town and ceremonial entry to ceremonial entry, she likely would have relished the opportunity to cement a relationship with her new people and to assume a public role, but that role was limited.

During Eleanor's tenure as queen, Marguerite was the intellectual luminary of the royal court. Although the *Heptameron* tells many tales of courtiers, it never mentions Eleanor. When factions emerged at court after Louise's death, the most influential group curried Francis's favor by supporting his mistress; a queen without power attracted no allies.

At several points, Eleanor attempted to take a more active political role. Her foreign policy initiatives focused on possible marriage alliances for the king's sons, designed to further cement the peace between her husband and brother. The dauphin Francis was the only member of the royal family who showed a marked affection for Eleanor and sometimes acted as her advocate with his father. When his engagement to her daughter, Marie of Portugal, was negotiated, Eleanor might have imagined a future where she would be honored as the mother of the queen and grandmother of future kings of France. These hopes were quashed by the dauphin's early death in 1536.

Eleanor then supported Charles, Francis's youngest son. Ironically, Eleanor's religious devotion first inclined her to Diane de Poitiers, the mistress of Francis's son Henry, as both were staunch Catholics. But by supporting Charles, Eleanor was allied with her husband's mistress Anne. (Anne allied with Charles as a counterweight to Henry and his mistress.) To forge a political alliance, Eleanor could support the faction of either her husband's mistress or her stepson's mistress, but the queen's attachment to either cause was relatively insignificant.

Eleanor also worked to bring to fruition Francis's efforts to gain a territorial base for his son Charles through a marriage to either Charles V's daughter or his niece. Francis fervently desired such a marriage to establish a base in Italy. It seems unlikely, given their history of warring over the peninsula, that Charles would have acceded except under duress—and Francis's position was more vulnerable than his. Nonetheless, throughout the late 1530s and 1540s, whenever peace led to diplomacy, marriage negotiations resumed. Eleanor was no doubt the most pleased member of any delegation that brought her husband and brother together.

In 1538, both the Valois and Hapsburg treasuries were empty and Eleanor again tried to negotiate peace. She suggested a meeting with Mary of Hungary, her sister and the governor of the Low Countries, no doubt hoping to replicate the noteworthy Ladies' Peace. When protracted negotiations produced an agreement, the English ambassador wrote to Henry VIII: "Queen Eleanor has been the principle instrument in managing these negotiations."[189] To her great joy, Eleanor persuaded Francis and Charles V to meet. While the emperor and the king exchanged gifts and signs of affection, likely only Eleanor believed that they cemented a genuine reconciliation. The agreement specified that Charles V would invest Francis's younger son, Charles, with the duchy of Milan and marry him to his daughter.

In 1539, when Francis gave Charles V the right to cross France in traveling from Spain to the Low Countries, the entire court went to meet him. The delegation included Eleanor, Anne, Marguerite, and Diane. All of the female powers behind the throne were united in the interests of peace. Francis spared no expense to impress the emperor as they traveled to all of his entrancing Renaissance chateaux—Amboise, Chenonceau, Blois, Chambord, Fontainebleau—and finally to Paris, with a lavish entry.

After two months of endless festivities, very much counter to his dour disposition, Charles left assuring Francis that their interests would be resolved to the king's satisfaction. But almost immediately, Charles suggested an agreement Francis considered less advantageous. He proposed marriage between his niece, Marie (instead of his daughter), and Francis's younger son, Charles. Her dowry would be the Low Countries and Franche-Comté, instead of the much-hoped-for Milan, and, it was stipulated, Francis would give his younger son Burgundy. This proposal infuriated Francis and led to renewed hostilities. Despite the failure of Eleanor's diplomatic efforts, the English ambassador wrote home: "No woman could have done better, with a better spirit."[190]

When Charles V threatened Paris in 1544 and its citizens were panicking, Eleanor worked for peace with her husband's mistress and his sister. Marguerite's confessor communicated with the emperor's confessor, and Eleanor wrote secretly to her brother. A female network again was crucial in attaining peace. When the Peace of Crépy was ultimately signed in 1544, it essentially reaffirmed Charles V's initial proposal. To cement the peace, the young prince Charles and Eleanor visited the emperor in the Low Countries—a triumphal tour and joyous reunion for her. But the young prince's death on September 9, 1545, again frustrated Eleanor's efforts. Her concerted attempts to arrange marriages for two of her husband's sons to cement peace had been stymied by their unexpected deaths.

Despite her prodigious attempts to reconcile king and emperor, Eleanor was such a negligible figure that when Francis I died no one even thought to inform her for several days. Charles V wrote to his ambassador at the French court: "She had not great reason to mourn the passing of the king in light of the little regard he had for her and the bad treatment she received."[191] Henry, her stepson and the new king, was particularly ungracious. He not only associated Eleanor with her brother but also with the disadvantageous terms of the Peace of Crépy. Nevertheless, after Eleanor returned to the Low Countries in 1548, she helped to negotiate the marriage alliance between Henry II's sister Marguerite and

Emmanuel-Philibert, prince of Piedmont. Eleanor remained willing to be deployed to foster peace between the Hapsburgs and the Valois. Eventually she returned to Spain, where she died in 1558. She had played the roles assigned to a royal sister—married twice to serve her brother's diplomatic interests and, in one case, to provide a brief peace between warring enemies.

Eleanor was a queen who never played a prominent role—a queen only by virtue of a treaty and almost written out of subsequent French histories. While she was queen, the other powerful and influential woman who dominated the court was Francis's mistress Anne de Pisseleu. After an initial, ineffective complaint, Eleanor was forced to accept Anne not only as her husband's mistress but also, after Louise's death, as the guardian of the royal children. The royal mistress thus eclipsed the queen, absorbing the public and private roles available to her, and shared the last twenty years of Francis's reign with his queen. Eleanor's diligent efforts to advance peace between the king and the emperor were consistently frustrated by Francis's desire for Italian conquest; Eleanor did not have Louise's authority. If a king did not allow his queen to play a productive role, she had little room to maneuver. Eleanor could not counter his mistress, who championed Francis's efforts for war and conquest. A king's support, as Anne's example reveals, gave a mistress great political authority.

A MISTRESS'S POWER

Anne de Pisseleu, selected by Louise of Savoy from among her ladies-in-waiting as a potential mistress for Francis, eagerly fell in with plans to bring her to Francis's attention.[192] Born in 1508, Anne was one of the youngest of twenty-three children (sixteen survived) born to Guillaume de Pisseleu, a minor, impoverished nobleman and his three successive wives.[193] (Anne's mother was his second.) With many sisters competing for very limited resources, Anne's prospects for a marriage dependent on a dowry were discouraging, to say the least. This situation might well have daunted many young women, but Anne made the best of it. Presenting Francis with a poem the day he was released from prison, she quickly impressed him and likely became his mistress that very day. Although Francis was willing to entertain two mistresses at the same time, Françoise, as we have seen, refused to become a secondary mistress and eventually retired from the court. Although Françoise deprecated herself as a brunette, Anne was a beauty whose looks corresponded to the standards of the day (fig. 3.11). Blond, blue-eyed, and renowned for charm, vivacity, and wit, she was conventionally extolled by her contemporaries as "the most beautiful of the

Fig. 3.11. Anne de Pisseleu, duchess d'Etampes, by Corneille de Lyon.
Private collection / The Bridgeman Art Library.

learned women and the most learned of the beautiful women"—a designation likely intended to slight the undeniably intelligent former mistress, Françoise. Immediately after his return from prison, Francis began to wear Anne's colors, and his relationship with her endured for the rest of his life.

Although their contemporaries never colored their relationship with romance, Anne had no serious rival for Francis's affection during her long tenure. Contemporaries instead noted Anne's obvious interest in power and wealth. Her long run as royal mistress gave her access to both, in part because she appropriated roles other royal women had played in Francis's court. Like other royal mistresses, Anne had a close association with other members of the royal family; she remained Louise's lady-in-waiting, the king's daughters' governor, and allied with Marguerite (fig. 3.12). Later, with Marguerite's frequent absences in Navarre, Françoise's departure, and Louise's death, Anne became the most important woman in Francis's court.

Anne's social background made her a far less appropriate royal mistress than Françoise had been. She had neither status nor a husband, either of which, perhaps peculiar by modern lights, would have made her a more credible royal mistress. Over time, Francis elevated her to befit her position as designated favorite. He appointed Anne as Eleanor's lady-in-waiting and then as governor of his two daughters. In 1534, he married her to Jean de Brosse, count of Penthièvre, which made her a countess. Two years later, he made her husband duke of Estampes, "in recognition," Francis put it, "of the exceptional consideration and pleasant services rendered to him daily by our dear and beloved cousin Jean . . . and also those of our dear and beloved cousin Anne," which made her a duchess.[194] Then he made her husband governor of Bourbonnais and Auvergne, positions that further elevated the couple's status and took Jean far from Anne.

Anne used her position to acquire goods, and Francis showered them on her. She confiscated the pensions and the revenues from her husband's estates and acquired a townhouse in Paris and two country chateaux. She did not hesitate to take every possible financial advantage of her position and used her standing with the king to reward her friends and to promote her large family. Her contemporaries charged that she was not discriminating in those whose careers she advanced. Reports of Anne's venality circulated almost as soon as she became the royal favorite, and they became increasingly vociferous over her long tenure as mistress. "The life of Madame has been so good in all things that, after her death, one is likely to find fourteen or fifteen thousand *écus*, as much in furniture as other things," reported Montmorency, her political adversary.[195] While

Fig. 3.12. This image from *La coche ou le débat d'amour* shows Marguerite d'Angoulême presenting her book to Anne de Pisseleu, suggesting their shared intellectual interests and patronage of the arts. Musée Condé, Chantilly / The Bridgeman Art Library.

Anne's actions provoked condemnation, she pursued the wealth and status that access to the kings later accorded their entrepreneurial royal ministers—Sully, Richelieu, and Mazarin, for example. Like them, she was not only accused of venality but also became a target for those who opposed the political positions she advocated.[196]

While the pursuit of wealth was a conventional way for a mistress to advance her interests, just as male favorites often did, Anne intervened more directly in political affairs. Spain's envoy reported to Charles V that she was "the real president of the king's most private and intimate council."[197] Her influence over Francis was so extensive that foreign diplomats recognized that to promote their interests they had to court Anne assiduously. Francis allowed Anne to influence his appointments and, as a result, offices were filled by men distinguished more by their support for her than their abilities. Because Anne so obviously trafficked in her influence with the king, she was surrounded by a circle of those seeking political favors. She dominated court functions, completely usurping the public role of the queen.

Her critics charged her with infidelity to the king. She took lovers, well over a dozen, according to Diane de Poitiers, who, as her rival at court, had no reason to be objective. Antoine Varillas reported in his *History of Francis I* (1685), written almost one hundred and fifty years later, that when the king found Anne in bed with Christian de Nancay, he said: "And, you, Monsieur de Nancay, who dare to enter into intrigues with a follower of Madame d'Etampes, go and reflect on the inconveniences of such conduct."[198] And Brantôme reported that his mistress provoked Francis to etch with a diamond on a glass window at the chateau of Chambord, "Women often change, woe to him who trusts them"[199]—where it can still be seen, although its authorship, of course, cannot be determined.

A mistress's sexuality was easily attacked to discredit her because it had gained her entry into the court. Some of Anne's contemporaries saw her as the epitome of the deleterious effects of giving women too much authority. She was especially vulnerable as she was not protected by her family's high status. Initially she was unmarried, insignificant, without good prospects. Both her marriage and elevation in status were due directly to the king's intervention. More generally, Anne was blamed for a decline in moral values toward the end of Francis's reign.[200] The vehemence of her critics' charges reflected her increasingly significant political role.

The court divided politically after the dauphin Francis died and Henry became heir apparent. With Henry in thrall to Diane de Poitiers, Anne had a serious rival contesting her preeminence, especially since Montmorency allied with the new dauphin and his mistress. The two mistresses warred for control from that time on. Each sought to place her favorites in positions of political and military power. But when Francis prepared to go to war with Charles V, Montmorency was repudiated and Anne's favorite the Admiral Philippe Chabot de Brion was placed at the head of the army. Long-standing rivals, Chabot and Montmorency were the king's boyhood friends and members of the highest ranks of the French nobility. They had both served with distinction in his military campaigns, married wealthy heiresses, and held important and lucrative positions. Each now attempted to displace the other. Their rivalry sharpened over whether France should pursue war or diplomacy with the emperor, Chabot favoring war and Montmorency peace.

When Francis subsequently pursued peace, Chabot fell from favor, and Francis relied again on Montmorency, who realigned French foreign policy, allying with the emperor and repudiating earlier alliances with the Turks and the German princes. The enticement of this reorientation was the much-sought prize of Milan. But the truce was irremediably broken when Charles V gave Milan to his son, Philip. Francis blamed Montmorency, who was again excluded from government. Anne had worked to discredit Montmorency for his opposition to her political positions. Those initiatives directly challenged those of Henry and Diane. Rivalry between Francis's sons Henry and Charles had begun in 1536 with the death of the dauphin Francis. It widened with the fall of Montmorency: Montmorency's friends rallied around Henry. Chabot, Marguerite, and Anne supported Charles. Their rivalry increased in 1542 when Charles's successful conquest of Luxembourg and Henry's retreat from Perpignan enhanced the younger prince's status at his brother's expense.

In the last years of Francis's reign, the court divided even more sharply. One camp supported Anne; the other looked to the future and supported Diane. Francis had been obviously ill since 1540; doctors treated him with guaiac and mercury, the conventional treatments for syphilis. As Francis put it, "God punished me where I have sinned."[201] He also experienced increasingly painful and debilitating attacks of gout. After the death of his youngest son in 1545, Francis was somewhat less engaged, likely because of his own failing health. His withdrawal from the political fray left the field to the two warring factions led by rival mistresses. Anne worried, quite justifiably, that Diane would supplant her. Francis's declining health threatened her status and led Anne to try to manipulate France's foreign policy to protect her future. To do so, she supported Francis's younger son, Charles.

Throughout the 1540s royal ministers had lined up behind either Henry and Diane or Charles and Anne. Sometimes their policies failed; other times they lost favor because a royal mistress discredited them with the king. For example, Montmorency, one of Henry's key supporters, had accused Anne's favorite Admiral Chabot of financial misdealing. But once Montmorency fell from favor, Chabot was exonerated and Anne helped restore him to royal favor. She was complicit in bringing down Guillaume Poyet, who had charged Chabot and was one of Henry's supporters. Poyet's infuriated response—"There is the good that women do at court. They are no longer content to exercise their empire, they undertake to violate the law and make examples of ministers most scrupulous in carrying out their duties"—was apt but did not advance his case.[202] In his *Critical Dictionary*, Pierre Bayle described this period as "a great disorder, one must acknowledge that the destiny of men—their favor, their disgrace—depended on the fantasy of a coquette, who scandalized the entire kingdom."[203]

Anne's interventions in foreign policy were not uncontested. When the town of Saint-Dizier, besieged by Spain from June to August of 1544, suddenly capitulated, the surrender was subsequently attributed to Anne's treason. The story behind the surrender is interesting. A scout intercepted a packet written in the code the duke of Guise used to correspond with his troops, and brought it to the Spanish chancellor Granvelle. He then used the code to urge the commander at Saint-Dizier to surrender because reinforcements would not be coming.[204] Some believed that Anne gave the code to the Spanish to promote an accord between the emperor and Francis's youngest son, Charles. Such an alliance might have led to a kingdom for the French prince and a refuge for Anne. Her rumored involvement ultimately led to charges of treason against her after Francis's death.

Although attacks on Anne became much more vociferous in the last years of Francis's reign, Marguerite d'Angoulême offered high praise: "For her good works, everyone praises her. They are known by all good men. For her friends, she spares nothing, and does not avenge her wicked enemies." Clement Marot, the beneficiary of Anne's patronage, extolled her: "Without prejudice to anyone, I give you the golden apple of beauty and steadfast loyalty to the crown." And Brantôme praised her as "a good and honest lady, who did not abuse her favor."[205] Anne also exercised a positive force in the cultural vitality of the twenty years she was Francis's favorite, commissioning artworks, promoting artists—Francesco Primaticcio, in particular—and paying their debts.[206]

When Charles V and Francis successfully negotiated peace, Anne was such an effective advocate that Charles wrote to thank her. From her position of strength, Anne renewed her efforts against Henry and Diane. Anne told Francis that Henry, at Diane's urging, wanted to reinstate Montmorency; Francis credited her report and exiled Diane, which led Henry and his supporters to withdraw to Diane's chateau of Anet. Francis did not reconcile with Henry or recall Diane until 1545, after the death of his youngest son, Charles, when his own health was in obvious decline and Henry his only remaining heir.

Anne, like most mistresses, was completely dependent on the health and goodwill of her royal protector. In the last years of Francis's life, she worried about her future, and with good reason. As a contemporary put it, "The court was weary of the domination of a favorite who made and unmade ministers, was suspected of intriguing with the enemies of France, and pursued with the utmost vindictiveness those who refused to abase themselves before her."[207] Saint-Mauris, the imperial ambassador, reported: "If the said lady were to appear in public, the people would stone her, which is what is demanded and what she deserves."[208]

When Francis died, the cry went up, "The king is dead, long live the new mistress," in recognition that Diane had displaced Anne, who had immediately lost access to power.[209] Henry forbade Anne any role in government and confiscated many of her goods and gave them to Diane, most notably the jewels Francis had given her (worth some fifty thousand *écus*) and her chateaux. Anne's prior political activities were then subjected to renewed scrutiny; the chancellor drew up an indictment, charging her with a treasonable correspondence with the enemies of France. She was never convicted, and some sources attribute the indictment to malign rumors circulated by Diane.[210]

Without Francis's protection, Anne's husband exacted vengeance as well. He sued to take away her goods and accused her of appropriating his funds and of ruining his family. Shut away in the gloomy castle of La Hardoinaye, Anne endured her uncongenial marriage until she died in 1580. As she remarked to friends, "Not everyone who wishes can be a widow."[211] Her precipitous fall from grace, after her long reign of unparalleled political influence, attested to the transitory and dependent nature of her power. Anne has almost entirely disappeared from historical accounts. Francis is generally considered the strongest and most impressive French Renaissance king. To acknowledge Anne's political power would diminish his reputation. But for errors of political judgment in his waning years, Anne has sometimes been blamed.

LEGACY

These women played varied and important roles in Francis's reign but are rarely acknowledged in the histories of the period. If they assumed limited or appropriate roles for women, they receive greater praise than for effective political actions for which they are more usually condemned. Most surprising, however, is that these influential women are so little known.

Francis's first wife, Claude, took only a maternal role and wins nearly universal praise, from her contemporaries to modern historians. But that appreciation is quite perfunctory. As her biographer Marie-France Castelain noted, "Claude, between a brilliant husband, an authoritarian mother-in-law, and an unconventional sister-in-law, has not been able to seduce historians."[212] So unobtrusive was Claude that she is best remembered with the variety of plum named for her. Eleanor, Francis's second wife, remains most associated with Francis's wars with Charles V. Likely as a result, she is as little acknowledged in histories as she was by her husband during her life.

Françoise garnered some appreciation as a stylish mistress who did not wield a political influence. Instead a story about her, which circulated in the early seventeenth century, transformed her into a moral lesson for straying wives. According to the story, after Francis's visit to Chateaubriant long after their relationship had ended, Françoise faced the less-than-tender mercies of her husband. Jean reverted to a particularly violent version of the jealous spouse, confining her in an entirely black room in their chateau.[213] Although she begged for pardon from her implacable husband, ultimately two masked men entered the room and, upon her husband's signal, opened the veins in her arms. The several contemporary reports of Jean the irate husband who beat his wife evolved much later into a frightening tale of a jealous husband who murdered an unfaithful wife in Varillas's history. This story gained greater currency when repeated in Mézeray's seventeenth-century *Histoire de France* and Pierre Bayle's eighteenth-century *Critical Dictionary.* In response, the Breton jurist Pierre Hévin vigorously defended Jean, making Breton honor the issue. The historian Dreux du Radier claimed that Jean avenged himself cruelly but justifiably on his faithless wife. These accounts disparaging Françoise rejected Albert Le Grand's seventeenth-century appreciation of Françoise as both beautiful and virtuous and victim of her husband's wrath on the mere suspicion of her infidelity. He included her in his *History of the Saints of Brittany.*[214] This story is still told no doubt because of its inherent drama and moral lesson.

Marguerite remains acknowledged more for her contribution to the cultural preeminence of sixteenth-century France rather than for her political actions. Rabelais dedicated the third book of *Gargantua and Pantagruel* "to the spirit of the queen of Navarre, a spirit abstract, ravishing and ecstatic."[215] Even Michelet, unflinchingly critical of Francis, praised Marguerite as "the pure elixir of the Renaissance."[216] He, however, repeated the charge, originally promulgated by François Génin earlier in the nineteenth century, that Francis and Marguerite had an incestuous relationship.[217] Modern historians discount the charges, as Génin's evidence was an adulatory letter from Marguerite to Francis in which she described herself as "more than a sister," but Michelet gave the story credibility and a long life.[218] Modern writers, Simone de Beauvoir among them, extol Marguerite as a source of inspiration and praise her contribution to women's writing. The debt of successful kings to women such as Marguerite who acted so ably in their interest is rarely acknowledged. Enhancing French literature was more acceptable and praiseworthy than the political roles Francis's mother and sister took.

Since Louise's role was overtly political, when she is treated in Renaissance histories, it is usually negatively. There are two crucial aspects of this criticism. First, there seems to be a supposition that, as a woman, she should not have assumed such power. To the degree that she did, it indicates a weakness in Francis's governance. Her role as a strong, politically engaged woman elicited denunciations of her as "a dry-hearted egotist." (Interestingly, the same terms were used to condemn other women, notably Anne of Brittany, for political involvement.) Second, critics blamed her for France's problems, especially for the treason of Charles, the constable of Bourbon. Louise became the explicit target of Bourbon historians intent on restoring the reputation of their relative at her expense.[219] They tried to rescue Charles from the taint of treason by indicting the Valois who had brought charges against him and attacking Louise's sexuality and venality. Speculation that Louise was romantically interested in Charles reduced her to an especially vindictive and powerful woman scorned whose actions precipitated the treason of one of France's most prominent noblemen and whose son then used the law to do her bidding.

Those nineteenth-century historians who criticized Francis for increasing the monarchy's power excoriated Louise even more severely. Michelet denounced her as "coarse, sensual, harsh, violent, avaricious and vindictive" and her son as having the character "of the swine and the ape." Michelet developed a coherent narrative, blaming Louise systematically for the failures of Francis's reign: She did not educate him for kingship; she lost Milan because she appropriated money intended for the troops; and the constable of Bourbon betrayed his country because his elderly mistress tried to entrap him with a wedding ring. Michelet also castigated Louise for the Ladies' Peace, wondering: "How is it that the mother does not see that she destroys her son? In making him more execrable, guiltier, she isolates him forever." According to Michelet, Francis allowed his mother to rule because he pursued women and war, and "war to please women."[220] Guizot indicted Louise for the persecution of the Protestants. Francis's imprisonment after his defeat at Pavia, he claimed, allowed Louise to implement a policy of repression. Most reprehensible were her motives; she was greedy and power hungry.[221]

For these historians, staunch proponents of the republic, monarchs who acquired greater power were even more objectionable than monarchs pure and simple. But women's roles in the acquisition of power were especially disturbing. Their motives were always assumed to be the worst possible; they were grasping and easily swayed by their passions. Venality was a kind of gateway vice for women in power; it highlighted their base, ignoble passions. These histories thus reinvigorated the issues that so dominated the "quarrel over women" of the Renaissance. Women should not exercise power because of their greater susceptibility to their passions. Men's motives were not only rational, they could also, particularly if they forcefully excluded women, be noble and act in the interest of France.

Such was not the case for Francis I, in these historians' views, because of his mother's corrupting effect. According to Guizot, "Louise of Savoy gave her son neither principles nor moral examples; for him the royal sovereignty, for her the rank, the influence, the richness of the queen mother, and for both the grandeur serving to satisfy their passions."[222] Sully Prudhomme described Louise as "this miserable prostitute, avaricious, false, cruel, and pleasure seeking."[223] Objecting to the concentration of power under Francis, these critics blamed Louise for it, and their harsh assessments have colored subsequent treatments of her.

It is worth pointing out how clearly gendered these criticisms are. Powerful men are rarely denounced as egotistic, but any politically involved royal mother was indicted as both an egotist and an obsessive mother, implicitly charged with emasculating her son and thus weakening the monarchy. A woman's exercise of power, no matter how effective, was deemed illegitimate and denounced as self-aggrandizing. "Bad mother" and "unnatural woman" were and remain epithets used to denounce her. For these critics, monarchy empowered women inappropriately, unlike the more democratic governments of nineteenth-century France, which appropriately restricted women's political opportunities.

Modern studies of the French Renaissance scarcely mention Louise. When they do, they sometimes blame her for the problems of her son's reign or repeat the charge that she inaugurated the persecution of Protestants. But Parlement demanded a court for burning heretics, and the Sorbonne condemned them and called for the burnings of witches, not Louise. She can be accused only of failing to override Parlement. Almost all of the persecution of Protestants during Francis's reign occurred after her death.

Louise's modern biographers assess her more positively, in particular dismissing the evidence used to tar her in the Semblançay and Bourbon cases as flimsy. They praise her for forming an outstanding king and for her critical role in both foreign and domestic policy.[224] Very recently, some scholars have acknowledged appreciatively her patronage of Renaissance arts.[225]

The women of Francis's court have rarely even provoked the interest of biographers, with the notable exception of Marguerite, extolled for her literary accomplishments but scarcely acknowledged for her political activities. Louise and Anne, who exercised real political power, were denounced as venal and self-serving despite the fact that Anne promoted the policies Francis favored and Louise attempted to position the crown advantageously vis-à-vis the nobility, financiers, Parlement, and foreign powers. While Francis is praised for these actions, these women are blamed for his failures or for his absolutist policies. Claude wins praise, ironically, for her lack of impact, and Eleanor is scarcely mentioned.

These oversights are particularly striking because these women were so significant. Admittedly, they divided the functions among them. Both of Francis's two mistresses positively channeled the sexual interest of the king, one enhancing his image, the other serving as a lightning rod for negative opinion. His wives divided childbearing and diplomacy. And most apparently, Francis benefited from the active political engagement of his mother and sister. What seems especially telling about the women of Francis's court is how successful they were in assuming conventional roles for royal women. Louise was a strikingly effective royal mother who essentially ruled with Francis. Marguerite was a deferential sister who also became a peer of the realm and a queen in her own right. Her literary and theological works enhanced the intellectual reputation of her brother. Francis's mistresses embodied larger-than-life examples across an emotional spectrum: Françoise was the king's love interest who cast an aura of romance over his early kingship; Anne offered a sobering example of a politically powerful and polarizing royal mistress. Even Francis's less-than-distinguished queens enhanced his reign—Eleanor by restoring peace and Claude by so prodigiously fulfilling her childbearing function. But if each woman took a conventional role, she did so in ways that expanded its scope.

While Francis might have cultivated these women as refined embellishments of his court, admirably serving conventional roles, they contributed much more.

Fig. 3.13. Francis I and Louise of Savoy accept a manuscript, emphasizing their interest in intellectual patronage and suggesting their shared governance. They are depicted by Symphorien Champier, in the *Grandes chronquies de Savoie*. BnF.

Louise proved an adept political partner; both Louise and Claude shared his passion for building and were involved in the construction of Renaissance architectural monuments. Louise was a discerning patron of the arts (fig. 3.13).[226] And Claude carried on her mother's use of illuminated manuscripts to develop and convey her images. Both Marguerite and Françoise were literary and intellectual ornaments of Francis's court. Anne and Eleanor shared the political and diplomatic stage during the final years of his reign, even if not always entirely effectively. All of these women were crucial to the reputation of Francis's court for sophistication, which made it preeminent in the West. Marguerite not only contributed to the "quarrel over women" as a writer but she and her circle of women, with their virtue and accomplishment, epitomized Christine de Pizan's model city of ladies. Louise offers a powerful example of an adept female ruler, even if merely as regent. Because Louise ruled, she also raised the hackles of those who insisted that women were incapable of doing so. Because Anne was so influential, she too provoked criticism for women's involvement in politics. The women of Francis's court offer compelling examples of power and influence. Their successes not only enhanced Francis's reign but also contributed to the perception of the first half of the sixteenth century as "la belle Renaissance." Those successes have not been sufficiently acknowledged. To do so would only tarnish Francis's image as the exemplary Renaissance monarch.

SIGNIFICANT DATES FOR CHAPTER 4

1500	Birth of Diane de Poitiers, January 9 (sometimes given as September 1499)
	Marriage of Diane and Louis de Brézé, March 29
1518	Birth of Françoise, Diane and Louis's daughter
1519	Birth of Henry II, March 31
1521	Birth of Louise, Diane and Louis's daughter
1523	Discovery of Jean de Poitiers, lord of Saint-Vallier's (Diane's father) involvement in plot
1531	Death of Louis de Brézé
1533	Marriage of Henry and Catherine de Medici
1547	Henry II's coronation
1548	Diane becomes duchess of Valentinois
1559	Henry II's death, July 10
1566	Diane's death at Anet, April 26

4

DIANE DE POITIERS

An Idealized Mistress

Diane de Poitiers, one of the most famous French royal mistresses, demonstrates just how successfully a royal mistress could assume a queen's roles and representations. Making strikingly effective use of Renaissance arts, literature, and rhetoric, Diane not only constructed an image of herself as a paragon of virtue but also presented a new image of Henry II, less as family man and more as model of chivalric romance. Renaissance artists were avid to depict a mistress renowned for her beauty, and Diane came to embody Diana, the goddess of hunting, and to epitomize the artistic glory of the French Renaissance. So proficient was she at defining and exploiting those representations that they became virtually synonymous with her, and in large part, Henry's association with this goddess/mistress defined his reign. Diane remains an especially evocative figure; she has been used to romanticize Henry II, his reign, and the French Renaissance.

Diane also offers a compelling model of the power of myth over history. Mistresses of the Renaissance have provided material for intriguing myths and legends. These stories take on lives of their own, offering captivating, dramatic renditions that displace more reliable accounts of historical events. They then shape the subsequent histories of the woman, her age, the monarchy, and even France itself. The power of myth over history is especially evident in the case of Diane. She used the myth she constructed to solidify her status. To an unprecedented degree, she controlled her image. Her myth gave her contemporaries and subsequent historians ways to praise not simply a royal mistress but also a monarch.

Although Diane provoked controversy much as Agnès Sorel had, she lived in the full flowering of the Renaissance. As a result, a much more extensive historical record, providing fuller documentation of her life, makes it somewhat easier to distinguish history from myth. But certain features of the historical record complicate the telling of her story. Her few surviving letters to Henry are businesslike rather than revealing about their relationship or her character, and only a few of Henry's verses and letters to her remain.[1] Conventions of the day required the gallant lover to destroy his lover's letters, and Henry apparently did so.[2] Thus we have few direct indications of the nature of their personal relationship.

Diane and Henry's thorough efforts to shape and control her public image were so effective that they continue to complicate the historian's work. That control dramatized her significance and crafted the public presentation of her character and her role. But historical writing immediately after Diane's life during the Wars of Religion was shaped by Catholic-Protestant polemics. Diane was a devout Catholic and a close associate of both the Guise and Montmorency families, two of the leading families during the religious wars of the late sixteenth century. As a result, she provoked some criticism from Protestants who used the indiscretions of French kings and their mistresses to claim the moral high ground and to argue that Catholics such as Diane were both immoral and intent on subverting the state. Finally, Diane is linked to stories so dramatic, compelling, and frequently repeated through the centuries that it is hard to assess them critically. Although readers might prefer to cherish these more romantic accounts, it is worthwhile to consider why these stories were told and how they were subsequently used in French history.

Diane raises some of the issues Agnès brought to the fore. Once again, contemporaries praised the mistress as extraordinarily beautiful. As we saw with Charles VII, physical description of monarchs could be unrelievedly harsh. Queens too were sometimes described in very unflattering terms. Contemporaries occasionally mentioned positive physical attributes or juxtaposed positive personal qualities against physical imperfections. But mistresses were almost always described in lyrical terms, perhaps to justify a king's infidelity. A mistress's stunning beauty allowed some contemporaries to counsel loyalty to the king or even adulation of his mistress. Just as Agnès did almost one hundred years earlier, Diane, tall and slender with very white skin, red-gold hair, and blue-green eyes, embodied contemporary standards of beauty (fig. 4.1).[3] She inspired artists who depicted her in full, classical glory; the display of her physical charms was no longer restricted to exposure of her breast.

One cannot help but wonder about the reports of Diane's beauty, which contemporaries proclaimed as not just extraordinary but also incredibly enduring, so that she was considered a great beauty until her death in her late sixties. Brantôme claimed that she would remain beautiful if she lived to be 110.[4] The

Fig. 4.1. *Diana the Huntress*. Fontainebleau school, sixteenth century. Louvre / The Bridgeman Art Library.

beauty of her skin was legendary and reputedly never touched by makeup. Such beauty, some insisted, could be due only to magic, which allowed her to bewitch men, especially to retain the interest of the king despite her advanced years. Others claimed no magic was necessary to preserve her looks: They cited instead a special beauty regime; Diane was devoted to exercise or bathed in milk or cold water. That alone, English writers gleefully noted, distinguished her from her unhygienic French contemporaries. Her recent exhumation revealed that her bones were full of gold, which she likely ingested as a beauty treatment.

But even this, perhaps her most enduring claim to fame, is debatable. The portraits and pen-and-ink drawings of the Clouet school do not show a woman of extraordinary beauty but instead a rather old, stern-faced woman. But they were done late in her life, and the artists may have been influenced by Protestant sympathies as well (fig. 4.2). The artists—Benvenuto Cellini, Francesco Primaticcio, and Jean Goujon—who created such beautiful representations of her may also have been more concerned to perpetuate her legend than to portray her accurately.

Regardless of how attractive Diane actually was or how attractive we might consider her, her contemporaries were virtually unanimous in extolling her beauty. For them, her beauty set her apart and sanctioned her status, just as Henry's favor elevated her above other court women. During Francis's reign, Diane, the half-recognized mistress of the young heir apparent, competed for political influence with Anne, Francis's acknowledged favorite. Her sway over Henry provoked hostility, fueled in part by misogynist objections to women's meddling in politics. Her critics had cause. The king's devotion and the duration of their relationship gave Diane great political authority as his most trusted advisor, and more influence than any previous mistress. When Henry reigned, Diane, his long-standing, publicly acknowledged mistress, was much more prominent than his queen, Catherine de Medici.

Diane offered a different model of a relationship between a king and his mistress than had Charles VII and Agnès Sorel. A young, unmarried woman, Agnès was chosen by the king from a group of ladies-in-waiting, but Diane was a widow twenty years older than Henry; her age gave her authority over him for the rest of his life. Their relationship provoked other questions for their contemporaries and subsequent historians about the nature of their relationship. Some legitimated it as platonic, akin to that between mother and child or a chivalric asexual relationship between an idealized lady and her devoted knight. Others saw it as purely sexual, based on the crass manipulation of a young man by a grasping, older woman. Less critical studies present the relationship as a great romance; this version reigns in the popular imagination.[5] Diane's life too has

Fig. 4.2. Diane de Poitiers. French school, sixteenth century. Musée Condé, Chantilly / The Bridgeman Art Library.

been the stuff of romantic fiction; novels and plays told her story. The relationship between Diane, Henry, and Catherine de Medici remains of perennial interest to both historians and novelists.

AN ADVANTAGEOUS MARRIAGE

Diane was born into an important noble family probably on January 9, 1500, although there is no exact record of the date or place of her birth.[6] The Poitiers family can be traced back to the estates they held in the twelfth century. In the Hundred Years War, they fought against the English and were richly rewarded with fiefs. Diane's father, Jean de Poitiers, was lord of Saint-Vallier and inherited numerous titles from his own father. He married Jeanne of Batarnay, a rich heiress.[7] The couple had five children—two sons and three daughters—and

Diane was their oldest daughter. At a time when daughters were generally considered liabilities because of the drain on family finances their dowries entailed, Diane had an unusually close relationship with her father, perhaps because she was a tomboy, devoted to hunting and vigorous exercise. Her entire life, she rose at dawn, bathed in cold water, and went for long horseback rides—practices cited as sources of her extraordinary beauty.

As a young girl, Diane was sent to Anne of Beaujeu's court. Noble daughters often went to the households of more prominent nobles to complete their educations and enhance their prospects, and Anne was an especially apt choice for Diane's family. As the daughter of one king and the sister of another, Anne offered access to the highest echelons of the French nobility. She was also interested in the education of girls and wrote a volume of advice to her daughter, Suzanne, on how a woman of her social class should behave.[8] As we have seen, Anne was one of the most remarkable women of her day. Her father, Louis XI, entrusted her with the governance of his kingdom in preference to his son (later Charles VIII). Anne molded the powerful women of her age. Both Louise of Savoy and Margaret of Austria were raised and formed at her court. Brantôme, in fact, claimed that there were no great ladies of the time who were not educated by her, including his own grandmother.[9] Anne's tutelage might well have cultivated the skills Diane later demonstrated in maneuvering through the intricacies of the royal court in her best interests. At twelve, Diane became one of Anne's maids of honor. Anne not only fostered Diane's education but also advocated her marriage to Louis de Brézé.

Throughout Diane's childhood, the fortunes of her family increased, which enhanced her prospects for an advantageous marriage. An honored and accomplished soldier, her father had fought in the Italian wars of Charles VIII and Louis XII. (Later Jean's outstanding military service during the Italian campaigns led Francis I to appoint him captain of one hundred gentlemen of the king's house, a commission of great honor.) When Diane accompanied her father to Saint-Germain-en-Laye, the royal chateau just outside Paris, for Francis I's marriage to Claude, Louis de Brézé caught sight of her and agreed to a marriage.

On March 29, 1515, Diane, an approximately fifteen-year-old legendary beauty, married Louis, fifty-six years old and described as old beyond his years, "ill-favored and a hunchback."[10] Although this marriage might strike modern sensibilities as a mismatch, it was a phenomenal success in contemporary terms. Louis and his family could expect to reap certain advantages from his alliance with the Poitiers family; the Poitiers had acquired power through their association with Anne of Beaujeu and their ties to the constable Charles of Bourbon. But the Poitiers family could expect even greater benefits.

Louis was a member of one of the greatest noble families and of royal blood. His family's preeminence had increased greatly over the course of the fifteenth century. His grandfather Pierre de Brézé's military activities gained royal favor, and his ties to Agnès Sorel enhanced his status at court. As her ally, Pierre had access to the king, which brought him great rewards and provoked jealousy and lawsuits. For valor in the battle at Formigny in 1450, Pierre was rewarded with status and wealth as grand steward of Normandy.[11]

Pierre's son Jacques married Charlotte, one of Charles VII's daughters by Agnès. Jacques and Charlotte's marriage was significant for several reasons. It reflected the great rise in status of the Brézé family: Pierre married into the royal bloodline. The fact that the daughter of a royal mistress married the grand steward of Normandy attested to the high status of a king's illegitimate daughter. This marriage came to a violent end when Jacques caught Charlotte *in flagrante* with his master of hounds and murdered them both in their bed. Jacques was imprisoned and so heavily fined that he had to forfeit his estates, although his sons, as nephews of the king, were entitled to regain them.

Diane's husband, Louis, was Charlotte and Jacques's oldest son. As the grand steward of Normandy, he was entitled to almost royal prerogatives. His wealth and prestige also gave his bride great status; she took precedence over most ladies of the court and became a lady-in-waiting to the queen mother, Louise of Savoy.[12] It might have been expected that such a misalliance in terms of age would soon make her a wealthy widow. But Louis lived another seventeen years, to the age of seventy-two, far beyond sixteenth-century life expectancy of about fifty. Insofar as the slight historical record can reflect the character of a marriage, it suggests that the couple lived in harmony.

Diane may well have absorbed Anne of Beaujeu's tutelage on marriage. Anne advised her daughter, Suzanne, that marriage "is a state of such beauty and so prized, provided it is honestly regulated, that it seems it cannot be honored enough or praised too much. And to achieve this state, you cannot devote yourself to it too much or conduct yourself too wisely or with too much gentleness, deference, and chastity . . . and you should not have any preferences, desires, or wishes of your own."[13] Anne, who had married a man twenty years older than she and chosen by her father, also claimed that fortunes were maintained and great houses made through carefully arranged marriages: Successful marriages enhanced powerful, noble families.

When Diane was pregnant with her first child, her husband wrote a letter to Montmorency, which reflected the couple's affectionate relationship and ties to the king. Louis commented that he did not believe that Diane, already in her ninth month, could get any bigger and noted with pleasure his elevated position in the coronation ceremonies for Queen Claude.[14] When the king and queen later visited Rouen, Louis presented them with the keys to the city. Louis and Diane were a wealthy, influential couple, graced with the king's favor.

Diane bore two daughters, Françoise in 1518 and Louise in 1521. Diane's marriage at such a young age also restricted her fertility, since she was less likely to bear a child until she attained full maturity (probably at about eighteen in the sixteenth century)—no doubt an unintended consequence. When she was widowed in 1531, Diane had borne only two children—one at the age of eighteen the other at twenty-one. When she became involved with Henry, she was thirty-six, beyond the age of prime fertility. Thus Diane did not suffer the risks to her health that many pregnancies could have entailed.

TO SAVE A FATHER

Louis de Brézé was prominent in the chronicles of the day primarily because of the involvement of his father-in-law, Jean de Poitiers, in Charles of Bourbon's plot against Francis I. Louis became involved when two of the plotters were overcome with pangs of conscience and told the bishop of Lisieux, who then informed Louis. When Louis notified the king of the impending English invasion with the aid of "an important personage of this kingdom,"[15] he implicated his father-in-law, although it is unclear whether Louis knew of his involvement. Charles escaped, but many of his co-conspirators were arrested, including Jean de Poitiers, who bore the brunt of Francis's ire. No doubt Jean's great wealth, status, and the favor Francis had shown him made his betrayal galling. Jean protested his innocence to Louis: "The king has ordered me to be arrested for no reason . . . as a traitor" and appealed to his son-in-law and daughter for assistance.[16] He confessed to attending meetings between Charles of Bourbon and representatives of Charles V and Henry VIII to arrange Charles of Bourbon's marriage to Eleanor, Charles V's sister and later Francis I's wife. Jean's signature witnessed incriminating documents in the case. Tried and convicted, his goods were confiscated, and he was sentenced to death. But he was ultimately granted a reprieve, and therein hangs a tale.

The document granting Jean's reprieve credits the efficacy of his son-in-law's appeal. But a rumor, which has regularly fueled historiographical speculation, claimed that the price demanded by Francis in exchange for her father's reprieve was Diane's honor. The *Journal of a Bourgeois of Paris* deemed it "a sweet exchange to one who esteems honor less than life."[17] Part of the fascination of this story is that, if it were true, Diane would have been the mistress of both father and son. The story also had great ideological value; anti-monarchists and Protestants could wring their hands over the debauchery of the Catholic king of France and his Catholic mistress. This story pitted the fidelity and virtue of a beautiful, young woman against the demands of a lustful king, with a father's life hanging in the balance. At issue was the king's reputation. For some, it was easy to believe that Francis, a notorious womanizer, would exact such a price. Several features of this story make it worth discussing.

Diane's immediate contemporaries rarely mentioned the incident. The most notable charge was made as early as 1552, at the height of Diane's political influence, by the Venetian ambassador Lorenzo Contarini: "Remaining young, widowed, and beautiful, Diane was loved and tasted by the King Francis I and others as well, as everyone says; then she came into the hands of King Henry II." Contarini insinuated that her public presentation was a fabrication: "Thus Diane the prude, Diane the inaccessible had dissimulated, under an apparent coldness and a chastity loudly proclaimed, a temperament of fire."[18] Francis inscribed a portrait of Diane as "beautiful to see, honest to frequent," which seems to exonerate her of any such charges.[19] Although their contemporaries were clearly impressed that Diane and her husband procured a reprieve for such serious charges, they did not generally suggest that it depended on the granting of sexual favors. The crime was grievous: Jean was clearly aware of a plot against the king; and the evidence of his involvement was compelling. Under these circumstances, the request of Louis and Diane to spare this traitor was audacious.

And what of Diane's husband? Is it at all conceivable that Louis would have pleaded for his father-in-law's life if his wife's honor were at stake? We know little about Louis beyond his high political and economic status. Many of his contemporaries allowed themselves to be married and ennobled to facilitate such liaisons. Louis could have seen the king's attachment to his wife as advantageous, as did Anne de Pisseleu's husband, but Louis was not likely a compliant husband. His own father had murdered his wife for her adultery. Nor is there reason to believe that Louis would have taken his wife's honor lightly. Diane, married to a man ten years older than her father, might have found it acceptable to be singled out by the king, especially to spare her father's life. But her sense of her own honor, so evident throughout her life, makes it highly unlikely that she would have agreed to be the king's passing fancy. So while some contemporary practices make the story credible, there are compelling reasons, based on the character of Diane and her husband, to doubt it. Nor does it seem likely, especially given Francis's passion for Françoise at the time and his success as a gallant, that he would have exacted such a price.

Who told this story? The Venetian ambassador's charge of 1552 was picked up shortly thereafter by Louis Regnier de la Planche, who gave the tale its most influential form in *The State of France under Francis I.*[20] The Protestant historian claimed that Diane began her career as a courtesan, bartering her chastity for her father's life, and used this presumed relationship to condemn her. Others told the story to praise her devotion to her father. In Brantôme's account, as Jean descended from the scaffold, he said, "God save the . . . [expletive deleted in original text] of my daughter who saved me so well." Brantôme believed that the sexual encounter occurred but did not condemn it, citing an analogous Christian example: Saint Augustine doubted whether a Christian of Antioch sinned when he, being held prisoner for a large sum, allowed his wife to pay his debt with her favors. Brantôme concluded, "If Saint Augustine is of this opinion, what may not be permitted various ladies, widows, and maidens, who redeem their fathers and husbands . . . what harm or scandal can arise from this?"[21] Dramatic and polemically useful, the story is now considered highly dubious.[22] An unsigned cache of letters from a woman to Francis I, previously believed to corroborate his relationship with Diane, was determined to have been written by Françoise de Foix.[23]

If this story of seduction was likely a useful invention, Francis nonetheless had a good political reason to grant Jean a reprieve: Louis controlled men at arms in Normandy, where France was susceptible to invasion from England. Jean's life was spared but he remained in prison until the Treaty of Madrid of 1526 stipulated that he be released along with other supporters of the constable of Bourbon. After Jean's reprieve, Louis defended France against the English in Normandy, and Diane served the court. The successful appeal for Jean's life cemented the couple's friendship with Francis. Francis went to Normandy, where Louis and Diane entertained him, and he visited Diane after Louis's death. On one visit, the marriage contract between Henry II and Catherine de Medici was drafted—an ironic twist in light of Henry and Diane's subsequent relationship. Louis and Diane also promoted political positions; they favored peace with the Hapsburgs and the marriage between Henry and Catherine de Medici.[24] Diane was related to Catherine (their grandmothers were sisters), and this marriage would bind Diane's family more closely to the royal family.

AN INDEPENDENT WIDOW

After sixteen years of marriage, Louis died in 1531, leaving a widow who was young, noble, beautiful, and prominent at court. Diane retained the financial assets of her husband, but without a male heir, her estates could have reverted to the crown.[25] To preserve them, she took her case to Parlement to maintain her rights of inheritance. She received from Francis the exceptional right not to have to account to a guardian during her widowhood.[26] Louis left her well provided with the means and the authority to dower and marry her daughters well. He had greatly enriched his family, increasing their land holdings and political connections. The further concentration of wealth and power in her family became one of Diane's chief concerns; she proved more than adept at the task.

Diane built a magnificent tomb for Louis, attributed to the famous sculptor Jean Goujon, in the cathedral in Rouen in the style of Renaissance royal tombs. That is to say, it had a carved figure of the deceased on a lower level with his living image above. In this case, Louis is on horseback flanked by four caryatids, representing victory, faith, prudence, and glory. The inscription proclaims his wife's devotion: OH! LOUIS DE BRÉZÉ, DIANE DE POITIERS, STRICKEN BY THE DEATH OF HER HUSBAND, HAS RAISED THIS SEPULCHER TO YOU. SHE WAS YOUR INSEPARABLE AND FAITHFUL WIFE IN THE MARRIAGE BED; SHE WILL BE THE SAME IN THE TOMB (fig. 4.3).

Diane seemed intent on being just as virtuous a widow as she had been a wife. Her husband's funeral was appropriate for the greatest nobleman, his funerary art impressive, and the conduct of his mourning widow exemplary. Diane was now thirty-one years old and showed no interest in remarriage. She would have been sharply aware of her high status, her independence, and her position as head of her family. Diane might have been inclined to follow the advice of Anne of Beaujeu to widows that "when it comes to the government of their lands and affairs, they must depend only on themselves; when it comes to sovereignty, they must not cede power to anyone."[27] Brantôme too pointed out the advantages noble widows enjoyed: "They have the use of their own money, the management of the estate. . . . Instead of being servants as before, they are in command; they can pursue their pleasures and enjoy companions who will do as they wish. They remain widows in order to keep their grandeur, dignity and possessions, titles and good treatment."[28]

Once widowed, Diane wore mourning clothes of black and white for the rest of her life. Particularly becoming to her fair skin and blond hair, they set her apart from other women. Not surprisingly, this romantic guise attracted the attention of poets, whose early appreciations of Diane foreshadow the mutually beneficial relationship between beautiful mistresses and Renaissance artists that she came to embody.

Diane retained her prominence in Francis's court. Before her husband's death, she participated in the festivities of Francis's reign, where she was esteemed for her beauty, intelligence, and virtue. Later, as the widow of a preeminent nobleman, Diane had both authority and independence. At the end of 1531, she returned to the court as a lady-in-waiting to Louise of Savoy and, after Louise's death, to the new queen, Eleanor.

Given her subsequent involvement in Henry's life, Diane's relationship with him can almost seem preordained, but their close association did not actually begin until Francis I recruited Diane to socialize the adolescent Henry to court

Fig. 4.3. Diane commissioned an extravagant tomb for her husband, Louis de Brézé. Photo by author.

life when he was eleven. Henry's childhood had been especially difficult. His mother died when he was five years old. His father was captured by Charles V in the French defeat at the Battle of Pavia. To gain his own release, Francis's two oldest sons became Spanish hostages. The dauphin Francis was nine years old; Henry was just seven. Diane was among the women of the court who accompanied the young princes to Spain and embraced them before turning them over to Spanish officials. Although Henry's attachment to Diane may date from that farewell kiss, the story may well be apocryphal—told to foreshadow their future relationship.

Imprisonment for more than four years marked Henry, who thereafter tended to be silent and uncomfortable in social situations, qualities either produced or exacerbated by his captivity.[29] Some twelve years after Henry's release, Matteo Dandolo, a Venetian ambassador, remarked that few had ever heard the young prince laugh.[30] Francis seemed particularly unattached to Henry, perhaps for the very qualities his captivity either underscored or induced.

The Ladies' Peace stipulated that Charles V's sister Eleanor would return his ransomed sons when she came to marry Francis. Diane accompanied the young princes and the future queen back to France. In the tournament held to honor the new queen, Diane won a prize for beauty, although she shared it with Anne, the king's mistress. For this honor, Brantôme dubbed Diane "the beautiful among the beautiful," since she won the prize for her beauty rather than by any need to curry favor with the king.[31] The young royal princes were dressed and armed as chevaliers, and each carried a standard; the dauphin Francis selected the new queen to champion, and Henry wore Diane's colors, probably in gratitude for escorting him on his return from Spain. When it was his turn, Henry knelt before Diane, indicating to all that he considered her his lady. Henry was smitten at a young age and remained so.

Despite Henry's chivalric gesture, Francis was concerned about his son's ability to assume a public position. As he came of age, Henry reveled in the life of a military camp more than that of the court. The Venetian ambassador Marino Cavalli emphasized, as did many of Henry's contemporaries, the brawn of the young prince (implying brawn at the expense of brains), describing him as "so well built that one would think he was made of muscle, indefatigable in exercises of arms or hunting." Henry was not considered particularly intelligent, and "his father the king did not love him much,"[32] the Venetian ambassador remarked. (Francis was devoted to his oldest son, Francis, and preferred his youngest son, Charles, known for his agreeable disposition.)

Legend has it that when Francis complained about Henry to Diane, she offered to transform Henry into a gallant and to initiate him into the ways of the court. She did so, it seems, by establishing between them a chivalric relationship, entirely chaste, in which she was his lady and he was her knight. Though this might seem a rather peculiar way to reeducate a young prince, Henry was a maladroit young man, deprived of his mother and neglected by his father. His relationship with Diane elevated him to fictional knighthood and gave him an intense personal relationship with a beautiful older woman. The invocation of chivalry also fit Francis's sophisticated court, which fostered both the Renaissance revival of the ancients and the new appreciation of women in court culture. The latter, which saw women as transforming feudal knights into Renaissance men, was so compelling, in part, because it could readily be grafted on to the older, courtly love tradition. Diane's chivalric approach to tutelage proved heady, as the young prince took his position as her devoted knight very seriously.

When Diane agreed to make Henry a gallant, what had she undertaken? She intended to help him develop a public persona appropriate to his station and to equip him for a more prominent position at court. When she took him in hand, Diane was thirty-one and Henry was eleven. Part of the reason Francis urged Diane to undertake Henry's social education was to prepare him for marriage. When Catherine de Medici was proposed as a bride, Diane spelled out for Henry some of the advantages of this marriage: The bride was rich and a descendent of Louis IX. Catherine's claims to territories in Italy would allow Henry a foothold from which to launch a crusade.[33] Such a venture would put him into the lists of the great crusading kings—a persona guaranteed to appeal to Henry's romantic self-image. Diane was later commissioned to guide Henry's young bride as well in the conventions of the French court.

Diane's involvement in Henry's marriage negotiations was not the only sign of her political involvement. She also advocated an alliance between France and the papacy, which would have made Francis the champion of orthodox Catholicism against the Protestant princes. To advance this plan, she worked with Montmorency to promote peace between Francis and Charles V. But Francis rejected these diplomatic designs. He instead opened negotiations with the Protestants, a preliminary move in the renewal of warfare with Charles V, which repudiated the political positions Diane advocated.

Moving toward war, the house of Valois suffered a devastating loss that changed the future for Henry and Diane. The young dauphin Francis had been playing tennis when he got caught in a storm, drank a glass of cold water given to him by Simon Montecucculi, and died.[34] Rumors that he had been poisoned warred with popular opinion that it was dangerous to drink cold drinks when overheated. The young heir had been popular, and great hopes for the dynasty had rested on him. Henry had not been viewed as a prospective heir; he had neither an engaging personality nor much to recommend him for the position thrust upon him. Suspicion for his brother's death fell on his young wife, Catherine de Medici, both because of the increase in her status and because of her Italian background. (Italians were considered especially adept poisoners.)

Diane immediately came to Henry's aid. As he took on new responsibilities, Henry could count on her to smooth his path and alert him to the dangers and traps of court life. With more than a hint of the pragmatic expediency that often guided the choices made by the women who became royal favorites, Diane seems to have singled out Henry for her sexual favors. Perhaps she had hesitated to sacrifice her virtue and reputation in a relationship with an awkward second son but would not refuse the heir apparent. By this time, Henry was sixteen years old to her thirty-six.

Up to this point, Henry had experienced short-lived liaisons with camp followers and almost three years of a less-than-successful marriage to Catherine. Henry's friend and Diane's ally Montmorency set the scene for the initial tryst at the chateau of Ecouen, in a room where the loves of Psyche were vividly depicted, although it seems unlikely that Henry required artistic inspiration to press his suit. He tied his destiny to devotion to his lady, writing,

> Alas, my God, how much I regret
> The time I lost in my youth
> How many times I wished
> To have Diane for my only mistress
> But I feared that she, who is a goddess,
> Would not want to abase herself
> To value me, who, without her esteem,
> Would have no pleasure, joy, or contentment. . . . [35]

In her new position as Henry's mistress, Diane was credited with transforming an awkward youth into a man who remained devoted to her for the rest of his life. Cavalli reported, "One affirms that this woman has undertaken to indoctrinate, to correct, and to counsel Monsieur the dauphin and to push him to all the actions worthy of him." Diane cloaked her relationship with Henry in discretion and mystery. Although some contemporaries noticed the new intimacy between them, others wondered whether she simply offered him friendship. So discreet was Diane that, even more than ten years after she became sexually involved with Henry, Cavalli reported, "while for conversation, he [Henry] confines himself to that of the Steward of Normandy [Diane], who is forty-eight years of age. He entertains for her a sincere affection; but it is not thought that there is anything lascivious about it and that this affection is like that between mother and son."[36]

One fundamental function that Diane assumed was to urge Henry to fulfill his conjugal duties. Henry neglected Catherine for his mistress's company, but Diane did not want Catherine set aside to be replaced by a queen who might stir his passions. Royal couples generally married earlier than their nonroyal contemporaries in hopes of bearing children earlier and more frequently to secure succession. Childless after years of marriage, it seemed that Henry and Catherine might never have children. Diane would brook no neglect of his wife by Henry; she not only insisted that he spend his nights with Catherine but was also involved in the intimate relations between the couple. She brought Henry talismans and love potions and consulted astrologers, alchemists, and sorcerers on his behalf. Finally in 1544, Catherine gave birth to a son, a development Henry credited to Diane's advice, giving her fifty-five hundred *livres* for the "good and recommendable services that she had previously done for the queen."[37]

Over the next ten years, Catherine bore nine more children. Nonetheless, she was forced to abase herself before Diane and to act as Diane's spy in the court, knowing full well that she owed her continued position as queen to the support of her husband's mistress. Catherine's many pregnancies ironically provided greater justification in their contemporaries' minds for Henry to spend more time with Diane, who even assumed a maternal role as Catherine's children's official governor.

As soon as Henry became the heir apparent, Diane's situation changed dramatically; she remained his most trusted advisor, guiding him through the political and social shoals of court life as he took on more prominent positions and proved himself on military campaigns.[38] Now dauphin and with Diane and Montmorency as allies, Henry was poised to assert himself. He took as his symbol the crescent moon with the motto, "When It Is Full, It Emulates the Sun."

RIVAL MISTRESSES, DIVIDED COURT

Diane's position as the acknowledged favorite of the future king brought her into direct conflict with Anne de Pisseleu, Francis's influential mistress. To discredit her emerging rival, Anne launched a campaign of personal invective against Diane in which she emphasized her rival's age, claiming inaccurately that Anne was born the day Diane wed.[39] (Anne was only nine years younger than Diane.) In this rivalry, Diane cited her position as lady-in-waiting and cousin to Catherine (although it seems rather tactless to tout her blood relationship with her lover's wife) and pointed to her ancient lineage and alliance with the powerful Brézé family. Anne disparaged Diane's looks and commissioned the poet Jean Voulté, whose verses described Diane: "her face painted with wrinkles, her false teeth, and her ruined complexion."[40] Diane launched a counterattack on Anne's fidelity.

Henry not only vociferously defended his mistress but also became her agent in the campaign against Anne, spreading the rumor that Anne had slept with her brother-in-law Guy Chabot, the chevalier of Jarnac. Because of Henry's rank, Jarnac could not challenge his royal accuser to a duel. But François de Vivonne, lord of La Châtaigneraie, wanted to accept the challenge in Henry's stead. Francis I had not permitted the duel to take place, but Henry allowed it immediately after his father's death. In a gruesome six-hour duel, Jarnac, despite pleas to Henry to end the gory contest, was essentially forced to kill Henry's stand-in. La Châtaigneraie ensured his own demise by refusing to have his life-threatening wounds treated because of the ignominy of his defeat.[41] Contemporaries saw this inglorious incident as a telling example of the destruction wrought by women in politics. As Blaise de Monluc remarked, "The king should stop the mouths of women who tattle-tale at court. . . . A gossip caused the death of M. de La Châtaigneraie."[42]

This battle between the two mistresses had significant political ramifications. Their supporters polarized the court. Anne's pronounced influence with Francis led Henry increasingly to turn against his father and to oppose his policies. Father and son were frequently and more sharply at odds during the last ten years of Francis's reign. When Anne persuaded Francis that Diane was fostering Henry's disloyal support of Montmorency, Francis ordered Diane to leave the court. Henry went with her, and the estrangement between father and son hardened. When Francis toured Normandy, he visited Diane at her chateau of Anet, where she interceded to make peace between father and son. Shortly thereafter, Henry was readmitted to Francis's council. When Francis fell ill, he sent his son into battle in his place; Henry distinguished himself as a soldier. Just as Henry gained greater credibility (and, by association, so did his mistress), Francis's mistress faced charges of disloyalty, a situation Diane exploited to her advantage.

Near the end of his life, Francis tried to carve out territory for his youngest son, Charles, by arranging his marriage alliance with a Spanish princess. Anne supported Charles and actively lobbied for this marriage. Once again, the rivalry between mistresses was politically significant; each mistress worked to foster the interests of the prince she supported. Diane overtly opposed both a Hapsburg marriage and the peace as antithetical to Henry's interests. This division of opinion heightened tensions between the two factions at court and divided the royal family. Henry urged his father to make no concessions to the emperor. But when Charles V proposed that Francis's son Charles should marry his niece and be given Burgundy as his territory, Henry saw this peace as antithetical to his interests as the future king, as it detached Burgundy from his control and allied it with Spain. Francis agreed to this arrangement even though he had earlier worked so assiduously against just this development. But in this case, his son would hold Burgundy. Henry may well have also seen the peace as reflecting Anne's undue influence and Francis's partiality toward his younger son. Henry was so aggrieved that he filed a formal protest with Parlement on December 12, 1544, insisting on the inalienability of crown lands—a legal challenge to his father and his brother. One evening, surrounded by his friends, Henry speculatively reconfigured the government as he would if he were king. Henry's jester characterized it as "selling the skin before the bear was dead," when he reported the event to an infuriated Francis.[43]

Despite the growing hostility between father and son, Henry inevitably assumed greater political preeminence after his brother Charles died in 1545. With only one surviving royal son, there was no other focus for a rival political party. Anne's prior commitment to Charles left her without much influence.

The rivalry between Diane and Anne not only attests to their great influence at court but also reveals in dramatic fashion the ways mistresses could complicate political issues and family relations. But it would be a mistake to construe this rivalry as that of two women simply jockeying for prominence. With a clear and consistent political position, supporting rival princes and policies, they were influential enough to shape politics in the last decade of Francis's reign. But Anne was invariably condemned for meddling. Diane was not, even though, as long as Francis reigned, her positions did not prevail.

By 1546, as it became increasingly clear that Henry would soon succeed his father, the Venetian ambassador Cavalli expressed great optimism about French prospects: "His [Henry's] qualities promise to France the most worthy king it has had in a hundred years." He noted that, although Henry was not well-spoken or given to repartee, he was nonetheless firm in his opinions. Even if "his intelligence was not the quickest," Cavalli concluded, "those men often succeed the best."[44]

Francis offered his son some dying words of wisdom. He warned Henry to be on guard against the Guises because "they will strip my children to their waistcoats and my poor people to their shirts."[45] He asked Henry to treat Anne with respect and urged him not to let ambitious individuals, especially Montmorency, into his council. These words suggest Francis's prophetic vision of the evils that would befall France during the Wars of Religion. Deathbed advice, which seemed to predict the future so accurately, gave chroniclers a compelling way to construct their narratives. But these words were first attributed to Francis many years after his death to indict Henry, who had not implemented its recommendations. Henry recalled Montmorency as grand master of the household and constable of France. He banned Anne from government, confiscated her goods, and dismissed her supporters from court. He used suspicions of Anne's treason as grounds to confiscate the duchy of Estampes and return it to the crown. In 1553 the duchy and the title went to Diane.

A KING'S FAVOR

Henry, at least according to the Venetian special envoy Matteo Dandolo, seemed to change with his accession to the throne: "He has become gay" and behaved "less as a good soldier and more as a captain." Dandolo further reported Henry's desire "that if the crown he was going to take would promise good government and assure the well-being of his people, God would give him the grace to let him have it for a long time, otherwise He would take it from him soon." Contarini too reported that the new king had a natural goodness and welcomed all. These reports were taken as signs of Henry's likely success as king. Several ambassadorial reports explicitly emphasized his relationship with Diane as indicative of Henry's seriousness of purpose. Contarini remarked, "As for the pleasures of the flesh, if we compare him to his father . . . one could call him chaste." Cavalli noted, "He is not given over to women; his [Diane] suffices."[46] In other words, Henry's devotion to his mistress enhanced his stature as king.

With Henry's accession to the throne, Diane wielded ever-greater power. Saint-Mauris, the Spanish ambassador, reported to Charles V: "As for the king, he continues to yield more and more to the yoke of Sylvius [Saint-Mauris's code word for Diane] and has become her subject and slave entirely, which his people lament." He complained further: "The worst is that the king lets himself be led and does everything that Sylvius and his lords advise, which drives the people to despair."[47] Diane was forty-eight years old, and her influence with the king was not simply that of a mistress over her lover but also of a trusted political advisor over an unsure king. As Cavalli noted, Henry was "born to be governed rather than to govern."[48] Saint-Mauris explicitly complained that Diane's preeminence was reflected in the way Henry spent his time. He had previously held audiences after dinner to hear the grievances of his subjects but now allowed no one to approach him, instead spending his time with Diane. "When he has given her an account of all of the business he has transacted in the morning and up to that moment, whether with the Ambassadors or other persons of importance, he seats himself upon her lap, a guitar in his hand, upon which he plays and inquires of the Constable or of Aumale [Francis of Guise] if the said Sylvius [Diane] 'has not preserved her beauty' touching her bosom from time to time and regarding her attentively, like a man who is ensnared by love."[49]

For her supporters Diane, like Agnès Sorel before her, epitomized the benefits of love: The king was more chaste, his court more praiseworthy, her effect on him salutary. On the other hand, Diane's critics charged, she distracted him from his duty, and her power superseded that of others—men who were implicitly more appropriate advisors. The love of a king for a mistress was thus a double-edged sword.

Diane did not allow her official status to undermine her reputation for respectability; she sought to be a model of propriety. Henry, less discreet than she and interested in proclaiming their relationship, made the illusion of her respectability difficult to maintain. To make their association clear, he adopted black and white as his colors (fig. 4.4). The letters that adorn virtually every surface associated with his reign, including the embroidery on his clothing, even his coronation robe, are themselves ambiguous. They should perhaps be considered an apt reflection of the triangulated nature of his personal life. There are almost as many opinions about what the letters are and what they mean as there are people who have written about them (fig. 4.5). The symbol has an *H*. Each *H* is crossed with something, but just what that is has produced contested interpretations. It might be crossed with the crescent moon, Henry's symbol of his growing power but also a symbol of the goddess Diana. And a crescent imposed on an *H* can also form *D*s on *H*s. That *D* could be for Diane but it could also connote Henri Deux or Henry II. The crescent itself is the same shape as a *C*. Some crescents, especially in Catherine's castles, are much more rounded into a shape closer to the letter *C*, with more prominent marks on the ends—more clearly *C*s than crescents or *D*s.[50] Thus debate over this emblem has persisted. The general division is between those who have seen it as an *H* and two *D*s and those who have seen it as an *H* with two *C*s.

Giovanni Capello, the nephew of the Venetian ambassador, remarked in his travel diary on his reading of the letters on Henry's clothing. "One sees at first an H. . . . One can see there also two Ds, which are the double initial of the Duchess of Valentinois. . . . Her true name is Diane, and the illusion is well manifested in these two crescents so united and so joined in the embrace of the two Ds, even as the two souls of the two lovers are united and reunited."[51] The *H*s and *D*s, the colors black and white, and the ubiquitous crescent moon were consistent features of Henry's iconography tying him to Diane.

Fig. 4.4. This image of Henry II by François Clouet shows him, as was typical, clothed in his mistress's colors of black and white. Musée Condé, Chantilly / The Bridgeman Art Library.

Fig. 4.5. *H*s and *D*s clockwise from top left, from a chimney at Chenonceau, a wall covering at Blois (modern recreations), a floor tile at Chenonceau, and from Anet. Photos by author.

Catherine used her initial with Henry's as well; it even adorned her tomb. She may have appropriated it to efface Diane's relationship with her husband. If so, this effort became more effective after Henry was dead and Diane gone from the court. Some historians insist that the symbol cannot be associated with anyone but Catherine and Henry because royal symbols could only refer to the queen. That argument is not entirely persuasive because the symbol so often appears in black and white, colors emphatically associated with Diane, because it is so prominent in Diane's chateau of Anet, and because Henry used it to sign his letters to Diane but not to his wife.[52] Henry was clearly willing to violate precedent in Diane's interest. Some distinguish two kinds of crests: an

H with two *C*s from an *H* with two crescent moons for Diane, although it is difficult to distinguish between them consistently or decisively.[53] If the letters remain ambiguous, that ambiguity is something Diane might have fostered; it underscored her importance but obliquely.

Once Henry became king, Diane epitomized the power that a royal mistress could exert. Within days of the new king's ascent, four of her supporters gained positions on the council—two members of the Guise family and Saint-André and Montmorency, who led factions during the subsequent Wars of Religion. Diane's supporters received rich rewards for themselves and members of their families—governorships of provinces, chateaux, honors, and pensions. In 1539, Diane's daughter Françoise married Robert de La Marck, prince of Sedan and member of the Montmorency family. In 1547, when Diane was at the height of her authority, her younger daughter, Louise, married Claude de Lorraine of the Guise family. This was not only a brilliant alliance; it also bound Diane to the Guise faction, later leaders of the Catholic party in the Wars of Religion. She then advanced the career of her son-in-law, to whom Henry gave command of the army. These marriage alliances connected Diane to the two most important families in Henry II's government.

Diane's support for Montmorency and the Guises, critics charge, was a gross misjudgment on her part. Her advocacy entrapped Henry in the clutches of those who later warred against his sons and tried to rob them of the crown. Their critics hold Francis's mistress Anne and Henry's mistress Diane responsible for the horrific unfolding of the Wars of Religion.[54] These men were indeed the most powerful nobles in France, and their sons later warred against Henry for political and religious reasons. But neither these mistresses nor any other political leader could have foreseen the development of several features essential to the outbreak of religious warfare. Most importantly, they could not yet have been aware of how politically divisive Calvinism would be. Its dramatic spread, especially among elites, with its inherent call to theocracy and its explicit justification of the overthrow of kings in the name of religion, occurred slightly later. These mistresses, by supporting powerful men, preserved their own power and neutralized that of their rivals by playing them off against each other. Nonetheless, Diane's support of the Guises might explain some of Catherine's later hostility toward them. Catherine might have also observed Diane's willingness to play Montmorency off against the Guises to prevent either of them from exercising more power over Henry than she did—a strategy Catherine later deployed.

Throughout Henry's reign, Diane's influence at court grew ever more obvious and extensive. After the ninety official days of mourning his father's death, Henry made a triumphal entry into Reims on July 24, 1547. Apparent everywhere was the silver crescent moon, symbol of the goddess Diana, which he had taken for himself. From the earliest days of his reign, the interlaced letters or symbols appeared on every new public building. Henry had a gold medal struck with Diane's head on one side and the goddess Diana on the other, with the legend I CONQUERED HIM WHO CONQUERED ALL.

When Henry made triumphal entries, cities were eager to show Diane the deference the king expected. These ceremonial occasions thus presented his relationship with his mistress in elaborate, allegorical, public tableaux (fig. 4.6). Most notably, on his entry into Lyon in 1548, the municipal leaders paid obvious tribute to Diane. As the king processed through a forest, he was met by an entrancing young woman dressed as the goddess Diana, accompanied by a group of lightly attired nymphs. "Diana" led a lion by a black-and-white leash. Representing both the city and the sovereign, it was tied by love to Diana. This was the first public presentation of the mistress as a goddess connected to the king.[55] On an obelisk, constructed in the center of town, victory crushed the furies and love extinguished the torches of discord. The beneficent effect of love on the kingdom was the overriding theme of this triumphal entry.[56] "One cannot say to what point has come the grandeur and omnipotence of the duchess of Valentinois"[57] (the latest and highest of Diane's many titles), the ambassador Contarini remarked on this occasion.

Catherine entered the city later that day. While it was customary for kings and queens to have separate entries to honor each, in this case, the Spanish ambassador reported the slight to the queen: "It is indeed true that little could be seen when the queen made her entry, because night came on and the people say that, as she is not good looking, the king gave orders that her pageant should be kept back until a late hour so that her highness should pass unnoticed."[58] Henry's love for his mistress, not his wife, elevated the kingdom.

Although Catherine again feared that she would be put aside, Diane still did not want a different wife who might be less indebted to her or of more interest to Henry. Catherine was useful as her spy within the court, not daring to refuse any service Diane exacted. Diane exerted her influence with Henry to ensure that Catherine was finally formally crowned queen of France in 1549.[59] Although this measure enhanced Catherine's status, Diane was as prominent as the queen at the coronation; the event clearly took place with her approbation.

Although Catherine's often-cited "Never did a wife who loves her husband love his whore"[60] is perhaps the most stinging indication of the hostility she felt for Diane, the relationship between the two women bears analysis. While there is no doubt that Catherine rankled under Diane's authority over her husband, the relationship in which they were both tied to Henry was one of mu-

Fig. 4.6. Royal entry festival of Henry II into Rouen, October 1, 1550. This image gives a good sense of Henry II's royal entries. It shows how extensive the royal party was as well as some of the allegorical representations, frequently evoking classical motifs. French school, sixteenth century. Bibliothèque municipale, Rouen / The Bridgeman Art Library.

tual benefit in ways that might seem peculiar to the modern reader. Diane, as much as anyone, prevented Catherine's repudiation and, as Henry explicitly acknowledged, fostered Catherine's pregnancies by insisting that he spend some nights with her. When Diane attained her greatest preeminence, she and Catherine seemed to have a rapprochement best reflected in the activities Diane undertook on behalf of Catherine's children. Diane was present at their births and baptisms. She concerned herself with their well-being, choosing their wet nurses and controlling appointments to their households. When there was an epidemic near the chateau of Blois, the royal children were sent to stay with Diane. When Catherine's son Charles did not tolerate milk, Diane had him nursed with cider and beer. She commissioned artists to paint the children's portraits, arranged the funeral of one of Catherine's sons, and even tended Catherine during her near-fatal bout with scarlet fever.[61]

Diane maintained her political influence over Henry by making sure that no one, especially Montmorency, could usurp it. Although Montmorency had been Diane's ally in her battle with Anne, he now seemed a threat, for she wanted political as well as personal control over Henry. In 1552 Contarini remarked on Montmorency's growing power and the enmity between the mistress and the constable.[62] Their enmity flared into open hostility when Montmorency sought to displace Diane by bringing to Henry's attention the lovely Jane Fleming, the illegitimate daughter of James IV of Scotland, who accompanied the young Mary Stuart when she arrived to marry the dauphin, Henry's son Francis. Although Diane benefited from Henry's great loyalty to his friends, so did Montmorency, and it was thus unlikely that Henry would repudiate him as Francis I had. But Diane secured her position and weakened Montmorency's by fostering the Guises as rivals to him and then working to hold the balance between them. The Spanish ambassador reported that Diane, "between the two enemies was a sort of all-powerful pivot."[63] Francis, the duke of Guise, and his brother Charles, the cardinal of Lorraine, were well positioned to enhance the status of their house, and they well understood the benefits of currying favor with the royal favorite. Diane advanced them to check rather than to negate Montmorency's power. She deployed this strategy more successfully than Catherine would later, largely because the religious conflict had not yet so clearly encroached on the political. Commenting further on the rivalry between the king's minister and his mistress, Contarini noted: "The person, without a doubt, whom the king loves and prefers is Madame de Valentinois [Diane]. . . . She is a woman of intelligence, who has always been the inspiration of the king." The king's attachment to Montmorency, he concluded, was much subordinated to his need for Diane, which had a love "more lively" as its source.[64]

Diane had unprecedented impact for a royal mistress—on the royal family, the court, and the politics of Henry's reign. She can reasonably be compared to Madame de Pompadour, Louis XV's powerful mistress, in that she ruled, or aspired to rule, the country as well as the king.[65] So extensive was her authority that all deferred to her. The king consulted with her on every issue, and ambassadors courted her: She knew all state secrets, all matters of council deliberation, and the content of all diplomatic dispatches and even signed some official correspondence *HenriDiane*.

Diane's political preeminence led Protestant polemicists to indict her for the renewed intensification of Protestant persecution during Henry's reign. Blaming Diane allowed Protestants to criticize royal policy indirectly but effectively. Henry was intent on persecuting heretics when peace allowed it, and Diane, as a staunch Catholic, doubtless supported his efforts. More reprehensible, she benefited directly from religious persecution; among her many sources of revenue were the confiscated goods of persecuted Protestants and Jews.

WEALTH AND STATUS

Diane's new titles and chateaux attested to her rising status. Not only had she profited from the confiscation of Anne de Pisseleu's goods, but she was also the beneficiary of an extraordinary tax collected explicitly on her behalf, which yielded three hundred thousand *écus*—revenue that ordinarily would have gone into the public treasury.[66] The *paulette*, a special tax on the French Church levied, in this case, on each church bell, also raised revenue for Diane. As François Rabelais commented, "The king had hung all the bells in the kingdom around the neck of his new mare."[67] Diane was already the grand steward of Normandy when Henry made her the duchess of Valentinois. The more besotted the king, the worse the state of the kingdom's treasury; Henry's willingness to divert state funds to her was unprecedented. He gave her the gem of Renaissance chateaux, Chenonceau, which belonged by law to the crown and was thus inalienable. The conditions of the gift reflected Henry's concern for his mistress. He was not giving away crown property, he insisted, but simply transferring to Diane the property rights of Thomas Bohier, the chateau's original owner, in recognition of her husband's service to the crown. (Despite Henry's care, the legal status of this gift was challenged after his death.) Diane's sons-in-law also received important positions, and she cultivated an extensive patron-client network.[68]

Unquestionably, Diane used her position to increase her wealth and the status of her family. Most of the sources we have in Diane's hand are accounts, demonstrating her meticulous attention to finances. She was as efficient a guardian of her financial interests as were male officeholders of the day. Even though Diane was one of the most successful royal mistresses in acquiring wealth, she was rarely condemned as venal, as Anne had been. Diane did not engage in the obvious influence peddling Anne had and was somewhat more subtle in her exercise of power. Equally significant, Diane's position as the king's mistress was not challenged by his son's mistress, as Anne had been. By the time Henry reigned, Diane's interest was completely aligned with his; his success as king magnified hers. Thus Diane retained her lofty reputation for great probity, virtue, and even purity.

Diane's charitable activities too contributed to her positive reputation; she, like Agnès, was to some degree redeemed by them. She founded and endowed a chapel, built a poorhouse for twelve women and six girls, and provided money for the girls' dowries. In her will, she left instructions for masses and ordered that one hundred poor persons be dressed at her expense. (The parish church in Anet still touts her piety.)

Diane was also extolled for her beneficial effect on the character of the court. Under her aegis, Henry's court was transformed from the freer court of Francis I. Diane introduced a new reign of austerity with fewer feasts and festivities. The court turned its attention to "thoughts, wise and virtuous," as the poet Ronsard put it, praising Diane as "a wise woman of wise counsel and gentle courage."[69] This striking transformation heightened Diane's irreproachable reputation. When Madame de Lafayette wanted to criticize the decadence of the court of Louis XIV in her novel *The Princess of Cleves*, she contrasted it with that of Henry II: "At no time in France were splendor and refinement so brilliantly displayed as in the last years of the reign of Henry II. The monarch was courteous, handsome, and fervent in love: though his passion for Diane de Poitiers, Duchess de Valentinois, had lasted far above twenty years."[70]

Diane had faced losing her personal influence over Henry only once when he was much taken by Jane Fleming. Catherine and Montmorency had encouraged the relationship to diminish Diane's ascendency.[71] While Montmorency sought greater political power, Catherine wanted a mistress who might both captivate her husband and threaten her status as queen less than Diane. If Henry spurned Diane, Catherine would no longer be beholden to her and might carve out a political arena for herself. It is disconcerting enough when a mother promotes a mistress, as Louise did for Francis, but even more so when a queen promotes a new mistress for her husband in hopes of gaining some greater legitimacy for herself.

When Diane learned of the relationship, she was able to force a definitive break, even though Jane, who bore a son whom Henry acknowledged and named Henry d'Angoulême, had clearly hoped to supplant her. When Jane returned to Scotland, the English ambassador reported, she "departed hence with child by this King and it is thought that . . . she shall come to fetch another. If she do so, [there] is like to be combat. . . . The old worn pelf [Diane] bears thereby to lose some part of her credit, who presently reigneth alone and governeth without impeach."[72] Neither this affair nor Henry's other short-lived sexual relations undermined Diane's influence.[73] His reliance on her showed no signs of abating. As Contarini reported, Diane had been Henry's inspiration, and he was bound to her and continued to love her despite her age.[74] Other ambassadors were tactless enough to comment on Diane's fading looks. Although Contarini claimed she was "far from looking as old as she is," Saint-Mauris noted that she was "very wrinkled and did not fool anyone."[75] Late in Henry's reign, when Diane was in her late fifties, she spent more time away from court, preferring to be at Anet. So throughout the 1550s, Henry and the court too spent much time there. Diane supervised the renovations of her holdings, including Chenonceau, notably building the bridge over the Cher River.

A decisive change occurred in Henry's reign when the long-standing conflict between Valois and Hapsburg, which Francis I and Charles V began and Henry II and Philip II continued, was finally set aside in 1559 so that both monarchs could more effectively stem the spread of Calvinism. Henry could dedicate himself to eradicating Calvinism, and Phillip II could try to halt its spread into the Low Countries. The marriage of Henry's daughter Elisabeth to Philip II would ratify the peace.

As part of the festivities celebrating the peace, a tournament was held in the Place Royale in Paris (now the Place des Vosges). Catherine de Medici, a great believer in astrology, tried to persuade Henry not to participate in the joust, because astrologers had warned her that the king should "avoid combat on a closed field in his forty-first year."[76] And Nostradamus predicted that "a young lion would overpower an old one on a field of battle in singular combat . . . his eyes gouged . . . to die a cruel death."[77] Diane, not much inclined to credit superstitions, did not try to dissuade Henry from participating. He went into pseudo-combat with Montgomery, the captain of the Scots Guard, wearing Diane's colors. As the two combatants approached each other, Montgomery's lance lifted Henry's visor and pierced his eye with its tip, accidentally inflicting the fatal wound. Henry lingered in agony for ten days. Ambrose Paré and Andreas Vesalius, respectively the most important surgeon and anatomist of the day, were called to his bedside but held out no hope of his recovery. During this time either Catherine prevented Diane from going to his side or Diane avoided going to Henry for fear of being shunted aside by the queen.[78]

With Henry's death, Diane, like other official royal mistresses, lost her influence, although her status was protected to some degree by her daughters' marriages into the Guise and Montmorency families. The chateau of Anet, although constructed with state funds, had been built on the property of the Brézé family, and thus Diane could retain it and retreat to it as a refuge. Some of her supporters, notably the Guises, rallied to the young king and his wife, their niece, and turned against Diane. The duke of Guise immediately appropriated her apartments in the Louvre. Catherine made sure that the crown jewels and the chateau of Chenonceau, which Henry had given Diane, again became crown property. (Catherine gave Diane the chateau of Chaumont-sur-Loire in exchange—an exchange financially advantageous to Diane.) Only after she attained firm control during Charles IX's reign could Catherine recoup some of the severe losses to the royal treasury due to Henry's favors to his mistress. But Diane retained most of the enormous wealth she had amassed.[79]

Diane retired to Anet, her spectacular Renaissance chateau in the center of Normandy. There she worked to preserve the goods she had acquired from her father, her husband, and her lover to enhance the position of her children and their offspring. She had accomplished much in pursuit of this goal; she was a very wealthy duchess, tied by marriage to some of the most powerful and influential families of France. Ultimately her offspring would be joined in marriage to the royal houses of Europe. A grandchild married a prince of Savoy. By the sixth generation, one of her descendants, Victor-Amadeus, was king of Sardinia; his daughter married Louis the duke of Burgundy; their son was Louis XV.[80]

When she was sixty-four, Diane had a serious riding accident from which she never fully recovered. She died two years later in seclusion at Anet.

DIANE IMAGINED

As prominent as Diane's political role was, her image as the goddess Diana, presented consistently throughout Henry's reign, was equally significant. It not only sanctified her but also ratified Henry's choice of her as a most fitting consort. His subjects either subscribed to this depiction of their relationship or considered it expedient to feign to do so.

Classical allusion was a significant feature of Renaissance literature and artistic representations, and depictions of Diana the huntress were common. But when Diane appropriated the goddess, she explicitly emphasized her virtue. As one of the twelve Olympians, the goddess Diana retained her virginity, which allowed her to exert authority over men—and, by association, so could the king's mistress. While Diane was often depicted in classical garb (or lack thereof) with bow and arrow, her body was not directly exposed to the viewer's gaze; instead it was usually slightly turned to suggest her reticence and chastity. Representations of her embodied sixteenth-century standards of beauty—tall, blond, and lithe. Depictions of Diane used these conventions to present her as ethereal, approaching the divine; the association of the mistress with the chaste, beautiful goddess heightened her authority.

Diane's appropriation of Diana the goddess not only played on classical tropes but also added new elements to create a cult particular to the French Renaissance, which underscored her relationship with Henry. She was frequently depicted in an affectionate relationship with a stag representing Henry, but the stag had fallen victim not to a hunter but to love. Several notable paintings, including one by François Clouet, depict Diane surrounded by other goddesses, as the king on horseback, clothed in black and white, looks on from afar, replicating the myth of the goddess Diana surprised by the hunter Actaeon (fig. 4.7).[81]

Diane was also associated with Venus, the goddess of love, and occasionally Minerva, the goddess of wisdom. These varied representations all placed her firmly in the realm of the ideal—of beauty, love, and wisdom. Some Catholic apologists even went so far as to compare her to the Virgin Mary, but poets firmly reattached her to love.[82] They waxed lyrical about her beauty and goodness, extolling her lofty status, generosity, hostility toward heretics, solicitude for widows and orphans, and piety.[83] Ronsard apostrophized her: "Your sun decorates you with its rays; you spread happiness everywhere on France."[84]

The goddess Diana offered Renaissance artists, poets, and courtiers, to say nothing of Diane herself, a rich array from which to choose. Her identification with the classical goddess elevated her above other royal mistresses and made her an important public symbol. The consistent emphasis on her chastity and virtue tied her to the integrity of the monarchy and the well-being of the kingdom. It suggested that the greater the appreciation of Diane's virtue, the more disinterested and beneficial her effect on the state, and as a result, the more appropriate and even commendable Henry's involvement with her.[85] The close relationships between the images of Diane, the idealization of her relationship to Henry, and the glory and credibility of his reign were ones she fostered, Henry endorsed, artists replicated, and the court embraced.

Fig. 4.7. This painting of *Diana Bathing* by François Clouet suggests Diane de Poitiers as the goddess, while the figure on horseback in black and white evokes her royal lover. Musée des Beaux-Arts, Rouen, France/The Bridgeman Art Library.

Thus Diane's image did not simply redound to her personal credit; it also fostered crucial dimensions of Henry's kingship. Especially compelling was the understanding of their relationship as a chivalric romance. Henry's notion of himself as king and partner in his relationship with Diane was firmly rooted in chivalry. His earliest association with Diane played on chivalric themes, but during his reign the court was completely captivated by its reading of the romance *Amadis de Gaula*. This multivolume novel by Garcia Rodriquez de Montalbo, published in 1508, was based on fourteenth-century tales by the Portuguese writer João de Lobiera. His protagonist, Amadis, epitomized the true knight; he was constant in love and in his defense of the defenseless. The book told the tale of two brothers, sons of a mythical king of Wales, who were abandoned, exiled to a foreign country, and enslaved by a magician. Amadis fell in love at the age of twelve with Oriane, the daughter of the king of the Britons who gave him a sword that allowed him to triumph over his enemies. He did not marry Oriane because of a conflict with her father. But, because his love was true, his sexual relations were blameless or even inspiring; his love inspired his feats of glory. Was this not, in essence, Henry's story?

Amadis had an immediate and obvious appeal to Henry, for he, like the king, was jousting, making war, or making love. Henry understood his role as the devoted knight of his ladylove and his relationship with Diane as a lived version of the chivalric romance. This fiction was then staged and ritually reenacted in the court. Brantôme reported that Henry and Diane spent afternoons reading the tales of Amadis aloud to each other. The French translator of the eleventh volume not only dedicated it to Diane but also took pains to compare her to the heroine.[86] Diane, like Oriane, recast the chivalric lady as both ideal and sexual. The novel played a crucial role in creating a literary representation of the royal relationship, and Henry was eager to promote this understanding. Each volume, as it appeared in French translation over the course of his reign, became an instant best seller, offering, as one literary scholar has suggested, "less a mirror in which a generation was reflected than a model it chose to emulate."[87]

Diane's image is perhaps most strikingly apparent today at Anet, her refuge (fig. 4.8). Constructed as a palace of love for a king and great lady, the chateau offered a veritable stage set on which to array the panoply of her images and to enshrine her relationship with Henry. Although it was built on land she inherited from her husband, Henry financed the ancient chateau's elaborate Renaissance reconstruction by Philibert Delorme, the most notable architect of the French Renaissance. The chateau was full of great artistic treasures, commissioned by Henry to portray his mistress, including Jean Goujon's famous sculpture originally in the courtyard of Anet, now on display in the Louvre (fig. 4.9). The famous relief by Benvenuto Cellini stands over the central entry, with the

Fig. 4.8. The entry to Diane's chateau of Anet. The stag at the top represents Henry II here, as it does in many representations of him with Diane. Photo by author.

Latin inscription, which translates as: THIS AMPLE DWELLING HAS BEEN CONSECRATED BY PHOEBUS TO THE GOOD DIANE WHO IS GRATEFUL TO HIM FOR WHAT SHE HAS RECEIVED (fig. 4.10). The chateau also housed a fabulous collection of books. Francis I had decreed that every book published in France be placed in the royal depository; Henry amended the decree so that a second copy went to Diane. Anet thus stands as a powerful example of the symbiotic relationship between Renaissance artists and a powerful, wealthy royal mistress.

Even more striking than the representations of Diane found in her chateau is her prominence in the décor of the royal chateau of Fontainebleau, where one of the side chapels, reserved for dignitaries, is decorated with hers and Henry's initials with the legend SHE ATTAINED EVERYTHING SHE ATTEMPTED. In the royal ballroom on either side of the throne, frescoes depict her virtues and her ability to overcome the vices afflicting the kingdom.

Unlike Agnès Sorel, who took several centuries to find a place in the historical literature, Diane remained prominent. Her positive image was created over Henry's lifetime and retained its allure. His contemporaries praised the refinement of his court, and Diane was credited with fostering Henry's appreciation of the arts. Diane's positive reputation was due to her assiduous cultivation of her image and to Henry's unwavering support both for her and dedication to

Fig. 4.9. Diana with a stag, in marble and bronze, attributed to Jean Goujon. Louvre/The Bridgeman Art Library.

burnishing her image. Protestant polemicists, like Théodore de Bèze and Jean Crespin, portrayed Diane as a dishonored woman, but they did so to discredit her religious views. Although he was a very young man when Diane reigned at court, Brantôme both praised her and recognized the religious basis for opposition to her: "Aside from her beauty, she was very clever and generous. . . . Being what she was, she could only persuade, counsel, and preach to the king things that were great, high, and generous. . . . And above all, she was a good Catholic and hated those of the [Protestant] religion; and this is why they so hated and maligned her."[88]

When a band of revolutionaries destroyed Diane's tomb and exhumed her, they reported that she remained beautiful. (The miraculous preservation of royal mistresses seems common to hagiographical treatments of them.) Diane

Fig. 4.10. Benvenuto Cellini relief with Diana embracing the stag, over the doorway to Anet. Photo by author.

has retained a reputation for sanctity—a mistress who redeemed a king, making him bolder, manlier, and a better ruler. Her emphasis on propriety cloaked her in virtue, and her ethereal beauty made her worthy of a king's devotion.

The dramatic story that Francis demanded her honor to save her father inspired literary interpretations. But the story redounded to her credit. In the nineteenth century, Victor Hugo used it to condemn the cruel exploitation of a beautiful, devout young woman by a rapacious, tyrannical monarch. In his *The King Amuses Himself*, her father denounced the king for having "tarnished, blighted, soiled, dishonored, and broken Diane de Poitiers"; but, by his actions, the king revealed himself as a tyrant.[89] The tale also was the basis of the libretto of Giuseppe Verdi's *Rigoletto*.

Fiction then shaped subsequent historical accounts. Rather surprisingly, Michelet was quite entranced by every laudatory, romantic story told about Henry II's mistress and could not resist the drama of this one. Accepting the story as valid, he enhanced the conventional account, suggesting that their relationship became one of mutual respect: "The Lady, who was twenty-eight years old, endowed with style and grace, with a very virile spirit, went straight to the king and walked with him. In saving her father, she took a solid political position as a friend of the king."[90] He was almost tolerant of Diane's preeminence, but significantly, because he saw it as primarily cultural and thus more benign than female political power. Once the mistress was safely consigned to the realm of romance, she could be extolled and her myth further burnished.

It is as an image that Diane remains a most distinctive royal mistress. Despite the extent of her influence and the duration of her reign over Henry's heart, the actual relationship between them remains somewhat obscure. Although Henry's devotion to her was obvious, Diane's sentiments and motives are less apparent. The historical record suggests little of the actual woman but instead details her impact and her acquisition of wealth. Diane's deliberate emphasis on her moral probity also protected her private sentiments from scrutiny. Her effective manipulation of her image in works of art and literature cloaked the emotional and the personal by presenting Diane as idealized and ethereal. She was unquestionably the mistress most adept in enhancing her status and creating her image. Diane's construction of her image not only protected her position but also played an important role in shaping Henry's cultural legacy. In important ways, the image became the reality. Diane constructed a court culture in which her relationship with the king embodied the ideals and, ironically, the moral authority of courtly love. Renowned for her virtue and probity, Diane was praised as a model of the beneficial effects of women on the Renaissance court.

Henry's association with Diane enhanced his image and shaped the understanding of his reign. For their contemporaries, Diane's virtue made Henry virtuous. This was not simply an example of myth triumphing over reality; Diane was deemed to have elevated the court by effectively regulating the king's sexuality. Henry was devoted to one mistress (with only a couple of other affairs documented with pregnancies). As a result, his court was less licentious than his father's had been. Appreciations of Diane's incomparable virtue legitimated her political advice, making it more credible and authoritative. Shaped by such advice, the political actions of the king too were more praiseworthy. Diane's virtue thus purified the court and elevated the monarchy.

The virtues of this mistress also recast the royal family. Henry's relationship with his wife, Catherine, was relegated to the merely prosaic, mundane, and pragmatic. To an almost unprecedented degree, Diane usurped the status and roles of the queen and reduced Catherine to royal consort. As Diane was idealized to the point of the ethereal, Henry's relationship with her was tinged by her divinity, and their adulterous relationship became the public face of the monarchy.

The idealized image, specifically of Henry as chivalric king, could be deployed to respond to the political realities of the sixteenth century as well. Late in his reign, Henry turned his attention from war with the Hapsburg monarchy to war on Protestants. As the chivalric king assumed the mantle of crusader against the new, Protestant infidels, Diane, a firm advocate of Catholic interests (and the beneficiary of all seized Protestant property), was heralded as the inspiration behind Henry's religious zeal.

What made these ways of presenting the king compelling to his contemporaries, especially since it is obvious to us that they offered a very particular, not to say peculiar, version of reality? These myths were so powerful because they reinforced an idealized vision of the monarchy that the king wanted to cultivate and that some Frenchmen were eager to believe—that their monarch was valiant and a fitting heir to a crusading past. In the sixteenth century, French kings were still trying to extend the territory under royal control and to challenge the feudal aristocracy for power. A crusading, chivalric king, cloaked in quasi-divinity, even if through association with his mistress, was clearly above mere mortal nobles. Such a king also gave France a privileged status among nations.

These public presentations of the mistress and her relationship with the king worked because they built on a heritage of myth and allegory shared by French elites. They used images that could be read by their contemporaries. Ability to "read" them then attested to one's education and sophistication. Images of the royal relationship used the newer cultural models of the Renaissance effectively. While we use the term *humanism* to describe the intellectual movement associated with the Renaissance absorption and adaptation of classical texts, in the sixteenth century the most influential form of humanism was a particular variant—courtly humanism, which moved out of Italy into the courts of northern Europe. Not surprisingly, it focused on the court as the purveyor of culture and the monarchy as the highest form of political life, explicitly rejecting the civic humanism of Italian republics. It was particularly indebted to Plato's idealization of the philosopher king.

Images of Diane and her relationship to Henry reflected courtly humanism by explicitly invoking Neoplatonism. Diane occupied the realm of Platonic ideals of the good, the true, and the beautiful. Her relationship with Henry was cloaked in myth, obscured by a literary and artistic veil, suggesting the Neoplatonic vision of this world as a reflection of the heavenly. This mystification could only work in a culture nourished by mythology—where elites and royals had themselves portrayed as Greek and Roman gods, for example, as in the depiction of courtiers as gods surrounding Diana (fig. 4.11).

The court of Henry and Diane clearly appreciated and assumed the moral authority courtly humanism ascribed to it. Castiglione famously presented the

Fig. 4.11. *Tour de la Ligue. Members of the Medici Court as the Gods of Olympus.* It depicts Catholics forging arms for the religious wars. The goddess Diana is prominent. French school, sixteenth century. Chateau Tanlay, Tanlay, France / The Bridgeman Art Library.

court, adjudicated by women, as the vehicle for civilizing society but especially for transforming the warrior into a veritable Renaissance man. In *The Book of the Courtier*, a man was not simply strong but also sophisticated, proficient in fighting and writing, wrestling and dancing.[91] Women who scorned earlier, feudal models of masculinity and endorsed those of the Renaissance courtier controlled this transformation. The benefits of Diane's tutelage first on the young Henry and then on the court were prime examples of the civilizing mission of courtly humanism. Their relationship not only epitomized the new authority of women in the Renaissance court but also allowed Henry to be seen as the model Renaissance prince.

Diane's image empowered her, shaped Henry's cultural legacy, and in important ways became the reality. She presented Henry to the court and ultimately the country as a valiant, devoted chivalric hero, and herself as his virtuous (almost chaste) lady worthy of devotion. These images enhanced Renaissance kingship, and the court ritually reinforced this morally and politically elevated notion. These images of Diane remain the most prominent and evocative of Henry's reign.[92] They serve still, as they did in his time, to define it. Although Diane's chastity, not surprisingly, has fallen out of current accounts, their relationship as a great royal romance retains its allure and captivates many—from French schoolchildren to modern popularizers.

The idealized depiction of the royal relationship may not reveal their actual relationship (or even Diane's actual physical appearance), but it is significant for several reasons. First, the French Renaissance constructed some of its most significant and durable images and myths around influential and powerful women, which proved effective ways to praise or disparage their power and authority and the men associated with them. Secondly, we should not assume that these images were powerful because sixteenth-century Frenchmen were naive. Instead, we should appreciate the very sophisticated cultural context required for interpreting the complex allegories and rich cultural allusions on which they relied. It would be a mistake to assume that those who produced these images or recognized their implications were anything but sophisticated interpreters of their culture and, indeed, their inheritance from classical antiquity. These images were successful in part because they relied on the effective presentation of persuasive ideas. They display the great skills of Renaissance artists and writers and the sophistication of mythmakers in using the media at their disposal, and we should not fail to recognize these qualities. But we might draw a more sobering lesson from this case: It is an example of the power and duration of images, constructed to serve personal and political interests, which over time solidify into myth. Images and the myths they enshrine remain most potent when they serve the interests of those who subscribe to them as well as those who promote them and when their constructors have great access to wealth and power—as did Henry and Diane.

Diane offered a much fuller image of the royal mistress and her roles than Agnès Sorel had. Subsequent idealizations of Agnès may be indebted to the larger role later played by Diane. Diane so enhanced the credibility of the royal favorite that Gabrielle d'Estrées will not only present herself as the goddess Diana but also be emboldened to envision a future as queen. After all, Diane was accorded the dignity of a queen, while Catherine was forced to assume, as long as Henry lived, the lesser role of legal concubine.[93]

SIGNIFICANT DATES FOR CHAPTER 5

1519	Birth of Henry II, March 31
	Birth of Catherine de Medici, April 13
1521	Death of Pope Leo X (Catherine's uncle)
1533	Marriage of Henry II and Catherine de Medici
1534	Death of Clement VII (Catherine's uncle)
1536	Death of dauphin Francis, August 10; Henry becomes dauphin
1544	Birth of Francis II, January 19
1545	Birth of Elisabeth, later wife of Philip II of Spain
1547	Birth of Claude, later duchess of Lorraine
	Death of Francis I, March 31
	Coronation of Henry II
1550	Birth of Charles, later Charles IX
1551	Birth of Edouard-Alexandre, later Henry III
1553	Birth of Marguerite, future queen of Navarre and France
1555	Birth of Hercules, renamed Francis
1559	Death of Henry II, July 10
1560	Conspiracy of Amboise, March
	Death of Francis II, December 5
1562	Massacre at Vassy
1564–66	Charles IX's grand tour
1567	Surprise of Meaux, September
1572	Attempted assassination of Admiral Coligny, August 22
	Saint Bartholomew's Day Massacre, August 24
1574	Death of Charles IX, May 30; Henry III becomes king
1584	Death of Francis, duke of Anjou, June 10
1588	Assassination of Henry, the duke of Guise, and his brother, the cardinal of Lorraine, December 23–24
1589	Death of Catherine de Medici, January 5
	Assassination of Henry III, August 2

5

Catherine de Medici

King in All but Name

When Catherine de Medici died on January 5, 1589, after being integrally connected to the French monarchy for nearly sixty years, Pierre de L'Estoile reported that the following verses, circulating in Paris, could well serve as her epitaph.

> The queen who lies here was a devil and an angel,
> Full of blame and full of praise:
> She upheld the state and brought it low;
> She made accords and no fewer debates:
> She bore three kings and five civil wars,
> Had chateaux built and towns destroyed,
> Made many good laws and bad edicts.
> Salute her passing, heaven and hell.[1]

These verses capture the contradictions of Catherine's life and subsequent reputation. They also moderate the vehement charges circulated by Protestant critics. These criticisms took shape in the immediate aftermath of the Saint Bartholomew's Day Massacre of Huguenots assembled in Paris to celebrate her daughter Marguerite's marriage to the Protestant prince Henry of Navarre. Their charges blamed Catherine for the massacre, made her evil incarnate, and remain embedded, particularly in Anglo-Protestant historiography. For her critics, the massacre was merely the most egregious example of Catherine's completely unscrupulous, Machiavellian politics, which led her to poison her enemies, betray her friends, and even corrupt her children. Her legend explicitly challenged Catherine's deliberate self-presentation as a devoted mother and protector of her children. Such charges discredited women rulers so effectively that similar criticisms were later deployed against Marie Antoinette. During the French Revolution, Catherine's myth was recycled as an especially damning example of the depravities of monarchy.

Of the women treated in this book, Catherine was the most powerful and has been the most thoroughly studied by historians. Her political actions made her the most controversial woman of this period. She faced the complications of a woman trying to rule without direct personal authority and preserve the throne for her sons, none of whom proved to be effective rulers. She contended with the greater complications faced by monarchs after the Reformation, where every existing source of political division was exacerbated by religious dissent. Integrally associated with the violence of this period, Catherine has not been rescued from the negative opinions of her contemporaries or subsequent mythologizers, despite the efforts of some recent historians to rehabilitate her.[2]

Until Henry II's death in 1559, Catherine's life can be read as almost the reverse of Diane de Poitiers's. Orphaned young, she was not the darling of a doting father, and her husband ignored her. For her first twenty-five years in France, her life was a series of humiliations, her marriage insecure, and her role negligible, as Diane went from triumph to triumph. Diane was the beloved mistress of her husband. Every new role for Diane meant an exclusion of Catherine from power or even from the conventional roles of a queen. Peripheral during her early years, Catherine exercised unprecedented power during the last thirty years of her life. She may have been at best only queen mother, regent, or the power behind the throne, but there was no doubt that, throughout much of her sons' reigns, Catherine was unquestionably the most important political actor in France. When she was not, as toward the end of Henry III's reign, it is certainly arguable that France would have been better served if she had remained so.

A MEDICI PAWN

Catherine de Medici was vulnerable from her birth on April 13, 1519. She was the only daughter of Lorenzo II, duke of Urbino, by his second marriage. Her mother was Madeleine de la Tour d'Auvergne, a descendant of Robert of Clermont, the youngest son of Louis IX of France. Their marriage was part of an ongoing strategy of pairing Medici money to French royal blood. Over the course of the Renaissance, French monarchs were intently interested in pursuing any claim to Italian territory that these marriages could assert.

Their union produced Catherine, even though her father had syphilis and tuberculosis and had infected her mother. Her mother died two weeks after giving birth to Catherine, and her father a few days later. (Michelangelo immortalized him as the shadowy figure poised between dawn and dusk in the Medici chapel.) The poet Ludovico Ariosto described Florence as a cradle between two coffins, and the orphaned Catherine as "the only green branch with few leaves, poised between fear and hope"[3]—the frail remnant of the Medici. Both Francis I and Leo X (the first Medici pope) professed great interest in the young girl, largely as a means to preserve the Franco-papal alliance.

A political pawn from her earliest youth, Catherine was raised in the tumult of early sixteenth-century Italian politics. Her fortunes reflected the vicissitudes of Florentine and Vatican political interests. As a young child, she was under the guardianship of her uncle Leo X, but her prospects declined sharply with his death. The election of Adrian VI, Emperor Charles V's former teacher, moved the Vatican into the Spanish camp. But after Adrian's death, the cardinals, who had found the reformer Adrian repressive, elected Giuliano de Medici (another of Catherine's uncles.) He took the name Clement VII and carried out a vigorous anti-Hapsburg agenda. But France's defeat in the Battle of Pavia in 1525 exposed the weakness of Clement's ally and ultimately led to the sack of Rome by imperial forces in 1527. Furthermore, Clement VII's election put Florence under the control of the autocratic Silvio Passelini, cardinal of Cortona. When Florence took advantage of the sack of Rome to overthrow him and establish a republic, Catherine, as a Medici and thus an implicit threat to the republic, was taken hostage and essentially imprisoned in a convent. After Clement VII signed a treaty with the emperor, the leaders of Florence, fearing a Medici resurgence, removed Catherine to Lucca, a town loyal to the republic. When Florence capitulated to the Medici, Catherine's utility as a hostage ended. Then, after eight years of upheaval in Florence, she enjoyed a period of relative stability at the papal court in Rome, where she was exposed to the art and culture of the Renaissance. Her presence there was commented upon: Venice's ambassador to the papacy, Antonio Suriano, described her as "small, thin, without fine features and with large eyes," but noted that she was "naturally vivacious, showing a charming spirit."[4] But Giorgio Vasari, who painted her portrait on the eve of her marriage at the age of fourteen, was charmed by her: "I was so affected by her particular qualities and by the affection she showed, not only to me, but to my whole country, that I adore her as one adores the saints of paradise."[5]

Her early experiences may have given the young Catherine an appreciation of the Renaissance, a cultural phenomenon far more advanced in Italy than elsewhere and in which her immediate forebears had been important patrons.

She may also have developed a horror of war and its devastating effects and a pragmatic sense of religion and politics and their relationship to each other. Her critics later suggested that Catherine's early experience made her not merely pragmatic but cynical or even Machiavellian, later willing to deploy extreme acts of political expediency, such as poisoning her enemies to advance her interests. Such assessments prejudged Catherine and fed into the xenophobia that indicted her "Italian" character. Faults later ascribed to her focused on her Italian roots; she was superstitious, devious, and a poisoner. Her early traumatic experiences might have made the young girl wary of political alliances and aware of their fragility.

To enhance the political position of both the Medici and the Vatican, Clement VII decided to use Catherine and his two illegitimate relatives, Alexander and Hippolyte, as political pawns. He intended to marry Catherine to France and Alexander to Austria but reserved Hippolyte (likely his own son) to succeed him as heir to Florence and ultimately perhaps as pope. Clement's plans to cover all his diplomatic bases were frustrated; Hippolyte died young, and some contemporaries suggested that Alexander poisoned him.[6] But the marriage between Catherine and the French prince Henry advanced the longstanding strategy of Franco-papal politics and brought great wealth to France. Catherine's dowry was one hundred thousand *écus*, and the pope also promised to carve out a state composed of Pisa, Livorno, Reggio, Modena, Parma, and Piacenza—all to be delivered to France. The dowry was important (the territory only promised), but the most preeminent attraction of this match was Francis I's political ambition in Italy.[7]

By any standard, except perhaps Clement's dynastic ambitions and Francis's Italian hopes, the marriage between Catherine and Henry was a misalliance, especially for a son who would unexpectedly inherit the throne. Catherine's paternal family did not belong to the traditional nobility but rather were practitioners of the vulgar trade of banking. For the French nobility, such activities revoked noble status, and thus, for some, Catherine's background made her an unworthy queen. Her commercial antecedents, the Italian character of her court, and even her accent were held against her. On the eve of her marriage, her looks were also found wanting (fig. 5.1). Negative physical descriptions conveyed disapproval;[8] diplomats, struggling to praise the young princess, noted her intelligence.

In preparation for marriage, Catherine traveled with an opulent entourage to Marseilles, where she was joined by her uncle Clement VII and Francis I, who came together to complete their negotiations. Clement wanted to thwart Hapsburg designs on Italy, and Francis wanted to garner Vatican support for

Fig. 5.1. This portrait of the young Catherine de Medici is a facsimile of a sixteenth-century drawing that appears in *Portraits of the Most Famous French Personalities of the 16th Century* by P. G. Niel. Paris. French school, nineteenth century. Bibliothèque des Arts Décoratifs, Paris / The Bridgeman Art Library.

his. Both Francis and Clement VII were so vitally concerned with Henry and Catherine's marriage that they made sure that it had indeed been consummated. According to the Milanese ambassador Antonio Sacco, Francis put the young couple to bed "to see them jousting, and indeed each of them did joust beautifully."[9]

THE STERILE WOMB

Despite the initial "jousting," the marriage was not a great success. Although Catherine could not provoke her fourteen-year-old bridegroom's interest, she made every attempt to adapt to her new life. She ingratiated herself with Francis I, recognizing upon whose goodwill her future depended. She joined the band of women who hunted with him, and he enjoyed her conversation. Francis turned her education over to his sister Marguerite, under whose guidance Catherine studied mathematics and poetry, improved her Latin, and began to study Greek. Catherine even emulated Marguerite's literary work. She tried to conform to Renaissance standards of the ideal court woman, but despite her efforts, her position became ever more tenuous.

Two years after the wedding, the Venetian ambassador Marino Giustiniano remarked that the marriage had taken place "to the dissatisfaction of the entire nation."[10] The death of Clement VII in 1534 negated Catherine's diplomatic value to France. Francis stated the reality of her situation: "I have a girl completely nude."[11] Catherine was always in danger of being ignominiously set aside. When rumors of an annulment grew louder, she begged Francis to be allowed to remain at court in some capacity even if she were no longer his daughter-in-law. He was moved enough to promise not to send her away.[12] Catherine needed powerful supporters, especially when talk of repudiating her increased with every year of childlessness. Her role in her husband's life was further marginalized when Diane de Poitiers became Henry's mistress.

In royal households formed by a triangle of king, queen, and mistress, no better example exists of its fraught nature and the convoluted family dynamics it produced than the triangle of Henry, Catherine, and Diane. Catherine was obviously devoted to Henry. While most queens took their husbands' relationships with their mistresses amiss, neither their attachment to the king was as obvious nor their grievance as palpable as Catherine's. She could not counter Diane's influence or compete with her in looks or charm and certainly not in her ability to provoke Henry's interest. So Catherine tolerated Diane, if only because objections to his mistress would further alienate her husband. In exchange for Diane's support of her marriage, Catherine was forced to act in Diane's interest at court. Their relationship gave the outward appearance of cordiality; Diane was discreet and Catherine masked her feelings. Diane's continued support was a crucial reason that Catherine was not sent back to Italy, especially as the years went by and she failed to fulfill her most essential role of bearing heirs.

Some four years into the marriage, Henry's fertility was demonstrated when he fathered a daughter by Filippa Duci, an Italian woman he encountered on campaign. Royal physicians had previously diagnosed hypospadias, a malformation of the seminal opening of the penis, as the cause of the couple's failure to conceive.[13] Sources debate whether Jean Fernel, the famous sixteenth-century physician, actually performed surgery on Henry or whether he simply suggested sexual positions more conducive to conception.[14]

Improbably by modern standards, Henry named the child after his mistress, and Diane delighted in the birth as proof of Henry's fertility and virility. (Royal failures to conceive were more often blamed on wives, despite the common belief that men played a much more crucial role in conception; men provided the seed and women merely the soil to nourish it.) The birth of Henry's daughter led the council to urge him to send back to Italy "this sterile womb." In 1542, Matteo Dandolo wrote back to Venice: "The most high *dauphine* is of a good complexion except for those physical qualities that allow women to have children, for not only has she not done so yet, but I doubt she ever will."[15]

Catherine availed herself of every remedy suggested by venerable medical authorities no matter how preposterous, including drinking mule urine each month. Finally after ten years of marriage, she bore a son named Francis on January 19, 1544, to great rejoicing. Catherine not only produced an heir, she bore ten children in twelve years, and seven of them lived to maturity. Some ascribed Catherine's new fertility to the black arts. Others, including Henry himself, attributed Catherine's ultimate success in bearing children to Diane's insistence that he spend some evenings with her.

Although a royal wife who bore no children was a serious liability and, indeed, might be repudiated, Catherine's inability to conceive from the time she was fourteen until she was twenty-five may have benefited her health. It may have allowed her to mature physically before being subjected to the rigors of childbirth and thus protected her own life. Catherine's greater maturity before the birth of her first child may also have enhanced her subsequent fertility. Her prodigious fertility seemed to guarantee the viability of the Valois dynasty (see fig. 2.5).[16]

The births of her children made it more difficult to set Catherine aside. Ironically, one of the people most pleased about the arrival of royal children was the king's mistress. Diane had urged Henry to perform his conjugal duties, and Catherine's successful maternity made it less likely that Henry would replace her with someone more to his liking. Greater security for his wife enhanced that of his mistress. Her pregnancies relegated Catherine to a maternal role. But she shared even that role with Diane.

With the death of Francis I's oldest son Francis in 1536, Henry became the acknowledged heir apparent. But his new prominence did not entail a more active or public role for Catherine, and it once again brought to the fore French dissatisfaction with her. Newly aligned court factions did not make room for

Catherine. Instead Henry and his brother, Charles, became embroiled in party politics, one faction revolving around Diane and the other around their father's mistress Anne de Pisseleu. The pivots of power and influence within the court were these two mistresses, with little role for the prospective queen, Henry's legitimate wife.

QUEEN (1547–1559)

After Henry II came to the throne in 1547, Catherine enjoyed higher status as queen but still had little opportunity to exercise a political role. Instead, Henry's reign made his mistress more powerful, his ties to her acknowledged at every turn. When he was crowned king of France in 1547, Henry wore his mistress's colors. Even when Catherine herself was crowned queen two years later, Diane was honored.

Several contemporaries reported Catherine's response to these insults. Some five years after Henry became king, Contarini noted that the queen could only "suffer such love and favor" as the king showed Diane, but added, "she is resigned to it and supports it patiently." He described this famous ménage à trois: "The queen even continually frequents the duchess [Diane], and she, for her part, does her [the queen] many favors in the interest of the king; it is she who exhorts him to sleep with her."[17] On the other hand, Brantôme's story that Catherine drilled holes in Diane's ceiling corroborates her contemporaries' sense of Catherine's jealousy.[18] Once, when Diane asked Catherine what she was reading, Catherine responded, "I have read the histories of this kingdom, and I have found in them that, from time to time at all periods, whores have managed the business of kings."[19] Whether resigned, jealous, or indignant, Catherine could not escape her husband's mistress and her influence. Diane was her children's guardian and her husband's most trusted advisor; signs of his affection for Diane could be read everywhere. Catherine did not publicly proclaim her grievances. Privately they must have festered, so much so that twenty-five years after her husband's death, Catherine wrote her most famous expression of indignation: "Never did a wife who loves her husband love his whore."[20]

Catherine's bitterness is understandable. She had little success in gaining her husband's love or in assuming more public roles during his reign. Henry looked to Diane or his chief minister Montmorency for political guidance. Disinclined to allow Catherine even the perquisites due a queen, Henry often put Diane into the queen's ceremonial roles. Law and convention minimally protected Catherine's status, but she remained largely in the background. Yet Henry's absence on military campaigns created a public space for Catherine. She was his regent, first in 1548 when he launched a military expedition in Italy, and then again in 1552 when he laid siege to Metz. The circumstances of the regency were not ideal. Catherine had to share the post with the guardian of the seals, a court functionary who owed his office to Diane. Catherine accepted this humiliating co-regency but did not promulgate the decree announcing it.[21] Nonetheless, the regency gave her a political role that she eagerly embraced, even though her power was strictly limited by the king's councilors. Her efforts to procure war finances were rebuffed, for example.[22] And she was still not Henry's confidant. Her letters to Henry expressed her desire to please him, but he wrote to Diane instead. When Montmorency inquired after Catherine's health, she begged for news of her husband.[23]

Henry suffered a great setback when the French army, besieged at Saint-Quentin (1557) by the allied forces of Mary Tudor of England and Philip II of Spain, was defeated. France lost three thousand men, with five thousand wounded and six thousand captured, including Montmorency. The defeat not only ended Henry's hopes for a successful Italian campaign (he was forced to call his army under Francis, duke of Guise, back from Italy to protect Paris) but it also left the road to Paris, a mere forty miles away, open to Spanish troops. Henry asked Catherine to raise revenue for the army. Addressing Parlement, she argued compellingly that funds were urgently needed to fend off the Spanish threat. As the Venetian ambassador Giovanni Capello reported, "With the most imposing form of words, she exposed the state of the needs of the moment" and urged cities to provide funds, "recognizing all the goods and graces of the king and expressing their gratitude to him."[24] Her great courage in the face of the threatened invasion and her persuasive appeal so moved Parlement that it approved the funds immediately. When the Spanish failed to follow up on their victory, they lost their opportunity to take Paris and the French captured Calais.

In 1558, the international situation changed dramatically with the death of the English queen Mary Tudor, the wife of Philip II. With the Protestant Elizabeth I now on the English throne, a Spanish-English alliance was inconceivable. So Philip proposed peace to contend with the spread of Protestantism in the Low Countries. Henry ultimately agreed to the Treaty of Cateau-Cambrésis, even though it precluded further French territorial expansion and, to Catherine's dismay, ended French aspirations in Italy. Henry too was interested in peace to address the dramatic spread of Protestantism in France.

Calvinism, a new, more aggressive form of Protestantism, was gaining converts. Its followers wanted to establish God's kingdom on earth; their political goal was a theocracy. Religious zeal thus fueled political dissent. The years of Henry's reign had seen a significant spread of these new ideas in France, due in part to the effective work of missionaries sent by John Calvin from Geneva.

Over the course of his reign, Henry enacted ever more repressive measures to eradicate heresy, but he could enforce them only inconsistently and sporadically, especially when military campaigns diverted him from domestic issues. His measures also provoked some judicial resistance. When, in October 1547, he established a tribunal to deal with heresy, popularly known as the "burning chamber," French religious courts contested it as a threat to their authority. And Henry's efforts to establish the Inquisition in France were thwarted by Parlement. On July 24, 1557, Henry issued the Edict of Compiègne, essentially a declaration of war on heretics, imposing the death penalty on anyone convicted of public or private expression of heterodox views. But executions for heresy only fueled Protestant fervor, and their numbers increased dramatically.

By 1558, Calvin claimed to have three hundred thousand followers in France. But Calvinism was also having a more pronounced political impact than the number of converts suggests. It attracted the nobility, among them the prince of the blood Condé, and developed territorial strongholds. La Rochelle, a Protestant fortress town on the Atlantic coast, cultivated connections to Protestant England, and the kingdom of Navarre openly supported Protestantism. Although Henry's actual repression of Protestants was only intermittent, the Treaty of Cateau-Cambrésis might well have enabled him, had he lived, to persecute Protestants more effectively. With Henry's death, they hoped for a more tolerant ruler.

Henry's death also increased Catherine's access to political power. The Venetian ambassador Contarini recognized her untapped potential: "She is not beautiful, but she possesses extraordinary wisdom and prudence. There is no doubt that she would be adept at governing, even though she is neither consulted nor considered to the extent she deserves to be, being that she is not of a blood equal to the king."[25]

QUEEN MOTHER (1559–1561)

Catherine's courage and ability would be tested in her role as queen mother. Henry had been the legitimate king and an accomplished soldier. His death exposed the dependence of the French monarchy on the personal qualities of its ruler as well as the festering political and religious divisions—difficulties the Italian mother of a young king would struggle to resolve. Henry's death left her a widow at the age of forty (fig. 5.2). Grief-stricken, she changed her emblem from a rainbow to a broken lance—"*Lacrymae Hinc, Hinc Dolor*" (From Which Comes My Tears and My Sorrow). Catherine commissioned an extravagant tomb at Saint-Denis to honor Henry. She subsequently identified herself with Artemisia II, devoted wife of King Mausolaus who, according to

Fig. 5.2. Portrait of Catherine de Medici, attributed to François Clouet. Musée Carnavalet, Paris / The Bridgeman Art Library.

legend, not only constructed a tomb proclaimed a wonder of the ancient world but also put her husband's ashes in wine and drank them, becoming a living tomb. Both Boccaccio and Christine de Pizan had praised Artemisia's ability to defend her country and govern effectively, and Catherine, like Artemisia, was a widow devoted to her husband's memory who intended to govern well.[26] Her status as widowed mother allowed her to consolidate her political authority and to emphasize her irreproachable moral probity during her sons' reigns. Her constant black attire reinforced this image, but conventional mourning was white, and a widowed queen, *la reine blanche*, wore it to show her powerlessness. Catherine's black asserted both power and grief.

Catherine was the widowed mother of four young sons; Francis was fifteen, Charles nine, Henry eight, and Hercules four. The Venetian ambassador Michele Soriano remarked that her daughters were "exquisite, gifted, charming, beautiful and intelligent," but her sons were "sad enough princes."[27] Yet three of them became kings of France. Unquestionably Catherine's greatest accomplishment was the preservation of the crown for them in the face of decades of religious dissent and civil war.

After Henry's death, Catherine emerged as a political force, although her position was initially ambiguous. Francis, at fifteen, had attained his majority, so Catherine could not act as his regent even though the young king was both politically and physically weak. Francis suffered from a congenital malformation that produced constant drainage from his ear. Even more disturbing, he was showing symptoms now identified as those of tuberculosis.[28] Young, ill, and disengaged, Francis reigned but did not rule. Catherine's efforts to direct his policies were thwarted by the influence of his young wife, Mary Stuart. Francis was under her sway, but she was influenced by her uncles, the Guises.

Francis the duke of Guise was one of France's greatest soldiers; his brother Charles controlled a number of bishoprics and abbeys as the cardinal of Lorraine (fig. 5.3). As sovereign princes in Lorraine and nobles of high rank in France, the Guises had attained positions of power under Henry II and had sometimes been Diane's allies. Now they assumed the powerful roles usually exercised by the princes of the blood by stepping into the void created by the weakness of the current princes:[29] Anthony of Bourbon, the prince with the best claim to be regent, was unreliable, and his brothers were too young to play the political role the Guises were eager to fill.[30] And the influence, power, and land holdings of the Bourbon family had been curtailed dramatically by the treachery of their relative, the constable. The Guises thus made steady inroads

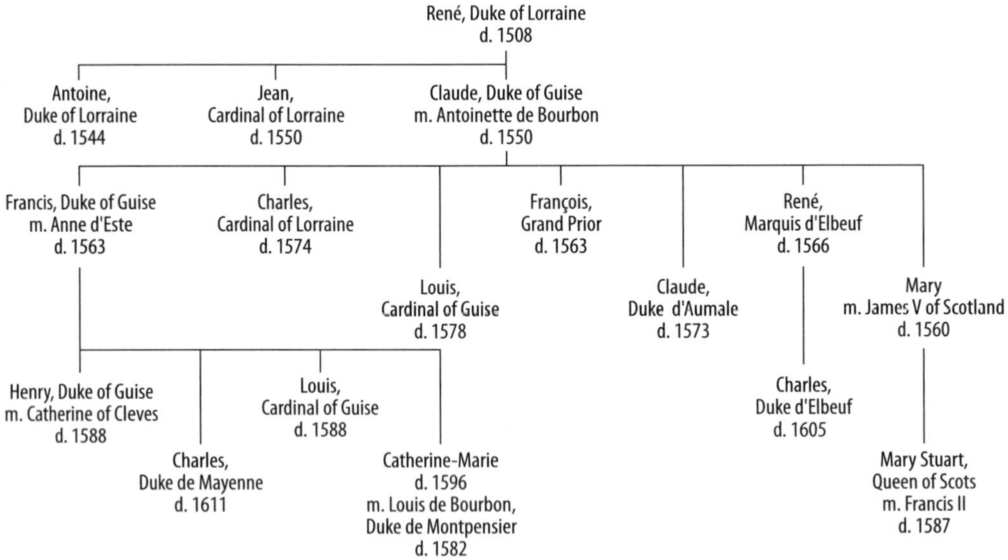

Fig. 5.3. Guise genealogy. Ian Aberle.

in establishing their power over the young king, as their contemporaries recognized. The English ambassador reported: "The house of Guise ruleth and doth all about the French king."[31] Etienne Pasquier, a prominent French jurist, commented, "They completely possess our young king . . . consequently all affairs of state pass through their hands."[32] And the Florentine Leon Ricasoli wrote home, "The Cardinal of Lorraine is both pope and king, wielding an authority greater than any that has ever existed in this kingdom."[33]

Protestants expected more-favorable treatment from Catherine than they had received from Henry II and were initially heartened by Francis II's new reign. The Reformed Church, as a follower reported to Calvin, had "much hope in her mildness and kindness."[34] But Catherine was not in control and, even more importantly, the Huguenots' interests were not hers. They wanted royal support for the expansion of their religious beliefs, but Catherine hoped both creeds would reconcile and accept the crown's authority. She even wrote to the pope to ask him to make concessions to Protestants on Catholic rituals, a request he no doubt considered audacious.[35] But the pronounced influence of the decidedly Catholic Guise family, who insisted on the rigorous enforcement of heresy laws, made it difficult for Catherine to advance a conciliatory policy.

Catherine's policy raised some doubts about her religious fervor. She was Catholic by tradition and practice. There is no evidence that she ever considered leaving the Church, although in her youth she found the religious reforms advocated by those who later became Protestants intriguing. When she arrived in France, she was influenced by Marguerite d'Angoulême who was openly receptive to the new religious ideas of Christian humanism and religious reform in the earliest days of the Protestant Reformation. Catherine also owned a Bible written in French and allowed her ladies-in-waiting to read it.[36] Bibles in the vernacular were taken as one sign of religious radicalism, since Protestants wanted everyone to read the Bible. As religious controversies sharpened, some Catholic critics charged that Catherine was a lukewarm Catholic. They pointed to advisors and ladies-in-waiting who seemed at best indifferent to religion. Toleration or conciliation was suspect as lack of fervor in this contested religious climate. Despite her critics, there are plenty of indications of Catherine's orthodoxy and religious devotion. As Contarini reported, "Her Majesty does not neglect her religious duties; she goes to Mass every day, attends vespers on feast days . . . and observes every principal feast."[37]

Catherine sought a Catholic-Huguenot reconciliation to resolve a political crisis and, as a result, was more tolerant of heterodox beliefs and more committed to religious dialogue than the other parties involved. She likely hoped that Catholic reform would allow Protestants to embrace the Church again.

Disinclined to persecute Protestants for heresy, Catherine was more than willing to repress them when they posed a political threat. She was equally inclined to favor them as a counterweight to other, opposing political forces. As the Venetian ambassador Suriano reported, "I don't know the true opinions of Her Majesty on it [religion], but I can affirm that she does not like tumult in the country, and that if she has not shown herself to be as ardent in repressing them [heretics] as one would like, it is because she fears seeing France destroyed by arms."[38] Catherine not only feared civil war but also recognized that religious division would likely fragment the country.[39]

During Francis II's reign, Catherine's goal was to gain the support of all parties for her son. Social and economic factors complicated her efforts. Throughout France, there were large numbers of unemployed men-at-arms, accustomed to looting and pillaging in warfare under Henry II, who now lived on the spoils of war. Protestant nobles who had fled France during Henry's reign hoped to regain their estates.[40] These groups, as well as those committed to the new religion, had more to gain from dissent than conciliation. The Protestants looked to the prince of the blood Condé as their leader and banded together to oppose the Guises. But in response to resistance, the Guises sharpened legislation against Protestants. Heresy became a crime punishable by death, and Protestant houses of worship were to be razed. These measures negated Catherine's conciliatory efforts.

Increasing religious repression provoked Protestants to try other means to influence the king. Some disgruntled Protestant nobles came together under the leadership of Jean de Barry, lord of La Renaudie, and hatched a plot to capture the king to remove him from the Guises' influence. Some of these conspirators wanted to make the king see the errors of Catholicism. For them, the conspiracy had a largely religious purpose. For others, the conspiracy cloaked a political rebellion against the power of the Guises. The timing of the plot was especially unfortunate, as the crown was pursuing conciliation. Catherine had just promulgated the Edict of Amboise, which distinguished between those who were Huguenots by religious conviction and those who were seditious. The former were to be tolerated and granted amnesty; the latter would be subject to the full weight of the law.

When one hundred Huguenot horsemen rode up the ramp to Amboise and penetrated into the courtyard of the royal chateau to carry out their plot, the royal guardsmen were taken unaware. With no clear plan, the plotters fired their pistols and fled. Albeit ill-conceived, this was an attack on a royal chateau and thus perceived as a serious threat. It changed the dynamics of the relationship between Catholics and Protestants and called into question Catherine's conciliatory policy. Some plotters were granted amnesty, but its leaders were executed and their heads festooned on the chateau's crenellations, high above the Loire for all to see. The Guises celebrated vanquishing the conspirators with the royal family to convey their control over the king. Reprisals against the plotters increased both religious violence and opposition to the Guises.

In the aftermath of the conspiracy, Catherine was able to pursue a policy of her own for the first time since Henry's death. Recognizing the danger the Guises posed to the monarchy, she advocated a more moderate policy toward Protestants and appointed as chancellor Michel de l'Hôpital, an honorable man and an adept politician known to advocate clemency toward Protestants.[41] Francis II endorsed the more conciliatory policy, noting that although he "had tried to separate the weeds from the wheat, now the weeds were grown so high that it was impossible to pull them out without pulling out the wheat as well."[42] The Edict of Romorantin (May 1560) reaffirmed the Edict of Amboise, again distinguishing heresy from sedition and offering Protestants liberty of conscience.[43] But the religious climate was hostile to peace. Both Protestants and Catholics perpetrated acts of violence against each other. It became less clear who could adjudicate religious issues or how political issues fraught with theological complications could be settled. Hôpital hoped an open council with Catholic-Protestant dialogue could resolve religious discord, but Pope Pius IV insisted that only a reconvened Council of Trent could address religious issues.

Catherine then convened an Assembly of Notables at Fontainebleau, where she hoped to use the authority of the princes of the blood to counter the Guises.[44] But the princes of the blood were led by the Protestant Condé, who had become the leader of the Huguenots. Much aggrieved by the Guises, he was not inclined to conciliate. He instead planned to seize Lyon, a staunchly Protestant city, as a base from which to march on Paris to assert the rights of Protestants. Catherine ordered Anthony of Bourbon to bring his brother Condé to court, where he was arrested. This act, the Venetian ambassador Giovanni Michieli claimed, was a guide to Catherine's politics: "She possesses well the art of dissimulation. That is seen in the detention of Condé, not only does she not speak harshly of him, she speaks in his favor."[45] Condé was tried, convicted of treason, and sentenced to death by a tribunal whose members represented the Guises' interests. (Hôpital refused to sign the edict. [46]) Condé's rebellion and conviction completely derailed Catherine's conciliatory policy. His rebellion likely emboldened Protestant opposition. His conviction weakened the princes of the blood and further confirmed the Guises' power. But the untimely death of Francis II on December 5, 1560, meant that Condé's death sentence was not immediately carried out. Perhaps improbably, the death of the young king held the best prospect for peace. A new reign might be less tied to the Guises and better able to keep them in check and thus allow a political reconfiguration more conducive to peace.

REGENT (1561–1574)

Francis's death, after a reign of only seventeen months, was a devastating blow to Catherine. In a letter to her daughter Elisabeth, Catherine acknowledged her difficulties: "God took your brother, whom I loved as you know, and left me three small children and a kingdom all divided, without a single person whom I can trust not to have some particular interest." Her second son, Charles, was only ten years old, and the age of majority for French kings was fourteen. While a minor king inevitably meant a weaker monarchy, Catherine was able to concentrate political power in her hands by pressing the preeminent prince of the blood Anthony of Bourbon to renounce any claim on the regency. Catherine appointed him lieutenant general of the kingdom, while making herself "governor of France." Regent in all but official title, Catherine reconfigured the royal council to counter the Guises; she included former members of Henry II's council, released Condé, and recalled Montmorency—all to counterbalance the Guises. As she wrote to her daughter, "My principal aim is . . . to preserve my authority, not for myself, but for the conservation of this kingdom and for the good of all your brothers." She intended to keep her son close to "help govern the state as a loving mother should."[47] This privately expressed aim was the rhetorical theme of her regency, which presented her as a vigilant mother, protecting her son and, through him, the state. During Charles's minority, Catherine was more independent of the Guises; she also presided over the council and controlled the domestic and foreign business of the state. Two days after Francis's death, the Venetian envoy reported that the queen mother's "will is supreme in all things" and that "she holds everything in her hand . . . she has the cachet of the king; . . . in the council . . . her opinion is the last word."[48]

Various Venetian ambassadors remarked with acute sensitivity on Catherine's difficulties. Michele Suriano reported that Charles IX's minority saw "a very young king, without experience or authority, a council full of discord, power in the hands of the queen, wise but timid, irresolute, and always a woman . . . she needed good councilors . . . but religious dissent among the nobility made everyone suspect." Marc-Antonio Barbaro described a more specific difficulty: "Each one on the council has his plan for himself."[49]

Catherine had greater authority during her son's minority, but it was contested. Kings too contended with dissident nobles and religious dissenters, but a female regent was especially vulnerable. The Guises and the princes of the blood explicitly challenged Catherine. If her strategy was to retain power by balancing the forces of opposition, those forces were not equally strong or reliable. Anthony of Bourbon, for example, was too vacillating, both politically and religiously, for Catherine to rely on him to check the politically astute and fervently Catholic Guises, who continued to conspire actively against her. In the spring of 1561, Guise, Montmorency, and Jacques d'Albon, lord of Saint-André and marshal of France, formed a triumvirate to try to control the young king. When they turned to Philip II of Spain for support, they opened the French Wars of Religion to direct foreign intervention.

The involvement of foreign powers in France, both Catholic and Protestant, continued until the end of the Wars of Religion in 1598 and greatly complicated Catherine's efforts to reconcile disparate religious groups and to retain the authority of the monarchy. With the Peace of Augsburg (1555), the German principalities had temporarily put aside religious warfare after almost thirty-five years, but France opened a new battleground. In the international sphere, Catholics feared the loss of France, while Protestants saw it as a territory to be gained for the new religion. When Catherine favored Protestants to thwart the Catholic faction's power, Catholic powers opposed her. In response, Elizabeth I then became her ally, offering troops and money. Protestants in the Low Countries too then favored Catherine and sought her support in their opposition to Spain. And Swiss troops might be forthcoming. When Catherine overtly favored Catholics because Protestants threatened the crown, as Condé had, for example, Philip II and the papacy offered her financial and military support. Whenever she seemed too tolerant of Protestants, Philip II presented himself as the supporter of the *truly* Catholic party in France. Not only were the various factions poised to intervene in the Wars of Religion, they were also willing to profit from dissent within the royal family, later recruiting Catherine's disaffected sons to serve their interests in plots against the brother who wore the crown.

Catherine had convened the Estates-General in 1560 to seek a remedy for ills of political and religious division afflicting the realm, but the meeting had been halted by Francis's death. Once Catherine had gained the Estates-General's acceptance of her regency, she endorsed a more conciliatory policy toward Protestants.[50] As a result, they became more overt in the practice of their faith, and Protestantism spread. At the same time, Catherine firmly embraced Catholicism and insisted that her ladies-in-waiting do the same under pain of being removed from the court. Early in Charles's reign, Catherine was determined to check the Guises. She hoped, perhaps naively, to reduce the role of religion in politics. Even though she and the royal council had agreed to allow Protestant religious practices in specified locations, they, like many, hoped for religious reconciliation. Two religions, it was almost universally believed, would divide a kingdom irrevocably.

Catherine remained optimistic that theological differences could be resolved through open discussion when she convened Protestant and Catholic clergy in the Colloquy at Poissy in the fall of 1561. Her optimism should perhaps have been checked when Philip II, Pope Pius IV, and the Sorbonne condemned the meeting in advance. Although the colloquy evinced an unusual spirit of conciliation, the question of the Eucharist proved to be an irresolvable sticking point. Catholics maintained the real physical presence of the body and blood of Christ in the Eucharist, whereas Calvinists insisted that Christ was only spiritually present. The issue immediately and irrevocably divided the two camps, and the colloquy ended without agreement. (This issue remains a crucial obstacle to current Catholic-Protestant ecumenical efforts.) The failure of the colloquy hardened positions on both sides. The Guises, proclaiming themselves standard-bearers of Catholic orthodoxy, left in protest. But first they tried to recruit Catherine's favorite son, Henry, to their cause.

Without a theological solution, Catherine's policy of toleration left her isolated, as both sides responded with greater intransigence. When Francis, the duke of Guise, was visiting his family estate at Joinville, his mother complained that Protestants worshipped at nearby Vassy within the city walls in violation of the current edict. Guise attacked Protestant worshippers; sixty some were killed and more than one hundred wounded. In response, Protestants mobilized around Condé, and the conflict threatened to spread to Paris. To calm the situation, Catherine persuaded Condé to leave Paris. But when Catholic leaders effectively placed the king and Catherine under house arrest, Protestants considered that war had essentially been declared on them.[51]

Condé then decided to liberate the king and his mother, for Protestants believed that the Guises held them captive. He led an army on Orléans, which he successfully captured, reigniting the Wars of Religion. Condé insisted that he had only taken up arms at Catherine's urging and disclosed her letters requesting his aid.[52] Catholics then believed that Catherine had betrayed them by allying with the Protestants. They even feared that she had changed her religion and possibly that of her sons. She was forced to defend herself to her ambassador in Madrid: "I have never either in fact, or in desire, or in my manner of life changed my religion."[53]

Catherine's policy of reconciliation became increasingly difficult to maintain as events inflamed religious passions. Not only had she failed to reconcile Catholics and Protestants, but each side now viewed her with suspicion. Concessions were increasingly seen as selling out one side for the other. Condé's open rebellion now pushed her into an alliance with Catholics. The triumvirate's power and Protestants' rebellion forced Catherine to espouse a less tolerant religious policy, decreeing the death penalty for those who fostered religious division. As it applied to both Catholics and Huguenots, it was unpopular and unenforceable. With Spanish funds, Catherine raised mercenary troops, and warfare became increasingly violent.

Both sides relied on foreign powers to finance their war efforts. When Catherine was forced by the triumvirate into a Spanish alliance, Condé allied with England. In exchange for money and soldiers, he agreed to turn over the port of Le Havre to Elizabeth I of England—the act of an enemy of the state. His brother, Anthony of Bourbon, led the Catholics (despite the firm commitment of his wife, Jeanne d'Albret, to the Huguenots) against him and laid siege to Huguenot-controlled Rouen. Catherine herself oversaw the operation. Rouen capitulated to royal forces, and Anthony died of wounds received during the siege. Protestant and Catholic armies then battled to a standstill at Dreux on December 19, 1562.

During this renewed warfare, a Huguenot identified as Jean Paltrot de Méré assassinated Francis of Guise on February 18, 1563. The Guises blamed the Protestant leader Admiral Gaspard de Coligny, who denied any involvement but admitted frankly that he considered the duke's death "the greatest benefit which could have befallen the kingdom."[54] Catherine too expressed her relief at the death of this powerful Catholic leader.[55]

These deaths removed a generation of Catholic leaders but produced a hiatus in the war, which allowed Catherine to negotiate a peace. But peace merely set a pattern for the resolution of future outbreaks of hostilities. That is to say, military hostilities produced standoffs, as neither side could prevail, and peace was declared by an edict the crown was powerless to enforce. In this case, the Edict of Amboise (March 19, 1563) granted Huguenots freedom of conscience and of religious practice but on restricted terms—only to nobles and urban elites, only on the outskirts of towns previously held by the Huguenots, and only in one town per district. To keep the peace, Huguenots were absolutely forbidden to practice in Paris. More restrictive than its predecessor, this edict was not popular with Protestants, who quite reasonably saw it as a setback.[56] However, when Elizabeth I was unwilling to cede Le Havre, Protestants and Catholics united to retake it.

Catherine capitalized on this success to have Charles IX declare his majority in 1563. Even though he was not yet fourteen, she hoped he would command more authority as king. On that occasion, Charles insisted that he would no longer tolerate the disobedience that had characterized his reign thus far. He claimed absolute authority with the significant exception of "the Queen, his mother, to whom he reserved the power of command."[57] Catherine, he insisted, would govern as usual. The ceremony ended with an edict of pacification, ordering those with weapons to dispose of them, and Catherine returned to her policy of trying to conciliate all sides. As she wrote at this time: "Women have a better will to conserve the kingdom than those who have put it in the state it is in."[58]

Shortly thereafter, Catherine, an avid horsewoman her entire life, took such a serious fall that she was not expected to live. Perhaps for that reason she wrote "Advice given by Catherine de Medici to Charles IX for the Policy of His Court and for the Government of His State." This document addressed the practical measures the young king should take to assert his authority over those who would challenge him and to win his people's loyalty. Catherine emphasized his need to "police the court." The king, she advised, should set an example and establish a clear schedule of his day's activities, some of which should allow nobles to attend him. A king should make himself accessible to the people; he could be seen out riding and offer diversions for the young people at court, for example.[59] The court, Catherine understood, could be used to exert political power and to neutralize opposition.

Any advice Catherine could give Charles should have been welcome. Slight, sickly, and very young, Charles was not an inspiring figure, and each illness debilitated him further. At fourteen, he was understandably not much interested in governing but instead avidly pursued hunting and outdoor activities and loved working as a blacksmith. Although the distinguished humanist and translator of Plutarch's *Lives*, Jacques Amyot, was his tutor, Charles was not a particularly apt student. He was, however, an accomplished musician who also composed several poems for Pierre Ronsard, his court poet. Tarred with his mother's Black Legend, which paints him as a madman subject to uncontrollable rages, Charles should be recognized first and foremost as an adolescent who left politics largely to his mother. The crown faced vehement religious and political opposition his entire reign.

Catherine planned a grand tour of the kingdom to reinforce Charles's kingship and enforce the peace. The royal family went to Fontainebleau to prepare for the upcoming travel. Peace provided a welcome opportunity to revel in lavish Renaissance festivities, as Catherine made her court a center of culture and diversion to keep war at bay and gain support for the monarchy. There were noteworthy Mardi Gras festivities; plays were performed in which members of the royal family took roles. A remarkable tapestry in the Uffizi Gallery in Florence, depicting the court's departure, shows the massive cortege of courtiers, domestic servants, entertainers, cooks, doctors, and nine dwarves—some of the more than ten thousand people accompanying the royal family.[60] Each stop on this tour required a grand ceremony to express the people's loyalty to the crown and their acceptance of the new edict of pacification. In every province and each town, the king was presented as embodying the restoration of royal authority and religious peace.

Catherine explicitly used the arts of the Renaissance, particularly court festivities, to emphasize the crown's unifying role (fig. 5.4). It alone could reconcile and harmonize forces as disparate as Christian and pagan and male and female. (Hence the androgynous dress at the royal transvestite balls.) In these festivities, Charles was depicted in many heroic guises—David battling Goliath, Perseus rescuing Andromeda, Theseus slaying the Minotaur, and Hercules killing Cerberus. Catherine used all available media to reinforce the positive qualities she wanted associated with her son's reign. Royal ceremonies also emphasized her role as a bringer of peace.[61]

Catherine and her family enjoyed much of this two-and-a-half-year tour. Important family events unfolded in public settings. In Toulouse, her children were confirmed. In Lyon, she met with Florentine banking families and with the pope in Avignon. At Bayonne in the Pyrenees, Catherine was reunited with her daughter Elisabeth, although her husband, Philip II, objected to Catherine's toleration of Protestants and refused to accompany his wife. When the duke of Alba, who acted as Philip's representative, met with Catherine, he tried to persuade Catherine to reverse her policy of toleration and commit to rooting out the Huguenots.

By tour's end, Catherine could point to her successes in presenting the Renaissance monarchy positively, but they obscured fundamental problems created by unprecedented religious division. Some communities were receptive to the royal visit, but others demonstrated just how necessary the tour had been to cultivate loyalty to the monarchy. Catherine made no headway with the intractable Jeanne d'Albret, whom she hoped to persuade to reestablish Catholicism in her territories—a completely fruitless mission. Huguenots' misgivings increased with every public royal celebration of Catholic feasts. But such manifestations of royal orthodoxy reassured neither Spain nor the papacy that the Huguenot threat had diminished.

And the meeting between Catherine and the duke of Alba may well have been her greatest diplomatic gaffe. Catherine pursued it as an opportunity to arrange Spanish marriages for her children.[62] But Alba used the meeting to persuade several Catholic nobles that Philip of Spain must be acknowledged as the "true father of French Catholics."[63] Alba denounced Catherine's policy of toleration and advocated stringent measures against the Huguenots, including the execution of the most prominent of them. While she did not agree

Fig. 5.4. This elaborate court tapestry, *Festival in Honor of the Polish Ambassadors in the Presence of Catherine de Medici* by François Quesnel, indicates Catherine de Medici's use of court festivities to cultivate support for the crown in a political and religiously divided France. Uffizi, Florence / The Bridgeman Art Library.

to Alba's harsh proposals, Catherine likely agreed to enforce the Council of Trent's decrees and punish religious dissenters.[64] But her meeting with him raised doubts among the Huguenots about her trustworthiness. Their mistrust complicated subsequent negotiations. While Catholics wanted Catherine to renounce toleration, Huguenots complained that her edicts provided insufficient protection. Catholic suspicions that Admiral Coligny had been involved in the assassination of the duke of Guise simmered as a source of grievance. Any illusion that Catherine might have had that the tour had helped resolve religious division was short-lived.

Catholic-Protestant conflicts exploded on the international scene. Protestants in the Low Countries revolted against Spain, and in response Catherine reinforced border garrisons. When Spanish troops moved from Milan through Lorraine, the French monarchy emphasized its firm adherence to Catholicism and, by implication, Spanish interests. These actions heightened Huguenot suspicion that Catherine had made a secret agreement to support the Spanish. (There is no evidence that there was such an agreement, despite the widespread belief in the sixteenth century that there was.)

In response, Condé again took up arms to lead the Huguenots. Protestant unease further increased when the king hired six thousand Swiss mercenaries as his own guard and did not disband them even after Alba had reached Brussels. Huguenots then feared that Alba might join forces with royal troops and attack them. They thus orchestrated a plan to capture the king to rescue him from the Spanish. When this plan, called the "Surprise of Meaux," was discovered, Catherine and Charles fled to Paris under the protection of the Swiss Guard. Huguenot forces then marched on Paris, getting close enough to capture the suburb of Saint-Denis. There they were defeated by royal troops under the leadership of Montmorency, who was wounded in the battle and died two days later. So vanished this mainstay of royal service from the beginning of Francis I's reign. The Huguenots were defeated, but they had demonstrated that they could mobilize a significant fighting force.

A horrified Catherine denounced the plot to kidnap her son as the "greatest wickedness of all time."[65] It made her see Huguenots more as dangerous political rebels than as religious reformers. Her position toward the Huguenots hardened, and for the first time she forbade the practice of the reformed religion. Her repudiation of her conciliatory policy provoked Hôpital to resign as chancellor.

The Huguenots had even more cause for disquiet. They had not "rescued" the king from the Spanish, but they had alienated the queen mother. They now faced serious threats from the emerging networks of Catholic leagues and the growing influence of the Guises, especially over Catherine's son Henry. Huguenots were especially concerned that France was aligning its foreign policy with the Spanish, who were stringently repressing Protestants in the Low Countries. These fears were confirmed when Charles IX declared war against them. Some Catholics then allied with the Huguenots, claiming they were freeing the king from more radical Catholics. The political situation was further complicated by Charles's illness—a severe bout of the pulmonary disease that would eventually kill him.

This war brought Catherine's son Henry to prominence as committed to the Catholic cause. At the battle of Jarnac on March 13, 1569, he earned a reputation for valor battling the Protestant forces led by Condé and Coligny. Condé was wounded, captured, and then assassinated in cold blood by the captain of Henry's guard. After Condé's death, Coligny led the successful Protestant forces against the royal army at Arny-le-Duc in June and then sued for peace.

Fearful that Protestant foreign powers would enter the war against her, Catherine ultimately signed the Peace of Saint-Germain in 1570, guaranteeing Protestants amnesty, liberty of conscience, and security of worship wherever it had been possible before the war. The peace allowed Protestants to occupy four fortified towns, which created bases for protection, arms, and alliance with foreign powers. While Protestants were relieved by these concessions, Catholics were disgruntled that the gains of their military victories had been lost.

A Venetian ambassador again provided an especially astute commentary on the difficulties Catherine faced. Giovanni Corer may well have been reflecting confidences Catherine shared with him when he reported that, as the queen was not in a strong position to challenge the Huguenots, "she tolerated them patiently and received them kindly, and favored them with apparent affection." She hoped to wear down their resistance, which she attributed "to ambition and love of vengeance more than to religious sentiments" and believed that "the obedience of the people to the king would increase with the age of the king." Catherine compared her situation to that of Blanche of Castille, the mother of Louis IX; she too had a minor son and had been forced to ally with heretics to succeed. However, as Corer pointed out, Catherine failed with both parties. "Huguenots said that Catherine deceived them with lies, and Catholics claimed that the Huguenots would not have gone so far if Catherine had not encouraged them." Corer nonetheless empathized with her plight, noting that "without the power to distinguish her friends from her enemies, she was obliged to make use of the men who were there even though they all had interests." He conceded that "any prince would have made mistakes in the middle of such confusion. How much more a woman, a foreigner without friends in which to confide . . . who never hears the truth."[66]

Despite these grave difficulties, Catherine remained the power behind the throne. On March 11, 1571, Charles acknowledged before the Parlement of Rouen the crucial role she played in preserving his kingdom: "After God, the Queen my mother is the person to whom I am most indebted. Her tenderness for me and for my people, her tireless work, energy, and wisdom have assured the running of state affairs so well during a time when, because of my age, I was unable to take charge of them myself, that even the tempests of civil war have been unable to harm my kingdom."[67]

Peace gave Catherine an opportunity to negotiate marriages for her children. Whenever Catholic-Protestant relations at home seemed at an impasse, Catherine turned to marriage negotiations to shore up France's international position. Just as her domestic policy pitted Protestant against Catholic, so too her foreign policy played Catholic against Protestant states, using marriage alliances to bind both without assuring either that they held the king in thrall. After her attempt to arrange a marriage between her son Charles and Elizabeth I of England, some fifteen years his senior, failed, Catherine then successfully negotiated Charles's marriage to Elizabeth of Austria, the daughter of Catholic Emperor Maximilian II. The wedding celebration not only cemented a crucial Catholic alliance but also revitalized the court. The pageantry emphasized that both the bride and groom were the descendants of Charlemagne and featured Catherine as Artemis, bringer of peace.

Catherine then tried to arrange a marriage for her son Henry to Elizabeth I of England. This plan, by allying France to Protestant England, would have provided a counterweight to Spain. But it faced many obstacles: Catholics were hostile to this marriage, and the twenty-two-year-old Henry had no desire to marry the Protestant thirty-nine-year-old virgin queen.[68] When this plan unraveled, Catherine proposed her youngest son, Francis, as a substitute groom. Elizabeth kept Francis dangling and continued to tout her marriageable virginity throughout her long reign without ever committing. Her marriage to Francis reemerged as a diplomatic gambit over the next decade.

Catherine also pursued a marriage between her daughter Marguerite and the Protestant Henry of Navarre.[69] This marriage, in the planning stage for several years, was intended as a masterstroke of Protestant-Catholic reconciliation. Both Coligny and Jeanne d'Albret, Navarre's mother and staunch Calvinist, resisted the match. [70] Jeanne's sudden death at the French court shortly after agreeing to the marriage raised suspicions of poisoning. Catherine's Italian connections heightened such suspicions. Although an autopsy revealed a lung disease, now identified as tubercular pleurisy, the suspicions revealed continuing hostility to Catherine.[71]

Although the proposed marriage was intended to reconcile Protestant and Catholic, both the domestic and international situation had become considerably more complicated by the Protestant rebellion against Spanish control of the Low Countries. Coligny's arrival at court heightened Catholic fears that he might persuade Charles to intervene in the Low Countries on behalf of the Protestant rebels. Charles's growing personal relationship with the Huguenot leader so alienated the Guises that they left the court. While Charles weighed Huguenot requests to aid the Protestant rebels in the Low Countries, Catherine tried to allay Spanish fears that France would intervene in their affairs.[72]

Rumors, repeated in ambassadors' reports and contemporary memoirs, swirled that Coligny was battling Catherine for influence over her son and attempting to persuade Charles to intervene in the Low Countries. Recent histories dispute such accounts, finding little evidence of Coligny's extensive influence over Charles.[73] But the long-planned wedding between Marguerite and Navarre further exacerbated Catholic concern. The ceremony at Notre Dame on August 18, 1572, also heightened anxiety. The Parisian populace was not pleased to witness a marriage between a Valois and a Protestant or to have such a large Protestant presence in the capital. The atmosphere could scarcely have been less propitious for Catholic-Protestant reconciliation.

THE SAINT BARTHOLOMEW'S DAY MASSACRE

On August 22, following four days of wedding festivities, Coligny was shot and wounded on the streets of Paris. All the evidence pointed to the complicity of the Guises. The shot was fired from a house the family owned, and the assassin, subsequently identified as Charles de Louviers de Maurevert, was a Guise client. But details of the event remain murky.[74] An agitated Charles promised a full inquiry. Coligny expressed his suspicion that Catherine was behind the attempt. If the Guises had undertaken it with Catherine's or her son Henry's approval of this act to avenge their father's assassination, an investigation might well have exposed their complicity. Catherine could have justified the attempted assassination as thwarting Coligny's influence over the king or preventing French entanglement in a war with Spain in the Low Countries. While these are plausible reasons Catherine might have condoned this act, they cannot be substantiated. Even after all this time and the work of many scholars, the question of Catherine's complicity remains impossible to determine.[75]

The attempt on Coligny roiled religious tensions, and the atmosphere in Paris became ever more ominous. The city was in the grip of a relentless heat wave, and the price of wheat had risen dramatically at the same time the crown spent on lavish wedding festivities. And Catholics and Protestants had been killing each other in the name of religion for more than a decade. Each saw the other not simply as heretics but also as contaminants of their communities. Both sides were regularly exhorted from the pulpit to expunge the other as sources of corruption.[76] In the aftermath of the failed assassination attempt, Catholics feared that Huguenots, massed in the city for the royal wedding, would seek vengeance. Rumors circulated that they intended to kidnap or kill Charles and the royal family. Charles himself was eager to avenge the attempt on Coligny's life.

Catherine had reason to fear not simply for the safety of her family but also that civil war would resume. If she were complicit in the attack on Coligny, she might have feared that the inquiry would reveal the role she or her family had played. To remove these possible threats to the crown, a plan was hatched to assassinate Protestant leaders. It remains unclear exactly who was involved in the plan, what was planned, or how many Protestants were targeted. The royal council met several times; the king attended at least one meeting, as did Catherine and the Guises, but there is no definitive record of its deliberations or decisions.[77]

The massacre began at 4:00 A.M. on August 24 (fig. 5.5). Catherine may well have believed that that she controlled the situation, but she reckoned without the fervor of Parisian Catholics. Members of the king's guard, led by Guise, murdered Coligny, threw his body from the window, and cut off his head to prove that he was dead and perhaps goad Catholics to further violence. Some Protestant leaders were murdered in the Louvre, where they were housed as wedding guests. Significantly, the lives of the young princes of the blood, Henry de Condé (son of the assassinated Louis de Condé) and Navarre, were spared. Although likely planned as a limited massacre of Protestant leaders (no surviving evidence suggests that wholesale slaughter of Protestants was endorsed), these attacks unleashed a spectacular wave of violence. Some believed they were carrying out royal wishes; Guise was heard to cry, "It is the king's command" during the melee. This cry legitimated settling private feuds between Catholic and Protestant as a public duty.[78] Some Catholics too no doubt believed that by exterminating Protestants they were carrying out God's will. The massacre raged in Paris for more than a week and spread to the provinces. The unchecked violence led to the deaths of at least two thousand in Paris and as many as thirty thousand in the provinces.[79] The king did not halt the massacre, but he may have been powerless to do so. (He later defended it as a response to a threatened coup.)

Whatever the massacre's intended scope, Catherine was held responsible for its initiation and the full extent of its horrors. Her presumed involvement in the massacre is the most significant source of her Black Legend. Those historians who have tried to rescue her reputation have insisted that there is no positive proof against her, or that she likely only endorsed the assassination of Huguenot leaders rather than the full-scale massacre, or that the limited assassination was a legitimate political expedient to rid the state of the leaders of dangerous dissidents. Others suggest that the plot was orchestrated by the Guises with the support of the young Prince Henry, which Catherine justified, only after the fact, to keep her son from being implicated in its excesses.[80]

Fig. 5.5. *St. Bartholomew's Day Massacre* by François Dubois. Catherine de Medici is the figure in black at the entrance to the castle, standing over dead bodies. Musée d'Archéologie et d'Histoire, Lausanne, Switzerland/The Bridgeman Art Library.

In the massacre's immediate aftermath, Catherine defended it to both Parlement and other European powers as necessary to preserve the monarchy from a Protestant plot against the royal family. Even if no one foresaw the devastating spread of mob violence, Catherine did bask in the adulation of Catholic leaders for her success in finally settling her Protestant problem. To some degree, she had. The massacre sharply reduced the number of Protestants and halted the growth of Protestantism in France; many more abjured their faith than were killed. Many Catholics and the Catholic powers saw the massacre as a long-awaited demonstration of the crown's resolve to carry out an implacable crusade against Protestants. Pope Gregory XIII ordered a *Te Deum* sung and a memorial medal struck. A room in the Vatican (no longer on view) depicts the massacre as glorious. Philip II had a *Te Deum* sung at the monastery of San Geronimo, and Catherine hoped the event would cement a Spanish alliance through her son Henry's marriage to Philip's oldest daughter.

When the massacre did not lead to a Spanish marriage, Catherine changed course and emphasized to Protestant powers that the massacre was a necessary, defensive action. She hoped to conciliate Elizabeth I's grievance over Protestants' deaths by again offering her son Francis as a husband. Catherine's foreign policy again shifted to reflect both the changing political situation and her maternal ambitions. She even allied with Protestant rebels in the cause of the liberation of the Low Countries from Spain—the very development that the attempt on Coligny may have been intended to prevent. But this was not the vacillation of a weak woman, rather part of a consistent effort to prevent the French king from being captive to any foreign power.

Although Catholics praised the massacre as a sign of her reinvigorated religious resolve, Catherine was, as always, more interested in eliminating any political threat the Huguenots posed than in regulating religious belief or practice. Consistently underestimating religious zeal as a motive for resistance, she believed that, deprived of their leaders, Protestants would be unable to mobilize. Instead, the massacre decisively alienated them from the crown. Prior to the massacre, they had been eager to negotiate, seeing the crown as a possible ally against more extreme Catholics. Now their political theorists developed arguments sanctioning their right to resist when a king impeded religious practice and questioning the authority of kings on the basis of religion. The Huguenots would never again trust Catherine, although she continued to try to conciliate them. Disaffected, they articulated the central charges of her Black Legend. Huguenots now warred against an illegitimate monarchy. Although many of their leaders had been killed, they continued to defend their fortress communities in the provinces. In response, troops under Catherine's son Henry besieged the Huguenot stronghold of La Rochelle. The city was spared only by his election as king of Poland.

This election must be recognized as one of Catherine's great diplomatic coups. Since the young prince Henry shared the blame for the massacre, Catherine worked for his election to take him out of harm's way. The Poles were flattered by the prospect of French royalty as their king, although they were less favorably disposed toward Henry after the massacre, which challenged their more tolerant religious views. Although Henry, a younger son without a crown, was pleased to be elected king of Poland, he found himself severely constrained by the Polish Diet (the representative body), which left him without much power or money or the means to acquire either. Even with limited opportunities to enjoy the trappings of kingship, he was king nonetheless.[81]

Catherine still had reason to be concerned about her family. Charles was ill with tuberculosis, and his younger brother Francis was eager to usurp power, profiting from Charles's illness and Henry's absence. No longer allied with the crown, Protestants mobilized around Francis and joined with moderate Catholics to oppose the crown. Some even advocated altering royal succession in Francis's favor. To avert this threat to legitimate succession, Catherine persuaded Charles to sign a decree proclaiming Henry as his heir.

Francis's supporters objected to the crown's concentration of power and its more stringent repression of Protestants. The massacre gave them cause for grievance and provided a flagrant example of political misdirection. It had, in their view, both empowered the Guises and allowed the crown to justify greater authoritarianism. Moderates asserted the authority of the nobility and the Estates to counter this unwarranted exercise of power. Influenced by the theory of government as a covenant between God and His people, articulated by Protestant political writers such as Philippe Duplessis-Mornay, these moderates wanted a contract between the monarchy and its subjects, an end to religious intolerance, and peace.[82] They supported Francis as the royal son they could attach to their cause. Francis would consistently play the role of the disgruntled younger son, avid for political power, around whom forces of opposition coalesced.

When Catherine and Charles learned of the plot, they arrested Francis and Navarre and confined them at the chateau of Vincennes on the outskirts of Paris to prevent Francis from seizing power as Charles's health precipitously declined. (He was by this point afflicted with subcutaneous hemorrhages.) Before he died on May 30, 1574, he affirmed his mother as regent until Henry could return from Poland. Catherine agreed: "Persuaded by the pressing request which my son made to me in his last words to take up the office of regent for the good of this crown to which I recognize I am bound by gratitude for all that which God has given me, I feel constrained to accept this office."[83] For Catherine, Charles's reign had been fifteen years of relentless struggle to hold the crown—through diplomacy, civil wars, and ultimately political violence.

HENRY III, HOPE OF THE VALOIS (1574–1589)

As Catherine awaited Henry's return from Poland, the inherent instability of the new regency afforded opportunities for the disgruntled to mobilize against the crown. In the face of mounting discontent, Catherine moved to the Louvre and kept Paris under strict guard. She was especially eager for Henry's return, but he lingered on a triumphal tour of Venice, which welcomed him as a counterweight to Spanish influence. When Henry finally crossed the Alps to meet Catherine, she looked forward to working with him to resolve the religious and political troubles and to reestablish royal authority.

Catherine was delighted that Henry, her favorite son, had come to power. She had always had a great affinity for him and now had great hopes for his reign. "This one is the right eye and the soul of the mother," the Venetian ambassador Giovanni Michieli said about Henry as he ascended the throne.[84] The strong connection between mother and son fueled stories that their relationship was incestuous, adding another salacious element to Catherine's Black Legend. Throughout his reign, Henry exploited his mother's love for him; he followed her advice when convenient and relied on her as his chief negotiator with disaffected parties.

Despite her hopes, Catherine was not unaware of Henry's deficiencies. The *Memoir* she addressed to him in August 1574 reflected her concerns and gave detailed instructions on how to be an effective prince.[85] Rule alone rather than depend on favorites, regain the loyalty of the provinces, and maintain a well-ordered court, she urged. Catherine could hope that this son who was older and accomplished might rule well, yet she feared the dangers he would face should he fail. His reign presented her greatest challenges.

Intelligent, sophisticated, well educated, and old enough to rule, Henry was the most promising of Catherine's sons. With an interest in philosophy, he surrounded himself with intellectuals in his Palace Academy. Industrious and attentive to bureaucratic detail, Henry understood that the court could assert royal authority. But despite his talents, his reign was jeopardized not simply by the religious and political complexities he faced but also by the way he attempted to redefine the monarchy. Henry's brief taste of kingship in Poland whetted his appreciation of his royal status. Asserting the perquisites of a monarch, he tried to concentrate political authority in his hands, which inevitably aroused noble opposition. His reign was also compromised from the outset by the blighted legacy of Saint Bartholomew's Day. But Henry's own willingness to isolate himself in a court surrounded by a small circle of devoted courtiers exacerbated his difficulties. From the beginning of his reign, Henry began to forfeit the political authority Catherine was trying to preserve for him.

Although Catherine had warned him about the dangers of fostering favorites at court, Henry surrounded himself with young men known as the *mignons*, or "cuties."[86] Although the term *mignons* was not initially pejorative, during Henry's reign it acquired the connotation of debauched and illegitimate usurpation of power and suspicion of sexual favors. His inner circle of favorites not only displaced other nobles, it excluded the royal mistress and female members of the court, who had been allowed great familiarity by earlier kings.[87] This exclusion further isolated Henry, separating him from a network of noble women, whose influence, ironically, might well have proved less controversial than that of the *mignons*. Favor still gained influence, positions, and access to the king, as Henry's *mignons* gained wealth and influential government positions from their association with him. But their prominence raised grave doubts about Henry's ability to rule. They feuded with each other and over women, defending themselves and asserting their loyalty to the king in numerous duels with supporters of the king's brother, Francis.[88] Their duels were an increasingly frequent public disturbance and led to the deaths of almost the entire first generation of *mignons*. The king loved finery, lapdogs, and all of the latest fashions, and his *mignons* aped him, making them figures of ridicule. This favoritism might also have been a deliberate strategy for the childless king to construct a new image of royal authority, not as father of his family and country but rather as a leader of men.[89] But, if so, it did not succeed in redefining his reign.

Beloved by the king who showered them with presents, these men diverted the king, who became more demoralized and morose over the course of his reign. Henry's extravagant affection for these men later fueled rumors, spread by both Catholics and Protestants, of his homosexuality, which were intended to discredit him and to explain the failure of his queen to conceive.[90] For a long time, Henry was assumed to have been either homosexual or bisexual, largely due to the charges of sixteenth-century polemicists. Recently historians have reconsidered. They now generally concede that Henry's bizarre personal behavior, which fluctuated so dramatically between the pursuit of pleasure and expressions of penitence, raised these suspicions among his contemporaries and made these charges credible. But even more significantly, these charges allowed both Protestant and Catholic critics to discredit him thoroughly.

Henry's excessive religious practices were equally disquieting.[91] He endlessly multiplied forms of religious devotion—going on pilgrimages, joining confraternities, and founding groups of penitents (fig. 5.6). His intense religious devotion was exacerbated by despair over his failure to produce an heir. Every crisis generated more extreme religious practices. Henry may have intended such practices to emphasize the religious authority of the French crown and his staunch Catholicism, but instead they were unsettling, certainly for Protestants and likely to some Catholics as well. For example, on the feast of the Assumption in 1583, the king and his *mignons* processed through Paris wearing pointed hoods over their faces, their robes blood-stained from self-flagellation. Henry's excesses—religious and hedonistic—provoked criticism and distanced him from his subjects. He did not present a recognizable model of kingship.

Clearly Henry's actions were the antithesis of Catherine's good advice upon his accession to the throne. Instead of making himself available to the nobility, he isolated himself by defining a rigid code of etiquette, emphasizing the deference due the king and the gulf between the king and the people. His intent to make the court a center of proper behavior and his own remoteness may have been a deliberate strategy to elevate the monarchy, but it instead distanced him

Fig. 5.6. An image of Henry III at a meeting of the Order of the Holy Spirit. French school, sixteenth century. Musée Condé, Chantilly, France / The Bridgeman Art Library.

from much of the nobility and alienated his countrymen. His method of governing was autocratic. For example, he outraged the council by granting land to the duke of Savoy without consultation, acting as if the French patrimony was his to dispense. He also reversed Catherine's generally conciliatory policy toward Huguenots, instead challenging them directly and immediately. Henry was determined to make Huguenot territories of Dauphiné and Languedoc bow to his authority, even if he had to use Spanish troops to do so. Negotiation now unfolded in an atmosphere of mutual mistrust.

Henry saw Henry Montmorency-Damville, the nephew of the recently deceased Montmorency and governor of Languedoc, who now led the united Huguenots and some disaffected Catholics, as his most immediate threat. Montmorency-Damville had openly challenged the royal family in a manifesto denouncing them for their role in the Saint Bartholomew's Day Massacre. Although Catherine professed to Montmorency-Damville her willingness to pursue peace, he suspected that she simply intended to detach him from his Huguenot supporters. In April 1575, the Huguenots met with the king to seek complete religious freedom and the prosecution of those guilty of the massacre. When the negotiations broke down, Montmorency-Damville sought military support from foreign Protestant princes.

Meanwhile, discontent permeated the royal household as Francis and Navarre, still under house arrest, plotted their escape. An English agent wrote: "It is a very hell among them, not one content or quiet with another, neither mother with son, nor brother with brother."[92] When Francis escaped in the fall of 1575, he again challenged his older brother. He joined the dissidents, and every day more armed men flocked to him. Catherine feared that Francis would go so far as to fight with Protestants, who, under Condé's leadership, had assembled an army of German and Swiss mercenaries. Although Catherine forced Francis to agree to a truce, he quickly broke it by going to war, claiming that an attempt had been made to poison him. The royal court was in such disorder that Navarre too escaped and assumed leadership of the Huguenots. Catherine urged the king to make peace, since he was in no position to lead a campaign against Francis, now supported by both Huguenots and disgruntled Catholics.

Catherine again proved to be an indefatigable negotiator in trying to restore peace in the face of religious division and dissension among her sons. Yet the peace she attained was perceived as a complete victory for Francis and the Protestants. By its terms, Henry had to make amends for the Saint Bartholomew's Day Massacre and grant territorial and financial concessions to the Protestants.[93] Protestants received freedom of conscience and worship, indemnity for victims of the massacre, and places of sanctuary. Protestant mercenaries were even paid three million francs to disband. This was beyond the crown's ability to pay, and the king and Catherine were caught between the demands of Protestants and those of financiers. Such a stringent peace could not last; its financial agreements were ruinous to the crown, and its concessions to Protestants alienated Catholics. The Parlement of Paris refused to register the edict, and the Parisian population demonstrated against it.

Henry immediately convened the Estates-General at Blois on December 6, 1576, hoping to procure funding for a new war on Protestants. Sympathetic to the Catholic cause, the Estates-General favored the resumption of war but would not agree to tax increases. It instead urged the crown to reduce expenses. When Henry publicly espoused religious uniformity, Catherine protested this policy as leading inevitably to civil war and addressed the Estates to dissuade them from war as a grave threat to the kingdom. Most disturbing, adamant Catholics organized to guarantee that severe measures would be taken against the Protestants if the king proved too weak to enforce them. Catherine recognized, as Henry perhaps did not, that having allied with these Catholics, he became beholden to a particular faction and thus could not mediate effectively between the various groups.

In the face of political crises, Henry resorted to the behaviors that had initially made him so unpopular. As he emphasized his power and status, his critics became more vehement. Derisive placards appeared in Paris proclaiming, "Henry by the grace of his mother, apathetic king of France, imaginary king of Poland, concierge of the Louvre."[94] His increasingly bizarre behavior offered an easy target. He collected menageries of exotic animals, wore lavishly bejeweled clothing, and spent more and more time with his young male favorites.[95] "There is beginning to be a lot of talk about the *mignons*, who are hated and scorned by the people, as much for their haughty manner as for their effeminate and immodest appearance, but most of all for the excessive liberalities of the king toward them. Popular opinion holds that this is the cause of the people's ruin," the contemporary journalist L'Estoile reported.[96]

In response to the dire situation he faced, Henry turned his attention to diversions such as theatrical events and masked balls, including a particularly noteworthy one that he attended dressed as a lavishly bejeweled woman. His attire scandalized the expense-conscious representatives to the Estates-General. This kind of Renaissance spectacle, intended not simply to entertain but also to depict a Platonic harmony of male and female, alienated rather than conciliated its viewers. While such allegorical depictions had been understood and appreciated by members of Henry II's court, viewers were now scandalized, and events like these generated hostile polemics. Even the generally sympathetic

Venetian ambassador Giovanni Michieli noted that Henry had lost his previous reputation for valor and "had abandoned himself to laziness to a degree that astounds everyone." He further remarked, "One has no idea of his expenses for beauty."[97] The king was now charged with frivolity, the pursuit of luxury, and inappropriate behavior, including sexual behavior—ironically, just the charges more usually leveled against mistresses (fig. 5.7). But if a prominent woman could be charged with emasculating a king, a horde of foppish male favorites suggested that the king himself had undermined the valor of French noble culture and the monarchy.

Fortunately, Catherine had brought her son Francis back into the family fold by the time Henry again went to war again the Huguenots. But the royal forces were too poorly funded to defeat them. This war too produced a short-lived peace, but it also exposed the weakness of the king's position; he could neither enforce a peace nor fund a war. Once again, Catherine's skills as a negotiator and peacemaker were necessary, but even she was not able to preserve the accord between her sons. When they again fell out, Catherine persuaded Francis to desist plotting against Henry only by fostering his ambition to be king of the Low Countries. The Low Countries had been hoping for French help against what they denounced as Spanish oppression since the time of Henry II; France had generally been willing to undermine Spanish power but not to intervene directly. Now Francis was willing to redirect his political aspirations there.

Catherine was again deployed as Henry's negotiator, this time with the Huguenots in the south of France, who were now mobilizing under the leadership of her son-in-law Navarre. With her daughter Marguerite's help, Catherine tried to bring Navarre into the royal camp, but it took six months of arduous travel and negotiation to wrest from him even a meeting to begin discussions. She ultimately negotiated truces in Languedoc and Dauphiné, but the peace remained fragile and unstable.

By the end of 1578, Catherine again had cause for concern about the disruption her son Francis was causing. He had not gotten enough support from either Elizabeth I or his brother to defeat the Spanish in the Low Countries. He had also alienated some of his former supporters with his autocratic behavior and his ineffective military ventures. After Catherine provided more money and troops for him, Francis decided to impose his will on the citizens of Antwerp; his soldiers went on a rampage, called "the Fury of Antwerp." The citizenry withstood the attack and in turn massacred Francis's troops. Chastened by this disaster, Francis slipped back into Paris, reconciled with his brother, and asked for funds to court the English queen.

Catherine remained concerned about the threat Francis posed to Henry's reign and the crown. When it became increasingly clear that Elizabeth was

Fig. 5.7. Ball at the court of King Henry III. French school, sixteenth century. Louvre/The Bridgeman Art Library.

more interested in using Francis as a bargaining chip to preserve an Anglo-French alliance than in marrying him, Catherine reversed her alliance strategy and proposed that Francis marry instead a Spanish princess who could bring the Low Countries as her dowry. Francis was willing to consider such a shift in his matrimonial fortunes, but his suit was rebuffed.

The fortunes of the Valois seemed to have hit a new low. Catherine was not well, and Henry, suffering from boils and toothaches, retreated into religious mania, manifested in penitential processions, making his disturbing behavior more obvious. As his health deteriorated, he suffered from delusions of persecution and ever more obviously favored his *mignons*. The Venetian ambassador Lorenzo Priuli wrote: "I lament that the king should take so little care for the dignity and the interests of the crown."[98] Henry's disengagement from the political realities around him also became more marked. Claude Haton, a Guise supporter, noted in his *Memoirs*, that by 1581, "the king has left the care of public affairs to his mother. . . . He has withdrawn to Saint-Germain-en-Laye, according to some, for the cure of the shameful disease which afflicts him."[99] The Florentine ambassador reported home, the king "rises before day and works his mind very hard. He is secret, patient, of tenacious memory and great powers of dissimulation . . . but when he wants to get out of doing anything, he has an admirable way of avoiding it."[100]

In June 1584, the fortunes of the Valois dynasty took a disastrous turn. Francis, Catherine's youngest son, died of tuberculosis, just as his brother Charles had. Catherine's response to his death must have been complex. He had consistently rebelled against her guidance and undermined Henry's authority and her hopes to strengthen the monarchy. Francis had threatened the stability of Henry's reign, requiring Catherine's constant mediation between her feuding sons. Rebels in the Low Countries and Elizabeth I had used Francis just as he had tried to use them. But his death was not simply a personal loss; it provoked a serious succession crisis.

CONTESTED POWER (1584–1588)

Henry III had been at odds with his brother his entire adult life and had been infuriated by Francis's many schemes to challenge his authority. But as Henry had no son of his own, Francis had been his heir.[101] The end of the Valois line exposed unequivocally the inherent vulnerability of Henry's own reign. As Catholics and Protestants alike focused on the future of the monarchy, they increasingly marginalized Henry and his mother's efforts to negotiate peace. Catherine nonetheless worked diligently to preserve Henry's diminishing authority in the face of powerful opposition.

Navarre now had the best claim to the throne. The great obstacle to his succession was his Protestantism. Even if Navarre converted to Catholicism, his conversion had to be accepted as genuine by the pope and French Catholics. At this point, Navarre refused to convert. There was no guarantee that Catholics would accept him even if he converted, and if he did so, he would lose credibility with his Huguenot supporters. The very willingness of Henry III to even acknowledge a Protestant heir to the throne was anathema to many Catholics. The Guises reanimated a much more vehement Catholic League, dedicated to keeping France Catholic and to preventing Navarre from inheriting. Insisting that Catholicism was a fundamental, defining character of the French monarchy, the Catholic League intended to gain the crown for a Catholic claimant.

Guise fomented Catholic agitation in the provinces and sought the support of Philip II of Spain, who agreed to subsidize a new war against the Huguenots. In November 1584, the king charged the League with treason because of its dealings with Spain, but he also tried to satisfy the League by taking harsh measures against the Huguenots.[102] Guise nonetheless signed a formal alliance with Spain the following Christmas. At this point, French Catholics under the leadership of the League worked to undermine the monarchy, and Protestants supported it, since their standard-bearer, Navarre, was now the heir apparent.

This reanimated League was much better organized, more centralized in Paris, and much better funded than its earlier manifestation. Its members supported Charles, the cardinal of Bourbon and Navarre's uncle, as the legitimate, Catholic heir to the throne. The League Manifesto of March 1585 insisted that it would take back the country from heretics and charged that the king's favorites had displaced the traditional nobility. Guise intended to reestablish a unified Catholic kingdom and to impose the articles of the Council of Trent as a foundation for Catholic unity. However, as the Tuscan envoy tellingly noted, "I do not believe their motive is zeal for religion, but vengeance, ambition, and greed."[103]

The League exploited the political situation to their advantage. It launched an effective pamphlet campaign in Paris against the royal family, explicitly attacking Catherine as a heretic. It raised an army and seized French cities with Spanish money and arms. The pope issued special indulgences for its members. When Catherine discovered that Guise's efforts were backed by Spanish soldiers who had entered France through the Low Countries, she demanded an explanation. The League's claimant to the throne, Charles, the cardinal of Bourbon, responded that non-Catholics and favorites would be excluded from power and that Catholicism would be reestablished throughout the kingdom.

Over the course of his reign, Henry became more inclined to defer to his favorites and to shut Catherine out of a more direct role in government, but he again turned to her in this crisis to negotiate with the Guises. Catherine and Henry were both concerned by the unsettled succession. Catherine agreed to try to resolve the stalemate, though she was so ill that she had to be transported by litter. After first refusing to meet with her, Guise finally agreed to a fifteen-day cease-fire. Catherine then offered an agreement she thought would satisfy the League, specifying that all state positions would be reserved for Catholics and that Protestants would have to renounce their faith or leave France. This was far and away the most stringent penalty imposed on French Huguenots, but the League wanted more—a new war against the Huguenots. As the League was popular, militarily successful, and well financed by Spain, Catherine could do little to negate its influence or to restore her son's authority.

Henry capitulated to the League. In July 1585, Catherine signed, in her son's name, a treaty with the cardinal of Bourbon and the duke of Guise, promising to abolish in perpetuity all liberty, even liberty of conscience, for Huguenots, who would be given six months to convert, emigrate, or face merciless repression. This treaty essentially established peace by making Guise the military leader, and the king their captive. As L'Estoile put it, "The king is on foot and the League on horseback."[104] Navarre contended that the treaty put the monarchy in jeopardy and condemned it as "a treaty with the House of Lorraine [the Guises] at the expense of the House of France"—emphatically asserting his legitimacy as heir apparent.[105] The League persuaded Pope Sixtus V to excommunicate Navarre and declare him ineligible to inherit the throne. (Paradoxically, this move increased his popularity, since even Catholics resented Vatican interference in French affairs.) The king, essentially the League's hostage, now faced a war with the Huguenots united under Navarre's leadership. At this tense juncture, Elizabeth I executed Mary Stuart in February 1587.

This event had an especially chilling effect on France. Not only was Mary the Guises' niece and the former queen of France but also one queen had killed another over a plot for treason, which surely gave pause to League members negotiating with foreign powers. The Guises, as relatives of the executed queen, proclaimed her a Catholic martyr and cited her execution as an example of the way Protestants would treat Catholics if they came to power.

Only Catherine, ill, exhausted, and enfeebled by age, lobbied for peace to prevent greater Spanish control of France. The king was in an unenviable position. The success of either the Huguenots or the League would have dire ramifications for him. The League's control of the crown was also a severe setback for the Protestants. The Parlement of Paris registered an edict outlawing Protestantism in France, proclaiming the Protestant princes Navarre and Condé heretics and denying their claim to the crown.

Protestant fortunes dramatically improved with the arrival of German and Swiss forces funded by Elizabeth I. The king, intent on preventing these Protestant forces from joining Navarre's, sent Guise to head off their arrival, but Guise's initial success further enhanced his reputation at the expense of the king's. But when Catholic forces engaged those of Navarre at the battle of Coutras on October 20, 1587, the Protestants achieved a decisive victory.

If the League could not prevail militarily, it could foment opposition to Henry with effective propaganda and mobilize Paris against him. In December 1587, theologians of the Sorbonne went so far as to decree that it was possible to depose a bad king.[106] As the positions of Protestants and Leaguers hardened, Catherine worked to prevent the League and the Guises from appropriating the Catholic position. The ambassador Busbecq wrote to Emperor Rudolf II: "I see that the respect for the majesty of the king has been weakened in a strange manner . . . [his subjects] having shaken off their respect for the name of the king just as animals shake off a strong yoke. . . . If, finally, there be war in France . . . the struggle will not be concerning religion or place or whose opinion ought to prevail or whose popularity will be preferred before the king, or who will manage the kingdom, but clearly who will reign."[107]

Even though Catherine's services were more necessary than ever, Henry relied on her less and accorded his favorites ever greater influence. When he reordered the government, he dismissed the officeholders Catherine had brought into government, dramatically reducing her influence; she still worked for conciliation but without authority or much support. To Bellièvre, she expressed her "regret at the wrong which has been done me in teaching the King that it is right to love his mother, as God commands, but not to give her enough authority and influence to make her able to stop them from doing what they want."[108]

So diminished was the king and so great the authority of the League that its members planned a future after his reign. It would appoint the cardinal of Bourbon, who, as a sixty-year-old clergyman, would probably not reign long and would have no legitimate heir. The League could then elect Henry of Guise. But the success of the Guise faction and the League depended on the financial and military support of Catholic Spain, which was poised to attack England with its powerful fleet—the Armada.

Henry was so fearful of the duke's growing popularity that he surrounded himself with a bodyguard of forty-five men for his own personal protection and forbade Guise to enter Paris. Guise defied him, claiming that he was simply defending his honor. When Catherine warned Henry that a tremendous crowd had gathered in the streets, he put a good face on it and met with Guise at the Louvre. Guise, despite having directly and publicly challenged the king, emerged unscathed. When the king called up the Swiss Guard to defend him, the capital rose against him. "One had never seen or heard of a foreign garrison deployed in Paris," L'Estoile indignantly noted.[109] Many of the Swiss Guard were killed, and the king fled, leaving Catherine to face the outraged Parisians. As Guise supporters took over the city, she negotiated with him as crowds cried "Long live the duke of Guise." The League, emboldened by the news that the Armada had sailed, demanded and received even greater concessions. By the Edict of Union of July 1, 1588, Henry agreed to root out heresy; Leaguers who had fought against him received amnesty; and Guise received the title of lieutenant general. Henry was forced to recognize Charles, the cardinal of Bourbon, as his heir and to convene the Estates-General to plan for war against the Huguenots. A *Te Deum* was sung at Notre Dame to celebrate the edict, and Catherine and the king's wife, Louise, were forced to attend. It was a humiliating reminder that the king had been captured by the League and that all of Catherine's efforts to preserve the independence of the monarchy had failed.

The edict, in essence, allowed Henry to keep his throne but gave political and military authority to the Guises.

The defeat of the Spanish Armada put Henry in a somewhat stronger position, as the League could no longer count on Spanish support. Henry convened the Estates-General, hoping they would support him against the Guises and help to reassert his authority.[110] Instead, the Estates demanded greater power at his expense. Henry's failure to gain their support and their overt challenge to royal authority confirmed his belief, held ever since Paris had risen against him, that the assassination of Guise was the only way to restore his authority. By the time Catherine learned of the plot, she was seriously ill with a lung infection and in no position to influence her son. Guise, who had so successfully defied the king that he no longer saw him as a threat, was easily lured into Henry's chambers at the chateau of Blois and attacked and killed by Henry's personal guard on Christmas Day, 1588. The assassination of Guise was followed immediately by that of his brother, the cardinal of Lorraine. When Henry III announced, "Finally I am the only king," L'Estoile reported that Catherine responded, "What have you done? God willing, it will turn out well for you."[111]

The assassinations, which enraged Catholics, did not enhance the king's political position. The theology faculty of the Sorbonne declared Henry deposed and urged Frenchmen to revolt.[112] The king tried to force the Estates-General to acknowledge his right to assassinate the Guises as threats to royal power, but it refused to sanction his acts. Catherine got up from her deathbed and tried one last time to conciliate the opposition. She approached the cardinal of Bourbon, whom Henry had confined under house arrest, but Bourbon saw her as complicit in Guise's assassination. Having failed in her final attempt to advance the interests of her son and the monarchy, Catherine concluded, "I can do no more" and prepared for death, which came on January 5, 1589.[113]

In his funeral oration, the bishop of Bourges heralded Catherine as "the most noble queen in race and generation who ever reigned in France" and praised her as "the most prudent in her administration, the gentlest in her conversation . . . but above all the most devout toward God."[114] A League preacher, on the other hand, wondered publicly whether Catholics should pray for her, since "she so often supported heresy."[115] The populace of Paris was so hostile that she was not buried at Saint-Denis until 1610, when, ironically, her husband's illegitimate daughter, Diane de France, arranged it.

THE EVIL QUEEN

Even before her death, Catherine had been encapsulated in myth.[116] Following the Saint Bartholomew's Day Massacre, Protestant polemicists leveled many of the defining charges against her as politically unscrupulous and morally reprehensible. These charges served the Huguenots as early as Catherine's regency for Charles IX. Between Charles's death and Henry III's return from Poland, Montmorency-Damville justified taking up arms against foreigners—the Medici and Guise princes of Lorraine. At the same time, *The Marvelous Discourse of the Life, Actions, and Deportment of Queen Catherine de Medici*, attributed to humanist and printer Henri Estienne, charged that Catherine was from a base, merchant family who practiced usury. Completely amoral, she thus allowed the ménage à trois with her husband and his mistress. Plotting against her sons to retain power herself, Catherine had set French history on a disastrous course.[117] In 1576, an exiled French Protestant Innocent Gentillet wrote *Anti-Machiavel*, which accused Catherine and her foreign advisors of the black arts. Pamphlets noted that astrologers had predicted that she would ruin her family, and indicted her, in particular, for having poisoned her brother-in-law, the young prince Francis; plotted the conspiracy of Amboise to destroy the Guises; and used her ladies-in-waiting to debauch her sons and Navarre. She traveled in order to urge Catholics to murder Huguenots and arranged Marguerite's marriage to wipe them out, such texts charged. Others used the particular situation to ground political arguments. François Hotman's *Francogallica* contended that ancient France had been a free state and constitutional monarchy, but it had been undermined by powerful, tyrannical women.[118] Following this theme, other satiric texts compared Catherine to a Turkish potentate, suggesting that the monarchy was both tyrannical and heretical.[119]

These charges against Catherine were articulated initially to undermine her. In the years that followed, they were deployed whenever women held power. It is worth noting that several important historians who lived during Catherine's life and whose histories appeared shortly thereafter, including de Thou and Aubigné, did not contribute to the legend. Perhaps because once Henry IV had, after a decade of warfare, successfully reconciled his countrymen to his reign and gained the throne, Bourbon historians were less concerned with the power of women or did not want to condemn Catherine's conciliation, which closely resembled that of the new king.[120] But her legend had new currency in the eighteenth century. In his *Essay on Manners*, Voltaire condemned Catherine as powerless, inconsistent, and her court as a "bizarre tableau" of "gallantry and fury, voluptuousness and carnage" in the aftermath of Saint Bartholomew's Day, "on which the contradictions of the human species were never [before] painted"—the result of her feminine qualities.[121] Later polemics cited Catherine to condemn Marie Antoinette on the eve of the Revolution.[122] After the French Revolution, Catherine's example reinforced the misogyny directed against women's power, which justified their exclusion from more-democratic governments. In the nineteenth century, the positive image of women was the submissive wife and mother. Representations of Catherine warned against both the powerful woman and the infamous "bad mother."

Fiction allowed authors even freer range to develop these charges against Catherine into a full-blown legend of evil incarnate. In the early seventeenth century, Madame de La Fayette drew on Mézeray's negative history of Catherine in her *Princess of Cleves* to praise the court of Henry II as a model of decorum, but, she claimed, under Catherine it became depraved.[123] Nineteenth-century novelists—Honoré de Balzac, Alexandre Dumas, Prosper Mérimée—looked back to the Renaissance to address their immediate political concerns. The Bourbon Restoration (1814–1830) had heightened interest in the period of the Wars of Religion, especially as the 1814 charter had made Catholicism the state religion and the Chamber of Deputies debated rooting out Protestant elementary schoolteachers in 1822. They thus found this period a particularly useful way to comment on current events. For Mérimée, the massacre was the outcome of religious extremism, and thus the negative example of Catherine warned against the current religious policy. For Balzac, who supported those policies, the massacre was a legitimate exercise of *raison d'état,* which exonerated Catherine.[124] Other novelists, most notably Dumas, sharpened the extreme aspects of her legend. He underscored Catherine's malevolence by emphasizing her superstitious reliance on astrology and poisoning (fig. 5.8).[125]

Catherine holds a firm place in both history and fiction; her power and her legend made her especially useful in casting aspersions on women in power. Surprisingly, Catherine is less of a villain in the canonical histories of the nineteenth and early twentieth centuries than one might expect. Those histories instead assign her a less central role than she actually played in the reigns of her sons. Still malign and Machiavellian, she was less politically influential than others had claimed. For Guizot, Catherine initially showed great promise as Henry II's regent toward the end of his reign but later "ceased to be judicious, dignified, and salutary." During Francis II's reign, neither the "sterling moderation of Chancellor de l'Hôpital" nor "the hypocritical and double-faced attentions paid by Catherine de Medici to both the Catholic and the Protestant leaders" could resolve the political and religious conflict. Note that these are descriptions of the same policy; the queen's motives were evil but her chancellor's were good. Weighing the failure of the age, Guizot concluded, "The great maladies and the great errors of nations require remedies more heroic than the adroitness of a woman." This is a key to Guizot's treatment of Catherine; she was vacillating and incompetent—as one would expect from a woman. Even the Saint Bartholomew's Day Massacre reflected female incompetence rather than moral failings. Catherine's ineptitude meant that its aftermath was characterized by "a confused mass of orders and counter orders, affirmations and denials, words and actions, incoherent and contradictory, all caused by a habit of lying and the desire to escape from the peril or embarrassment of the moment." In essence, Catherine pursued "violent and timorous, incoherent and stubborn" policies.[126]

For Michelet, Catherine was not as influential as her sons or the men who surrounded them. And he warned his readers to mistrust her letters, which presented her too favorably—a deliberately distorted, positive self-presentation.[127] Following his nineteenth-century predecessors, Lavisse condemned Catherine's pursuit of power to contrast her sharply with her heroic chancellor. Hôpital was "a wise and good Frenchman, who believed Protestants should be allowed to practice their religion and that all the French should love each other." For these classic historians, Catherine, fearful that Coligny would usurp her power over her son, determined to kill him. To cover up this plot gone awry, she authorized the massacre, which made her "a wicked woman" who committed "an

Fig. 5.8. This image of the astrologer Cosimo Ruggieri (d. 1615) with Catherine de Medici by J. Lemard (fl. 1913), indicates the persistence of the association of the queen with the occult. Bibliothèque des Arts Décoratifs, Paris / The Bridgeman Art Library.

abominable and cowardly crime." But Lavisse focused on Henry III, a "very bad prince" whose government of favorites led to the end of the Valois. Henry, in effect, pursued the kind of government inaugurated by a woman, and to the same bad effect.[128] Although Catherine's Black Legend persists in the popular histories and imagination, recent histories have appreciated her efforts to save the Valois monarchy.[129] Even the Saint Bartholomew's Day Massacre can be understood as based on clearheaded *raison d'état.*

To balance the persistence of her Black Legend, one must acknowledge the many factors that worked against Catherine's success as queen. She became the power behind the throne only after the unexpected death of her husband. But foreign and female, she had serious liabilities. Not even a royal princess, she came from a family engaged in trade. As such, she could not invoke the mythic elements of Renaissance kingship with much success and so relied instead on a rhetoric of motherhood to anchor her political authority. Catherine also used the full range of Renaissance imagery to present a compelling allegory of her sons' reigns. But such artistic images became less compelling when undermined by both incomprehension and polemical counterarguments.

As the power behind her sons' reigns, Catherine would have faced the inherent instability and concerted noble opposition characteristic of regencies. But her regency inevitably provoked fears in all those wary of the exercise of power by a woman, especially a foreign woman. (Marie de Medici and Anne of Austria later faced the same kind of opposition.) Most importantly, Catherine had to contend with the political and religious complexities wrought by the spread of Protestantism, which further divided the nobility and fueled their opposition. Thus Catherine had to overcome noble opposition and unify religious factions opposing royal authority. Some factions were empowered by a new political ideology that endorsed resistance to a king in the name of religion.

Whenever there was peace, Catherine presented elaborate entertainments to center culture in the court and to both divert and overawe the nobility. She was particularly adept in developing Renaissance motifs in court festivals. She fostered a distinctly French school of painting and directly promoted the careers of Jean and François Clouet, commissioning a large number of family portraits. She brought new arts into the court, including ballet and Italian comedic theater. The Italian cuisine she introduced formed the basis of what we now consider French cooking. She deserves greater recognition as well for her role in bringing science to the court and fostering its role as an agent of the state. During her sons' reigns, the monarchy had a greater presence in Paris, which led to the commissioning of architectural monuments. Much of the Ile Saint-Louis was rescued from landfill to become the site of elegant town homes for royal officeholders, for example. Catherine began a royal building campaign worthy of her father-in-law, Francis I (fig. 5.9). Buildings designed and constructed under her auspices to assert the importance of the monarchy in Paris include a wing of the Louvre, which still exists, and the palaces of the Tuilleries and of the Reines, which no longer do. Catherine and her son Henry III clearly understood that a Renaissance monarch had a responsibility for and interest in the development of French culture. If not for the Wars of Religion, Catherine might be best known not as a Machiavellian queen but rather as a central figure in the development of the Renaissance in France and a worthy successor to Francis I.

One might also wonder how much more politically effective Catherine might have been if even one of her sons had proved capable of ruling. Each not only had fatal flaws but also worked to undermine the others. Notably, her sons were the only French Renaissance kings who ruled with living brothers to challenge their hold on power. Catherine was unable to procure political, religious, or even familial peace. Nonetheless, she well understood the threats posed to the continued rule of her young sons, especially by the Guises. If they controlled her sons, they might wrest the crown from the Valois. Catherine, who likely would have moderated her husband's intransigent stance toward the Protestants in any case, needed to make significant concessions to them to prevent her sons from becoming puppets of the Guises. She has quite frequently been criticized for her failure to acknowledge the intense religious sentiments of both Catholics and Protestants or to understand the theological complexities that divided the adherents of the two religious sects. As a result, she was unfailingly confident that religious differences could be negotiated away in councils or papered over by edicts. Acutely aware of the political danger religious dissent posed, she nonetheless remained unwavering in her pursuit of peace and her belief that peace could be produced by a settlement. Some of Catherine's most appealing qualities were her indefatigable efforts on behalf of peace and her unflagging optimism that it could be achieved. When settlements invariably proved unsatisfactory to Catholics or Protestants, the aggrieved party protesting that too much had been granted to the other, Catherine adopted a policy designed to keep the peace by conciliating all parties. This policy was less and less effective as political and religious positions hardened. Both Protestants and Catholics had cause for grievance, and neither trusted her. Both believed that a weak king could be captured, quite literally, to support their side. Catherine's strategy of trying to balance these forces has frequently been criticized. However, with the exception of her belief that the two warring religious communities could resolve their theological differences, Catherine's failed policies were essentially those followed with much better results by Henry IV. The terms of Henry's great

Fig. 5.9. A design for a tapestry of Catherine de Medici as part of a series on the history of Queen Artemis, one of the associations Catherine wanted to reinforce. In this particular image, Catherine, as Artemis, is meeting with artists. The background shows their work and emphasizes Catherine's role as a patron. BnF.

Edict of Nantes were already included in Catherine's earlier edicts. Henry IV, to his great credit, was able to enforce his edict and make it the foundation of a lasting religious peace. But Henry did not have the blood of Saint Bartholomew's Day on his hands, which had so compromised Catherine's efforts to conciliate religious and political dissent.

Catherine's difficulties in effecting her policies must also be set in the context of the international struggle between Catholics and Protestants across the European continent. During the second half of the sixteenth century, France was *the* crucial battleground. Noble opposition, religious division, and shifting international alliances complicated the entire period when Catherine played her role as the most significant power behind the throne. Her sons all relied on her, but Catherine was not the only influence on them: Francis II was captured by the

Guises; Charles IX was influenced by Coligny and the Protestants; Henry III was frequently under the influence of his *mignons* and was eventually merely the Guises' figurehead king. Catherine is blamed for their failings and gets little credit for ultimately preserving the inheritance of her sons or as a good queen dedicated to preserving the French monarchy. A surprisingly sympathetic assessment of Catherine was given by Henry IV, as recorded by Claude Groulart, the president of the Parlement of Normandy. The king reputedly said of her in 1599: "But I ask you, what could the poor woman do, left with five children to provide for after the death of her husband, and with two families, ourselves and the Guises, who thought about usurping the crown. Wasn't it necessary that she play many roles to fool both while protecting her children, who reigned one after the other, thanks to the guidance of so shrewd a woman? I am surprised that she never did worse!"[130]

Catherine understood the Wars of Religion as an intense political contest and her quest to preserve the throne for her sons as enmeshed in domestic and international political and religious dissent. The survival of the monarchy was due to a significant degree to her efforts at conciliating feuding factions. She tried to restore the monarchy to its strength under Henry II and, in so doing, passed it on to Henry IV. Although she aspired to the power of a centralizing monarch, neither the abilities of her sons nor the conditions of the time allowed her to succeed. Catherine, nonetheless, asserted the necessity of the personal dominance of the king, which monarchs with absolutist pretensions later implemented. She tried to use the court to control the nobility and to dissipate dissent, and she clearly saw it as an institution that could foster a monarch's authority. Her aspirations foreshadow Louis XIV's effective control of the court at Versailles. Catherine's valiant efforts were often undermined by her children, for whom the political turmoil of the day unfolded not simply within a political crisis but also a contested family dynamic.

SIGNIFICANT DATES FOR CHAPTER 6

1553	Birth of Marguerite de Valois, May 14
1569	Marguerite acts as her brother Henry's agent
1572	Marguerite's marriage to Henry of Navarre, August 18
	Saint Bartholomew's Day Massacre, August 24
1574	Marguerite plots with her husband and her brother Francis
1575–1576	Marguerite under surveillance in the Louvre
1577	Marguerite's mission to Flanders for her brother Francis
1578	Marguerite travels to Navarre
1580	Marguerite meets Champvallon
1582	Marguerite returns to court
1584	Return to Nérac
	Death of Francis, June 10
1585	Marguerite flees to Agen and then to Carlat
1586	Marguerite incarcerated at Usson
1589	Death of Catherine de Medici
	Assassination of Henry III, August 2
1593	Henry IV begins annulment discussions with Marguerite
1594	Marguerite writes her *Mémoires*
1598	Edict of Nantes, April 15
1599	Marguerite's marriage annulled
1605	Marguerite returns to Paris
1610	Henry IV assassinated, May 14
	Death of Marguerite, May 27

6

Marguerite de Valois

Scandalous Queen, *Femme Savante*

Marguerite de Valois, daughter of Henry II and Catherine de Medici, wife of Henry IV and, more popularly, the notorious "Queen Margot," was a most unusual queen of France. Queen by virtue of her marriage to Henry IV, she was estranged from him before he became king. An accomplished princess, political actor, and renowned intellectual, she may also be one of the most maligned women in French history. *The Satiric Divorce*, a pamphlet published in 1660, defined an image of Marguerite that has prevailed for centuries, of a woman of deranged, aberrant sexuality. This pamphlet purports to be an account by the long-suffering Henry IV of the trials he endured because of his wife's promiscuity. In it he complained that when Charles IX married Marguerite to him, saying he was giving her to the Huguenots, he should have explained that he meant it literally, since she was so indiscriminate in satisfying her sexual appetites. She traveled widely, the pamphlet charged, to pursue sexual depravity with greater liberty, and the monastery she supported should have registered as a brothel. The pamphlet legitimated the annulment of their marriage on the grounds of her "monstrous lubricity" and listed fifteen of her lovers, including all of her brothers.[1]

This lurid account is the source of many stories told about Marguerite. It has had enduring credibility largely because it has been assumed for centuries that the distinguished humanist, historian, and Henry's staunch Huguenot supporter Théodore Agrippa d'Aubigné was its author. (This text is still most readily found in his collected works.) Recent studies challenge this account, positing less authoritative authors, offering political motives for its charges, and suggesting that many of Marguerites's supposed sexual partners were actually political allies.[2] Ultimately, the pamphlet may be better understood as personal vendetta or political propaganda than history. Nonetheless, the flagrantly promiscuous woman Henry was forced to divorce for her degrading sexuality remains the most prominent view of Marguerite.

In his nineteenth-century novel *Queen Margot,* Alexandre Dumas mythologized the charges of indiscriminate sexual activity, accepting as true Marguerite's avid pursuit of anonymous sex in the streets of Paris but depicting her as redeemed by her love for Joseph Boniface, lord of La Molle. Dumas's novel and many other fictional works, including *La Reine Margot,* the recent French movie based on the novel, reinforced the most salacious elements of Valois myths.[3] To mention just a few: According to myth, Catherine's ladies-in-waiting were a group of prostitutes able to bend men to her diabolical political purposes; Catherine poisoned Navarre's mother, Jeanne d'Albret, and all other political enemies who died unexpectedly at the Valois court. In addition, all Valois family relations were completely depraved, and Marguerite had incestuous relations with all of her brothers and indiscriminately took lovers from all walks of life, keeping the hearts of those who met untimely ends in the pockets of her voluminous petticoats. Fiction both perpetuated and exaggerated the inflammatory charges of *The Satiric Divorce.*

In sharp contrast to these stories, Marguerite's contemporaries extolled her as unusually beautiful and accomplished. Montaigne, the great sixteenth-century essayist, dedicated the first edition of his *Essays* to her. She was, like her great-aunt of the same name, a writer of some distinction, the patroness of an academy, and a serious student of Neoplatonic philosophy. She is yet another royal woman who exerted an important cultural influence. But even if not to the degree detailed in her myth, Marguerite acted on her sexual desires. Perhaps most disconcerting to her contemporaries, Marguerite took political action, behaving more as if she were a royal son than a daughter.

Setting Marguerite's actions in the political context and the royal family dynamic not only complicates the simplistic sexuality of her myth but also exposes the frustrations that awaited an elite woman who attempted to act independently of male support. Intent on preserving the crown for her sons, Catherine used her daughters to serve political interests, as was conventional with all royal daughters. But Marguerite sought a direct political role by allying with one brother or another, supporting her husband, or attempting to mediate between factions. Ultimately she helped to effect the transition from the Valois to the Bourbon dynasty, not least by saving Navarre's life in the immediate aftermath of the Saint Bartholomew's Day Massacre. When Marguerite died, she was not initially demonized as sexually promiscuous but rather praised for her grace and learning and appreciated for her cultural activities. Her life and her legend thus offer disparate and multifaceted views of this intriguing woman.

A ROYAL CHILDHOOD

Marguerite, the seventh child of Henry II and Catherine de Medici, was born in 1553 just outside Paris at Saint-Germain-en-Laye, a favorite country residence of her family. She experienced an idyllic childhood in the Valois court during the fullest flowering of the French Renaissance. In her memoirs, Marguerite remembered her father especially fondly, telling a story of his teasing her about which young courtier she would marry. She chose the marquis of Beaupréau over the prince of Joinville [Henry of Guise] because "the prince is always making mischief and will be master over everybody." Even as a child, she claimed, she was at odds with her brother Henry because she resisted his early efforts to convert her to Protestantism. Her brothers figured large in her young life because her sisters married early and went abroad, while she remained at the French court. These childhood stories underscored her forthright character, wisdom, and staunch Catholicism, which subsequent events would corroborate. As she put it, "They [the stories] gave proof of the early ripeness of my judgment and my courage."[4] These particular stories also forecast the complex role these two Henrys—Henry of Guise and Henry III—would play in her life.

At the age of six, Marguerite attended her sister Elisabeth's wedding by proxy to the king of Spain as part of the Treaty of Cateau-Cambrésis. Her father's mortal wound at the celebratory tournament and his subsequent death altered her childhood as well as the future of France. In September 1559, her fifteen-year-old brother was crowned Francis II. Just a year later, Marguerite witnessed the mass executions, bodies hanging from the parapets of Amboise, following the conspiracy whereby some Huguenots tried to wrest the young king from the Guises' control. A year later, when she was seven, Marguerite attended the Estates-General meeting that proclaimed her mother as regent for the new king Charles IX.

Much of what we know about Marguerite's early years is gleaned from her memoirs, which were probably written about 1594.[5] They treat her life from childhood until her return to the French court in 1582 but were not published until 1628, thirteen years after her death. Written from a mature perspective rather than that of the young woman living through these dramatic events, her memoirs end before the denouement of the Wars of Religion. Equally significant, they were written after all other members of her immediate family were dead. She could thus tell her story more freely, recast her own actions in a more favorable light, and depict the past as portentous. Significant events receive scant attention as she focused on the drama of her life. She presented herself as an engaged and principled young woman, and, most notably, as a conscientious, credible actor in the Wars of Religion and a loyal supporter of Henry IV. This perspective was deliberate; she wrote her memoirs as Henry was trying to claim the throne and as she, isolated in Usson, was seeking his permission to return to Paris. Despite these caveats, Marguerite's memoirs remain a crucial source about her life.

With the outbreak of the Wars of Religion in 1562, Marguerite and her youngest brother, Hercules (later renamed Francis), were sent to Amboise (see fig. 2.5). With peace, she joined her family on their tour of France (1564–1566), during which Catherine courted the Hapsburgs, hoping to arrange marriages for both Charles IX and Marguerite. Marguerite was both attractive and accomplished. Although her education was rather haphazard, she had acquired a reputation for learning, on several occasions amazing her audiences with her abilities in Latin.[6] Fluent in Spanish and Italian, she was well-read, even learned, in French. Marguerite nonetheless found her education deficient and worked assiduously to overcome its superficialities.

As Marguerite came of age, she was heralded as a young woman of stunning beauty and great refinement. Don Juan, who detoured in his travels specifically to see her, proclaimed, "The beauty of that princess is more divine than human, but she is made to damn and ruin men rather than to save them." A Neapolitan nobleman delayed his trip home for several months saying, "If I had returned without seeing this princess, I could hardly have claimed to have seen France" (fig. 6.1).[7]

Her beauty and intelligence may have made her an attractive spouse, but they gave her no greater autonomy than any other princess. Instead, the need to balance alliances with Protestant and Catholic powers complicated her marriage negotiations and made them crucial to Charles IX's foreign diplomacy. Later, as her brothers Henry and Francis jockeyed for position and exploited Charles's weakness and declining health, they recruited Marguerite to serve their ends.

Marguerite experienced her first heady taste of politics when Henry asked her to protect his interests while he was on military campaign, reporting that he needed "a confidential person about the Queen my mother, who shall always be ready to espouse and support my cause." He enlisted Marguerite, telling her: "I know no one more proper for that than you or as attentive to my interest as I should be myself. You have wit, discretion, and fidelity." Marguerite clearly relished her role as a political player. "His [Henry's] words inspired me

Fig. 6.1. Marguerite de Valois as a young woman, ca. 1572, by François Clouet. Musée Crozatier, Le Puy-en-Velay/The Bridgeman Art Library.

with resolution and powers I did not think I possessed before. I had naturally a degree of courage, and, as soon as I recovered from my astonishment, I found I was quite an altered person."[8] Marguerite would be neither passive spectator nor mere supporter.

One key to Marguerite's tempestuous family relationships was her willingness, indeed eagerness, to play a political role. She passionately threw herself into any venture suggested to her. As a result, her brothers used her against each other. An eager ally, she often effectively carried out others' projects but without sufficient self-interest. Her brother Henry proved to be especially adept at manipulating her, but her mother, husband, and brothers all used her to serve their interests. It is telling that these family relationships are appropriately described in political terms. They had political ramifications and unfolded with the ruthlessness of war.

Marguerite's service to her brother Henry quickly came to naught. When Louis de Berenger, the baron de Guast, reported to Henry that she was corresponding with Henry of Guise, it precipitated the first crisis of her young life. This correspondence was likely a mere flirtation, although the legend of the sexually overcharged Margot posited Guise as her first lover. But no matter how innocuous the relationship might have been, any rumor tarnished her value on the royal marriage market. Although Marguerite claimed that Guast invented the story, and described him as "born to do evil," her interest in Guise fueled gossip in European courts.[9] When Henry warned his mother not to trust her, Marguerite felt unjustly betrayed. She expected Henry to be grateful for her service, but he, allied with Guast, treated her coldly.

The handsome, charismatic Guise might well have attracted Marguerite, and a relationship with her would have been politically advantageous for him. In fact, his relative, the cardinal of Lorraine, had been advocating their marriage. But there were pressing political reasons for Catherine to intervene: She was hoping to arrange Marguerite's marriage to a Catholic prince. More importantly, any increase in the Guises' power diminished the crown's authority. Marguerite's suspected impropriety led Charles IX and Catherine to beat her and to send Guise from court. Their harsh response reveals the royal family's control and the primacy of a daughter's reputation to her value on the marriage market. (When Guise immediately married Catherine of Cleves, Marguerite reported that she urged him to do so to dissipate her mother's anger.)[10]

Immediately after her disgrace, Marguerite fell gravely ill. She saw the illness as a reaction to the alienation of her mother's affection. Their relationship was somewhat repaired by her mother's conscientious care. Marguerite ultimately blamed Guast for her disgrace. In her account, he was a vindictive Machiavellian, jealous of her political influence.[11] This denunciation expressed Marguerite's frustration that both her political activities and personal desires had been stymied by Guast's talebearing—her independence denied and her brother and mother's authority violently imposed.

MARRIAGE PLANS

Marguerite's rumored correspondence with Guise derailed her mother's marriage negotiations with Sebastian of Portugal. Despite his value in cementing a Catholic alliance for France, the sickly Sebastian was an especially unappealing prospective spouse for the beautiful not-yet-twenty-year-old princess. The papal envoy reported that the monks who tutored him "have made the king conceive a perfect horror of women."[12] Catherine then proposed a Spanish marriage to Charles, the son of Philip II of Spain by his first wife. (Marguerite's sister Elisabeth was Philip's second wife. Catherine even later proposed, after Elisabeth's death, that Marguerite take her sister's place.) Charles, an epileptic with a hunched back and a stammer, was another unattractive groom. Plans for even this inauspicious union were thwarted when the duke of Alba reported Marguerite's correspondence with Guise.[13] In her memoirs, admittedly written some thirty years later, Marguerite proclaimed her willingness to serve her mother's political aims by accepting any spouse she proposed.[14]

Even mothers whose own marriages were difficult because their husbands did not return their love, like Catherine's, arranged their daughters' marriages solely for political advantage. For royal daughters, the personal inevitably bowed to the political. And Marguerite's memoirs consistently portray her as a dutiful daughter despite her often-contentious relationship with her mother.

Catherine then dramatically reversed course and arranged Marguerite's marriage to Henry, the Protestant king of Navarre to balance Charles's marriage to the Catholic Elizabeth of Austria (fig. 6.2). Although Navarre's staunchly Protestant mother, Jeanne d'Albret, ultimately agreed to the marriage, she warned her son that his prospective bride, while beautiful, had been raised in a dissolute court. "Not for anything on earth would I want you come to live there. Although I knew it [the corruption] was great, I find it even greater. There, it is not men who prey on women, but women who prey on men. If you were here, you would never escape without special intervention from God."[15]

The wedding was a most peculiar affair. The bride attended Mass, her Protestant groom waited outside, and, according to some accounts, the bride wept

Fig. 6.2. Henry of Navarre and Marguerite de Valois as king and queen of Navarre about the time of their wedding. BnF.

throughout the ceremony. The evening celebration featured a ballet in which the bride's brothers defended Paradise against the bridegroom and other Huguenots who, depicted as devils, were defeated and sent back to hell. This allegorical depiction was perhaps not the most conciliatory message to forge peace, even though the heretics were ultimately rescued from hell by angels played by Catherine's sons.[16] The ballet was intended to represent Protestant-Catholic reconciliation and hopes for peace. But those hopes were immediately nullified by the Saint Bartholomew's Day Massacre.

Marguerite expressed little emotional reaction in her memoirs to either her wedding or the massacre, even though these linked events were so pivotal to her life and the Valois monarchy. Marguerite excused Catherine's complicity in manipulating Charles to authorize the attack on Huguenot leaders as due to her fear that the Huguenots would assassinate the royal family. Mistrusted by both Catholic and Protestant, Marguerite had no advance knowledge of the impending massacre. Her mother sent her to bed, as her sister Claude, who knew about the plot, "dissolved in tears." Marguerite thus suggested that her mother put her at risk to avoid arousing Huguenot suspicions. Later Marguerite and Navarre, roughly roused from sleep, were ordered from their beds. As the violence penetrated even the halls of the Louvre, Marguerite protected wounded Huguenots and interceded with the king to save some of her husband's closest associates.[17]

Immediately after the massacre, Marguerite sought Catherine's reassurance that her marriage had not been deliberately arranged to facilitate it. Marguerite was apparently willing to wed for reasons of state but not to provide a cover for political assassination, or so she insisted in her memoirs, which placed her on the side of the massacre's intended victims. Most importantly, she maintained, her actions alone saved her husband's life. When her mother pressured her to have her marriage annulled, presumably so that Navarre could be added to the list of targeted Huguenot leaders, Marguerite refused to repudiate her marriage and thus saved him. To her mother's pressure to end her marriage, Marguerite responded, "I am content to remain as I am."[18] Her support for Navarre demonstrated her loyalty and her honor, or so her memoirs insist.

Both Marguerite's and Navarre's circumstances had obviously been altered for the worse by the massacre. The initial hope that the marriage might reconcile a Huguenot leader to the Valois monarchy and so forge peace had been completely destroyed. Any increase in status or independence Marguerite might have enjoyed as a wife had been negated. Although his marriage protected his life, Navarre was even more seriously disadvantaged than his bride. He was a prince humbled by his forced conversion to Catholicism but mistrusted by Catholics. His associates had been massacred with the cooperation and likely direct involvement of the royal family. He and his wife were now essentially under house arrest in the Louvre.

FRACTURED FAMILY (1574–1578)

The Saint Bartholomew's Day Massacre, as we have seen, derailed prospects for peace. It also heightened the intense competition between Catherine's sons. As Charles IX's health sharply declined, Francis and Navarre served as rallying points for discontent. Henry's likely accession worried both moderate Catholics and Protestants, as he was too closely allied with the Guises.[19] In February 1574, Francis and Navarre plotted their escape from court and, according to contemporary rumors, worked to prevent Henry from assuming the throne should the king die. Francis seemed capable of leading a party in alliance with Navarre and his cousin Condé, the other Huguenot prince of the blood.

Marguerite responded favorably to Francis's attempts to recruit her to serve his interests: "Now that he had made the first advances, in so respectful and affectionate a manner, I resolved to receive him into a firm friendship and to interest myself in whatever concerned him."[20] Again Marguerite's memoirs present her as an insightful person and loyal ally.[21] But when she learned of the plot, she informed her mother but urged that the plotters face no recrimination, doubtless trying to remain in everyone's good graces.

When Navarre and Francis again plotted to flee and that plot too was exposed, their confederates, Joseph Boniface de La Molle and Hyacinthe-Boniface de Anibal de Coconat, became scapegoats. On this occasion, Charles, at Catherine's urging, took a harsher line. He accused La Molle and Coconat of suborning the two princes to undermine his authority.[22] Charles pardoned Francis and Navarre but condemned the two nonroyal conspirators to death for treason. They were executed and their bodies displayed to deter future dissent.

According to Marguerite's legend, she was romantically involved with La Molle.[23] This attachment, as with many of the lovers attributed to her, is supported by bits of contemporary gossip, some subsequent historical speculation, and fictional accounts. If she was, he was the first of her presumed lovers after her marriage. Francis might have used La Molle to attract her to his cause, or Marguerite might have feigned a relationship with La Molle to allow Navarre to escape. Her memoirs do not corroborate a relationship but simply report his death perfunctorily. But her text is characteristically discreet; any explicit discussion of a sexual relationship would have been beyond the pale. Marguerite justified her involvement in this plot on political grounds, insisting that she "acted to impede the bad effect which could have brought so much evil to them [presumably Navarre and Francis] and to the state."[24]

When Parlement investigated Navarre's involvement in the plot, Marguerite wrote the "Supporting Statement for Henry of Bourbon" to defend him. She described the history of faithful relations between the house of Navarre and the royal family and then justified Navarre's attempts to flee with Francis in fear for their lives. To corroborate these fears, Marguerite cited rumors of a "second Saint Bartholomew's," threats that any son she might bear would be killed, and suspicions that Navarre would be imprisoned in Vincennes. With great persuasive force, this text expressed Navarre's grief at his friends' demise in the massacre; they had, after all, come to celebrate his wedding with the crown's assurance of safety. Navarre now doubted such guarantees, especially since the queen and her son granted the Guises privileged access. Conceding that Navarre had plotted to escape, the document insisted that he acted justifiably to save Francis's life (and his own).[25]

In this text on which Navarre's future or even life might have depended, Marguerite's arguments were sufficiently compelling that he avoided punishment. She reported with great delight that the commissioners were astonished to find her text so well prepared.[26] The text stands up to modern scrutiny. Navarre's recent biographer, Jean-Pierre Babelon, cited it as the product of "an expert pen and a brilliant spirit."[27] It attests to Marguerite's zest for a political role. In this instance, Navarre treated her as a reliable political ally. (He had, of course, lost most of his other allies in the massacre.)

Charles's death liberated Navarre from house arrest, but Marguerite contended that with his death she "lost in him all that I could lose."[28] The sentiment was less an expression of grief than dread of Henry's return from Poland, when she would pay a price for her collusion with Francis and Navarre. Just as Marguerite made Guast the villain responsible for her early disgrace, so too in the looming crisis with her brother Henry, now the king, she again blamed Guast. She did not admit that she had plotted with Francis and her husband to escape or even possibly to alter royal succession at Henry's expense. Instead, she claimed, she had supported them because of the ills done to her by Guast.[29]

Marguerite's correspondence undermines this exculpation. It reveals instead that she was on good terms with Henry until the winter of 1573, when she shifted her allegiance with the sudden decline in Charles IX's health. This shift was likely based on her assessment of her future political prospects. If Henry became king, the Guises would return, the Wars of Religion would resume, and Marguerite's own position would be so compromised that a future political role for her would be inconceivable. If instead Francis succeeded in altering the royal succession, she would become an indispensable link between Francis's moderate Catholic supporters and her husband's Huguenot supporters.[30] Marguerite could not convincingly cloak her alliance with one brother and betrayal of another with noble or even defensible motives, so her memoirs offer no rationale for her disloyalty to Henry. They instead consistently present her as a loyal, conscientious actor on the political stage, occasionally undone by the deeds of others—in this case, again by the perfidy of Guast.[31]

Once Henry III became king, Marguerite suffered the consequences of her disloyalty. Marguerite, Navarre, and Francis were all confined to the Louvre. Henry was determined to punish Marguerite for allying with Francis against him and chose to retaliate by attacking her reputation. He linked her with Charles de Balzac, baron d'Entragues, and reported this relationship to Catherine (another example of siblings telling tales to their mother), and tried to provoke her husband's jealousy. Marguerite insisted that her brother manufactured this relationship to discredit her.[32] And both he and her mother eventually apologized to her for the calumny against her.[33] Such episodes amply demonstrate the siblings' personal as well as political antagonism.

Marguerite's implacable enemy Guast remained Henry's trusted advisor. At the time, Guast was romantically involved with Charlotte de Baune, baroness de Sauve, one of Catherine de Medici's ladies-in-waiting, who was also being pursued by both Marguerite's husband and her brother Francis.[34] Catherine deployed her ladies-in-waiting to good political effect as part of her network of spies. Catherine's Black Legend—which transformed these women, referred to as the "flying squadron," into a group of especially adept prostitutes—is not entirely credible, despite Sauve's many romances. Catherine banished from her court any lady-in-waiting whose sexual activity was exposed by pregnancy and insisted on proper behavior.[35] But she did use these women to advance her political interests and likely had earlier used Sauve to report on Navarre during Marguerite's marriage negotiations. Now Sauve put Catherine's son Francis and son-in-law at odds, thwarting their united opposition to the king and separating Marguerite from both of them.[36]

With the foreshadowing Marguerite frequently used as a narrative device in her memoirs, she noted that this "abominable plan" was the source of many evils. When Sauve persuaded Navarre that his jealous wife might betray him, Marguerite contended that "mistrust was a forerunner of hatred," pointing the reader toward future conflicts and the alienation of affection between husband

and wife.[37] Her husband's loyalty had been subverted by his interest in Sauve, suggesting to Marguerite that Navarre was personally and politically disloyal, that he could be manipulated by her enemies, and that he would pursue his own political interests without regard for her.

When Marguerite recruited Louis de Clemont, lord of Bussy d'Amboise, away from Henry's circle to Francis's cause, the king again condemned their relationship as inappropriate. Bussy d'Amboise was a brilliant, dangerous figure. With great military successes to his credit, he was much admired by his contemporaries. Brantôme proclaimed him as the nonpareil of his century.[38] That such an admired figure now numbered among Francis's gentlemen made him a threat to Henry, who was trying to drive his brother's supporters from court. Unlike some linked to Marguerite, this relationship seems credible. She expressed admiration for him: "He was born to be the terror of his enemies, the glory of his masters, and the hope of his friends." The king, with Guast's connivance, attempted to expose her relationship with Bussy d'Amboise with such glaring evidence that Navarre would be forced to repudiate her. But Navarre was either not perturbed or not persuaded of her infidelity. And Marguerite praised her husband's "amiable disposition."[39] Catherine commented on the situation with unusual moderation: "My daughter is unfortunately born in such a century. In my younger days, we were allowed to converse freely with everyone. . . . Bussy d'Amboise is a person of quality. What grounds are there for such calumny?"[40]

Nonetheless, Marguerite likely began a sexual relationship with Bussy d'Amboise by the spring of 1575, when their relationship was widely rumored. (Both her most sympathetic and her most critical biographers agree.)[41] The rumors were lent credence when Navarre's men united with the king's men to attack him. If Marguerite neither feared her husband nor was much concerned with honor, it may have been because she saw her status as higher than his; and Bussy d'Amboise had high enough status to be an acceptable lover of a royal princess. Navarre was likely more seriously aggrieved that Marguerite now served her brother Francis's interests rather than his.[42] She had retaliated for Navarre's personal and political disloyalty. In this family saga, any personal relationship inevitably had political ramifications.

This first public disagreement between Navarre and Marguerite was likely less about adultery than politics. Their marriage seems never to have been a love match. A story circulated that Marguerite felt such aversion for Navarre that she had to be shoved to blurt out "I do" during their wedding. But Marguerite actually knew Navarre quite well before their marriage; he had been at court from 1557 until he joined the Huguenots in 1568.[43] Her supposed aversion might derive from the striking differences between them their contemporaries could not fail to note. Reared as the product of a sophisticated court, Marguerite was accustomed to the finest that Renaissance culture had to offer. Navarre, in contrast, had been brought up in a rustic court with a rather austere Protestant sensibility; he was "neither fastidious in his person nor circumspect in his habits."[44] His clothes were often worn and dirty, and he rarely bathed. As the historian R. J. Knecht baldly noted, "He reputedly stank like carrion."[45] Navarre's sexual exploits became legendary, and his appetites indiscriminate. As another historian has remarked with some bemusement, Marguerite and Navarre "did not enjoy together what each found pleasurable and rewarding in different company."[46] Ultimately they both had reputations for the pursuit of sexual pleasure but not with each other. This reputation defamed Marguerite but proclaimed Navarre's virility.

Both parties at this time were involved with others, so much so that the modern historian Jacqueline Boucher suggests that they agreed to mutual adultery.[47] According to the standards of the day, Navarre, like other noblemen, was allowed, perhaps even encouraged, to vaunt his female conquests. Marguerite, on the other hand, could pursue such relationships only if she was completely discreet and no hint of scandal touched her. It is telling that, according to her memoirs, her conduct was blameless; rather she suffered from her brother's repeated attempts to sully her reputation.

The case of Marguerite suggests an evolving standard of sexual behavior toward greater tolerance of the discreet affairs of elite women. This sense is corroborated by memoirs, novels, and even confessors' manuals, which allowed married women "secret sins" if their husbands' honor remained protected.[48] But a queen's behavior had to be above suspicion to guarantee the legitimacy of her children, and Marguerite had not yet produced an heir.

Henry's attempts to discredit his sister were not simply malicious; he wanted to derail the growing political opposition coalescing around his younger brother. He was also diverting his critics from their attacks on his male favorites. Bussy d'Amboise not only offered an alternative, strong male model of the courtier, he also ridiculed Henry's *mignons.* Once again, Henry was especially concerned that Marguerite was working with Francis against him. Navarre, still under house arrest, remarked: "At court we are all ready to kill each other."[49] Marguerite's memoirs expose the period after Henry ascended the throne as filled with contentious family battles fueled by conflicting political agendas. The reverse was equally true—political conflicts played out in family feuds.

At this time, Marguerite reported that her husband had a fit and lost consciousness, a condition she attributed to "his excesses with women." Navarre credited his recovery to her care, and she noted, "treated me with more kindness." Although Marguerite periodically expressed grievance at Navarre's neglect, she enjoyed several periods of curious harmony and even affectionate relations with him during their generally inharmonious marriage. Francis acknowledged to Marguerite that, in this disagreement, he and Navarre had been outmaneuvered by Henry, who had successfully fomented dissension between them. As a result, according to Marguerite, he [Navarre] "resolved to love me and give me greater contentment with him."[50] Their rapprochement was fleeting and insubstantial. Almost twenty years later, in his annulment proceedings, Navarre testified that in the seven months before he fled the court in February 1576, he and his wife had shared a bed without talking, feigning reconciliation to avoid scandal.[51]

When Francis finally escaped house arrest, he became a rallying point for opposition to Henry III. When the king was forced to recognize that he could not fight both his brother and the Protestants, he reconciled with Francis. But, as Marguerite noted, this reconciliation had successfully separated the interests of her husband and Francis. When Navarre too escaped from court, expressing his regret at leaving Marguerite without saying good-bye, he declared himself a Huguenot again and rallied Huguenot opponents of the crown. Henry accused Marguerite of aiding Navarre's escape and, as a result, kept her a virtual prisoner. Henry was so intent on vengeance that Marguerite credited only Catherine's intervention with saving her life.[52]

Left alone under virtual house arrest in the Louvre, the twenty-three-year-old Marguerite turned to intellectual pursuits, a pattern that would characterize her entire life. She became one of the nine muses of the Countess of Retz's Salon Vert (Green Salon), which focused on poetry, especially Petrarchan sonnets. She also attended meetings of Henry III's Palace Academy and began her lifelong study of Neoplatonic philosophy.

MISSION TO FLANDERS (1577)

As we have seen, neither the Huguenots nor the Catholics were satisfied by the peace, which temporarily reconciled the two feuding brothers. The formation of a Catholic League to overturn it led to war, with the crown allied with the League against Navarre. Her position at court increasingly untenable, Marguerite proposed to take the waters at Spa, in the Low Countries. Her pretext was seeking treatment for a skin inflammation, but this trip covered a diplomatic mission undertaken at Francis's behest. Cultivating a base of political power in Flanders, Francis recruited Marguerite to test the waters.

On this trip, Marguerite not only served her brother's interest but also enjoyed her mother's rare support. Catherine encouraged this venture so that Francis, if he gained a crown of his own, might cease to foment opposition to his brother. Marguerite found it gratifying to be considered important enough to undertake this mission, reassuring her mother, "I would never prefer my own well-being to that of my brothers or this state."[53]

At every stop, Marguerite was greeted with elaborate festivities held to welcome her. She was making the case to Flanders of the advantages of French support in its battle against Spain. When Don Juan, Charles V's illegitimate son and the new Spanish governor of the Low Countries, entertained her, Marguerite assumed she had charmed him.

But Marguerite's position in Flanders took a dramatic turn for the worse. Don Juan violated the truce that he had signed with the Estates of Flanders, provoking hostilities in the very area Marguerite had to cross. Indeed, the mere appearance of her cortege was enough to provoke popular uprisings along her route. Fleeing to safety, Marguerite faced a flooded river, an insurrection of citizens who believed that she had betrayed them by allying with the Spanish, and rumors that Don Juan's soldiers were coming to arrest her.

Marguerite nonetheless saw this venture as a great success that furthered her brother's aspirations in Flanders. She had recruited some nobles to Francis's cause. It was now up to him to raise an army to challenge the Spanish there. A mere footnote in the histories of the period, this mission is highly significant in her memoirs. Marguerite reveled in her reception in Flanders, where she was honored as the daughter, sister, and wife of kings, and, she believed, taken seriously in the political and diplomatic spheres. Having served her brother Francis well, the two siblings were united in their opposition to their older brother.

Although modern historians have been rather dismissive of Francis, many of his contemporaries considered him a rising star, the likely next heir to the French crown, or perhaps even the usurper of his brother's throne.[54] But most of his political ventures were unsuccessful, and his allies often found him unreliable. Willing to seize any opportunity, Francis invariably took entirely pragmatic political positions and was never staunch in support of a religious or political cause. In this case, he lost interest in Flanders when his mother proposed a Spanish marriage. (He could not aid the resistance against Spain in Flanders.) But he, like many younger royal brothers, had no clearly defined role and became a source of dissension.

Even if Francis was inconstant, Marguerite remained his staunch ally from the time of the Saint Bartholomew's Day Massacre, describing him as a "perfect knight." After this mission, she returned to Paris and again supported Francis in his conflicts with Henry's *mignons*. When Henry again detained Francis in the Louvre, Marguerite helped him escape. Implicated, she denied involvement, even though Francis had descended by rope from the palace and Marguerite was caught burning a rope in her fireplace. Francis's escape left her completely isolated.[55] Her memoirs are completely and uncharacteristically silent about this six-month period. Her circumstances were likely uncongenial enough that being queen *in* Navarre began to seem attractive. She would have high status in a new setting where she might play a more significant role.

Over the more than two years of their separation, Navarre had repeatedly requested that his wife be returned to him, largely to ensure that she serve his interests rather than Francis's. But the king refused to allow it. He claimed that Marguerite was married to a Catholic, not a heretic, referring to Navarre's coerced conversion to Catholicism after the Saint Bartholomew's Day Massacre. Marguerite too complained that she was being denied her rights as a wife and asked to rejoin her husband.[56] When Henry sought peace with Navarre, he finally agreed to return his wife. As Marguerite left Paris, she no doubt had mixed feelings. For better or ill, she was now traveling to a remote area full of Protestants to rejoin her husband after a long separation. But she began this journey with her mother's full approval.[57]

QUEEN IN NAVARRE (1579–1582)

Catherine accompanied her daughter on the long and difficult journey south. They left on August 2, 1578, ostensibly to unite Marguerite and her husband and to negotiate a peace between the two kings. The journey also allowed Catherine to assess the Huguenot threat. Marguerite saw herself as a mediator between her husband and the king: "I am determined to do everything in my power for him [the king] in whatever will not be prejudicial to the greatness and maintenance of my husband . . . in order to persuade him [Navarre] always toward peace . . . for I would prefer death to war."[58] Marguerite could see her role as serving peace and thus the best interest of her brother, mother, and husband. On this particular mission, she was not forced to choose a side.

To negotiate the agreement, Marguerite and her mother first met with Navarre in Gascony on October 3, 1578. It is interesting to speculate on the effects of the two-year separation upon this unconventional marriage (even by royal standards) and the expectations the couple might have had for their reunion. Marguerite must have seen it as a way for her to regain greater autonomy after her virtual imprisonment in the Louvre and to enjoy greater status as a queen. Navarre too must have viewed her return with mixed emotions. He no doubt enjoyed his status as king of his own territory and as the sought-after leader of the Huguenots. His independence had also allowed him to cultivate a penchant for sexual adventure. When his wife and mother-in-law joined him, Navarre immediately became involved with Victoria de Ayata, a new Spanish lady-in-waiting to Catherine. Whatever its personal dynamic, religion and politics further complicated their relationship.

After rejoining her husband, Marguerite continued to travel with her mother to seek an agreement between the Huguenots and the crown. Months of negotiation were required even to arrange the meeting between Protestant and Catholic representatives that finally produced the Articles of Nérac. Protestants gained fourteen new secure towns in which to practice their religion but on condition that Catholic practices be allowed in them within six months. Marguerite might well have considered this period of travel and negotiation another political success. But even if she had exerted a moderating influence, it diminished abruptly when her mother departed and she went with her husband to Navarre.

Marguerite's own religious fervor complicated both the delicate political balance between Catholics and Protestants and her marriage. She was a devout Catholic, and her stay in these Huguenot strongholds increased her commitment to her faith. Religious differences with her spouse proved daunting. When they traveled together, they could not even stay in the same town: Navarre could not enter Catholic towns, and Marguerite was not welcome in Protestant ones. Ultimately their religious differences produced personal conflict. When Marguerite practiced her religion at Pau (Navarre's birthplace and the heart of Huguenot country), other Catholics in the area took heart and joined in the services. When Navarre's secretary, Jacques Lallier du Pin, saw Catholics attending Mass there, he arrested them. Marguerite complained to Navarre and expected him to support her over his secretary, but her husband refused. His refusal may well have reflected his personal interests as much as his religious convictions. He was pursuing Mademoiselle de Revours, one of Marguerite's ladies-in-waiting, whom Marguerite described as "a malicious girl, who did not like me and who wished for me all the evil offices she could produce."[59] As Marguerite's biographer Eliane Viennot has noted, whenever Navarre was in love, he neglected and mistreated his wife and failed to take her concerns seriously.[60] But Marguerite's stay in Pau, a city contemporaries dubbed a "little Geneva" for its Protestant fervor, disillusioned her about the possibility that she, a staunch Catholic, could live there. Navarre was also acutely aware that Marguerite's open practice of her religion in this Huguenot bastion adversely affected his own standing with his supporters.

When Navarre failed to support her, Marguerite left for Nérac, Navarre's other royal chateau. Intent on making the best of her situation, Marguerite enjoyed her time in Nérac as perhaps the most brilliant during her problematic reign as queen of Navarre. Still sufficiently in Navarre's good graces that he allowed her to indulge her taste for luxury, she created a court "so beautiful and so pleasant that we did not envy that of Paris."[61] This claim was no doubt hyperbolic, but this court was one she created and which revolved around her. Others acknowledged its charms as well. Henry IV's prime minister, Maximilien de Bethune, first baron then marquis de Rossy, who took the name *Sully* when he became a peer of France in 1605, proclaimed: "The court there was a sweet and pleasant time; because one spoke only of love and of the pleasures and pastimes on which it depends."[62] Marguerite again pursued her interest in Neoplatonic philosophy and to that end commissioned a new translation of Marsilio Ficino's *Commentary on Plato's Symposium.* Her account books show purchases of both classical texts and works of French humanists.[63] Some were purchased for educational institutions in Navarre, reflecting Marguerite's desire to spread humanism. Her time at Nérac was a pleasant interlude in both the Wars of Religion and her tempestuous relationship with her husband. When Navarre fell ill, Marguerite nursed him; he was again grateful, and they had a genuine reconciliation.[64]

Initially Marguerite and Navarre presented a united front, and she consistently reaffirmed her intention to "share her husband's fortune."[65] Whenever Marguerite was offered an opportunity to dissolve their marriage (and surely their religious incompatibility would have elicited a sympathetic hearing from the Vatican), she demurred. She worked conscientiously to diminish hostilities between Catholics and Protestants and to persuade the king that Navarre was not exacerbating them. When Navarre became embroiled with Armand de Gontaut de Biron, the governor of Guyenne, because Biron refused to extend privileges to Protestants, Marguerite urged the king to remove Biron to preserve the peace. But Henry would not.

Both sides were poised for war. Neither Catholics nor Protestants were abiding by the terms of the Articles of Nérac (the agreement that Catherine had just negotiated), and both were eager to redress their grievances. The immediate conflict was provoked by the crown's demand that Huguenots turn over certain Protestant towns and by Navarre's request that Protestants be allowed freedom of worship. On April 15, 1580, Navarre wrote "To Lords of the Nobility," justifying his taking up arms. On a more personal note, he wrote to Marguerite:

"It is my extreme regret that instead of the contentment I want to give you and to make you receive some pleasure in this peace, that the contrary was necessary."[66] When, just a few weeks later, Navarre successfully captured the town of Cahors, the king believed that Marguerite had misled him into believing that her husband opposed war.[67]

War, Marguerite recognized, made her position more difficult: "I could not, in conscience, wish success to either side; for if the Huguenots got the upper hand, the religion which I cherished as much as my life was lost, and if the Catholics prevailed, the king, my husband, was undone."[68] Despite her religious misgivings, she threw her lot in with her husband and urged the king to send her brother Francis to reach an accord. (This suggestion served the king's interests as well by distracting Francis.)

When Francis came to negotiate a peace on behalf of the crown in December 1580, in his entourage was a squire, Jacques de Harlay, lord of Champvallon, with whom Marguerite became romantically involved.[69] He had qualities she appreciated: He was handsome, brave, cultivated, and a poet. Their love affair was reported by the Parisian chronicler L'Estoile, the Florentine agent Busini, and Busbecq, Emperor Rudolf II's ambassador. Her correspondence declared her love for him and decried their desperate circumstances. She cast their relationship as an idealized Neoplatonic love, although she was troubled by Champvallon's lack of discretion and eventually had to contend with love's disillusionments.

The strained relations between Marguerite and her husband were further complicated by Navarre's affair with Françoise de Montmorency.[70] The fact that she was Marguerite's lady-in-waiting made the situation stickier than some of Navarre's other affairs. (Initially Marguerite even believed that Françoise was loyal to her and might be a good source of information.) When Françoise became pregnant, Navarre sought Marguerite's help in keeping her condition a secret. He sent his mistress to take the waters at Béarn and asked Marguerite to accompany her. When Françoise went into labor, Navarre again sought Marguerite's assistance. After a daughter was born dead, he urged Marguerite to visit his mistress to preserve the remnants of her reputation. Despite their mutual tolerance, this was too much for Marguerite, who refused.

It must have rankled that Navarre's mistress was pregnant at the same time Marguerite was going to the baths, the waters of which were believed conducive to conception. The secretary of state, Bellièvrre, reported to Catherine Marguerite's "extreme desire that she had to give this contentment to the king her husband to have children."[71] Now that Marguerite had reunited with her husband, no matter how unsatisfactory or sporadic their sexual relations, her failure to conceive was deeply troubling. The pregnancy of any mistress raised the possibility that Marguerite would be set aside. And Françoise was just the first of the mistresses Navarre promised to marry if she bore him a male child.

With Navarre an ever-more-dangerous rival to the king, Catherine urged Marguerite to return to Paris, "if only," she wrote, "to deprive his [Navarre's] court of the prestige, which she, as daughter of France, represented."[72] Despite this flattery, Catherine and Henry were most intent on bringing Marguerite and her husband under the crown's control. But Navarre recognized that his return might cede leadership of the Huguenots to his cousin Condé. So he delayed and sent his wife to the court. Marguerite, caught between the competing interests of her husband and the crown, assured the king that Navarre would join her once a peace was signed.

RETURN TO COURT (1582–1583)

Marguerite finally arrived at court in the spring of 1582, perhaps seeking a more congenial setting in light of her husband's flagrant and unabashed infidelity, but primarily bowing to Catherine and Henry's pressure. Marguerite dutifully continued to urge Navarre to join her, but it became increasingly clear that her pleas would have no effect. Marguerite's return to court did not improve her situation. Received with "enough coldness," she immediately recognized that she should have mistrusted Henry's motives, noting that he had neither forgotten nor forgiven her support for Francis. Henry recalled her to court "to make me as miserable as he wanted," she complained.[73] He increasingly blamed her for failing to persuade Navarre to come to Paris. A first crisis occurred when Henry, having realized that not even Françoise de Montmorency's presence could lure Navarre, urged Marguerite to send her home.

When she did so, Navarre wrote to Marguerite, requesting that she love his mistress as he did. Marguerite responded to Navarre's outraged letters by reminding him that she came to court to serve his interests and that such a request was appropriate when asking for a favor for a servant or *serviteur* but not for a mistress.[74] Navarre's request seemed to have forced Marguerite to recognize how humiliating and intolerable her situation had become. Catherine's expressed outrage that Marguerite's lady-in-waiting had been her husband's mistress may have also heightened Marguerite's grievance. When a furious Navarre berated Marguerite for dismissing his mistress, Catherine denounced him for taking up with a "public prostitute." She wrote: "You are not the first young husband who has been imprudent in affairs of this kind, but I think you must be the first and indeed the only one, who has, after such a thing has occurred, used such language to his wife. This is not the way to treat women of her house, to upbraid them publicly on the whim of a little courtesan." Catherine warned Henry that as long as she lived she would not tolerate such treatment of her daughter, and she contrasted his treatment of his wife with Henry II's respect for her honor.[75] That she did so, given her own long ménage à trois with Diane de Poitiers, seems quite peculiar and no doubt reflected both sympathy for Marguerite's situation and exasperation with Navarre's failure to return to court.

But Navarre was not particularly concerned to remain in his wife's good graces. He was completely captivated by Diane d'Andoins, countess of Grammont, called "Corisandre" after the heroine of *Amadis de Gaula*. Mature and intelligent, drawn from the ranks of the highest nobility, Corisandre was the first of Navarre's long-standing mistresses.[76] His promise to marry her and subsequent neglect of Marguerite broke their marriage irretrievably. As the daughter of a king, Marguerite expected deference, which Navarre no longer gave her. She would make only one more desperate attempt to reconcile with him.

Catherine's letter berating Navarre emphasized that her husband had been particularly attentive when she was pregnant. Indeed, there were intimations that Marguerite was pregnant immediately after she arrived at court. Whatever the grounds for this hope, it was soon dashed. The Tuscan envoy reported that Marguerite no longer wished to live with her husband, a rumor likely based on her purchase of a private residence.[77] Her independent establishment underscored the reality that she was, in essence, a spurned wife. But, defying the conventions of the day, she did not then return to her brother's household and authority. Marguerite's decision to live independently fueled the sexual rumors that circulated about her.

After an absence of almost three years, Marguerite found both the court and Paris uncongenial. Parisians, as L'Estoile reported, were disaffected with the king and his excessive religious and sexual behavior. The court, under the control of Henry's *mignons*, was actively hostile to Marguerite. She was, after all, Francis's ally and wife of Navarre, now a Huguenot leader. But her return to Paris did allow Marguerite to renew her relationship with Champvallon in December 1582.[78] (Her fourteen letters to him date from their eighteen-month separation.)

Marguerite was remarkably indiscreet about her sentiments for Champvallon, and she made it entirely too obvious that she considered him the love of her life. According to her lyrical letters, he embodied the Platonic ideas of goodness, truth, and beauty. She described her relationship with him as analogous to that of the Italian humanist Petrarch for the idealized Laura. Marguerite was rather quickly disabused of her illusions both by his marriage and by his involvement with Sauve, the very woman who earlier enthralled her husband. Marguerite bemoaned her fate: "There is no justice in heaven or fidelity on earth! O God! You boast that you have wronged me and you mock me with her from whom I receive the sole consolation that her little merit will be a just remorse for your wrong."[79]

That spring, rumors reported that Marguerite was pregnant, speculation due not simply to her obvious interest in Champvallon but also to her dramatic exodus from court. This development, like many in her life, has both a possible political explanation and more than a hint of sexual scandal. Henry, increasingly frustrated by his sister's failure to persuade her husband, was obviously angry with her already by May 1583. He no doubt disapproved of her life in Paris; her independence alone would have irritated him, but her continued support for Francis infuriated him.

In June, Marguerite was ill. This health crisis may well have been triggered, like others, by her realization of the untenability of her situation. She had angered the king and had no support in Paris. She was allied with her brother Francis, but he was quite ill. Her husband had no interest in her, and indeed the harshness of his letters to her likely reflected his mistress's sway over him. Marguerite's illness (and no doubt her behavior) again fueled rumors of pregnancy. The Tuscan envoy reported that Marguerite was heavy and thus either pregnant or suffering from hydropsy (an abnormal fluid retention now called edema). Informants even told the English ambassador that she had delivered a son in June, but he expressed skepticism in his report home.[80] While a pregnancy was possible, a full-term birth seems less likely: Champvallon had arrived in December, not early enough for Marguerite to have a full-term birth in June. Marguerite was also out in public throughout the spring, and a full-term pregnancy would have been difficult to hide. It is possible that she miscarried or even had an abortion. Her legend has built on these rumors to posit several, hidden-away, illegitimate children.[81]

By the end of July, Henry's fury with his sister erupted. He had ordered her to rejoin her husband in May. With no means to undertake the long journey, she made no plans to do so. The siblings' antagonism was deep and long-standing; any incident could prove inflammatory. Busbecq reported that the situation took an ugly and dramatic turn when Henry, at a court ball, berated Marguerite for the lovers she had taken since her marriage, citing times and places and accusing her of having had an illegitimate child. This oft-repeated story should be viewed more skeptically than it has been; not only does no other source report it, but no royal balls were held that year.[82]

But Henry had several causes for outrage with Marguerite. She had fallen afoul of several of his favorites. When the duke de Joyeuse, acting as Henry's confidential courier to Rome, was intercepted, Henry blamed Marguerite. (Busbecq later indicated that the king had gotten false reports.[83]) Marguerite's denunciations of Henry's favorites and her ongoing support for Francis, corroborated by their correspondence (copies of which Henry had received), exacerbated hostilities. Another favorite, Epernon, reported to Henry that Marguerite's court was scandalous. In a penitential phase, Henry, atoning for his own excesses and praying desperately for an heir, found his sister's behavior even more reprehensible than usual. His ire focused most directly on two of her ladies-in-waiting as the presumed intermediaries between Marguerite and Francis. Henry described the two women to Navarre as "pernicious vermin and insupportable near a princess of such state" and on August 6 ordered them to leave.[84] Catherine, who now regretted recalling Marguerite to court, urged her to mollify Henry by leaving. When Marguerite finally did so on August 9, she was accompanied by the two objectionable women. Henry was so furious that he sent troops after her and arrested the two ladies-in-waiting. The story became even more lurid when it was reported that the king's patrol stopped the two women and grilled them about Marguerite's conduct, with Henry III inquiring "with his own lips" about the "honor of the queen his sister." L'Estoile, who reported the incident, construed the questions as asking if Marguerite had borne a child by Champvallon or even whether her ladies-in-waiting had facilitated an abortion.[85]

This event was obviously a great humiliation for Marguerite, an attack on both her person and her rank. Catherine was further concerned that Henry's outbursts against his sister would make reconciliation with Navarre impossible. Marguerite was cut off from her family and her husband and left without funds. And her husband had personal and political reasons not to take her back.

Initially, the political prevailed. Navarre, committed to the Huguenot cause, could exploit this situation for its benefit. He sent Duplessis-Mornay to investigate the insult to his wife and to demand justice. Duplessis-Mornay concluded that either Marguerite had committed an unspeakable crime to be treated so badly or Henry had committed a grievance against her for which Navarre should be compensated.[86] It is telling that Navarre was the one to be compensated for an attack on his wife's honor. The situation was complicated: Navarre could not take Marguerite back and save face unless she was exonerated or he had been sufficiently compensated.

Marguerite existed in this nebulous state, scorned by her brother and spurned by her husband, unwelcome in both Paris and Nérac, for eight humiliating months. Her letters reveal her desperation. She wrote to her mother: "Although he [Henry III] cannot love me for my merits or my service or my very humble affection, I hope, Madame, that, as I am burdened with so many evils and problems, he will love me out of pity." She wrote in conciliatory tones directly to the king: "Sire, your judgment must be my true judge. . . . Put aside your anger and consider what I have had to endure in order to obey you. . . . I am still your servant and your sister and you are my only comfort."[87]

Navarre's letters suggest that he was not entirely unsympathetic to his wife's plight, although his conciliatory tone may have reflected his appreciation of the strategic gains the situation might produce.[88] He recognized that Henry could not allow Marguerite to return to Paris without a humiliating recantation. Thus Navarre was able to demand the strategically important fortresses of Agen and Condom as recompense for the attack on his wife's honor. The two kings thus reconciled but left Marguerite without an ally.

As she prepared to return to Navarre, Marguerite seems to have been unrealistically optimistic about their reconciliation. Perhaps she was hopeful that she might bear a son. If she had earlier miscarriages, she might have had some confidence in her fertility. Although she was aware that her husband's mistress Corisandre was in residence with him, Marguerite might have hoped, given the affectionate tenor of Navarre's correspondence, that they would revive their marriage.[89]

When Marguerite rejoined her husband, she initially expressed her contentment.[90] But the reality of their reunion, sympathetically described by Michel de Huguerye, was grim: "The king and the queen his wife arrived. I have never seen a face more washed by tears or eyes redder from tears. And it made me pity this princess, seated next to her husband in a discourse of gentlemen . . . none of whom said a word to her."[91] Only the birth of an heir might restore Marguerite to her husband's favor, but Navarre, in love with Corisandre, had no interest in his wife. Marguerite visited spas in hopes of becoming pregnant, but she scarcely saw her husband, so preoccupied was he with his mistress. The Tuscan ambassador reported that Navarre had a love for Corisandre beyond measure. And L'Estoile claimed that Navarre had not spent a single night with Marguerite, his neglect enraging both Marguerite and her mother.[92] Her husband's treatment ended Marguerite's hopes of producing an heir, and at thirty-one, she abandoned hope of being a wife in anything but name.[93] The breakdown of this marriage, initially intended to forge a political and religious unity, would have a decisive impact on the further unraveling of both.

RENEGADE QUEEN: FROM NÉRAC TO AGEN TO CARLAT (1584–1585)

Francis's death on June 10, 1584, not only isolated Marguerite further but also dramatically altered and complicated the political situation. Forced to address the question of royal succession, Henry recognized Navarre as not only his presumptive but also *likely* heir. That recognition also made Marguerite the likely queen of France. This new situation highlighted Marguerite's failure to produce an heir and made her more vulnerable and even, for some, expendable. Her family expected her to persuade Navarre to convert again to Catholicism to be an acceptable heir. When Marguerite failed to do so, Catherine complained to Bellièvre. "Tell my daughter that she is simply increasing my anguish"; and later, "If she keeps acting like this, she must realize that the king would never wish to hear her spoken of again."[94] In this latest crisis, when Navarre should have acted in the interest of state and recognized his Catholic wife's value in bolstering his claim to the throne, he instead pursued pleasure and Corisandre.[95]

Marguerite had spent the winter in Nérac in miserable isolation; her personal and political situation became intolerable. At odds with both the king and Navarre and without allies or means, she chafed with no role to play. She had previously served as a bridge between various factions. She had consistently sought a political role and had seen herself as an important political agent and an ally worth cultivating, as crucial to whomever's interest she served. Marguerite feared that both her brother and her husband now considered her negligible—personally and politically. Rumors of expedient poisonings circulated. L'Estoile spread the story that Marguerite's secretary had tried to poison Navarre, and Marguerite believed that Corisandre was trying to poison her.[96]

At this point, Marguerite took a highly unusual and decisive act. She began negotiations with Guise and the League, which had emerged as powerful enough to challenge her husband's status as heir apparent and which were attempting to wrest control of the monarchy from her brother. Her negotiations thus undermined them both. Her relations with Navarre were so tense that he might have repudiated her. But Marguerite preempted the move by conspiring against him. Her decision was a striking departure from her earlier loyalty to him and willingness to mediate between him and the king.[97] With this action,

Marguerite could claim to serve Catholic interests. She appealed to the Spanish for cash subsidies for her support of the League. As she prepared to defect in March of 1585, Marguerite told her husband that she wanted to go to Agen to prepare spiritually for Easter.

Marguerite's behavior at this juncture, especially in light of its denouement, has seemed at the very least ill-considered. Was this an act of revenge directed against an unfaithful husband and a vindictive brother, a decisive measure to regain control over her desperate circumstances, or even an act of self-preservation? Marguerite's situation was unquestionably dire. Alienated from her mother and the king, she had been unable to reestablish relations with her husband. She feared that she would be set aside in favor of his mistress. She had lost the brother who had been, despite his inconstancy, her ally (admittedly more in his interest than hers). No doubt recognizing her growing vulnerability, she chose to act. As her biographer Viennot notes, Marguerite offers the unique example of a sixteenth-century queen refusing to share her husband's fate. Marguerite was not an abandoned queen but rather a queen who abandoned the king.[98]

When Marguerite defected to the League, the crown was as threatened by the League as by the Huguenots, and thus her alliance with the League was a rebellion against her family and the crown as well as her husband. Henry even considered trying her for treason. Horrified by her daughter's conduct, Catherine wrote to Bellièvre the letter frequently cited to indicate the breakdown of mother-daughter relations: "I see that God has left me this creature as punishment for my sins in the afflictions she gives me every day. . . . I assure you that I am so afflicted that I do not know what remedy to find."[99]

Marguerite began to fortify Agen against both her husband and the king. (Guise was counting on commanding Agen as an axis of circulation from south to west for the League.) Marguerite may have thought that she controlled this complex situation, but the League was using her to undermine both her husband and her brother and to gain strategically important towns. She may have also believed that she was now allied to the likely winner. Perhaps her decision was a simple political calculation; the towns under her control offered her the surest refuge, and they were loyal to the League.

Indeed, the king, caught between Catholic and Protestant opposition, was ultimately forced to concede the League's strength and enter into an uneasy alliance with it. But Henry's agreement with the League made no provision for Marguerite, isolated in Agen, now surrounded by royal troops.

Marguerite's efforts to fortify Agen ultimately provoked opposition from the local populace. She had been given Agen as part of her dowry, made a triumphal entry into the city in 1578, and doubtless hoped for a welcome on her return. To fortify it, she razed the dwellings of some of the town's most influential residents, and to provision it, she raised taxes. These actions produced great resentment. Eventually the town revolted, opening its gates to Henry's army and begging to be taken over by the crown.[100] Marguerite was forced into hasty flight, just ahead of the king's forces. Her flight was a boon for Henry; it allowed him to regain the strategically important Agen. Henry was displeased when Marguerite sought refuge at Carlat, a castle sufficiently well fortified that she remained too independent and, no doubt from his perspective, a disloyal loose cannon. On her flight, Robert de Lignerac, the head of the League in the region, accompanied Marguerite on Guise's orders.

From September 1585 to October 1586, Marguerite remained at Carlat.[101] This fifty-four week period of her life remains obscure. She arrived after being driven out of Agen and left immediately after a murder. For a time, Carlat offered refuge, but Marguerite's last days there precipitated the disastrous end to her quest for independence.

Marguerite urgently needed funds to fortify Carlat and to provision troops against a potential Huguenot attack. She sent an emissary to Spain, and Guise wrote to Philip II on her behalf, but funds were not forthcoming. In addition, for several months in the spring of 1586 Marguerite was so seriously ill that rumors swirled at the French court that she was at death's door. Indeed, a physician attended her for forty days. For the king, her death might afford greater opportunity to resolve the succession crisis: Navarre could remarry, and rumors of a proposed marriage to Catherine's granddaughter Christine circulated.[102] Catherine may have been interested in trying to keep the crown in the Valois family and perhaps hoped that, if Navarre agreed to convert as part of a new marriage alliance, her son's reign too would be more secure. The king expressed no regret at the prospect of Marguerite's death: "The more I think back, the more I am aware of the ignominy this miserable [creature] has done to us. It would be better for her and for us that God take her."[103] When Marguerite recovered by early June, this illness too became a rumored pregnancy.

Lack of funds and threats of attack no doubt made Marguerite's months at Carlat difficult, especially because the governor of the chateau, Lignerac, and her brigade commander, Jean de Lart, lord of Aubiac, were soon at odds.[104] (Like other League nobles, Aubiac had entered Marguerite's service when she defected to the League.) Hostility between the two men erupted when Marguerite encouraged Aubiac to take over from Lignerac. In an incident that remains unclear, the dispute between the two men ended in the death of a bystander—the young deaf son of Marguerite's apothecary. When Lignerac found the boy in Marguerite's bedchamber, he stabbed him to death.[105] This event, like many in Marguerite's life, is best known through her legend, which explained it as a jealous feud between her two lovers. While we know little about Aubiac, as compared to other supposed lovers, the poem Marguerite wrote a year later expressed affection for him. But Lignerac and Aubiac were also rivals for influence. Aubiac had shared the command of the queen's troops with Lignerac, and the two were in competition for the captaincy of Carlat. How that antagonism might have led to an attack on the young man remains unknown, as well as whether the two men were at odds over love or power.[106]

No matter the provocation, the murder clearly revealed that Marguerite had lost control of Carlat. Her impetus to seek security became even more compelling when she learned that the king's army, under the command of her old enemy Joyeuse, was coming to arrest her. In her hasty retreat, Marguerite first sought refuge at the chateau of Ibois. Begging Phillip II for funds, she described her ordeal there: "The night I arrived without the leisure to provide food or powder . . . I was besieged. After two days without eating or hope of rescue . . . and having no means because of lack of powder to defend us, the soldiers forced me to surrender."[107]

Henry ordered Jean de Beaufort Canillac to "seize the person of the Queen of Navarre" without consideration "for the quality of our sister or the closeness of the blood bond between us." Henry gave Canillac further instructions: "to hang Aubiac and in the presence of this miserable one [Marguerite]."[108] Aubiac was arrested and summarily tried, convicted, and executed for treason.[109] His death entered Marguerite's legend as the tragic end of yet another of her inappropriate relationships. However, as Robert Sealy has persuasively argued, Aubiac's execution should best be seen as punishment for Marguerite's dealings with Spain.[110] His execution was part of the king's attempt to quash rebellious Catholic Leaguers. Henry further ordered Canillac to "take and shut up the Queen of Navarre at Usson."[111] Catherine's comment on her daughter's imprisonment was harsh: "I read what my son the king wrote to me concerning that poor wretched creature whom God had me put into the world to be the scourge of my old age. . . . Now she is where I want her to be, provided we can retain the upper hand."[112] Marguerite implored her mother: "I fall at your feet and beg you most humbly."[113] But the royal family no longer had any sympathy for this renegade daughter. Tales of her inappropriate behavior again circulated in Paris—this time that she had borne a child to Aubiac. On November 13, 1586, Marguerite was confined at Usson, one of the most impregnable chateaux in France. There she would remain for almost twenty years (fig. 6.3).

Fig. 6.3. The impregnable chateau of Usson, razed at the end of the sixteenth century, where Marguerite de Valois was confined for nearly twenty years. BnF.

EXILE IN USSON (1586–1605)

As the Wars of Religion devolved into the conflict between Henry III, Guise, and Navarre, Marguerite remained a prisoner at Usson, under the orders of her brother, with Canillac as her jailer. Any thought that Marguerite would be consigned to oblivion failed to recognize her remarkable powers of reinvention. Her jailer defected from the king to the League and became her protector. Contemporaries credited her charms. Brantôme, for example, claimed that

Canillac was so besotted by Marguerite that he "became her prisoner in a short time even though he was brave and valiant. Poor man! What could he do?"[114]

Any man who allied with Marguerite has been cast as a lover—including Aubiac and Canillac. Such claims were characteristic of contemporary polemics. In Marguerite's case, her behavior was unorthodox enough to provoke such charges, but their vehemence likely masks hostility to her violation of conventional, female *political* roles as much as sexual mores.

In this case, Canillac had clear political reasons to defect from the king and to ally with Marguerite. He felt ill-used by the crown; he did not have sufficient funds for his men; and Guise offered him both protection and money.[115] Canillac also found his own situation increasingly precarious: He was the king's representative in territories held by the League, and he had learned of several plots to free Marguerite by killing him. He also found his role as Marguerite's jailer unpalatable. He reported to Catherine that Marguerite "has fallen into despair, convinced of her death, which no consolation that I was able to offer can dispel. For three days now, she has done nothing but weep and torture herself, eating and drinking nothing. . . . I beg you to let me be responsible neither for the death of your daughter nor for any part in so final an act."[116] After Canillac defected from the crown, he continued as Marguerite's warden.[117] But as he no longer served the king, Marguerite was more the queen of Usson than a royal prisoner.

While Marguerite remained isolated at Usson, the Wars of Religion raged ever more bloody, and the Valois monarchy was ever more threatened as the League essentially captured the king and controlled Paris.[118] At this low point, Henry and his sister reconciled. Although rumors circulated in Paris that she would be returning, that possibility became less likely in the aftermath of Henry's desperate assassination of the duke and the cardinal of Guise, and impossible after Henry was assassinated. While Marguerite remained incarcerated at Usson, her mother, her brother, and Canillac all died.[119]

Marguerite's nineteen-year stay in Usson had several distinct stages. For the first ten years, she faced considerable financial hardship. Her brother had cut off her pensions. She repeatedly begged Philip II for support, but he no longer saw her as a political asset.[120] Only the generosity of her sister-in-law, Elizabeth of Austria, the widow of her brother Charles IX, sustained her. After 1594, when Henry IV sought Marguerite's support for an annulment, more funds were forthcoming and her financial situation less dire.

Even to this remote site, Marguerite attracted artists and prominent intellectuals, who offered courses in mathematics and philosophy.[121] The historian Dupleix described her court as "the Parnassus of Usson," where "the queen caused the formation of a system of philosophic harmony so highly developed that it resonates everywhere in France and Europe."[122] In his play *L'Astrée*, Honoré d'Urfé made Marguerite his protagonist, Galatea, and painted her court there as the realization of a Platonic ideal. Secluded in Usson, Marguerite reflected on her past life as she composed her memoirs, while her estranged husband battled the remnants of the League to claim his throne.[123] She was the last of her immediate family and free to tell her story, but she did not illuminate her life after she left her husband.

Although Marguerite was generally out of the fray, she became important again when her husband sought her cooperation for an annulment. By 1593, Navarre (now Henry IV and referred to as Henry hereafter) had abjured Protestantism, which might have also sparked a decisive change in Marguerite's attitude toward him. Eventually the two of them worked toward what became a successful annulment and reconciliation. Marguerite agreed on the mutual benefits of dissolving their marriage when Henry first raised the issue, but desperate for money, she requested property, considerable financial resources, and the retention of her prerogatives.[124] The resources of the kingdom were too limited for Henry to meet her demands. When he considered the issue more pressing because he wanted to marry his pregnant mistress, Marguerite insisted on a lucrative financial settlement and proved a wily negotiator.[125] Eventually Henry settled a large pension on Marguerite, allowed her to assume the title "Queen and Duchess of Valois," and paid her considerable debts. She, in turn, agreed to request an annulment from the pope. In a letter to Sully, Henry's prime minister, Marguerite expressed her desire to be accommodating: "I desire the good success to enhance the contentment of the king and good Frenchmen, who, you have written, desire so ardently to have the legitimate children of the king."[126]

When the pope annulled their marriage on December 17, 1599, both parties rejoiced. Henry sent Marguerite an affectionate letter, assuring her that "I do not wish to cherish and love you less . . . on the contrary, to have greater care than ever in all that concerns you."[127] In response, Marguerite praised "the generosity of a [his] beautiful soul . . . in the assurance of his good grace and protection."[128] The end of their marriage paved the way for Marguerite to request that she be allowed to return to Paris.

RETURN TO PARIS (1605)

When Marguerite lobbied to return, Henry IV was not pleased initially at the prospect of a Valois in Paris before the Bourbons were well established. He was also suspicious of Marguerite's connections to former Leaguers. But ever since he had ascended the throne in 1589, Marguerite had assured him of her loyalty: "The power that your majesty has over me is absolute and entire. . . . I am entirely yours; that you can dispose of me in any way and in any fashion that pleases you."[129]

As events made Henry's dynasty more stable—France was restored to relative peace and most of his enemies reconciled to his reign—Marguerite's return became conceivable. By 1601 Henry had attained his annulment, married Marie de Medici, and finally had an heir, the future Louis XIII. But he still had cause for concern. Plots to displace him revealed pockets of resistance to the Bourbon dynasty. As Henry considered allowing her to return, Marguerite demonstrated her loyalty.

Even isolated at Usson, Marguerite was sufficiently well connected to warn Henry that her nephew Charles d'Angoulême, the son of Charles IX by his mistress Marie Touchet, was plotting against the new dauphin in favor of his nephew, Henry's illegitimate son by Charles's sister Henriette d'Entragues. The Tuscan ambassador reported on this dangerous situation: "Some claim that the marriage of the king to Marguerite de Valois is still valid, and in their eyes the dauphin is illegitimate. The marquise de Verneuil [Henriette d'Entragues] with the authorizing promise of the king, considers her own son as the only legitimate one and the dauphin as a bastard."[130] Marguerite too emphasized the danger her "evil nephew" posed.[131]

Marguerite understood that the situation could be used to her advantage, both to regain the territory of Auvergne from her disloyal nephew (Catherine de Medici had willed it to him) and to arrange her return to Paris on advantageous terms. The legal process against Charles d'Angoulême would take time and elicit public interest, and Marguerite could participate most effectively if she were on site, or so she persuaded the king. Her return and her life in Paris were funded by the concessions Henry granted. He allowed her to sue Parlement to have her mother's will broken and to gain the territories Charles forfeited by his treachery. This arrangement was not simply beneficial to her; it ultimately returned lands to the crown. Most importantly, her bequest to the dauphin reinforced the legitimacy of Henry IV's second marriage and the new dynasty, emphasizing the connection between Bourbon and Valois. Marguerite purchased land across from the Louvre on the rue de Seine and built a palace, writing to Henry, "I esteem it worthy of being offered to the dauphin."[132]

Henry faced her return with some trepidation about how his new queen or the Parisian population would respond to this repudiated Valois queen after her long exile. This startling reversal in Marguerite's fortunes had to be carefully orchestrated. She was received with respect and greeted by Caesar, Henry's son by Gabrielle d'Estrées (the king's former mistress). Shortly thereafter, she was presented to both the queen and the dauphin. Marguerite quickly went from being a pariah living in isolation to becoming a significant personage in Paris—one of the most remarkable transformations of her eventful life.

After her long absence, Marguerite was much intrigued by the changes she found in Paris. But if Paris had changed, she seemed unaware that time had passed her by. When she had left Paris, she was a great beauty acknowledged for her intellectual accomplishments. When she returned at the age of fifty-two (elderly by the standards of the day), her appearance was much altered. Her skin was now red and raw, the result of the bleaches she applied; she wore an extravagant blond wig and clothes twenty years out of date. She might have been dismissed as a caricature of her young self, a figure ripe for ridicule, but instead she won the affection of Parisians.

Marguerite's life in Paris was occasionally tinged by scandal.[133] Her name was linked to several lovers—all appreciably younger than she. The first was rumored to be Gabriel Dat Saint-Julien, and scandal followed immediately. He was assassinated by Vermont, the son of one of Marguerite's ladies-in-waiting.[134] Vermont likely felt that Saint-Julien had supplanted his mother's (the former Mademoiselle de Thorigny) influence with Marguerite. The death, rumored to be yet another case of one lover attacking another, provided her critics with food for doggerel, but once again the grievance was more likely political rather than romantic.[135] Marguerite feared that she had been the target of the attempted assassination to prevent her testimony against Charles d'Angoulême. That very day (April 5, 1606), she addressed the king: "Monseigneur: An assassination has just taken place before the entrance to my residence, before my eyes, next to my carriage, a son of Vermont, who fired a pistol at one of my gentleman whose name is Saint-Julien. I humbly beg Your Majesty order that justice may be done and no pardon given. If this wickedness is not punished, no one can live securely." Three days later she thanked him for his "swift justice" and requested that the mother and brothers of the would-be assassin be exiled "in order to protect my life." She added: "This evil woman is devoted to my nephew Charles Monsieur. Since he knows I am now seeking your permission to bring him to trial [to break Catherine's will], I fear he will make use of the malice of that woman and of her children [the Vermonts] to attack me, which is why I beg you to protect me by their banishment."[136] When Henry granted her request, Marguerite expressed both her gratitude and her fear that there would be other attempts on her life.[137]

Even if this event likely had a political cause, Marguerite's life in Paris included other young male favorites. As she was no longer married, there was less cause for scandal and less political capital could be made by excoriating her. She was involved with the handsome young nobleman Hector Regnault du Dufort, lord and baron de Baujaumont.[138] In 1609, when he was ill, Marguerite cared for him. Although she was lampooned for the young men she attracted, it was taken as a sign of her eccentricity. But Marguerite was admired for her great generosity and renowned for her intellectual interests. Her palace on the rue de Seine attracted prominent intellectuals who shared her interests. Not surprisingly, given her previous history, Marguerite immersed herself in the cultural delights of Paris. Rather more surprisingly, she played a central role in the new royal family.

Without the burden of inharmonious conjugal relations, Marguerite and Henry were able to be friends who could express the affection, respect, and amusement they provoked in each other. The potential political and personal discomfort Marguerite posed for the king did not materialize. Henry's wife, Marie de Medici, had good reason to mistrust any woman associated with him; she had just won her battle with her husband's mistress, Henriette d'Entragues. Henriette had believed that Henry would ultimately abandon Marie for her, an illusion no doubt fostered by both his written promise to marry her and his practice of moving between their beds and having children with both of them. But Henriette's patent disloyalty brought her influence to an end. To Henry's relief, Marie and Marguerite, his current and former queens, became friends. Marguerite's acceptance by the royal family reinforced the continuity of the monarchy and also suggested to the public that the Bourbon dynasty was stable enough to welcome remnants of the former dynasty. When Marie was crowned queen of France, Marguerite, garbed in crown and royal mantle, followed behind the queen and her young daughter (fig. 6.4). Marguerite also acted as a kind of honorary aunt to her former husband's children; she was godmother to his daughter Henriette, and the dauphin (later Louis XIII) called her *maman-fille*, literally mama-girl.

Marguerite was increasingly significant as the new queen's advisor, serving explicitly as Marie's guide to royal protocol. As mistress of "feasts and ceremonies of the court," she orchestrated the royal ball held when the young princess Elizabeth was engaged to Philip IV of Spain.[139] After Henry's death at the hands of an assassin in 1610, Marguerite continued to serve the crown, most notably in 1614, when nobles fomented dissent to challenge Marie's regency. In these dangerous circumstances, Marie had confidence in and relied on Marguerite.

Fig. 6.4. *The Coronation of Marie de Medici at St. Denis* by Peter Paul Rubens. Louvre, Paris/The Bridgeman Art Library.

As she aged, Marguerite, always devout, became even more so. She attended as many as three masses a day, made substantial gifts to convents, and actively supported the Catholic Reformation, allowing the Jesuits into all of her territories.[140] Next to her palace, she founded a monastery of the reformed, discalced Augustinians, popularly known as "the *petits-Augustins* of Queen Marguerite."

When Marguerite died in 1615, at the age of sixty-two, her body lay in state and the entire court wore mourning clothes. Paul Phelypeaux de Pontchartrain eulogized her: "There died in Paris Queen Marguerite, the sole survivor of the race of Valois, a princess full of kindness and good intentions for the welfare of the state and who was her only enemy."[141] Dupleix proclaimed her "cherished and honored by all orders of the kingdom, for her piety, devotion, and affection for the state."[142] She was buried in the mausoleum of the Valois in the basilica of Saint-Denis.

Marguerite's myth, especially the most salacious and sexually explicit charges against her, did not circulate widely until after her death. During her lifetime, despite the rumored scandals, she was best known as a legendary beauty, as her brother Francis's ally, then as Henry's set-aside wife, and finally as the flamboyant woman who returned to Paris in her old age, respected for her intellectual and cultural activities. Even more significantly, she was appreciated for solidifying the Bourbon dynasty. She had agreed to have her marriage annulled, then aided her husband's fertile new wife, and finally bequeathed her goods to the young dauphin.

INTELLECTUAL LUMINARY

In sharp distinction to her highly sexualized myth, Marguerite was particularly respected by her contemporaries as a woman of intellectual distinction. She was not known for her writings, because most appeared only after her death.[143] But Brantôme praised Marguerite as much for her literary accomplishment as for her beauty: "She herself composed well, as much in prose as in verse. . . . Her compositions are very beautiful, learned, and pleasing, because she knows well the art."[144] In her lifetime, Marguerite was most appreciated for her poetry. Most of it was lost, but the remaining poems have provoked recent scholarly attention.[145]

Modern literary scholars cite Marguerite's *Mémoires* as the first written by a woman and as an important Renaissance work. Her text invoked the humanist tradition, explicitly using Plutarch as her model to recreate her own life as heroic.[146] Her first editor proclaimed, "Rome praised so highly the *Commentaries* of its first emperor, France now has those of a great queen, which cede nothing to it."[147] A popular success, this work offered an absorbing firsthand narrative of the decades of religious and political warfare.

Marguerite's intellectual accomplishments reflect her dedication to the study of philosophy. After a rather unsystematic early education, she first cultivated her intellectual development by attending the academy her brother Charles IX had established. When left in isolation at the royal court after her husband and brother had fled, Marguerite attended Henry III's Palace Academy, where she heard lectures by Jean Bodin and Pontus de Tyard, likely discovered the philosophy of Raymond Sebond and Michel de Montaigne, and began to explore Neoplatonism as more congenial than the Petrarchan emphasis of Madame de Retz's salon. Marguerite dated her interest in philosophy to that time. "I had found a secret pleasure . . . from the perusal of good books, to which I had given myself up with a delight I never before experienced. . . . My captivity and its consequent solitude afforded me the double advantage of exciting a passion for study and an inclination for devotion."[148]

When Marguerite went to Navarre, she once again studied Neoplatonic philosophy, commissioning a translation of Marsilio Ficino's *Commentary on Plato's Symposium* and receiving works written by French Neoplatonists and their translations of ancient texts. She was also intrigued by Pico della Mirandola's works, which reconciled ancient and Christian texts.

Marguerite studied philosophy intently during her long exile at Usson, where, even isolated, she played a role in disseminating Neoplatonism in France. She commissioned translations of Pico della Mirandola's *Discourse of Honest Love* and his *Oration on the Dignity of Man*. These works were not only fundamental in bringing Neoplatonism to a French readership but also in introducing hermetic literature. This literature offered a privileged knowledge to its devotees and promoted a syncretic appreciation of a wide array of intellectual traditions as contributing to an ennobling quest for truth.[149] Late in life, Marguerite was especially interested in Stoic philosophy and commissioned French translations of Epictetus and Seneca. Her philosophical interests thus extended beyond her well-known study of Neoplatonism.

The influence of Neoplatonism, especially in its syncretic and mystical form, is evident in Marguerite's writings, most strikingly in her letters to Champvallon. In them, Marguerite used Platonism to represent earthly love in a spiritualized form. The human experience of love is akin to "those in perpetual contemplation awaiting the hour of perfect glory." Her love is "a divine being to whom nothing is unknown." Champvallon's name is "imprinted on her soul as if on wax." So strong is his effect on her that, when separated from him, "her soul takes on another form." Through love, Marguerite notes, "the soul ascends above the earthly" and experiences "such admirable effects as happy spirits receive in the breast of eternity." Her soul, she protests, is now "so focused on beautiful thoughts that it cannot be diverted." As a lover transformed by love, she has a "soul that will adore you eternally." She confides to Champvallon: "I am no longer myself." Midway through this series of letters, just after citing her fidelity as oil to love's fire, she warns him: "A fire has to be fed, and fire absent its heat loses its fire." She then berates him, asking, "If her sincere and faithful passion does not merit love, should it be recompensed with such cruel hatred?" Books, she says to him, are "full of the perfidy of your sex." She was thus mistaken when she called him a god; she should have instead called him "Icarus," no doubt for flying too close to the fire of her love. Realism sets in, as she notes, that the perfection of love is the union of two souls, but it, like Achilles' immortality, can be subject to "a fatality of certain accident."[150]

Marguerite's intellectual development is reflected in these letters. Plato offered the idealized model applied to Champvallon, her earthly love. In her disillusionment, she moved away from invoking a male model of heroism as when she earlier compared herself to Plutarch's heroes.[151] She highlighted instead men's faithlessness, while her own behavior invoked mythical female models—Dido, Venus, and Echo—in the tradition of Christine de Pizan's *The Book of the City of the Ladies*. Marguerite cast Champvallon in the more conventional female role, that is to say, as an idealized love unresponsive to the devoted lover. Her self-ascribed role as the devoted but scorned lover was conventionally taken by a male writer.[152]

With her last prose text, *The Learned and Subtle Discourse* (sometimes called "Discourse on the Excellence of Women"), Marguerite took an avowedly feminist position and entered the lists of the defenders of women in the "quarrel over women" by denouncing *The Flowers of Moral Secrets* of the Jesuit Father Loryot.[153] When he suggested that women should be honored by men for their weakness, Marguerite was goaded to respond to "his scorn for her sex." Weakness, she notes, inspires not honor but pity. Characterizing his text as misogynist, she explicitly challenges Loryot to read works written by women and points to the many cases of female excellence.[154] She assigns idealized characteristics unequivocally to women. Her arguments repeat time-honored tropes in the long-standing "quarrel over women" and are explicitly indebted to Heinrich Cornelius Agrippa von Nettesheim's *On the Preeminence of Women* (1529). Marguerite insists that just as God proceeded in creation from inferior to superior, so too did nature proceed from crude to fine. As the interior invariably replicates the exterior, so the delicacy and fine features of the female face reflect her greater development.

For Marguerite, this view inevitably had social ramifications. In earlier societies, it perhaps made sense to empower men to defend against savage beasts, she considered. But now that human beings live in societies, it is much more reasonable to regulate "the most beautiful spirits," those "most capable of reason, justice, and equity, who would make them live most happily." Thus man must yield to woman and "honor her and almost adore her, as the holiest and most vivid image of divinity." The world is not, as conventional wisdom would have it, "made for man and man for God, but rather the world is made for man, man made for woman, and woman made for God." This relationship, she adamantly contends, is obvious. Women's bodies are more beautiful, more delicate, and more elaborate than men's. Their spirits are "tranquil, restful, and devout"; those of men are "tumultuous and bloody." Women, as the culmination of creation, surpass men in all that is "excellent, perfect, and worthy."[155] These arguments, neither subtle nor deferential, staunchly assert women's intellectual abilities, qualities on display in the gatherings Marguerite fostered throughout her life.

Marguerite's writings might have been sufficiently influential to gain her a place in French Renaissance literature. But her use of patronage and the intellectual gatherings she held made her central to the intellectual movements of the day and placed her at the forefront of the emerging classical age. Marguerite had a defining role as an early *salonière.* While confined at court in the mid-1570s, she had a circle composed primarily of court poets. In her later salons at Nérac and Usson, she encouraged a generation of writers, many of whom gratefully acknowledged her crucial role in fostering their work.[156]

The salon she held in Paris during the last ten years of her life (1605–1615) was a veritable center of intellectual life.[157] With Plato's *Symposium* as her model, Marguerite often gathered a group at table to discuss a particular topic. She took a directive role, somewhere between *salonière* and *philosophe,* as her contemporary Etienne Pasquier described: "She dedicated herself to a manner of life so serious and royal that in all of her actions, even at table, she was surrounded by people accomplished in all sorts of sciences, because although dinners and suppers were principally dedicated to the nourishment of the body, every time she did more to nourish the spirits."[158]

Marguerite's activities were influential beyond her immediate circle, as her salon sought to disseminate its findings. Women were central to her gatherings, and she established a broader network by sending the works of the authors she patronized to prominent women in various towns, "to elevate their spirits and those of others in their communities."[159] As Marguerite's *Learned and Subtle Discourse* demonstrated, Plato's *Symposium* received a distinctive reading in the context of the French court. It both offered an inspiring model for intelligent discourse and fueled Marguerite's quest to disseminate knowledge more broadly. She shared with her Valois ancestors the ambition to enhance their legitimacy by promoting high culture, but her desire to do so extended beyond the court. Philosophy gave Marguerite a public role.

Her gatherings focused on the full range of topics generated by the humanist understanding of human nature—the importance of learning to virtue and the cultivation of all facets of human nature, for example.[160] They were thus particularly significant in the transition from Renaissance humanism to early seventeenth-century learning. Her cultivation of Neoplatonism underscored the moral significance of all learning and thus points toward some concerns of seventeenth-century academies. Her salon not only put the intellectual prestige of the Valois on display but also made Marguerite's commitment to philosophy concrete.

Marguerite, like her famous great-aunt Marguerite d'Angoulême, also wrote about sex and love. Neoplatonism provided a way to treat these issues and to cope with the challenges of being a sixteenth-century royal woman. Why would this have been the case? Neoplatonism in Renaissance France was less wedded to the ideal physical specimen as male and offered the possibility of a feminine ideal. Neoplatonism may have also been a way for Marguerite to interpret her personal life, particularly her failed sexual relations, especially with her husband. If women were the higher form of human life, then the difficulties of their sexual relationships with men became more understandable; men, it was clear, were not to be idealized. If the beautiful Champvallon was the antithesis of her rustic spouse, he too failed to be worthy of her love. Neoplatonism offered a means to elevate her extramarital sexual relations, empowering women in love relationships as mystical guides. Neoplatonism, particularly as it was grafted onto the intellectual tradition of courtly humanism, privileged the intellectual accomplishments of women and female discourse and sociability. With Plato's *Symposium* as her model, Marguerite established groups where women were welcome and encouraged to play these roles, even though, in the famous Platonic dialogue, women left before the discussion.

Neoplatonism saw faith and reason as mutually reinforcing and was readily integrated into orthodox Catholicism. For Marguerite, her learning enhanced her strong Catholic faith: "By tracing nature in the universal book which is opened to all mankind, I was led to knowledge of the Divine Author. Science conducts us, step by step, through the whole range of creation, until we arrive at length at God."[161]

How does this woman of intellectual distinction correspond to the sexualized woman of *The Satiric Divorce* or even Dumas's more romanticized Queen Margot? Her writings are clearly not of the "kiss and tell" variety; they are, as would befit her station and the standards of the day, discreet. As scholars continue to explore her real and supposed sexual relationships by setting them in their political contexts and by considering the political and religious motives of those who defamed her, more of the claims of *The Satiric Divorce* seem entirely invented. In light of this erosion of her myth, one must acknowledge the great efficacy of sexual denunciation in the polemics of the Wars of Religion, detach Marguerite from the excesses of her myth, and study the myth itself, as Viennot has done in her important works.

But what is one to do, if anything, with the sexual life of this Valois princess? Marguerite did have extramarital sexual relations, certainly during the last sixteen years of her life after her marriage was annulled, perhaps during the almost twenty years she was separated from Henry, and likely before. Some modern scholars do not find it inconceivable that she may, as her myth contended, have been pregnant or even have borne an illegitimate child. Some scholars, most notably Viennot and Madeleine Lazard, have urged a reappraisal of Marguerite as one of the first modern women, especially with respect to her attitude toward sex.[162] But instead of recasting her in modern guise, one might more appropriately reappraise her writings. Even if her letters perhaps give too ethereal a cast to her relationship with Champvallon, they also reveal ways in which she personally integrated sex, love, and Neoplatonism. Her writing set her extramarital sexual relations in the full context of her life. They offer a view of Marguerite as an integrated personality and serve as an important corrective to the mythical, sexual predator described in *The Satiric Divorce.* Marguerite is then comprehensible as a Renaissance woman who engaged in extramarital sexual relations but saw them as ennobling and even spiritual. If one pays more attention to her voice than to those of her critics, Marguerite reveals herself as a woman who took advantage of her status and every opportunity she had to act according to her talents and her desires—be they sexual, political, or intellectual. And she used her literary skills to tell her side of her story.

MARGUERITE'S MYTH

Despite the drama of Marguerite's life story, myths associated with her have proved even more engaging.[163] They include some of the most salacious stories of the Renaissance—from petticoat pockets filled with lovers' hearts to illegitimate sons who became misanthropes or traitorous priests. Dupleix, the historian to whom Marguerite had given a rich sinecure and who wrote a laudatory *éloge,* later bit the hand that fed him. His *Histoire générale de France,* written after Marguerite's death, lent historical credibility to every rumor associated with her. But his denunciations served a clear political purpose. His history was written at the behest of Cardinal Richelieu to discredit Marie de Medici by raising doubts about politically powerful women.[164] Through it, the most salacious stories told about Marguerite passed into the more authoritative works of Bourbon historians.

As this book has documented, critics regularly condemned the court for its moral failings, from Charles VII's pursuit of luxury and women to Henry III's bizarre behavior and devotion to young men. The court thus rarely stood as a model of Christian moral behavior. But the charges against Marguerite have been particularly vociferous and enduring. The question remains as to what degree her behavior contributed to her myth. While royal men had never been held to marital fidelity, royal women were expected to conform to a higher standard. If men were unlikely to incur any penalty for sexual transgression, elite women had some leeway, too. Over the course of the sixteenth century, sexual liaisons outside of marriage became somewhat more acceptable for elite women, provided they were conducted after marriage and the birth of legitimate heirs and with discretion. Marguerite d'Angoulême's *Heptameron* might well be considered as a mid-sixteenth-century commentary on courtly manners and behavior, and illicit sexual relations are a central topic, and while the tales idealize love, love is rarely found in marriage.

But Marguerite was likely an adulterous queen—a charge leveled with less foundation at any number of her predecessors. Even if the charge of adultery was likely legitimate, her legend distorts her into a woman of insatiable sexual appetites. The most lurid tales were told about her lovers from inferior social ranks. Reputed lovers of high social standing, such as Bussy d'Amboise, elicited less outrage or even gained approbation. Many tales of reputed lovers may have had little to do with her sexual behavior and actually be compelling ways to indict her political activities and allies.[165] Many rumors of love affairs were circulated by her brother Henry to discredit her, just as his critics used sexual innuendo to discredit him.

Even though Marguerite quickly entered legend, the earliest accounts of her were laudatory. Like other royal children, she was the beneficiary of extravagant praise by court poets. She was heralded first for her beauty and then for her intellectual accomplishment. Later, when Guy Le Febvre de La Boderie translated Ficino's commentary on Plato's *Symposium*, he dedicated it to Marguerite, claiming that she was a model of perfect Platonic love. Montaigne put himself in dialogue with her in his *Apologie de Raymond Sebond*, clearly denoting his esteem. Even if Shakespeare's *Love's Labour's Lost*, written between 1592 and 1595, did not portray her court in an entirely flattering way, his use of it as his setting attested to its renown abroad.

Negative comments about Marguerite first attacked her for debauchery of an unspecified nature, consistent with broad-brush attacks on her family and characteristic of Protestant polemics against the Catholic Valois. Such attacks were intended to distinguish dissolute Catholic royalty from virtuous Protestants who would, by implication, be better guardians of the state. If Catherine and her children were first charged with rather vague failings, the charges later became specific sins, especially sexual sins. The tone of these attacks became more vehement, and their content, lurid catalogs of depravity. By the seventeenth century, such attacks on the reputation of the Valois were an especially effective means to praise the Bourbons.

In the immediate aftermath of the Saint Bartholomew's Day Massacre, the inflammatory pamphlet *A Wake-Up Call for the French*, denouncing Catherine, included the charge that Marguerite had incestuous relations with three of her brothers.[166] It also called her "Margot," a name that came from this usage to connote her sexual activities. This attack on Marguerite typified what became a conventional feature of pamphlet literature, that is to say, a predilection to attack both royal men and women for their debauchery. These pamphlets launched extreme charges that bore no connection to actual activities but were simply the strongest delegitimizing denunciations one could make. For example, League pamphleteers went so far as to accuse Navarre of incest with his mother, Jeanne d'Albret, despite her reputation for great spirituality. Marguerite was not generally indicted in such pamphlets, but once the League was at war with both Henry III and Navarre, she could be tarred by Catholics and Protestants as a Valois-Medici. Briefly, at the end of the sixteenth century, Marguerite enjoyed an enhanced reputation. She was, after all, unlike Gabrielle d'Estrées, the mistress Henry IV planned to marry, a legitimate queen, a Catholic, and, at that point, still married to the king.

The myth of Margot waxed and waned as political anxieties about women in politics increased or abated. It was systematically revived and revised to serve the interests of the monarchy or, later, the state. In the 1630s, in response to the threat posed to his power by the alliance of the dowager queen, Marie de Medici, with the queen Anne of Austria, historians revived Marguerite's myth to show the dangers of women in power. For the historian Dupleix, for example, Marguerite was an unstable political force whose actions reflected her runaway passions. He not only claimed that she had two illegitimate children but also that she and Marie de Medici shared "that tenderness which easily ties women together," intimating that they, like other women interested in political power, were lesbians.[167] Early in Louis XIV's reign, Marguerite was invoked to crystallize emerging bourgeois anxieties about the prominence of women in political life and the cultivation of luxury by the nobility. This period also saw an increased appreciation of Henry IV as the king with a common touch. As Henry took on his legendary character, Marguerite was castigated as a wife who had been an impediment rather than a good bourgeois helpmate to him.

The dissolution of her marriage also provoked some sympathy. But this appreciation was short-lived, as *The Satiric Divorce* played an almost immediate and central role in creating the mythic Queen Margot. Although not published until 1660, this text circulated much earlier in manuscript among disaffected nobles to discredit Henry IV, even while sympathizing with his marital woes. After his death, Marguerite was targeted by both the anti-aristocratic attacks of the Parisian population and the anti-Valois charges of Bourbon historians. This text lent support to both camps. While early histories of Henry IV's reign cited a marriage between cousins of too close proximity as the justification for the annulment, others picked up the charges in *The Satiric Divorce* and amplified them. For example, Jacques-August de Thou's *Histoire universelle* accused Marguerite of having Guast murdered as just one example of the dangerous consequences of a woman's passion.[168] Such charges have been central to historical writing about Marguerite ever since.

By the nineteenth century, the queen disappeared almost entirely into her legend. One particularly striking example was the famous fictional version of her relationship with La Molle. In Dumas's *Queen Margot*, La Molle, about to be executed for plotting against Charles IX, begged spectators gathered at the scaffold to commend him to the good graces of the queen of Navarre. Other versions of the story heightened the drama. In one, Marguerite transported La Molle's severed head to the churchyard of Saint Martin of the Martyrs and buried it. Dumas's fully developed romance built on earlier texts. Brantôme referred to the story obliquely when he wrote, "I know two beautiful and honorable women, who having lost their gallants in battle, made such lamentation, affected such extravagant mourning . . . [that] they gave great scandal and damaged their reputations."[169] Gédéon Tallement des Reaux, a seventeenth-century collector of scandals, embellished this part of Marguerite's legend, including her petticoat pockets full of her lovers' hearts.[170] Stendhal's character Mathilde de La Molle's reenactment of the event in *The Red and the Black* added to the story's popular currency.

Queen Margot, as Marguerite has come to be known, reveals, as did Diane de Poitiers, the power of myth over history. But Diane constructed a long-lived, consistent, and powerful myth that defined her from her lifetime to our day. Marguerite's myth, in contrast, was not established until the end of her life. She thus played little role in its construction. If her memoirs were intended to mythologize her positively, they were ineffective against the inflammatory charges of texts such as *The Satiric Divorce*. Instead her critics, or even possibly her aggrieved enemies, defined her myth.

As historians focused recently on other members of her family, it became clear that in many respects the negative reputations that still adhere to them were often based on a few telling (and perhaps compelling) stories. New studies call into question elements of Catherine de Medici's Black Legend or tales of Henry III's sexual profligacy by documenting the creation and evolution of such myths and by pointing out the ways they served the propaganda campaign of Protestants, the Catholic League, or the Bourbons against the last Valois monarchs.

Marguerite's myth has proved so enduring that it has only just begun to be eroded by scholarly scrutiny. Even if every salacious element of her myth were completely credible, the myth neglects her political roles and intellectual accomplishments. Perhaps now, Marguerite's sexual history, so much exaggerated over the centuries, can no longer be deployed quite as effectively to argue for the exclusion of women from politics. Perhaps too her history can be better differentiated from the powerful and politically effective myth that still surrounds her.

Marguerite was highly unusual among royal women. She had extramarital relations not as a mistress but as a queen. Her temperament led her to both politics and scandal, and she fled from neither, a proclivity she shared with her brother Henry III—but he was a king and she was a royal daughter. Her tendency to follow her instincts and to abandon good sense or even self-interest threw her into adventure. Her unconventional behavior made her an inspiration for romance novelists and an easy target for political polemicists. Marguerite was ambitious, avid for glory, and eager for a public role even when, as they frequently did, her actions embroiled her in scandal. Her brothers easily persuaded her to participate in their political schemes. Despite her obvious intelligence, they often manipulated her. Her marriage, arranged for peace between Protestants and Catholics, instead provided the occasion for the Saint Bartholomew's Day Massacre, one of the most violent of all the violent events of sixteenth-century religious warfare. While royal marriages were intended to cement alliances and produce heirs, Marguerite's marriage to Henry was a failure on both counts. Saint Bartholomew's Day destroyed its diplomatic purpose, and she bore her husband no heirs.[171] Henry used Marguerite as a diplomatic stalking horse, the same way he would later use his mistress Gabrielle d'Estrées. It is certainly worth considering whether some of his much-vaunted political success was due to the women who ably served his political purposes.

Marguerite's political failures are obvious, at least in hindsight. She supported Francis against Henry III, but so did many astute politicians of the day. Her alliance with the League against her husband and her brother certainly seems rash in retrospect. But the League was strong enough to control Paris and subsequently the king. And she, like all political actors during the Wars of Religion, played one faction against others for personal advantage and survival. When there was a price to pay for political failure or treachery, she paid it more often than her co-conspirators. But even more adept politicians—her brothers, mother, and her husband, for example—often proved no better able to weigh accurately the ramifications of their political acts in the face of the complexities and shifting allegiances of the Wars of Religion. Her defection from her husband and the king was a highly unusual act of political independence by a sixteenth-century woman, but it may have saved her life, just as her role during the Saint Bartholomew's Day Massacre may have saved Henry's. Marguerite's rashest acts may thus have been acts of self-preservation. She was a political survivor in dangerous times.

Equally significant, Marguerite played an important role in the development of the court and French culture at the end the sixteenth century. She proved adept at using the court as an instrument of intellectual development and cultural diffusion. She likely has not been as appreciated as she warrants, at least in part, because she functioned far more independently than most royal women. Although she did not have royal revenue to use the arts to enhance the monarchy, Marguerite was nonetheless a significant figure in French cultural patronage and the development of letters and philosophy. Her cultural success provokes one to wonder: What sort of cultural phenomena might the Bourbon court have fostered had Marguerite presided when Henry IV became king? Like her great-aunt, Marguerite contributed her own writings to the "quarrel over women," and her study of philosophy led her to assert the superiority of women.[172] She had, over the course of her long and drama-filled life, carved out a distinctive and unusually independent course as author, wife, and queen.

SIGNIFICANT DATES FOR CHAPTER 7

1553	Birth of Henry of Navarre, later Henry IV, December 14
1573	Birth of Gabrielle d'Estrées, December 23
1590	Gabrielle and Henry meet
1592	Gabrielle marries Nicholas d'Amerval, lord of Liancourt
1593	Henry abjures Protestantism, July 25
1594	Coronation of Henry IV at Chartres, February 27
	Henry enters Paris, March 22
	Birth of Caesar to Gabrielle and Henry, June 7
	Triumphal entry, September 15
1595	Gabrielle's marriage to Liancourt annulled, January 7
	Parlement registers letters legitimating Caesar, February 3
1596	Birth of Catherine-Henriette, November 11
1598	Edict of Nantes, April 13
	Birth of Alexandre, April 19
	Peace of Vervins, May 2
1599	Death of Gabrielle, April 10
1610	Henry IV assassinated, May 14

7

Gabrielle d'Estrées

Nearly a Queen

Gabrielle d'Estrées, an officially acknowledged mistress of Henry IV, was preparing for her wedding the Sunday after Easter 1599, when she died on Holy Saturday. Unlike Marguerite, who had often challenged her husband, Gabrielle made Henry's cause hers and, as a result, nearly became the queen of France. The object of the king's devotion for nine years, she was the only woman to keep Henry even remotely faithful. She bore him three children and died a gruesome death on the eve of their controversial and problematic marriage. Gabrielle lived a vibrant life in a public setting and, like Marguerite, appears in contemporary memoirs. Her attitude toward the king evolved from an almost scornful disinterest in the face of his obvious attraction to her to a relationship that seemed based on mutual affection, respect, and trust. So too, Gabrielle evolved from a spoiled, carefree young woman into the king's full personal and political partner. This relationship also opened up more significant and extensive roles for her in the political arena than that played by other mistresses or by virtually any queen. Gabrielle, like all mistresses, depended completely on the favor of the king for such opportunities, but Henry made hers an expansive position. She frequently acted as the king's representative in important political and diplomatic negotiations.[1] As it took Henry more than a decade to win his disaffected kingdom, these negotiations were critical to his success.

Over the course of their relationship, Gabrielle grew in stature—so much so that Henry could present her as an appropriate queen, even though she did not have the status, blood, or diplomatic standing of a princess. She, like other mistresses, provoked criticism. But Gabrielle was neither blamed for the Wars of Religion nor subjected to attacks as scurrilous as those heaped on Marguerite.

Gabrielle no doubt benefited from Henry's great political skills in reconciling opposing groups at the end of the Wars of Religion. Some accounts of Gabrielle's influence on Henry's reign suggest that she too was an adept diplomat, so much so that she was seen as working to pacify and unify a war-ravaged France. Some of her contemporaries appreciated her effectiveness in advancing the political interests of the new Bourbon king.

Gabrielle has also been the happy beneficiary of the positive image that adheres to Henry as one of France's most popular kings. Identified almost entirely with favorable developments, Henry neither provides grist for the mills of critics of monarchy nor serves the purposes of anti-republican, monarchist narratives. Gabrielle is thus identified with the popular Bourbon monarch and the improving political and religious situation under Henry.

Equally important, the Bourbons, the new dynasty effectively concentrating its authority in the hands of the king, exerted greater control over the writing of history. For historians apotheosizing Henry and the Bourbons, Gabrielle became simply one of Henry's string of sexual conquests, although their polishing of Henry's image redounded to her benefit.[2] As the wedding approached, the vehemence of attacks on her increased, but with her death, her critics fell silent. Not until Enlightenment critiques of the monarchy would Gabrielle be a target of Voltaire's wit, for example. But such attacks were much blunter than those of religious polemicists and no doubt softened somewhat by her death. For Bourbon historians, a mistress could enhance Henry's authority and heroic masculinity, but a female political partner diminished him. Thus Gabrielle, more than any other women in this history, has been virtually expunged from narratives of this period. But her story adds distinctive elements to the saga of royal mistresses.

As a mistress planning her royal wedding, Gabrielle raises questions about the nature of kingship and the expected relationship between the king and queen. Did the possibility of a mistress-queen indicate a change in the perception of royal marriages? To the degree that the proposed marriage was accepted, was acceptance rooted in war weariness or simply cynicism about royal morals and monarchs?

Gabrielle's death on the eve of her marriage saved France from having to confront the many problems such a union would have produced, particularly for Church-state relations. Some French bishops might have endorsed Henry's marriage to Gabrielle, but the pope adamantly opposed it. If Henry had gone forward with a marriage sanctified in Paris but repudiated by Rome, what would have happened to the tense relations between Henry and the Vatican and the fragile religious peace in France? A marriage to Gabrielle could have also raised serious issues for royal succession. She had two sons by Henry. Even though Henry legitimated them, they were born out of wedlock and would not have been considered legitimate heirs to the crown. To the shock of many of his contemporaries, Henry seemed willing to do so. If Henry had died leaving a young legitimate son, might his reign have been contested by an older, legitimated brother? The French state might have faced the contested succession that plagued many Italian city-states during the fifteenth century, as rulers inserted illegitimate or legitimated-after-the-fact sons into the line of succession.

Gabrielle also raises questions about the relative advantages of a mistress's fertility. Had she not borne the king children, and male children at that, it is highly unlikely that Henry would have considered her an appropriate wife. But Gabrielle had borne two sons and a daughter and was pregnant with her fourth child when Henry announced their upcoming marriage, and his wife had borne him no children. Surely the desire to have this fourth child be legitimate had a decisive impact on his wedding plans. After all, Henry had promised to marry previous mistresses if they bore him a son. The other obvious advantages to Gabrielle of having her children legitimated by the crown were the income and estates they received. Through the king's gifts to her oldest son, Gabrielle acquired great wealth as well as the political positions attached to administering those estates during his minority. This wealth has produced a discrepancy in the way biographers have treated her. Was she a gold digger or was she the king's true love? For some, she grew from a rather amoral young woman into the king's partner. For others, she was an adventuress who weighed her chances at every point and took them when the advantages were clear—a femme fatale who captured the king.[3]

The best-known image of Gabrielle is the frontispiece to this volume. As noted in the introduction, this image of her with her sister, in which they engage the viewer with straightforward gazes, was not that of a respectable woman. Although the image seems to consign her to the status of mistress, it is also ambiguous. Gabrielle holds out Henry's coronation ring, given in promise of marriage. The painting explicitly points to her fertility (her sister's pinching of her breast) to convey Gabrielle's transformation from courtesan to the mother of his child. The painting indicates Henry's great challenge in presenting Gabrielle as his choice to be queen of France.

Another version of this image on display in the museum at Montpellier projects different images and recasts Gabrielle (fig. 7.1). The setting is the same, but crucial elements have been modified. The servant is now Gabrielle's child's wet nurse, the rather lascivious image of a naked man above the fireplace has been replaced with a conventional classical nude; and there is no blank mirror.

Fig. 7.1. Gabrielle d'Estrées and her sister, the duchess of Villars. Fontainebleau school, sixteenth century. Musée de la Société Archéologique, Montpellier, France/The Bridgeman Art Library.

Most strikingly, Gabrielle and her sister are clothed; and neither looks directly at the viewer. This more conventional image transforms Gabrielle into an alluring woman in a maternal setting, but the similarity of the two images suggests that the new image is not intended to efface the earlier, sexualized image of Gabrielle in her bath, but rather, by modifying it, to refine it. The juxtaposition of these two paintings raises the crucial question of whether the mistress could become respectable or even an acceptable queen—questions that defined Gabrielle's tenure as royal mistress.

THE SEVEN DEADLY SINS

Gabrielle became Henry IV's mistress almost as a family tradition. Her maternal lineage was renowned for both beauty and the wealth and influence that trade in sexual favors could gain. Late in the seventeenth century, Louis de

Rouvroy, the duke of Saint-Simon, dubbed Gabrielle and her six sisters "the seven deadly sins."[4]

The Estrées family was descended from Jean d'Estrées, who began his public career as a page to Anne of Brittany and then followed a conventional career of military service to the king, which led to titles, wealth, and advantageous marriages. Jean served Louis XII in the Italian wars; Francis I rewarded him with a position as captain of fifty men at arms; and under Henry II, Jean became grand master of the artillery. While in Italy, he rescued Jacques, the illegitimate son of Jean of Bourbon, for which he was given Jacques's daughter in marriage. Gabrielle and Henry were thus four generations removed from a common Bourbon ancestor.

Antoine, Gabrielle's father, was proud of this connection.[5] Antoine attached himself to Francis, Henry III's younger brother, who appointed him a gentleman of his chamber and then rewarded him with royal governorships. Henry III, to detach him from Francis's service, made Antoine governor of several other territories and a chevalier of the Order of the Holy Spirit (see fig. 5.6). Antoine was also one of the earliest nobles to ally firmly with Henry IV after the assassination of Henry III. On the paternal side, Gabrielle belonged to a high-ranking noble family with long and profitable service to the crown throughout the Renaissance.

Gabrielle's maternal progenitors had greatly enhanced the family through their extramarital liaisons. Marie Gaudin, Gabrielle's great-grandmother and the wife of Philibert Babou, was one of Francis I's many unofficial mistresses, which led to the elevation of the Babou family and the gift to Marie of the chateau of La Bourdaisière in the Loire Valley. Marie's son Jean de Babou advanced the family considerably in more orthodox ways; he was grand master of the artillery, served as ambassador to Rome under Catherine de Medici, and made an advantageous marriage to Françoise Robertet, the daughter of one of Henry II's ministers. Their daughter and Gabrielle's mother, Françoise, and her sisters were renowned for their beauty and bad reputations. Françoise, who served as lady-in-waiting to Mary Stuart when she became Francis II's bride, was notorious for her extramarital affairs. Although she took a series of lovers immediately after her marriage to Antoine d'Estrées, she later settled into a period of maternity, bearing ten children in ten years, nine of whom lived.

Then Françoise became grist for the sixteenth-century scandal mill. She had an affair with Louis of Berenger, lord of Guast and Marguerite de Valois's nemesis. When Guast was assassinated in one of the many duels of Henry III's *mignons*, Yves, the marquis of Allègre, subsequently killed Guast's assassin in a duel. Françoise, grateful that Allègre had killed her lover's assassin, offered him money then herself as a reward. When Allègre accepted the latter, Françoise left her husband and children, taking only her youngest daughter with her. The abandonment of her family provoked quite a scandal, exacerbated when Françoise bore a daughter out of wedlock. The saga came to a satisfying end by contemporary standards, when Allègre's disgruntled tenants murdered him and Françoise in their beds.

Perhaps not surprisingly, Gabrielle, born into this scandal-plagued family in 1573, was less well trained in proper comportment than in feminine wiles. Her own mother, it was claimed, offered her to Henry III, although there is no evidence beyond the fact that Françoise presented Gabrielle at court. According to the often-repeated story, Henry III evinced no interest in Gabrielle, reputedly remarking that if he were interested in a thin blonde, he would seek out his wife.[6] Gabrielle's father, perhaps with more desperation than good sense, turned the education of his daughters over to his wife's sister Isabelle Babou de Sourdis, wife of the former governor of Chartres and mistress of the chancellor Philippe Hurault de Cheverny.[7]

Most of Gabrielle's sisters were associated with sexual misconduct. Neither Gabrielle nor her sister Diane was a model of propriety, but two other sisters were notorious: Françoise had many conspicuous affairs; Angelique, an abbess, conducted many sexual affairs at her convent and, until she was exposed, encouraged other nuns to do the same. In Gabrielle's case, some accounts attributed lovers to her or insisted that she was, in fact, Henry III's mistress. Stories of her family's dissolute past were intended to tar Gabrielle as an adept courtesan before she became Henry's mistress; she thus could never be an appropriate queen. Whether or not these rumored affairs had any substance, contemporary Parisians were amused that the Estrées family home in Paris was on the rue des Bons-Enfants (the Street of Good Children).

Likely reflecting her disordered family life, Gabrielle seems to have had a rather poor education and to have been an indifferent student. But early on, she was recognized as a young woman of staggering beauty (fig. 7.2): "Her eyes were of a celestial color so luminous that it would be difficult to judge if they borrowed from the sun their vivid clarity or if a beautiful star reflected hers. With that she had two equally round eyebrows of a pleasing darkness, a slightly aquiline nose, her mouth the color of rubies, a throat so white . . . of the color of lilies, of a proportion so admirable that one would take her for a masterpiece of nature."[8] Louise-Marguerite de Lorraine continued her extravagant description of each of Gabrielle's features in this vein in her *History of the Loves of Henry IV*, doubtless intending to sanction Gabrielle's elevation to royal mistress.

Fig. 7.2. Portrait presumed to be Gabrielle d'Estrées by François Quesnel. Musée Condé, Chantilly, France / The Bridgeman Art Library.

ROYAL PURSUIT

Despite her maternal heritage, Gabrielle did not pursue Henry and initially did not even respond to his interest in her. She was instead enamored of Roger de Saint-Larry, the duke of Bellegarde, with whom she had been involved since 1587 (when she was fourteen) and whom she hoped to marry. When presented at court by the duke of Eperon, his relative and one of Henry III's favorites, Bellegarde too joined their ranks, becoming in short order grand master of the *garde-robe*, first gentleman of the chamber, and finally grand squire of France. When Henry III's reign was jeopardized by the League, he asked Henry of Navarre to take care of Bellegarde, who then became one of his most influential officials.[9] Bellegarde brought Gabrielle to Henry's attention.[10]

When Henry met Gabrielle in November 1590, he had recently become the legitimate heir to the throne and begun his quest to claim it. He was thirty-seven years old and Gabrielle was a seventeen-year-old beauty. It was a *coup de foudre* (lightning bolt) for him; she captivated him for the rest of her life. Henry's fortunes—personal and political—were at an especially low point. He had just failed to take Paris from the Catholic League. His mistress Corisandre no longer aroused his passions, but initially he could not detach Gabrielle from Bellegarde. As Henry pursued Gabrielle, he was taking camp followers to bed. From these inauspicious beginnings, it seemed unlikely an enduring relationship and real partnership would develop.

Although it is uncommon for a man, especially a king, to be pilloried for his sexual adventures, Henry was far more indiscriminate than usual. Those who have tried to track his sexual liaisons have recorded more than fifty known sexual partners. His later popularity and the pens of Bourbon historians meant that his sexual adventures did not detract from his reputation. To some degree they added to his allure as a virile alternative to the last Valois kings, who were perceived as effeminate and degenerate. It is still somewhat surprising that so little opprobrium attaches to Henry's behavior, especially since, on occasion, he neglected his political interests to pursue his passions.

While Gabrielle was preoccupied with youthful indiscretions, the political situation in France degenerated. It remained unclear whether French Catholics would accept Henry as their king and even less likely that the Vatican would endorse his claim. Indeed his initial efforts to bring France under his control did not go well. Henry failed to win over significant portions of the French nobility, who were vital to his efforts to pacify the country and retain the crown. He faced great resistance from the remnants of the League in staunchly Catholic areas and, above all, in Paris. And Catholic dissent was funded and encouraged by Spain and the Vatican. It would ultimately take Henry ten years to win over or conquer the opposition and solidify his claim to the throne. It was by no means certain that he would prevail.

While Henry sought to regain France, he also campaigned to win Gabrielle. His camp was in Compiègne, not far from her home. Initially Bellegarde begged Henry to go with him to meet her. Bellegarde had so often praised Gabrielle's beauty that Henry was eager to see for himself. In retrospect, Bellegarde acknowledged, "It is so true that we have more to guard against ourselves than our real enemies."[11] Once Henry had seen Gabrielle, he could not be diverted from pursuing her. He took advantage of his camp's proximity to court her as he besieged Chartres. The territory was not even safe for him. On one visit to her, he disguised himself as a woodsman. The fact that she and Bellegarde planned to marry made no difference to Henry, who, as a modern historian noted, had "the mentality of an oriental despot when it came to women."[12] It is generally believed that Gabrielle succumbed to Henry's suit during the siege of Chartres in April 1591.

Why did Gabrielle become involved with this man she initially found unattractive and much less appealing than her lover? Perhaps the urgings of her well-placed relatives, well aware of the great advantages that could accrue to a royal mistress's family, were persuasive. Her father, one of the earliest noble converts to Henry's cause, might have expected to profit even more from his daughter's relationship with the king. Her father had many daughters to marry well and sons to promote. Gabrielle's Aunt Isabelle might also have wanted to promote her lover Cheverny's interest. Despite his previous allegiance to the League, Cheverny had just returned to Henry's favor and may have promoted Gabrielle's relationship with the king to advance himself. Contemporaries commented that it was less that Henry persuaded Gabrielle of his charms than that the entire Estrées family laid siege to the king.[13]

Whether or not her family persuaded Gabrielle, they immediately benefited from the new relationship. Cheverny found greater favor with Henry. Henry focused his military campaign on besieging Noyon to capture it from the League, in part so that Gabrielle's father, who had just been appointed governor of the territory, could enjoy its benefits—one of several occasions when Henry neglected his best military opportunities to pursue Gabrielle.[14] This dallying provoked criticism that Henry was not acting decisively against the League, and recriminations from Elizabeth I that he was not making progress sufficient to warrant her financial support. The English ambassador Unton reported to her that "the king chose this town because of the great love he bore the governor's daughter who has all power over him."[15]

At this stage of their relationship, Henry was an avid pursuer, while Gabrielle was at best somewhat cavalier. Willing to exercise the power of her sexual attraction over him, she was frequently and unrepentantly late to meet him, a trait that infuriated him. By August 1591, the relationship had become official, but Gabrielle may have remained involved with Bellegarde. Henry's frustration with this situation is evident in his letters to Gabrielle: "There is nothing to prolong or increase my suspicions save the manner in which you act toward me. . . . To begin, I protest to you, my dear mistress, that whatever I may assert respecting the offenses I have received, is not intended to stir up any remnants of bitterness, for I am satisfied with the trouble you have taken to content me; but only to show you that my cause for suspicion was just."[16]

Early in their relationship, Gabrielle's father arranged a marriage for her to the widower Nicolas d'Amerval, lord of Liancourt, but Antoine's motives remain unclear. Perhaps he believed the situation required decisive paternal action. He had borne the burden of his own wife's defection and must have worried about his daughters. Bellegarde had been interested in marrying Gabrielle, but he had left the field to the king. Her father might well have thought that her relationship with Henry would be fleeting. Henry's prospects too were not entirely encouraging, despite some military success. His religion remained a serious impediment to his quest for the crown, as many would only accept a Catholic claimant. And Henry was unquestionably still married to Marguerite of Navarre, in exile in Usson since 1586. Thus by arranging Gabrielle's marriage, Antoine may have been attempting to salvage her reputation, to sequester her in the country, or to provide a measure of protection should her royal lover lose interest. The marriage could have also shielded Gabrielle from the scandal of her mother's recent murder. Both her brother and her sister contended that the marriage was arranged to keep Gabrielle away from Henry, but this ex post facto account might have been necessary to preserve her reputation. That is to say, the case for a subsequent annulment might have required that the marriage be genuine. It is equally plausible that the marriage was carried out at Henry's behest; a married mistress was more respectable.[17]

Other considerations too may have shaped these marriage plans. Marriage would have reduced Gabrielle's father's authority over her, and she might well have imagined that any marriage would give her greater freedom. Henry might have presumed that marriage would make her more accessible to him. (Prior to her marriage, Gabrielle often insisted to Henry that she could not join him because her father objected to their relationship.) Immediately after her marriage, Henry gave Gabrielle two estates. Such gifts could have been wedding presents. But they also seemed to substantiate both the king's relationship with Gabrielle and Liancourt's assent to a *mariage blanc* (a phony marriage) to disguise it. Henry's gifts made Gabrielle more financially independent. Marriage served her father's interests as well; he benefited from Henry's gifts to him, and his daughter had a more respectable status.

For whatever reason, Antoine selected Liancourt as suitable. Twelve years older than Gabrielle, Liancourt's contemporaries considered him physically and personally unattractive; his peasants described him as an especially rapacious overlord. Both her sister and her brother described Gabrielle's resistance to the match; she did not speak for three days. This situation underscores an unpleasant reality of sixteenth-century marriages, that is to say, the extent of a father's authority over his daughter. One might hope that a father would take his daughter's wishes into account, but whether or not he did, he had complete authority until he ceded it to her husband. In this case, however, Gabrielle's relationship with Henry diminished her husband's authority over her.

A ROYAL RELATIONSHIP

Despite its inauspicious beginnings, the nature of the relationship between Henry and Gabrielle seemed to change quite dramatically sometime in 1593. The question is Why? Did Gabrielle weigh her options and decide that a position as mistress of the king was a good opportunity for her? In other words, had she become a true heir of the Babou tradition—a femme fatale? Or had Henry made her see him differently and she had come to love him? It is also entirely possible that it is only *our* sense that the relationship changed, because we have Henry's letters to Gabrielle from this period. Since he was such an inveterate letter writer, it is likely that he wrote to her from the beginning of their relationship, and that those letters, which could well document an earlier, passionate relationship, have been lost. Whatever her motives at this time, Gabrielle was thereafter devoted to Henry's interests. Henry's cause was hers, and she was his staunch and effective partisan.

Gabrielle accompanied Henry on his military campaigns, where Bellegarde noted, her living conditions in camp were "as mean as those of a fishwife."[18] Acting as Henry's partner, Gabrielle seemed to share his courage and ambition. Her devotion endeared her to him, and he showered her with expensive gifts. Henry even imposed a special head tax; its revenues went directly to Gabrielle, reviving the practice of Henry II, who had levied taxes for Diane de Poitiers.[19]

Gabrielle suddenly became a wealthy woman. Her wholehearted support might indicate the beginning of her aspirations to be queen, although there is no evidence that these hopes underlay her change of attitude or, indeed, that Henry had given any thought to marrying her. They were, after all, both married to others. Gabrielle's marriage could be annulled by appeal to the local ecclesiastical authority. (Her brother, François-Anibale, was bishop of Noyon at this time and might have presided over annulment proceedings.) But an annulment of Henry's marriage to Marguerite required papal approval. Likely not coincidentally, Henry made his first overtures to Marguerite to attempt to procure an annulment. His councilor Philippe Duplessis-Mornay also expressed concern that Henry's many love affairs were damaging his reputation and urged him to "regularize" his marital situation.[20]

As Gabrielle's relationship with Henry became more public, their future also began to seem more secure. Henry seems to have considered her his lucky star, since their relationship coincided with an improvement in his fortunes. He had courted her from his base in Normandy as important nobles rallied to his cause. As royal forces increasingly thwarted League troops, Henry became more confident (fig. 7.3). But Paris remained a significant holdout, and the Estates-General convened to challenge Henry's claim to the throne.

As Henry sought noble support, Gabrielle cultivated female noble allies, among them Louise of Lorraine, the widow of Henry III; Louise of Coligny, the daughter of the assassinated admiral; and Louise of Guise. Somewhat sur-

Fig. 7.3. Equestrian portrait of Henry IV before the walls of Paris, 1594. French school, sixteenth century. Musée Carnavalet, Paris/The Bridgeman Art Library.

prisingly, Gabrielle forged these important connections with the female representative of Catholic, Protestant, and ultra-Catholic interests. With such connections, she helped to bridge Henry's still-significant hurdles in claiming the throne. Such efforts were essential as Henry remained unacceptable to many Catholics.

When the Estates convened to elect a king (usually simply to ratify hereditary succession), they intended, in this case, to set aside Henry III's designation of Henry as his heir. There were other possible claimants. The League supported Charles, the cardinal of Bourbon. But the cardinal of Bourbon was not eager to contest his cousin's claim, and his own was neutralized when Henry's army guard surrounded him. Catholics then supported the duke of Mayenne (the brother of the two assassinated Guises, Henry and Louis) (see fig. 5.3). The duke was willing to withdraw his claim if Henry agreed to a number of conditions, including converting to Catholicism. Spain claimed the French throne for the infanta Isabel, the daughter of Henry II's daughter Elisabeth and Philip II of Spain. This claim violated Salic law and, as significantly, raised the specter of Spanish influence in France.

Henry's religion made his situation unusually complex. His Huguenot supporters feared that he would convert. The League continued to reject his claim to the throne. Other Catholics sought a rapprochement with Henry and sent out feelers to the Vatican. The pope rebuffed them, saying, "How can we put faith and confidence in Henry of Navarre, when even one of his adherents has told us that, if Saint Peter himself looked upon the conversion of that prince as certain, we ought not to believe it."[21] But the pope damaged the League's cause by threatening to excommunicate all Catholics who did not repudiate Henry—a move seen as an attack on the autonomy of the French Church. The king of Spain lobbied for the Spanish princess and attempted to solidify her claim by betrothing her to the Hapsburg Archduke Ernst. This alliance was seen as overt and unpalatable Hapsburg control of the crown. The archduke then proposed the duke of Mayenne as king, a collusion that discredited both of them. Many members of the Estates-General objected to the Protestant Henry but also deeply resented Spanish pressure. A popular song mocked the Estates:

> Come on, my ass! through the gates
> To Monsieur de Mayenne's Estates;
> So you can turn, without a wrench,
> Into Spaniard instead of French.[22]

Opposition to Mayenne greatly enhanced Henry's position, which was further strengthened when the Parlement of Paris condemned any intent to confer the crown on a foreigner. This decree excluded the Spanish infanta as well as members of the Guise family, who, as rulers of Lorraine, could be considered foreign.[23] Henry, committed to ridding France of Spanish influence, began to work toward reconciliation with his Catholic subjects. In this, as in so many of his political endeavors, Gabrielle proved an effective ally.

Gabrielle urged Henry to convert (yet again) to Catholicism.[24] She advised that the League strongholds of Paris and Rouen would rally to him *only* if he renounced Protestantism. Their citizens could be persuaded, she insisted, to prefer Henry to the League and to see the League as a pawn of foreign powers. Even Sully, Henry's chief minister, who wrote the history of Henry IV's reign to emphasize, often beyond plausibility, his own contributions and to denigrate other influences, nonetheless acknowledged Gabrielle's importance to Henry's decision to convert. Henry himself cited as crucial the supplication of "his closest and most tender servant" who had moved him to tears.[25] The seventeenth-century historian Mézeray too credited Gabrielle, noting that she spoke to Henry of the misery of his people and the prospect of spending the rest of his days at arms "far from the rest and sweetness of life."[26] She, of course, embodied that sweetness, but also appealed to Henry's sympathy for his people. Gabrielle also persuaded Henry's devoutly Protestant sister, Catherine of Bourbon, not to oppose Henry's conversion.[27] Whatever role her entreaties played in Henry's decision, his Huguenot supporters blamed Gabrielle: They saw her efforts as a step in her quest to have Henry's marriage annulled.[28] As early as April 1592, Henry announced his intention to be instructed in the Catholic faith, although he insisted, paradoxically, that religion, as a matter of the heart, "was not taken off like a shirt"[29]—despite his own many necessary and politically expedient changes.[30]

Once Henry agreed, Gabrielle also worked to "sell" his conversion to French Catholics. Her ability to negotiate this complex situation is all the more impressive given that we have no evidence that she had any strong religious views or previously honed political sensibilities. Her family had been Huguenots during the Wars of Religion, became Catholic again under the League, but were early supporters of Henry.[31] Perhaps Gabrielle's religious expediency allowed her to negotiate with both sides when she took on this most difficult issue. Unlike Catherine de Medici, whose religious tolerance perhaps made it difficult for her to appreciate the intensity of religious sentiments, Gabrielle proved an adept negotiator, likely because of her own lack of strong commitment to a particular faith. She was in the no-win situation of anyone who grappled with these contentious issues, and her efforts provoked criticism. A disgruntled Calvinist preacher, Gabriel d'Amours, exhorted Henry: "Did you but listen to Gabriel d'Amours, your minister, as you listen to Gabrielle, your *amoureuse*, I would see a generous king victorious over his enemies."[32] Members of the Catholic League too excoriated Gabrielle. Parisian placards ridiculed her with verses such as:

> Neither the high learning of the old Sorbonne,
> The bravado of the Spanish, nor the clamor of the Legate,
> Have as much power to make a renegade,
> As the inviting eyes of an angelic face.[33]

A Protestant wit remarked: "Do you remember the old days when Gabriel [the archangel] announced the message of salvation? Now it is another Gabrielle by whom the king renounces his salvation."[34] Although Gabrielle's efforts provoked satiric responses, Henry's abjuration of Protestantism would be *the* crucial step, along with Pope Clement VIII's acceptance of it as genuine, in gaining Catholic support for his kingship.[35] (Sixtus V had previously excommunicated Henry and written an open letter to the people of Paris claiming that he was not fit to reign.)

Henry wrote to Gabrielle that he was taking the "perilous leap," and some Protestants blamed her when he solemnly abjured his Protestant beliefs at Saint-Denis on July 25, 1593. Aubigné, the Protestant scholar, inveighed against her, but Sully, who often blamed Gabrielle for things he disapproved, positively credited her with Henry's conversion.[36] Some Catholics then espoused Henry's cause. Others were bought off through "treaties of capitulation," offering tax relief or even cash payments.[37] Henry's conversion obviously heightened his Protestant supporters' anxieties. But Gabrielle proved surprisingly effective in reconciling the Huguenot nobility to him. Each Protestant noble who came to reconcile with Henry also met with his mistress. She also worked behind the scenes as a liaison to those League members ready to make peace with the king. Gabrielle thus proved pivotal in gaining both Protestant and Catholic support for Henry.

Henry's conversion was decisive in solidifying his claim to the throne. Now Catholic and unquestionably the legitimate king of France, he was crowned on February 27, 1594, at Chartres (Reims was not yet under his control). That year too the military campaign to bring Paris under royal control finally turned in Henry's favor: Mayenne, the former Catholic claimant to the throne, left Paris under a truce; Spanish troops withdrew; some League regiments simply joined Henry's army; and, finally, the Parlement of Paris accepted Henry as king. Resistance to Henry remained confined to radical remnants. He entered Paris, attended Mass, and watched the Spanish leave. His mistress was less welcome:

"Isn't it a strange thing to see a great king being the servant of a woman, living without honor and making an angel of a whore," was just one of the verses circulating.[38]

September 15, 1594, marked Henry's triumphal entry into Paris and Gabrielle's first public appearance as a member of the royal entourage. Henry chose to present her in a highly advantageous way, as L'Estoile described: "The King made his entry into Paris by torchlight. . . . It was eight o'clock when his Majesty crossed over the Pont Notre Dame, accompanied by a large body of cavalry and surrounded by a magnificent nobility. He, with a laughing face, well pleased at seeing all the people crying *Vive le Roy!* so gaily, kept his hat constantly in his hand, principally in order to salute the dames and damsels, who were at the windows. . . . Madame Liancourt [Gabrielle] went a little before the King, in a magnificent litter, which was quite open, and she was covered with so many pearls and such brilliant gems that they outshone the torch light; and her gown was of black satin, tufted all over with white."[39]

Although royal processions offered important occasions for the royal family to shape public perception and to convey messages about the monarch to a broader audience, this one offered a novel, disconcerting perspective.[40] Remarkably, Gabrielle actually preceded Henry. This was the only occasion on which *anyone* preceded him, indicating Henry's desire to announce her importance. The procession marked Gabrielle's increasingly public status; she was no longer primarily behind the scenes. On earlier occasions, including the famous "Mass for Paris," celebrating Henry's reconciliation with the Church, Gabrielle attended but remained hidden behind a screen.

This entry into Paris was just one of many public occasions on which Gabrielle was presented essentially in the queen's place. This privileged position distinguished Gabrielle from Henry's previous mistresses and put her on the plane of previous officially designated mistresses. But Henry's presentation of Gabrielle, which contemporaries read as indicating his intention to share power, made her political influence much more overt than that of earlier official mistresses. In addition, Henry put Gabrielle into positions a queen would ordinarily have filled. Groulart, president of the Parlement of Normandy, complained that Henry required all magistrates to treat Gabrielle as if she were actually a royal princess. When Gabrielle arrived in Rouen, he commented, "I went to pay her my respects, and again on the following Sunday, having received the king's command to that effect."[41] Presenting a mistress in Paris also provoked more concerted opposition than simply presenting her to the court. For better or ill, with the king's return to Paris, his private life and relationship with his mistress were both more evident and more remarked upon.

Even as Henry accorded her greater prominence, Gabrielle's position remained tenuous, and Henry's political position still insecure. In December, only a few months after Henry's triumphal entry, a young Jesuit-trained student attempted to assassinate him. Henry was chastened by the renewed sense that his troubles were far from over, and his councillors were distressed to have to contemplate the issue of succession should an assassin succeed. Duplessis-Mornay urged him to set Gabrielle aside and to marry a woman who would be an appropriate queen. Henry resisted strongly. For him, the reasonable thing to do was to marry his mistress, and he began to take steps to that end. He again raised the issue of annulment with Marguerite, worked to annul Gabrielle's marriage, and moved to legitimate Caesar, the son she had borne him on June 7, 1594. The Florentine ambassador reported that Henry already treated Gabrielle as if she were his wife.[42]

Gabrielle's greater public prominence coincided roughly with Caesar's birth, an event no doubt decisive in altering both Henry's public presentation of her and their personal relationship. Henry certainly wished to acknowledge Caesar's paternity, but the situation was complicated by the fact that Gabrielle was still married. The conventional practice would have been to have Gabrielle's husband acknowledge the child as his. Such an arrangement was not ideal because, if Henry had no legitimate son and if Liancourt claimed Caesar, neither Gabrielle nor Henry could later make a convincing counterclaim on his behalf. Liancourt might also have been able to control the goods Henry gave to his child or claim Gabrielle's rapidly increasing wealth.

Crucial in Henry's fervent desire to acknowledge this child was that his birth allayed fears of his sterility. Henry and Marguerite had no children, and, perhaps as significant, doctors had declared after Henry suffered an especially serious bout of venereal disease in 1592 that he would be unable to father children.[43] No wonder that the arrival of Caesar, a healthy male child, was greeted with both joy and relief.[44] These concerns made Henry especially eager to legitimate his son.

The Parisian population remained mistrustful of Gabrielle and even doubted her son's royal blood. L'Estoile remarked on the sudden death of the king's physician Jehan Ailleboust and speculated that Gabrielle had poisoned him to prevent his reporting that her newborn son was not the king's. She had, however, been the king's constant companion the entire autumn before his birth in June.[45]

To safeguard Caesar's paternity and the king's gifts to him against any claim by Liancourt, Gabrielle initiated annulment proceedings. The proceedings were conducted in Amiens, a former League stronghold now interested in demonstrating its loyalty to the king. When Henry arrived to accept League members' surrender, he clearly hoped to influence Gabrielle's annulment proceedings. She presented a petition claiming that she had been married against her will and asserted that her marriage had not been consummated because her husband was impotent. The latter charge would have been sufficient grounds for annulment, but it was difficult to prove. In investigating Gabrielle's marriage, the bishop of Amiens discovered that Liancourt's first wife was Gabrielle's father's cousin. This offered a more clear-cut rationale for annulment, since Church law forbade remarriage to a relative of a previous spouse. The situation became more complicated and more bizarre when Liancourt not only refuted Gabrielle's claims of his impotence but also tried to bequeath her property to his children by his first wife. He claimed that his initial statement supporting Gabrielle's case was false, signed in fear for his life.[46] (His fear may have been real, but it was likely groundless, as Henry did not use assassination as a state tool.) The annulment was granted on the grounds that Liancourt had previously been married to Gabrielle's relative, but the grounds were not made public. It was generally assumed that Liancourt's impotence had been decisive, but that was not a compelling rationale, at least not in the popular imagination. The situation was ripe for satire; a risqué story told most notably by Sir Walter Raleigh recounted that Liancourt and his third wife had eight daughters![47]

After the annulment, Gabrielle more clearly assumed the status of *maîtresse en titre*. She began to be attended by a court, as Henry decreed on January 8, 1595, the day after the annulment was granted. A suite of rooms was prepared for her at the Louvre; although sensitive to public opinion, Gabrielle occupied them only when Henry was in residence.[48] He further decreed that foreign dignitaries pay their respects to her as "Titular Mistress of his Majesty, the King of France." Henry called upon the Parlement of Paris to register the letters patent by which he acknowledged Caesar's paternity and legitimated him. The wording of this document is quite significant: "Whereas We have desired to have issue and to leave it after Us to this Kingdom, and whereas God has not yet allowed Us to have any in lawful wedlock, since the Queen, Our spouse, has been for ten years separated from Us, it has been Our desire, pending the time when He may graciously endeavor to have children elsewhere." Furthermore, he claimed, Caesar, like other legitimated royal children, "will be obliged to serve this State, as has happened in the past, with others of the same quality, who served the State well, and rendered great and notable services."[49]

Henry thus set his progeny by Gabrielle against his childless state with his queen. He wanted offspring. God had not given him legitimate children because his wife was separated from him. The irregularity of his marital situation and the resulting failure to produce legitimate offspring were, seemingly, grounds to sanction a different, albeit extramarital, relationship. His declaration continued:

> Having recognized the many great graces and perfections, as much of mind as of body, that abide in the person of Our very dear and well-beloved, Gabrielle d'Estrées, We, for some years past, have sought her to that effect, as being the subject whom We judged to be the most worthy of Our friendship; which We held We might do with all the less scruple and burdening of conscience, as We know that the marriage, which she had previous contracted with the Lord of Liancourt, was null, and had never had effect, as is testified by the judgment of separation and annulment of the said marriage, which has since ensued. And whereas the said Lady, after Our long suit and by exercise of such authority as We brought to bear, did condescend to obey Us and do Our pleasure, and whereas it has pleased God that she should not long since give Us a son, who has hitherto borne the name of Cesar Monsieur, now, in addition to the natural charity and paternal affection in which We hold him, both because he is Our issue and by reason of the particular graces which God and nature have bestowed upon him in his early infancy, and which induce Us to hope they increase with his years, so that he, coming from such a stock, may some day yield much good fruit to the State.[50]

Here Henry argued that no opprobrium should be attached to Gabrielle. Her marriage had not been valid, as her annulment proved. Gabrielle succumbed to Henry and to his authority. Their sexual relationship, he suggests, was an appropriate recognition of his kingship. Not only did God give him a son but one so favored by Him and nature that he would serve the state well. Henry thus cast Caesar as a fitting heir. With this decree, Henry not only proclaimed his son's legitimacy but also asserted that Gabrielle was not a fallen woman and that his relationship with her was fitting, almost divinely sanctioned.

The statement also seems to assert a fortuitous conjunction of Henry's desires and God's wishes and begs for a theological interpretation. It seems both overweening and theologically unorthodox for a king to declare that an illicit relationship with his mistress did not make her a fallen woman or a sinner. No doubt this stance was controversial, but one wonders whether it or any part of it was credible to anyone and, if so, to whom? It suggests, despite Henry's recent conversion to Catholicism, an abiding "Protestant" tendency to interpret or challenge Church teachings.[51] It was an act of great temerity to make such a theologically charged pronouncement, especially since Henry had been reconciled to Rome for only two years. Legitimating his son too was somewhat unusual and doubtless reflects Henry's overriding concern to have progeny.[52]

COMPANIONATE MARRIAGE

While Henry's justification of his extramarital relationship might simply reflect royal presumption, it also suggested a Protestant notion of marriage as dependent on the commitment of the two parties to each other. This notion perhaps allowed both Henry and Gabrielle to dismiss their marital entanglements rather cavalierly. Whether or not they viewed their relationship as rooted in Protestantism, Henry and Gabrielle took their respective marriages lightly. So successful was this presentation of their relationship as a kind of marriage that even austere Calvinists commended Gabrielle's behavior as "that of a wife rather than a concubine."[53] Henry treated her with the dignity due a wife (not that he accorded his own wife much dignity) and expected others to do the same.

After the fall of Amiens in 1597, Henry made peace with Spain and the Catholic opposition. He could now begin reconciling with Catholics and Protestants in his kingdom. Peace warranted another triumphal welcome into Paris. The king himself lit a huge bonfire, burning "war" in effigy in the Place de Grève in front of the Hotel de Ville. At the celebratory feast, Gabrielle sat next to the king, and the duchess of Guise waited on her. With one hand Gabrielle selected delicacies from the plates the duchess presented to her and held out her other for Henry to kiss.[54] This was socially unconventional enough to provoke comment. The women of the Guise family, in close proximity to the crown by rank and blood and of much higher status than Gabrielle, nonetheless marched behind her, were seated behind her, and behaved in other ways that clearly inverted the conventional social order to endow Gabrielle with greater status.[55] When the duke of Mayenne was entertained at Fontainebleau, Gabrielle and Henry shared a table for two, and the duke occupied a side table.[56] This arrangement violated precedent by placing Gabrielle in the position the queen should have held.

Even more unconventional was Henry's public display of the intimate character of their relationship. L'Estoile expressed disgust that during a masked ball held at Fontainebleau, Henry and Gabrielle kept raising their masks to exchange kisses.[57] Gabrielle was a constant presence, and the couple spent as much time together as possible. When she accompanied him on military campaigns, she was praised for both her commitment to Henry's cause and her courage. Her public closeness to Henry meant that she received some credit for his successes and ultimately for peace and the resolution of religious conflict. Henry's letters to Gabrielle are familiar, expressing his love and devotion and notably his "fidelity to the tomb."[58] The letters explicitly detail his hopes and plans for the military campaigns that kept them apart, highlighting both their close relationship and Gabrielle's role as his confidant. The letters, not part of the public character of the relationship, nonetheless corroborated what the public saw.

The couple engaged in prosaic activities together. They enjoyed hunting; they shopped at the Foire Saint Germain (a Parisian bazaar). On one such occasion, Henry refused to buy a ring for Gabrielle because he considered it overpriced.[59] These public presentations of their relationship, whether by design or not, fostered Henry's populist reputation, solidifying a public impression of the king as a man of the people. This engaging facet of his public persona both enhanced his appeal at the time and remains a source of his continuing popularity as the king who wanted a chicken in the pot of every Frenchman on Sundays. But such everyday activities and disregard for protocol discredited Gabrielle; her behavior was not fitting for a queen.

Gabrielle's political functions were more extensive than those exercised by previous mistresses. Henry defined a privileged position for her; their close personal relationship gave her access to greater political power. Sully complained: "The d'Estrées thought of herself as a minister of state, and acted with as much authority as though she held the king's commission and seal."[60] In contrast, Pierre Matthieu, Henry's official historian, praised Gabrielle's beneficial influence on the king, his politics, and his court: "He confided to her the opinions and reports he received. . . . Whenever he revealed to her his mental wounds, she at once applied herself to quieting their pain. . . . The Court confessed that the great favor she received . . . sustained all and oppressed none."[61] Henry expressed confidence in Gabrielle's diplomatic abilities, even delegating her to deal with his own annulment. This decision interjected Gabrielle into international politics and gave her the unenviable task of negotiating with the pope, who resisted Henry's matrimonial plans.[62]

The pope's interest in authorizing Henry's annulment would be, in part, to ensure that any future marriage reinforced France's connection to the Church. Clement VIII also recognized that Henry now had the support of most of the French clergy and laity. After Henry's conversion, he might have been more inclined to favor his annulment, and he would, at the very least, consider the issue within his authority. But there was still the problem of Gabrielle.[63]

The pope might also have recognized that Gabrielle had helped to bring the monarch back into the Roman Catholic Church. Even before Henry had reconciled hard-core members of the League to his reign, Gabrielle had corresponded with the bishop of Rennes in his interest. Now, as she worked to develop the case for Henry's annulment, she expressed her loyalty to the Church. Gabrielle emphasized that Henry's annulment had ramifications for the relationship between France and the Church and her hopes to reconcile them.[64] The French monarchy and the Vatican were now engaged in an elaborate diplomatic dance to begin the process of reconciliation. Clement VIII signaled his acceptance of Henry by writing to the heads of religious orders urging them to pray for Henry's health and well-being. In turn, Henry agreed to publish decrees of the Council of Trent in France, to restore Catholicism in his own Protestant territories, and to appoint only Catholics to political office. Henry acknowledged Gabrielle's diplomatic efforts to reconcile him with the Church, for which Catholics praised her and Huguenots blamed her.

Gabrielle's diplomatic efforts were strikingly unsuccessful in dealing with an intransigent League holdout. Jean de Monluc Balagny was an adventurer, opportunist, and lifelong friend of Antoine d'Estrées. He was married to Renée of Amboise, who had a well-deserved reputation as a schemer. In 1593, Balagny was the League's governor of Cambrai, and he wanted to become the permanent ruler. Cambrai was strategically important to Henry, because if Reims were loyal to him, he could take it with its great symbolic value as the traditional coronation site. Renée went to Gabrielle to propose terms on her husband's behalf. Balagny would hold Cambrai for the king if he were made a prince and marshal of France. As a sweetener, clearly intended to heighten her zeal for this arrangement, Balagny proposed that, as he was childless, Gabrielle's offspring be named his heirs. Henry accepted these terms, which made Balagny very rich. But Balagny failed to secure Cambrai for Henry. When the Spanish besieged the town, the citizens surrendered to them, complaining of Balagny's tyranny. Gabrielle's advice had not been good in this case. Her personal interests likely led her to support Balagny; he offered wealth, security, and status to her son. Indeed, these negotiations, like most of her diplomatic ventures, enhanced her wealth and status as well. As a result, her motives are often impugned.

Gabrielle's other diplomatic ventures were equally complex but more successful. She was especially important in reconciling others who resisted Henry's reign. She made peace with the Guise family, in the course of which Louise of Guise became her friend. It was more difficult to reconcile male members of the family. Their leader, the duke of Mayenne, was powerful enough to threaten Henry. Gabrielle negotiated this delicate situation. Again, she used her diplomatic clout to her own advantage. The agreement included a secret clause, specifying that if Gabrielle and Henry married, Mayenne would support her children's right to the throne. This agreement is the first explicit indication that Gabrielle hoped to marry the king and to have their children succeed him. Henry acknowledged Gabrielle's assistance during the ceremony recognizing their reconciliation.

Henry took steps to further enhance Gabrielle's status. When he legally acknowledged his son Caesar, he gave Gabrielle the chateau of Montceaux, which had belonged to Catherine de Medici, with its attendant title of marquise. Once Gabrielle became a marquise, the way was paved to give Caesar a duchy, which Gabrielle then could be appointed to administer. She acquired this position by letters patent in December 1595, whereby Henry named Gabrielle as her son's heir should he predecease her. These letters patent ignored legal precedent and once again demonstrated Henry's willingness to violate it for his mistress's sake. Surprisingly, Parlement did not object to registering the letters patent.[65] These appointments greatly raised Gabrielle's position and wealth. In July 1596, Henry made her a member of the royal council.

Caesar's status enhanced Gabrielle's. Henry's support distinguished her from other unwed mothers. Courts would have conventionally recognized neither her legal ties to her son nor rights to his property, and the unwed mother would have had to rely, ultimately, on the favor of her sons or other male relatives.[66] But Henry gave Gabrielle the unusual right to administer her son's great wealth and extensive landholdings. Through the king's gifts to him, Gabrielle acquired wealth and the political offices attached to the administration of those estates during his minority. She always wore the keys of her office on the royal council to reinforce her political status.

When a daughter, Catherine-Henriette (named for Henry and his sister Catherine) was born to Gabrielle in 1596, the infant's baptism was celebrated on a scale appropriate to legitimate royalty. Henry's sister and the duke of Montmorency served as her godparents, and Catherine-Henriette was immediately engaged to the duke's son.[67]

Although Henry continued to give Gabrielle titles, gifts, and offices, sometimes in direct recompense for her extraordinary service, their relationship was a mutually supportive partnership. When Amiens fell to the Spanish, Henry needed funds but the treasury was empty. Gabrielle stepped into the breach. She gave Henry all of her cash (some fifty thousand *écus*) and persuaded other nobles to contribute directly to his cause. She pledged her jewelry as security and accompanied the army. These actions were among the few that produced no criticisms from Sully, and some of Gabrielle's former critics, such as the Huguenot leader Aubigné, became her supporters.[68] In this crisis, her actions were entirely and perhaps uncharacteristically disinterested. As the king's partner, she contributed funds, nursed Henry, and shared the dangers of the siege with him. She was later richly rewarded for her efforts. Henry purchased land from the Cleves and the Foix families to form the duchy he gave Gabrielle, making her the duchess d'Estampes and elevating her rank in the social and political hierarchy to just below the constable, the first duke of the realm. This was, ironically, the same title ultimately conferred on Francis I's mistress, Anne de Pisseleu.

Gabrielle exercised direct political power over several French territories. She was the king's deputy to Beaufort and Etampes, but these were small landholdings. Her greatest power was due to her position as Caesar's guardian. Her son was governor of Brittany-Vendôme, and she administered it in his name. On July 10, 1597, Parlement registered letters patent in which Henry announced that his son "at the age of three had such extraordinary ability that he was able to confer on his mother all of the honors associated with his titles."[69] By this decree, Gabrielle became the duchess of Beaufort, although the Parisian public renamed her duchess of *ordure* (excrement).[70] Other members of her family exercised control over other parts of France, giving Gabrielle an extensive political network. Her father was crown deputy to Picardy and the Ile de France, and her brother-in-law was lieutenant general of Normandy. Adept and thorough in her administrative work, Gabrielle kept four secretaries employed. She had considerable political influence to deploy. Mayenne, for example, thanked her for getting his son's estate elevated to a duchy. As Gabrielle worked to reconcile Protestants and Catholics to Henry, both groups acknowledged her influence: The Huguenots gave her a pension of ten thousand *écus* a year; the Jesuits petitioned her to be allowed back into France.

In 1598, Gabrielle deployed her notable diplomatic skills to resolve a touchy situation in Brittany. Philippe Emmanuel, duke of Mercoeur, held the duchy with the assistance of his exceedingly wealthy wife, Marie of Luxembourg. He hoped to make Brittany more autonomous, an effort the Parlements of Rennes and Nantes supported. To this end, Mercoeur first deserted Henry III in favor of the League and then opposed Henry IV's efforts to extend royal authority over Brittany. In 1597, Henry demanded that Mercoeur take an oath of fealty. When he refused, Henry prepared to attack, but Gabrielle hoped to arrange a peace. She first negotiated with members of the Breton nobility, detaching them from Mercoeur and winning them over to Henry. After her success, both the duke and his wife surrendered and agreed to a marriage between their infant daughter and Gabrielle's son, Caesar. Gabrielle thus used her children as diplomatic markers much like legitimate royal children, although they cemented peace with recalcitrant French nobles rather than enemy states. Henry gave Gabrielle full credit for the ultimate agreement, which again reconciled Brittany to the crown.

In June 1598, all Paris celebrated the peace, which acknowledged that Henry had brought the League into line, retained Brittany, regained Cambrai, and compelled the exodus of Spanish troops. This peace, which finally confirmed Henry's hold on the crown, must have seemed an unimaginable boon. This achievement became an important foundation of Henry's enduring, highly positive reputation. His mistress had proved an effective ally.

But the central problem of religious division had not been settled. To establish a foundation for religious peace, Henry issued the Edict of Nantes, his famous decree granting some toleration for Huguenots, on April 13, 1598. The edict granted Protestants the right to practice their religion where they already practiced and on the estates of Huguenot nobility (not in Paris, the court, or episcopal cities) and to hold all offices except ecclesiastical ones. Henry was confident that it would be accepted, but Gabrielle was more dubious. Indeed, the edict provoked great papal opposition from Clement VIII. Gabrielle participated in ongoing talks between Catholics and Protestants in hopes of implementing a lasting peace acceptable to both. The complex situation had frustrated many adept negotiators. Henry relied on his sister and Gabrielle, both of whom worked assiduously to gain support for the edict; Catherine met with Huguenot leaders, and Gabrielle with the Catholic nobility.[71] Contemporaries such as Scipion Dupleix acknowledged Gabrielle's crucial impact, and the Protestant Aubigné gratefully acknowledged Gabrielle's pivotal role in the successful promulgation of the edict. At this point, estates and wealth were no longer the appropriate rewards for her services; both the king and his mistress had marriage as a goal.

MARRIAGE PROSPECTS

Although it is not clear exactly when Henry decided to marry Gabrielle, Sully described his conversation with Henry about the merits of various princesses as prospective brides. When Henry said that the ideal bride must be "beautiful, of agreeable temper, and capable of bearing me children," he clearly wanted Sully to confirm Gabrielle as the ideal choice (fig. 7.4). Instead Sully raised obstacles to the match: The people would object; Caesar was the product of double adultery (both father and mother were married to others); the other two children, Catherine-Henriette and Alexandre (born in 1598), were born to an adulterous father (Henry was still married to Marguerite); any children of this union could produce a contested succession, perhaps even a civil war. The discussion, ac-

Fig. 7.4. Gabrielle d'Estrées at about the time she was to marry Henry IV, French school, sixteenth century, private collection, The Bridgeman Art Library.

cording to the story, came to a halt when Henry announced his determination to marry Gabrielle.[72] Despite the sense of Sully and other advisors that such a marriage was too problematic, Henry began to present Gabrielle to the French public as a "wife," the mother of his children, his partner, and even an appropriate queen. Gabrielle's fertility also allowed Henry to present her as a "better" queen than the infertile Marguerite. A poem Henry wrote to Gabrielle, urging her to "share my crown," became the lyrics of a popular song.[73]

On the occasion of the baptism of her son Alexandre, Gabrielle was presented as queen in all but name. Sully explicitly contended that by having the baptism at Saint-Germain-des-Prés with all honors due to "the infants of

France," Gabrielle was preparing the French for the change in her children's status she envisaged.[74] An agent of the Tuscan grand duke reported he feared that the king's "love for this lady would become an incurable evil . . . if God did not put His holy hand to it."[75] On November 17, 1598, Gabrielle moved into the queen's apartments in the Louvre and began to be attended in a manner befitting a queen.

Henry was setting the stage for this marriage and recognition of Gabrielle as queen. He gave her the ring he had received to mark his coronation. Cardinals and nobles were sent to the Vatican to plead his case for an annulment, and Henry began to press his wife to cooperate in this quest. But an annulment remained politically fraught. Clement VIII remained mistrustful of Henry's religious sincerity. (He had waited two years to accept Henry's abjuration of Protestantism as genuine.) But the problem of succession made an annulment more urgent and more compelling, perhaps even for the Vatican.

Henry's heir apparent was his cousin Henry, the prince of Condé and the son of the former Huguenot leader. This prince was not an appealing future monarch. His mother was believed to have killed her husband, and there was widespread suspicion that Henry was not even Condé's son, and fear that he could emerge as a Huguenot leader. He thus embodied the prospect of renewed religious war.

As a result, when Henry again sought the annulment in 1598, Clement VIII was more favorably inclined, fearing that the French crown might pass to the reputedly Protestant Condé, but remained unalterably opposed to Henry's plan to marry Gabrielle. The French papal legate commented that Henry was "in her toils" and said, "No one speaks to him about this, because no one has the courage."[76] On January 20, 1599, Henry wrote personally to the pope, as he put it, "not only from my hand but also from my heart," entreating him to grant the annulment.[77]

The pope was not alone in resisting this match. Despite the king's positive presentation, Gabrielle had provoked opposition, especially in Paris. Attacks on her became more vehement as her status increased and it seemed more likely that Henry would indeed marry her. Pamphlets attacked her as a whore. Parisian clergymen preached against her; one declared that "a lewd woman in the court of the king was a dangerous monster and caused much evil, especially when she was encouraged to raise her head." Popular epigrams circulated about Gabrielle; one pointed out that a Turk won a great victory over his enemies immediately after he killed his young mistress (with the implicit suggestion that Henry do the same). Henry responded to advice to distance himself from Gabrielle, saying that he would not only continue to kiss his mistress, but he would do so in public, even during council meetings. His plans to marry Gabrielle provoked explicit attacks on her suitability to be queen. Some objected to her low birth; others cited with disapproval what was known about her life before Henry, her conduct as his mistress, and the excessive wealth she had acquired. Gabrielle's entire family was denounced as leeches, gorging themselves at public expense. Parisian public opinion condemned her birth, her avarice, and her political activities.[78]

Henry's fervor did not abate, and his letters to Gabrielle would have corroborated his contemporaries' sense of his captivation. He wrote to Gabrielle: "My beautiful love . . . you will see a courtier who loves you dearly and who is called King of France and of Navarre. It is an honorable enough title, but . . . that of your subject is much to be preferred."[79] Gabrielle was seen, as mistresses often were, as "unmanning" the king—especially a military man like Henry. It would be preferable, in popular opinion, to have a "love 'em and leave 'em" king than one ensnared by love. Henry's sexual activities were less problematic than his desire to marry his mistress, his sexual relationship less disturbing than his love. Many, including the pope, Henry's critics, and his advisors, worried about the lengths to which he might go in pursuit of love.

Opprobrium directed against a royal mistress often deflected criticism from a king who was appreciated as her antithesis. In this case, Gabrielle was criticized for extravagance in a time of economic hardship. Her spending was then juxtaposed to the king's fiscal restraint or, some would say, stinginess. Two popular stories recounted by L'Estoile made this distinction. The king met a peasant on his way to market who complained about taxes. When Henry said that the king must be mad to tax his people so, the peasant remarked, "Well, they say that he is not the worst, but there is one 'Belle Gabrielle,' who tickles him and ruins us all." Another story took the same tack. A poor boatman ferrying the king across a river complained that peace brought no relief from taxes but conceded, "I don't think the taxes are his doing, but there is a bad whore whom he keeps. He gives her beautiful dresses and knickknacks every day, and the poor folk suffer, as they pay for it all."[80]

The most serious issue provoked by Henry's proposed marriage was its possible effect on royal succession. His actions suggested that he might consider his "legitimated" sons, conceived out of wedlock, eligible for succession. Jurists of the realm worried explicitly about how succession might unfold. They were specifically concerned that Henry's two "legitimated" sons might insert themselves into the succession against French law or, if they were unable to do so, pose a threat of civil war. They counseled Henry that an illegitimate son could not inherit, even if the king had legitimated him. Nicolas de Harlay de Sancy, the finance minister, always aggrieved by Gabrielle's influence, reported later and from the safety of his memoirs that when Henry consulted him, he objected vehemently: "The sons of a whore are always bastards."[81]

Henry became even more eager to marry Gabrielle when he faced a serious health crisis in 1598. He had contracted venereal disease in his youth and now had a severe attack of gonorrhea, which left him depressed, debilitated, and worried about succession.[82] Marriage might give him a legitimate heir, as Gabrielle was again pregnant. Alternatively, Caesar might ultimately be accepted as his heir. Concerned too about what would become of Gabrielle and their children if he died, Henry decided on an Easter wedding. He tried to protect his mistress and his sons by forming alliances with various nobles to forestall opposition to the marriage and gain support for Caesar's possible succession. He also made secret arrangements to compel members of the clergy to dissolve his marriage to Marguerite and to perform the ceremony that would make Gabrielle the queen.[83]

Plans for marriage were moving forward, but significant obstacles remained. Neither Henry nor Gabrielle was aware that Clement VIII had decided to oppose the marriage and promote instead Henry's marriage to Marie de Medici. Unaware of papal intransigence, Henry was nonetheless in negotiations with Italian representatives who hoped to successfully arrange this alternative.[84] He at least seemed to be entertaining marriage to one of two possible brides, perhaps as a diplomatic ruse or a contingency plan.

Gabrielle, in a very advanced state of pregnancy, focused on the upcoming wedding with some consternation. She consulted astrologers and fortune-tellers, but their prognostications, reported after the fact, were not at all reassuring: One said, "Her destiny was within reach but that a small child would keep her from it"; another that she would only be married once (to Liancourt); a third that she would die young. The days just before Easter were full of portents, which contemporaries saw as especially significant, at least after the fact. L'Estoile repeated a fortune-teller's assurance that "the marriage would never take place" and that "Gabrielle would never see Easter Sunday."[85]

On the advice of the king's confessor, Henry and Gabrielle separated for two weeks before the wedding; he remained at Fontainebleau, and she returned to Paris.[86] On the Tuesday before the wedding, she went to dinner at the house of the Swiss finance minister, Sebastian Zamet. That evening she had convulsions and the next morning was overcome with stomach pains. By Thursday morning, she was well enough to attend Mass but later that day experienced great pains. Her condition deteriorated precipitously and dramatically. Gabrielle again suffered convulsions; her faced turned black; her fetus was pried from her womb in pieces. Her appearance was so horrifying that, when her friends and relatives saw her, they fainted. After several days of horrifying agony, Gabrielle died on April 10, 1599.

Her manner of dying was so dreadful that some of her contemporaries saw it as the work of the devil. Others expressed relief that her death had averted a political crisis. The physician La Rivière pronounced, "Here is the hand of God." Groulart expressed relief: "God has remedied when men despaired of it." Sully wrote, "We were on the edge of a precipice. God alone could pull us back from it."[87] Gabrielle's contemporaries were most struck by the fortuitous timing of her death as preventing a political crisis. Just before her death, the Venetian ambassador Contarini had expressed his fears of a "fatal accident" in light of Henry's "indubitable inclination" to marry his mistress, "something of which everyone has an extreme horror."[88] Seventeenth-century historians raised the possibility of poison, specifically that "a corrupt lemon" Gabrielle had eaten at Zamet's had killed her.[89] Modern historians suggest *placenta previa* as the most likely cause. But Gabrielle's remains, unlike those of Agnès and Diane, have not been exhumed and tested for poison.

After her death, Henry went into such deep mourning that his councilors feared for his life and begged him to reengage for the good of France. In a letter to his sister, Henry claimed that his "affliction was incomparable" and that "his grief would accompany him to his tomb," concluding, "The root of my love is dead, and it will never grow again."[90] Gabrielle was buried in her sister's abbey with the funeral of a royal princess. Henry promised to build a monument to her at Montceaux but never did.

Henry's obvious grief might have been a satisfying end to the romantic saga of this royal relationship. But Gabrielle's death did not end or even produce much of a pause in Henry's passionate pursuit of royal mistresses. Gabrielle was not even the last mistress he promised to make queen. A mere three months later, he proclaimed to Henriette d'Entragues: "This heart dreams only of your charms; you are my only love."[91] Gabrielle's immediate successor was so scheming and so overt in her quest to advance her interests through her pregnancies that Gabrielle became, in comparison, the mistress of blessed memory, sanctified by love and an early death. Intensely ambitious to be queen of France and single-minded in pursuit of that goal, Henriette was a woman about whom little good could be said. As Sully put it, "The lady was no novice."[92] Henriette too came from a family accustomed to what royal favors could gain; her mother, Marie Touchet, had been Charles IX's mistress and borne his illegitimate son. Henriette adroitly exploited the king's infatuation. He was so completely besotted that even as he went forward with his marriage to Marie de Medici, he promised *in writing* to marry Henriette if she bore him a son. Henry's letter gave Henriette grounds for a breach-of-promise suit, but he did not learn his lesson from her first attempts to entrap him: Any of her three pregnancies could have plunged the kingdom into a succession crisis, given the king's written promise to marry her.

By the time Henriette bore him a son, Henry's legitimate son (later Louis XIII) had already been born to his queen Marie de Medici. His marriage brought more frustration than happiness. Henry complained to Sully: "I receive from my wife neither companionship, nor gaiety nor consolation, she either cannot or will not show me any kindness or pleasant conversation, neither will she accommodate herself to my moods and disposition."[93] His passionate pursuit of Henriette continued unabated. She was an especially flagrant example of the ill-advised nature of Henry's sexual relationships, as Henriette participated in treasonous plots against Henry to gain recognition for her son as the heir to the French throne. Only by threatening the plotters with the death penalty did Henry finally regain the promissory note he had so foolishly signed.

Henry continued to pursue sexual conquests even against his political interests and those of France. His flagrant extramarital affairs continued. The Tuscan ambassador wondered: "Has anyone ever seen anything more like a bordello than this court?"[94] It is ironic that Henry, who was so concerned that he might not be able to father sons, ultimately had a house full of illegitimate children, whom he raised along with his legitimate heirs. (In addition to his children by Gabrielle and Henriette, he had a son by Jacqueline de Bueil, and another by Charlotte des Essart.)

The last and most discreditable of Henry's romantic escapades was his pursuit of the young princess of Condé, Charlotte de Montmorency, the sixteen-year-old daughter of the constable Montmorency-Damville. She had been promised to another, but Henry married her instead to the prince of Condé, reputedly "a man who prefers hunting to women."[95] When Condé refused to play the compliant husband and asked instead to leave the court with his wife, Henry refused. Denouncing Henry as a tyrant, Condé sought safe passage from France through the Netherlands.[96] This maneuver provoked an international incident as France prepared to go to war with the Hapsburgs, and Henry's intention to pursue the young woman into Spanish-held territory both heightened tensions and his eagerness for war. But an assassin's knife felled Henry on the streets of Paris and brought an end to his quest for the princess and France's plans for war. Henry's reputation, like Gabrielle's, was to some degree redeemed or at least spared by his unexpected and early death. His contemporaries appreciated his reign as having ended civil war, won peace with Spain, and promulgated the Edict of Nantes.

Their appreciation shaped the "Good King Henry" legend which eulogized him as a man of the people—a king of largesse and humanity who brought peace and the beginnings of prosperity before his reign was tragically cut short—certainly no small accomplishments. His Bourbon descendants built on his positive reputation to assert the value of monarchy. They did not treat his sexual peccadilloes, except as they reinforced his masculinity. Since Gabrielle did not enhance the legend, she was largely overlooked by them and by subsequent historians. Despite her greater political role, Gabrielle is rarely mentioned and certainly never attained the mythic status of Diane or Agnès. Instead, she has been either relegated to a simple sexual liaison or successfully expunged from the historical record.

Disparate views of Gabrielle circulated during her nine-year reign over Henry's heart. Either she was venal and self-interested, grasping and ambitious, a woman whose unusual beauty ensnared the king and whose fertility threatened a nation. Or she was Henry's angel, guiding and aiding his destiny with

Fig.7.5. Henry IV and Gabrielle d'Estrées, French school, nineteenth century, Musée Carnavalet, Paris, The Bridgeman Art Library.

her purse, her advice, and her personal charm (fig. 7.5). She was either an effective political actor or she merely held positions the king created for her. Either she acutely assessed the complex contemporary political realities of Henry's reign or she was merely the pawn of Cheverny or other men who manipulated her. Whatever her motives or abilities, Gabrielle was unique as the only woman ever to inspire Henry's fidelity. She had the undeviating love, support, and admiration of the notoriously faithless king.

Gabrielle's story adds a number of particular elements to the history of royal mistresses. As her early life and family history more than amply demonstrate, she felt no inclination to be a model of probity or to mask the sexual character of her relationship with Henry; Gabrielle seems to have worried very little about her reputation. She, like other earlier mistresses, gained status and wealth, and like later mistresses, she advanced her children by the king. Unlike other prominent mistresses, Gabrielle left no mark on French culture in the arts or literature of the French Renaissance. Admittedly, her ascendancy was during a period of war and instability, but she did not demonstrate intellectual interests or sophistication but deployed instead pragmatic talents. She, like her royal lover, faced and navigated the shoals of political and religious division. Like Diane de Poitiers, she made the king's interests hers and benefited from their alliance. And Henry must have found it a considerable relief to have a mistress who, unlike his wife, did so. As a result, Gabrielle's relationship with the king also seems quite different from those who preceded her as royal titular mistress. The political challenges Henry faced opened unusually extensive political roles for his mistress; she became the king's full partner both politically and personally. Such an extensive partnership suggests a close personal relationship akin to a modern marriage. Indeed, Michelet later vehemently objected to Gabrielle's part in promoting Henry's image as a doting "husband." Such a portrayal, he contended, demeaned the king.[97] It was also highly unusual for the king to present the sexual and personal nature of the relationship with his mistress so overtly. Nor were her political roles in any way obscured. Henry was an unconventional king in many respects; his mistress respected convention as little as he.

Despite the unusual character of the partnership, the traditional issue of royal succession shaped it. Henry wanted to marry Gabrielle so as to have a legitimate male heir. Her fertility made her an ideal prospective wife. On the other hand, the high risks of maternal mortality that characterized early modern childbirth kept this mistress from becoming queen, virtually on the eve of her wedding.

If Gabrielle had lived to marry Henry, the relationship would certainly have produced great challenges to Church-state relations. Their marriage might have altered the dynamics of royal marriages, making them personal rather than political relationships. Instead, for French kings and queens of the seventeenth and eighteenth centuries, marriages produced even more uncongenial personal relationships than those of the Renaissance. The political implications of Gabrielle and Henry's proposed marriage might have been disastrous for France. By the time Henry died in 1610, would there have been legitimate male children borne of their union? Would questions of succession have arisen because Henry had legitimated his sons borne before marriage? Might there have been internecine warfare between the supporters of legitimate children as opposed to illegitimate ones? In light of these complex scenarios, Gabrielle's early death forestalled any number of religious, political, and diplomatic crises the marriage might have produced. As a result, she, like Agnès Sorel, remained a royal mistress associated with the restoration of peace and stability—Agnès at the end of the Hundred Years War and Gabrielle at the end of the Wars of Religion. Ironically, Gabrielle's greatest contribution to stability and peace was her death, which forestalled all the complications an unorthodox marriage with legitimated sons might have entailed. Gabrielle's sudden, unexpected death erased, to a large degree, prior opprobrium and instead enshrined her as a tragic young beauty, dead too soon, on the eve of her greatest triumph.

Although Bourbon historians quickly reduced Gabrielle to insignificance, Henry's biographers, no doubt because of the prominence of mistresses in his life, sometimes take a position for or against the "right" mistress. Several insist that the mistress he should have loved was Diane de Grammont (Corisandre), for she was, in their accounts, the most appropriate of Henry's mistresses—high social standing, less self-interested, better for Henry, more astute, and so on.[98] But even those biographers look back on Gabrielle with something approaching nostalgia when they contemplate the venality of Henriette. Some praise for Gabrielle is provoked by horror at her replacement. The implicit recognition that Henry's judgment could be so poor redounds to Gabrielle's credit. In pursuing her own interests, she did not abuse Henry's. Gabrielle then became the "good mistress" by comparison. Despite her conspicuous political role and personal partnership that prefigures a modern marriage based on mutual love and support, Gabrielle has largely been reduced in subsequent histories to a figure of romance and beauty—two qualities that effectively consign her to the category of mere mistress. She has not found a place in the pantheon of idealized mistresses, likely because she acted as a partner—both personal and political—or, in other words, as a wife. For Bourbon historians, no woman should be acknowledged as a partner of their heroically masculine king Henry IV.

Conclusion

Gabrielle d'Estrées's death is an appropriate place to end this history of the Renaissance as told through the lives of some of its most prominent queens and mistresses. By 1599, Henry IV was poised to launch the period of political consolidation and cultural preeminence we associate with royal pretensions to absolutism. The year of Gabrielle's death coincided with the inauguration of a new period in French history, with much stronger state control of politics, economics, and culture and with less openness to politically active women, although, as in all times, there were notable exceptions.

There are obvious comparisons between Agnès and Gabrielle, the mistresses who begin and end this history. Both were legendary blond beauties who had more power than previous illicit sexual partners of kings. Their political activities not only provoked opposition but also brought other men into prominence in their wake. Each mistress preempted many of the queen's conventional functions. Each was praised and excoriated, held sway for a relatively short time, and died very young under somewhat suspicious circumstances after bearing her fourth child. Despite a king's protestations of love, each was speedily replaced in his affection.[1] Perhaps their most striking difference was in their posthumous reputations. Agnès became a heroine who saved a king. Gabrielle, because her political role did not burnish Henry IV's legend, was reduced simply to a sexual interest and scarcely mentioned.

Gabrielle's death marked the end of the immediate possibility that a mistress would become queen of France. The roles of queen and mistress never again blurred in quite the same way. Although Louis XIV would later have a morganatic marriage with his mistress Madame de Maintenon, he did not make it public even at that high-water mark of royal authority, despite the fact that, at her age (fifty), potential heirs were not a complicating factor. But Gabrielle's death did not end the reign of powerful mistresses or the triangulated French royal family relations between king, queen, and mistress, nor a mistress's challenge to a queen's preeminence. All of these were marked features of Louis XIV's and Louis XV's reigns. But Gabrielle's death seemed to quash the romantic possibility of a mistress's elevation to queen, a king's marriage for love, or a royal marriage that was a political and personal partnership. Rather, the role of mistress and prime minister were more likely to blur under later kings, most notably in the case of Madame de Pompadour, the premier example of a powerful mistress under an absolutist monarch. Queens were often relegated to ever-narrower domestic and ceremonial functions, only to emerge as powerful regents wielding the greater power of a more centralized state, as did Marie de Medici and Anne of Austria during the minorities of Louis XIII and Louis XIV respectively.

What has this history of Renaissance queens and mistresses told us? The women profiled here undertook important political and cultural activities during the French Renaissance, making them more central to the unfolding of French history than one might expect or than most histories of the period acknowledge. They belong to the political, social, and cultural history of the French Renaissance.[2] Royal women exercised significant power only if their lovers, husbands, sons, or brothers bestowed it or, at the very least, did not impede them from acquiring it. But with such support, they were accomplished political actors during the French Renaissance. Those royal women who were especially noteworthy expanded their circumscribed positions. At times their impact was so pronounced they defined reigns, as Diane de Poitiers and Catherine de Medici did. A mistress might create and foster a king's image, as Agnès showed, or enhance it through positive representations, as Diane did most clearly. Other women added crucial dimensions to kings' reigns. Françoise de Foix cloaked Francis's reign in romance, and his sister Marguerite enhanced its intellectual credibility. A queen might protect a throne for her son, as both Louise of Savoy and Catherine de Medici did. Ironically, the greater their role, the more vehemently it had to be denounced or their motives discredited as malign and distinctly female.

Queens such as Anne of Brittany, Catherine de Medici, and even to a limited degree Marguerite de Valois, deployed their access to revenue, public position, and high social status to their advantage. But a mistress could be a force for novelty or iconoclasm, and her lover's interest could open unprecedented opportunities. Queens and mistresses not only reflected the complementary faces of the exercise of power but were often central figures in each other's lives. The waxing power of one could displace the waning influence of the other. A queen or mistress could challenge the other; in rare cases they worked in concert; more often they established parallel networks. In many ways, queens and mistresses used their opportunities just as their male counterparts did. They, like powerful nobles or male favorites respectively, worked to increase the status and wealth of their families and to build more powerful and extensive client networks.

But for each woman featured in this study, perhaps the defining feature of her life was one over which she had almost no control—her fertility. It was *the* crucial determinant of her life expectancy. Diminished fertility made it much more likely that a woman might attain the average life span of slightly more than fifty years. The sexual attractions of a mistress or the dynastic duties of a queen frequently led to an early death—Agnès Sorel and Gabrielle d'Estrées both died before the age of twenty-eight, each having borne four children. Claude de France died at twenty-four, having borne seven children. Anne of Brittany died at the age of thirty-six, having had at least eleven pregnancies. These young women all bore large numbers of children in a relatively short time. In this history, women who had long lives had few children or none at all. Marguerite d'Angoulême (fifty-seven) and Eleanor of Austria (fifty-nine) each bore two children. Louise of Savoy (fifty-five) and Diane de Poitiers (sixty-six) each had had two children when they were very young, were widowed, remained widows for most of their childbearing years, and lived longer than the normal life expectancy. Anne de Pisseleu (seventy-two) and Marguerite de Valois (sixty-two) lived to a greater age than was common and had no children (although this is disputed for Marguerite). Catherine de Medici, who had ten children and died at the age of sixty-nine, is the only significant exception.

While fertility largely defined their life expectancy, it had other personal and political ramifications. It is unclear whether Charles VII or Agnès saw their daughters as boons; they gave them to other noble families to raise. Charles likely did not, as he had fourteen other children by his queen. Agnès's pregnancies may have also led to Charles's rumored straying toward the end of their relationship. The fact that Diane de Poitiers did not bear Henry II's children during their twenty-year relationship no doubt gave her greater staying power as a mistress. Pregnancy likely would have cast doubt on the chivalric, almost ethereal image of the relationship she cultivated. On the other hand, Gabrielle d'Estrées's prodigious fertility assuredly enhanced her attractions for Henry IV as a possible queen. She was indisputably able to produce heirs for the kingdom. While fertility could shorten a queen's life, infertility posed even greater risk to her position. Early years of infertility threatened Catherine de Medici's position, and infertility provided a rationale (although not the grounds) for the eventual annulment of Henry IV's marriage to Marguerite de Valois. Other demographic factors also affected a queen's or a mistress's opportunities as well. If she were widowed young, she might have power through a young son, as Catherine de Medici did. If a royal woman had a long life, she might have a chance to reinvent herself, as Catherine and her daughter Marguerite both did.

Although these women could not control their fertility and its incontrovertible effect on their life expectancy or its implications for their status, they were not simply passive captives to their biological fate. Despite their essential biological role, their activities were in no way restricted to the maternal, with the notable exception of the much-appreciated Claude. They instead took action and assumed roles that made them prominent actors in the history of the Valois dynasty from the end of the Hundred Years War to the ascension of the first Bourbon king. The fluidity of the Renaissance monarchy offered them a wide scope for action and a variety of possibilities for "self-fashioning." Some, including Marguerite d'Angoulême and Anne de Pisseleu, advocated war. Anne of Beaujeu and Catherine de Medici made war, while others, Louise of Savoy, Catherine de Medici, and Eleanor of Austria among them, worked for peace. Despite the prohibition on female rule of the Salic law, many of them—Louise, Catherine, and Anne of Beaujeu—ruled as regents in place of kings. They did so effectively enough that the role of regent was recast as more appropriately female.[3] A female regent could nurture the kingdom and protect it from civil war waged by powerful men, as the uncles of Charles VII did during the Hundred Years War, or as Catherine de Medici's sons did during the Wars of Religion.

Royal women advanced their political goals by many of the same means as their male counterparts but shaped by their gender. They too cultivated a male network but also often worked within female networks as well. Their power often came at the expense of other women. They negotiated marriages for other women and their own children to make political and diplomatic alliances in their political interests. Sometimes their political plans even worked at cross-purposes to the king's—as did Anne of Brittany's and Marguerite d'Angoulême's marriage plans for their daughters. They had public functions as negotiators, diplomats, writers, theologians, and patrons of the arts. They had private or less overtly public roles as wives, lovers, and mothers. Their actions provoked debate, and thus they were prominently cited in the "quarrel over women" as examples, both positive and negative. They also contributed their voices to the quarrel, always in defense of women. Involved in the religious controversies of the day as theologians—Marguerite d'Angoulême, for example—or as supporters of a creed, they became targets for polemical attacks. The religious zeal of a queen might garner praise or blame, but a mistress's devotion could redeem her.

Virtually every exercise of power by a queen or a mistress provoked criticism. Anne of Brittany's political interests were seen as misdirected to her territory rather than to France. Attempts by Louise of Savoy and Catherine de Medici to preserve the throne and royal authority for their sons were denounced as the self-aggrandizing pursuit of power, despite their obvious concern for the welfare of their sons. A queen mother's political activity was decried, from the Renaissance to our own day, as the untoward influence of a mother over her son. Failures of a royal son were frequently attributed to his mother but almost never to his father. Maternal love was highly suspect, and when the mother was a queen, her love could make her son effeminate and emasculate him and the kingdom.

Women who wielded political power overtly were condemned as unnatural or praised as masculine. Henry IV's mother, Jeanne d'Albret, according to her contemporaries, had the intelligence of a man. Catherine de Medici was described as "more minister than woman." Francis I praised his mother as "having nothing of the heart of a woman."[4] For good or ill, a woman with intelligence, political savvy, or, worst of all, political power was not entirely female.

Thoroughly reprehensible in a queen were any signs of sexuality except pregnancy. Any thought that Louise, in her forties, might have wanted to marry a man thirteen years her junior merited derision. Catherine de Medici was accused of many sexual transgressions, even though she remained a circumspect widow dedicated to the memory of her husband. And Marguerite de Valois was cast as sexually depraved. Other royal women, most often mistresses, have been reduced to a single, sexual dimension—even if the intent was to praise them. Agnès's sexual allure, for example, allowed her to rescue the feckless Charles VII, and Diane's tutelage helped to transform the young Henry II into a king. So by constraining a king's sexuality, a mistress could be a positive influence. A king's selection of a mistress could add the complications of love, fueling Renaissance discourse about the passions and raising doubts about the king's manhood. But love could also elevate a king, as it did Henry II, or even enhance his masculinity as it did Henry IV.

Queens, even when their marriages cemented a peace or forged an alliance, remained targets for discontent, as Anne of Brittany and Catherine de Medici demonstrate. Even if fertility was their most appreciated attribute, the queens profiled here also assumed active political roles, developed their own political agendas, and promoted the cultural avant-garde of the Renaissance. But such activities could be divisive and generate criticism or even harsh political propaganda. Especially as directed against Catherine de Medici and Marguerite de Valois, such criticism hardened into legends or caricatures in popular media. Since the sixteenth century, fictionalized accounts have regularly denounced the political actions of a particular woman and, by extrapolation, sanctioned the exclusion of women from politics or even public life. They relegated Renaissance women to the sexual sphere, even though their lived experience was more expansive.

Each royal mistress offered a somewhat different model of what the position entailed, although all shared certain attributes. All were heralded as stunningly beautiful, perhaps to justify a king's dalliance. A king's love for his mistress gave her access to him, which in turn gave her greater status and often more opportunity to act politically. The mistresses treated in this book used their positions, to a greater or lesser degree, to acquire wealth and status for themselves and their families. They inspired kings; the love of a good woman made him better than he might have otherwise been, or so some have believed. Mistresses sometimes altered a king's reign by glamorizing his image or complicating his political and domestic life. Over the course of the Renaissance, royal mistresses demonstrated more overt political involvement and had more pronounced effect on culture. As they took ever more prominent positions in the court, in all of its dimensions, they presented more public evidence of their sexual relationship with a king and thus contributed to ongoing discussions of sex and love. Mistresses, more than queens, challenged conventional views of women and thus provoked their contemporaries to comment on women in politics. Although their activities were frequently disparaged, they were unquestionably political actors. But it was also easy for some commentators, particularly in the nineteenth and twentieth centuries, to rob their activities of any real import. Agnès became merely a beautiful inspiration to Charles VII; Diane an idealized guide for a young king; and Gabrielle, whose political partnership with Henry IV was clearly problematic, disappeared or became simply another notch on the belt of the virile king.

Focusing on Renaissance queens and mistresses directs our attention to issues often seen as conventionally feminine—peace and diplomacy, religion and charity, literature and art, for example. And unquestionably, a woman's political activities could be thwarted by a king's opposition (Marguerite de Valois's conspicuous failures are perhaps most revealing). Royal women's cultural activities were less controversial and less overtly challenged. And the rise of the Renaissance arts gave royal women great opportunities to define and present their images and views and ultimately to shape the French Renaissance.

But Renaissance royal women also challenged gendered conventions of women's more-appropriate activities. Anne of Beaujeu led an army; Catherine de Medici conducted war and weighed the political implications of religious conflicts; and both Marguerite d'Angoulême and Marguerite de Valois pursued the distinctly masculine study of philosophy.

These Renaissance women impel us to look ahead to future queens and mistresses. Marie de Medici, Henry IV's second wife, became the regent for her nine-year-old son, Louis XIII, much on the model of Catherine de Medici. They were both targets of the popular distrust of a foreign woman, especially an Italian woman, tarred by an unfortunate association with commerce. Marie, politically insignificant during her husband's reign and deeply aggrieved by his infidelities, emerged as a strong regent.[5] Her regency was no doubt strengthened by Catherine's earlier exercise of the position, but Marie also benefited from the fact that Henry IV officially conferred the title of regent on her as he prepared to go to war against the Hapsburgs. Her tenure was complicated by the greater need for reliable and capable ministers since the monarchy was by then both more centralized and much more bureaucratic. Marie's initial choice of Concino Concini almost undid her regency; her appointment of Richelieu was fortuitous, although he later allied with her son against her. So strong did Marie become as regent that she eventually refused to relinquish power to her son, who was forced to defeat her on the battlefield.

By the time Madame de Pompadour, Louis XV's most powerful mistress, became *maîtresse en titre* (1745), the position had become quasi-institutional. Like all of the mistresses in this book, she carved out a distinctive role. The extent of Pompadour's power was broader in all areas of state policy than that of her predecessors. She, like Anne de Pisseleu, Diane de Poitiers, and Gabrielle d'Estrées, promoted a political agenda. But Pompadour had to work much harder than they had to be accepted, because her social status was lower and because the court had become more acutely aware of social distinctions under Bourbon kings than ever before. Pompadour also had to strive to retain her position; both Louis XIV and Louis XV had made the position of titular mistress one of shorter duration and more abrupt replacement than characterized the tenure of Anne de Pisseleu or Diane de Poitiers. Rapid turnover made it harder for the mistresses under absolutist kings to use their positions to gain political power as well as the sexual interest of a king, although Pompadour certainly did so.

Later mistresses assumed the politically useful role of lightning rod to deflect criticism from the monarch. A contemporary guide to court conduct announced that a mistress or male favorite was to serve as a "shield against hatred."[6] As the target of vituperative verses making specific criticisms, named *poissonades* for her (Jeanne Antoinette Poisson), Pompadour served this function admirably. She had distracted the king from his fundamental concern for the people; her bourgeois background had degraded the court from the highest noble standards; and she had displaced the nobility from their rightful positions by giving financiers access to the court[7]—all charges leveled at Renaissance mistresses as well. Pompadour was accused too of profligacy and blamed for the crown's spending. Extravagant expenditure to the detriment of the country was a royal sin often ascribed to a king's mistress from the time of Agnès Sorel, sometimes with some justification. Pompadour was also charged with patronizing the outlandish arts of the Rococo and thus corrupting French culture, very much like attacks on Agnès's excesses of style.

While Pompadour may well represent the absolutist apogee of a royal mistress's political influence, she also attempted to epitomize the positive qualities their contemporaries had attributed to Renaissance mistresses. She explicitly identified with Agnès Sorel's reputation of doing good for the kingdom, aiding the poor, and cultivating intellectual activities, as had Françoise de Foix. Pompadour was certainly a figure around whom political parties coalesced, as with Agnès, Diane, and Anne de Pisseleu. Pompadour, like Diane, was preoccupied with her image and patronized artists depicting her as a youthful beauty, just as Diane had done. And Pompadour is tied to the great painters of the Rococo period in the same way Diane is connected to Renaissance artists.

Just as Pompadour carries the saga of the Renaissance mistress forward into a more powerful yet rigidly circumscribed role, so Marie Antoinette raises the most extreme example of the difficulties a French queen could face. Her Austrian background led critics to see her as a traitor to France. Her beauty and femininity were associated with "deceit, seduction, and the pursuit of private interest." Such an association put the queen into the category of the mistress.[8] Marie Antoinette offered a more clearly defined target for opposition to the monarchy than the women treated here, in part because of the emergence of print culture and the growing hostility toward the monarchy as France moved closer to revolution. Marie Antoinette was especially vulnerable both because of the international tensions between France and Austria and because of the new popular expectation that politics be open. Critics of monarchy promulgated the sense that "politics behind closed doors was epitomized by a politics of the bedroom."[9] So critics readily fastened on the royal bedroom and a problematic sexual relationship between the king and the queen as symptomatic of the nation's ills. (The marriage of Louis XVI and Marie Antoinette was not consummated until years after the wedding.) Ironically, the fact that Louis XVI was not a womanizer and had no mistress made Marie Antoinette's position even less tenable. No mistress deflected criticism from him. Such a woman could have been an obvious scapegoat for fears that an impotent king was emasculating a monarchy. But in the absence of a mistress, the legitimate queen was criticized and, by extension, her husband as well.

Royal women thus continued to be important to the unfolding of French history and to its interpretation. But greater political and cultural centralization created a less fluid situation that was less amenable to their influence. Later queens were more constrained, but as regents they availed themselves of the opportunity. After the Renaissance, queens would be weaker when their husbands reigned and stronger as regents in their sons' minorities. But no queen was a partner to her husband as Anne of Brittany had been, or even had a congenial relationship with her spouse. The women featured in this book are not simply forerunners of later figures. They set forth the parameters of these positions and made them politically and culturally significant in the new context of Renaissance France.

Equally important, from the time of the Bourbons, French political theorists emphasized the king's patriarchal role as the head of the French family and his French blood.[10] Foreign queens were thus increasingly suspect for both their foreignness and femininity. Aspersions could be cast on the social origins of mistresses such as Madame de Pompadour and Madame du Barry. The horrors of the Wars of Religion were retrospectively laid at the feet of prominent women.

When Joan Kelly-Gadol answered her famous question of whether women had a Renaissance in the negative, she asserted that the Middle Ages offered better opportunities for women. Subsequent scholars have highlighted the impact of elite women of the Middle Ages. But this study suggests that the women featured here were as prominent and powerful as their medieval counterparts. This study then raises the question of whether the view that the Renaissance entailed the greater subservience of women to patriarchy is due, in large measure, to the patriarchal lenses through which subsequent historians saw their Renaissance subjects. In other words, did the nineteenth century distort Renaissance women in its own image? This history suggests that our understanding of Renaissance queens and mistresses has been shaped and constrained significantly by nineteenth- and twentieth-century historians. As their views became canonical in French national histories, they undermined elite women's contributions to the Renaissance.

Discomfited by France's monarchist past, these historians could express their hostility to the monarchy by denouncing the women associated with it—mother, wife, or mistress. These women thus were distorted from credible actors on the

Renaissance stage into villains complicit in the monarchy—a particularly despicable form of parasitism. Criticisms of royal women could, as they perennially did, stand in for denunciations of a king. Such charges were then reinforced by the assumption that kings' failures were due to their insufficient diligence in keeping women out of politics. Weak kings gave women access to power; strong kings acted without their interference. Women in politics were dangerous because they were dominated by their passions. When royal women took on prominent, political functions, they unleashed their passions with devastating results for the nation, or so these historians asserted. Nor did these historians appreciate royal women's efforts to form future kings. They were especially harsh on royal mothers, who had the greatest opportunity to have a malign effect. This particular construction of the royal past doubtless further justified the greater exclusion of women from political power in republican France. Renaissance elite women were reinterpreted through nineteenth-century views of the biological essentialism or separate spheres that rigidly differentiated male and female roles both by nature and in society. Specific objections to the political actions of royal women were not confined to indictments of monarchy or particular kings but expanded to female involvement in politics more generally.

Nineteenth- and twentieth-century historians singled out the Renaissance for especially harsh criticism for several reasons. First, they found the criticisms by their predecessors persuasive and drew on the generally negative remarks of early chroniclers. Those views had been moderated to some degree by somewhat more appreciative, later assessments, including those images constructed or promoted by Renaissance women themselves. But more-positive images fell to the onslaught of religious polemics, which added many scurrilous tales about royal women to the predominant narrative of the Renaissance. Second, some of these historians saw the Protestant Reformation as a development that would have been beneficial to France had it not been quashed by absolute monarchy; and royal women had generally buttressed Catholic monarchs. Third, they accepted the accounts of Bourbon historians, who criticized Valois kings as weak and their reliance on women as a compelling sign of that weakness, to bolster the new dynasty. Bourbon historians polished an image of Henry IV as unequivocally autonomous and masculine. Later historians eagerly embraced their predecessors' positive sense of Henry IV and negative views of powerful women.

When some of the most significant historians of the nineteenth century turned to the pre-Revolutionary monarchy, they told a very distinctive story, with the women of the Valois dynasty playing an important but peculiar part. Michelet and Guizot generally disparaged the Renaissance and thoroughly indicted queens. Their idiosyncratic interpretations were set in stone for generations of French schoolchildren in textbooks, particularly those of Ernest Lavisse.

When Michelet, Guizot, and Lavisse treated the period from the fifteenth century to the advent of the Bourbons, Joan of Arc became the definitive representative of the national identity and political liberty they saw in the Middle Ages. Lavisse offered the clearest articulation of this view: "In no country, does one find as beautiful a story as that of Joan of Arc."[11] Notably, Joan's faith in France, rather than her religious faith, saved it. French history became an enthralling morality play in which good warred against evil. Lavisse made Joan's status as a national saint explicit: "All the French should love and venerate the memory of this young girl who loved France so much and died for us."[12] Lavisse was merely canonizing Joan after her distinctive position had been well established by earlier histories. Guizot, for example, took Joan's religious motives seriously and emphasized her deep devotion, her voices, and her ability to predict the future, but religion and patriotism were inextricable in his account. Joan urged her troops: "In the name of God fight. Even if the English were suspended from the clouds, we should take them, for God has sent us to punish them." Accordingly, she was for Guizot the "heaven-sent interpretess of the nation's feeling, the hope of the people of France," who ultimately "sacrificed herself for France."[13] Michelet emphasized the distinctiveness of her virginity, which both distinguished her from other women and gave her political credibility. Joan's politicized and secularized sanctity was thus admirable but also so unconventional as to be unattainable by any other woman.

Unquestionably, the Valois of the fifteenth and sixteenth centuries fit much less well than the mythologized Joan into these heroic, national narratives. Not only was writing about the pre-Revolutionary monarchy more politically charged than the more remote Middle Ages, but the Renaissance also seemed to defy heroic treatment. Its denouement in the bloody Wars of Religion exposed violence and betrayal more than the noble deeds of heroes. (It is no accident that this period romanticized the Middle Ages as both safely remote from current political issues and peopled with romantic heroes.) Unlike the Hundred Years War, the Wars of Religion could not be redefined as a valiant battle against a foreign aggressor, at least not until Henry IV repulsed the Spanish and saved France.

Guizot and Michelet identified and developed a set of specific charges against the Valois: They were the kings who set France on the road to absolutism by systematically curtailing the liberty of the people, pursuing destructive foreign policies, and unleashing religious intolerance. For Michelet, medieval feudalism had allowed greater liberty and more collective action, which advanced the French nation. But the Renaissance thwarted these positive developments. Guizot praised the artistic glories of the Renaissance but bemoaned its political failures. Michelet condemned the Renaissance monarchy for its impact on French character, concluding that "it courted the people and made them the king's courtiers."[14]

Although they held a jaundiced view of Valois monarchs, these historians' harshest criticisms focused on royal women. In Michelet's idiosyncratic history, the Renaissance concentrated power in the hands of monarchs, but this malign development was engineered by royal women. He singled out for condemnation without reservation Marguerite of Austria, Anne of Brittany, and Louise of Savoy. For him, they were three almost diabolical Machiavellian women whose "sweet love of family, their scorn for nations, made them complicit in the great crimes of diplomacy." The marriages they tried to arrange for their children were "intended to create a universal empire to unite the people under a yoke."[15] For Michelet, the political machinations of these three women were responsible for the entire debacle of the French pursuit of Italy and ultimately for the two centuries of warfare that ensued.

Guizot too criticized Anne of Brittany. He saw her character as difficult and her relations with her two French royal husbands as uncongenial. He discounted other, romantic versions of her marriage to Louis XII. "Anne was haughty, imperious, sharp-tempered, and too much inclined to mix in intrigues and negotiations at Rome and Madrid, sometimes without regard for the king's policy,"[16] he claimed. But Guizot held Louise of Savoy, Francis I's mother and regent, responsible for the great evils of the sixteenth century, especially for the persecution of the Protestants, which Francis's imprisonment allowed her to implement.[17] Most reprehensible in Guizot's account were her motives for repression of religious dissent: She was greedy and avid for power.

Only the advent of Henry IV allowed these three historians to return to a heroic, national narrative. They eagerly embraced him in his most legendary dimension. Henry was heroic because he was so male. None of them acknowledged that any woman played any role in his reign and rarely even mentioned women, even in his personal life. Strikingly, none used the example of Marguerite de Valois, whose life and certainly whose legend could have further tarred women as political actors. This omission suggests that it was better for Henry's heroic legend to excise women rather than make polemical use of his queen.

Lavisse distilled the elements of Henry IV's legend for students at all levels. They learned that in war Henry was "brave among the brave." He pardoned his enemies and brought peace to a troubled land, demonstrating that he was "as able as he was brave."[18] Lavisse emphasized Henry's great concern for the people, most notably his desire to have a chicken in the pot every Sunday. He underscored Henry's masculinity; he was educated as a soldier and, as Lavisse explicitly contended, "This male education saved him." Most praiseworthy was his early espousal of religious tolerance. "France was the first country where one recognized that a man should not be badly treated because of his religion. It is a great honor for France." As a result, Henry was "not only one of the greatest kings but also one of the greatest Frenchmen that history has known."[19]

Guizot too praised Henry as tolerant beyond his age, which was not yet elevated "up to the higher principle of religious peace, the distinction between the civil and intellectual order, freedom of thought, and of faith guaranteed by political liberty."[20] Guizot distinguished Catherine's ineffective policies from Henry's successful ones which, for him, foreshadowed the highest accomplishments of the republic. Unlike Catherine, Henry did not try to play one side against the other. Instead "he set his thoughts higher, upon the general and national interests of France." He was adept in both foreign and domestic policy: "Abroad the policy of Henry IV was as judicious and farsighted as it was just and sympathetic at home." Michelet too admired Henry for his courage, but he ultimately indicted the sixteenth century as a blighted opportunity for France. The Renaissance, he claimed, promoted an ideal too weak to inspire men. The Reformation too inspired Frenchmen but offered martyrdom rather than enfranchisement and was ultimately co-opted by the monarchy.[21]

The interpretation of the Valois monarchy and women's role in it by these influential post-Revolutionary historians are worth discussing because it has proved especially enduring. Their histories entailed the disparagement of women as they asserted the heroic character of the national history and people of France. Its heroes valiantly served the national interest, and its history was a tale of increasing liberty. But the Renaissance was not easily integrated into this heroic saga. Under Valois kings, heroism yielded to venal self-interest and conventional ideas about women's weaknesses explained their failures. Inappropriately politically active women thus distorted France's history. Their evil and petty motives were unworthy of France's heroes or national character. They exerted a destructive force by acting in personal and familial interests instead of the public or national good. Strong enough to stymie kings and emasculate them, royal women weakened the nation, according to these historians. Ironically, powerful women were to be denounced, but politically inactive women could be praised for inspiring a king or promoting culture.

Novels proved even more powerful than these histories in defining the ways queens and mistresses were remembered. Catherine de Medici rather peculiarly became both sexually depraved and an unwomanly woman. Novels no doubt made the plight of some, Marguerite de Valois, for example, more sympathetic, but they also weakened women as historical actors, making them victims of their passions. Women were sentimentalized, and in both histories and novels, sexual stereotypes defined them. Novels in turn influenced subsequent histories, and fictions have proven especially hard to excise from Renaissance histories.

As this book attests, royal women have had surprisingly long and influential historiographical lives. Canonical histories, written in a period of patriarchal democracy, remade the Valois monarchy in its image, and that interpretation remains powerful. Royal women have remained defined by older historiography to a degree that their male counterparts have not. In the late twentieth century, some of these women have found sympathetic biographers, but they still have not generally been acknowledged for their importance to the Renaissance. Their histories should be further disentangled from the systematic misogyny that has sometimes defined them.

Ironically, fictional and romanticized views of royal women largely explain their modern allure. They are featured in songs, legends, and children's stories. The sudden deaths of beautiful mistresses by violent means, like that of Françoise de Foix, remain chilling and overloaded with moral lessons about women who violate sexual conventions. Marguerite de Valois offers a warning about female sexuality and passion run amok, and Catherine de Medici can still be cited as an example of overweening maternal ambition and involvement in the lives of her sons. Royal women hold a prominent place in stories defining French national identity—the intrepid Agnès who saved a king, and Diane who molded another, for example. Their images remain in Renaissance artifacts of the national patrimony readily available to the public in museums and chateaux. The works they commissioned stand as their most prominent and enduring cultural legacy. In their single romanticized dimensions, these women warrant passing remarks in French schoolbooks.

In very recent times, royal women have been the focus of local interest and tourism. They embody romance and offer early models of fashion and celebrity. They have sometimes been singled out as prescient proponents of modern ideas, including internationalism or regionalism (ironically, both for Anne of Brittany), religious ecumenism (Marguerite d'Angoulême), sexual liberation (mistresses in general and Marguerite de Valois in particular), and feminism. They retain this fascination, for instance in a series of thirteen (and counting) popular novels by Robert Merle that follow the exploits of a Huguenot physician through the Wars of Religion. Interestingly, in them Henry III has been rescued from the excesses of his legend and rehabilitated as a conscientious king, but neither Catherine de Medici's nor Marguerite de Valois's myths have been reconsidered. The picture of Gabrielle d'Estrées, which introduces this book, provoked the best-selling German novel *Die Purpurlinie* by Wolfram Fleischhauer in 2002.[22] Diane de Poitiers graced the cover of an issue of *Le Nouvel Observateur* in summer 2009 that focused on women of power, ending with French First Lady Carla Bruni-Sarkozy.[23]

Royal women of the French Renaissance were the celebrities of their day. They lived quasi-public lives and acted in public settings; their personal triumphs and tragedies were common knowledge. They not only had significant impact on kings' reigns but also left deep traces of their lives in Renaissance arts and literature. The ways they transgressed expectations of women's lives, worked to break free of limits placed on them, or took conventional roles and molded them to fit the challenges they faced continue to intrigue us—as personalities, as actors on the historical stage, as promoters of cultural innovation, and as means to understand and interpret the French Renaissance and the subsequent history of France.

Notes

INTRODUCTION

1. Paola Tinagli, *Women in Italian Renaissance Painting: Gender, Representation, and Identity* (New York: Manchester University Press, 1997).
2. If accurately dated 1594, the painting could not suggest Gabrielle's death.
3. About this painting, see Janine Garrisson, *Gabrielle d'Estrées: Aux marches du palais* (Paris: Le Grand Livre du Mois, 2006), 112–13; Katherine Crawford, "The Politics of Promiscuity: Masculinity and Heroic Representation at the Court of Henry IV," *French Historical Studies* 26: 2 (Spring 2003), 234.
4. Catherine's portrait shares elements with Marie Leszcinska's portrait. See Mary Sheriff, "The Portrait of the Queen," in *Marie Antoinette: Writings on the Body of the Queen*, ed. Dena Goodman (New York: Routledge, 2003), 45–52.
5. On the examination of Marie Antoinette, see Caroline Weber, *Queen of Fashion* (New York: Holt, 2006), 24–47.
6. Jacob Burckhardt, *The Civilization of the Renaissance*, trans. S. G. S. Middlemore (Vienna: Phaidon Press, 1937).
7. Joan Kelly-Gadol, "Did Women Have a Renaissance?" in *Becoming Visible*, ed. Renate Bridenthal, Claudia Koonz, and Susan Stuard, 2d ed. (Boston: Houghton Mifflin, 1987), 175–202.
8. Thierry Crépin-Lebond and Martha Wolff, "The Kings and Their Artists," in *Kings, Queens, and Courtiers: Art in Early Renaissance France*, ed. Martha Wolff (London and New Haven: Art Institute of Chicago and Yale University Press, 2011), 77.
9. Throughout this book, dates for kings specify their reigns, except where indicated otherwise.
10. The extent of French territory increased considerably during the Renaissance. Dauphiné was acquired in 1349. The French monarchy expanded by annexing the lands of princes without male descendants: Burgundy after Charles the Bold's death in 1477 and the lands of René of Anjou. In the sixteenth century, it annexed the constable of Bourbon's land on the same principle and Brittany through marriage. During the

sixteenth century, it incorporated the lands brought to the crown by holders of the crown: Louis XII, Francis I, and Henry IV. By Louis XI's reign, the royal domain was 60 percent of the kingdom. By the seventeenth century, it included virtually all of contemporary France. See Emmanuel Le Roy Ladurie, *The Royal French State, 1460–1610* (Oxford: Blackwell, 1987), 33–38. Fig. 2.1 shows these additions.

11. Pair de France, or "peer of the realm," a medieval title denoting the highest nobility, was more restricted in number and higher in status than in England. Marguerite d'Angoulême was one of only twenty-one.
12. John Knox, *First Blast of the Trumpet against the Monstrous Regiment of Women* (Geneva, 1558).
13. Pierre de Bourdeille, lord of Brantôme, *Oeuvres complètes*, ed. Ludovic Lalanne, 11 vols. (1848; repr., New York: Johnson Reprint, 1968).

CHAPTER 1. AGNÈS SOREL

1. Aeneas Sylvius Piccolomini, *Pii secondi pontificis maximi commentarii rerum memorabilium* (Rome, 1584), 163.
2. In the eighteenth century, both Agnès and Joan were used to criticize the clergy and the monarchy. Nora Heimann, *Joan of Arc in French Art and Culture, 1700–1855: From Satire to Sanctity* (Aldershot, UK: Ashgate, 2005).
3. Honoré Capfigue, *Agnès Sorel et la chevalerie* (Paris, 1896), 56.
4. Jules Michelet, *Histoire de France*, 19 vols. (Paris, 1876–1877), 6: 176.
5. Gonzague Saint Bris, *Agnès Sorel: Dame de Beauté et première maîtresse royale* (Tours, France: Nouvelle République, 1998), 29.
6. The Hundred Years War was longer than the name, coined in the nineteenth century. Anne Curry, "France in the Hundred Years War," in *France in the Later Middle Ages*, ed. David Potter (Oxford: Oxford University Press, 2002), 93–94.
7. Emmanuel Le Roy Ladurie, *The Royal French State, 1460–1610* (Oxford: Blackwell, 1987), 35–38.
8. Fanny Cosandey argues that Salic law paradoxically allowed queens to define their roles. *La reine de France: Symbole et pouvoir (XVe-XVIIIe siècle)* (Paris: Gallimard, 2000), 19–54; Sarah Hanley places Salic Law within the "*querelle des femmes.*" *Les femmes dans l'histoire: La loi salique* (Paris: Indigo Editions des Femmes, 1994). Craig Taylor considers Salic law crucial to Valois claims. "The Salic Law and the Valois Succession to the French Crown," *French History* 15 (2001), 358–77. The fundamental text, *Pour ce que plusiers*, likely written by Guillaume Cousinot II de Montreuil (ca. 1400–1484), is reproduced in *Debating the Hundred Years War: Pour ce que plusieurs; A declaracion of the trew and dewe title of Henry VIII*, ed. Craig Taylor (Cambridge: Cambridge University Press, 2006).
9. For Charles VI's mental state, see R. C. Famiglietti, *Royal Intrigue: Crisis at the Court of Charles VI, 1392–1420* (New York: AMS Press, 1986), 1–21.
10. Princes of the blood traced direct male descent back to Louis IX.
11. Thomas Basin, *Histoire des règnes de Charles VII et de Louis XI*, ed. J. Quicherat, 4 vols. (Paris, 1855–59), 1: 312.

12. On Charles's neuroses, see Georges Chastellain, a Burgundian chronicler later attached to the French king, *Oeuvres,* 6 vols. (1827; repr., Geneva: Slatkine, 1971), 2: 181, 185–86.
13. Isabeau had six sons: Three died very young; two others, expected to reign, died; only Charles VII survived to reign. Tracy Adams, *The Life and Afterlife of Isabeau of Bavaria* (Baltimore, MD: Johns Hopkins University Press, 2010), 230.
14. For Chastellain, guilt was the source of Charles's diffidence. *Oeuvres,* 2: 181.
15. Two items are especially telling: Article 6—"The crown and kingdom of France, with all of their rights and appurtenances, will remain and will belong to us, King Henry cited above, and our heirs in perpetuity"; and Article 29—"Item, considering the horrendous and enormous crimes and wicked deed perpetrated in this kingdom of France by Charles, who styles himself dauphin of Vienne, it is agreed that neither our beloved father, nor we, King Henry . . . shall begin or make any treaty of peace or accord with this Charles." Text reproduced in *English Medieval Diplomatic Practice,* ed. Pierre Chaplais, 2 vols. (London: Hambledon, 1982), 2: 629, 636.
16. According to Adams, to condemn Isabeau for repudiating her son posits an anachronistic sense of the nation. *The Life and Afterlife of Isabeau of Bavaria,* 40, 190–94. Marie-Véronique Clin sees Isabeau's alliance with the English and Burgundians as intended to defeat the Armagnacs and attain peace through her daughter's marriage. *Isabeau de Bavière: La reine calomniée* (Paris: Perrin, 1999), 212, 216, 258, 261.
17. Reported immoral activities at the queen's court led Charles VI to disband it and close Isabeau's accounts. John the Fearless claimed that such treatment legitimated his actions. R. C. Famiglietti, *Royal Intrigue,* 183.
18. Gaston du Fresne de Beaucourt, *Charles VII: Son caractère* (Paris, 1872), 4.
19. Such charges circulated in the Burgundian pamphlet *Le pasorelet* but were not taken seriously. Craig Taylor, ed., *Joan of Arc: La Pucelle: Selected Sources* (New York: Palgrave Macmillan, 2006), 12.
20. Chastellain, *Oeuvres,* 1: 50–51.
21. Auguste Vallet de Viriville posits Charles's protracted adolescence or hereditary madness. *Nouvelle recherches sur Agnès Sorel* (Paris, 1856), 47–48.
22. Enguerrand de Monstrelet noted that famine deaths among the poor led to "a great and sorrowful perplexity." *Chroniques d'Enguerrand de Monstrelet,* ed. J. A. Bouchon, 8 vols. (Paris, 1826), 7:1–2.
23. Jean Chartier reported that although the king had changed clothes with another, Joan was not deceived. *Chronique de Charles VII, roi de France,* ed. Auguste Vallet de Viriville, 3 vols. (Paris, 1858), 1: 67. A similar report is found in *Procès de condamnation de Jeanne d'Arc,* ed. Pierre Champion, 2 vols. (1920; repr., Geneva: Slatkine, 1976), 2: 36.
24. Joan's witnesses cited her prophesy that a virginal figure would redeem France from the sins of Eve, construed as Isabeau. Taylor, *Joan of Arc,* 18, 78–9.
25. Georges de la Trémoille was intent on avenging the Armagnacs. Paul Kendall, *Louis XI: The Spider King* (New York: Allen & Unwin, 1971), 41.
26. Christine de Pizan, *Le ditié de Jehanne d'Arc,* ed. Angus J. Kennedy and Kenneth Varty (Oxford: Oxford University Press, 1977), 28–29.

27. Pierre Champion, *La dame de Beauté, Agnès Sorel* (Paris: Honoré Champion, 1931), 13.
28. Taylor disputes that Charles could have ransomed Joan and contends that Charles betrayed her because his supporters were indifferent to her fate. *Joan of Arc*, 20.
29. Chastellain, *Oeuvres*, 4: 465.
30. Olivier de La Marche, *Mémoires*, in *Choix de chroniques et mémoires sur l'histoire de France*, ed. J. A. C. Buchon (Paris, 1854), 7: 407; Chastellain, *Oeuvres*, 4: 365.
31. Marcel Frager, *Marie d'Anjou: Femme de Charles VII* (Paris: Editions de Paris, 1948).
32. Beaucourt differentiated two views of Charles VII: The more prominent described him as mediocre and pleasure seeking; the other, when he associated with Agnès, praised him as the courageous savior of the monarchy. *Charles VII*, 2. Colette Béaune explains this divergence as Burgundian versus Armagnac. "L'Historiographie de Charles VII: Un thème de l'opposition à Louis XI," *La France à la fin du XVe siècle–Renouveau et apogée*, Colloque de Tours, 1983 (Paris: CNRS, 1985), 265–81.
33. Eric Inglis sees Fouquet's works as asserting an emerging French nation but concedes that this particular image is often considered to reveal Charles's weakness. *Jean Fouquet and the Invention of France* (New Haven and London: Yale University Press, 2011), 73.
34. Robert Philippe, *Agnès Sorel* (Paris: Hachette, 1983), 30.
35. Saint Bris, *Agnès Sorel*, 28
36. By the sixteenth century, the entry included the procession of various corporations, the king, the court, and theatrical elements. Robert J. Knecht, *Renaissance Warrior and Patron: The Reign of Francis I* (Cambridge: Cambridge University Press, 1994), 47. See also Lawrence M. Bryant, *The King and the City in the Parisian Royal Entry Ceremony: Politics, Ritual, and Art in the Renaissance* (Geneva: Droz, 1986).
37. Christian marriage had not yet displaced Frankish, easily dissolved sexual relationships. Alessandro Barbero, *Charlemagne: Father of a Continent* (Berkeley, CA: University of California Press, 2002), 129–31.
38. La Marche, *Mémoires*, 7: 407; Jean Le Clerc, *Chronique Martiniane*, ed. Pierre Champion (Paris: H. Champion, 1907), 97; Basin, *Histoire des règnes de Charles VII et de Louis XI*, 1: 313.
39. Pierre de Bourdeille, lord of Brantôme, *Oeuvres complètes*, ed. Ludovic Lalanne, 11 vols. (1848; repr., New York: Johnson Reprint, 1968), 9: 393–94. His grandmother's attachment to Anne of Beaujeu's and Marguerite d'Angoulême's courts, and his aunt's status as Louis XII's goddaughter gave Brantôme access to documents that no longer exist. His reports are important but not completely credible. Pauline Matarasso, *Queen's Mate: Three Women of Power in France on the Eve of the Renaissance* (Aldershot, UK: Ashgate, 2001), 19n10.
40. Heiress to the duchy of Lorraine, wife of René, duke of Anjou, and the sister-in-law of the queen Marie of Anjou, Isabelle had a sophisticated court at the juncture of French, Italian, and Spanish influences, which exposed Agnès to early manifestations of the Renaissance.
41. Chartier insisted that the relationship was not sexual. *Chronique de Charles VII*, 2: 181–82.

42. Vallet de Viriville dated the relationship to 1435 following Jean Le Clerc's chronicle, which divided Charles's life into two parts—before 1435, when he lived chastely, and after, when he was involved with Agnès—and explained Agnès's absence from the historical record before 1443 as due to French reticence. *Nouvelle recherches sur Agnès Sorel*, 15.
43. See, for example, www.esrf.eu/news/general-old/general-2005/sorel/index_html/ and http://pathographie.blogspot.fr/2007/06/ltude-scientifique-des-restes-dagns.html.
44. In 1444 Agnès's name is found in the "Gages des dame et officiers de la Reyne de Sicilie, Isabelle de Lorraine," reprinted in Champion, *Dame de Beauté*, 173 ; and later that year in "Table des Ordonnances et Etats des Maisons des Roys, Reynes, Dauphins, Enfants ets Autres Princes de France," reprinted in Vallet de Viriville, *Recherches sur Agnès Sorel*, 304.
45. *Journal d'un bourgeois de Paris (1405–1449)*, ed. Alexandre Tuetey (Paris, 1881), 387. This collection of anonymous texts, compiled from manuscripts, was written by a clerical eyewitness who took a partisan, Anglo-Burgundian position until 1436. Afterward he identified with the crown.
46. Champion, *Dame de Beauté*, 36.
47. La Marche, *Mémoires*, 7: 407.
48. Jeanne de Vendôme, lady-in-waiting to the queen and debtor to Coeur, accused him. Malcolm Vale, *Charles VII* (Los Angeles: University of California Press, 1974), 173.
49. Agnès's detractors were Burgundian partisans. Vallet de Viriville, *Nouvelles recherches sur Agnès Sorel*, 59.
50. Basin, *Histoire des règnes de Charles VII et Louis XI*, 1: 313.
51. Brantôme, *Oeuvres*, 9: 717.
52. *Journal d'un bourgeois de Paris*, 387.
53. Falsely attributed to Antoine de la Salle.
54. Christine de Pizan asserted the value of women, supported the Valois monarchy, defended Charles VII, and argued that Joan was God's agent sent to save France. *Ditié de Jehanne d'Arc* (Clermont-Ferrand, France: Paleo, 2010).
55. *The Chronicles of Enguerrand de Monstrelet*, trans. Thomas Johnes, 13 vols. (London, 1805), 9: 382. Monstrelet was a Burgundian and a witness against Joan. His *Chronicles* end at 1444. An additional book by an unknown author related events between April 1444 and the duke of Burgundy's death in 1467.
56. Piccolomini, *Commentarii*, 292.
57. Kendall details Louis's antagonism, *Louis XI*, 67, 160.
58. The cages in which Louis kept his prisoners are displayed in the chateau of Loches.
59. Jean V de Bueil idealized chivalric, military culture during the Hundred Years War in, *Le jouvencel*, ed. Guillaume Tringant (1923; repr., Geneva: Slatkine, 1996).
60. Chartier, *Chronique de Charles VII*, 2: 181.
61. Le Clerc, *Chronique Martiniane*, 98.
62. Chartier, *Chronique de Charles VII*, 2: 186–87.
63. Jacques Du Clercq, *Mémoires de J. Du Clercq*, ed. Frédéric Reiffenberg, 3 vols. (Brussels, 1825), 3: 141–42; Claude de Seyssel, *Histoire singulière du roy Loys XII* (Paris, 1558), 35.

64. Chastellain, *Oeuvres*, 3: 17–18.
65. Marie married the lord of Coëtivy; Charlotte married Jacques de Brézé; Jeanne married Antoine de Bueil. Agnès's fourth daughter survived her by only a few days.
66. Gifts to Agnès included La Roquiercezière, Issoudun en Berry, Vernon, and Anneville, a pension of three thousand *livres* a year, and houses at Chinon, Beaulieu, and Orléans.
67. Chartier, *Chronique de Charles VII*, 2: 181.
68. Chastellain, *Oeuvres*, 2: 365.
69. On sumptuary laws, see Georges Duby, ed., *Revelations of the Medieval World*, in *History of Private Life*, ed. Philippe Aries and Georges Duby, vol. 2. (Cambridge, MA: Belknap Press of Harvard University, 1987), 569–75.
70. Jean II Juvénal des Ursins, *L'epître sur la réformation du Royaume*, cited in Champion, *Dame de Beauté*, 40.
71. Chastellain, *Oeuvres*, 4: 366.
72. Marina Warner, *Joan of Arc: The Image of Female Heroism* (New York: Knopf, 1981), 172–73.
73. Quoted in Champion, *Dame de Beauté*, 39.
74. Basin, *Histoire des règnes de Charles VII et Louis IX*, 1: 177.
75. Chastellain, *Oeuvres*, 4: 365.
76. Bref de Nicolas V, April 11, 1448, *Archives du Vatican, Register of Nicholas V*, 385, fol. 275. Reproduced in Etienne Caravay, *Archives des missions scientifiques*, 3rd series, 7: 467.
77. Saint Bris, *Agnès Sorel*, 31. The anonymous writer who continued Monstrelet's *Chronicle* noted that Agnès often remembered Mary Magdalene. *The Chronicles of Enguerand de Monstrelet*, 9: 98. The gift is noted in "Inventaire de la fabrique de l'église collègiale de Loches en 1749," in Gaspard Thaumas de La Thaumassière's 1699 *Histoire du Berry*, 2 vols. (Bourges, 1865) 1: 94; Viriville, "Recherches historiques sur Agnès Sorel," in *Bibliothèque de l'Ecole des Chartres* (1849), 3rd series, 1: 319.
78. Chartier, *Chronique de Charles VII*, 2: 186–87.
79. Documents about Agnès's tomb are "pièces inédites et justificatifs" in Joseph Delort, *Essai critique sur l'histoire de Charles VII, d'Agnès Sorelle, et de Jeanne d'Arc* (Paris, 1824), 208–24.
80. Marina Warner, *From Beast to Blonde* (New York: Farrar, Straus and Giroux, 1996), 367–69.
81. Philippe, *Agnès Sorel*, 86; Joanna L. Laynesmith, *The Last Medieval Queen* (Oxford: Oxford University Press, 2004), 141.
82. A king and queen's relationship was depicted iconographically as analogous to that of Christ and his Church. Marina Warner, *Alone of All Her Sex: The Myth and Cult of the Virgin Mary* (New York: Vintage, 1983), 113–16. This theological association with Agnès was not made.
83. Laynesmith, *Last Medieval Queens*, 49.
84. On Agnès's legend, see Champion, *Dame de Beauté*, 110–70.
85. Bernard de Girard Du Haillan, *Histoire générale des roys de France, contenant les choses mémorables advenues tant au royaume de France qu'ès provinces étrangères sous la domination des François*, 2 vols. (Paris, 1627), 2: 1253.

86. Baïf's poem, *Agnès Sorelle,* is reproduced in Delort, *Essai critique,* 277–82.
87. Charles Sorel, *La solitude et l'amour philosophique de Cléomède* (Paris, 1640). This text is reproduced by Champion in *Dame de Beauté,* 186–97.
88. On the poem's influence, see Heimann, *Joan of Arc,* 13–21.
89. Voltaire's earlier, obscene version (1730) circulated in manuscript to amuse his friends. A sanitized version (1762) was frequently republished.
90. François Marie Arouet de Voltaire, *Oeuvres de Voltaire,* vol. 11: *La Pucelle* (Paris, 1832), 17.
91. Ibid., 64.
92. Jean-François Dreux du Radier, *Mémoires historiques, critiques et anecdotiques des reines et régentes de France,* 6 vols. (Amsterdam, 1776), 3: 181–82.
93. Friedrich Schiller, *The Maid of Orleans* (1801; New York: Ungar, 1967), 23.
94. Ulric Güttinger, *Charles VII à Jumiège* (Paris, 1827), 15.
95. Vallet de Viriville saw Agnes as a nationalist heroine and her opponents as anti-nationalists. *Nouvelles recherches sur Agnès Sorel,* 59.
96. Philippe, *Agnès Sorel,* 100.

CHAPTER 2. ANNE OF BRITTANY

1. For Isabeau's defenders, this was a credible response to dire circumstances. Tracy Adams, *The Life and Afterlife of Isabeau of Bavaria* (Baltimore, MD: Johns Hopkins University Press, 2010), 194–198, 201–07, 212–17.
2. Margaret of Scotland and Charlotte of Savoy.
3. Laudatory Bretons include: Emile Gabory, *L'Union de la Bretagne à la France: Anne de Bretagne, duchesse et reine* (Paris: Plon, 1941); Jean Markale, *Anne de Bretagne* (Paris: Hachette, 1980); Michel de Mauny, *Anne de Bretagne: Ce coeur qui a tant aimé la Bretagne* (Plérin, France: Brittia, 2000). Critics include: Georges Minois, *Anne de Bretagne* (Paris: Grand livre du mois, 1999); Bernard Quilliet, *Louis XII: Père du people* (Paris: Arthème Fayard, 1986); Hervé Le Boterf, *Anne de Bretagne* (Paris: France-Empire, 1996).
4. Le Boterf, *Anne de Bretagne,* 19–20.
5. Bertrand d'Argentré, *Histoire de la Bretagne* (Paris, 1611), 1005.
6. If accounts of Anne's intellectual accomplishment were accurate, she would have been better educated than Erasmus, Minois notes. *Anne de Bretagne,* 48–49.
7. Ballad 10 of 25 satiric ballads directed against Louis XI, in Arthur de La Borderie, *Jean Meschinot: Sa vie et ses oeuvres* (Paris, 1896), 63.
8. Francis reigned as the son of Jean V's brother instead of Jean's daughter because of this treaty's preference for a male descendant.
9. Frederic J. Baumgartner, *Louis XII* (New York: St. Martin's Press, 1994), 19.
10. This remark is always cited without attribution.
11. Minois claims that Charles traveled with the *Roman de la rose* and other romances, which cultivated his chivalric ideas. *Anne de Bretagne,* 296–97. Yvonne Labande-Mailfert concedes that Charles's education was not substantive but denies that he read only romances. *Charles VIII et son milieu: 1470–1498* (Paris: C. Klincksieck, 1975), 21–22.

12. Claude de Seyssel, *Histoire singulière du roy Loys XII* (Paris, 1558), 39.
13. Bernard de Mandrot, ed., *Dépêches des ambassadeurs milanais en France sous Louis XI et François Sforze*, 4 vols. (Paris: H. Laurens, 1916–23) 2: 135.
14. Francesco Guicciardini, *The History of Italy*, trans. Sidney Alexander (Princeton, NJ: Princeton University Press, 1969), 95.
15. Philippe de Commynes, *Mémoires*, ed. Joel Blanchard, 2 vols. (Geneva: Droz, 2007), 1: 529.
16. Guicciardini, *History of Italy*, 49.
17. Pierre de Bourdeille, lord of Brantôme, *Oeuvres complètes*, ed. Ludovic Lalanne, 11 vols. (1848; repr., New York: Johnson Reprint, 1968), 2: 284. Minois, *Anne de Bretagne*, 520–21.
18. Anne of Beaujeu relinquished power only after her husband, Pierre, became duke of Bourbon. Thierry Wanegffelen, *Le pouvoir contesté: Souveraines d'Europe à la Renaissance* (Paris: Payot, 2008), 182–86.
19. On Anne of Beaujeu's exercise of power, see Pauline Matarasso, *Queen's Mate: Three Women of Power in France on the Eve of the Renaissance* (Aldershot, UK: Ashgate, 2001), 41–49, 55–59.
20. Antoine Le Roux de Lincy reproduced ledgers listing Bretons receiving money from Charles VIII, including Anne's guardians, Rieux and Françoise de Dinan. *Vie de la reine Anne de Bretagne, femme des rois de France Charles VIII et Louis XII*, 4 vols. (Paris, 1860), 3: 189–90.
21. Several months later, these same nobles swore to "sustain and defend" Francis. Minois, *Anne de Bretagne*, 93.
22. As a Penthièvre widower, Albret might have unified Bretons.
23. Minois, *Anne de Bretagne*, 114.
24. Argentré, *Histoire de la Bretagne*, 1112.
25. Minois, *Anne de Bretagne*, 152.
26. Pierre-Hyacinthe Morice, *Mémoires pour servir de preuves à l'histoire de Bretagne*, 3 vols. (Paris, 1756), 3: 14.
27. Minois, *Anne de Bretagne*, 244–45.
28. Albret's mother was the granddaughter of Jean IV, Anne's grandfather's brother.
29. Document reprinted in Le Roux de Lincy, *Vie de la reine*, 4: 208.
30. Argentré, *Histoire de Bretagne*, 1119.
31. Didier Le Fur, *Anne de Bretagne: Miroir d'une reine, historiographie d'un mythe* (Paris: Guénégaud, 2000), 14.
32. On November 12, Louis of Orléans and Pierre and Anne of Beaujeu examined the duchess. Yvonne Labande-Mailfert, "Le mariage d'Anne de Bretagne avec Charles VIII vu par Erasme Brasca," *Mémoires de la société d'histoire et d'archéologie de Bretagne* 55 (1978), 26.
33. Le Roux de Lincy, *Vie de la reine*, 1: 78–81.
34. Commynes, *Mémoires*, 1: 476–79.
35. Matarrasso cites Anne's many engagements as unusually cynical. *Queen's Mate*, 51–2.
36. Argentré reproduced her marriage contract with Charles VIII. *Histoire de Bretagne*, 1128–33.

37. Quoted in Yvonne Labande-Mailfert, *Charles VIII: Le vouloir et la destinée* (Paris: Fayard, 1986), 146.
38. Eugenio Albèri, ed., *Relazioni degli ambasciatori veneti al Senato,* 2nd series, 5 vols. (Florence, 1839–1863), 4: 15–16.
39. Le Roux de Lincy maintains that Anne immediately influenced Charles. *Vie de la reine,* 1: 89. Others are more skeptical; see Philippe Tourault, *Anne de Bretagne* (Paris: Perrin, 1990), 102–3.
40. Le Fur, *Anne de Bretagne,* 67–71.
41. Albèri, *Relazioni degli ambasciatori veneti,* 4: 15–16.
42. Ibid., 26.
43. Lawrence M. Bryant, *The King and the City in the Parisian Royal Entry Ceremony: Politics, Ritual, and Art in the Renaissance* (Geneva: Droz, 1986), 128. Anne's iconography as bringer of peace and justice complemented her husband's. Le Fur, *Anne de Bretagne,* 17–38.
44. Minois, *Anne de Bretagne,* 312–13.
45. The papal dispensation, produced after Innocent VIII's death, was backdated to December 15. Labande-Mailfert, *Charles VIII: Le vouloir et la destinée,* 152.
46. Francis de Paule, founder of the Minims in France and Anne's confessor, espoused this hope when he proposed the name.
47. In the thirteenth century, Charles of Anjou conquered Sicily and Naples. In 1480, his descendent René of Anjou claimed Naples and Jerusalem. René lost Naples to the Aragonese in 1442 and never pressed his claims to Jerusalem. Louis XI assumed those claims. Matarasso, *Queen's Mate,* 86.
48. Ibid., 83n9. Matarraso accepts Le Roux de Lincy's count as the most most credible. *Anne de Bretagne,* 1: 134. A number of other pregnancies were never subsequently reported or recorded as births, so there are conflicting accounts as to the number of Anne's pregnancies.
49. Discovered in 1940, the Rhesus factor is a blood antigen (positive if present, negative if absent). If a woman who is Rh-negative has a baby who is Rh-positive, she will develop antibodies to the Rh factor in subsequent pregnancies, and they will attack the fetus.
50. Quilliet, *Louis XII,* 136; Labande-Mailfert, *Charles VIII et son milieu,* 271.
51. Anne Denis, *Charles VIII et les Italiens: Histoire et mythe* (Geneva: Droz, 1979), 119–42.
52. Robert J. Knecht, *The Rise and Fall of Renaissance France* (Oxford: Blackwell, 2001), 38–40.
53. Robert J. Knecht notes that Francis was reported to have syphilis as early as 1524 and treated for it during the last five years of his life. *Renaissance Warrior and Patron: The Reign of Francis I* (Cambridge: Cambridge University Press, 1994), 112, 495–97.
54. Minois, *Anne de Bretagne,* 357.
55. François Marie Arouet de Voltaire, "Epigramme 95," *Oeuvres complètes de Voltaire,* 54 vols. (Paris, 1877–95), 10: 569.
56. Knecht, *Rise and Fall of Renaissance France,* 44–45.
57. Commynes was devoted to Louis of Orléans: He joined rebels against Anne of Beaujeu. Restored to royal favor, he served Charles VIII during the Italian campaign,

praised Charles for bravery in battle, and noted that Savonarola prophesied that "God led him by the hand." *Mémoires,* 1: 634, 639, 654.

58. Commynes commented, "The queen was not one in whom he [Charles VIII] took great pleasure, but she remained a very good lady." *Mémoires,* 1: 529.
59. Between forty-seven and fifty-three women were attached to Anne's court. Robert J. Knecht, *The French Renaissance Court* (New Haven and London: Yale University Press, 2008), 59.
60. Ibid., 143.
61. Speculation about the causes of Charles's death ranges from apoplexy to poison; an embolism seems most likely. Labande-Mailfert, *Charles VIII et son milieu,* 477–83.
62. In August 1497, Charles was ill and the following month cleaned up his court. Minois, *Anne de Bretagne,* 371–72.
63. Anne wrote "Nos Ames et Feaulx," August 20, 1498, reproduced in Le Roux de Lincy, *Anne de Bretagne,* 3: 25–26.
64. Louis might not have reigned: The peers affirmed the king, and Louis's earlier rebellion supporting Brittany against Charles VIII did not endear him to them. The Bourbons, especially Anne of Beaujeu, had to be appeased. Anne demanded that crown rights to Bourbonnais and Auvergne be waived and that her daughter, Suzanne, be allowed to inherit these territories. Matarasso, *Queen's Mate,* 145–47. This resolution set up the contested inheritance under Francis I.
65. Minois, *Anne de Bretagne,* 392.
66. Meaning that there will be no children. My italics.
67. René de Maulde La Clavière, ed., *Procédures politiques du règne de Louis XII* (Paris, 1885), 915–16.
68. Ibid., 1050.
69. Reported by the bishop of Orléans. Ibid., 1018.
70. For full documentation, see ibid., 787–1132. Louis cited four grounds: his blood relationship (as second cousin of Jeanne's father); their spiritual relationship; (Louis XI was Louis's godfather); Louis XI's intimidation; and Jeanne's inability to perform the marriage act. Jeanne's defense claimed that the first two had the requisite dispensations and the last two were negated by subsequent sexual intercourse. Louis claimed that Jeanne was so deformed that the marriage had not been consummated; Jeanne explicitly denied it. *Ibid.,* 825, 835. Abel Destefanis weighed the judicial evidence and concluded that compelling grounds was Louis XI's coercion. *Louis XII et Jeanne de France étude historique et juridique sur une cause en nullité de marriage à la fin du XV siècle* (Avignon, France: Les Presses Universelles, 1975), 161–64, 175–78.
71. Maulde La Clavière, *Procédures politiques,* 835.
72. Pierre-Hyacinthe Morice, *Mémoires pour servir de preuves à l'histoire écclesiastique et civile de Bretagne,* 3 vols. (Paris, 1742–1746), 3: 808–9.
73. Jeanne has attracted relatively little attention from biographers. See Ann M. C. Forster, *The Good Duchess: Joan of France (1464–1505)* (New York: P. J. Kennedy and Sons, 1950); and Henri Pigaillem, *Jeanne de France: Première épouse de Louis XII* (Paris: Pygmallion, 2008.
74. Commynes, *Mémoires,* 1: 530–31.

75. Anne of Brittany, "Nos Amez et Feaulx," reproduced in Le Roux de Lincy, *Anne de Bretagne*, 3: 21.
76. Brantôme claimed that Louis was smitten by Anne when she was seven. *Oeuvres*, 7: 308.
77. The text of the marriage contract with Louis, chapter 365, spelled out the rights and privileges accorded Brittany in this new contract. Argentré, *Histoire de Bretagne*, 1154–56. Louis ignored this clause and made his oldest daughter duchess of Brittany.
78. Le Fur emphasizes Brittany's ephemeral autonomy. *Anne de Bretagne*, 153–55.
79. Brantôme, *Oeuvres*, 7: 313.
80. Seyssel, *Histoire singulière*, 45.
81. Jean de Saint-Gelais, *Histoire de Louys XII* (Paris, 1622), 97–98; Commynes, *Mémoires*, 1: 693; repeated by Brantôme, *Oeuvres*, 7: 312.
82. Louis XII reportedly made this remark to the duke of Lorraine. Edward Le Glay, ed., *Négociations diplomatiques entre la France et l'Autriche*, 2 vols. (Paris, 1845), 1: lii. Matarasso considers it apocryphal. *Queen's Mate*, 147.
83. René de Maulde La Clavière praises Louis's attention to his peoples' needs. *Louise de Savoie et François Ier, trente ans de jeunesse (1485–1515)* (Paris: Perrin, 1895), 116–17. According to Nicole Hochner, Seyssel's construction of Louis as the "Father of His People" was intended to counter the negative image produced by his rebellion, imprisonment, and annulment. *Louis XII: Les dérèglements de l'image royale 1498–1515* (Seyssel, France: Champ Vallon, 2006), 21, 176–213. Le Fur contends that Louis, without a son, could be the father of his people. *Louis XII, 1498–1515* (Paris: Perrin, 2001), 154–57.
84. Quilliet, *Louis XII*, 111.
85. Albèri, *Relazioni degli ambasciatori*, 4: 15–16
86. Devices, often allegorical, were important means to convey the individual and his or her concerns.
87. Hochner, *Louis XII*, 258
88. Seyssel, *Histoire singulière*, 47.
89. Brantôme, *Oeuvres*, 7: 316.
90. Anne was conscious of her Foix family connections. Matarasso, *Queen's Mate*, 207.
91. Wanegffelen, *Pouvoir contesté*, 107–14.
92. His family sided with the French against the Bretons in the "crazy war."
93. Maulde La Clavière, *Louise de Savoie et François Ier*, 134–35.
94. Jean d'Auton, *Chroniques de Louis XII*, 4 vols. (Paris, 1889–1895) 3: 77–79, 117. For d'Auton, this anecdote emphasized Louis's compelling personal attractions. Hochner, *Louis XII*, 257. Seyssel, *Histoire singulière*, 47.
95. Commynes criticized Louis's war leadership: He failed to take advantage of military opportunities or evaluate his opponents' strength. *Mémoires*, 3: 159, 151.
96. Hochner, *Louis XII*, 263.
97. A queen was not necessarily crowned. If she were, it was after the king and at Saint-Denis rather than Reims. Knecht, *French Renaissance Court*, 97.
98. My italics. Anonymous contemporary, *Récit de ce qui s'est passé lors de la remonstrance faict au Roy Louis XII par les états du royaume, pour l'engager à consentir*

au mariage de Madame Claude de France avec Monsiegneur François, recounts that Thomas Briçot made the above speech, quoted in Minois, *Anne de Bretagne*, 498–99. For an extensive discussion of this document, see Quilliet, *Louis XII*, 327–33.

99. Maximilian noted to Henry VII. *Letters and Papers Illustrative of the Reigns of Richard III and Henry VII*, ed. James Gairdner, 2 vols. (London, 1861), 1: 301.
100. Baumgartner, *Louis XII*, 139.
101. Maulde La Clavière, *Procédures politiques*, 582.
102. Maulde La Clavière, *Louise de Savoie et François Ie*, 190.
103. Military reversals jeopardized Louis's Italian campaign. When Haute-Navarre was lost to Spain, he abandoned Italy to defend France.
104. On September 24, 1511, Andrea da Borgo wrote to Margaret of Austria that physicians reported signs assuring a male child. On January 1, 1512, Jean Leveau wrote, "Some would be disappointed if it were a male child." *Lettres du roi Louis XII et du cardinal Georges d' Amboise, avec plusieurs autres lettres, mémoires et instructions*, 4 vols. (Brussels, 1712) 3: 56, 111.
105. Knecht, *French Renaissance Court*, 118–19.
106. Niccolò Machiavelli, *The Prince*, trans. George Bull (London: Penguin, 2003), 13–15.
107. Gabory, *L'Union de la Bretagne à la France*, 242.
108. Anne's library likely went first to Diane de Poitiers then to Pierre Séguier. Pascale Thibault, *Les manuscrits de la collections d'Anne de Bretagne* (Blois, France: Les Amis de la Bibliothèque de Blois, 1991).
109. Baldassare Castiglione, *The Book of the Courtier*, trans. George Bull (London: Penguin, 1967), 237.
110. Jean-Claude Bologne, *Histoire de la pudeur* (Paris: Olivier Orban, 1986), 158.
111. Brantôme, *Oeuvres*, 7: 314.
112. Jean-François Solon, *La cour de France* (Paris: Librairie Générale Française, 1996), 22.
113. Anne likely followed the injunctions of Anne of Beaujeu, who condemned excessively ornate clothing as "offensive to the Creator." Sharon L. Jansen, *Anne of France: Lessons for My Daughter* (Woodbridge, Suffolk, UK; Rochester, NY: D. S. Brewer, 2004), 37–38.
114. Marguerite d'Angoulême, *Heptameron*, trans. P. A. Chilton (New York: Penguin, 1984), 236–54.
115. Minois, *Anne de Bretagne*, 423
116. For analysis of the complexities and ambiguities conveyed through manuscript illumination about the role and status of women, see Cynthia Brown, *The Queen's Library: Image Making at the Court of Anne of Brittany, 1477–1514* (Philadelphia: University of Pennsylvania Press, 2011); see also Brown, ed., *The Cultural and Political Legacy of Anne de Bretagne: Negotiating Conventions in Books and Documents* (Cambridge, UK: D. S. Brewer, 2010).
117. According to Michelle Szkilnik, Dufour associated Anne with influential women to assert his own authority. "Antoine Dufour's Vies des femmes célèbres," in Brown, ed., *Cultural and Political Legacy*, 78–9.
118. Thibault, *Manuscrits de la collections.*
119. Louis passed the first law fostering printing in 1513.

120. Le Roux de Lincy, *Anne de Bretagne*, 2: 37. On Anne's interest in Brittany's history, see Thibault, *Manuscrits de la collections*, 20–23. On Troy's mythic significance, Le Fur, *Anne de Bretagne*, 35–8; Minois, *Anne de Bretagne*, 518–21.
121. Matarasso, *Queen's Mate*, 249.
122. Geneviève-Morgane Tanguy, *Les jardins secrets d'Anne de Bretagne* (Paris : Fernand Lanore, 1990) 116–27.
123. André de La Vigne, *Epitaphes en rondeaux en honneur de la reine* (Paris, 1874), unpaginated.
124. Jean de Saint-Gelais, *Histoire de Louys de France* (Paris, 1622), 154.
125. The crucial source was Commynes, *Mémoires*, 1: 693. Brantôme emphasized her vindictiveness. *Oeuvres*, 7: 310–17.
126. Le Boterf, *Anne de Bretagne*, 9.
127. For Breton historiography, see Le Fur, *Anne de Bretagne*, 152–99. Songs and poems are reproduced in ibid., 190–97.
128. Nicolas de Montfaucon de Villars, *Anne de Bretagne ou l'amour sans foiblesse* (Paris, 1671).
129. Jules Michelet, *Histoire de France*, 19 vols. (Paris, 1876–1877), 9: 220, 244–47, 312.
130. François Guizot and Mme. Guizot de Witt, *France*, 8 vols. (New York: Collier, 1902), 2: 478.
131. Ernest Lavisse, *Histoire de France*, 9 vols. (Paris: Hachette, 1900–1911), 5: 42.
132. Michelet, *Histoire de France*, 9: 244–47; Geneviève-Morgane Tanguy, *Au fil de la Loire: Anne de Bretagne et l'art sacré* (Paris : Maison de Vie, 2001), 11; Minois, *Anne de Bretagne*, 522.
133. Quilliet, *Louis XII*, 454.
134. Tanguy, *Jardins secrets*, 8–10; Tanguy, *Au fil de la Loire*, 10–12. Matarasso disputes the claim. *Queen's Mate*, 179–80.
135. Elizabeth L'Estrange, "Le mécènat d'Anne de Bretagne," in *Patronnes et mécènes en France à la Renaissance*, ed. Kathleen Wilson-Chevalier (Saint-Etienne, France: Presse Universitaire de Saint-Etienne, 2007), 169–93; Cynthia Brown, "Le mécènat d'Anne de Bretagne et la politique du livre," in *Patronnes et mécènes*, 194–224.
136. Tanguy, *Au fil de la Loire*; Tanguy, *Jardins secrets*; Gabory, *L'Union de la Bretagne à la France*.

CHAPTER 3. THE WOMEN OF THE COURT OF FRANCIS I

1. Gaspard de Saulx Tavannes, *Mémoires de très-noble et très-illustre Gaspard de Saulx, seigneur de Tavannes* (Paris, 1838), 337.
2. Pierre de Bourdeille, lord of Brantôme, *Oeuvres complètes*, ed. Ludovic Lalanne, 11 vols. (1848; repr., New York: Johnson Reprint, 1968), 3:127.
3. Paule Henry-Bordeaux, *Louise de Savoie: "Roi" de France* (Paris: Perrin, 1971), 13.
4. Her grandniece Marguerite, who married her grandson Henry of Navarre, is also Marguerite de Navarre. To distinguish them, I refer to the former as Marguerite d'Angoulême, the latter as Marguerite de Valois.

5. Francis I, *Poésies du roi François Ier, de Louise de Savoie, duchesse d'Angoulême, de Marguerite, reine de Navarre et correspondance intime du roi avec Diane de Poitiers et plusieurs autres dames de la cour,* ed. Aimé Champollion-Figéac (repr.; 1847, Geneva: Slatkine, 1970); Francis I, *Oeuvres poétiques,* ed. J. E. Kane (Geneva: Slatkine, 1984).
6. Louise, *Journal* (Clermont-Ferrand, France: Paleo, 2006), 13. Louise's *Journal* notes important dates without much commentary and was arranged initially by the date on which events took place, for astrological reasons. When first published at the end of Martin and Guillaume du Bellay's *Memoirs,* it was reordered chronologically.
7. Henry-Bordeaux, *Louise de Savoie,* 13.
8. Anne was Louise's cousin on her father's side and her aunt by marriage on her mother's.
9. Philippe de Commynes, "Lettre de Jean Bossioau duc de Milan," in *Lettres et négociations de Philippe de Commynes,* ed. Kerwyn de Letthove, 3 vols. (1881; repr., Geneva: Slatkine, 1972) 1: 203.
10. Scholars disagree about the number and the names of the mistresses and their offspring. Sharon Jansen provides a historiographical overview. *The Monstrous Regiment of Women: Female Rulers in Early Modern France* (New York: Palgrave Macmillan, 2002), 278n8.
11. René de Maulde La Clavière, *Louise de Savoie et François Ier, trente ans de jeunesse (1485–1515)* (Paris: Perrin, 1895), 35–43.
12. Myra Dickman Orth, "Louise de Savoie et le pouvoir du livre," in *Royaume de fémynie: Pouvoirs, contraintes, espaces de liberté des femmes, de la Renaissance à la Fronde,* ed. Kathleen Wilson-Chevalier and Eliane Viennot (Paris: H. Champion, 1999), 71–92. Louise's collection included Petrarch and Boccacio. Paris Paulin, *Etudes sur François Ier,* 2 vols. (1885; repr., Geneva: Slatkine, 1970), 2:38.
13. Louise of Savoy, *Journal,* 12.
14. Guillaume de Jaligny, *Histoire de Charles VIII,* ed. Théodore Godefroy (Paris, 1617), 109.
15. Louise of Savoy, *Journal,* 12.
16. Réné de Maulde La Clavière, ed., *Procédures politiques du règne de Louis XII* (Paris, 1885), 716–22. This act exerted royal control and isolated the family. Patricia F. Cholakian and Rouben C. Cholakian, *Marguerite de Navarre: Mother of the Renaissance* (New York: Columbia University Press, 2006), 16.
17. Niccolò Alamanni reported the eight-year-old Francis's interest to Francesco Gonzaga of Mantua. Robert J. Knecht, *The French Renaissance Court* (New Haven and London: Yale University Press, 2008), 168. Paulin credits Louise with introducing her children to the rules of rhyme and meter. *Etudes sur François Ier,* 1: 41.
18. Baldassare Castiglione, *The Book of the Courtier,* trans. George Bull (London: Penguin 1967), 88.
19. Guillaume Budé, *La correspondance d'Erasme et de Guillaume Budé,* ed. Marie-Madeleine de la Garanderie (Paris: Vrin, 1967), 98–99.
20. Louise of Savoy, *Journal,* 14.
21. Francis was not the dauphin; he was neither Louis's son nor heir to Dauphiné.
22. Maulde La Clavière, *Louise de Savoie et François Ier,* 314.

23. Louise of Savoy, *Journal*, 20.
24. Ibid., 22.
25. Brantôme, *Oeuvres*, 9: 640–41.
26. Henry VIII agreed that, if Mary outlived Louis, she could marry Suffolk for love. Robert J. Knecht, *Renaissance Warrior and Patron: The Reign of Francis I* (Cambridge: Cambridge University Press, 1994), 17.
27. Louise of Savoy, *Journal*, 23–24.
28. Antonio de Beatis, *The Travel Journal of Antonio de Beatis: Germany, Switzerland, the Low Countries, France and Italy, 1517–1518* (London: Hakluyt Society, 1979), 107–108.
29. J. S. Brewer, J. Gairdner, and R. H. Brodie, eds., *Letters and Papers, Foreign and Domestic of the Reign of Henry VIII* (London, 1862–1910) vol. 2, pt. 1, no. 82: 28.
30. Armand Baschet, ed., *La diplomatie vénitienne. Les princes de l'Europe au XVIe siècle, François Ier, Philippe II, Catherine de Médicis. Les papes, les sultans, etc., . . . d'après les rapports des ambassadeurs vénitiens* (Paris, 1862), 367.
31. Abel Desjardins, ed., *Négociations diplomatiques de la France avec la Toscane*, 6 vols. (Paris 1859–1886), 1: 52, 55.
32. Beatis, *Travel Journal*, 107.
33. Henri Pigaillem, *Claude de France* (Paris: Pygmailion, 2006), 72. This quote is frequently reproduced without attribution, like other such apt quotations.
34. Francis's relationship with Mme. Dishommes provoked ribald farces in Paris, reported in *Journal tenu par un bourgeois de Paris pendant le règne de François Ier*, 2 vols. (Clermont-Ferrand, France: Editions Paleo, 2001), 1: 12; it was also featured as a story in Marguerite d'Angoulême, *Heptameron*, trans. P. A. Chilton (New York: Penguin, 1984), 286–92.
35. Beatis, *Travel Journal*, 107.
36. Baschet, *Diplomatie vénitienne*, 385.
37. Brantôme, *Oeuvres*, 3: 242–43.
38. Claude vowed to name her son after Francis de Paule and to promote his canonization. Paule was beatified after Louis XII and Anne of Brittany's petition, and Louise took credit for his canonization: "Brother Francis de Paule was canonized by me: at least I paid the taxes for it." *Journal*, 30.
39. Kathleen Wilson-Chevalier uses Claude's patronage to assert a more influential role for her. But it is always difficult to assign agency to the commissioner of works, and in Claude's case, her images replicate those of her mother. "Claude de France: In Her Mother's Likeness, a Queen with Symbolic Clout?" in *The Cultural and Political Legacy of Anne de Bretagne: Negotiation Conventions in Books and Documents*, ed. Cynthia J. Brown (Cambridge, UK: D. S. Brewer, 2011), 123–45.
40. Marguerite d'Angoulême's poem is a conversation with her recently deceased niece, Charlotte, on the happiness of the blessed in the afterlife. *Dialogue en forme de vision nocturne* (Alençon, 1533).
41. Beatis, *Travel Journal*, 107.
42. Knecht notes the debate about the cause of Francis's death and Francis's treatment for syphilis. *Renaissance Warrior and Patron*, 544–45.

43. Reported by Marguerite d'Angoulême, in Christine Martineau, Michel Veissière, and Henry Heller, eds., *Guillaume Briçonnet/Marguerite d'Angoulême Correspondance*, 2 vols. (Paris: Imprimerie Lahure, 1975–1979), 2: 271–72.
44. Robert Fleuranges III de La Marck, *Mémoires du maréchal de Florange*, ed. Robert Goubaux and André Lemoisne, 2 vols. (Paris: H. Laurens, 1913–1924), 2: 148.
45. *Journal tenu par un bourgeois de Paris*, 1: 150. Emmanuel Le Roy Ladurie identifies the self-styled bourgeois of Paris writing at this time as Nicolas Versoris, an advocate of the Parlement of Paris. *The Royal French State, 1460–1610* (Oxford: Blackwell, 1987), 132. Brantôme reported reading in the *Chroniques d'Anjou* about miracles produced by her intercession. *Oeuvres*, 8: 107.
46. Brantôme, *Oeuvres*, 8: 106.
47. Georges Toudouze, *Françoise de Chateaubriant* (Paris: Fleury, 1948), 26.
48. The evidence that they were not married is the document recording their daughter's baptism on March 19, 1507, which lists Françoise as *socie seu dilecte (compagne or amie)*, in other words, as unmarried. Toudouze cites the archival record from the parish church of Saint Jean de Béré. *Françoise de Chateaubriant*, 27.
49. Ibid., 28–29.
50. This story is found in Antoine Varillas's *Une Histoire de François Ier*, 2 vols. (Paris, 1685), 1: 177. Toudouze includes her letters. *Françoise de Chateaubriant*, 171–202.
51. Toudouze, *Françoise de Chateaubriant*, 174.
52. Brantôme, *Oeuvres*, 3: 128.
53. Part of the epitaph inscribed on her tomb at Chateaubriant.
54. Marguerite d'Angoulême, *Lettres de Marguerite d'Angoulême, soeur de François Ier, reine de Navarre*, ed. F. Génin (1851; reprt., New York: Johnson Reprint, 1965), 149.
55. Cited in Pacal Arnoux, *Favorites et "dames de coeur": D'Agnès Sorel à Mme de Pompadour, quand l'amour triomphe de la raison d'État* (Monaco: Rocher, 2005), 46.
56. Toudouze, *Françoise de Chateaubriant*, 173.
57. Brantôme, *Oeuvres*, 9: 18.
58. Alain Decaux, *Histoire des Françaises* (Paris: Perrin, 1998), 373.
59. Brantôme, *Oeuvres*, 9: 19.
60. Toudouze, *Françoise de Chateaubriant*, 24.
61. *Journal tenu par un bourgeois de Paris*, 1: 52–53.
62. Joycelyne G. Russell, *The Field of Cloth of Gold: Men and Manners in 1520* (London: Routledge & Kegan Paul, 1969).
63. Jean Jacquart, *François Ier* (Paris: Fayard, 1994), 177.
64. Henry-Bordeaux, *Louise de Savoie*, 123. This was just one of the many marriages proposed for Charles, and Renée ultimately married Ercole II d'Este.
65. Baschet, *Diplomatie vénitienne*, 385.
66. Francis renewed Louise's authority October 7, 1524. Documents from Louise's regency and Francis's subsequent captivity are collected in Aimé Champollion-Figéac, *Captivité de roi François I* (Paris, 1847), 29.
67. Louise of Savoy, *Journal*, 25. She noted that celestial prognostications predicted "a great affair against the Swiss." Ibid., 21.

68. Jean Barrillon, Duprat's secretary, discussed the Concordat's ramifications and Louise's role. *Journal de Jean Barrillon,* 2 vols. (Paris, 1899), 2: 1–77.
69. The Pragmatic Sanction gave French clergy the right to choose bishops, limited clerical appeals to Rome, and denied the pope rights to various taxes, granting the French church considerable independence vis-à-vis Rome. Pope Leo X sought a more-favorable agreement. Knecht, *Renaissance Warrior,* 91–92.
70. Antoine Duprat, chancellor of France, won Anne of Brittany's favor by persecuting Gié; he became chancellor with Louise's support. According to Knecht, Duprat was hardworking, shrewd, grasping, and universally despised. *Renaissance Warrior,* 42.
71. One hundred bishops owed their position to the king. Le Roy Ladurie, *Royal French State,* 119
72. Frederic J. Baumgartner, *Henry II, King of France 1547–1559* (Durham, NC: Duke University Press, 1988), 13.
73. Louise wrote to the electors, promoting Francis's qualifications. Henry-Bordeaux, *Louise de Savoie,* 188.
74. Louise, *Journal,* 31.
75. See Denis Crouzet, *Charles de Bourbon, connétable de France* (Paris: Fayard, 2003).
76. Hedwige de Chabannes, *Marguerite de Valois: Grande princesse, grand écrivain* (Paris: Pensée Universelle), 44.
77. Henry-Bordeaux, *Louise de Savoie,* 215–16.
78. The codicil reflected Charles's foresight. Henry-Bordeaux, *Louise de Savoie,* 216.
79. Louise might have considered this marriage to reattach these lands to the crown.
80. Henry-Bordeaux, *Louise de Savoie,* 217.
81. The story that Louise was Charles's mistress was first mentioned only ten years later in Adriaan von Baarland *Un Flamand des Pays d'En Bas tout dévoue à Charles Quint.* See Henry-Bordeaux, *Louise de Savoie,* 217.
82. Robert J. Knecht, *The Rise and Fall of Renaissance France* (Oxford: Blackwell, 2001), 151. Pierre Jourda, Marguerite's most reliable biographer, contends that marriage between Marguerite and Charles was proposed during negotiations for Francis's release. *Marguerite d'Angoulême, reine de Navarre, 1492–1549: Etude biographique et littéraire,* 2 vols. (Paris: Champion, 1930), 1: 108. Louise became involved because Charles spurned her sister, according to *Journal tenu par un bourgeois de Paris,* 106.
83. Francis's own marriage to Eleanor forged just this Hapsburg alliance.
84. Henry-Bordeaux blamed Anne of Beaujeu for Bourbon's treason because of her bequests to him. *Louise de Savoie,* 246. For the fullest account, see Crouzet, *Charles de Bourbon.*
85. Louise's mother Marguerite had renounced her inheritance in her brothers' favor, but they died without issue. Henry-Bordeaux, *Louise de Savoie,* 219–20.
86. Louise's claim would have enriched her but ultimately returned those lands to the crown.
87. The emperor would receive Burgundy; Henry VIII, Picardy, the Ile-de-France, and Paris; and Charles, Poitou, Champagne, and Provence.

88. Martin du Bellay, *Mémoires de Messire Martin du Bellay,* in *Choix de chroniques et mémoires de l'histoire de France,* ed. J. A Buchon (Paris, 1836), 381.
89. Cholakian and Cholakian see the Semblançay affair as a "gluttonous grab for power." *Marguerite de Navarre,* 90.
90. Henry-Bordeaux, *Louise de Savoie,* 129.
91. Ibid., 213.
92. For an extensive discussion of this case, see Henry-Bordeaux, *Louise de Savoie,* 392–408.
93. Quoted in Henry-Bordeaux, *Louise de Savoie,* 233.When the council of state convened, it concluded that 480,000 *livres* would not cover the predicted 600,000 of expenses for the following trimester.
94. Quoted in *ibid.*, 229.
95. Louise of Savoy, *Journal,* 407.
96. Henry-Bordeaux, *Louise de Savoie,* 395.
97. Ibid., 398.
98. The declaration of the judges of August 9, 1527, is reproduced in ibid., 404–5.
99. Henry-Bordeaux refutes this account as without foundation. She cites Louise's letter to Robertet saying 364,000 francs had been sent to Italy. *Ibid.*, 236–40.
100. Semblançay never raised in his defense the four hundred thousand *écus* supposedly owed by Louise, suggesting that it was without foundation. Ibid., 270, 395–98.
101. The document making Louise regent is included in Champollion-Figéac, *Captivité de roi François I,* 1–10.
102. Louise's letter of August 30, 1524, is reproduced in ibid., 11.
103. See Knecht, *Renaissance Warrior,* 218–24.
104. Francis I, *Lettre de François I à sa mère après la bataille de Paris* 1525, ed. Luc Merlet (Chartres, 1858), 3–4.
105. The Treaty of Moore (1525), negotiated with Cardinal Wolsey, lasted until 1541.
106. "Dissentiment entre le Grand Conseil de la Régente et le Parlement de Paris," in Champollion-Figéac, *Captivité de roi François* I, 307.
107. "Lettre du chancelier du Prat au Roi," in ibid., 377–78.
108. Knecht cites a combination of depression, anorexia, and a nasal abscess. *Renaissance Warrior,* 245.
109. Marguerite d'Angoulême, "Le Navire," in *Les Dernières poésies,* ed. Abel Lefranc (Paris: 1896), 413–14.
110. Baumgartner traced the conflict over Burgundy to the rivalry between Louis of Orléans and John the Fearless, which produced the Armagnac-Burgundian civil war. Francis, descended from Louis of Orléans and Charles V, was related to John the Fearless. The negotiations of 1523 involved retribution for John the Fearless's murder, almost a hundred years earlier. Charles insisted on the restoration of Burgundy as the heritage of his great-grandfather Charles the Timid, given to his daughter Mary of Burgundy and taken illegitimately by Louis XI. *Henry II,* 11. (See fig. 2.1.)
111. Francis I, "Lettres Patentes du Roi François I pour faire couronner Roi de France de jeune Dauphin François," in Champollion-Figéac, *Captivité de roi François I,* 416.

112. Payments were made to the English, the Swiss, and the Italians for their support.
113. Francis praised obedience to the regent as evidence of their loyalty. "*Aux grands de Royaume et aux campagnies souveraines*," in Campollion-Figéac, *Captivité de roi François I*, 159–60.
114. This marriage forced Charles to renege on his prior commitment of his sister in marriage to Charles of Bourbon.
115. Clement VII's document condoning Francis's reneging is found in Champollion-Figéac, *Captivité de roi François I*, 530–31.
116. Brantôme, *Oeuvres*, 1: 120.
117. Henry-Bordeaux, *Louise de Savoie*, 375.
118. Louise might have objected to Françoise as a member of the Foix family and ally of Anne of Brittany. Toudouze, *Françoise de Chateaubriant*, 43.
119. Tavannes, *Mémoires de Gaspard de Saulx*, 337.
120. Toudouze, *Françoise de Chateaubriant*, 108–9.
121. Ibid., 111.
122. Ibid., 129.
123. Francis I, *Les Ordonnances faictes par le roy nostre sire sur le faict des hostelliers, taverniers et denrées qu'ilz vendent* (Paris, 1531).
124. Christiane Gil, *Les femmes de François I* (Paris: Flammarion, 2005), 165.
125. The two were Clement Marot and François Sagon; Françoise decided in Sagon's favor.
126. Montmorency's prominence suggests that Francis took the charges seriously.
127. Brantôme, *Oeuvres*, 8: 320.
128. Edward Le Glay, ed., *Négociations diplomatiques entre la France et l'Autriche durant les trente premières années du XVIe siècle*, 2 vols. (Paris, 1845), 2: 710.
129. J. Bodin, *Rapport de l'huissier Bodin*, ed. M. Jubinol, in *Journal de Institut historique*, 2nd series, 4 (1844): 347.
130. Francis ordered Louise's funeral modeled on Claude's state funeral. Knecht, *French Renaissance Court*, 119.
131. Decaux argues that Louise practiced *raison d'état*, as this peace protected France but betrayed its alliances with Italy and Turkey. *Histoire des Françaises*, 346.
132. Quoted in Henry-Bordeaux, *Louise de Savoie*, 475.
133. Henry-Bordeaux assessed what Louise gave the nation: a united, prosperous kingdom the union of the domains of duke of Bourbon with the crown, and her extensive goods worth 1.5 million *écus*. *Louise de Savoie*, 471.
134. Dorothy Mayer, *The Great Regent, Louise of Savoy, 1476–1531* (New York: Funk & Wagnalls, 1966), 291.
135. Clement Marot, *Oeuvres*, ed. Pierre Jannet, 3 vols. (Paris, 1868–1872), 3: 6.
136. When Louise was dying, Marguerite begged Francis to write to Louise saying, "She is not contented with me." *Nouvelles Lettres de la Reine de Navarre*, ed. F. Genin (Paris: Jules Renouard, 1842), 116–17.
137. Marguerite de Navarre, *Heptameron*, 122–52. For an extensive discussion, see Maulde La Clavière, *Louise de Savoie et François Ie*, 201–17. Henry-Bordeaux notes that there is no conclusive contemporary source. *Louise de Savoie*, 87.

138. Marguerite de Navarre, *Heptameron,* 90–97.
139. Henry-Bordeaux, *Louise de Savoie,* 87. See discussion in Maulde La Clavière, *Louise de Savoie et François Ie,* 201–17. Marguerite's recent biographers Patricia F. Cholakian and Rouben C. Cholakian see her preoccupation with rape in the *Heptameron* as due to this attack. *Marguerite de Navarre: Mother of the Renaissance* (New York: Columbia University Press, 2006), 34–39.
140. For a discussion of the proposed English marriages, see Jourda, *Marguerite d'Angoulême,* 1: 12–15. Maulde La Clavière notes that the state council discussed the issue for fear that Marguerite would overturn Salic law, but only the chronicler Jean d'Auton made this claim. *Louise de Savoie et François Ier,* 199.
141. The disagreement was over their respective rights as heirs of Marie d'Armagnac.
142. Marie Cerati, *Marguerite de Navarre* (Paris: Sorbier, 1981), 28.
143. Quoted in Toussaint du Wast, *Marguerite de Navarre: La Perle des Valois* (Paris: Max Fourny, 1976), 32.
144. *Letters and Papers, Foreign and Domestic of the Reign of Henry VIII,* eds. J. S. Brewer, J. Gairdner, and R. H. Brodie (London: Public Record Office, 1862–1910), 2: 34–49.
145. Marguerite was devoted to Francis's children but spent little time with her daughter because, Nancy Roelker suggests, she knew that her daughter was hostage to Francis I's interests. *Queen of Navarre: Jeanne d'Albret, 1528–1572* (Cambridge, MA: Belknap Press, 1968), 9–21. Cholakian and Cholakian present Marguerite as an enigmatic mother who nonetheless was her daughter's advocate. *Marguerite de Navarre,* 145–47, 152, 246–47, 261–62, 303–5.
146. Toussaint du Wast, *Marguerite de Navarre,* 33
147. For the gift's significance, see Barbara Stephenson, *The Power and Patronage of Marguerite de Navarre* (Aldershot, UK: Ashgate, 2004), 3, 4, 189.
148. Castiglione, *Book of the Courtier,* 88.
149. Marguerite studied Greek and Hebrew to read Scripture in original languages.
150. Luther's pamphlets arrived in France in 1519 but were not condemned until 1523. Le Roy Ladurie, *Royal French State,* 121.
151. Marguerite protected communities of nuns subjected to sexual abuse by male clergy. Cholakian and Cholakian, *Marguerite de Navarre,* 135–37, 147–49, 258–59.
152. Cerati, *Marguerite de Navarre,* 69.
153. Mario Sanuto, *Diarii,* ed. R. Fulin, 58 vols. (Venice, 1879–1903), 40: 79.
154. Toussaint du Wast, *Marguerite de Navarre,* 116.
155. Marguerite d'Angoulême, *Lettres,* 209.
156. Brantôme credited Marguerite with saving Francis's life. *Oeuvres,* 8: 119.
157. Gifts included the titles and rights of her former husband, Charles of Alençon. Francis rewarded her with lavish gifts. Stephenson, *Power and Patronage,* 120–121, 126.
158. Marguerite d'Angoulême, *Lettres,* 245–54.
159. Brantôme, *Oeuvres,* 8: 58.
160. Marguerite d'Angoulême, *Heptameron,* 119, 187, 202.
161. In 1542 when Marguerite was fifty, she reported feeling a child move but later wrote, "Contrary to the hope I had that God would give you something of service to you and

yours. But he wished otherwise." "Lettres de Marguerite de Navarre à François Ier" in *Lettres de femmes: Textes inédits et oubliés du XVI*[e] *au XVIII*[e] *siècle*, ed. Elizabeth C. Goldsmith and Colette H. Winn (Paris: Champion, 2005), 25, 28.

162. Baschet, *Diplomatie vénitienne*, 404, 412.
163. Knecht, *Renaissance Warrior and Patron*, 282–83.
164. Charles Samaran and H. Patry, *Marguerite de Navarre et le pape Paul III, lettres inédites* (Nogent-le-Rotou, France: Daupeley-Gouverneur, 1907).
165. Knecht, *Renaissance Warrior*, 318–19.
166. *Journal d'un bourgeois de Paris, (1405–1449)*, ed. Alexandre Tuetey (Paris, 1881), 173.
167. Although Marguerite's departure suggests a loss of influence, she still belonged to the *conseil secret* and exercised power through her networks. Stephenson, *Power and Patronage*, 28, 79–111.
168. Briçonnet and Marguerite exchanged 123 letters. Guillaume Briçonnet, *Correspondance*, 1521–1524, 2 vols. (Geneva: Droz, 1975).
169. Toussaint du Wast, *Marguerite de Navarre*, 153.
170. Brantôme, *Oeuvres*, 8: 116–17.
171. Ibid., 3: 134.
172. *Ibid.* For a balanced presentation of Marguerite's religious interests, see Cholakian and Cholakian, *Marguerite de Navarre*, 48–51, 135–58.
173. The Treaty of Madrid specified that Francis would "neither assist nor favor the king of Navarre to reconquer his kingdom even though he married his only and much loved sister." Quoted in Toussaint du Wast, *Marguerite de Navarre*, 188. The roots of the conflict over Navarre were long-standing and embroiled Charles V and Francis I. The de Foix family had controlled Navarre until it passed to the d'Albrets when Jean d'Albret married Catherine de Foix in 1484. But Ferdinand of Spain supported the claim of his second wife, Germaine de Foix, to Navarre and seized the southern part of it in 1512. Strategically important, this acquisition closed off an invasion route from France but threatened France by giving Spain control of strategic mountain passes. Baumgartner, *Henry II*, 11.
174. Hilarion de Coste praised Marguerite for cultivating her territories. *Les Eloges et les vies des reynes, des princesses, et des dames illustres en piété, en courage, et en doctrine*, 2 vols. (Paris, 1647), 2: 260–77.
175. Stephenson, *Power and Patronage*, 190.
176. Marguerite wrote to Montmorency justifying her behavior. *Nouvelles Lettres*, 344. See Stephenson, *Power and Patronage*, 131–34.
177. Marguerite d'Angoulême, *Nouvelles Lettres*, 177.
178. Ibid., 289–91, 292–93.
179. On the composition of Marguerite's court, see Cerati, *Marguerite de Navarre*, 158–62.
180. Antoine Héroët was a humanist, a poet, and bishop, ca. 1492–1568.
181. Francis is sometimes excused by his illness. Cerati, *Marguerite de Navarre*, 148–51.
182. Chabannes, *Marguerite de Valois*, 159.
183. Henry did not want d'Albret lands to pass into foreign hands.

184. Marguerite d'Angoulême, *Les dernières poèsies de Marguerite de Valois* (Paris, 1865).
185. Ghislaine De Boom, *Eléonore d'Autriche: Reine de Portugal et de France* (Brussels: Le Cri, 2003), 72.
186. Ibid., 29. Charles Moeller described her as a "true Flammande." *Eleanore d'Autriche et de Bourgogne: Reine de France* (Paris, 1865), 191–92.
187. Brantôme, *Oeuvres*, 9: 272.
188. *Calendar of Letters and Papers, Foreign and Domestic of the Reign of Henry VIII*, 22 vols. (London, 1862–1932), 6: 682.
189. Ibid.
190. Ibid., 14, pt. 1: 300.
191. Quoted in De Boom, *Eléonore d'Autriche* , 153.
192. Louise expanded the number of young women in her court and took young women under her wing; Anne was one of them. Paulin, *Etudes sur François Ier*, 2: 205.
193. On Anne's family, see Paulin, *Etudes sur François Ier*, 2: 204–19.
194. Ibid., 251.
195. Quoted in Gil, *Femmes de François I*, 161.
196. Paulin challenges the charges against Anne and sees criticism of her as intended to catalog Francis's vices. *Etudes sur François Ier*, 1: 1–25.
197. *Calendar of Letters, Dispatches, and State Papers*, 10 vols. (London: Longman, 1862), 6: 117.
198. E. Desjardins cites Varillas. *Anne de Pisseleu: Duchesse d'Etampes et François Ier* (Paris: Champion, 1904), 53.
199. Brantôme, *Oeuvres*, 9: 715–16.
200. As Ivan put it: "She incarnated at court liberty of manners and openness of spirit." *Diane de Poitiers* (Paris: Fayard, 1997), 91.
201. Reported in 1524 about Francis I. *Calendar of Letters, Dispatches, and State Papers*, 4: 606. Several doctors suggest that the evidence points to a urinary tract infection, likely the result of gonorrhea. Knecht, *Renaissance Warrior and Patron*, 544–46. Some, notably Paris Paulin, argued that tales that Francis had contracted syphilis in Italy from La Belle Ferronière were invented by supporters of Charles of Bourbon. *Etudes sur François Ier*, 1: 21–25.
202. Guillaume Ribier, *Lettres et Mémoires d'état des rois, princes, et ambassadeurs*, 2 vols. (Blois and Paris, 1666), 1: 561. Poyet attempted to curry favor, writing a groveling letter to Anne. Charles Porée, *Un Parlementaire sous François Ier: Guillaume Poyet, 1473–1548* (Angers, 1898). Poyet received a light sentence because of his vigorous self-defense. Knecht, *Renaissance Warrior and Patron*, 500–01.
203. Pierre Bayle, *Dictionnaire historique et critique de Pierre Bayle*, 16 vols. (Paris: 1820–1824), 6: 182.
204. Du Bellay reported that reinforcements would not be coming. *Mémoires de Messire Martin du Bellay*, 1: 722. Brantôme repeated the story. *Oeuvres*, 6: 154.
205. Decaux, *Histoire des Françaises*, 382–83; E. Desjardins, *Anne de Pisseleu*, 25; Brantôme, *Oeuvres*, 3: 24.
206. Eugenie Pascal, "Princesses épistolières au tourant du XVI au XVII siècle: Consommatrices de culture, mécènes, et/ou propagandistes?," in *Patronnes et mécènes en*

France de la Renaissance, ed. Kathleen Wilson-Chevalier (Saint-Etienne, France: University of Saint-Etienne, 2007), 127–28.

207. Brantôme, *Oeuvres*, 9: 512–13.
208. Charles Paillard, "La mort de François Ier et les premiers temps du règne de Henri II d'après des dépêches de Jean de Saint-Mauris," *Revue historique* 5 (1877): 103.
209. Quoted by Colin Jones, *Madame Pompadour: Images of a Mistress* (London: National Gallery Publications, 2002), 34.
210. Cloulas, *Henri II*, 143–44.
211. Brantôme, *Oeuvres*, 9: 676
212. Marie-France Castelain, *Au pays de Claude de France* (Romorantin: Société d'art, d'histoire et d'archéologie de Sologne, 1986), 2.
213. Marot's poem claimed that she was imprisoned. Toudouze, *Françoise de Chateaubriant*, 140–41.
214. On her historiography, see ibid., 66–70.
215. François Rabelais, *Gargantua and Pantagruel* (London: Penguin Books, 1955), 280.
216. Jules Michelet, *Histoire de France*, 19 vols. (Paris, 1876–1877), 10: 158.
217. Marguerite d'Angoulême, *Nouvelles lettres*, 42. This thoroughly repudiated charge is still repeated. Knecht, *Renaissance Warrior and Patron*, 86n15.
218. Michelet, *Histoire de France*, 10: 159.
219. As Maulde La Clavière notes, Bourbon historians condemned Louise for the very actions for which they praised Marguerite of Austria. *Louise de Savoie et François Ier*, 63–64. See Antoine de Laval, "Continuation d'Antoine de Laval (1612)," in Guillaume de Marillac, "Vie du Connetable de Bourbon, 1490–1512," ed. J. A Buchon, *Choix de chroniques et mémoires de l'histoire de France*, vol. 10 (Paris, 1836).
220. Michelet, *Histoire de France*, 9: 358–59.
221. François Guizot and Mme. Guizot de Witt, *France*, 8 vols. (New York: Collier, 1902) 2: 38–39.
222. Ibid., 79.
223. Sully Prudhomme is the pseudonym for René-François-Armand Prudhomme. *Les Crimes des reines de France* (Paris, 1791), 226.
224. Henry-Bordeaux, *Louise de Savoie*, 113–14.
225. See Mary Beth Winn, "Louise de Savoie, ses enfants et ses livres: Du pouvoir familial au pouvoir d'état," in *Patronnes et mécènes en France à la Renaissance*, ed. Kathleen Wilson-Chevalier (Saint-Etienne, France: Presse Universitaire de Saint-Etienne, 2007), 251–83.
226. Louise and Francis wanted Leonardo da Vinci to make Romorantin a new Venice, and Louise commissioned Andrea del Sarto.

CHAPTER 4. DIANE DE POITIERS

1. See Diane de Poitiers, *Lettres inédites Dianne de Poytiers*, ed. Georges Guiffrey (Geneva: Slatkine, 1970). Henry was devoted; Diane's sentiments are less apparent. Guiffrey sees their relationship as the product of Diane's deliberate manipulation; intro., 64–65.

2. Sabine Melchior-Bonnet, *L'art de vivre au temps de Diane de Poitiers* (Paris: NiL, 1998), 71–74.
3. This painting by the Fontainebleau school is an idealized representation of Diane de Poitiers, presumed to be inspired by Primaticcio's painting at Fontainebleau, which was based on a Greek sculpture.
4. Pierre de Bourdeille, lord of Brantôme, *Oeuvres complètes,* ed. Ludovic Lalanne, 11 vols. (1848; repr., New York: Johnson Reprint, 1968), 9: 682–83.
5. See Jehanne d'Orliac, *Diane de Poitiers, gran' sénéchalle de Normandie* (Paris: Plon, 1930); Princess Michael of Kent, *The Serpent and the Moon: Two Rivals for the Love of a Renaissance King* (New York: Simon & Schuster, 2004).
6. This date is disputed. Ivan Cloulas, *Diane de Poitiers* (Paris: Fayard, 1997), 21.
7. Her dowry was twenty thousand gold *écus;* the marriage contract assured Jean's inheritance of his wife's goods. Cloulas, *Diane de Poitiers,* 18.
8. Sharon L. Jansen, *Anne of France: Lessons for My Daughter* (Woodbridge, Suffolk, UK; Rochester, NY: D.S. Brewer, 2004). Anne advised women to mask their sentiments. Thierry Wanegffelen, *Le pouvoir contesté: Souveraines d'Europe à la Renaissance* (Paris: Payot, 2008), 131.
9. Brantôme, *Oeuvres,* 8: 105.
10. Louis is so described in every source that mentions him but never with attribution. His looks struck his contemporaries as marked contrast to his young bride's beauty.
11. Cloulas, *Diane de Poitiers,* 12–14.
12. Melchior-Bonnet, *L'art de vivre,* 18.
13. Jansen, *Anne of France,* 41.
14. Reproduced in Cloulas, *Diane de Poitiers,* 374n40.
15. Georges Guiffrey, ed., *Procès criminal de Jehan de Poitiers, seigneur de Saint-Vallier* (Paris, 1867), 1–5.
16. Diane de Poitiers, *Lettres inédites,* x.
17. *Journal tenu par un bourgeois de Paris pendant le règne de François Ier,* 2 vols. (Clermont-Ferrand, France: Editions Paleo, 2001) 1: 112–13.
18. Armand Baschet, ed., *La diplomatie vénitienne. Les princes de l'Europe au XVIe siècle.* (Paris: H. Plon, 1862), 438.
19. Purportedly written about Diane by Francis I in an album of portraits belonging to Mme. de Boisy about 1520. Diane de Poitiers, *Lettres inédites,* xxxiv.
20. Louis Regnier de la Planche, writing under the pseudonym François de l'Isle, published in 1576 his *Histoire de l'Etat de France* (Paris, 1884).
21. Brantôme, *Oeuvres,* 9: 104.
22. The story's history is documented by Diane de Poitiers, *Lettres inédites,* x–xxiv.
23. Cloulas, *Diane de Poitiers,* 61.
24. Ibid., 78.
25. Ibid., 87.
26. Melchior-Bonnet, *L'art de vivre,* 34.
27. Jansen, *Anne of France,* 41.
28. Brantôme, *Oeuvres,* 9: 636–37.
29. The two princes left on February 17, 1526, were imprisoned on March 17, and returned to France on July 7, 1530.

30. Eugenio Albèri, ed., *Relazioni degli ambasciatori veneti al Senato*, 2nd series, 5 vols. (Florence, 1839–1863), 1: 4.
31. Brantôme, *Oeuvres*, 9: 316.
32. Baschet, *Diplomatie vénitienne*, 429–30.
33. Cloulas, *Diane de Poitiers*, 78–79.
34. Found with incriminating documents, including safe conduct from the emperor and a book of poisons, Montecuccoli initially confessed, then retracted it but was brutally executed. Robert J. Knecht, *Renaissance Warrior and Patron: The Reign of Francis I* (Cambridge: Cambridge University Press, 1994), 337.
35. Poem reproduced in Cloulas, *Diane de Poitiers*, 102–3.
36. Baschet, *Diplomatie vénitienne*, 429.
37. Cloulas, *Diane de Poitiers*, 110.
38. Didier Le Fur, *Henry II* (Paris: Tallandier, 2009), 172–92.
39. Saint-Mauris's dispatch is reproduced in Charles Paillard, "La mort de François Ier et les premièrs temps du règne de Henri II, d'après les dépêches de Jean de Saint-Mauris (April–June 1547) *Revue historique* 5 (1877), 89.
40. Joannis Vulteii Rhenensis, *Hendecasyllaborum*, cited in Diane de Poitiers, *Lettres inédites*, lv.
41. This gruesome event is cited to indict Diane's malign influence. Presumably Henry's attachment to her led him to allow the duel to continue beyond the bounds of decorum.
42. Blaise de Monluc, *Commentaries de Blaise de Monluc*, ed. Paul Courteault (Paris: Gallimard, 1964), 178.
43. François de Scepeaux, *Mémoires de la vie de Scepeaux, lord of Vieilleville*, ed. Vincent Carloix (Paris, 1757), 71.
44. Baschet, *Diplomatie vénitienne*, 430.
45. This ex post facto reasoning circulated to discredit the cardinal of Lorraine late in the Wars of Religion. Jacques-Auguste de Thou, *Histoire universelle de 1543 jusqu'à 1607*, 16 vols. (London, 1739), 1: 183.
46. Baschet, *Diplomatie vénitienne*, 432–33, 434, 436.
47. Paillard, "La mort de François Ier," 112.
48. Baschet, *Diplomatie vénitienne*, 287.
49. Paillard, "La mort de François Ier," 111.
50. Iconography linked Henry and Diane so firmly that it left little space for his queen. Even after Henry's death, when Diane left the court, Catherine could not separate her husband's iconography from that of his mistress.
51. Baschet reproduces an unedited section from Giovanni Capello's diary, *Diario del viaggio ed arrivo di Giovanni Capello, ambasciatore veneto al Re Christianissimo*, in *Diplomatie vénitienne*, 442–43.
52. Diane de Poitiers, *Lettres inédites*, lxxxix.
53. Françoise Bardon insists that the crossed *D* and *H* are simply Henry's emblems, but by adopting the crescent, he honored Diane. *Diane de Poitiers et le mythe de Diane* (Paris: Presses Universitaires de France, 1963), 45.
54. Claude de L'Aubespine's repeated phrase attributed to Henry II's reign the disasters that followed. *Histoire particulière de la court de Henry II*, in *Archives curieuses de*

l'Histoire de France depuis Louis XI jusqu'à Louis XVIII, ed. L. Cimber et F. Danjou, 1st series, vol. 3 (Paris, 1855), 279, 283.

55. Cloulas, *Diane de Poitiers*, 182.
56. Diane explicitly requested that the governor of Lyon honor her. Brantôme, *Oeuvres*, 3: 250. The citizens of Lyon went too far, even for Diane. Thierry Wanegffelen, *Catherine de Médicis: Le pouvoir au féminin* (Paris: Payot, 2005), 15.
57. Baschet, *Diplomatie vénitienne*, 437.
58. Paillard, "La mort de François Ier," 115.
59. The status of queen does not depend on her coronation.
60. Catherine de Medici wrote to the secretary of state, Bellièvre, in 1584. *Lettres de Catherine de Médicis*, ed. Hector de la Ferrière, 11 vols. (Paris, 1880–1943), 8: 181.
61. Diane's correspondence documents her involvement with Catherine's children. *Lettres inédites*, 20–24, 31–39, 45–50, 83–88.
62. Baschet, *Diplomatie vénitienne*, 434–47.
63. Paillard, "La mort de François Ier," 84–120.
64. Baschet, *Diplomatie vénitienne*, 437.
65. Baschet develops this comparison. Ibid., 431.
66. These taxes were paid by venal office holders to retain their offices, and by the corporations of towns to be confirmed in their privileges, according to Saint-Mauris, ed. Paillard, "La mort de François Ier," 175–76.
67. François Rabelais, *Gargantua*, trans. J. M. Cohen (New York: Penguin, 1969), 7.
68. Melchior-Bonnet, *L'art de vivre*, 213–15.
69. Pierre de Ronsard, *Oeuvres inédites de P. Ronsard* (Paris, 1855), 205.
70. Madame de Lafayette, *The Princess de Clèves*, trans. Robin Buss (London: Penguin, 1962), 23.
71. Baschet, *Diplomatie vénitienne*, 440.
72. *Calendar of Letters, Dispatches, and State Papers Relating to Negotiations between England and Spain*, ed. Royal Tyler, 15 vols., (1914; repr., Nendelm, Liechtenstein: Kraus-Thomson, 1969), 10: 588.
73. When his affair with Nicole de Savigny produced a son, Henry did not acknowledge him.
74. Eugenio Albèri, ed., *Relazioni degli ambasciatori veneti al Senato*, 2nd series, 5 vols. (Florence, 1839–1863), 4: 77–78.
75. Paillard, "La mort de François Ier," 112.
76. Luca Guarico, a bishop and an astrologer, predicted this. Wanegffelen, *Catherine de Médicis*, 155.
77. This prophecy was presented to Henry II in 1555. Edgar Leoni, *Nostradamus: Life and Literature* (New York: Nosbooks, 1961), 141.
78. Popular accounts cite Catherine's cruelty in keeping Diane from Henry. See Michael of Kent, *Serpent and the Moon*, 361. Other sources suggest that Diane feared that she would be barred. Cloulas, *Diane de Poitiers*, 302.
79. Francis Allaman, accused of diverting royal funds with Diane's complicity, was condemned to death, and his goods were confiscated. Ultimately, he paid a fine but did not forfeit his life. Cloulas, *Diane de Poitiers*, 315–16.

80. Ibid., 326.
81. In the myth, the goddess turns the hunter into a stag for spying on her; the stag is then hunted and killed by his dogs. Diane's enemies noted this allusion to underscore her malign influence.
82. Bardon, *Diane de Poitiers et le mythe de Diane*, 7.
83. Melchior-Bonnet, *L'art de vivre*, 202. Bardon notes that the number and range of allegories and allusion was without precedent. *Diane de Poitiers*, 88. Joachim Du Bellay, *Regrets* (Paris: R. Laffort, 1958), sonnets 159, 179; Olivier de Magny, *Odes Amoureuses de 1559* (Geneva: Droz, 1964), 181–82.
84. Pierre Ronsard, *Oeuvres complètes*, ed. Paul Laumonier, 8 vols. (Paris: Hachette, 1914–1946), 8: 339.
85. Bardon, *Diane de Poitiers et le mythe de Diane*, 65.
86. The French translation of this volume did not appear until just after Henry II's death. Garcia Rodriquez de Montalbo, *L'onziesme livre d'Amadis de Gaula* (Paris, 1560), unpaginated dedication.
87. See H. I. Martin, "What Parisians Read in the Sixteenth Century," *French Humanism*, ed. Werner L. Gundersheimer (London: Macmillan, 1969), 183.
88. Brantôme, *Oeuvres*, 3: 246–47.
89. Victor Hugo, *Le roi s'amuse* (Paris, 1866), act 1, sc. 5, p. 15.
90. Jules Michelet, *Histoire de France*, 19 vols. (Paris, 1876–1877), 10: 201–2.
91. *The Book of the Courtier* presented the court of Urbino as a model. Translated into French in 1537, the text had some 130 vernacular editions. On its phenomenal success and impact, see Margaret King, *The Renaissance in Europe* (New York: McGraw-Hill, 2003), 235–40.
92. Emmanuel Le Roy Ladurie complains that Henry's reign has been reduced to a romance. *The Royal French State, 1460–1610* (Oxford: Blackwell, 1987), 143.
93. Baschet makes this point. *Diplomatie vénitienne*, 472–73. Paris Paulin, *Etudes sur François Ier*, 2 vols. (1885; repr., Geneva: Slatkine, 1970), 2: 204–19.

CHAPTER 5. CATHERINE DE MEDICI

1. Pierre de L'Estoile, *Mémoires de Pierre de L'Estoile pour servir à l'histoire de France et journal de Henri III et de Henri IV*, in *Collection complète des mémoires relatifs à l'histoire de France*, 4 vols. (Paris, 1825), 1: 382. This chapter is particularly indebted to the work of R. J. Knecht, which I have frequently used to teach this period, especially *Catherine de' Medici* (New York and London: Longmans, 1998); and *The Rise and Fall of Renaissance France, 1483–1610* (Oxford: Blackwells, 2001).
2. See Nicola M. Sutherland, *Princes, Politics, and Religion, 1547–1589* (London: Hambledon Press, 1984); *The Massacre of St. Bartholomew and the European Conflict* 1559–1572 (London, Basingstoke: Macmillan, 1973); Jean-Louis Bourgeon, *L'assassinat de Coligny* (Geneva: Droz, 1992).
3. Ludovico Ariosto, *Opera Minore* (Milan: Rizzoli, 1964), 216.
4. Antonio Suriano, *Relazione della Crote di Roma, 1531*, in *Le Relazioni degli ambasciatori veneti al Senato*, ed. Eugenio Albèri, 2nd series, 5 vols. (Florence, 1839–1863) 4: 30.

5. Cited in Alfred de Reumont and Armand Baschet, *La Jeunesse de Catherine de Médicis* (Paris, 1866), 172.
6. That rumor inspired Alfred de Musset's play *Lorenzaccio* (1834) and a story in Marguerite d'Angoulême's *Heptameron*, trans. P. A. Chilton (New York: Penguin, 1984), 158–66.
7. The documents negotiating their marriage are reproduced in Reumont and Baschet, *Jeunesse de Catherine de Médicis*, 273–318.
8. The Venetian ambassador, Giovanni Capello, described Catherine: "A beautiful woman when her face is veiled. . . . Many say she is the image of her uncle [Pope] Leo X. Armand Baschet, ed., *La diplomatie vénitienne. Les princes de l'Europe au XVIe siècle.* (Paris: H. Plon, 1862), 480.
9. Antonio Sacco to the president of Milan on October 30, 1533, as well as the "Lettre italienne écrite de Marseille au Duc par un témoin des cérémonies qui aurent lieu pour célébrer le mariage de Catherine de Medicis avec Henri d'Orléans," which announced baldly that the marriage was consummated, are reproduced in Reumont and Baschet, *Jeunesse de Catherine de Médicis*, 319–24.
10. Baschet, *Diplomatie vénitienne*, 469.
11. Pierre de Bourdeille, lord of Brantôme, *Oeuvres complètes*, ed. Ludovic Lalanne, 11 vols. (1848; repr., New York: Johnson Reprint, 1968), 7: 341.
12. Baschet, *Diplomatie vénitienne*, 478.
13. Ivan Cloulas, *Catherine de Médicis* (Paris: Fayard, 1992), 96.
14. So speculated the surgeon, Pierre Dionis, *Traité général des accouchements, qui instruit de tout ce qu'il faut faire pour être habile accoucheur* (Paris, 1718), 70.
15. Albèri, *Relazioni degli ambasciatori*, 4: 47.
16. So many children might have assured the Valois dynasty, but all except Marguerite and Henry predeceased Catherine, and Henry outlived her only by months. Her son Louis died young, and twin daughters Jeanne and Victoire, shortly after birth. Her daughter Elisabeth, queen of Spain, died in childbirth in her early twenties. Her daughter Claude died at twenty-seven, but gave Catherine her only legitimate grandchild. Her sons suffered serious illnesses. Francis died at sixteen, probably of tuberculosis and mastoiditis. Charles died at twenty-three, and Hercules (renamed Francis) at twenty-nine, both likely of tuberculosis. Henry III was assassinated at thirty-seven and had no offspring.
17. Baschet, *Diplomatie vénitienne*, 474.
18. Brantôme, *Oeuvres*, 9: 283–84.
19. Cited in Lucien Romier, *La royaume de Catherine de Médicis: La France à la veille des guerres de religion* (1925; repr., Geneva: Slatkine, 1978), 9. The statement was also reported to the duke of Ferrara by his ambassador Alvarotti. Thierry Wanegffelen, *Catherine de Médicis: Le pouvoir au féminine* (Paris: Payot, 2005), 153.
20. Catherine de Medici, *Lettres de Catherine de Médicis*, ed. Hector de la Ferrière, 11 vols. (Paris, 1880–1943), 8: 181.
21. Catherine asked that the document not be read to Parlement. Guillaume Ribier, *Lettres et memoirs d'états des rois, princes, et ambassadeurs*, 2 vols. (Blois and Paris, 1666) 2: 387–88.

22. Thierry Wanegffelen, *Le pouvoir contesté: Souveraines d'Europe à la Renaissance* (Paris: Payot, 2008), 158–60.
23. Catherine de Medici, *Lettres,* 1: 64.
24. Baschet, *Diplomatie vénitienne,* 481.
25. Ibid., 478.
26. Margriet Hoogvliet, "Princely Culture and Catherine de Médicis," in *Princes and Princely Culture, 1450–1650,* ed. Martin Gosman, Alasdair A. MacDonald, and Arie Johan Vanderjagt (Leiden and Boston: Brill, 2003), 111.
27. Baschet, *Diplomatie vénitienne,* 487.
28. Cloulas, *Catherine de Médicis,* 37.
29. The Guises formed a powerful faction in Paris and the provinces, and in aristocratic, clerical, and governmental circles. Jean-Marie Constant, *Les Guises* (Paris: Hachette, 1984). Stuart Carroll emphasizes the Guises' dynastic interests and sees their commitment to ultra-Catholicism as primarily political. *Martyrs and Murderers* (Oxford: Oxford University Press, 2009).
30. His brothers were Louis, prince of Condé, and Charles, cardinal of Bourbon.
31. Patrick Forbes, ed., *A Full View of the Public Transactions in the Reign of Queen Elizabeth,* 2 vols. (London, 1740), 1: 160.
32. Etienne Pasquier, *Lettres historiques,* ed. D. Thickett (Geneva: Droz, 1966), 35.
33. Abel Desjardins, ed., *Négociations diplomatiques de la France avec la Toscanne,* 6 vols. (Paris, 1859–1886), 3: 404.
34. François Morel to John Calvin, cited in Wanegffelen, *Catherine de Médecis,* 182–84.
35. Catherine's letter commissioned Monsieur de L'Isle to gain Paul IV's support for the Cardinal of Lorraine's measures to calm religious dissent at the Colloquy. *Lettres,* 1: 404–5.
36. Robert J. Knecht, *The Rise and Fall of Renaissance France* (Oxford: Blackwell, 2001), 54.
37. Baschet, *Diplomatie vénitienne,* 436.
38. Ibid., 518.
39. Admiral Coligny proposed dividing France along confessional lines, an anathema to Catherine, as the Venetian ambassador Giovanni Michieli recognized. Baschet, *Diplomatie vénitienne,* 506.
40. Knecht, *Rise and Fall of Renaissance France,* 287.
41. Hôpital is credited with great toleration but followed Catherine's policies for which she is less recognized. See Wanegffelen, *Catherine de Medicis,* 203; Knecht, *Rise and Fall of Renaissance France,* 100, 272.
42. Francis II, *Edict de Romorantin* (n.p., n.d.).
43. It moved heresy cases to Church courts, which could not impose the death penalty, and banned illicit assemblies. Robert J. Knecht, *Catherine de' Medici* (London: Longman, 1998), 288.
44. It included the royal council, officers of the crown, and princes of the blood.
45. Baschet, *Diplomatie vénitienne,* 501.
46. Cloulas, *Catherine de Médicis,* 150.
47. Catherine de Medici, *Lettres,* 1: 568.

48. Baschet, *Diplomatie vénitienne*, 508, 510.
49. Ibid., 511, 518.
50. The Edict of Saint-Germain of July 11, 1561, pardoned all offenses from the time of Henry II. Knecht, *Catherine de' Medici*, 289.
51. Alain Decaux charges that Condé thwarted an opportunity for Catherine to ally with Protestants. *Histoire des Françaises* (Paris: Perrin, 1998), 407.
52. Catherine wrote letters to Condé saying: "I will never forget what you have done for the king. . . . I beg you to trust what one will say to you on behalf of one who can reassure you as well as your own mother. . . . I will never forget what you have done to conserve the children and mother of the kingdom. . . . Burn this 'incontinent' letter." *Lettres*, 1: 281–84.
53. Ibid., 1: 296.
54. Cited by Sutherland, who suggests that Poltrot assassinated the duke because he had been La Renaudie's friend. *Princes, Politics, and Religion*, 148–49.
55. Knecht insists that Catherine's statements do not prove her complicity. *Catherine de' Medici*, 91–92.
56. Condé accepted it, but Coligny and some Protestant clergy did not.
57. Charles IX, *Déclaration du roy Charles IX sur sa majorité* (n.p., 1563).
58. Catherine de Medici, *Lettres*, 2: 17.
59. Ibid., 2: 90–95.
60. Jean Boutier, Alain Dewerpe, and Daniel Nordman estimate the numbers, ranging from six thousand to twenty thousand. *Un tour de France royal: Le voyage de Charles IX (1564–1566)* (Paris: Aubier, 1984), 108–10.
61. On Charles's images, see ibid., 324–45; Wanegffelen, *Catherine de Médicis*, 245–64.
62. Knecht claims that Catherine's pursuit of these marriages wasted an opportunity for peace. *Catherine de' Medici*, 272.
63. Antoine Perrenot, cardinal de Granvelle, asserted Philip II's desire "to remedy the evils of France." *Papiers d'état du Cardinal de Granvelle*, ed. C. Weiss, 9 vols. (Paris, 1841–1852), 9: 289.
64. Paul Van Dyke, *Catherine de Médicis*, 2 vols. (New York: Scribner's, 1923), 1: 324–25.
65. Knecht cites this event as fundamental to Catherine's rejection of conciliation. *Catherine de' Medici*, 272.
66. Baschet, *Diplomatie vénitienne*, 521–24.
67. Charles IX to Parlement, March 12, 1571. *Harangue du Roy Charles IX à Messieurs de la Cour de Parlement, tenant sa Siège Royale et son lit de Justice* (Rouen, 1547), unpaginated.
68. Catherine expressed regret to her ambassador in England at Henry's stubbornness. *Lettres*, 4: 27.
69. This chapter will refer to Henry of Navarre as Navarre to distinguish him from his brother-in-law Henry III. Henry of Guise will be referred to as Guise.
70. Catherine threatened to pressure the pope to reexamine Jeanne's annulment, which, if overturned, could have called her son's legitimacy into question. Nancy Roelker, *Queen of Navarre: Jeanne d'Albret 1528–1572* (Cambridge, MA: Harvard University Press), 358–59.

71. Knecht, *Catherine de' Medici*, 357.
72. Huguenot forces, led by Jean de Hangest, lord of Genlis, crossed into the Low Countries, where the Spanish decimated them. Although Charles professed ignorance of the intended invasion, Genlis produced Charles's imprudent letter to Louis of Nassau. Michel Simonin, *Charles IX* (Paris: Fayard, 1995), 279.
73. Sutherland contends that neither Charles nor Catherine objected to Protestant plans to intervene in the Netherlands. *Princes, Politics, and Religion*, 180.
74. Guise, Catherine, Henry, or Charles de Louviers de Maurevert, acting on his own mission of vengeance, are blamed. Carroll advances the last to exculpate the Guises. *Martyrs and Murderers*, 219.
75. Without new evidence, Catherine's involvement in the initial plot cannot be proved. Knecht, *Catherine de' Medici*, 272.
76. Wanegffelen, *Catherine de Médicis*, 352–53. See Barbara Diefendorf, *Beneath the Cross: Catholics and Huguenots in Sixteenth-Century Paris* (Oxford: Oxford University Press, 1991) 173–75.
77. A document dated August 23—"Royal order taken in secret council attended by the Queen Mother, the two brothers of the king, and several other private councilors which ordered the Massacre of St. Bartholomew"—records a meeting wherein such a plan might have been developed. "Extrait registres et croniques du bureau de la ville de Paris," *Archives curieuses*, series 1, vol. 7 (Paris, 1835), 213. This document corroborates that Charles, not initially included, concurred after he was persuaded that the Huguenots were plotting vengeance against the royal family. Three distinct meetings were held; Catherine attended at least one, the king one, and the Guises at least one. Stuart Carroll contends that these meetings were held to develop a list of those to be killed and to plan the killing. *Martyrs and Murderers*, 213.
78. Ibid., 218.
79. Mack P. Holt, *The French Wars of Religion, 1562–1629* (Cambridge: Cambridge University Press, 2005), 95.
80. Wanegffelen, *Catherine de Médicis*, 358–60.
81. Eliane Viennot sees Henry's Polish experience as formative. *Marguerite de Valois: Histoire d'une femme, histoire d'un mythe* (Paris: Payot, 1995), 75.
82. Philippe Duplessis-Mornay, *Vindiciae contra Tyrannos* (n.p., 1589). Duplessis-Mornay is still the most common way to refer to the Protestant leader and advisor to Henry IV, but Mornay du Plessis, de Mornay du Plessis, and Mornay Duplessis are other forms. The massacre was crucial in demystifying the monarchy. Emmanuel Le Roy Ladurie, *The Royal French State, 1460–1610* (Oxford: Blackwell, 1987), 189
83. Catherine de Medici, *Lettres*, 5: 1.
84. Baschet, *Diplomatie vénitienne*, 566.
85. Catherine de Medici to Cheverny. "Mémoire pour montrer à Monsieur le roy mon fils," *Lettres*, 5: 73–75.
86. On favorites, see Robert J. Knecht, *The French Renaissance Court* (New Haven and London: Yale University Press, 2008), 291–95. See Nicolas Le Roux, *La faveur du roi: Mignons et courtisans au temps des derniers Valois* (Seyssel, France: Champ Vallon, 2001), 200–8; 528–33.

87. Positions these nobles might have expected were held instead by the sons of less-prominent or provincial nobles.
88. Knecht describes the duels and assassinations. *French Renaissance Court,* 318–23.
89. Katherine Crawford, *The Sexual Culture of the French Renaissance* (Cambridge: Cambridge University Press, 2010), 216–30.
90. Claude Haton explicitly charged the king with sodomy. *Mémoires de Claude Haton,* ed. Felix Bourquelot, 2 vols. (Paris, 1857), 2: 1070–71. As Le Roy Ladurie notes, recent studies do not credit stories of Henry III's homosexuality. *Royal French State,* 191.
91. Henry presented himself as a conqueror of heretics, emphasizing his sacerdotal function. Jacqueline Boucher, *Louise de Lorraine et Marguerite de France: Deux épouses et reines à la fin du XVIe siècle* (Saint-Etienne, France: Publications de l'Université de Saint-Etienne, 1995), 153–54.
92. Valentine Dale wrote to Francis Walsingham. *Calendar of State Papers Foreign, Elizabeth,* vol. 11: 1575–1577 (London: 1880), 40.
93. Montgomery-Damville became governor of Languedoc; Henry of Navarre received Guyenne and an indemnity of 622,000 *livres;* and Francis received Tourraine, Berry, and d'Anjou.
94. Pierre de L'Estoile,*Mémoires,* 1: 140–41.
95. These activities fueled intense anticourt literature, portraying the court as Sodom. For an example, see Nicolas Barnaud, *Le réveille-matin des François, et de leurs voisins* (1574; repr., Paris: EDHIS, 1977).
96. L'Estoile, *Mémoires,* 1: 153.
97. Baschet, *Diplomatie vénitienne,* 572. Baschet contends that Henry's behavior led to ridicule of a French king for the first time; 574.
98. *Ibid.*
99. Haton, *Mémoires,* 2: 1047.
100. Desjardins, *Négociations diplomatiques,* 4: 639.
101. Louise, according to Knecht, had an early miscarriage and never again conceived, perhaps because of the medical treatment she received. *French Renaissance Court,* 282.
102. Holt, *French Wars of Religion,* 126.
103. Desjardins, *Négociations diplomatiques,* 4: 635.
104. L'Estoile, *Mémoires,* 2: 199.
105. Henry IV, "Addressed to Various Princes," dated "toward the end of August 1585," *Recueil des letters missives,* ed. Xivrey et Gaudet (Paris, 1843–1876), 2: 129.
106. Calvin and his French followers justified Protestant revolt against Catholic rulers. Francis Hotman in *Franco-Gallica* (1573) claimed that the Estates-General had a right to choose the king.
107. Ogier Ghiselin de Busbecq, *Lettres d'Auger de Gislen, seigneur de Busbec,* vol. 10, *Archives curieuses de l'histoire de France,* eds. L. Cimber and F. Danjou (Paris, 1836), 58.
108. Catherine de Medici, *Lettres,* 9: 382.
109. L'Estoile, *Mémoires,* 1: 359.
110. The nobility divided into supporters of the monarchy and the League. The clergy considered the crown insufficiently diligent in battling heresy. The third estate was concerned about finances, especially rising wheat prices.

111. L'Estoile, *Mémoires*, 1: 381.
112. Holt, *French Wars of Religion*, 132.
113. L'Estoile, *Mémoires*, 1: 381.
114. Regnault de Beaune, archbishop of Bourges, "Oraison funèbre faicte aux obsèques de la Royne Mère du Roy," in Catherine de Medici, *Lettres*, 9: 498.
115. L'Estoile, *Mémoires*, 1: 383.
116. About her legend, see Cloulas, *Catherine de Médicis*, 11–21; Nicola Sutherland, "Catherine de Medici: The Legend of the Wicked Italian Queen," in *Princes, Politics, and Religion*, 236–48; Wanegffelen, *Catherine de Médicis*, 25–43. Katherine Crawford traces these criticisms through successive foreign queens. "Constructing Evil Foreign Queens," *Journal of Medieval and Early Modern Studies* 37 (2007) no. 2, 393–418.
117. Henri Estienne, *Discours merveilleuse de la vie, actions, et deportmens de la reyne Catherine de Médicis*, in *Archives Curieuses*, ed. M. L. Cimber and F. Danjou, vol. 9 (Paris, 1836). R. J. Knecht challenges this attribution, contending that it is an anonymous text whose author was conciliatory. *Catherine de' Medici*, 164–65.
118. Innocent Gentillet, *Anti-Machiavel*, ed. C. Edward Rathé (Geneva: Droz, 1968); François Hotman, *Francogallica*, ed. and trans. Ralph Giesey and J. H. Salmon (Cambridge, MA: Cambridge University Press, 1972), 123–24.
119. *La France-Turquie* (Orléans, 1576). This text lists a fictional press; instead it was likely printed in the Low Countries or Geneva.
120. Robert J. Sealy, S.J., *The Myth of the Reine Margot: Toward the Elimination of a Legend* (New York and Washington, DC: Peter Lang, 1994), 9.
121. François Marie Arouet de Voltaire, "Essai sur les moeurs," *Oeuvres complètes de Voltaire*, 54 vols. (Paris, 1877–1895), 12: 503–11.
122. Catherine was used to attack Marie Antoinette in Marie-Geneviève-Charlotte Thiroux d'Arconville, *Histoire de Francois II* (Paris, 1783), and in Marie-Joseph Chenier's play, performed on November 4, 1789. *Charles IX, ou la Saint Barthélémy* (Paris, 1826).
123. Madame de Lafayette, *The Princess de Clèves*, trans. Robin Buss (London: Penguin, 1962), 23.
124. Honoré de Balzac praised Catherine as a "man of state." *About Catherine de Medici*, trans. Katherine Prescott Wormeley (Boston, 1864), 4. For Jean Solnon, Catherine was dedicated to civil peace and might today be a likely peace-prize recipient. *Catherine de Médicis*, 14–15.
125. A prominent theme in Alexandre Dumas's *La Reine Margot* (Paris: Gallimard, 2008) and *La Dame de Montsoreau* (Paris: Gallimard, 2008), and in Balzac's *About Catherine de Médici*. Dumas's novels remain popular and can be found in many editions.
126. François Guizot and Mme. Guizot de Witt, *France*, 8 vols. (New York: Collier, 1902), 3: 205, 248, 274–84, 304–5; 328–29; 353.
127. Jules Michelet, *Histoire de France*, 19 vols. (Paris, 1876–1877), 9: 159–62, 258–59, 307, 308–15. Michelet was sympathetic to Catherine's difficulties under Henry II and saw her as an early advocate of reform. Ibid., 6: 28–31, 35; 4: 121–25; 6: 244–47.
128. Ernest Lavisse, *Histoire de France*, 9 vols. (Paris: Hachette, 1900–1911), 6: 35.

129. Sutherland, "Catherine de Medici," 237–50.
130. Henry IV's conversation in 1599 with Claude Groulart, who blamed Catherine, a Medici, as evil, warned Henry against marriage to Marie de Medici. Wanegffelen, *Catherine de Médicis,* 400.

CHAPTER 6. MARGUERITE DE VALOIS

1. Théodore Agrippa d'Aubigné, *Divorce satyrique ou les amours de la reyne Marguerite,* in *Oeuvres complètes de Théodore Agrippa d'Aubigné,* ed. E. Reaume and F. de Caussage (Paris, 1873–1879), 2: 653, 657, 661, 681.
2. Robert Sealy, S.J., *The Myth of the Reine Margot: Toward the Elimination of a Legend* (Baltimore, MD: Peter Lang, 2004). Eliane Viennot's generally sympathetic study of Marguerite's life and her myth is crucial to the reappraisal of Marguerite. *Marguerite de Valois: Histoire d'une femme, histoire d'un mythe* (Paris: Payot, 1994). Viennot has edited Marguerite's writings and correspondence. Her work is central to this chapter.
3. *La Reine Margot,* Patrice Chéreau's film of 1994.
4. Marguerite de Valois, *Mémoires,* in *Mémoires et autres écrits, 1574–1614,* ed. Eliane Viennot, (Paris: Honoré Champion, 1999), 74.
5. A minority view contends that her memoirs were written between 1599 and 1603. Janine Garrisson, *Marguerite de Valois: La Reine Margot* (Paris: Fayard, 1994), 11.
6. Marguerite alone of her siblings responded in Latin to a visiting archbishop. Brantôme, *Oeuvres complètes,* ed. Ludovic Lalanne, 11 vols. (1848; repr., New York: Johnson Reprint, 1968), 8: 31.
7. Brantôme reported these remarks. Ibid., 24–26.
8. Marguerite de Valois, *Mémoires,* 81–83.
9. Ibid., 84.
10. Ibid., 86, 89.
11. Ibid., 86–87. Her *Memoirs* do not blame her mother, but Marguerite's correspondence documents Catherine's neglect. Marguerite de Valois, *Correspondance, 1569–1614,* ed. Eliane Viennot (Paris: H. Champion, 1998), 48.
12. Reported by France's ambassador to Spain. Raimonde de Fourquevaux, *Dépêches de M. de Fourquevaux, ambassadeur du roi Charles IX en Espagne, 1565–1572,* ed. Célestin Douais, 3 vols. (Paris, 1896–1904), 2: 153.
13. On July 29, 1570, Catherine wrote to Fourquevaux to deny the rumors. *Lettres de Catherine de Médicis,* ed. Hector de la Ferrière, 11 vols. (Paris, 1880–1943), 3: 321–23.
14. Marguerite de Valois, *Mémoires,* 88. Viennot claims that Marguerite initially protested that she would marry Catherine's choice. *Marguerite de Valois,* 32.
15. Included in Henry IV, *Lettres d'amour et écrits politiques,* ed. Jean-Pierre Babelon (Paris: Fayard, 1988), 44.
16. Théodore Agrippa d'Aubigné, *Histoire universelle,* ed. Alphonse de Ruble, 10 vols. (Paris: Beauvais, 1834–1840), 3: 303. The allegory was misread by the wedding guests: Protestants were offended; for Catholics, it highlighted the marriage's illegitimacy. Thierry Wanegffelen, *Catherine de Médicis: Le pouvoir au féminin* (Paris: Payot, 2005), 354–55.

17. Marguerite de Valois, *Mémoires*, 95–98, 100.
18. Ibid., 101.
19. Francis became duke of Anjou when his older brother Henry became king. In this text, he will be referred to as Francis so that the reader does not have to keep track of his evolving titles.
20. Marguerite de Valois, *Mémoires*, 103.
21. Viennot claims that Marguerite's memoirs were written to assert her husband's consistent loyalty to the crown and thus support his later quest to claim it. *Correspondance*, 67. But the memoirs focus on *Marguerite's* loyalty.
22. La Molle was Francis's chief advisor and negotiator for his proposed marriage to Elizabeth I of England. He kept English Protestants informed about the French court. Michel Simonin, *Charles IX* (Paris: Fayard, 1995), 403, 425.
23. Viennot does not find a relationship with La Molle credible. *Marguerite de Valois*, 65–69. Jacqueline Boucher credits the relationship and believes that Marguerite's poems about Hyacinthe refer to La Molle. *Louise de Lorraine et Marguerite de France: Deux épouses et reines à la fin du XVIe siècle* (Saint-Etienne, France: Publications de l'Université de Saint-Etienne, 1995), 153–54.
24. Marguerite de Valois, *Mémoire justificatif pour Henri de Bourbon*, in *Mémoires*, 243.
25. Ibid. 239–49.
26. Marguerite de Valois, *Mémoires*, 105.
27. Jean-Pierre Babelon, *Henri IV* (Paris: Le Grand Livre du Mois, 1997), 104.
28. Marguerite de Valois, *Mémoires*, 106.
29. Although there is a lacuna in Marguerite's memoirs from September 1572 to November 1573, her letters show that she was on good terms with Henry during this period. *Correspondance*, 101n132. Viennot cites this as the great lie of the text. Marguerite de Valois, *Mémoires*, 47.
30. Viennot, *Marguerite de Valois*, 65–66.
31. Marguerite de Valois, *Mémoires*, 106 ; Marguerite de Valois, *Correspondance*, intro., 51. Marguerite's letters to William of Orange also assert her loyalty to Henry III. *Correspondance*, 70–73.
32. Marguerite de Valois, *Mémoires*, 110–11. Brantôme dismissed the relationship. *Oeuvres*, 6: 312.
33. Marguerite de Valois, *Mémoires*, 114.
34. Viennot, *Marguerite de Valois*, 76.
35. Jean-François Solnon, *La Cour de France* (Paris: Librairie Générale Française, 1996), 25.
36. Marguerite de Valois, *Mémoires*, 115.
37. Ibid.
38. Brantôme, *Oeuvres*, 6: 192.
39. Marguerite de Valois, *Mémoires*, 121.
40. Catherine de Medici wrote to the secretary of state, Bellièvre, in 1584. *Lettres de Catherine de Médicis*, ed. Hector de la Ferrière, 11 vols. (Paris, 1880–1943), 6: 16.
41. Marguerite de Valois, *Mémoires*, 121, 117–18. If she wrote to Bussy, no letters survive. Marguerite claimed that she saw Bussy only because he frequented her brother

Francis and that rumors to the contrary were spread by Le Guast. Ibid., 117. Viennot, *Marguerite de Valois,* 77–79.

42. Boucher, *Louise de Lorraine et Marguerite de France,* 195. Viennot emphasizes Marguerite's prior loyal service to Navarre. *Marguerite de Valois,* 74.
43. For Viennot, their differences were religious and political rather than personal, their supposed incompatibility invented after the fact. *Marguerite de Valois,* 42. Bourbon historians cited Marguerite's refusal to assent, but her contemporary, the Marshal de Retz, testified that nothing seemed unusual about the ceremony. Boucher, *Louise de Lorraine et Marguerite de France,* 22.
44. Aubigné, *Divorce satyrique,* 66.
45. Robert J. Knecht, *The Rise and Fall of Renaissance France* (Oxford: Blackwell, 2001), 480.
46. Mark Strage, *Women of Power: The Life and Times of Catherine de Medici* (New York: Harcourt, Brace, Jovanovich, 1976), 203.
47. Boucher, *Louise de Lorraine et Marguerite de France,* 88.
48. *Colloque Marguerite de France, Reine de Navarre et son temps,* Agen, 11–13 October, 1991 (Agen, France: Centre Matteo Bandello, 1994), 331. Neither Marguerite's memoirs nor her correspondence substantiates any other relationship, but discretion was essential.
49. Henry IV, "Letter of Navarre to Miossens," which Xivrey dates to January 1576, in *Recueil des Lettres missives,* ed. Jules Berger de Xivrey and Joseph Guadet, 9 vols. (Paris: 1843–1876), 1: 81. According to Boucher, Marguerite's promotion of Francis's interests explains Henry's anger over Mlle. de Thorigny as their go-between. *Louise de Lorraine et Marguerite de France,* 88.
50. Marguerite de Valois, *Mémoires,* 121–24.
51. This testimony was much later and intended to support their annulment case.
52. Marguerite de Valois, *Mémoires,* 131, 127.
53. Ibid., 133. This adventure constitutes a sixth of her *Mémoires.*
54. Mack Holt's study addresses this question. *The Duke of Anjou and the Politique Struggle during the Wars of Religion* (Cambridge: Cambridge University Press, 2002).
55. Marguerite de Valois, *Mémoires,* 127.
56. Ibid., 142.
57. Catherine de Medici, *Lettres,* 6: 28.
58. Marguerite de Valois, *Correspondance,* 90–91.
59. Marguerite de Valois, *Mémoires,* 198.
60. Viennot, *Marguerite de Valois,* 116.
61. Ibid., 199.
62. Maximilian de Bethune de Sully, *Memoirs of Maximilian de Bethune, Duke of Sully,* 5 vols. (London: Lackington & Allen), 1: 43. Sully wrote the history of Henry's reign to highlight his role. His history was distorted by its transmission; he dictated it (extracts of which became his *Memoirs*) to many secretaries, who ultimately produced the *Economies royales.*
63. Marguerite purchased Plutarch's works, Joachim du Bellay's *Memoirs,* Du Haillan's *History of France,* and Cicero's *Discourses.* Viennot, *Marguerite de Valois,* 135.
64. Marguerite de Valois, *Mémoires,* 198.

65. Ibid., 139, 202.
66. Henry IV, *Lettres missives,* 1: 285–93.
67. It is sometimes called "la guerre des amoureuses" on the assumption that Marguerite was involved with Turenne, but Viennot claims that the rumored relationship was unsubstantiated court gossip. *Marguerite de Valois,* 129–35.
68. Marguerite de Valois, *Mémoires,* 202.
69. Aubigné charged that he surprised Marguerite "en ses privautez" with Champvallon and that this was the source of her antipathy toward him. *Histoire universelle,* 6: 158.
70. The fifth daughter of the baron of Fosseux, she was derogatorily called "La Fosseuse" (the grave digger), revealing the double standard. She was disparaged, but little opprobrium attached to her male lover.
71. Boucher, *Louise de Lorraine et Marguerite de France,* 169.
72. Catherine de Medici, *Lettres,* 7: 373, 472.
73. Marguerite de Valois, *Mémoires,* 213.
74. Marguerite de Valois, *Correspondance,* 222–25. Françoise's dismissal provoked an uncharacteristically harsh response from Navarre. His letter no longer exists, but we know something of its tenor from Marguerite's deeply offended response.
75. Catherine de Medici, *Lettres,* 8: 36–37.
76. Their affair might have begun as early as 1581, but they were certainly lovers by January 1583.
77. Catherine believed the rumor despite the denials of well-informed court women. *Lettres,* 7: 420. Abel Desjardins, ed., *Négociations diplomatiques de la France avec la Toscanne,* 6 vols. (Paris, 1859–1886), 4: 407.
78. Boucher argues that Francis promoted the seduction to bind Marguerite to him and that she, overcome by passion, was oblivious to the impact of her actions. *Louise de Lorraine et Marguerite de France,* 176.
79. Marguerite de Valois, *Correspondance,* 226.
80. ("Alcuni vogliono che la sia gravida, altri idropica.") Desjardins, *Négociations diplomatiques,* 4: 466.
81. Viennot, *Marguerite de Valois,* 152. The English ambassador reported that Marguerite was said to have borne a son on June 13, 1583. *Calendar of State Papers. Foreign Series of the Reign of Elizabeth,* vol. 18 (London: 1863), 163.
82. Viennot, *Marguerite de Valois,* 152.
83. Ogier Ghislain de Busbecq reported that it was rumored. *Lettres du baron de Busbec,* 3 vols. (Paris, 1748) 3: 230. Scipion Dupleix, *Histoire de Henri le Grand, IVe du nom* (Paris, 1632) 595; Brantôme said the rumors were false. *Oeuvres,* 8: 72.
84. Henry III complained to Navarre that the two ladies-in-waiting "lived very freely and participated in the political intrigues of the queen of Navarre." August 4–5, 1583, no. 4992, in *Lettres de Henri III,* ed. Jacqueline Boucher, vol. 6 (Paris: H. Champion, 2006), 105–6.
85. Pierre de L'Estoile, *Mémoires de Pierre de L'Estoile pour servir à l'histoire de France et journal de Henri III et de Henri IV,* in *Collection complète des mémoires relatifs à l'histoire de France,* 4 vols. (Paris, 1825), 2: 262–63.

86. Philippe Duplessis-Mornay, *Mémoires de messire Philippes de Mornay, seigneur Du Plessis*, 2 vols. (La Forest, 1625), 2: 372–73.
87. Marguerite de Valois, *Correspondance*, 256.
88. Henri IV, *Lettres d'amour et écrits politiques*, 78–79.
89. These letters of Henry's are included in Marguerite de Valois, *Correspondance*, 267–68, 271–72.
90. Marguerite de Valois, *Correspondance*, 292.
91. Michel de la Huguerye, *Mémoires inédits*, ed. A. de Ruble, 2 vols. (Paris: Société de L'Histoire de France, 1877–1880), 2: 316.
92. L'Estoile, *Mémoires*, 1: 263.
93. No one spoke about the queen of Navarre, and her husband had no interest in taking her back, reported the Tuscan ambassador. Desjardins, *Négociations diplomatiques*, 4: 478.
94. Catherine de Medici, *Lettres*, 8: 180–82.
95. Boucher, *Louise de Lorraine et Marguerite de France*, 286.
96. Navarre's partisans could have plotted Marguerite's murder, a common treatment of unfaithful wives. Ibid., 346–47. Scipion Dupleix claimed, "Most of her foibles proceeded from her extreme and continual fear." *Histoire de Henri le Grand*, 367. According to J. J. Scaliger, Marguerite ate only what had previously been tasted, for fear of being poisoned. *Scaligerana* (Cologne, 1667), 164.
97. June–September 1584, Marguerite sent forty-two letters to gentlemen of the southwest, likely exploring her options with the League. Garrisson, *Marguerite de Valois*, 231.
98. Viennot, *Marguerite de Valois*, 154.
99. Catherine de Medici, *Lettres*, 8: 318.
100. Lucille Bourrachot defends Marguerite's actions in Agen: Her fortifications were well conceived; Marguerite likely believed that the explosion of an arms depot was an attack; her efforts were complicated by an outbreak of the plague. "Agen et Marguerite de Valois," in *Colloque Marguerite de France*, 61–80.
101. It became a royal chateau when Francis I seized Charles of Bourbon's goods.
102. Rene Lucinge reported to the duke of Savoy. *Lettres sur la cour de Henri III en 1586*, ed. Alain Dufour (Geneva: Droz, 1966), 298, 606. The Tuscan ambassador Cavriana reported on December 8, 1586, that Marguerite was ill and that if she died, Navarre would marry Christine of Lorraine. Desjardins, *Négociations diplomatiques*, 4: 663.
103. Henry III, *Lettres de Henri III*, ed. Jacqueline Boucher, vol.6 (Paris, 2006), 320.
104. Aubiac, a squire attached to Marguerite's household since 1584, is described as unattractive and undeserving of "finding himself in the bed of a daughter of France." Aubigné, *Divorce Satyrique*, 668. According to the Tuscan ambassador, he was "noble, young, handsome, but audacious and indiscreet" and Marguerite had borne a child by him. Desjardins, *Négociations diplomatiques*, 4: 661. Dupleix claimed that he knew of this son. *Histoire de Henri le Grand*, 409–10. Michel Moison disputes this because shortly before this illness, Marguerite had taken a two-hundred-mile trip on horseback. He contends that Aubiac's punishment was appropriate to having been Marguerite's lover but not severe enough to punish hiding a royal birth. *L'Exile*

auvergnat de Marguerite de Valois, la reine Margot (Nonette, France: Editions Cler, 1999), 59.

105. The letter of Mendoza, Philip II's ambassador, is quoted in Philippe Lauzun, *Itineraire raisonée de Marguerite de Valois en Gasgogne, d'après ses livres de* compte (1578–1586) (Paris: Picard, 1902), 351.
106. Moison contends that Henry III appropriately pursued Aubiac because Marguerite had turned him against him. *L'Exile auvergnat de Marguerite de Valois*, 88. The event was reported by foreign ambassadors but not by Parisian sources. Sealy, *Myth of the Reine Margot*, 57n10. Pierre Vaissière speculates that the king may have detached Lignerac from his sister, which put him at odds with Aubiac. "Marguerite de Valois et la Ligue en Auvergne: Carlat-Usson," *Revue des questions historiques* 66 (1938), 34.
107. Marguerite de Valois, *Correspondance*, 328–32.
108. Henry III, *Lettres de Henri III*, ed. Jacqueline Boucher, vol. 4 (Paris: Société de l'histoire de France, 1984), 109.
109. Pierre Vaissière says he was condemned for his liaison."Marguerite de Valois et la Ligue en Auvergne: Carlat-Usson," *Revue des questions historiques* 66 (1938), 27. Sealy insists that it was for treason. *Myth of the Reine Margot*, 55.
110. Sealy, *Myth of the Reine Margot*, 4.
111. Henry III, *Lettres de Henri III*, 4: 109.
112. Catherine de Medici, *Lettres*, 9: 108–9.
113. Marguerite de Valois, *Correspondance*, 324–25.
114. Brantôme, *Oeuvres*, 8: 149.
115. Jean de Beaufort-Montboissier, marquis de Canillac, became lieutenant-general for Haute-Auvergne in 1584. Catherine had urged Henry to reward him for his service in arresting Marguerite. *Lettres*, 9: 92.
116. Reproduced in Sealy. *Myth of the Reine Margot*, 66n50.
117. Canaillac made a formal request to join Guise. He assumed that the Estates-General would meet and asked for consideration of Marguerite as an issue of state. Ibid., 77–80.
118. Desjardins, *Négociations diplomatiques*, 4: 778.
119. Marguerite de Valois, *Correspondance*, 333. By March there was an accord on returning Marguerite. Viennot, *Marguerite de Valois*, 178.
120. *Treasorie et Recepte générale des finances et maison de la Reine de Navarre*—twenty-eight volumes of Marguerite's expenses—are incomplete for the years of exile. Sealy reproduces the documents whereby Marguerite and her allies sought funding. *Myth of the Reine Margot*, 115–29.
121. François Humblot gave a course in mathematics; Jean de Champaignac and Scipion Dupleix offered courses in philosophy.
122. Dupleix, *Histoire de Henri le Grand*, 140.
123. Her letters to Fourquevaux document that Marguerite had constructed a cultural center there. *Correspondance*, 429–33, 438–40, 442–45, 493–94.
124. Ibid., 484–88.

125. Marguerite wrote to Gabrielle d'Estrées in hopes of gaining her support for her campaign to return to Paris. Ibid., 396–98.
126. Ibid., 341–43. Marguerite's correspondence reveals that she did not oppose the annulment but rather was concerned to establish her proper place. Viennot "Marguerite de Valois et le comte d'Auvergne: Stratégies pour la reconquête du pouvoir," in Kathleen Wilson-Chevalier and Eliane Viennot, eds., *Royaume de fémynie: Pouvoirs, contraintes, espaces de liberté des femmes, de la Renaissance à la Fronde* (Paris: Champion, 1999), 90–102. The financial arrangements are spelled out in Marguerite de Valois, *Correspondance*, 341–43, 345, 422–23.
127. Henri IV, *Lettres missives*, 5: 194–95.
128. Marguerite de Valois, *Correspondance*, 436.
129. Ibid., 349–50.
130. Desjardins, *Négociations diplomatiques*, 5: 520.
131. Marguerite warned Henry of plots and pockets of resistance in her territory and suggested that well-fortified areas, including Usson, should be razed. *Correspondance*, 450, 485, 496.
132. Catherine's bequest to her illegitimate grandson was confirmed by Henry III and Henry IV. See Eliane Viennot "Marguerite de Valois et le comte d'Auvergne," 90–102.
133. Marguerite de Valois, *Correspondance*, 490–607. For Marguerite's activities in Paris, see Viennot, *Marguerite de Valois*, 204–29.
134. Boucher notes the grievances of the family. *Louise de Lorraine et Marguerite de France*, 355. The attempt may have been to prevent Marguerite from testifying against her nephew. Viennot, *Marguerite de Valois*, 211.
135. Vassière cited popular verses. "Reine sans couronne: Les dernières années de la reine Margot à Paris," 21. Sealy claims both that the Vermonts wrote *Le divorce satyrique* and that Dat's assassin was the Vermonts' son. *Myth of the Reine Margot*.
136. Marguerite de Valois, *Correspondance*, 511–15.
137. Ibid., 586–90.
138. Ibid., 433–34.
139. Vassière, "Reine sans couronne," 19.
140. Marguerite de Valois, *Correspondance*, Viennot, ed., intro., 11.
141. *Mémoires de Pontchartrain*, in *Collection des mémoires relatifs à l'histoire de France*, vol. 17 (Paris, 1822), pt. 2: 78.
142. Scipion Dupleix, *Histoire de Louis le Juste* (Paris, 1633), 72.
143. For Marguerite's association with literary figures, see Marie-Madeleine Fragonard, "La reine Marguerite au rang des illustres," in *Colloque Marguerite de France*, 193–204.
144. Brantôme, *Oeuvres*, 8: 43.
145. Marguerite de Valois, *Album de Poésie*, ed. Colette Winn and François Rouget (Paris: Garnier, 2004).
146. Viennot traces Marguerite's classical allusions in her footnotes to Marguerite's text. *Mémoires et autres écrits*, 69–214.

147. Auger de Mauléon de Granier edited the first edition of Marguerite's memoirs, published in 1628.
148. Marguerite de Valois, *Mémoires*, 134.
149. For example, Jerome d'Avost expressed the optimistic view that human beings had the capacity to connect the secular and the Christian, in *Dialogues on the Graces and Excellences of Man* (1583), which he dedicated to Marguerite.
150. Marguerite's letters to Champvallon, *Correspondance*, 167–68, 173–75, 176–78, 183–84, 221–22, 226–29, 232–236, 240–54.
151. Marguerite de Valois, *Mémoires*, 70–71. Viennot contends that Marguerite's Neoplatonic personality was initially androgynous but later became distinctly feminine. *Correspondance*, intro., 53.
152. See Madeleine Lazard, *Images littéraires de la femme à la Renaissance* (Paris: Presses Universaires de France), 1985).
153. François Loryot, *Les fleurs des Secretz Moraux* (Paris, 1614). Boucher rejects Marguerite as a feminist and instead sees her as driven by passion. *Louise de Lorraine et Marguerite de France*, 267.
154. Marguerite de Valois, *Discours docte et subtile*, in *Mémoires et autres écrits*, 213.
155. Ibid., 217–19.
156. All three Urfée brothers dedicated work to her: Antoine d' Urfée, *Epistre première de la beauté*; Anne d' Urfée, *Hyme de Sainte Suzanne*; and in Honoré d' Urfée's third book of his *Epistres morales*. On Marguerite's philosophical patronage, see Jean Balsamo "Marguerite de Valois et la philosophie de son temps," in *Colloque Marguerite de France*, 269–82.
157. Marguerite attracted literary and philosophical figures, including Marie de Gournay, Philippe Duportes, François Maynard, Etienne Pasquier, Mathurin Regnier, and Theophile de Viau.
158. Etienne Pasquier, *Oeuvres*, 2 vols. (Amsterdam, 1723), 2: 666–67.
159. Pierre Matthieu, "*History de Louys XIII*," in *Histoire de Henry IIII roy de France et de Navarre*, 2 vols. (Paris, 1631), 2: 40.
160. Evelyne Berriot-Salvadore, "Le temps de malheurs, le temps de la philosophie: Marguerite et la vulgarization des sciences," in *Colloque Marguerite de France*, 255–68.
161. Marguerite de Valois, *Discours docte et subtile*, 270.
162. Viennot hopes for greater appreciation of Marguerite in a century "worthy of her." *Marguerite de Valois*, 394. Madeleine Lazard presents Marguerite as a modern woman. "Le discours docte et subtil," in *Colloque Marguerite de France*, 231.
163. Viennot thoroughly discusses the treatment of Marguerite from her time to the present. *Marguerite de Valois*, 233–394.
164. Sealy notes that Dupleix's use of *Le divorce satyrique* gave it such historical validity that seventeenth-century historians like François Eudes de Mézeray used it uncritically. *Myth of the Reine Margot*, 23–25.
165. Viennot lists the sources of her legend and when they became part of it. *Marguerite de Valois*, 407–8.
166. Nicolas Barnaud, *Le réveille-matin des François, et de leurs voisins* (1574, repr.; Paris: Editions d'Histoire Sociale, 1977).

167. Dupleix, *Histoire de Henri le Grand*, 409–10.
168. Jacques-Auguste de Thou implicated Marguerite in Guast's death, claiming she persuaded Viteux to avenge Guast's tales about her. *Histoire universelle*, 14 vols. (Paris, 1734) 7: 300–1.
169. Brantôme, *Oeuvres*, 9: 122.
170. Gédéon Tallement de Reaux, *Historiettes* (Paris: Gallimard, 1990), 60.
171. Viennot concludes that Marguerite probably was not sterile, but it is not clear on what basis. *Correspondance*, intro., 14.
172. Marguerite's memoirs are self-serving, as are Bourbon histories; their accounts have been accepted and hers have not.

CHAPTER 7. GABRIELLE D'ESTRÉES

1. Her two most important biographers take antithetical views: For Raymond Ritter, Gabrielle was Chancellor Cheverny's pawn. *La Charmante Gabrielle* (Paris: Albin Michel, 1947). For Adrian Desclozeaux, she was an effective political agent. *Gabrielle d'Estrées, marquise de Montceaux, duchesse de Beaufort* (Paris, 1889).
2. See *La Légende d'Henri IV: Actes de Colloque Société Henri IV* (Paris: J & D Editions, 1995).
3. Philippe Erlanger, *Gabrielle d'Estrées, femme fatale* (Paris: Perrin, 2000).
4. Voltaire's comment is best known, but he cited Tallement de Reaux, who quoted Saint-Simon. Louis de Saint-Simon, *Mémoires*, 10 vols. (Paris: J. Tallandier, 1980), 10: 345.
5. Ritter, *Charmante Gabrielle*, 54–57.
6. Janine Garrisson, *Gabrielle d'Estrées: Aux marches du palais* (Paris: Le Grand Livre du Mois, 2006), 15.
7. Cheverny was chancellor from 1581 until his death, except for his period of disgrace, 1588–1590. Isabelle's husband's reputed homosexuality may have made her conduct more acceptable. Garrisson, *Gabrielle d'Estrées*, 13–14.
8. Louise-Marguerite de Lorraine, *Histoire des amours de Henry IV* (Leiden, Netherlands, 1664), 11.
9. Erlanger, *Gabrielle d'Estrées*, 21–22.
10. Biographers generally dismiss other rumored love affairs and consider Bellegarde as Gabrielle's only sexual relationship before Henry. Ritter, *Charmante Gabrielle*, 21.
11. Reported by Louise-Marguerite de Lorraine, *Histoire des amours de Henry IV*, 8.
12. Erlanger, *Gabrielle d'Estrées*, 29.
13. David Buisseret, *Henry IV* (London: Allen & Unwin, 1984), 249.
14. For military advantage, Henry should have besieged Rouen rather than Chartres in Cheverny's interest, or Noyon in Gabrielle's. Erlanger, *Gabrielle d'Estrées*, 38. The duke of Sully noted Henry's "secret" motive. *Memoirs of Maximilian de Bethune, Duke of Sully*, 5 vols. (London: Lackington & Allen), 1: 266.
15. Henry Unton, *Correspondence of Sir Henry Unton, Ambassador from Queen Elizabeth to Henry IV*, ed. Joseph Stevenson (London, 1848), 106.

16. Henry IV, *Lettres d'amour et écrits politiques*, ed. Jean-Pierre Babelon (Paris: Fayard, 1988), 143. The letter was previously dated 1594 and is now dated early 1593.
17. Scholars remain divided about Gabrielle's marriage: For Erlanger, the marriage was a facade to protect her reputation. *Gabrielle d'Estrées*, 44–46. For Desclozeaux, Antoine arranged the marriage to keep her from Henry. *Le mariage et le divorce de Gabrielle d'Estrées après les documents nouveaux* (Paris, 1886), 65–75. For Murat, the marriage allowed Gabrielle to continue her relationship with Bellegarde. *Gabrielle d'Estrées* (Paris: Fayard, 1992), 68–80.
18. Louise-Marguerite de Lorraine, *Histoire des amours de Henry IV*, 10.
19. Gifts to Gabrielle included: 400 crowns per month when the liaison began, then raised to 500 and 1,000 after Henry decided to marry her. In 1593, he allotted to her 20,000 crowns to be levied on the dues payable for the transfer of judicial offices and for the guardianship of nobles under age in Normandy. In 1594, she received a gift of 33,000 crowns for the purchase of property.
20. Philippe Duplessis-Mornay, *Mémoires de Messire Philippe de Mornay*, 2 vols. (La Forest, France, 1625), 2: 301.
21. Ludwig van Pastor, *Histoire des papes depuis la fin du Moyen-âge*, 22 vols. (Paris: Plon, 1924–1962), 22: 68.
22. Cited in Irene Mahoney, *Royal Cousin: A Life of Henry IV* (New York: Doubleday, 1970), 270.
23. Robert J. Knecht, *The Rise and Fall of Renaissance France* (Oxford: Blackwell, 2001), 480.
24. Born Catholic, Henry became Protestant under the influence of his mother, Jeanne d'Albret, Catholic under duress after the Saint Bartholomew's Day Massacre, and then a Protestant leader.
25. Sully, *Memoirs*, 1: 332–33.
26. François Eudes de Mézeray, *Histoire de France depuis Faramond jusqu'au règne de Louis le juste*, 3 vols. (1685; repr.; Cambridge, MA: Omnisys, 1990), 3: 1164.
27. Louise-Marguerite de Lorraine reported that Catherine of Bourbon was jealous of Gabrielle's beauty but considered her an appropriate mistress because of it. *Histoire des amours de Henry IV*, 27. Scholars debate Catherine and Gabrielle's relationship: Ritter says they hated each other. *La Charmante Gabrielle*, 141. Desclozeaux claims that they got along well. *Gabrielle d'Estrées*, 95. And Garrisson says that they tolerated each other. *Gabrielle d'Estrées*, 26–27.
28. Théodore Agrippa d'Aubigné, *Divorce satyrique ou les amours de la reyne Marguerite*, in *Oeuvres complètes de Théodore Agrippa d'Aubigné*, ed. E. Reaume and F. de Caussage (Paris, 1873–1879), 8: 303; Pierre de L'Estoile, *Mémoires-journaux*, 12 vols. (1877–1899; repr., Paris: Tallandier, 1982), 6: 67.
29. As Henry wrote to Charles of Bourbon. Cited by Jean-Pierre Babelon, *Henri IV* (Paris: Le Grand Livre du Mois, 1997), 333.
30. The religious and political motives behind Henry's conversion remain sharply debated. See Michael Wolfe, *The Conversion of Henri IV: Politics, Power, and Religious Belief in Early Modern France* (Cambridge, MA: Harvard University Press,

1993); Ronald S. Love, *Blood and Religion: The Conscience of Henri IV, 1553–1593* (Montreal: McGill-Queen's University Press, 2001).

31. Ritter, *Charmante Gabrielle*, 18.
32. Gabrielle d'Amours, *Bulletin de la Société d'histoire de Protestantisme*, 1: 280–85.
33. Reprinted in Henry IV, *Lettres d'amour*, 106.
34. Pierre de Vaissière, *Henri IV* (Paris: Fayard, 1928), 426.
35. To accept the abjuration of someone excommunicated, French clergy used the absolution *de futurum caustelam,* that is to say, one in mortal danger could be absolved, subject to papal ratification. See Wolfe, *Conversion of Henri IV*, 122.
36. Henry IV, *Recueil des lettres missives*, ed., Jules Berger de Xivrey and Joseph Guadet, 9 vols. (Paris: 1843–1876), 3: 821. Some Huguenots charged that Gabrielle pushed for the conversion to make possible the annulment of Henry's marriage. Sully, *Memoirs,* 1: 360; Théodore Agrippa d'Aubigné, *Histoire universelle*, ed. Alphonse de Ruble, 10 vols. (Paris: Beauvais, 1834–1840), 8: 302.
37. Knecht, *Rise and Fall of Renaissance France*, 466.
38. Quoted in Murat, *Gabrielle d'Estrées*, 70.
39. Pierre de L'Estoile, *Mémoires de Pierre de L'Estoile pour servir à l'histoire de France et journal de Henri III et de Henri IV*, in *Collection complète des mémoires relatifs à l'histoire de France,* 4 vols. (Paris, 1825), 3: 80–81.
40. On Henry IV's ceremonial entries, see Lawrence Bryant, *The King and the City in the Parisian Royal Entry Ceremony: Public Ritual and Art in the Renaissance* (Geneva: Droz, 1986); S. Annette Finley-Croswhite, *Henry IV and the Towns: The Pursuit of Legitimacy in French Urban Society*, 1589–1610 (Cambridge: Cambridge University Press, 1999), 47–62.
41. Claude Groulart, *Mémoires et voyages en cour*, 1588–1600, in *Nouvelle collection pour servir l'histoire de France*, ed. Michaud and Poujoulat, vol. 11. (Paris, 1838), 561.
42. Abel Desjardins, *Négociations diplomatiques de la France avec la Toscane*, 6 vols. (Paris 1859–1886), 5: 320–21.
43. Murat, *Gabrielle d'Estrées*, 148; Erlanger, *Gabrielle d'Estrées*, 191. The doctor La Rivière persuaded Henry that his sexual pursuits could make him less able to have children and shorten his life, according to Cheverny. Garrisson, *Gabrielle d'Estrées*, 356.
44. Despite fears about his virility, Henry ultimately had fourteen children. His legitimate children were the dauphin Louis XIII (1601), Elizabeth (1602), Christine (1606), Nicholas (1607), and Gaston (1608), Henrietta Maria (1609). His illegitimate children were, by Gabrielle: Caesar, Catherine, Alexandre; by Henriette: Henri de Verneuil, Gabrielle; by Jacqueline de Bueil: Antoine; by Charlotte des Essart: Jean-Baptiste and Marie Henriette.
45. L'Estoile, *Mémoires*, 3: 72. Sully suggested that Gabrielle passed off Liancourt's son as Henry's and that Sancy, who reported it, suffered professionally as a result. *Memoirs*, 2: 32–33.
46. See relevant documents in Desclozeaux, *Gabrielle d'Estrées*, 27–50.
47. This anecdote is recounted by Noel Gerson in his popular history, *Lady of France* (New York: Funk & Wagnalls, 1963), 286.

48. Desclozeaux, *Gabrielle d'Estrées*, 78.
49. Henry IV's "Lettres de légitimation de César de Vendosme" (January 1595), reprinted in translation in Ernest Vizetelly, *The Favorites of Henry of Navarre* (Boston: Gorham Press, 1910), 141.
50. Ibid.
51. When Henry VIII of England sought to annul his marriage to Catherine of Aragon, he questioned the papal dispensation that allowed him to marry his brother's widow.
52. Only three French kings had previously legitimated children born of adulterous relationships: Charles VII, his three daughters by Agnès Sorel; Henry II, his daughter Diane by Filippa Duci, and his son, Henri d'Angoulême, by Jane Fleming; Charles IX, his son by Marie Touchet, Charles duke d'Angoulême.
53. P. F. Willert, *Henry of Navarre and the Huguenots of France* (London, 1893), 232.
54. L'Estoile, Mémoires-*journaux*, 7: 122.
55. Honoré Capfigue, *Gabrielle d'Estrées et la politique de Henri IV* (Paris, 1859), 143.
56. Ibid., 126–27.
57. L'Estoile, *Mémoires-journaux*, 7: 476.
58. Henry IV, *Lettres d'amour*, 123.
59. L'Estoile, *Mémoires-journaux*, 7: 455, 463.
60. Sully, *Memoirs*, 217.
61. Pierre Matthieu's praise cited in ibid., 2: 294n.
62. Sully saw Gabrielle's involvement in negotiation with the papacy as inappropriate. Ibid., 211–12.
63. Clement VIII owed his election to the Spanish faction and was expected to align the papacy against the heretical king of France. Desclozeaux, *Gabrielle d'Estrées*, 118.
64. Sully, *Memoirs*, 2: 211.
65. Ibid., 177.
66. Merry Weisner, *Women and Gender in Early Modern Europe*, 2nd ed. (New York: Cambridge University Press, 2000), 35–41.
67. Henri IV, *Lettres missives*, 4: 961. Sully objected. *Memoirs*, 2: 212.
68. Sully, *Memoirs*, 2: 167.
69. Letters patent registered on January 28, 1596, gave Gabrielle "all rights and privileges of guardianship, and likewise all gifts and other benefits and emoluments proceedings from us and the kings our successors." The text is reproduced by Desclozeaux, *Gabrielle d'Estrées*, 129–32.
70. L'Estoile, *Mémoires-journaux*, 7: 99.
71. Emmanuel Le Roy Ladurie acknowledges that the appeasement lobby, led by Gabrielle, supported Henry's resolve to impose the edict. *The Royal French State, 1460–1610*, trans. Juliet Vale. (Oxford: Blackwell Publishers, 1994), 239.
72. Sully, *Memoirs*, 2: 192–202.
73. Henry IV, *Lettres d'amour*, 151–52.
74. Sully, *Memoirs*, 2: 212.
75. Desjardins, *Négociations diplomatiques*, 5: 356.
76. *Lettres du cardinal de Florence sur Henri IV et sur la France*, ed. Raymond Ritter, *La Charmante Gabrielle* (Paris: Albin Michel, 1947), 111.

77. Henry IV, *Lettres missives*, 5: 86–87.
78. These stories are reported in Vizetelly, *Favorites of Henry of Navarre*, 197; Erlanger, *Gabrielle d'Estrées*, 149–50; Henry Sedgewick, *Henry of Navarre* (Indianapolis, IN: Bobbs-Merrill, 1930), 252.
79. Henry IV, *Lettres d'amour*, 152.
80. L'Estoile, *Mémoires-journaux*, 7: 543–44.
81. Nicolas de Harlay de Sancy, *Discours sur l'occurrence de ses affaires*, ed. Gilbert Schrenck (Paris: H. Champion, 2000) 116–17.
82. Knecht, *Rise and Fall of Renaissance France*, 479.
83. Desclozeaux, *Gabrielle d'Estrées*, 226–29.
84. Marie de Medici had been considered ever since an annulment had been broached. Her father, Ferdinand of Tuscany, lobbied Clement VIII in his daughter's interest. Desjardins, *Négociations diplomatiques*, 5: 368, 374–407.
85. Aubigné, *Histoire universelle*, 9: 258; L'Estoile, *Mémoires-journaux*, 7: 186.
86. Sully, *Memoirs*, 2: 286.
87. Ibid., 2: 291. La Rivière's reaction was reported by d'Aubigné, *Histoire universelle*, 9: 4.
88. Eugenio Albèri, ed., *Le Relazioni degli ambasciatori veneti al Senato*, 15 vols., 2nd series (Florence, 1839–1863), 4: 356.
89. Sully reported that Gabrielle left Zamet's because she feared she had been poisoned. *Memoirs*, 292. See extensive discussion in Desclozeaux, *Gabrielle d'Estrées*, 257–70.
90. Henri IV, *Lettres missives*, 175–76.
91. Ibid., 177–78.
92. Sully, *Memoirs*, 2: 305.
93. Henry IV, *Lettres d'amours*, 295.
94. Desjardins, *Négociations diplomatiques*, 5: 405, 476.
95. Ibid., 5: 568.
96. Le Roy Ladurie sees this event as extending the Montmorency family's grievances against the Valois to the Bourbons in "a fairly absurd novelette framework." *Royal French State*, 243.
97. Jules Michelet, *Histoire de France*, 19 vols. (Paris, 1876–1877), 12: 343.
98. Henry's letters to Corisandre are more campaign reports than declarations of love. He was unfaithful; she was already aggrieved by mid-1589, although their break did not come until 1592. See Henri IV, *Lettres missives*, 2: 487–88.

CONCLUSION

1. Janine Garrisson makes these comparisons. *Gabrielle d'Estrées: Aux marches du palais* (Paris: Le Grand Livre du Mois, 2006), 114.
2. See Kathryn Norberg, "Incorporating Women/Gender into French History Courses, 1429–1789: Did Women of the Old Regime Have a Political History?" *French Historical Studies* 27 (Spring 2004), 243–92.
3. Crawford, Katherine, *Perilous Performances: Gender and Regency in Early Modern France* (Cambridge, MA: Harvard University Press, 2004).

4. Sharon Jansen, *Debating Women, Politics, and Power in Early Modern Europe* (New York: Palgrave Macmillan, 2008), 204.
5. See Jean-François Dubost, *Marie de Medici: La reine devoilée* (Paris: Payot, 2009).
6. Guy Chaussinand-Nogaret, *La vie quotidienne des femmes du roi, d'Agnès Sorel à Marie Antoinette* (Paris: Hachette, 1990), 233.
7. Colin Jones, *Madame de Pompadour, Images of a Mistress* (London: National Gallery, 2002), 42.
8. See Sarah Maza, "The Diamond Necklace Affair Revisited (1785–1768): The Case of the Missing Queen," in *Marie Antoinette: Writings on the Body of the Queen*, ed. Dena Goodman (New York: Routledge: 2003), 73–97.
9. Dena Goodman, "Introduction: Not Another Biography of Marie Antoinette," in *Marie Antoinette: Writings on the Body of the Queen*, 4.
10. Michel De Waele notes this development in "La fin des guerres de religions et l'exclusion des femmes de la vie politique française, *French Historical Studies* 29, no. 2 (Spring 2006), 199–226.
11. Ernest Lavisse, *Histoire de France*, 9 vols. (Paris: Hachette, 1900–1911), 4: 63.
12. Ibid., 80.
13. François Guizot and Mme. Guizot de Witt, *France*, 8 vols. (New York: Collier, 1902), 2: 250, 261, 279.
14. Jules Michelet, *Histoire de France*, 19 vols. (Paris, 1876–1877), 9: 245.
15. Ibid., 244–47.
16. Guizot, *France*, 2: 478.
17. Ibid., 38–39.
18. Lavisse, *Histoire de France*, 358–64.
19. Ernest Lavisse, *Histoire de France: Cours moyen* (Paris: Armand Colin, 1912), 103–107.
20. Guizot, *History of France*, 3: 402.
21. Michelet, *Histoire de France*, 12: 280–85.
22. Wolfram Fleischhauer, *Die Purpurlinie* (Munich: Schneekluth, 2002).
23. François Reynaert, "Les femmes de pouvoir en France," *Le Nouvel Observateur*, no. 2333 (July 23–29, 2009), 8–12.

Index

Italicized page numbers indicate figures.